T0220779

Lecture Notes in Computer Science 12526

More information about this subseries at http://www.springer.com/series/7411

Olga Galinina · Sergey Andreev ·
Sergey Balandin · Yevgeni Koucheryavy (Eds.)

Internet of Things, Smart Spaces, and Next Generation Networks and Systems

20th International Conference, NEW2AN 2020
and 13th Conference, ruSMART 2020
St. Petersburg, Russia, August 26–28, 2020
Proceedings, Part II

 Springer

Editors
Olga Galinina 🆔
Unit of Electrical Engineering
Tampere University
Tampere, Finland

Sergey Andreev 🆔
Unit of Electrical Engineering
Tampere University
Tampere, Finland

Sergey Balandin 🆔
FRUCT Oy
Helsinki, Finland

Yevgeni Koucheryavy 🆔
Unit of Electrical Engineering
Tampere University
Tampere, Finland

ISSN 0302-9743   ISSN 1611-3349   (electronic)
Lecture Notes in Computer Science
ISBN 978-3-030-65728-4   ISBN 978-3-030-65729-1   (eBook)
https://doi.org/10.1007/978-3-030-65729-1

LNCS Sublibrary: SL5 – Computer Communication Networks and Telecommunications

This Springer imprint is published by the registered company Springer Nature Switzerland AG
The registered company address is: Gewerbestrasse 11, 6330 Cham, Switzerland

Preface

We welcome you to the joint proceedings of the 20th International Conference on Next Generation Teletraffic and Wired/Wireless Advanced Networks and Systems (NEW2AN 2020) and the 13th Conference on the Internet of Things and Smart Spaces (ruSMART 2020) held in St. Petersburg, Russia, during August 26–28, 2020.

Originally, the NEW2AN conference was launched by the International Teletraffic Congress (ITC) in St. Petersburg in June 1993 as an ITC-Sponsored Regional International Teletraffic Seminar. The first edition was entitled "Traffic Management and Routing in SDH Networks" and held by the R&D Institute (LONIIS). In 2002, the event received its current name, the NEW2AN. In 2008, NEW2AN acquired a new companion in Smart Spaces, ruSMART, hence boosting interaction between researchers, practitioners, and engineers across different areas of ICT. From 2012, the scope of ruSMART conferences has been extended to cover the Internet of the Things and related aspects.

Presently, NEW2AN and ruSMART are well-established conferences with a unique cross-disciplinary mixture of telecommunications-related research and science. NEW2AN/ruSMART are accompanied by outstanding keynotes from universities and companies across Europe, the USA, and Russia.

The NEW2AN 2020 technical program addresses various aspects of next-generation data networks, while special attention is given to advanced wireless networking and applications. In particular, the authors have demonstrated novel and innovative approaches to performance and efficiency analysis of 5G and beyond systems, employed game-theoretical formulations, advanced queuing theory, and stochastic geometry. It is also worth mentioning the rich coverage of the Internet of Things, cyber security, optics, signal processing, as well as business aspects.

ruSMART 2020 provided a forum for academic and industrial researchers to discuss new ideas and trends in the emerging areas of the Internet of Things and Smart Spaces that create new opportunities for fully-customized applications and services. The conference brought together leading experts from top affiliations around the world. This year, we have seen participation from representatives of various players in the field, including academic teams and industrial companies, particularly representatives of Russian R&D centers, which have a solid reputation for high-quality research and business in innovative service creation and development of applications. The conference was held virtually due to the COVID-19 pandemic.

We would like to thank the Technical Program Committee members of the two conferences, as well as the invited reviewers, for their hard work and important contributions to the conference. This year, the conference program met the highest quality criteria, with an acceptance ratio of around 35%. The number of submissions sent for peer review was 225, while the number of full papers accepted is 79. A single-blind peer-review type was used for the review process.

The current edition of the conference was organized in cooperation with IEEE Communications Society Russia Northwest Chapter, YL-Verkot OY, Open Innovations Association FRUCT, Tampere University, Peter the Great St. Petersburg Polytechnic University, Peoples' Friendship University of Russia (RUDN University), The National Research University Higher School of Economics (HSE), St. Petersburg State University of Telecommunications, and Popov Society. The conference was held within the framework of the "RUDN University Program 5-100."

We believe that NEW2AN 2020 and ruSMART 2020 conferences delivered an informative, high-quality, and up-to-date scientific program.

August 2020

Olga Galinina
Sergey Andreev
Sergey Balandin
Yevgeni Koucheryavy

Organization

Technical Program Committee

Torsten Braun	University of Bern, Switzerland
Paulo Carvalho	Centro ALGORITMI, Universidade do Minho, Portugal
Chrysostomos Chrysostomou	Frederick University, Cyprus
Roman Dunaytsev	The Bonch-Bruevich Saint-Petersburg State University of Telecommunications, Russia
Dieter Fiems	Ghent University, Belgium
Alexey Frolov	Skolkovo Institute of Science and Technology, Russia
Ivan Ganchev	University of Limerick, Ireland
Jiri Hosek	Brno University of Technology, Czech Republic
Alexey Kashevnik	SPIIRAS, Russia
Joaquim Macedo	Universidade do Minho, Portugal
Ninoslav Marina	UIST, North Macedonia
Aleksandr Ometov	Tampere University, Finland
Pavel Masek	Brno University of Technology, Czech Republic
Edison Pignaton de Freitas	Federal University of Rio Grande do Sul, Brazil

Publicity Chair

Nikita Tafintsev	Tampere University, Finland

Contents – Part II

Contents – Part I

Next Generation Wired/Wireless Advanced Networks and Systems

Detection and Recognition of Moving Biological Objects for Autonomous Vehicles Using Intelligent Edge Computing/LoRaWAN Mesh System

Volkov Artem[1], Malik Al-Sveiti[1], Ibrahim A. Elgendy[2], Alexey S. Kovtunenko[3], and Ammar Muthanna[1,4(✉)]

[1] St. Petersburg State University of Telecommunications, 22 Prospekt Bolshevikov, St. Petersburg, Russia
artemanv.work@gmail.com, aldonasmar@gmail.com, ammarexpress@gmail.com
[2] School of Computer Science and Technology, Harbin Institute of Technology, Harbin, China
ibrahim.elgendy@hit.edu.cn
[3] Ufa State Aviation Technical University, Ufa, Russia
askovtunenko@mail.ru
[4] Peoples' Friendship University of Russia (RUDN University), 6 Miklukho-Maklaya Street, Moscow 117198, Russia

Abstract. Currently, 5G/IMT-2020 networks with their possibilities become more and more services of new areas. These services are integrated into different human life activities. And in several cases, human life depends on Artificial Intelligence technologies, Autonomous Systems, and the Internet of Things (IoT), etc. Autonomous vehicles provide very strict requirements to the network in terms of ultra-low latency, high throughput, and wide coverage. To support these requirements, additional technologies must be employed. The current paper discusses the possibility of the use of airborne platforms aiming to support the terrestrial networks for autonomous vehicles realization as a part of delay-critical applications. Airborne platforms will help in the provisioning of safe road trips by delivering time-critical information to the vehicles globally, even in remote areas. In this paper, we discuss requirements and potential solutions for supporting the autonomous vehicle infrastructure, as a part of an intelligent transportation system. It's proposed to use a sensor network along the road, consists of energy-efficient sensors that can connect in a Mesh network. Also, a novel approach for the detection of biological objects activity on the roadside, based on Artificial Intelligence technologies are suggested.

Keywords: 5G/IMT-2020 · IMT-2030 · LoRaWAN mesh · Autonomous vehicles · AI · IoT · MEC

O. Galinina et al. (Eds.): NEW2AN 2020/ruSMART 2020, LNCS 12526, pp. 3–15, 2020.
https://doi.org/10.1007/978-3-030-65729-1_1

1 Introduction

5G networks are designed to increase the speed of the wireless network so that it can transfer data that may reach 20 GB per second, and it's also can achieve a significant increase in the amount of data sent through non-wired systems that increase the circular range [1, 2]. 5G/IMT-2020 offers very important features, low latency (more responsive), big channels (speeds up data) and connecting more than one device at once (e.g. sensors, smart devices) [3, 4]. Software-Defined Network (SDN) is designed to make networks more flexible, it's also decoupling control and data plane. SDN provides much more efficient resources allocation and it's keeping in to in eye on the network services [5]. Also the network in SDN much more programmable, centrally managed and agile for any need, that means, we can use the SDN concepts in 5G to make the network more flexible [7, 8]. The main motivation to use SDN in 5G is that the system can be modified from a separating utilizing some consistent interfaces. Network Functions Virtualization is a virtualization technology for the physical network elements of a telecommunication network, when network functions are executed by software modules running on standard servers and virtual machines in them. These software modules can interact with each other to provide communication services that previously involved hardware platforms. The relationship between NFV and SDN is that the concepts of NFV originated from SDN, NFV and SDN are complementary, that means one does not depend upon the other, both have similar goals but, approaches are very different, SDN needs new interfaces, control modules and applications but NFV requires moving network applications from dedicated hardware to virtual containers on commercial off the shelf (COTS) hardware. The concept of MEC is to provide the placement of cloud IT resources for network virtualization closer to end users, on the edge of the carrier network. MEC uses the same principles as NFV and optimizes them for a radio access environment in mobile networks. MEC and NFV have in common the standard platform, open environment and Focus on programmability. Autonomous vehicles (AV) now use the 5G technology benefits to achieve low latency in data transmission [6]. In order to achieve low latency for AV, the network management entity must be proactive to make decisions about services that come from vehicles in time. Network Function Virtualization (NFV) release new possibilities within the network, and requires the addition of latest management and orchestration functions within the current model of operations, administration, maintenance and support. Older networks implement network functions (NFs), often associated with the infrastructure which they operate. NFV extracts software implementations of network functions from computing, storage, and network resources.

The rest of the paper is organized as follows: In the next section we overview the related works on 5G standardization with AV and MEC structures. In the problem statement clause we define the problem that we are going to solve in this work. In the proposed solution section we describe the architecture of our proposed solution for detection and recognition of biological objects activity, present the Mesh Network architecture, describe how it works and analyzing Mesh topologies and the functional diagram of the proposed solution. In Sect. 5 the main proposed Algorithm for recognition of biological objects was described. Section 6 shows the algorithm modeling to test the performance of the proposed method. In addition, Sect. 7 concludes the paper and discuss our future works.

2   Related Works

With the advancement of technology and the emergence of artificial intelligence, Autonomous vehicles have become the focus of attention of many industries. There has been a lot of research on autonomous vehicles in recent years. Projections indicate that autonomous vehicles will appear on the road further in the coming years [9]. Autonomous vehicles combine many technologies without the need for human intervention, help solve the traffic crisis, reduce accidents that may happen on the road caused by humans, reduce pollution caused by ordinary cars and reduce energy consumption [10]. MEC technology enables us to use cloud computing services and information technology environment on the edge of the core network and this would provide a quick response to autonomous vehicle services and improve the resource utilization. Road maps can also be stored and processed on MEC network servers. The MEC server can control computing services for a large number of autonomous vehicles, as the enhanced service area of the MEC server will support autonomous vehicles.

In [11] authors consider the achievements in the MEC networks development, as well as the main problems that arise when organizing a network architecture with MEC. Also three scenarios of interaction in networks with MEC were considered. In the first scenario, in addition to the three levels of network architecture represented by the end-user level, the level of the radio access network edge with the MEC servers associated with the base stations, the remote cloud server level, there is an additional level between the MEC servers and the remote computing cloud, which enables end-users to interact with MEC servers, remote cloud and with each other.

3   Problem Statement

Since the advent of cars, express roads between cities, there has been a problem of collisions with animals that suddenly cross the road. Because of that, terrible accidents occur, where people, animals and property suffer. Given the trend and the next step in the development of road transport, namely unmanned vehicles, it is worth considering the problem of accidents with animals from a new angle. In the case when someone is driving, he may notice unusual phenomena (shadow, bushes, etc., as well as warning oncoming drivers), which will allow him to reduce speed in advance and be prepared for an unexpected situation, including a collisions with animals. However, even considering human capabilities, animal accidents are not uncommon.

Therefore, as part of the development of the concept of autonomous vehicles and its infrastructure, it is necessary to consider the problem of accidents and develop an appropriate solution that will improve autonomous vehicles, as well as save the lives of people, animals and preserve property (vehicles, etc.).

Considering the technological advantages of 5G networks described above, in particular SDN /NFV network technologies, as well as cloud-based MEC and FoG Computing, there is a possibility of realizing our task, within the framework of the set requirements for the speed of the solution (delay from the trigger to autonomous transport), further forecasting the activity of biological objects. It is worth noting that this article considers the case of remote roads from residential areas (cities, villages, etc.), the length of the roads themselves, various weather conditions, the durability of the system, the possibility of its flexible configuration, scaling, and also the requirements for recognition type of biological object. In addition, in addition to the above-described capabilities that are laid down at the stage of developing the solution, it is necessary to provide for the possibility of further development of appropriate software modules for the tasks of predicting the movement of biological objects, taking into account digital models of infrastructure and autonomous transport.

4 Proposed Solution

4.1 Part One. The Common Architecture of Proposed Solution for Detection and Recognition of Biological Objects Activity

In the paragraphs of this article, which are described above, technological trends in 5G communication networks are defined, the capabilities of these technologies are described in a certain way, and a problem was described as a separate paragraph, the solution of which (the beginning of the solution) is the aim of this work. The posed problem of detecting biological objects in the roadside zone includes many complex system tasks, the solution of which, in turn, will allow to achieve a new level of road safety, especially in the framework of the concept of unmanned vehicles. This article discusses the concept of solving the problem, as well as the proposed method for organizing the infrastructure part and one of the analytical module that implements the methods of Artificial Intelligence.

Therefore, within the framework of the problem under discussion, a solution was proposed to use the technology of organization the cloud structures - MEC. This technology will ensure the feasibility of the criterion for the speed of the system, minimizing network and other delays introduced by an unnecessary part of the information and communication infrastructure. As a reader, it is proposed to use a network of low-cost sensors with LoRa MESH communication modules. The use of this radio technology will allow fulfilling the criterion for the remoteness of individual sections at roads from Base Stations, for energy conservation. As part of the task of processing the incoming data and the criterion of high reliability of analytical data, in this paper we propose the using the neural networks to recognize types biological objects.

Figure 1 shows the general architecture, including elements of the physical world (car, road, animals, etc.). Considering that this solution is proposed as part of an information system that includes two areas of analytical digital models: road and roadside infrastructure, autonomous transport. As already been found out in practice, an autonomous vehicle itself, with all the computing capabilities and machine vision technologies available today, will not be able to take into account a number of combinations of external phenomena and provide absolute safety for both passengers and everyone else. As a result, it is proposed to develop and considering data from digital models of roads and infrastructure, where autonomous transport is partly an independent structure. Interaction with each other should just provide the network and computing infrastructure of 5G communication networks.

Figure 1 shows the elements within the framework of this issue, as well as their possible interaction. One of the principles that was laid down in the requirements for the solution being developed is the feasibility within the remoteness of roads and, as

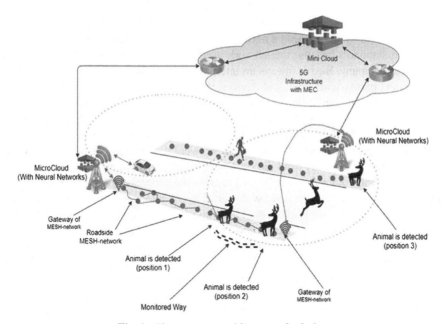

Fig. 1. The common architecture of solution

was already determined above, to fulfill this requirement, we proposed a new generation of LoRa technology. Thus, it is possible to transmit data from remote sensors that are located along the road along its curbs in several rows. After the sensor is triggered, its data is transmitted to the nearest MEC cloud, which is located at the nearest Base Station, so the entire roadside can be divided into "zones", which are also highlighted in circles with a dashed line in Fig. 1. When sensors are triggered and after data is transmitted to the nearest cloud, the primary data processing occurs, which allows to create the necessary data structure for the analytical module for object recognition implemented using Machine Learning technology. After that, certain messages are sent in a broadcasting manner to the nearest base stations, which broadcast the corresponding messages to the autonomous vehicles. In turn, these vehicles already knows in advance about the possibility of meeting a biological objects, determine their speed and time parameters and predict a further model of their movement. Thus reducing the likelihood of accidents that could have occurred if the autonomous vehicle relied only on the on-board sensor system and on-board video analytics system with machine vision. also noting that the proposed solution will just bypass the limitations of accident prevention, which are provided by the limited range of cameras and sensors. In the proposed solution, the car will know about the objects before the lidar or radar can notice, analyze and react, given the high speeds of modern and future automotive vehicles.

4.2   Part Two. The MESH Network Architecture and Protocols

Lora is Low Power Wide Area Network Standard (LPWAN), this term consist of three parts: 1) low power 2) wide area 3) network. The difference between a normal small device and an IoT device is its capability to connect to the internet, and because we expect millions of them, we need a network to connect all of them, this network has to be based on standards because the network itself and the IoT devices will not be built by the same company. Best is always an international standard accepted by everybody [12]. The next part is Wide Area, our devices can connect to our wi-fi network which is part of LAN or local area network, we all know that it's reach is limited to a few meters around our access points, wide area networks need to bridge much bigger distances. This is necessary for IoT devices because we are using them everywhere. The AM Radio Station is an example of wide areas, we were able to receive AM even in the middle of nowhere, far away from the station, but these transmitters were huge, usually they were emitting kilowatts of energy so it seems to be quite easy to bridge big distances using high power. The third part is Low Power, if we want to work on batteries, we don't have lots of power for transmission. And here we see the dilemma, we want kilometers of reach, but have no power to spend. Fortunately, physics gives as a third parameter to ease this dilemma a bit, it is called Bandwidth. The Physical laws say that if we want to create radio connection for a certain distance, we can either increase transmission power or decrease the bandwidth of the channel. We should bother about bandwidth because bandwidth and maximum capacity of a channel are directly related, the smaller the bandwidth, the lower the capacity of our channel. Today our wireless LANs are capable of transferring millions of characters per second, and they are still always too slow.

To understand how LORAWAN Mesh Network works, In the figure below sensor 1 is an intermediate link between sensor 4 and Network Server. When sensor 1 fails, sensor 5 takes the role as an intermediate and the connection between the server and sensor 4 is restored (Fig. 2).

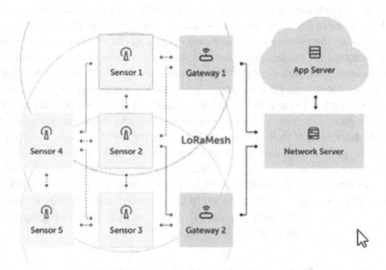

Fig. 2. LoRaWAN mesh topology

LoRaWAN Mesh network offers a reliable way to transfer data. The technology allows you to create large, flexible networks that consume little power. This makes the LoRaWAN grid one of the best ways to collect data from multiple remote sensors simultaneously.

4.3 Part Three. Computing Infrastructure

In Fig. 1, a generalized architecture of the proposed solution was given. Within the framework of the architecture under consideration, a number of elements have been identified that implement certain computing and network functions. The following Fig. 3 shows the functional diagram of the solution.

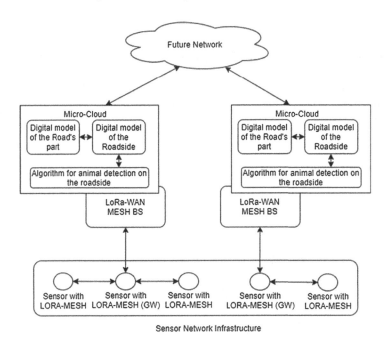

Fig. 3. The functional scheme of the suggested solution

Figure 3 shows the following elements:

1. Sensors with the LoRaWAN MESH module, for reading and subsequent data transfer via the Mesh network to the base station and to the virtual server;
2. LoRaWAN MESH base stations for aggregation of LoRa traffic and subsequent transportation of data to roadside clouds (Micro-cloud in MEC structure);
3. Within the framework of the Micro-Cloud, the corresponding server analytic application is deployed, which consists of the following main modules:

   – Algorithm for animal detection on the roadside. This algorithm is implemented on the basis of the architecture of recurrent neural networks, pre-trained to detect the corresponding biological objects;

- Digital model of the roadside. This module is a software package that implements roadside mathematical models, stores data, processes them for further transmission, as well as higher-order analytical models - for example, a forecasting system;
- Digital model of the road's part. This module is a software package that implements mathematical models of a part of the road infrastructure controlled by the cloud. This software provides, stores, processes data on the entire traffic situation and management of dynamic road elements (for example, a railway crossing, etc.). Based on these data, certain predictive analytical data are generated for the development of the corresponding section of the road, any incoming autonomous vehicles are informed, by transmitting the requested data by the vehicle's on-board system.

5   Proposed Algorithm for Biological Objects Recognition

Here, we propose a new algorithm that help recognising the biological objects when one if those cases is beside the road and trying to cross it. Cases that we are going to recognize:

1. One person
2. A group of people
3. Deer

The figure below shows sensors map in two adjacent zones (Fig. 4).

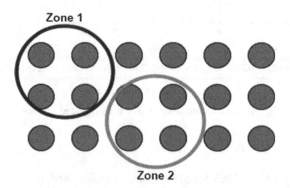

Fig. 4. Map of the sensor's zones

5.1   Data Processing

The number of active pushed sensors in one zone (4 m).

$$N, N \in M$$

$$M := [x, y] = [3, 4] = 12;$$

T (Response Time) Delta between sensors from adjacent areas:

$$Ts = Ts\_(1\_1) - Ts\_(1\_2);$$

Ts 11 - response time of the first sensor in the first zone, *Ts* 12 - response time of the first sensor in the second zone.

Sum of Forces (F) of pressed sensors in one zone: $F = \sum\_(n=0)^N F\_(n), N \in M$

Average sensor press time in one zone: $\Delta T\_avrg = (\sum\_(n=0)^N \Delta t\_n)/N, N \in M$

The distance between the first pressed sensor in the first zone and the last pressed sensor in the second zone:

$$S = \sqrt{((N\_12 - N\_11)^2 + (N\_(22) - N\_21)^2)}$$

5.2 Neural Network

Today, an artificial neural network is widely used to solve various problems in various aspects in our life. For example, the areas of speech recognition, computer vision (a complex integrated video analytics of graphic objects), recently - complex engineering systems and their modules (for example, oil refineries automobile plants and so on). Such complex tasks of analyzing large volumes of information are solved by developing tools belonging to the Artificial Intelligence class. One of the most developing methods for predicting models based on large amounts of data is artificial neural networks, a variety of which is already large at this stage of development of these technologies [13].

At the moment, there is a large variety of neural networks. One of the typical tasks is classification. One of the most common classification methods is a method based on descriptions objects using signs, in which each object is characterized by a set of numerical or non-numerical signs. However, for some types of data, open features do not give a classification accuracy, for example, the color of image points or a digital audio signal. The reason is that this data contains hidden features. Deep Learning is a set of machine learning algorithms that try to model high-level abstractions in data, in other words, extract hidden features from data [14]. Therefore, considering the features of the object (traffic) and its attributes (numerical - statistical series), a neural network with Deep Learning was chosen.

To solve the recognition of a biological object, considering the peculiarity of the incoming data for our task, as well as the requirements for the system under study and development, a recurrent neural network was chosen as NN.

Since the chosen architecture for the neural network implements the principle of training with the involvement of a teacher, it is required to compose training Datasets with marked data, then save the state of the trained network. To train the neural network, the input $DataSet_{ML}$ was converted to $DataSetML_{train}$ by adding a new data column, each row had the identifier of the statistical sample. Accordingly, for training to recognize a larger type of traffic, this training Dataset needs to be expanded by marking the corresponding statistical sample with a label of a biological object, e.g. Deer, Human or Human Groups. Thus, the structure of the training $DataSetML_{train}$ is as follows:

[Type of BO]	[ActiveSensZone]	[TimeFirstSen]	[ForceSumm]	[deltaTime]	[distance]
Deer	N_{11}	Ts_{12}	F_{13}	ΔT_{avrg24}	T_{15}
Humm	N_{21}	Ts_{22}	F_{23}	ΔT_{avrg24}	T_{25}
Group.Humm	N_{31}	Ts_{32}	F_{33}	ΔT_{avrg34}	T_{35}
...	...	...	...	...	...
...	N_{N1}	Ts_{N2}	F_{N3}	ΔT_{avrgN4}	T_{N5}
others	$N_{(N+1)1}$	$Ts_{(N+1)2}$	$F_{(N+1)3}$	$\Delta T_{avrg(N+1)4}$	$T_{(N+1)5}$

The network model contains 4 fully connected RNN layers, each of which contains 12 hidden nodes.

The hyperparameters of learning:

– Optimizer: Adam;
– Number of epochs: 60;
– Number of samples per iteration: 1024;

Learning speed: 0.0025

6   Results

To test the operability of the proposed method for detecting a biological object on the roadside, a data generator was developed according to the formulas and tolerances defined above. As a simulation, a simulation model was developed in Python programming language, with an artificially recurrent neural network implemented. After the Dataset was created, the developed neural network was activated, after its successful training, the state of the neural network was preserved (the resulting architecture, weights, and other parameters). This neural network has the ability to further refine and implement on the stand, in order to pilot the solution.

Using the model data generator with subsequent processing, a DataSetML_train was formed, and fed to the input of a neural network, the configuration of which is shown in the article above.

During training, the parameter 'accuracy' was monitored - the function inverse to the error function in recognition of activity and the parameter 'loss' - cross entropy determining a slightly near-predictable distribution to the true one.

It is expressed as follows (Fig. 5):

Also, in addition to the graphs shown in Fig. 5, the Confusion Matrix of neural network training was calculated and built. The matrix is displayed in Fig. 6.

In the figure, where the Confusion matrix is displayed, it is clearly seen that for the task, the network has successfully completed the training process. As a result of training the developed neural network and testing its operation on test Datasets, in a trained state, the developed neural network can identify the type of biological object with a probability of 99.8%. Using the Confusion matrix, you can see that the network made a mistake 3 times. It is also worth noting that the selected architecture was an effective

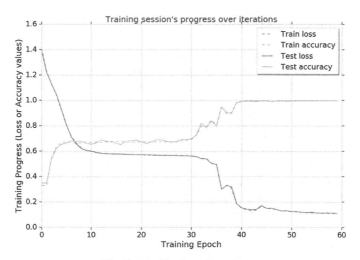

Fig. 5. Machine learning process

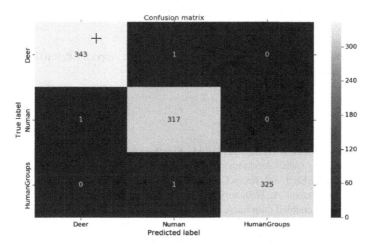

Fig. 6. Confusion matrix

solution to the task. With a lower value of neurons in the embedded layers, the artificial neural network does not work stably, and it also does not reach the appropriate level as an object detection and makes a significant number of errors. With a larger value of the number of nested neurons, the network also does not work stably and the effect of "retraining" the network occurs, it was possible to judge those graphs that were obtained as part of the study of the NN architecture and its training on test data. It is also worth noting that the schedule of the learning process contains a sharp jump in the quality of training an artificial neural network at the time of the 40th era. The graph should have a smoother character. However, in this task, various characteristics of the neural network were investigated and those that are given in this article are more efficient and fulfill the task of testing the proposed solution.

7   Conclusion and Future Work

In this paper, we present a solution to detect and recognize the biological objects activity on the roadside. This solution can help alleviate accidents caused by animals or people on the road. We have used MEC technology that has system speed specifications and reduces network delays when transmitting data through it. LoRa mesh wireless technology was used to provide data transmission between highway remote networks and the main station. We proposed an algorithm to identify the movement of people and animals on the highway, in this algorithm we used the neural network, a network that is widely used in various fields. This network solves many complex tasks that contain large amounts of data. Artificial neural networks are one of the most sophisticated methods for predicting models based on large amounts of data. We also proposed an algorithmic model to test the operability of the algorithm that we proposed by developing a simulation model in the Python programming language, with the implementation of an artificial neural network. This work aims to develop a new mechanism to detect the movement of people and animals on the highway and their roadsides, expand the digital roads models for provides the new AV possibilities. In the upcoming works, we will aim to use the proposed algorithm by analyzing the data in more detail, which would help to further mitigate the accidents that could happen on the road.

Acknowledgment. The publication has been prepared with the support of the "RUDN University Program 5-100" (recipient Ammar Muthanna).

References

1. Galinina, O., Andreev, S., Gerasimenko, M., Koucheryavy, Y., Himayat, N., Yeh, S.-P., Talwar, S.: Capturing spatial randomness of heterogeneous cellular/WLAN deployments with dynamic traffic. IEEE J. Sel. Areas Commun. **32**(6), 1083–1099 (2014). art. no. 6824742
2. Ateya, A.A., Muthanna, A., Koucheryavy, A.: 5G framework based on multi-level edge computing with D2D enabled communication. In: International Conference on Advanced Communication Technology, ICACT, vol. 2018-February, pp. 507–512. Institute of Electrical and Electronics Engineers Inc. (2018) https://doi.org/10.23919/ICACT.2018.832381
3. Ometov, A., et al.: Toward trusted, social-aware D2D connectivity: bridging across the technology and sociality realms. IEEE Wirel. Commun. **23**(4), 103–111 (2016). art. no. 7553033
4. Volkov, A., Ateya, A.A., Muthanna, A., Koucheryavy, A.: Novel AI-based scheme for traffic detection and recognition in 5G based networks. In: Galinina, O., Andreev, S., Balandin, S., Koucheryavy, Y. (eds.) NEW2AN/ruSMART -2019. LNCS, vol. 11660, pp. 243–255. Springer, Cham (2019). https://doi.org/10.1007/978-3-030-30859-9_21
5. Muthanna, A., Volkov, A., Khakimov, A., Muhizi, S., Kirichek, R., Koucheryavy, A.: Framework of QoS management for time constraint services with requested network parameters based on SDN/NFV infrastructure. In: International Congress on Ultra Modern Telecommunications and Control Systems and Workshops, vol. 2018-November). IEEE Computer Society (2019) https://doi.org/10.1109/ICUMT.2018.8631274
6. Petrov, V., Samuylov, A., Begishev, V., Moltchanov, D., Andreev, S., Samouylov, K., Koucheryavy, Y.: Vehicle-based relay assistance for opportunistic crowdsensing over narrowband IoT (NB-IoT). IEEE Internet Things J. **5**(5), 3710–3723 (2018). art. no. 7857676

7. Volkov, A., Khakimov, A., Muthanna, A., Kirichek, R., Vladyko, A., Koucheryavy, A.: (2017) Interaction of the IoT traffic generated by a Smart city segment with SDN core network. In: WWIC 2017 International Conference on Wired/Wireless Internet Communication, pp. 115–126, 0302-9743 eISSN: 1611-3349. Springer-Verlag GmbH, Heidelberg (2017)

8. Volkov, A., Proshutinskiy, K., Adam, A.B.M., Ateya, A.A., Muthanna, A., Koucheryavy, A.: SDN load prediction algorithm based on artificial intelligence. In: Vishnevskiy, V.M., Samouylov, K.E., Kozyrev, D.V. (eds.) DCCN 2019. CCIS, vol. 1141, pp. 27–40. Springer, Cham (2019). https://doi.org/10.1007/978-3-030-36625-4_3

9. Tran, T.X., Hajisami, A., Pandey, P., Pompili, D.: Collaborative mobile edge computing in 5G networks: New paradigms, scenarios, and challenges. IEEE Commun. Mag. **55**, 54–61 (2017)

10. Gerla, M., Lee, E.K., Lee, U.: Internet of vehicles: from intelligent grid to autonomous cars and vehicular clouds. In: 2014 IEEE World Forum on Internet of Things, WF-IoT 2014, pp. 241–246. IEEE Computer Society (2014) https://doi.org/10.1109/wf-iot.2014.6803166

11. Bonnefon, J.F., Shariff, A., Rahwan, I.: The social dilemma of autonomous vehicles. Science **352**, 1573–1576 (2016). https://doi.org/10.1126/science.aaf2654

12. Ometov, A., et al.: Feasibility characterization of cryptographic primitives for constrained (wearable) IoT devices. In: 2016 IEEE International Conference on Pervasive Computing and Communication Workshops, PerCom Workshops, art. no. 7457161, (2016)

13. Rathore, H., Agarwal, S., Sahay, S. K., Sewak, M.: Malware detection using machine learning and deep learning. In: International Conference on Big Data Analytics, pp. 402–411. Springer, Cham (2018)

14. Sewak, M., Sahay, S.K., Rathore, H.: An investigation of a deep learning based malware detection system. In: Proceedings of the 13th International Conference on Availability, Reliability and Security, p. 26. ACM (2018)

Method of Constructing Node Map
in Wireless Mesh Sensor Network

Van Dai Pham[1(✉)] 🆔, Ilya Grishin[1], Darina Okuneva[1], and Ruslan Kirichek[1,2]

[1] Bonch-Bruevich Saint-Petersburg State University of Telecommunications,
Saint Petersburg 193232, Russia
`fam.vd@spbgut.ru`, `msp_sut@list.ru`, `darina_okuneva@mail.ru`, `kirichek@sut.ru`
[2] V.A. Trapeznikov Institute of Control Sciences of Russian Academy of Sciences,
Mosscow 117997, Russia

Abstract. Widely usage of LPWAN networks allows us to think about
the further development of this technology, which develops networks to
work not only with the star topology but also with a mesh topology.
With such development, a procedure should be provided for determining
the coordinates of nodes in the network. In this article, we propose a
method for constructing a map of sensor nodes in the wireless mesh
network. In particular, we analyzed rangefinder methods based on the
received signal strength or the signal propagation duration to calculate
the distances between nodes. With determined distances, a method is
considered for constructing a three-dimensional model of each network
fragment, then spatial transformations are carried out for the subsequent
construction of a three-dimensional model of the whole network.

Keywords: Mesh network · Localization · Positioning · Wireless
sensor network · LPWAN · Multidimensional scaling

1 Introduction

Nowadays, Low-Power Area Networks (LPWANs) are popularly chosen to deploy
the Internet of Things (IoT) applications. Such networks provide abilities of long-
range transmission and saving energy consumption while most IoT devices are
powered by batteries. In recent years, there are various technologies proposed
for LPWANs such as LoRa technology from Semtech, ultra-narrow band (UNB)
technology from Sigfox, and random phase multi-access (RPMA) technology
from Ingenu [1]. Most LPWANs have developed to provide a large coverage area
in the urban environment, which is one of the aims in the process of developing
Smart Sustainable Cities.

Successful experience of using LPWAN networks allows us to think about
the subsequent development of this technology, which provides for the transition
from a star topology to mesh networks. A mesh or multi-hop communication can
be supported in the LPWANs with the end nodes can become the relay nodes to
transmit the data from remote nodes to the gateway [2]. With such a transition,

O. Galinina et al. (Eds.): NEW2AN 2020/ruSMART 2020, LNCS 12526, pp. 16–27, 2020.
https://doi.org/10.1007/978-3-030-65729-1_2

a procedure should be provided for determining the nodes' coordinates in the wireless mesh network located at significant distances from each other.

In most cases, solving the problems of determining the coordinates of nodes is based on the geographic approach. When processing the received signals, physical quantities are extracted that depends on the location of the radiating antenna, based on which this location can be determined by geometric methods. Thus, we can specify the goniometric, rangefinder, difference-rangefinder methods, and their combinations. This paper discusses the most common rangefinder methods in wireless networks.

Moreover, the rangefinder method is based on calculating the distance between the emitting and receiving antennas according to the signal strength or signal propagation time. In this paper, we consider mesh LPWAN networks with the gateways located on street lighting poles at a level above a person, but below the average level of roofs, and other nodes located lower than the average level of roofs.

2 Distance Determination Methods

2.1 RSSI-Based Method

When determining the distance between nodes based on the level of the RSSI (Received Signal Strength Indicator) signal received in the city, it should be taken into account that the radio signal propagation is carried out in conditions of dense urban development. This invariably leads to the effect of multipath propagation, which manifests itself in the fact that an additive mixture of the useful signal and its many copies arising as a result of diffraction, scattering, and reflections of the radio signal from objects irradiated by the transmitting antenna and having different delay times proportional to the path length.

Moreover, the channel parameters are a function of time, since scattering and reflecting the radio wave can move in space, introducing a Doppler shift into the reflected radio waves. In this case, receiving an accurate signal propagation model is not possible, and generalized path loss models are applied [3]:

$$PL(d, f) = 10\alpha lg(d_{m,n}) + \beta + 10\gamma lg(f) + N(0, \sigma), dB \qquad (1a)$$

$$\hat{d}_{m,n} = 10^{\frac{PL(d_{m,n}, f) - (\beta + 10\gamma lg(f) + N(0, \sigma))}{10\alpha}}, m \qquad (1b)$$

where $d_{m,n}$ – Euclidean distance between nodes m and n, m; $\hat{d}_{m,n}$ – estimated Euclidean distance $d_{m,n}$, m; f - carrier frequency, GHz; $\alpha = 2, 12$ – coefficient of increasing path loss with the distance; $\beta = 29, 2$ – coefficient associated with the path loss offset value; $\gamma = 2, 11$ – coefficient of increasing path loss with frequency; $N(0, \sigma)$ – Gaussian random variable with zero mean and standard deviation $\sigma = 5, 16$. Coefficient values α, β, γ and standard deviation σ are chosen for the urban zone of multi-story or low-rise buildings under the conditions of signal propagation in the line of sight.

Figure 1 shows the dependence of the radio signal attenuation on the distance according to the formula (1a) with $N(0, \sigma)$ and value $PL(d, f)$ obtained as a

result of distance measurements corresponding to the pico-urban dense zone
and microcells [3].

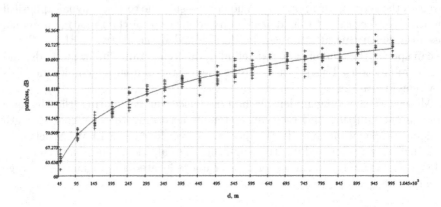

Fig. 1. The dependence of the radio signal attenuation on the distance

For each distance, the graph shows 11 values of the path loss obtained by
averaging 15 measurement results. The results of the calculation of distances
according to the path losses (1b) are presented in Fig. 2.

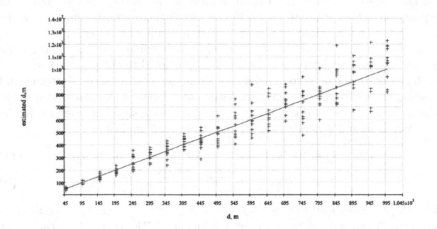

Fig. 2. Calculated distances according to path loss values

Obviously, the presence of a random variable $N(0, \sigma)$ leads to an error in
calculating the Euclidean distance between the transmitting and receiving stations: $\hat{d}_{m,n} = d_{m,n} + \triangle d_{m,n}$. According to the expression (1b), the results of
the distance difference obtained from the Euclidean metric and from the data
received during the experiment are presented in Table 1.

Table 1. Distance measurement errors using RSSI-based method

$d_{m,n}$, m	20	40	60	80	100	120	140	160	180	200	250	330
$\triangle d_{m,n}$, m	15.5	−2.1	−3.9	38.7	12.4	12.9	87.7	91.1	68.4	163.2	159.3	230.9
$\frac{\lvert \triangle d_{m,n}\rvert}{\lvert d_{m,n}\rvert}$	0.78	0.05	0.07	0.48	0.12	0.10	0.63	0.57	0.38	0.82	0.64	0.70

According to graphs and Table 1, it can be seen that although the model (1a) fully complies with the experimental data; when determining the distances between nodes based on the path loss, calculation errors turn out to be very significant, which implies the use of the RSSI-based method in conjunction with other methods based on the signal propagation time.

2.2   TOA-Based Method

In the method based on the time of arrival (TOA) signal, the distance is measured according to the radio signal propagation time from a transmitter to a receiver and the condition that the radio waves propagate in a homogeneous medium with a constant speed of v m/s:

$$\hat{d}_{m,n} = v(t_n - t_m) = v\hat{t}_{mn} \tag{2}$$

where $v = 299792458$ m/s – electromagnetic wave propagation speed, t_n— receiving time, t_m—sending time (indicated in the message), $\hat{t}_{mn} = t_{mn} + \triangle t_{mn}$ – estimated propagation time between nodes.

As the disadvantage of this method, it is required to synchronize internal clocks of nodes, which is not possible for mesh networks. Systematic and random changes in the parameters of quartz clock resonators such as aging of the resonator or environmental conditions will lead to a deviation of time scans. For instance, according to the LoRa specification [4], if the time error is $\pm 10\,ppm$, then for 128 s the deviation of the clock will be 1.3 ms. And, since the difference between the clocks of the nodes m and n is $\triangle t_{mn} = 0.1\,\mu s$, the distance measurement error $\triangle d_{m,n}$ is already 30 m, it becomes obvious that errors are unacceptable with using the TOA-based method.

2.3   TDOA-Based Method

In the case of determining the distance between nodes using the TDOA (Time Difference Of Arrival) that is based on measuring the difference in the arrival time of the radio signal, it should be considered that the effectiveness of this method directly depends on the bandwidth allocated for transmission. According to the report ITU-R SM.2211-1, it is indicated that for signals with a frequency bandwidth of 30 kHz, the root-mean-square error of determining the location of terminal devices was about 100 m [5]. Thus, referring to the parameters of modern LPWAN networks, it can be argued that this method can provide acceptable location accuracy in networks using the frequency band recommended for standard LoRaWAN networks - 125 kHz, but for networks with a bandwidth 100 Hz determining the location of the signal source is not possible.

2.4 SDS-TWR-Based Method

According to the SDS-TWR-based (symmetric double-sided two-way ranging) method, each of nodes that are not synchronized with each other measures the signal travel time in the forward and reverse directions, as well as the response message generation time $t_{r\,m}$, $t_{r\,n}$, significantly longer than the signal travel time, i.e. the measurement is carried out in two cycles with a duration $t_{c\,m}$ and $t_{c\,n}$. Estimation of the travel time of the radio signal between the nodes m and n will be:

$$\hat{t}_{mn} = \frac{(\hat{t}_{c\,n} - \hat{t}_{r\,n}) + (\hat{t}_{c\,m} - \hat{t}_{r\,m})}{4}$$

$$= \frac{(t_{c\,n} - t_{r\,n})(1 + \delta_n) + (t_{c\,m} - t_{r\,m})(1 + \delta_m)}{4} \quad\quad (3)$$

$$\approx t_{mn} + \frac{(t_{r\,n} - t_{r\,m})(\delta_m - \delta_n)}{4}$$

where $\hat{t}_{c\,m}$, $\hat{t}_{c\,n}$ – estimated cycle time of nodes $t_{c\,m}$ and $t_{c\,n}$; $\hat{t}_{r\,m}$, $\hat{t}_{r\,m}$ – estimated response time of nodes $t_{r\,m}$ and $t_{r\,n}$; δ_m, δ_n – the deviation of the time of nodes m and n.

As can be seen from the expression (3), the method allows SDS-TWR to compensate for the shift of the time scales and the deviation of the time, which significantly increases the accuracy of determining the distance between the nodes.

Table 2 below shows the distance measurement results between two nodes, the time clock of which is described as: $t \cdot (1 + 20\,ppm)$ for node 1 and $t \cdot (1 - 20\,ppm)$ for node 2, verifying the truth of these statements.

After receiving data about distances between nodes, the calculation of their coordinates can be implemented in two stages:

– at the first stage, using the available data from the network nodes, a three-dimensional network model is restored,
– and at the second stage, spatial transformations of the obtained model are carried out using the anchor points, which are the nodes located on the street lighting poles, and whose coordinates are known.

Mesh networks deployed for the implementation of Smart Sustainable City projects imply a sufficiently large number of nodes and a high density, which makes it possible to distinguish network fragments with a fully connected topology. Therefore, initially, the question of restoring three-dimensional models of given fragments of the network as a basis for the subsequent construction of a three-dimensional network model as a whole can be considered.

Table 2. Distance measurement using SDS-TWR-based method

$d_{m,n}$, m	t_{mn}, ns	$\hat{t}_{mn}$, ns	$\hat{d}_{m,n}$, m	$d_{m,n}$, m	t_{mn}, ns	$\hat{t}_{mn}$, ns	$\hat{d}_{m,n}$, m
50	166.782	166.781	49.9997	550	1834.603	1834.602	549.9997
100	333.564	333.563	99.9997	600	2001.385	2001.384	599.9997
150	500.346	500.345	149.9997	650	2168.167	2168.166	649.9997
200	667.128	667.127	199.9997	700	2334.949	2334.948	699.9997
250	833.91	833.909	249.9997	750	2501.731	2501.73	749.9997
300	1000.692	1000.691	299.9997	800	2668.513	2668.512	799.9997
350	1167.474	1167.473	349.9997	850	2835.295	2835.294	849.9997
400	1334.256	1334.255	399.9997	900	3002.077	3002.076	899.9997
450	1501.038	1501.037	449.9997	950	3168.859	3168.858	949.9997
500	1667.82	1667.819	499.9997	1000	3335.641	3335.64	999.9997

3   Three-Dimensional Model of a Mesh Network Fragment

Assume a fragment of a wireless mesh network consisting of N nodes with a fully connected topology, regarded as some set $S := s$, power $N : |S| = N$. Each node of a given network fragment has a designation s_n, where $n = 1, 2...N$ – node number.

The fully connected topology allows us to estimate the distances between all nodes of the fragment of $\hat{d}_{mn}$, based on which the square matrix of distances $\hat{\mathbf{D}}$ can be compiled. The matrix $\hat{\mathbf{D}}$ is symmetric and has the dimension N. This matrix is a feature space of the network fragment, where a separate matrix column represents a cathedral is a set of features of a wireless node with a number corresponding to the column number of the matrix $\hat{\mathbf{D}}$.

The solution to the problem of reconstructing a three-dimensional model of the network fragment S based on the matrix of squares of distances $\hat{\mathbf{D}}$ can be found by the method of metric multidimensional scaling [6] designed to reduce the dimension of a set of attributes (in this case, to 3).

Since the matrix $\hat{\mathbf{D}}$ is symmetric, it can be expanded as $\hat{\mathbf{X}} \cdot \hat{\mathbf{X}}^T$, where the rows of $\hat{\mathbf{X}}$ can be considered as the coordinates of the nodes. Since the matrix $\hat{\mathbf{D}}$ can be represented through spectral decomposition, then:

$$\hat{\mathbf{D}} = \mathbf{U} \cdot \mathbf{\Lambda}_D \cdot \mathbf{U}^T = \hat{\mathbf{X}} \cdot \hat{\mathbf{X}}^T \tag{4}$$

where $\mathbf{U}$ – orthogonal matrix; $\mathbf{\Lambda}_D$ – diagonal eigenvalue matrix of $\hat{\mathbf{D}}$.

It should be noted that since $tr\hat{\mathbf{D}} = 0$, there will be at least one negative element in the matrix of eigenvalues of $\mathbf{\Lambda}_D$. Since $\hat{\mathbf{X}} = \mathbf{U} \cdot \mathbf{\Lambda}_D^{1/2}$, negative eigenvalues give the complex matrix $\dot{\mathbf{\Lambda}}_D^{1/2}$, therefore, the coordinate values will also not be real. The solution to this problem is possible by double centering the matrix $\hat{\mathbf{D}}$ by alternately centering the matrix in columns and rows:

$$\mathbf{J} \cdot \hat{\mathbf{D}} \cdot \mathbf{J} = \left(\mathbf{E} - \frac{1}{N}\mathbf{I}^T \cdot \mathbf{I}\right) \cdot \hat{\mathbf{D}} \cdot \left(\mathbf{E} - \frac{1}{N}\mathbf{I}^T \cdot \mathbf{I}\right) = \mathbf{Z} \tag{5}$$

where $\mathbf{E}$ - identity matrix of dimension N; $\mathbf{I} = (1, 1...1)$ - N-dimensional row vector.

Since the double-centered matrix $\mathbf{Z}$ is also symmetric, it can be represented as a spectral decomposition:

$$\mathbf{Z} = \mathbf{U} \cdot \boldsymbol{\Lambda}_Z \cdot \mathbf{U}^T \tag{6}$$

where $\boldsymbol{\Lambda}_Z = diag(\lambda_1 \lambda_2 ... \lambda_N)$ - diagonal eigenvalue matrix $\mathbf{Z}$, $\lambda_1 \geq \lambda_2 \geq ... \geq \lambda_N \geq 0$; $\mathbf{U} = (\mathbf{u}_1 \mathbf{u}_2 ... \mathbf{u}_N)$ - $N \times N$ - column eigenvector matrix $\mathbf{u}_n$.

The choice of three maximum eigenvalues and the corresponding column vectors allows you to form a matrix of coordinates of nodes in three-dimensional space.

$$\hat{\mathbf{X}} = (\mathbf{u}_1 \quad \mathbf{u}_2 \quad \mathbf{u}_3) \cdot \begin{bmatrix} \sqrt{\lambda_1} & 0 & 0 \\ 0 & \sqrt{\lambda_2} & 0 \\ 0 & 0 & \sqrt{\lambda_3} \end{bmatrix} = \mathbf{U}_3 \boldsymbol{\Lambda}_3^{1/2} \tag{7}$$

4   Spatial Transformations

The construction of the three-dimensional model of the mesh network fragment gives the coordinates of each nodes $s_n \in S$: $(x_n^* \quad y_n^* \quad z_n^*)$ with the center of mass subnet at the origin. Figure 3 shows the nodes in the fragment of a wireless mesh network. Representation of the network fragment in the form of a graph allows us

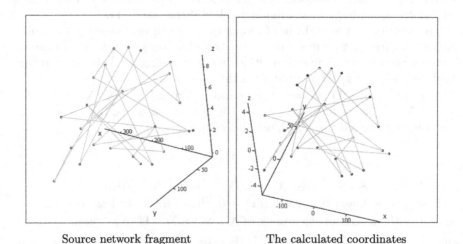

Source network fragment   The calculated coordinates

Fig. 3. Location of nodes in three-dimensional space

to see that reconstructed from the data on distances obtained by the SDS-TWR method, the three-dimensional model of the network fragment corresponds to the initial one, but is located in a different coordinate system. We denote the coordinate system of the network fragment as CS1, and the coordinate system of the network fragment obtained from the calculated results as CS2.

Thus, to find the nodes's coordinates, it is necessary to shift and rotate around a certain axis of the nodes of the network fragment, which can be described by the matrix of spatial transformations:

$$\mathbf{x}_n = (x_n^* \quad y_n^* \quad z_n^* \quad h) = (x_n \quad y_n \quad z_n \quad 1) \cdot \mathbf{T} \tag{8}$$

where h – homogeneous coordinate factor; $\mathbf{T}$ – spatial transformation block matrix [7,8]:

$$\mathbf{T} = \left(\frac{3 \times 3 \mid 3 \times 1}{1 \times 3 \mid 1 \times 1} \right) = \left(\frac{\mathbf{R} \mid \mathbf{P}}{\mathbf{S} \mid \mathbf{M}} \right) \tag{9}$$

where $\mathbf{M}$ – scaling matrix; $\mathbf{P}$ – vector of perspective transformation; $\mathbf{R}$ – resulting matrix of arbitrary rotation in three-dimensional space; $\mathbf{S}$—shift row-vector.

Arbitrary sequential spatial transformations are described by the resulting matrix:

$$\mathbf{T} = \prod_{k=1}^{K} \mathbf{T}_k \tag{10}$$

The matrix of spatial transformations describing a shift in three-dimensional space has the form: $\mathbf{S} = (\triangle x \quad \triangle y \quad \triangle z)$, where $\triangle x, \triangle y, \triangle z$ are the displacement values along the coordinate axes Ox, Oy, Oz.

An arbitrary rotation matrix can be received as a result of a non-commutative product of the rotation matrices $\mathbf{R}_x, \mathbf{R}_y, \mathbf{R}_z$ around the principal axes by the angles $\alpha_x, \alpha_y, \alpha_z$:

$$\mathbf{R}_x = \begin{pmatrix} 1 & 0 & 0 \\ 0 & cos(\alpha_x) & sin(\alpha_x) \\ 0 & -sin(\alpha_x) & cos(\alpha_x) \end{pmatrix}, \mathbf{R}_y = \begin{pmatrix} cos(\alpha_y) & 0 & sin(\alpha_y) \\ 0 & 1 & 0 \\ -sin(\alpha_y) & 0 & cos(\alpha_y) \end{pmatrix},$$

$$\mathbf{R}_x = \begin{pmatrix} 1 & 0 & 0 \\ 0 & cos(\alpha_x) & sin(\alpha_x) \\ 0 & -sin(\alpha_x) & cos(\alpha_x) \end{pmatrix}$$

The vector $\mathbf{P}$ and the matrix $\mathbf{M}$ are taken: $P = (0 \quad 0 \quad 0)^T$, $\mathbf{M} = (1)$.

It can be seen that the implementation of these transformations is possible if the network has nodes with known coordinates – N_{kc}. For three-dimensional space, the number of such nodes should be $N_{kc} \geq 3$, the nodes should not lie on one straight line, which is possible if such nodes are placed on the street lighting poles. Thus, the procedure for finding nodes' coordinates can be described as:

1. introduce the third coordinate system CS3;
2. move coordinate system CS1 so that one of the nodes with known coordinates Y_{kc1} is at the origin of coordinates CS3;

3. perform the required turns so that the second node with the known coordinates Y_{kc2} is located on one of the main axes;
4. move the coordinate system CS2 so that the node corresponding to the node Y_{kc1} is at the origin of coordinates CS3;
5. perform the required turns so that the coordinates of the nodes of the calculated network fragment corresponding to the nodes with known coordinates Y_{kc2}, Y_{kc3}, coincided with the coordinates Y_{kc2}, Y_{kc3} in CS3;
6. perform the inverse transformations described in this section.

The result of these transformations over a network fragment obtained as a result of calculations (Fig. 3b) is shown in Fig. 4. Here, the nodes of the network whose coordinates are to be determined are marked in red, and the nodes obtained as a result of the calculations are blue.

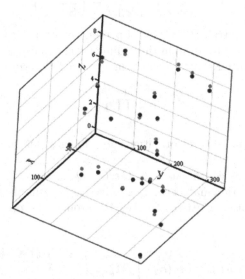

Fig. 4. The location of the nodes of the network fragment in space: (red - the source location, blue - calculated location) (Color figure online)

5   Simulation Evaluation

Assuming that a network fragment is composed of 100 nodes in 3-dimensional space with coordinates (x, y, z) generated randomly in (0, 1000 m), (0, 1000 m), and (0, 100 m), respectively. In this fragment, all nodes can receive signals from each other, therefore it is possible to determine distances between each pair of nodes. The actual distances between nodes are denoted by the matrix **D**.

Adding the noise values to the actual distances represents the errors when determining distances between nodes. A noise coefficient k is used in (11) to represent the noise. Noise values N are added to the distance matrix as follows:

$$\mathbf{N} = k \times rand_{100 \times 100}$$
$$\mathbf{N} = \mathbf{N} + \mathbf{N}^T \; and \; diag(\mathbf{N}) = 0 \tag{11}$$
$$\mathbf{D}_{noise} = \mathbf{D} + \mathbf{N}$$

First of all, we use a goodness-of-fit statistic based on the differences between the actual distances and the distances between the found coordinates after spatial transformations. A stress value was presented by Krusal in his paper about multidimensional scaling [9]. The distances are compared according to the stress value calculated by (12). According to Krusal's experience, the stress values (Table 3) are used as a recommendation to evaluate the difference of distances between actual and found coordinates. Therefore, it is necessary to use the additional methods for comparing the results. With each simulation run, the different noise values are generated. The received stress values obtained from the simulation results are presented in Fig. 5.

$$stress = \sqrt{\frac{\sum \left(d_{m,n} - \hat{d}_{m,n} \right)^2}{\sum d_{m,n}^2}} \tag{12}$$

Table 3. Evaluation of stress values

Stress	Goodness-of-fit
Stress $\geq$ 0.200	Poor
$0.100 \leq$ stress < 0.200	Fair
$0.050 \leq$ stress < 0.100	Good
$0.025 \leq$ stress < 0.050	Excellent
$0.000 \leq$ stress < 0.025	Perfect

As shown in Fig. 5, with the stress values are in the perfect interval with the noise coefficient $k = \{1, 2\}$. That means that they found coordinates might be close to the actual coordinates. The distance differences of each node are shown in Fig. 6, where with $k = \{1, 2\}$ distances between the actual and calculated nodes are small (Fig. 6a). However, with $k = 3$ (Fig. 6b) these distances are bigger, though the stress value is in the good interval in this case. In our purpose, the stress values may be considered in the other intervals. Thus, it is necessary to consider the differences between X and $\hat{X}$, Y, and $\hat{Y}$, Z, and $\hat{Z}$. As shown in Fig. 7 with $k = \{1, 3\}$, the differences are much related to Z values while there are small differences in X and Y. The calculated coordinates of (X, Y) are close to the actual values. Thus, the latitudes and longitudes of nodes were found with the errors less than the altitudes.

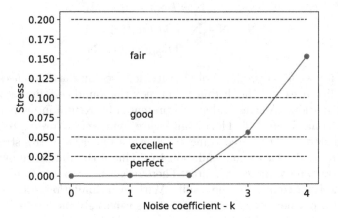

Fig. 5. Stress value

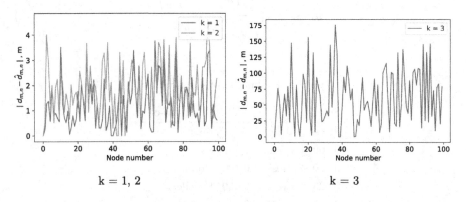

k = 1, 2   k = 3

Fig. 6. Distance differences, m

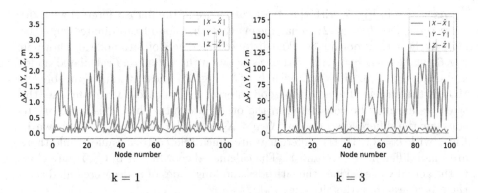

k = 1   k = 3

Fig. 7. Differences $\triangle X, \triangle Y, \triangle Z$, m

6 Conclusion

Thus, based on the results of the computational experiment, we can draw the following conclusions:

1. The metric multidimensional scaling (MDS) method allows to restore a three-dimensional model of a wireless mesh network with a high degree of accuracy.
2. The efficiency of the MDS method is ensured in the case of constructing a matrix of differences between objects (distance between nodes) by the method of symmetric bilateral bidirectional measurement of distance SDS-TWR. The considered methods RSSI, TDOA, TOA and others introduce a significant error and limit the dimension of the space to 2, or cannot be used in radio systems with a narrow frequency band.
3. For the final calculation of the coordinates of nodes in space, there must be at least 3 nodes with previously known coordinates located on more than one line.

Acknowledgments. The publication has been prepared with the support of the grant from the President of the Russian Federation for state support of leading scientific schools of the Russian Federation according to the research project HIII-2604.2020.9.

References

1. Queralta, J.P., Gia, T., Zou, Z., Tenhunen, H., Westerlund, T.: Comparative study of LPWAN technologies on unlicensed bands for m2m communication in the IoT: beyond LoRa and LoRaWAN. Proc. Comput. Sci. **155**, 343–350 (2019). https://doi.org/10.1016/j.procs.2019.08.049
2. Kirichek, R., Vishnevsky, V., Pham, V.D., Koucheryavy, A.: Analytic model of a mesh topology based on LoRa technology. In: 2020 22nd International Conferenceon Advanced Communication Technology (ICACT), pp. 251–255. IEEE (2020). https://doi.org/10.23919/ICACT48636.2020.9061519
3. ITU. Recommendation ITU-R P.1411-9 Radio wave propagation data and prediction methods for planning outdoor short-range radio communication systems and local radio networks in the frequency range 300 MHz to 100 GHz. ITU (2017)
4. Semtech Corporation: datasheet SX1276/77/78/79 LoRa Transciever, p. 132 (2019)
5. ITU. Report ITU-R SM.2211-1 Comparison of methods for determining the geographical location of a signal source based on differences in arrival times and arrival angles. International Telecommunications Union, Geneva (2015)
6. Davison, M.L., Kamensky, V.S., Ayvazyan, S.A.: Multidimensional scaling: visual presentation methods. Finance and Statistics, Moscow (1988)
7. Lloyd, E., Lederman, W.: Handbook of Applied Statistics, vol. 2. Finance and Statistics, Moscow (1989)
8. Rogers, D., Adams, J.: Mathematical Foundations of Machine Graphics. World, Moscow (2001)
9. Kruskal, J.B.: Multidimensional scaling by optimizing goodness of fit to a nonmetric hypothesis. Psychometrika **29**, 1–27 (1964). https://doi.org/10.1007/BF02289565

Applying the Concept of Software-Defined Networking in Wireless Mesh Network

Ekaterina Kuznetsova[1], Yulia Avakyan[1], Van Dai Pham[1(✉)] [ID],
and Ruslan Kirichek[1,2]

[1] Bonch-Bruevich Saint-Petersburg State University of Telecommunications,
193232 Saint Petersburg, Russia
cotti31@gmail.com, avakyanyulia@gmail.com, fam.vd@spbgut.ru,
kirichek@sut.ru
[2] V.A. Trapeznikov Institute of Control Sciences of Russian Academy of Sciences,
117997 Moscow, Russia

Abstract. Nowadays, many networks are deployed in a mesh topology. Especially, most wireless sensor networks also use multi-hop or mesh communication to exchange sensor data between devices. Increasing the number of nodes leads to the requirement of flexible deployment and configuration in such networks. Taking advantage of software-defined networking (SDN), this article discusses applying the SDN concept to manage wireless mesh sensor networks, in which the network management is carried out with the assisted SDN controller. Based on the simulation models, a series of computer experiments was performed to evaluate the network performance with and without SDN support. Based on the simulation results, the wireless mesh network supported by the SDN controller showed more efficiency in bandwidth, jitter time, and packet loss.

Keywords: IoT · Wireless sensor network · Wireless mesh networks · SDN · Controller · Modeling

1 Introduction

Nowadays, wireless technologies are becoming one of the most widely used technologies in everyday life. The wireless communication technologies enable to exchange information quickly, without using a cable transmission medium. As a part of the Internet of Things (IoT), most IoT devices are communicated with each other via wireless networks. As known-well wireless sensor networks such as ZigBee, Z-Wave, Bluetooth Low Energy, all nodes can exchange data in the mesh or multi-hop topology, which are flexible to add or remove nodes in the networks. It can be seen that wireless technologies are widely used in all aspects of life, from the industrial field to a small area of home use.

© Springer Nature Switzerland AG 2020
O. Galinina et al. (Eds.): NEW2AN 2020/ruSMART 2020, LNCS 12526, pp. 28–38, 2020.
https://doi.org/10.1007/978-3-030-65729-1_3

However, wireless technology is especially vulnerable to data transmission, because it sends electromagnetic waves to transmit signals. The transfer process will not proceed optimally if there is an obstacle between the sender and the receiver. Buildings are one of the most common obstacles in wireless technology, even when passing through one wall, the signal weakens. Trees and people can also interfere. To minimize signal attenuation, a decision was made to reduce obstacles. The right placement and choice of devices will help overcome obstacles. Moreover, when the receiver is far from the transmitter, it is required to have additional nodes to relay the data between them. In wireless sensor networks, multi-hop communication is often used to transmit the data to the gateway. A mesh-based network is characterized by high reliability, high throughput, and reduced power consumption. High reliability is ensured by a redundancy of nodes (in the event of a failure of one node, data will be bypassed differently). Using multiple alternative routes increases network bandwidth. Reducing power consumption is achieved by reducing the power of the signals by transmitting data through a larger number of nodes separated by shorter distances. The use of mesh topology in wireless wide (WWAN) and metropolitan (WMAN) networks is being actively studied [11].

In recent years, the emergence of various types of networks and data requires the networks are more flexible, scalable, and reusable for various applications. Especially in the wireless mesh networks used for IoT applications, there are requirements for network management such as device management, routing traffic management, data management, etc. A concept of Software Defined Networking (SDN) is considered as a solution for managing the network. SDN enables configuring and managing the networks at the centralized controller [7,12]. Applying the SDN approach to IoT networks has shown various improvements in network and service management [4,13].

As well, it enables developing different network solutions for the networks based on the collected information. In this work, we consider an approach of using SDN assisted for the wireless mesh network collecting data sensor. To evaluate the network performance, we use a network simulation to compare the networks with and without using SDN-controller.

2   Technologies Overview

2.1   Mesh Network

Wireless networks, in particular Wireless Mesh Networks (WMN), are one of the most promising wireless technologies for building highly scalable wireless transport networks for energy saving systems [14], renewable energy sources [1] and solar energy collection stations [3]. Mesh networks are used to solve a wide range of problems. Depending on the task requirement, the behavior of the mesh topology can be configured most appropriately.

Mesh network is a distributed data transmission system. In such a network, all nodes connect and exchange information without using a central server. Mesh topology enables long-distance data transfer by dividing the entire route into several short hopes. Thus, the intermediate nodes contribute to the amplification of the signal and its transmission to the destination point. This mesh routing principle can provide high throughput in the coverage area [2]. The mesh topology provides the ability to rebuild the network at any given time while maintaining connectivity. The network is obliged to continue working, despite the movement of participants or their exit from the network.

The mesh network consists of the following components:

- Node – is an equal participant in the network.
- Route – a chain of intermediate nodes needed to transmit a data packet. The choice of route depends on the routing algorithm for transmitting traffic.
- Gateway – the device that receives and extracts useful data from packets and then encapsulates them and forwards it to the other networks.

Theoretically, traffic goes from the host to the gateway, or from the gateway to the host along a certain path. But nodes can also exchange traffic within the network.

The network coverage area is divided into cluster zones, in each of which access points are located. The number of clusters is theoretically unlimited. A fragment of a mesh network is shown in Fig. 1.

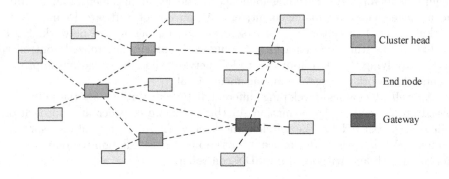

Fig. 1. A fragment of a mesh network

One of the access points is the head node and it is connected to the trunk information channel. The connection is via cable or radio channel. The head nodes are interconnected via a transport radio channel. The connection takes place between the nearest neighbors. The remaining nodes and gateways in the cluster are also connected. Each access point can create network subscriber tables with control of the transport channel and support for dynamic traffic routing along the optimal path through neighboring points, using routing protocols in the mesh network [10]. If any of the access points fail, then traffic will be automatically redirected along the new route, which ensures the delivery of data to the addressee in minimum time.

2.2   Software-Defined Networking

The main feature of the SDN is the separation of the control plane from the data plane. A typical network device consists of three components (Fig. 2):

1. Administration level (Management Plane) provides device management.
2. The level of traffic control (Control Plane) contains various algorithms and functionality that automatically respond to traffic changes.
3. Traffic transmission (Data Plane) contains functionality providing physical data transmission.

Fig. 2. Typical SDN architecture

The logical model is shown in Fig. 3.

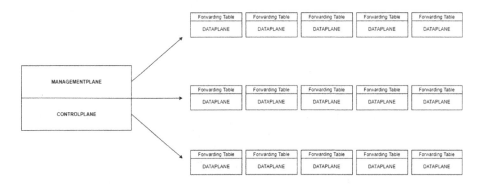

Fig. 3. The logical model of network devices in the SDN

All intelligence in SDN (Management Plane and Control Plane) is transferred to a separate central device called the SDN controller. Thus, the network device only serves the data stream (Data Plane traffic transfer level), becoming simpler and cheaper. The network device cannot be completely deprived of intelligence, but it is enough to replace it with a simple forwarding table.

Different logics are developed in the controller to support the entire network based on various types of network information, such as status information, topology, statistics, and much more. The main element that enables the controller to interact with network devices is the standard protocol for SDN – Openflow. The first effort of approaching SDN in wireless sensor networks (WSN) in [6] presented the SDN architecture for WSNs and the key challenges in research. The authors proposed Sensor OpenFlow that has many changes compared with OpenFlow in the wired network. The controller is used to manage switch flow tables. Based on them, a decision is made to transfer the received packet to a specific port on the switch. Thus, direct network connections are formed in the network with minimal data transmission delays and the necessary parameters. Applying the concept of Software Defined Networking to WSNs has attracted wide attention with more overview in surveys [5,9].

Applying the SDN concept to sensor networks, we can manage and control all networks through a centralized controller. Since the SDN was originally conceived for wired networks, the controller in the traditional case statically sets the paths to each switch so that it can run centralized routing algorithms. However, in wireless networks, the controller must detect all the switches before it can run centralized routing algorithms.

The advantage of SDN-based management in sensor networks is the centralized management of the entire network, simplifying the deployment of control protocols and applications across the network on demand. SDN in mesh networks has found application in the management of unmanned aerial vehicles [8] and many other areas [9].

3   Network and Simulation Modeling

3.1   SDN-assisted WMN

SDN principles are integrated into wireless mesh networks using OpenFlow switches with wireless interfaces, based on IEEE 802.11 protocols. The OpenFlow protocol is used to manage network switches and routers from a central device that is a network controller.

The software-defined wireless mesh network can take advantage of OpenFlow and use the Optimized Link State Routing (OLSR) protocol routing OpenFlow traffic data. Software-defined wireless mesh network consists of a POX controller, OLSR, software tiered switch Open vSwitch, Python scripts. A wireless mesh router is required to allow connectivity to various networks and to provide Internet connectivity and work as a gateway. The router is linked up to the OpenFlow controller via a wireless or wired interface.

SDN concept, which is implemented using OpenFlow, provides easy management and network flexibility. The use of wireless resources can be increased by the central server.

Figure 4 presents the concept of a wireless mesh network using the SDN concept. This network includes several mesh routers to provide Internet access, as well as a connection interface for end-users SDN connections are presented from the OpenFlow controller to each router. Such connections may be wired or wireless.

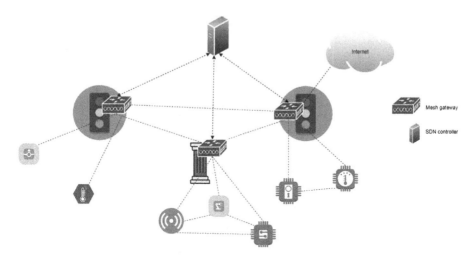

Fig. 4. SDN over Wireless Mesh Network

3.2 Simulation Model

Using only the mesh topology in LPWAN, the network is overloaded with service traffic and stops working. Therefore, the possibility of using an SDN controller to separate control traffic is considered, thereby unloading the network there.

For comparison, two network models are presented. The first is a regular auto-routed mesh network. The topology will consist of 100 end nodes - sensors for collecting indicators and 10 gateways for communication within the network. A fragment of the topology is shown in Fig. 5.

The second model network also consist of 100 end nodes - sensors, 10 gateways, and one SDN controller, which will set the routing logic. A fragment of the topology is shown in Fig. 6.

The network was implemented using an SDN emulation platform called Mininet. The main Mininet does not provide wireless support, but there is a branch of the Mininet network emulator called Mininet-WiFi. Contains virtualized Wi-Fi stations and access points based on standard wireless drivers. The Mininet-WiFi extension provides basic support for modeling wireless lines, so simulation of the previously described models was performed in it. The Mininet-WiFi emulator, like Mininet, runs on the Linux operating system, and network-scripts are written in Python.

To measure network parameters, a traffic generator simulating data transmission was also written. The basis was the cross-platform client-server program Iperf, which allows testing the network performance.

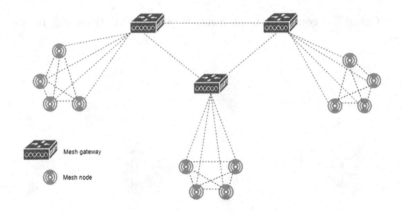

Fig. 5. Fragment of a regular mesh topology

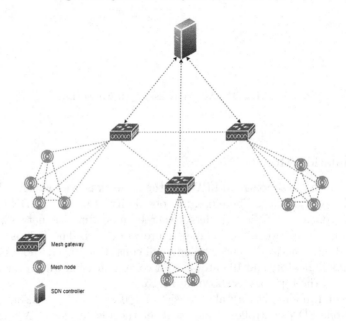

Fig. 6. Fragment of a mesh topology with an SDN controller

During the simulation, iperf clients and servers were launched on several devices to represent the operation of a real network, and the results were collected from only one iperf client-server connection.

Data transmission was carried out for 200 s with a measurement interval of 1 s and transmitted each datagram with a size of 200 bytes. As a result of the simulation, we get a log file from the results of the iperf utility.

4   Modeling Results

To evaluate the effectiveness of networks, the parameters collected and analyzed during the experiment using the Ipeft utility are considered. Simulation results are compared in three ways: bandwidth, jitter time, and packet loss.

Figure 7 shows the results of measuring the bandwidth of the two models. A mesh network with SDN controller support showed higher bandwidth than a mesh network without an SDN controller. The network managed by the controller shows that the amount of traffic is effectively transmitted through the transit nodes. In particular, in a mesh network, the bandwidth of 1.07 Mb/s has a probability of 0.3. At the same time, in a mesh network with an SDN controller, the bandwidth can be 1.07 Mb/s with a probability of 0.8. Thus, the delay time and jitter of data transmission can be reduced in the proposed network model.

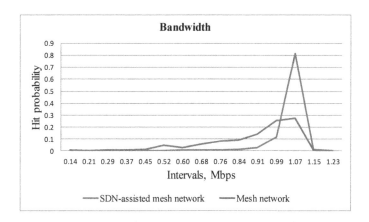

Fig. 7. Probability distribution of bandwidth

Figure 8 and Fig. 9 show the results of measuring the jitter of two models, as well as the number of lost datagrams during the simulation time. The jitter parameter represents a variance of datagram latencies. The lower jitter shows that the data transmission delay is more stable in the network-assisted by SDN. Based on the measurement results obtained in the probability distribution, we can see that jitter of 2.15 ms has a probability of 0.9 in the SDN-assisted mesh network while it has a probability of less than 0.4 in the mesh network without supported SDN, i.e. about 90% transmitted datagrams have the latencies with a variance of 2.15 ms. Moreover, the network assessment also is considered in the number of lost datagrams measured every second. According to the measurement results shown in Fig, the SDN-assisted mesh network provides a lower loss rate while the number of lost datagrams is proximally double higher in the network without assisted SDN.

The network with the SDN controller has lower jitter and packet loss rates, which is an indicator of efficiency. The average values of simulation results are presented in Table 1.

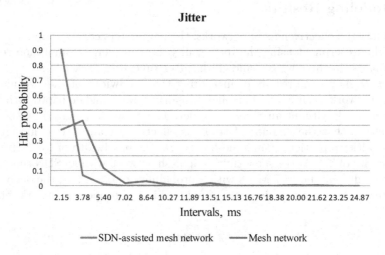

Fig. 8. Probability distribution of jitter

Table 1. Average values of simulation results.

Network	Bandwidth (Mbps)	Jitter (ms)	Lost/Total Datagrams	Lost datagrams (%)
SDN-assisted mesh network	1.01	0.605	4355/130743	3.3
Mesh network	0.875	0.848	21789/131073	16.6

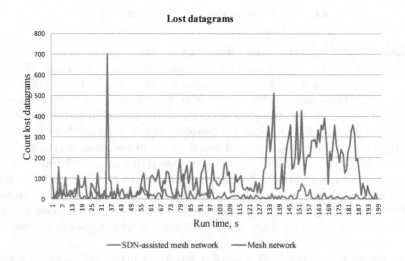

Fig. 9. Datagram loss statistic

5 Conclusion

In this article, we proposed the use of the concept of software-defined networks for the wireless mesh network collecting sensor data. Two simulation models were developed - with an SDN controller and a regular auto-routed mesh network. The results of the analysis of these models and experiments have shown the effectiveness of using the concept of software-defined networks in the mesh networks. This concept allows us to achieve the best performance in terms of bandwidth, packet loss, and jitter. The use of software-defined networks helps to solve the problems that arise in the mesh networks. Looking into the future, we plan to expand our work and compare the performance.

Acknowledgments. The publication has been prepared with the support of the grant from the President of the Russian Federation for state support of leading scientific schools of the Russian Federation according to the research project No. HIII-2604.2020.9.

References

1. Cai, L.X., Liu, Y., Luan, T.H., Shen, X., Mark, J.W., Poor, H.V.: Sustainability analysis and resource management for wireless mesh networks with renewable energy supplies. IEEE J. Sel. Areas Commun. **32**(2), 345–355 (2014). https://doi.org/10.1109/jsac.2014.141214
2. Cheng, S.M., Lin, P., Huang, D.W., Yang, S.R.: A study on distributed/centralized scheduling for wireless mesh network. In: Proceeding of the 2006 International Conference on Communications and Mobile Computing - IWCMC. ACM Press (2006). https://doi.org/10.1145/1143549.1143668
3. Fadlullah, Z.M., Nakajo, T., Nishiyama, H., Owada, Y., Hamaguchi, K., Kato, N.: Field measurement of an implemented solar powered BS-based wireless mesh network. IEEE Wirel. Commun. **22**(3), 137–143 (2015). https://doi.org/10.1109/mwc.2015.7143337
4. Kirichek, R., Vladyko, A., Zakharov, M., Koucheryavy, A.: Model networks for internet of things and SDN. In: 2016 18th International Conference on Advanced Communication Technology (ICACT). IEEE (2016). https://doi.org/10.1109/icact.2016.7423280
5. Kobo, H.I., Abu-Mahfouz, A.M., Hancke, G.P.: A survey on software-defined wireless sensor networks: challenges and design requirements. IEEE Access **5**, 1872–1899 (2017). https://doi.org/10.1109/access.2017.2666200
6. Luo, T., Tan, H.P., Quek, T.Q.S.: Sensor OpenFlow: enabling software-defined wireless sensor networks. IEEE Commun. Lett. **16**(11), 1896–1899 (2012). https://doi.org/10.1109/lcomm.2012.092812.121712
7. Masood, M., Fouad, M.M., Seyedzadeh, S., Glesk, I.: Energy efficient software defined networking algorithm for wireless sensor networks. Transp. Res. Proc. **40**, 1481–1488 (2019). https://doi.org/10.1016/j.trpro.2019.07.205
8. McCoy, J., Rawat, D.B.: Software-defined networking for unmanned aerial vehicular networking and security: a survey. Electronics **8**(12), 1468 (2019). https://doi.org/10.3390/electronics8121468

9. Ndiaye, M., Hancke, G., Abu-Mahfouz, A.: Software defined networking for improved wireless sensor network management: a survey. Sensors **17**(5), 1031 (2017). https://doi.org/10.3390/s17051031
10. Popkov, G.: Mesh-networks: development prospects, possible application. Probl. Inf. **3**, 74–79 (2012)
11. Shemchuk, Y.: LPWAN and other wireless technologie. Control Eng. Russ. IIoT **1**, 54–58 (2019)
12. Vladyko, A., Muthanna, A., Kirichek, R.: Comprehensive SDN testing based on model network. In: Galinina, O., Balandin, S., Koucheryavy, Y. (eds.) Internet of Things, Smart Spaces, and Next Generation Networks and Systems. Lecture Notes in Computer Science, vol. 9870, pp. 539–549. Springer, Cham (2016). https://doi.org/10.1007/978-3-319-46301-8_45
13. Volkov, A., Muhathanna, A., Pirmagomedov, R., Kirichek, R.: SDN approach to control internet of thing medical applications traffic. In: Vishnevskiy, V., Samouylov, K., Kozyrev, D. (eds.) Distributed Computer and Communication Networks. Communications in Computer and Information Science, vol. 700, pp. 467–476. Springer, Cham (2017). https://doi.org/10.1007/978-3-319-66836-9_3
14. Xu, Y., Wang, W.: Wireless mesh network in smart grid: modeling and analysis for time critical communications. IEEE Trans. Wirel. Commun. **12**(7), 3360–3371 (2013). https://doi.org/10.1109/twc.2013.061713.121545

Analytical Model for Software Defined Network Considering Memory Node for Routing Rules

Evgeny Mokrov[1]([✉]) [iD], Dmitry Poluektov[1] [iD], Egor Machnev[1] [iD],
Sergey Shorgin[2] [iD], Abdukodir Khakimov[1] [iD], and Jiri Hosek[3] [iD]

[1] Peoples' Friendship University of Russia (RUDN University),
6 Miklukho-Maklaya st., Moscow 117198, Russian Federation
{mokrov-ev,poluektov-ds,machnev-ea,khakimov-aa}@rudn.ru
[2] Federal Research Center "Computer Science and Control" of the Russian Academy
of Sciences, 44-2 Vavilov St., Moscow 119333, Russian Federation
sshorgin@ipiran.ru
[3] Brno University of Technology, Technicka 3082/12, Brno, Czech Republic
hosek@feec.vutbr.cz

Abstract. In this work a software defined network (SDN) is studied as a
queueing network. The main point of the system is that the switch memory node, storing routing rules is modeled separately. The memory node
impacts the distribution of the newly arrived packets among the other
nodes. In this work we propose analytical and simulation model to analyze the performance of the considered network. Analytical model covers
a simplified network case with one flow type, while simulation model let
us analyze a general-case of SDN network segment with multiple flow
types.

Keywords: Software-defined networking · Queueing model · SDN
controller · OpenFlow · Analytical model · Simulation

1 Introduction

Nowadays, 5G network receives focused attention in the scientific community.
This research topic gives rise to study in different areas. Some of the current studies include the possibility of using wireless radio-frequency (RF) power transfer
considered in [5] or the problem of network traffic offloading addressed in [12].
Some papers focus more on socio-technical aspect, like [11], where they consider

The publication has been prepared with the support of the "RUDN University Program
5-100" (recipients D. Poluektov, A. Khakimov, Sections 1, 2, 5). The reported study
was funded by RFBR, project number 18-00-01555(18-00-01685) (recipients E. Mokrov,
Section 4). The reported study was funded by RFBR, project number 20-37-70079
(recipient E. Mokrov, Section 3). For the research, infrastructure of the 5G Lab RUDN
(Russia) was used.

© Springer Nature Switzerland AG 2020
O. Galinina et al. (Eds.): NEW2AN 2020/ruSMART 2020, LNCS 12526, pp. 39–55, 2020.
https://doi.org/10.1007/978-3-030-65729-1_4

social aware device-to-device network performance. The fundamental concept of SDN (Software Defined Networking) changes the legacy understanding of network architecture by entering the terms of programmable networks and abstracting from the physical network infrastructure. The original definition of SDN is the separation among network management functionality and traffic flow management (Control Plane) and packet data switching functionality (DataPlane). Functions for calculating network topology and traffic routing tables are performed on a separate device – the network controller. All network intelligence is located on the network controller. Packet switching and routing (Data Plane) functions are performed on network equipment that supports loading switching tables from a central network controller, usually using the OpenFlow Protocol. This allows you to scale the resources required for traffic control, regardless of the resources required for packet switching, in order to ensure the most efficient hardware load. Besides, centralizing the control level reduces the number of managed smart devices, simplifies network operation, and makes it possible to organize the services. The development of the idea of centralizing network control functions allows us to define SDN more widely. This is the development of standard protocols and data models that will allow you to organize logically centralized management of multi-vendor and multi-level networks. SDN controllers provide higher-level systems with an abstract topology and service models, simplifying service organization and enabling to create new applications that use network programming capabilities.

For analytical modeling of OpenFlow based SDN a queueing theory with feedbacks was used in [2,7] to display the interaction between the control plane and the data plane, where the switch is modeled as a $M/M/1$ queue, and the controller – as a $M/M/1/S$ queueing system with feedbacks. Work [7] is the first attempt to reflect the interaction between the controller and the switch. The subsequent work of these authors [8] uses the Jackson network to model the data plane. The controller is separately modeled as an $M/M/1$ queue (taking into account both infinite and finite buffer scenarios). Based on the OpenFlow standard [13], traffic coming from the controller to the switch should not be able to go back to the controller. However, this important aspect has not been taken into account by both models [7,8]; they do not distinguish between signaling and data traffic.

In [14] the requests for flow type determination from switches to controller are modeled as a process of $M^K/M/1$ series of requests to get the average time of flow service. Given the limited time to define a rule for flow transmission, the maximum number of switches per controller can be defined. However, the feedback between the data plane and the controller is not taken into account in this work.

The most accurate simulations of OpenFlow protocol on the switch is given by authors of [9,10] and the authors of [6] by dividing the packets that just recently came into the system and the packets that returned from the controller, which combines extensive work in queuing models for SDN.

However, extensive research does not accurately describe the work of the SDN network and does not allow an analytical assessment of all performance parameters. Based on approach used in [6,8,14] we have considered the system with division of incoming flows by traffic types and added the node responsible for the rule storage in the flow table.

Another effective analytical method besides queueing theory is network computation which is also used for SDN and OpenFlow networks analysis [3,4]. This approach allows to define the upper limits of event processing and SDN controller buffer size.

In this work we studied SDN network using queueing theory. First, in Sect. 2, we describe the SDN architecture and its main characteristic. Then, in Sect. 3 we propose an analytical model for a segment of the considered network in general case and later provide solution for a simplified case. Section 4 contains numerical analysis of the performance metrics for the single flow type case analytical model. That section also contains description of the constructed general-case simulation model and its results for multiple flow case.

2   System Model

We consider the case of using the SDN outband network as depicted in Fig. 1. The constructed network consists of a controller and four sequentially connected switches, each of the switches has a dedicated channel for signal traffic from the controller. The system receives packets of different types of services. The controller stores a table of all rules for forwarding packets according to the types of services. Each switch has a limited memory that stores information about the most frequent types of services that arrive at it.

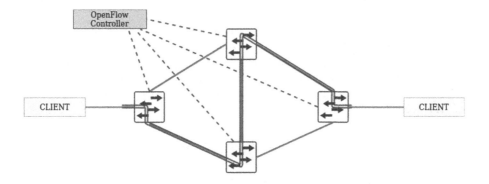

Fig. 1. Outband network architecture

When a new packet arrives at the switch, if the information about its type of service is present in the switch's memory, the packet is forwarded to the next switch according to a known route. If there is no route information for this type of service in the memory of the switch, the packet is redirected to the controller. When a packet arrives at the controller, the search for a rule to build a route for this packet is carried out, and then the packet is returned back to the switch that transmitted it, at the same time all the switches that enter the route for this type of service, the signal channel transmits a rule to build a route for this type of service. A rule on a switch can be deleted for two reasons: first, if there is insufficient memory for a new rule coming from the controller, or after a specified time has elapsed. In the first case, the switch deletes one of the old known rules according to a certain algorithm - the rule either for the oldest or for the rarest type of service. In the second case, the rule is deleted if for some specified time there were no packets of this type of service coming to the switch, and each new call updates this timer.

3   Analytical Model

3.1   General Case

This system can be represented as a queueing network consisting of $L + 1$ nodes, where L is the number of network switches. K incoming flows correspond to the number of different types of services are supposed to be Poisson distributed with means λ_k, $k = 1, ..., K$. Each node of the switch has a memory buffer, which can contain up to $M \leq N$ rules and processes the application for some time $T_s(n_m)$, and the rule memory is exactly T_m time units, the controller node processes each application for a constant time T_c. Here m is the number of rules stored in the memory of the switch when it serves a new packet.

Due to the restrictions imposed, namely, the fact that the controller sends signal information to all nodes of the network at once, we believe that, with the considered architecture, interlocks can only occur at the first node of the network, so we introduce the following simplified model.

In the model presented in Fig. 2 we consider only the controller and one of the network switches for which we allocate its memory as a separate node. It should be noted, that while all types of service share controller and switch queues each of them has its own memory slot, represented as a separate node.

Let the system input K Poisson's incoming flows with intensity $\lambda(k), k = 1, ..., K$. According to the delta function

$$\delta(n_m(k), j) = \begin{cases} 1, n_m(k) = j, \\ 0, n_m(k) \neq j. \end{cases}$$

Incoming flow applications follow either to the Switch node corresponding to the switch or to the Controller node corresponding to the controller.

A) The Switch node structure corresponds to the $G/G/1/S$ system. At the time of request for this node, the package knows its rule, so it is serviced according to the service discipline. We also enter a simplistic assumption that there are no losses in the system due to rule loss during the time when the request

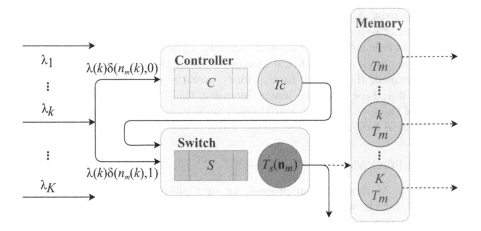

Fig. 2. Queueing Model of the system

was in the service queue – if the request is on the switch, it is guaranteed to be serviced. This simplification correlates sufficiently with the technical model [1], because in practice this situation is very rare.

The duration of service on the device is a random value with the $S_k(\mathbf{m})$ distribution function, which generally depends on the number of rules in the Memory node (the more rules, the more time it takes to search for it). After the service at the Switch node is over, the request goes to the Memory node, updating the rule storage timer.

B) The Switch node structure corresponds to the $G/G/1/S$ system. At the time of request for this node, the package knows its rule, so it is serviced according to the service discipline. We also enter a simplistic assumption that there are no losses in the system due to rule loss during the time when the request was in the service queue – if the request is on the switch, it is guaranteed to be serviced. This simplification correlates sufficiently with the technical model [1], because in practice this situation is very rare.

The structure of the Controller node corresponds to the $G/G/1/C$ system. At the moment the request is received on this node, the package queues up to search for the advisory rule. The search duration is the duration of servicing the request on the device. In general, it is a random value with infinitely small dispersion, which can be approximated by some constant T_c. After completion of service on the Controller node, the request is sent to the Switch node to transfer the information packet, as well as to the Memory node to update knowledge about the rule and start the storage timer.

C) Structure of the Memory node. The node consists of K devices, and no more than M devices can be occupied at the same time ($M << K$). The incoming request of the k-th thread stands on the k-th device, respectively. In this case, the request will find the device free if the rules for this traffic type have not been in memory before, or the request located on it will be supplanted if the rule existed and it is necessary to update the timer for its storage. By duration of request service here we understand the duration of rule storage in the switch memory – constant value T_m. The request coming from the Controller node can catch the Memory node in the state when M devices are occupied, then it will have priority over the request that corresponds to the flow type with the lowest intensity, thus displacing it. Denote the state of the k-th device in the Memory node as $n_m(k) =\{1$, device is busy; 0, device is free$\}$.

3.2 Simplified Model

To acquire a Markov random process, let us make the following simplifying assumption. Let the service duration at each node of the network be random values with an exponential probability distribution and the distribution parameters:

1. at the Switch node – μ_s,
2. on the Controller node – μ_c,
3. on the Memory node – μ_m,

are the same for all types of threads.

Table 1 contains descriptions for all the main parameters used to describe the model.

In that case, we can introduce random process $\mathbf{X}(t) = (\mathbf{n}_c, \mathbf{n}_s, \mathbf{n}_m)(t)$ to describe the considered system. Its state space is given in (1).

$$\mathbf{X} = \{(\mathbf{n}_c, \mathbf{n}_s, \mathbf{n}_m) : \mathbf{n}_c = (n_c(1), ..., n_c(K)), \sum_{k=1}^{K} n_c(k) \leq C,$$

$$\mathbf{n}_s = (n_s(1), ..., n_s(K)), \sum_{k=1}^{K} n_s(k) \leq S, \mathbf{n}_m = (n_m(1), ..., n_m(K)),$$

$$n_m(k) \in \{0, 1\}, \sum_{k=1}^{K} n_m(k) \leq M\} \tag{1}$$

Table 1. Parameter

Parameter	Description
K	The number of traffic types in the queueing network
$\lambda(k), k = 1, ..., K$	Arrival rate of the k-th traffic type
S	Switch queue length
C	Controller queue length
M	Number of memory slots
$n_m(k) \in 0, 1$	State of the k-th memory node server
μ_s	Switch node service rate
μ_c	Controller node service rate
μ_m	Memory node service rate

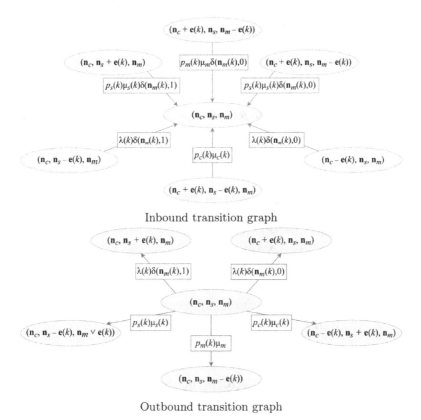

Fig. 3. Transition graphs for the central state

For the given process transition graphs can be acquired as shown in Fig. 3 an equilibrium system can be derived and the equation for its central state can be seen in (2).

$$p(\mathbf{n}_c, \mathbf{n}_s, \mathbf{n}_m) \sum_{k=1}^{K} (\lambda(k) + p_c(k)\mu_c(k) + p_s(k)\mu_s(k) + \mu_m) =$$

$$\sum_{k=1}^{K} (p(\mathbf{n}_c, \mathbf{n}_s - \mathbf{e}(k), \mathbf{n}_m)\lambda(k)\delta(n_m(k), 1) +$$

$$p(\mathbf{n}_c - \mathbf{e}(k), \mathbf{n}_s, \mathbf{n}_m)\lambda(k)\delta(n_m(k), 0) +$$

$$p(\mathbf{n}_c + \mathbf{e}(k), \mathbf{n}_s - \mathbf{e}(k), \mathbf{n}_m)p_c(k)\mu_c(k) +$$

$$p(\mathbf{n}_c, \mathbf{n}_s + \mathbf{e}(k), \mathbf{n}_m)p_s(k)\delta(n_m(k), 1)\mu_s(k) +$$

$$p(\mathbf{n}_c + \mathbf{e}(k), \mathbf{n}_s, \mathbf{n}_m - \mathbf{e}(k))p_s(k)\delta(n_m(k), 0)\mu_s(k) +$$

$$p(\mathbf{n}_c, \mathbf{n}_s, \mathbf{n}_m + \mathbf{e}(k))\delta(n_m(k), 0)\mu_m, \quad (\mathbf{n}_c, \mathbf{n}_s, \mathbf{n}_m) \in X \qquad (2)$$

where

$$p_i(k) = \frac{n_i(k)}{\sum\limits_{j=1}^{K} n_i(j)}, \; i \in \{c, s\}.$$

For the described system, the following parameters are studied: an average number of packets on controller and switch (3), average waiting time on the controller (5) and switch (7). Equations (4) and (6) gives us the average number of packets and average waiting time in the whole system.

$$N_i(k) = \sum_{(\mathbf{n}_c, \mathbf{n}_s, \mathbf{n}_m) \in \mathbf{X}} n_i(k) p(\mathbf{n}_c, \mathbf{n}_s, \mathbf{n}_m), \; i \in \{c, s\}, \tag{3}$$

$$N(k) = N_c(k) + N_s(k), \tag{4}$$

$$W_c(k) = \frac{N_c(k)}{\lambda(k)\hat{p}_c(k)}, \tag{5}$$

$$W(k) = \frac{N(k)}{\lambda(k)}, \tag{6}$$

$$W_s(k) = W(k) - \hat{p}_c(k)W_c(k), \tag{7}$$

where

$$\hat{p}_c(k) = \sum_{(\mathbf{n}_c, \mathbf{n}_s, \mathbf{n}_m) \in \mathbf{X}} p(\mathbf{n}_c, \mathbf{n}_s, \mathbf{n}_m)\delta(n_m(k), 0),$$

$$\hat{p}_s(k) = \sum_{(\mathbf{n}_c, \mathbf{n}_s, \mathbf{n}_m) \in \mathbf{X}} p(\mathbf{n}_c, \mathbf{n}_s, \mathbf{n}_m)\delta(n_m(k), 1),$$

and $\hat{p}_c(k) + \hat{p}_s(k) = 1$.

Here $\hat{p}_c(k)$ and $\hat{p}_s(k)$ are probabilities that a newly arrived packet would be sent to the controller or to switch correspondingly.

4   Simulation and Performance Analysis

4.1   Single Flow Numerical Analysis

In a view of the fact that the overall state space exponentially grows with the number of different traffic types, in the current study, we only aim to prove the derived mathematical model. Thus, we consider a single type of traffic and relatively small queue lengths, since each additional traffic type leads to the exponential extension of the state space. All the initial data for the analysis is presented in Table 2.

Since controller and switch nodes are mainly responsible only for searching for the routing rule and sending the packet and the packet doesn't change while in the system, we consider the times needed to serve it on the controller and on

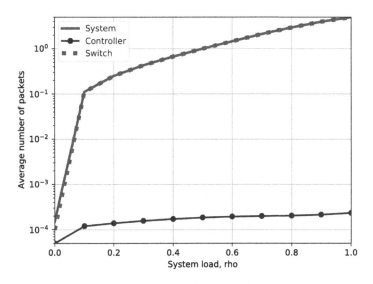

Average number of packets

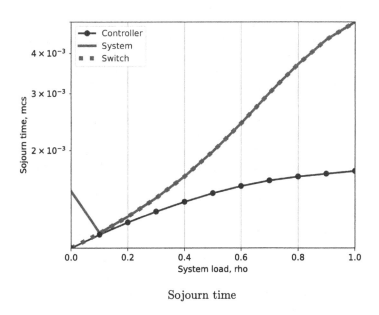

Sojourn time

Fig. 4. Performance metrics with respect to load

Table 2. Initial Data

Parameter	Value	Description
K	1	A single traffic type
M	1	Number of memory slots
$\mu_s = \mu_c$	1000	Controller and switch nodes service rate
μ_m	0.1	Memory node service rate
ρ	$0 < \frac{\lambda(1)}{\mu} \leq 1$	System load
$S = C$	10	Controller and switch queue lengths

switch identical. The average time a rule stays in memory is long enough so that to minimize controller load. The system is studied in the non-overloaded state.

Figure 4a shows the plots of the average number of packets on the controller, on the switch and in the system. The exponential scale of the y-axis used to depict the values for the controller since the values are much smaller than these on the switch. Figure 4b shows the average time a packet spends on the controller on the switch and in the system. Both plots are given dependant on the load of the first traffic type.

Figure 5 shows the same parameters under load $\lambda = 800$ dependant on the service rate of the memory node. One can see that both plots reflect similar behavior since the more packets are in the node the longer the average time to be served on this node is. Also, the less time a rule is kept in the memory node, the more frequent a packet is sent to the controller, resulting on one hand in an increase of the average number of packets and average time on the controller and in the system and on the other hand in decline of these values for the switch. The increase of packets in the system is due to the fact the part of the load is redirected to the controller.

It can be seen that for the listed data almost all the packets are immediately forwarded to the switch, resulting in its load being extremely close to that of the system. In this scenario, the controller is left largely unutilized.

Additionally, a generalized simulation model was developed for the considered system. In this model, Switch was divided into two additional nodes: *FlowTable* that performs the function of routing rule search, and *Processing*, responsible for sending packets.

This generalization allows using the model to get insight into the undergoing processes inside Switch, e.g., add rule search time in FlowTable before being forwarded either to Processing or to Controller. That time corresponds to the time necessary to confirm if the rule is currently present on Switch.

In order to better reflect analytical model, rule search time in the FlowTable node is assumed to be zero in the simulation model results provided in the current subsection. The initial data for the calculations, the results of which are given in this section are presented in Table 2. This analysis will verify compliance with the constructed models and then consider using a simulation model of a more complicated case of the network.

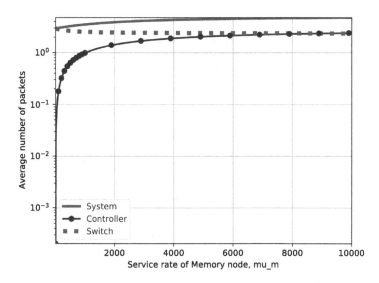

Average number of packets

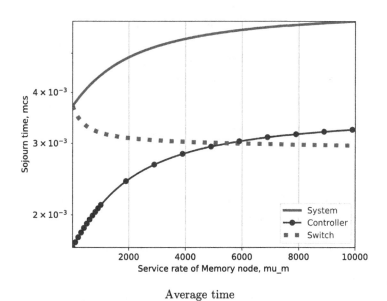

Average time

Fig. 5. Performance metrics with respect to memory node service rate

The main disadvantage of the proposed analytical model is the complexity of the calculation for a large number of incoming flows due to the increase in the state space. However the developed simulation model of the system does not suffer such a drawback.

The behavior of the plot obtained during simulation for the same initial data as the analytical model is very similar to the behavior of the analytical results with average divergence of about 1%. That allows us to confirm the correct operation of the developed simulator.

4.2   Multiple Flow Simulation

In practical SDN implementations, traffic is divided into many types. Therefore, we also consider scenario, where the number of incoming flows has been increased. For this scenario we also consider the processing time on the FlowTable node to be non-zero. The initial simulation data are shown in Table 3.

Table 3. Initial data for the multiple flow case.

Parameter	Value	Description
K	100	Number of different traffic types
M	100	Number of memory slots
μ_s^{-1}	0.01	Service time on Processing (mcs)
μ_c^{-1}	0.05	Service time on Controller (mcs)
μ_f^{-1}	0.05	Rule search time on FlowTable (mcs)
μ_m^{-1}	1000	Rule storage time in Memory (mcs)
S	30	Total buffer size on FlowTable and Processing
C	100	Buffer size on Controller
ρ	$0 < \frac{\sum_{k \in K} \lambda_k}{\mu_f} \leq 2$	Intensity of packet service (rule storage) in Memory

To begin with, we will carry out a trial similar to the previous one but with increased number of incoming flows. Thus, we can observe the correct operation of the system.

The plot of the average number of packets in the network nodes is presented in Fig. 6a.

It can be noted that the behavior of the plots does not differ much from those for a single flow, with the exception of the obtained values, since the total load and buffer sizes in the system nodes have changed. On Switch, the average number of packets increases until the system load increases to $\rho = 1$, then it tends to 30 - the total buffer size on Switch.

Figure 6b shows sojourn time on Switch. Here we see that the time on Switch increases evenly with increasing packet arrival rate, since the FlowTable node

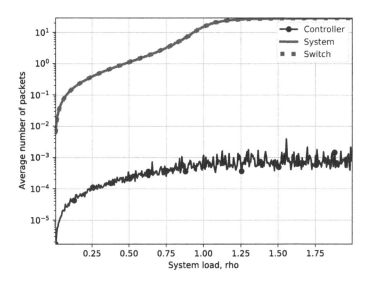

Average number of packets

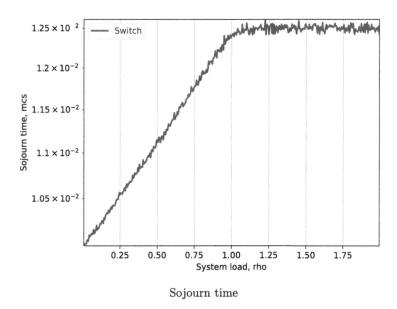

Sojourn time

Fig. 6. Performance metrics with respect to load for 100 traffic types.

successfully copes with the load. Then, under continuous increase of the load the buffer starts to overflow and some packets are being blocked in the system. Switch node sojourn time begins to tend to a constant value of 0.0125. The plot for system sojourn time is not present, since it will coincide with Switch plot as can be concluded from the previous plots. As for Controller, its sojourn time is almost constant since for the considered system the bottleneck is Switch, due to FlowTable being also located on it. Thus, for most figures in this section only plots for the Switch node are present.

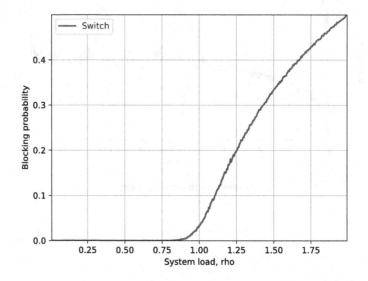

Fig. 7. Blocking probability with respect to load for 100 traffic types.

The blocking probability in the system is illustrated in Fig. 7. Blocking probability on Controller here tends to zero, since there are practically no packets for it. The main bottleneck in this case is Switch, or specifically, FlowTable since it is the first node where the packets arrive. Thus the plot behaviour closely resemble one for a simple single service model

Finally we consider the average number of packets in the system and its dependency on the rule storage time previously denoted as μ_m^{-1} in the analytical model. We fix the system load at a value of $\rho = 0.9$. Thus we get the system in a loaded state, while having a low level of blocking probability as can be seen from Fig. 7. Then we vary the rule storage time in Memory to get the corresponding plot for the average number of packets. All the other parameters are the same as in the previous trial. The plots of the average number of packets on Controller and Switch are given in Fig. 8.

The nearly stationary behavior of the average number of packets on Switch is expected, since the load on FloWTable is at a constant value $\rho = 0.9$. The average number of packets on Switch during the entire trial is about 8 packets. At the same time, one should notice a change in the number of packets on

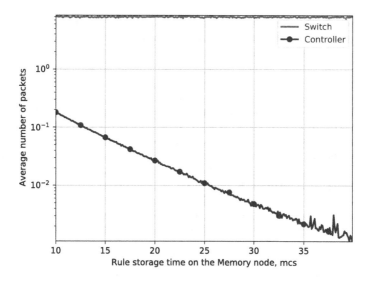

Fig. 8. Number of packets with respect to rule storage time.

Controller, since we lower the rule storage time, thus increasing rate of forwarding new packets on Controller. With a rule storage time of 10 mcs, an average number of packets on Controller equals 0.18. This makes up 10% of the total load on the system and 16.6% of the total number of packets passing through the system. At point 20 mcs, Controller receives 2.8% of the load, which meets the recommendations of the OpenFlow protocol and is a suitable value for this system.

5   Conclusions

In this paper we studied a software-defined network segment performance, consisting of a controller and several switches. To describe the behaviour of this network a mathematical model using queuing theory was proposed. In this model a memory node responsible for flow rule storage on the switch was modeled as a separate node with limited storage time. For the proposed model a state space, equilibrium equation system and equations to calculate main system parameters were derived. The proposed analytical model only covers single flow type case due to the exponential rise of state space elements with addition of flow types. To better analyze the considered system a simulation model was constructed. The results for the average packet number and sojourn time for analytical and simulation models are very similar in single flow type case. The constructed simulation model allowed us to use analyze system performance in multiple flow case. Based on the acquired results an existing analytical model can be improved to analyze multiple flow case. In Future works we plan to also verify the results given by the presented models by performing a trial using a SDN testbed. Also, we plan to formulate and solve an optimization problem to minimize end-to-end latency with respect to the flow rule storage time.

References

1. 5G PPP Architecture Working Group white paper, View on 5G Architecture. Technical report (2016)
2. Ateya, A., et al.: Chaotic salp swarm algorithm for SDN multi-controller networks. Eng. Sci. Technol. **22**(4), 1001–1012 (2019). https://doi.org/10.1016/j.jestch.2018. 12.015
3. Azodolmolky, S., Nejabati, R., Pazouki, M., Wieder, P., Yahyapour, R., Simeonidou, D.: An analytical model for software defined networking: a network calculus-based approach. In: 2013 IEEE Global Communications Conference (GLOBECOM), pp. 1397–1402 (2013). https://doi.org/10.1109/GLOCOM.2013. 6831269
4. Azodolmolky, S., Wieder, P., Yahyapour, R.: Performance evaluation of a scalable software-defined networking deployment. In: 2013 Second European Workshop on Software Defined Networks, pp. 68–74 (2013). https://doi.org/10.1109/EWSDN. 2013.18
5. Galinina, O., Tabassum, H., Mikhaylov, K., Andreev, S., Hossain, E., Koucheryavy, Y.: On feasibility of 5G-grade dedicated RF charging technology for wireless-powered wearables. IEEE Wirel. Commun. **23**(2), 28–37 (2016)
6. Goto, Y., Masuyama, H., Ng, B., Seah, W.K.G., Takahashi, Y.: Queueing analysis of software defined network with realistic openflow-based switch model. In: 2016 IEEE 24th International Symposium on Modeling, Analysis and Simulation of Computer and Telecommunication Systems (MASCOTS), pp. 301–306 (2016). https://doi.org/10.1109/MASCOTS.2016.30
7. Jarschel, M., Oechsner, S., Schlosser, D., Pries, R., Goll, S., Tran-Gia, P.: Modeling and performance evaluation of an openflow architecture. In: Proceedings of the 23rd International Teletraffic Congress, ITC '11, International Teletraffic Congress, pp. 1–7 (2011)
8. Mahmood, K., Chilwan, A., Østerbø, O., Jarschel, M.: Modelling of openflow-based software-defined networks: the multiple node case. IET Netw. **4**(6), 278–284 (2015). https://doi.org/10.1049/iet-net.2014.0091
9. Miao, W., Min, G., Wu, Y., Wang, H., Hu, J.: Performance modelling and analysis of software-defined networking under bursty multimedia traffic. ACM Trans. Multimedia Comput. Commun. Appl. 12(5s) (2016). https://doi.org/10.1145/2983637
10. Muthanna, A., Khakimov, A., Gudkova, I., Paramonov, A., Vladyko, A., Kirichek, R.: Openflow switch buffer configuration method. In: Proceedings of the International Conference on Future Networks and Distributed Systems, ICFNDS '17. Association for Computing Machinery, New York, NY, USA (2017). https://doi. org/10.1145/3102304.3102327
11. Ometov, A., et al.: Toward trusted, social-aware D2D connectivity: bridging across the technology and sociality realms. IEEE Wirel. Commun. **23**(4), 103–111 (2016)
12. Pyattaev, A., Johnsson, K., Surak, A., Florea, R., Andreev, S., Koucheryavy, Y.: Network-assisted D2D communications: implementing a technology prototype for cellular traffic offloading. In: 2014 IEEE Wireless Communications and Networking Conference (WCNC), pp. 3266–3271 (2014)

13. The Open Networking Foundation: OpenFlow Switch Specification. Technical report (2012)
14. Yao, L., Hong, P., Zhou, W.: Evaluating the controller capacity in software defined networking. In: 2014 23rd International Conference on Computer Communication and Networks (ICCCN), pp. 1–6 (2014). https://doi.org/10.1109/ICCCN.2014.6911857

Secure MBR Array Codes in the Presence of Special Type Eavesdropper

Stanislav Kruglik$^{(\boxtimes)}$ (iD)

Skolkovo Institute of Science and Technology, Moscow 121205, Russia
`stanislav.kruglik@skoltech.ru`

Abstract. Minimum bandwidth regenerating (MBR) array codes are a class of regenerating codes that provide reliability of data while ensuring low repair bandwidth or, in other words, the amount of information downloaded for the repair of temporally unavailable node. An important aspect of all distributed storage systems is security. In this paper, we address the security issues of MBR array codes in the presence of eavesdropper with access to limited number of elements from each node. We provide an explicit construction of MBR array codes secure against such eavesdropper and prove the bound on the total amount of information stored in such a system.

Keywords: Distributed storage · Secure networks · Information-theoretic security · Regenerating codes · Network coding.

1 Introduction

Distributed storage systems are designed to store a big amount of data among nodes in a corresponding network. As a reflection of the exponential growth of the amount of data stored by humanity, the importance of such systems significantly increases. OceanStor, Dropbox, and Apache Hadoop are few examples of them [1, 15]. One of the problems system designers regularly face is nodes failure. The straightforward solution is to duplicate data several times becomes irrelevant for practical scenarios as it causes a significant increase in the introduced redundancy. This fact attracts the attention of system designers and research community to codes for distributed storage. The main goal is to design special classes of codes that optimize node failure correction in different terms. One of them, introduced in paper [18], proposes to optimize the total amount of nodes accessed during the data recovery. This metric is called locality and corresponding codes are termed locally recoverable codes (LRC). The second measure, called repair bandwidth, proposes to optimize the amount of data transmitted in the system to accomplish repair [3]. Corresponding codes are called regenerating codes and are the main focus of this paper.

The research was partially funded by RFBR, projects no. 19-01-00364, 19-37-90022, 20-07-00652, and joint RFBR and JSPS project no. 20-51-50007.

O. Galinina et al. (Eds.): NEW2AN 2020/ruSMART 2020, LNCS 12526, pp. 56–66, 2020.
https://doi.org/10.1007/978-3-030-65729-1_5

Formally speaking, regenerating codes are class of codes over a finite field of q elements that stores B uniformly and independently distributed message symbols over this field among n storage nodes. Each of them stores α field symbols. Data collector can reconstruct initial message by downloading all data stored in any subset of k nodes. In case of a node failure, replacement node can recover its' content by downloading β symbols from any subset of $d\,(d \geq k)$ remaining nodes. The total amount of data downloaded for repair termed *repair bandwidth* and is equal to $d\beta$. Note that this value is significantly smaller than the message size B.

In the initial paper [3] authors established a bound on the message size that formed a trade-off between the storage space at each node α and the repair bandwidth $d\beta$

$$B \leq \sum_{i=1}^{k} min(\alpha, (d - i + 1)\beta) \tag{1}$$

The case of minimizing α and consequently β is called minimum storage regenerating point (MSR). There are a lot of papers that proposed constructions of MSR codes for a different set of parameters, among them [8,11,12,17]. Another extreme point in bound (1) is minimum bandwidth regenerating (MBR). In such a case we first minimize β and only after it α. There are also a number of papers that investigates such case, see [4,9,11,12] and references in them. Despite significant importance of protecting storage systems against permanent or occasional node failures this paper focuses on another important aspect of distributed storage systems – security of the data. With increase of distributed storage system spreading, untrusted storage providers or communication channels are used more often. These facts enhance the risks of data leakage and make security issues the state of the art in distributed storage system designs [5–7,14].

Typical storage systems have multiple nodes distributed among different physical locations that leads to possible presence of adversarial that gain full access to some subset of nodes. Also adversarial can gain additional information by accessing data transmitted for repair of these nodes. Such eavesdropper model is extensively studied in literature and there are many generalizations of regenerating code constructions for this scenario [5,13,16].

In this paper we consider a special type of an eavesdropper that can access all nodes in a distributed storage system but only a small number of symbols stored in them. This model corresponds to case when eavesdropper controls communication infrastructure in the system and can insensibly access a small portion of stored data. To illustrate the difference between various eavesdropper models, we show an example of MBR array code with $n = 3$, $k = 2$, $d = 2$ over ternary field that provides optimal security against the eavesdropper with access to one node from [13]. Note that z_1 and z_2 are random symbols drawn uniformly and independent from ternary field. This scheme is depicted in Fig. 1, where the eavesdropper gains no information about a from two symbols stored in any node, but in case of the eavesdropper with limited access to all nodes, two symbols from two different nodes will be enough to recover a. For instance, it can be done by accessing z_2 from node 1 and $z_2 + a$ from node 2.

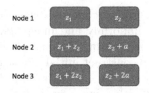

Node 1 z_1 z_2

Node 2 $z_1 + z_2$ $z_2 + a$

Node 3 $z_1 + 2z_2$ $z_2 + 2a$

Fig. 1. Example of MBR array code secure against eavesdropper with access to one node

The main contribution of this paper is as follows. We proposed an explicit construction of MBR array codes that are secure in the presence of eavesdropper with access to limited number of elements from each node. Also we obtained an amount of data that can be securely stored in such a system and showed that our schemes reach this bound.

2 Preliminaries

2.1 Notations

Let $\mathbb{F}_q$ be a finite field with q elements and let $\mathbf{X} = (X_1, \ldots X_n)$ be a vector over that field. Let C be an $a \times n$ matrix with elements from $\mathbb{F}_q$. To address the i-th row or i-th column of C we write $C_{i,:}$ or $C_{:,i}$ respectively. We use the notation $[n] \triangleq \{1, \ldots, n\}$ and denote by $\mathbf{X}_\tau$ the restriction of $\mathbf{X}$ to the positions indexed by $\tau \subseteq [n]$. By $C_{i,\tau}$ we denote the restriction of $C_{i,:}$ to the same set of positions. Superscript t means matrix transpose operation.

By $H(X)$ we denote the entropy of a discrete random variable (RV) and by $I(X;Y) = H(X) - H(X|Y)$ we denote the mutual information between discrete RVs X and Y.

2.2 MBR Codes

Let us consider a distributed storage system that consists of n storage nodes each having storage capacity of α over $\mathbb{F}_q$. This system stores B uniform and independent message symbols $\mathbf{S} = (S_1, \ldots S_B)$ over this field, that can be reconstructed by downloading all the data stored in any subset of k nodes. In this paper we consider MBR codes that achieve the minimum possible repair bandwidth $d\beta = \alpha$. This means that for a failed node repair we need to download exactly the same amount of data that it initially stores. In the absence of secrecy requirements from the bound (1) we get that MBR code must have parameters

$$B = (kd - \binom{k}{2})\beta, \quad \alpha = d\beta.$$

Following the notations from [16] let us describe MBR array code in terms of an $(n \times \alpha)$ code matrix C in which α elements in i^{th} row correspond to α

elements stored in a node i $(1 \leq i \leq n)$. We set $\beta = 1$ since for larger values of β codes can be obtained by a concatenation of codes with $\beta = 1$. In such a case $\alpha = d$.

The code matrix C is determined as matrix product of a $(d \times d)$ message matrix M with an $(n \times d)$ encoding matrix Ψ

$$C = \Psi M. \qquad (2)$$

Note that all elements in above-mentioned matrices belong to the field $\mathbb{F}_q$, elements stored at i^{th} storage node can be found as $\Psi_{(i,:)}M$ and M and $\mathbf{S}$ are linked by bijection mapping.

To ensure regenerating properties we denote encoding and message matrices as follows:

$$\Psi_{n \times d} = [\Phi_{n \times k} \; \Delta_{n \times (d-k)}],$$

$$M = [\begin{matrix} L_{k \times k} & T_{k \times (d-k)} \\ T^t_{(d-k) \times k} & 0_{(d-k) \times (d-k)} \end{matrix}].$$

Matrices Φ and Δ are chosen in such a way that any k rows of Φ are linearly independent and any d rows of Ψ are also linearly independent. It can be ensured by choosing as Ψ a corresponding Vandermond matrix with an additional requirement of $q \geq n$. Matrices L and T in message matrix M are formed from $B = kd - \binom{k}{2} = k(d-k) + \frac{k(k+1)}{2}$ message symbols $\mathbf{S}$ as follows. Upper triangular part of $(k \times k)$ symmetric matrix L is formed from $\frac{k(k+1)}{2}$ message symbols. The rest $k(d-k)$ message symbols form matrix T. Note that in this choice of L and T matrix M will be symmetric.

Let us illustrate reconstruction and repair process of constructed code.

- *Reconstruction* Let a data-collector has an access to k storage nodes that corresponds to $k \times \alpha$ submatrix C_{DC} of code matrix C. C_{DC} can be found as $\Psi_{DC}M$, where Ψ_{DC} is submatrix of Ψ that corresponds to k nodes to which data-collector connects. By construction of matrix Ψ, $\Psi_{DC}M = [\Phi_{DC}L + \Delta_{DC}T^t \; \Phi_{DC}T]$, where Φ_{DC} and Δ_{DC} are submatrices of Φ and Δ corresponding to nodes available for data-collector. As any k rows of matrix Φ are linearly independent its' sub-matrix Φ_{DC} is invertible and by multiplying C_{DC} on left by Φ_{DC}^{-1} one can recover sub-matrix T, after it he can compute $\Delta_{DC}T^t$ and, as a result, matrix L and message $\mathbf{S}$.

- *Repair* Let the failed node has index f thus α symbols stored in it can be found as $\Psi_{(f,:)}M$. For repair procedure replacement node connects to an arbitrary set $\{h_i | 1 \leq i \leq d\}$ of d remaining nodes and computes $(\Psi_{(h_i,:)}M)(\Psi_{(f,:)})^t$ on each of them. By collecting these d symbols replacement node we obtain $\Psi_{rep}M(\Psi^f)^t$, where $\Psi_{rep} = [(\Psi_{(h_1,:)})^t \dots (\Psi_{(h_i,:)})^t]^t$. Because any d rows of Ψ are linearly independent matrix Ψ_{rep} is invertible and multiplying $\Psi_{rep}M(\Psi_{(f,:)})^t$ on left by Ψ_{rep}^{-1} one can obtain $M(\Psi_{(f,:)})^t$. Since matrix M is symmetric the content of the failed node can be repaired.

2.3   Eavesdropper Model

Let eavesdropper has access to up to l elements from each node in the set-up of SubSect. 2.2. This means that it can access $E_i \subseteq [n]$, $|E_i| \le l$ symbols $C_{(i,E_i)}$ from i-th row of the code-matrix C. We are interested in information-theoretic security that requires that such eavesdropper gains no information about stored message symbols $\mathbf{S}$. This condition can be formulated as

$$I(S; C_{(1,E_1)}, ... C_{(n,E_n)}) = 0 \tag{3}$$

and system for which this condition is true is called information-theoretic secure.

Secure coding schemes usually mixes information symbol to be stored with random symbols that are independent from them [5]. There are two typical ways to ensure secrecy in distributed storage literature. First of them is precoding information and random symbols by maximum rank distance (MRD) codes, for example Gabidulin codes [2,14]. Unfortunately, the required field size is exponential with number of nodes. Another one is direct mixing of information and random symbols using the storage code [2,5,16]. In this paper we will modify the last techniques to ensure information-theoretic security of MBR array codes against the introduced eavesdropper.

3   Secure MBR Codes

Let us construct MBR array codes secure against eavesdropper with access to up to l elements from each node. In what follows we will use previously introduced framework. To ensure secrecy let us add to the code matrix of MBR array code matrix $Z_{n \times l}$ that consists of uniformly and independently distributed random symbols over $\mathbb{F}_q$ and jointly encode them by rate one code with generator matrix $G = \begin{bmatrix} G_1 \\ G_2 \end{bmatrix}$ as follows

$$C^{(s)}_{n \times (d+l)} = [\Psi M \ Z] \begin{bmatrix} G_1 \\ G_2 \end{bmatrix}.$$

By $C^{(s)}$ we denote the secure version of MBR array codes. In such a case each server stores $\alpha^{(s)} = \alpha + l = d + l$ symbols. Note that all operations are done over $\mathbb{F}_q$ and all elements of G belongs to $\mathbb{F}_q$. By this fact we can independently encode each row of matrix $[\Psi M \ Z]$.

Let us choose as matrix G the generator matrix of $(d+l, d+l)$ Reed-Solomon code over $\mathbb{F}_q$ and assume that $q \ge (d + l)$. This matrix is a square Vandermond matrix and hence invertible. Corresponding Reed-Solomon code has a $(d + l, l)$ Reed-Solomon code over the same field as a subcode so we can distinguish its' generator matrix G_2 in the matrix G. As it will be the generator matrix of maximum distance separable (MDS) code any l of its' column will be linearly independent. Let us formally prove the information-theoretic security of this scheme.

Theorem 1. *Let for any row i, $(1 \leq i \leq n)$ of code matrix $C^{(s)}$ eavesdropper has an access to $E_i \subseteq [d+l]$, $|E_i| \leq l$ symbols $C^{(s)}_{(i,E_i)}$ from it. MBR code defined above is information-theoretical secure against such eavesdropper.*

Proof. As we independently compute each row of $C^{(s)}$ we can write the following condition for i-th row

$$C^{(s)}_{(i,:)} = [\Psi_{(i,:)} M \, Z_{(i,:)}] \cdot G$$

From it follows:

$$C^{(s)}_{(i,:)} = (\Psi_{(i,:)} M_{(:,1)}, ..., \Psi_{(i,:)} M_{(:,d)}, Z_{(i,1)}, ..., Z_{(i,l)}) \cdot G$$

$$= \underbrace{(\Psi_{(i,:)} M_{(:,1)}, ..., \Psi_{(i,:)} M_{(:,d)}) \cdot G_1}_{C_1^{(s)}} +$$

$$\underbrace{(Z_{(i,1)}, ..., Z_{(i,l)}) \cdot G_2}_{C_2^{(s)}} \,.$$

As any l columns of G_2 are linearly independent for any set of elements $E_i \subseteq [d+l]$ with $|E_i| \leq l$ choosing $Z_{(i,1)}, ..., Z_{(i,l)}$ i.i.d. random gives $C^{(s)}_{(i,E_i)} \in \mathbb{F}_q^{1 \times |E_i|}$ distributed uniformly over the vectors of length l and therefore independent of $\Psi_{(i,:)} M$. It follows that

$$I(\Psi_{(i,:)} M; C^{(s)}_{(i,E_i)}) = I(\Psi_{(i,:)} M; C^{(s)}_{1,E_i} + C^{(s)}_{2,E_i}) = 0$$

As $\mathbf{S}$ and M are linked by bijection mapping and $C^{(s)}_{(i,:)}$ depends only on $\Psi_{(i,:)} M$ we can write

$$I(\mathbf{S}; C^{(s)}_{(i,E_i)}) = I(M, C^{(s)}_{(i,E_i)}) = I(\Psi M, C^{(s)}_{(i,E_i)})$$

$$= I(\Psi_{(i,:)} M, C^{(s)}_{(i,E_i)}) = 0 \tag{4}$$

As matrix Z consists of uniformly and independently distributed random symbols over $\mathbb{F}_q$ $C^{(s)}_{(i,E_i)}$ for all i $(1 \leq i \leq n)$ can be considered as mutually independent. This fact together with (4) gives the theorem statement.

3.1 Reconstruction

Let $C^{(s)}_{DC}$ be $k \times (d+l)$ sub-matrix of $C^{(s)}$ corresponding to k rows to which data-collector connects. Because we independently encode each row of matrix $[\Psi M \, Z]$ we can write the following equation

$$C^{(s)}_{DC} = [\Psi_{DC} M \, Z_{DC}] \cdot G,$$

where Ψ_{DC} is a $(k \times d)$ submatrix of Ψ and Z_{DC} is a $(k \times l)$ submatrix of Z corresponding to rows to which data-collector connects. Because matrix G is invertible we can extract $\Psi_{DC} M$ from $C^{(s)}_{DC}$ and recover message matrix M and consequently $\mathbf{S}$ as it is done in SubSect. 2.2.

3.2 Node Repair

Let $C_{(f,:)}^{(s)}$ be the row of matrix $C^{(s)}$ that corresponds to the failed node f and $C_{(h_i,:)}^{(s)}$ be the rows that correspond to arbitrary set $\{h_i | 1 \leq i \leq d\}$ of d remaining nodes. Because we independently encode each row of matrix $[\Psi M \; Z]$ we can write the following equation

$$C_{(f,:)}^{(s)} = [\Psi_{(f,:)} M \; Z_{(f,:)}] \cdot G,$$

where $\Psi_{(f,:)}$ and $Z_{(f,:)}$ are rows of matrices Ψ and Z that correspond to the failed node f.

$$C_{(h_i,:)}^{(s)} = [\Psi_{(h_i,:)} M \; Z_{(h_i,:)}] \cdot G,$$

where $\Psi_{(h_i,:)}$ and $Z_{(h_i,:)}$ are rows of matrices Ψ and Z that corresponds to remaining node h_i.

By connecting to any set $\{h_i | 1 \leq i \leq d\}$ of d remaining nodes and using the fact that G is invertible legal user can compute $\Psi_{(h_i,:)} M$, determine the inner product $(\Psi_{(h_i,:)} M)(\Psi_{(f,:)})^t$ and pass it to the replacement node. Replacement node obtain d symbols that form $\Psi_{rep} M (\Psi_{(f,:)})^t$, where $\Psi_{rep} = [(\Psi_{(h_1,:)})^t ... (\Psi_{(h_d,:)})^t]^t$. Based on the techniques from SubSect. 2.2 one can reconstruct the information content of the failed node $\Psi_{(f,:)} M$ and consequently repair it as $[\Psi_{(f,:)} M \; \hat{Z}] \cdot G$, where row $\hat{Z}$ consists of l uniformly and independently distributed random symbols over $\mathbb{F}_q$. Note that content at replacement and failed node will differ while information part used in regenerating algorithms will remains the same.

3.3 Example

We illustrate proposed framework with an example of MBR array code over $\mathbb{F}_3$ with $n = 5$, $k = 2$, $d = 2$ and $\alpha = 2$, $\beta = 1$, $B = 3$ secure against eavesdropper with access to $l = 1$ out of $\alpha^{(s)} = d + l = 3$ symbols form each node. The message symbols $\mathbf{S} = (a, b, c)$. (3×2) encoding matrix Ψ and (2×2) message matrix M takes the following values

$$\Psi = \begin{bmatrix} 1 & 0 \\ 0 & 1 \\ 1 & 1 \end{bmatrix}, \; M = \begin{bmatrix} a & b \\ b & c \end{bmatrix}.$$

The MBR array code with the absence of secrecy requirements presented in Fig. 2. It can be seen that repair of failed node can be accomplished by downloading $\beta = 1$ symbols from two remaining nodes as well as reconstruction of $\mathbf{S}$ can be accomplished by downloading the data stored in any two nodes.

To add the security from eavesdropper we augment the code matrix $C = \Psi M$ by random (3×1) matrix Z so that $[C \; Z]$ is the new code matrix. Then, to

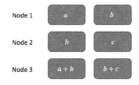

Fig. 2. MBR array code with absence of secrecy requirements

distribute the noise, $[C\ Z]$ is multiplied by generator matrix G of $(3,3)$ Reed-Solomon code. Matrices G and G^{-1} have form:

$$G = \begin{bmatrix} 1 & 1 & 1 \\ 1 & 2 & 1 \\ 1 & 1 & 2 \end{bmatrix}, \ G^{-1} = \begin{bmatrix} 0 & 2 & 2 \\ 2 & 1 & 0 \\ 2 & 0 & 1 \end{bmatrix}.$$

Code obtained after such operation is presented in Fig. 3. Clearly eavesdropper with access to any single symbol from any node gains no information about $\mathbf{S}$. It can be seen that repair of failed node can be accomplished by downloading $\beta = 1$ symbols from two remaining nodes in case of access to all symbols from them. For example, to repair node 3 we compute $[a+b+z_1, a+2b+z_1, a+b+2z_2]G^{-1} = [a, b, z_1]$ and $[a, b]\Psi_{(3,:)} = a+b$ on node 1 and $[b + c + z_2, b + 2c + z_2, b + c + 2z_2]G^{-1} = [b, c, z_2]$ and $[b, c]\Psi_{(3,:)} = b + c$ on node 2. By downloading $a + b$ and $b + c$ we repair information part of node 3 and can repair it as $[a + b, b + c, z_4]G$, where z_4 is a new random variable. The reconstruction of $\mathbf{S}$ can be accomplished by downloading $\alpha = 2$ symbols from any two nodes. For example, by the same argument as before, we can compute $[a, b]$ on node 1 and pass it to the data collector. Also we compute $[b, c]$ on node 2 and pass it to the data collector. So it receives all components of $\mathbf{S}$ and can reconstruct it.

Fig. 3. MBR array code secure against eavesdropper with access to any single symbol from any node

4   Bound on Message Size

Let us consider array codes framework and eavesdropper model introduced in Sect. 2. Note that the derivation techniques are similar to [10] but for convenience of the reader we provide a detailed proof. A bound on a message size that can be securely stored in such a system is as follows

Theorem 2. *Number of message symbols $B^{(s)}$ that can be securely stored by regenerating codes in presence of eavesdropper with access to l out of $\alpha^{(s)}$ symbols from each node satisfy the bound*

$$B^{(s)} \leq \sum_{i=1}^{k} min(\alpha^{(s)} - l, (d - i + 1)\beta)$$

Proof. Message reconstruction property of regenerating codes can be formulated as

$$H(\mathbf{S}, C_B^{(s)}) = 0$$

where C_B is $\{B_1, B_2, ...B_k\}$ rows of matrix $C^{(s)}$ that correspond to k rows available for legal user.

Secrecy condition can be reformulated from (3) in terms of entropy as

$$H(\mathbf{S}|C_{(1,E_1)}^{(s)}, ...C_{(n,E_n)}^{(s)}) = H(\mathbf{S}),$$

We can therefore write

$$H(\mathbf{S}) = H(\mathbf{S}|C_{(1,E_1)}^{(s)}, ...C_{(n,E_n)}^{(s)}) - H(\mathbf{S}|C_B)$$

$$\leq H(\mathbf{S}|C_{(1,E_1)}^{(s)}, ...C_{(n,E_n)}^{(s)}) - H(\mathbf{S}|C)$$

$$= H(\mathbf{S}|C_{(1,E_1)}^{(s)}, ...C_{(n,E_n)}^{(s)}) - H(\mathbf{S}|C_{(1,:)}^{(s)}, ...C_{(n,:)}^{(s)}).$$

Defining by $C_{(i,\bar{E}_i)}^{(s)}$ the elements of i-th row of matrix $C^{(s)}$ unavailable to the eavesdropper we can write

$$H(\mathbf{S}) \leq H(\mathbf{S}|C_{(1,E_1)}^{(s)}, ...C_{(n,E_n)}^{(s)}) -$$

$$H(\mathbf{S}|C_{(1,E_1)}^{(s)}, C_{(1,\bar{E}_1)}^{(s)}, ...C_{(n,E_n)}^{(s)}, C_{(n,\bar{E}_n)}^{(s)})$$

$$= I(\mathbf{S}; C_{(1,\bar{E}_1)}^{(s)}, ...C_{(n,\bar{E}_n)}^{(s)}|C_{(1,\bar{E}_1)}^{(s)}, ...C_{(n,\bar{E}_n)}^{(s)})$$

By message reconstruction property we can write

$$H(\mathbf{S}) \leq H(C_{(B_1,\bar{E}_{B_1})}^{(s)}, ...C_{(B_k,\bar{E}_{B_k})}^{(s)}|C_{(B_1,E_{B_1})}^{(s)}, ...C_{(B_k,E_{B_k})}^{(s)})$$

Because information content of each node can be repaired by downloading β symbols from any subset of d remaining node we can obtain the following bound for message size securely stored in such a system

$$B^{(s)} = H(\mathbf{S}) \leq \sum_{i=1}^{k} min(\alpha^{(s)} - l, (d - i + 1)\beta)$$

Corollary 1. *In case of secure MBR codes introduced in Sect. 3 $\alpha^{(s)} - l = d\beta = \alpha$. That means that the replacement node for node recovery downloads only information content that it stores keeping MBR property.*

5   Conclusion

In this paper, we introduce the notion of eavesdropper with limited access to all nodes in a distributed storage system to regenerating codes and prove the bound on the maximum amount of information that can be securely stored. We also propose an explicit construction of MBR array codes resistant to such eavesdropper and prove that it securely stores the maximum possible amount of information in case of minimum repair bandwidth. In further research, we will extend the notion of MSR array codes to such a scenario as well as consider the stronger eavesdropper model who has not only limited access to all nodes but also full access to a small subset of them.

Acknowledgments. Authors thanks A. Frolov and G. Kabatiansky for introducing this problem to him and for numerous fruitful discussions during work on this paper.

References

1. Aftab, U., Siddiqui, G.F.: Big data augmentation with data warehouse: a survey. In: 2018 IEEE International Conference on Big Data (Big Data), pp. 2785–2794 (2018)
2. Agarwal, A., Mazumdar, A.: Security in locally repairable storage. In: 2015 IEEE Information Theory Workshop (ITW), pp. 1–5 (2015)
3. Dimakis, A.G., Godfrey, P.B., Wu, Y., Wainwright, M.J., Ramchandran, K.: Network coding for distributed storage systems. IEEE Trans. Inf. Theory **56**(9), 4539–4551 (2010)
4. Han, Y.S., Pai, H., Zheng, R., Varshney, P.K.: Update-efficient error-correcting product-matrix codes. IEEE Trans. Commun. **63**(6), 1925–1938 (2015)
5. Kadhe, S., Sprintson, A.: Security for minimum storage regenerating codes and locally repairable codes. In: 2017 IEEE International Symposium on Information Theory (ISIT), pp. 1028–1032 (2017)
6. Kruglik, S.: Ph.d. forum: Security issues in distributed storage networks. In: 2020 IEEE 21th International Symposium on A World of Wireless, Mobile and Multimedia Networks (WoWMoM), pp. 1–2 (2020)
7. Kruglik, S., Rybin, P., Frolov, A.: On the secrecy capacity of distributed storage with locality and availability. In: 2019 IEEE 90th Vehicular Technology Conference (VTC2019-Fall), pp. 1–5 (2019)
8. Li, J., Tang, X., Tian, C.: A generic transformation for optimal repair bandwidth and rebuilding access in MDS codes. In: 2017 IEEE International Symposium on Information Theory (ISIT), pp. 1623–1627 (2017)
9. Lin, S., Chung, W.: Novel repair-by-transfer codes and systematic exact-MBR codes with lower complexities and smaller field sizes. IEEE Trans. Parallel Distrib. Syst. **25**(12), 3232–3241 (2014)
10. Pawar, S., El Rouayheb, S., Ramchandran, K.: On secure distributed data storage under repair dynamics. In: 2010 IEEE International Symposium on Information Theory, pp. 2543–2547 (2010)
11. Rashmi, K.V., Shah, N.B., Kumar, P.V.: Optimal exact-regenerating codes for distributed storage at the MSR and MBR points via a product-matrix construction. IEEE Trans. Inf. Theory **57**(8), 5227–5239 (2011)

12. Rashmi, K.V., Shah, N.B., Kumar, P.V., Ramchandran, K.: Explicit construction of optimal exact regenerating codes for distributed storage. In: 2009 47th Annual Allerton Conference on Communication, Control, and Computing (Allerton), pp. 1243–1249 (2009)
13. Rashmi, K.V., Shah, N.B., Ramchandran, K., Kumar, P.V.: Information-theoretically secure erasure codes for distributed storage. IEEE Trans. Inf. Theory **64**(3), 1621–1646 (2018)
14. Rawat, A.S., Koyluoglu, O.O., Silberstein, N., Vishwanath, S.: Secure locally repairable codes for distributed storage systems. In: 2013 IEEE International Symposium on Information Theory, pp. 2224–2228 (2013)
15. Rhea, S., Eaton, P., Geels, D., Weatherspoon, H., Zhao, B., Kubiatowicz, J.: Pond: the oceanstore prototype. In: 2nd USENIX Conference File Storage Technol. (FAST), pp. 1–14 (203)
16. Shah, N.B., Rashmi, K.V., Kumar, P.V.: Information-theoretically secure regenerating codes for distributed storage. In: 2011 IEEE Global Telecommunications Conference - GLOBECOM 2011, pp. 1–5 (2011)
17. Ye, M., Barg, A.: Explicit constructions of high-rate MDS array codes with optimal repair bandwidth. IEEE Trans. Inf. Theory **63**(4), 2001–2014 (2017)
18. Yekhanin, S.: Locally decodable codes. Found. Trends Theor. Comput. Sci. **6**(3), 139–255 (2012)

Improvement of a Dactyloscopic Authentication Security Using Polarimetric Technique

Pavel Trubin$^{(\boxtimes)}$ ⓘ, Aleksandr Murashov ⓘ, Dmitry Suntsov ⓘ, and Elena Velichko ⓘ

Higher School of Applied Physics and Space Technologies, Peter the Great St. Petersburg Polytechnic University (SPbPU), Polytechnicheskaya Street 29, Saint Petersburg 195251, Russia
ptk4815@yandex.ru, alexander790@mail.ru,
dima.suntsow416@gmail.com, velichko-spbstu@yandex.ru

Abstract. The development of an optical polarimetric scheme for improvement of fingerprint systems is presented in this paper. It is based on Mueller matrix imaging (with 36 measurements) of scattering object using Lu-Chipman polar decomposition algorithm for calculation of polarimetric characteristics. Experiments were made with real fingers and several dummies made of gelatin and white glue. The proposed scheme and the algorithm have showed promising results for solving the problem of improving the security of fingerprint sensors.

Keywords: Polarimetry · Mueller matrix · Biotissue · Dactyloscopy · Infosec

1 Introduction

Authentication, authorization, and administration are some of the classic tools for managing IT security. Ongoing researches by software development companies con-firms that the use of unique human characteristics is one of the best solutions to ensure privacy, confidentiality, proper authentication, secure access control.

Biometric technologies attract the attention of many researchers from various sectors of the economy, as well as government agencies. Biometric systems are significantly superior to traditional authentication methods using a password system or identification cards. The undoubted advantage of biometrics is the authorization method, in which the system does not need to create passwords and identification cards because the person always carries everything needed for authentication.

Nowadays it is difficult to imagine a person who does not have a smartphone. Almost all modern smartphones and most laptops use a fingerprint-based security system. Significant advantages of the fingerprint scanning method are the presence of a unique "key" for each user, the miniature device for authentication, the simplicity of the authentication process for the user, and, as a result, the high potential for integration into various devices [1]. However, fingerprints can be easily faked using com-mon material such as gelatin or PVA glue [2].

© Springer Nature Switzerland AG 2020
O. Galinina et al. (Eds.): NEW2AN 2020/ruSMART 2020, LNCS 12526, pp. 67–73, 2020.
https://doi.org/10.1007/978-3-030-65729-1_6

Despite the variety of existing solutions, they have drawbacks enough to crack the security of the system so developers are constantly looking for new protective methods.

Due to the advantages of optical technologies, such as contactlessness, radiation safety, and many biometric data available for calculation, they are one of the most popular for research.

The problems of existing methods, such as OCT [3] is high cost, complexity of implementation, low integration capabilities, or lack of accuracy, as in the case of oxy-gen saturation method [4].

The paper considers polarimetric methods – analysis of the polarization characteristics of light multiply scattered by the medium. The methods of polarimetry show promising results in biomedical research in the problems of differentiating different types of scattering tissues [5–10]. It is known that biological tissues can exhibit polarization properties, for example, anisotropy, dichroism, and optical activity [11, 12]. Common artificial finger models are made of materials that have a significantly more uniform structure compared to biological tissue, which is why significant differences in polari-metric parameters are expected [13–16]. Polarimetry methods can provide additional information on biological tissue, which is essential for deter-mining fake prints [9].

Thus, the Muller matrix provides information on the polarimetric properties of living tissue. This method can be applied both for studying and diagnosing cancer cells [17], and for analyzing the features of the subcutaneous structure of the finger; the second application will be discussed in this article.

2 Theory

To describe the polarization properties of the scattered light beam and its conversion, the Stokes vector method and Mueller matrices are preferable in comparison with others, because it is applicable for partially polarized incoherent radiation [17, 18].

The polarization of light is described using the Stokes vector containing the intensity parameter I and 3 parameters that are responsible for the degree of polarization of various types (parameter Q describes the preponderance of linear horizontal polarized light over vertical polarized light; the third parameter U describes the preponderance of +45 polarized light over −45 polarized light and, finally, V describes the preponderance of right circular polarized light over left circular polarized light).

The Mueller matrix fully characterizes the optical polarization properties of the sample. In the general case, the matrix has a 4 × 4 dimension with 16 independent elements (determined by 36 dimensions). The input S_{in} Stokes vector relates to the output Stokes vector S_{out} of the optical system through the matrix M of this system:

$$S_{out} = MS_{in} \tag{1}$$

$$S_{out} = \begin{pmatrix} I_{out} \\ Q_{out} \\ U_{out} \\ V_{out} \end{pmatrix} = \begin{pmatrix} M_{11} & M_{12} & M_{13} & M_{14} \\ M_{21} & M_{22} & M_{23} & M_{24} \\ M_{31} & M_{32} & M_{33} & M_{34} \\ M_{41} & M_{42} & M_{43} & M_{44} \end{pmatrix} \begin{pmatrix} I_{in} \\ Q_{in} \\ U_{in} \\ V_{in} \end{pmatrix} \tag{2}$$

Using the Mueller matrix, one can determine: birefringence, optical activity, dichroism.

The polarimetry of biological tissue is associated with problems arising from multiple scattering, which complicates existing computational methods developed for transparent media. Various effects due to different components of an inhomogeneous biological tissue overlap each other, which makes quantitative analysis difficult. For quantitative analysis, various methods of decomposition of Mueller matrices are used. In this paper, we use the Lu-Chipman algorithm [19], which is based on polar decomposition of the Mueller matrix into three matrices, each describing certain properties of the object:

$$M = M_\Delta M_R M_D, \tag{3}$$

where M_Δ describes the depolarizing parameters of the medium, M_R is responsible for the effects of linear birefringence (phase delay) and optical activity, M_D includes the effects of linear and circular dichroism.

The value of dichroism is a potentially important biometric characteristic, calculated as the module of the dichroism vector d:

$$\left|\vec{d}\right| = d = \frac{1}{M(1,1)}\sqrt{M(1,2)^2 + M(1,3)^2 + M(1,4)^2}. \tag{4}$$

Depolarization parameter Δ can be calculated from the elements of the matrix M_Δ:

$$\Delta = 1 - \frac{|tr(M_\Delta) - 1|}{3}, 0 \le \Delta \le 1. \tag{5}$$

The value of the linear retardance δ is expressed with the matrix M_R:

$$\delta = \cos^{-1}\left\{\sqrt{(M_R(2,2) + M_R(3,3))^2 + (M_R(3,2) - M_R(2,3))^2} - 1\right\}. \tag{6}$$

3 Experiment

A system for calculating the Muller matrices of biological tissues that backscatter polarized light was developed. The block diagram of the set-up is shown in Fig. 1.

The principle of operation of the scheme: the sample is illuminated by the light of the source (1) passing through the optics defining the input polarization (2–4), scattered by the sample, and collected by the optics of the output analyzing elements (5–6) to the detector (7). One of the 6 states of polarization at the input corresponds to 6 polarization states at the output. 36 measurements are carried out, each of which corresponds to an image that carries information about the effect of the sample on the light of a certain

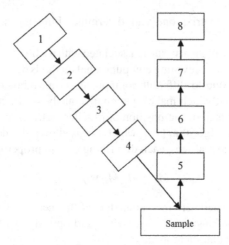

Fig. 1. The block diagram of the laboratory setup. 1 – He-Ne laser, 2 –polarizer, 3 – half-wave plate, 4,6 – a quarter-wave plates, 5 – collecting lens, 7 – analyzer, 8 – CCD camera.

polarization. Subtracting and adding these images according to the scheme in Table 1, we can obtain a matrix of images corresponding to the Mueller matrix.

Table 1. Calculation of matrix elements M_{ij} for a method of 36 measurements [20]. Here the first and second terms represent the input and output polarization states respectively: H = horizontal, V = vertical, P = +45°, M = −45°, R = right circular, L = left circular.

M_{11} HH + HV + VH + VV	M_{12} HH + HV-VH-VV	M_{13} PH + PV-MH + MV	M_{14} RH + RV-LH-LV
M_{21} HH-HV + VH-VV	M_{22} HH-HV-VH + VV	M_{23} PH-PV-MH + MV	M_{24} RH-RV-LH + LV
M_{31} HP-HM + VP-VM	M_{32} HP-HM-VP + VM	M_{33} PP-PM-MP + MM	M_{34} RP-RM-LP + LM
M_{41} HR-HL + VR-VL	M_{42} HR-HL-VR + VL	M_{43} PR-PL-MR + ML	M_{44} RR-RL-LR + LL

4   Results and Discussion

For experiments, gelatin and PVA (white) glue samples imitating a human finger were used [2]. Obtained dummies were very poor quality, but even in this form they were able to overcome the protection of smartphones.

Figures 2 and 3 show calculated images for a live finger and glue dummy. Similar matrices were obtained for all models. The difference in images may indicate a different internal structure of human skin and artificial material. Inhomogeneities of the structure of glue are clearly visible on images, the papillary pattern is worse distinguished.

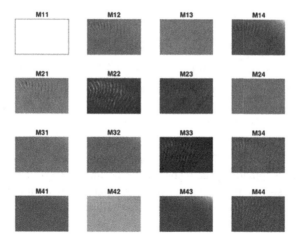

Fig. 2. Muller matrix (images) measured for a real finger.

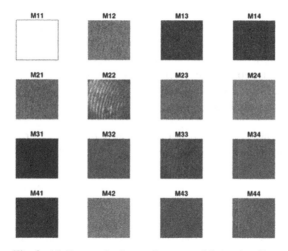

Fig. 3. Muller matrix (images) measured for a glue film.

Experiments were carried out to calculate the Muller matrices at different scattering angles. The polarimetric parameters for glue, gelatin and fingers were calculated (Table 2). Significant difference in the elements can be seen, considering the measurement error.

According to the results, it is possible to say that the living tissue of the finger depolarizes light much more strongly than the material of the fake finger, has a greater dichroism parameter and linear birefringence. Gelatin samples may differ in density of the mixture, uniformity of solidification, therefore, the error of the parameters for gelatin is often an order of magnitude larger than the glue.

Comparing these parameters, we can separate the living biological tissue from a fake one. It should also be noted that the obtained parameters of real biological tissue are

Table 2. Measured polarimetric parameters.

Parameter	Finger	Glue	Gelatin
Δ, depolarization	0.913 ± 0.004	0.713 ± 0.002	0.750 ± 0.070
d, dichroism	0.072 ± 0.004	0.029 ± 0.002	0.040 ± 0.010
δ, linear retardance	1.270 ± 0.050	0.417 ± 0.016	0.550 ± 0.040

close to the known values [11]. This method can be used outside the laboratory after the development of an automatic tissue recognition algorithm. One of the most promising solutions is the measurement and analysis of specific elements of the matrix, which make it possible to determine the type of tissue with enough accuracy. This will simplify the setup and reduce analysis time.

5 Conclusion

The results obtained show that the developed method is applicable to the task of increasing the security of fingerprint scanners, and it can be used for user authentication. Future research should be aimed to determine the possibilities of integration, miniaturization of the set-up, simplification of measurements, search and testing of other algorithms for matrix decomposition and calculation of biometric parameters, organization of a database of biometric parameters.

Acknowledgments. This research work was supported by Peter the Great St. Petersburg Polytechnic University in the framework of the Program "5-100-2020".

References

1. Marasco, E., Ross, A.: A survey on antispoofing schemes for fingerprint recognition systems. ACM Comput. Surv. **47**(2), 28 (2015)
2. Matsumoto, T., Matsumoto, H., Yamada K., Hoshino, S.: Impact of Artificial Gummy Fingers on Fingerprint Systems, In: Proceedings of SPIE 4677 (2002)
3. Marcel, S., Nixon, M., Li, S.: Handbook of Biometric Anti-Spoofing. 1st edn. Springer (2014)
4. Drahanský, M., Kanich, O., Březinová, E., Shinoda, K.: Experiments with Optical Properties of Skin on Fingers. International Journal of Optics and Applications **6**(2), 37–46 (2016)
5. Sviridov, A., Chernomordik, V., Hassan, M.: Intensity profiles of linearly polarized light backscattered from skin and tissue-like phantoms. J. Biomed. Optics **10**(1), 12–14 (2005)
6. Chen, Y., Hsu, H., Khaleel, M., Chang, Y., Wu, C., Wu.: Study of biological reaction in cancer cell with spectroscopic imaging ellipsometry. In: Proceedings of SPIE 9925 (2016)
7. Bachinskiy, V.: Perspectives of laser-polarimetric methods of biological tissue investigation in forensic medicine. Russian J. Forensic Med. **2**(3), 4–8 (2016). (In Russian)
8. Bulykina, A., Ryzhova, V.: Skin research by scattering ellipsometry method. Sci. Techn. J. Inf. Technol. Mech. Optics **17**(5), 753–760 (2017). (in Russian)

9. Trubin, P., Savchenko, E., Velichko, E.: Development of polarimetric sensor for identification system. In: 2018 IEEE International Conference on Electrical Engineering and Photonics (EExPolytech), IEEE, pp. 279–282 (2018)

10. Putintseva, M., Aksenov, E., Korikov, C., Velichko, E.: Non-invasive research of biological objects by the method of laser polarimetry. In: Journal of Physics: Conference Series, IOP Publishing, vol. 1124 (2018)

11. Ghosh, N., Vitkin, A.: Tissue polarimetry: concepts, challenges, applications, and outlook. J. Biomed. Opt. **16**(11), 110801 (2011)

12. Tuchin, V.: Tissue Optics: Light Scattering Methods and Instruments for Medical Diagnosis, 3rd edn. SPIE Press, Bellingham (2015)

13. Davydov, R., Antonov, V., Yushkova, V.: A new algorithm for processing the absorption and scattering signals of laser radiation on a blood vessel and human tissues. J. Phys. Conf. **1236**, 012079 (2019)

14. Bohidar, H., Maity, S.: Polarized light scattering study from gelatin solutions and gels. European Polymer J. **34**, 1361–1370 (1998)

15. Busch, K., Busch, M.: Chiral Analysis. 1st edn., pp. 320–321, Elsevier Science (2006)

16. Calixto, S., Ganzherli, N., Gulyaev, S., Figueroa-Gerstenmaier, S.: Gelatin as a photosensitive material. Molecules **23**(8), 2064 (2018)

17. Davydov, R., Mazing, M., Yushkova, V.: A new method for monitoring the health condition based on nondestructive signals of laser radiation absorption and scattering. In: Journal of Physics: Conference Series, vol. 1410 (2019)

18. Darlow, L., Webb, L., Botha, N.: Automated spoof-detection for fingerprints using optical coherence tomography. Appl. Opt. **55**(13), 3387–3396 (2016)

19. Lu, S., Chipman, R.: Interpretation of Mueller matrices based on polar decomposition. J. Opt. Soc. Am. A **13**, 1106–1113 (1996)

20. Baba, J.: The Use of Polarized Light for Biomedical Applications. Ph.D. Dissertation, Texas A&M University (2003)

Method of Comparison of Neural Network Resistance to Adversarial Attacks

Alexey Nemchenko[1](✉) (iD) and Sergey Bezzateev[2](✉) (iD)

[1] ITMO University, St. Petersburg 197101 Kronverksky Pr. 49,, Russia
nemc_aleks@mail.ru
[2] Saint Petersburg State University of Aerospace Instrumentation, St. Petersburg 19000 B. Morskaya 67,, Russia
bsv@aanet.ru

Abstract. The vulnerability of neural networks to adversarial attacks has long been revealed. However, the structure of neural networks is not given due attention during the attack. The article deals with the impact of different parameters of a neural network on its resistance to adversarial attacks. The main purpose of this research is to determine which parameters increase resistance to attacks. The way by which neural networks can be compared has been proposed. Several neural networks were selected for comparison and a number of adversarial attacks were conducted on them. As a result, certain conditions were identified under which the attack took place over a longer time. It was also found that different changes in neural network parameters were required to protect against different attacks.

Keywords: Neural networks · Information security · Training finder · Machine learning

1 Introduction

Recent advances in the field of machine learning have significantly expanded the scope of artificial neural networks. Particularly great success has been observed in the application of convolution neural networks. Thanks to them, incredible performance in the recognition of objects has been achieved. In this case, the recognition accuracy reaches 95% and sometimes exceeds the human abilities.

However, neural networks have disadvantages not inherent in humans. It is on the basis of such disadvantages are built adversarial attacks on the neural network [1]. For example, for a convolution neural network used to classify images, adding perturbations to the recognition object can be critical. Such distortions can lead to classification errors. At the same time, a person will not even notice such perturbations. In this work we investigate the possibility of determining ways to increase the resistance of convolution neural networks to adversarial attacks. We considered a neural network in which changes were made during the experiment. Training was conducted on the same data and the same attacks were performed.

© Springer Nature Switzerland AG 2020
O. Galinina et al. (Eds.): NEW2AN 2020/ruSMART 2020, LNCS 12526, pp. 74–79, 2020.
https://doi.org/10.1007/978-3-030-65729-1_7

The main objective of the study was to characterize how various factors influence the effectiveness of adversarial attacks. Such as changing the size of the training sample, changing the number of cores, changing the activation functions, and combining these methods. Based on the results obtained, a method was formed that allows comparing different neural networks by their degree of resistance to competitive attacks.

2 Related Work

To affect neural networks, attacks are used either during training by manipulating the data in the training sample [2] or during the operation of the neural network by affecting the data to be classified [1]. To prevent such attacks, adding noise [3], using high-level representation guided denoiser [4], learning on data containing competitive examples [1] are used. Researches in this area are mainly aimed at counteracting attacks at a specific stage, without assessing the impact of the parameters of the neural network itself on its overall security. In this paper, the study of the influence of various parameters of the neural network on the degree of its resistance to competitive attacks is considered.

3 The Proposed Way to Compare Different Neural Networks

Exposure to a normal neural network means attacks that use information to recognize. Due to the fact that it is impossible to control such information, the methods of protection adopted must be designed with the potential attacks in mind.

The first step is to determine if the neural network parameters are compromised. Most adversarial attacks use the white box principle when there is complete information about the neural network. If the information about the parameuters of the neural network used in the system is publicly available, the range of attacks on it is increased. It takes very little time from the moment an attacker receives the network's data to the moment he is able to submit a competitive example to the neural network's entry.

If the parameters of a neural network are not considered fully protected from receiving them by an intruder, due to receiving them from a third party source or for other reasons, the security of the neural network can be analyzed by determining the variability of neural network parameters. In cases where it is impossible to hide the original parameters, their variability will significantly complicate the attack. The moment an attacker generates an image, the neural network parameters will already change and the attack will not be so successful. However, retraining is possible if the training sample is different from the original one. Achieving such a result is also possible with constant retraining of the neural network, in this case it is not necessary to determine the time when the parameters were disclosed, but only to determine the time required to change the parameters of the Artificial Neural Network.

The second step is to analyze the parameters of the training sample. Increasing the size of the training sample allows increasing the accuracy of the neural network. Adding special noise or examples of competitive attacks to the training sample makes it more resistant to FGSM and DeepFool attacks. However, simply increasing the size of the training sample has almost no effect on the FGSM attack. At the same time, when the size of the tutorial sample is reduced, it increases the duration of attacks in which the attack method targets a minimum number of modified pixels, such as JSMA and OnePixel. The assessment is performed by performing a DeepFool attack, due to the fact that this attack is the fastest among those considered, which can be influenced by changing the size of the training sample.

The third step is to define the activation functions of the neural network. For several attacks, their effectiveness depends on the selected activation function. The analysis will be performed by determining the activation function used, if the activation function has an upper value limit of the parameter, then it is considered vulnerable. Such function is Bounded ReLU [3], neural networks with such function become more resistant to JSMA and OnePixel attacks. This is because if this type of function is used, the ability to assign excessive weight to one or more pixels will be limited.

The fourth step Determine the number of parameters processed by the neural network. The increase in the number of parameters leads to an increase in the duration of an attack such as PGD. Neural networks that have increased the number of cores and therefore the number of parameters can better withstand DeepFool attacks.

Step five, conduct a series of adversarial attacks on the neural network. In this case it is not recommended to conduct those attacks that were used to train the neural network. Using the same attack during training and testing is dangerous and can overestimate the reliability of protection. This step will determine which neural network is more vulnerable to attack.

4   Object of Study and Methods of Exposure

To determine the degree of influence of neural network parameters on its resistance to adversarial attacks, a convolution neural network was used. The main feature of such neural networks is the presence of convolution layers. They act as a filter that sequentially passes through all parts of the image and performs the operation of multiplication with the part of the input data above which it is now. Then it summarizes all the obtained values, thus forming the core [5]. It is the convolution core that is the most vulnerable part of the neural network.

As part of this work, the objects of classification were images. The impact on the subject of the study was carried out through competitive attacks using the principle of "White Box". Among the attacks used to affect the subject of investigation, such as FGSM [6], PGD [7], DeepFool [8], JSMA [9] were used. All these attacks usually focus on maximizing some measure of harm caused by adversarial perturbation, limited by some perturbation size limit designed to make it less visible to the human observer. For research purposes, we used methods that require a large amount of computational operations. This was done in order to determine the degree of influence of parameters on the speed of attacks.

5 Experiment

The results were assessed by influencing five neural network models. Each of the neural networks has different parameters. The same training sample CIFAR-10 [10] was also used for each of them. Changing the size of the training sample was performed by excluding the same training examples. In the course of attacks, 1000 competitive images were generated for each case. The images for the attack were selected from the test set CIFAR-10 of images. Simulation of the object of investigation was carried out using TensorFlow machine learning libraries in the Jupyter Notebook software environment.

From the results of the experiment we can see that as the size of the training sample decreases, the time of JSMA attack increases. As a result, it was determined that when using 15000 images in training, JSMA allows to conduct the process of neural network training in less time than the adversarial attack. It is assumed that there are no other countermeasures are applied against the JSMA attack (Fig. 1).

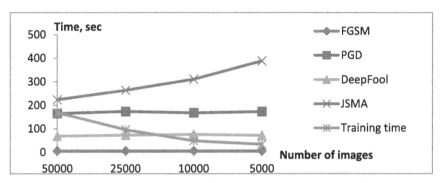

Fig. 1. The dependency of the attack time and the size of the training sample.

There is also a dependence of increasing the amount of time for PGD attacks with a significant increase in the number of parameters in the neural network. However, this had almost no effect on other attack methods.

By comparing the data obtained during the analysis of the considered neural networks, it was determined that the use of more convolution cores, as well as the use of Bounded ReLU, allows to increase the time of the attack. The increase in the number of cores leads to an increase in the number of signs detected by the neural network, thus making it difficult to select parameters during attack by attackers. The use of Bounded ReLU also makes it difficult to select parameters. At the same time, the training time changes slightly. Use of the considered methods of protection together has not shown improvement of results, and in the considered case even has shown less efficiency, than each of methods separately. This is most clearly demonstrated for the DeepFool attack. A comparison table for this attack is shown in Table 1.

Table 1. Time of DeepFool attack in seconds depending on the training sample on different neural network variants

The size of the training sample	Artificial Neural Network	Artificial Neural Network with increased number of the cores	Artificial Neural Network with Bounded ReLU	Artificial Neural Network with Bounded ReLU with increased number of the cores
50000	69	177	350	152
25000	73	185	306	124
10000	76	185	250	122
5000	72	170	244	106

6   Discussion and Future Work

The data obtained allow us to confirm that the method of neural network security assessment, which is being developed based on neural network parameters assessment, can be used. As the experiment has shown that combination of various methods of protection can either not increase safety, but even reduce it. This research is an important direction for future developments in the field of countering attacks on neural networks. Further research will be aimed at more precise identification of the dependence of various parameters of the neural network and the timing of competitive attacks.

Acknowledgements. This paper is supported by Government of Russian Federation (grant 08-08).

References

1. Szegedy, C., et al.: Intriguing properties of neural networks. https://arxiv.org/abs/1312.6199 (2013). Accessed 21 May 2020
2. Shafahi, A., et al.: Poison frogs! targeted clean-label poisoning attacks on neural networks. In: Advances in Neural Information Processing Systems, pp. 6103–6113 (2018)
3. Zantedeschi, V., Nicolae, M.I., Rawat, A.: Efficient defenses against adversarial attacks. In: Proceedings of the 10th ACM Workshop on Artificial Intelligence and Security, pp. 39–49 (November 2017)
4. Liao, F., Liang, M., Dong, Y., Pang, T., Hu, X., Zhu, J.: Defense against adversarial attacks using high-level representation guided denoiser. In: Proceedings of the IEEE Conference on Computer Vision and Pattern Recognition, pp. 1778–1787 (2018)
5. Gu, J., et al.: Recent advances in convolutional neural networks. Pattern Recogn. **77**, 354–377 (2018)
6. Goodfellow, I.J., Shlens, J., Szegedy, C.: Explaining and harnessing adversarial examples. https://arxiv.org/abs/1412.6572 (2014). Accessed 21 May 2020

7. Madry, A., Makelov, A., Schmidt, L., Tsipras, D., Vladu, A.: Towards deep learning models resistant to adversarial attacks. https://arxiv.org/abs/1706.06083 (2017). Accessed 21 May 2020
8. Moosavi-Dezfooli, S.M., Fawzi, A., Frossard, P.: Deepfool: a simple and accurate method to fool deep neural networks. In: Proceedings of the IEEE conference on computer vision and pattern recognition, pp. 2574–2582 (2016)
9. Papernot, N., McDaniel, P., Jha, S., Fredrikson, M., Celik, Z.B., Swami, A.: The limitations of deep learning in adversarial settings. In: 2016 IEEE European symposium on security and privacy (EuroS&P), pp. 372–387. IEEE (March 2016)
10. Krizhevsky, A., Hinton, G.: Learning multiple layers of features from tiny images, Master's thesis, Department of Computer Science, University of Toronto (2009)

Comparative Analysis of Cryptographic Key Management Systems

Ievgeniia Kuzminykh[1,4][✉] ⓘ, Bogdan Ghita[2] ⓘ, and Stavros Shiaeles[3] ⓘ

[1] King's College London, Strand, London WC2R 2LS, UK
ievgeniia.kuzminykh@kcl.ac.uk
[2] University of Plymouth, Drake Circus, Plymouth PL4 8AA, UK
bogdan.ghita@plymouth.ac.uk
[3] University of Portsmouth, Portsmouth PO1 3RR, UK
stavros.shiaeles@port.ac.uk
[4] Kharkiv National University of Radio Electronics, Nauky av. 14, Kharkiv 61166, Ukraine

Abstract. Managing cryptographic keys can be a complex task for an enterprise and particularly difficult to scale when an increasing number of users and applications need to be managed. In order to address scalability issues, typical IT infrastructures employ key management systems that are able to handle a large number of encryption keys and associate them with the authorized requests. Given their necessity, recent years have witnessed a variety of key management systems, aligned with the features, quality, price and security needs of specific organisations. While the spectrum of such solutions is welcome and demonstrates the expanding nature of the market, it also makes it time consuming for IT managers to identify the appropriate system for their respective company needs. This paper provides a list of key management tools which include a minimum set of features, such as availability of secure database for managing keys, an authentication, authorization, and access control model for restricting and managing access to keys, effective logging of actions with keys, and the presence of an API for accessing functions directly from the application code. Five systems were comprehensively compared by evaluating the attributes related to complexity of the implementation, its popularity, linked vulnerabilities and technical performance in terms of response time and network usage. These were Pinterest Knox, Hashicorp Vault, Square Keywhiz, OpenStack Barbican, and Cyberark Conjur. Out of these five, Hachicorp Vault was determined to be the most suitable system for small businesses.

Keywords: Cryptography · Key distribution · Key management service · Secret handling

1 Introduction

The complexity and reliability of any cryptosystem is based on the use of cryptographic keys. The key exchange is one of the mechanisms at core of the process and it ensure confidentiality when exchanging information between users and its behaviour is well-explained for small systems. However, in larger IT infrastructures, reaching hundreds or

© Springer Nature Switzerland AG 2020
O. Galinina et al. (Eds.): NEW2AN 2020/ruSMART 2020, LNCS 12526, pp. 80–94, 2020.
https://doi.org/10.1007/978-3-030-65729-1_8

thousands of users, the process of handling the cryptographic keys for individual business applications is an increasingly difficult task and poses significant challenges as manual decentralized control is expensive and error prone. Such complex environments, including a large number of systems, group accounts, and users associated with them require a convenient and effective way to manage them. The solution is to use a cryptographic key management system (KMS) that provides a unified interface for managing keys, increase security of the enterprise network, provide scalability, and minimize human errors [1]. If an IT infrastructure does not include a sufficiently reliable management of key information then, having taken possession of it, an attacker may also gain access to the stored information, user accounts, their associated information and any databases [2].

A cryptographic KMS is a centralized system that provides key generation, key storage and key distribution, as well as automatic expiration, updating, re-placement, back-up and revocation of keys, all for a wide range of applications [3, 4]. A typical example of a large scale KMS is a public-key infrastructure PKI, which uses hierarchical digital certificates for authentication and public keys for encryption.

Given their necessity for current IT infrastructure, several key management methods and tools are available on the market, varying in terms of cost, complexity and use cases. In this context, selecting the most suitable option becomes a challenge, since some of these solutions may be impractical or difficult to implement; as a result, the process of selection can be time consuming or unfeasible for an organisation that does not have enough resources to conduct such an assessment. This study aims to address this problem by comprehensively comparing the existing key management systems that match a set of attributes important for small businesses, such as simplicity of installation, ease of usage, performance and price, that may take precedence over scalability and security.

2 Key Management System Architecture and Features

A Key Management System is used to centrally distribute and store all keys used by an organisation and may take various forms, ranging from free small applications that run on conventional computer equipment to complex hardware solutions. Simple, open source solutions often rely on a regular database server for storage that stores keys encrypted in the database. However, due to the importance of the key management system, an appropriately designed system should include a hardware security module for key processing, or at least consider such an option [5].

The typical components of a KMS include the KMS Server, the KMS Client, the Hardware Security Module (HSM) and a database [6, 7], as summarised in the architecture on Fig. 1.

The *KMS Server* is the central part of the system, where the actual key management takes place; this module is also responsible for the all operation related to the encryption key lifecycle, from generation, then activation, expiration and then destruction, as well as the key allocation against targets [8]. In order to deliver its functionality, the KMS Server connects to its dedicated HSM and a database to provide key management and key requesting services.

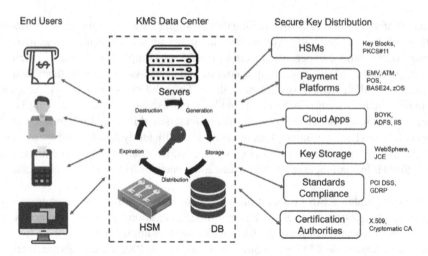

Fig. 1. Architecture of KMS with functions and applications.

The *KMS Client* provides a graphical user interface for users to manage and operate the KMS server. While less critical in terms of process and security provision, this entity is essential for the customer, because it reflects system usability, attractiveness, and simplicity.

The *Hardware Security Module* is used by KMS to ensure the quality of keys generated and the protection of these keys while in storage or in transit. HSM can perform a number of important security-related cryptographic operations such as encryption, hashing, digital signing, and Message Authentication Codes (MAC). Additionally, sophisticated techniques can be used to ensure that keys are never present in unencrypted form in server memory or client machines [5]. Typically, an HSM is installed inside a server or within an Ethernet cluster within corporate network.

The *Database* stores all data, but sensitive information such as keys and key components are also encrypted under the master key generated by the HSM. Keys only exist in clear text inside the HSM. Other sensitive data, for example settings and logs, are integrity protected by a hardware MAC key so that the data cannot be edited without the server. Different solutions may choose to implement their respective databases using any preferred database management systems, such as Oracle, MySQL, PostgreSQL, DB2, Redis, etc.

The variety of use case where a KMS can be deployed and where keys are necessary to be securely handled makes it likely that customers have many reasons to use KMS in their business-critical processes. Some typical use cases include payment platforms, such as ATM or POS systems with Remote Key Loading (RKL) [9], Europay, MasterCard and Visa (EMV) keys for card issuance and authorization [10], cloud applications such as Bring Your Own Key (BYOK) to cloud environments [11, 12], HSM application keys, e.g. Atalla, Thales, etc., keys for data protection [13], e.g. PCI DSS, GDPR compliance, and Identification and Authentication Management Systems (IAMS) [14, 15], or X.509 certificates for PKI, web servers, IoT devices [16–18].

3   Research Methods

The previous section provided an overview of the underlying concepts of KMS. Aside from highlighting a number of necessary characteristics, such as the presence of the four main entities, it also raised a number of issues that do not war-rant an increased level of security but provide other desired or supporting functionality, such as protection of the KMS infrastructure itself or improved usability and user experience.

Based on these concepts, this section proposes a three-stage process to identify, reduce, and comparatively analyse the existing KMS solutions. The identification stage will involve an extensive search to highlight existing solutions. In order to reduce the analysis task, the second stage will use a consistent set of the security attributes to investigate their impact for a typical organisation to shortlist and quantitatively assign their importance for a unified score. Finally, the third stage will involve a combination of feature analysis and benchmarking of the shortlisted solutions.

3.1   Literature Review

For literature review, various search queries were used to look for scientific articles and technical documentation regarding key management systems that currently available to handle software secrets. For searching both scientific and non-scientific search engines were used. The keywords used to derive start set were: "encryption key management system", "cryptographic key management system", "software key management system", "enterprise key management system". Among the scientific papers, only a few publications describing the KMS were found, the main part of the search results was either on the websites of the manufacturers of this software KMS tool, or on specialized source code sharing platform with software, such as Github.

The following inclusion and exclusion criteria were used to identify a set of KMS for screening the results of the search:

- IC1: The KMS solution should be software based.
- IC2: The KMS solution should be currently available for download, subscription or purchasing.
- IC3: There should exist description of the system, minimal documentation/specification.
- EC1: The project (e.g. on the GitHub) is apparently dead (i.e., no recent comments, updates or support contact information).
- EC2: the KMS tool is not presented in English.

3.2   Selection Process

As previously mentioned, a large number of existing KMS products have been proposed and are currently available as implemented solutions for organisations to adopt. The search proposed in the previous section would therefore yield a large number of results, all matching the context of a small organisation, but without considering the actual abilities of the respective products. In order to prime the process of evaluating them, a number of discriminating criteria are proposed in this section to derive the systems that are likely to best align to the requirements of typical small and medium organisations; these criteria are summarised below:

1. Cost. While technical capabilities are critical, small organisations are likely to face a more pragmatic challenge in terms of affordability. This criterion may exclude indeed more mature, complex solutions, but it will also represent the prime selection choice for smaller organisation.
2. REST API. A KMS must be integrated with the existing IT infrastructure, interface, and messaging, more specifically with the existing applications and users that must be connected. Having a REST API does not guarantee a smooth interconnectivity, but without it most organisations will perceive the integration task as a rather daunting one and may decide to opt out.
3. Perform an authentication of users and inside itself (who logged in and what actions are performed). All access to systems is required to be authenticated, preferably using client certificates.
4. Access control policy (how, when and by whom a key is accessed). Beyond key handling, a KMS must have the ability of authorization the subject of access using an access control list.
5. Logging. A complete solution should not only successfully manage keys but also be able to review and audit them against the authentication and access control list.
6. Secure communication. This is an expected criterion, as it links directly with the strict requirement for encryption, preferably suing a prior, approved standard.
7. Local storage. This is unlikely to provide substantive performance improvements, but it will reduce the dependency for external resources.
8. Backup. Given keys underpin the entire infrastructure, it is vital to have in place backup mechanisms that can ensure the survivability of the keys as part of the disaster management policy.
9. Scalability. The scalability challenges closely correlate with the size and complexity of business; one typical example is the computational requirements while performing cryptographic operations as the number of keys, users and applications increase.

The aim of these criteria is to reduce the number of solutions to a manageable figure and follow with a comparative analysis only on these systems.

3.3 Comparative Analysis

The KMS tools selected in the previous step were analysed using a set of attributes. Each attribute corresponded to a question with an assigned score, ranging from 1 point for low-impact, to 2 points for relevant, and 3 points for critical attributes. Given the paper focuses on the small and medium business needs, financial resources were highlighted as a priority and, hence, the analysis was restricted only to free-of-charge solutions. Similarly, the complexity of the KMS tool installation and managing process was also perceived as a significant issue and hence associated with a significant impact.

To measure installation and managing complexity, performance, and usability, each key management system was integrated in a C# test application which represents unit tests.

The complexity of the implementation was defined as the time, steps and knowledge necessary for the complete implementation of the solution, and whether additional actions such as changing or adapting the initial source code are required. Performance was measured based on the response time—the time it takes for retrieving a key from the KMS's storage—and network usage that shows amount of data that is sent over the network when retrieving a key. Ease of use implies qualitative indicators of how easy it is to use the system after its implementation, to monitor, read the logs, how convenient the user interface is. In order to evaluate usability, it is necessary to conduct a survey with physical respondents who used or currently are using the encryption key management tools and who can help to estimate an usability, as well as pros and cons of the solution. However, conducting a survey on each tool requires more time for research and, thus, was deselected.

The list of the attributes is presented in Table 1.

Table 1. List of attributes for comparative analysis of KMS.

3 points	2 points	1 point
Secure storage	Multiple authentication methods	Is the KMS beneficial of having unit tests in the source code?
Audit logs	Automated start	Popularity in the developer community (based on the number of stars and watches)
Access control	Comprehensive documentation	
No known vulnerabilities	HSM support	
High impact in the community (low ratio of open/total issues)	Available for commercial use	
Actively maintained and developed? (based on the number of recent commits)	Technical support for developers	

Each KMS can be evaluated by adding the scores from each attribute. If the answer yes to the question then the points are added to the score, otherwise nothing is added. In relation to the ratio of open/total issues, the points are added when the ratio is below average, calculated among all the compared KMS. Similarly, the popularity points are awarded for systems that have a number of commits higher than the average. Performance results are evaluated with high score of 3 points each in case when values are less than average for response time and network usage.

3.4 Experimental Environment

In order to evaluate the parameters of the installation speed and performance of key management tool, each of the five KMSs was installed on a virtual machine Ubuntu 18.04

that had characteristics with one CPU, 4096 GB RAM and 60 GB operative memory. The physical machine for running VMs had hardware characteristics with i7-8550U CPU and 16 GB RAM. Key management tools were configured, and had a way to interact with test applications via REST API. The REST calls were initiated by the console test applications in order to perform different operations as requesting a key, storing a key, retrieving a key, authentication of the communication with the specific KMS. The execution performance was measured during retrieving a key operation, and was marked using BenchmarkDotNet tool [19]. Another performance metric, the network usage, was measured using Process Monitor, as well as all network traffic that was sent between the key management system and test application.

4   Results and Analysis

The comprehensive search based on the IC and EC criteria from Sect. 3.1 produced a list of 58 software based key managements tools, of which 32 were open source code and 26 were closed source.

Further assessment of key management tools was made on matching important requirements for generating, storing, providing access and transmission of secrets, as described in Sect. 3.2. An analysis of these requirements provides an idea of how well key management systems may fit the needs of small and medium-sized businesses. Table 2 and Table 3 show a general comparison of the functions of all identified KMSs with respect to the SME requirements.

Table 2. Open source KMSs evaluation. Empty cells mean Yes.

	Free of charge	REST API	Auth with certificate	Access control policy	Audit logs	Secure communication	Keys on-premises
Ansible Vault		No	No	No	No	N/A	
Bastillion-io Bastillion		No	No				
Chef Vault	No	No	No		No	N/A	
Cloudflare Red October			No		No		
Codahale Sneaker	No	No	No				No
Cyberark Conjur			No				
Docker Biscuit	No	No	No		N/A	N/A	
Docker Secrets		No	No	No			
EnvKey	No		No				No

(continued)

Table 2. (*continued*)

	Free of charge	REST API	Auth with certificate	Access control policy	Audit logs	Secure communication	Keys on-premises
Flix- Keeto		No	No			N/A	
FreeIPA		No			No		
Fugue CredStash	No	No	No			N/A	No
GnuPG		No	No				
Hashicorp Vault							
LatFchset Custodia			No	No			
Lyft Confidant		No	No				
Manifold Torus		No	No		No		No
Meltwater Secretary		No	No				
Mozilla SOPS	No	No	No			N/A	
Neat S.r.l. Kmc-Subset137		No	N/A	N/A	N/A	N/A	N/A
Oleiade Trousseau		No	No	No	No	N/A	
OpenSSH					No		
OpenStack Barbican							
Pinterest Knox		No					
Poise Citadel	No		No		No		No
PrivacyIDEA		No	No				
Schibsted Strongbox	No	No	No				No
Shopify EJSON		No	No		No	N/A	
Shyiko Kubesec		No	No				
Square Keywhiz							
T-Mobile T-Vault			No				
XOR Data Exchange Crypt		No			No		

Table 3. Evaluation of closed source KMSs regarding to the requirements of small businesses. Empty cells mean Yes.

	Free of charge	REST API	Auth with certificate	Access control policy	Audit logs	Secure communication	Keys on-premises
Amazon AWS KMS	No						No
Amazon AWS Secrets Manager	No						No
AppViewX CERT+	No		N/A				N/A
Bloombase KeyCastle	No		N/A				
Chef Vault	No	No	No		No	N/A	
CipherCloud Key Management	No		N/A		N/A		N/A
Cryptomathic Crypto Key Management System	No		N/A				N/A
Egnyte	No					N/A	
Fornetix Key Orchestration	No		N/A				N/A
Futurex Key Management Servers	No		N/A	N/A	N/A	N/A	
Gemalto Safenet Virtual KeySecure	No		No				
Google Cloud KMS	No						No
Hancom SKM	No		N/A				
Hytrust KeyControl	No		N/A				
IBM Security Key Lifecycle Manager	No		N/A		N/A		N/A

(continued)

Table 3. (*continued*)

	Free of charge	REST API	Auth with certificate	Access control policy	Audit logs	Secure communication	Keys on-premises
KeyNexus Key Management as a Service	No		N/A				
Kryptus KNET	No		N/A		N/A		
Microsoft Azure Key Vault	No	No					No
Oracle Key Manager	No	No	N/A		N/A		
Oracle Key Vault	No	No	N/A				
Quintessence qCrypt	No		N/A				
SSH.com Universal SSH KeyManager	No	No	N/A				
Thales Vormetric Data Security Manager	No		N/A				
TokenEx	No				No	N/A	
Townsend Security Centralized Encryption KMS	No		N/A				
Unbound KeyControl	No		N/A				
Zettaset Xcrypt	No		N/A		N/A	N/A	

The information in Table 2 and 3 allowed selecting the systems that satisfy all the mandatory requirements: be open source and free of charge, include a REST API for user communication and other tools for analysis and visualization of acquired data in real time, support user access control, be able to record audit logs that allow a timely responses when an incident takes place, provide secure communication for key exchange, store keys locally cached on the client ma-chine to prevent outages if server side is unavailable. The authentication through certificates is considered preferable but not a requirement.

The analysis of key management systems summarised by Table 2 determined that only six tools correspond to the requirements and are suitable for further more comprehensive analysis: Cyberark Conjur, Hashicorp Vault, OpenStack Barbican, Pinterest Knox, Square Keywhiz, and T-Mobile T-Vault. Given that the T-Mobile T-Vault is an extension of the Hashicorp Vault, it was excluded from the comparison.

Following the shortlisting, the selected five key management systems were analysed for a set of attributes and for the complexity of implementation, discussed in Sect. 3.3. The analysis was based on data from the research studies [20, 21], Github repositories and technical documentation of each tool [22–27]. The comparison results are summarised in Table 4, where the attributes are arranged in order of their weight.

Table 4. Comparison of the KMS. Empty cells mean Yes. The data was collected 2020-06-07.

	Conjur	Vault	Barbican	Knox	Keywhiz
Secure storage (3p)					
Audit log (3p)			No		No
Access control (3p)					
No known vulnerabilities (3p)			No	No	No
Open/total issues (3p)	27	14.1	17.3	0	27.7
Recent commits (3p)	74	158	16	6	39
Response time (ms/op.) (3p)	6.95	1.56	83.37	0.78	2.31
Network usage (kB/op.) (3p)	3.63	3.93	1.76	3.65	2.86
Multiple auth methods (2p)	No			No	
Start automatically (2p)		No			
Well-written documentation (2p)				No	No
HSM support (2p)				No	No
Open for commercial use (2p)					
Technical support (2p)				No	No
Unit tests (1p)					
Popularity (1p)	422	165552	226	870	2294
Total score	29	33	25	23	20

The analysis shows that all KMSs can be easily integrated in the existing infrastructure through an API client, perform access control and logging information about client actions and secrets, as stated during the selection criteria for the full list of KMSs. There is a small variation, as Keywhiz and Barbican do not log information regarding the client identity who access the resource or request the secret. In addition, all of the KMSs could be used for commercial purposes, allow to test source code with unit tests and support multiple secure storage backends, as databases (MySQL, PostgreSQL, etc.), cloud storages and file system.

From a safety perspective, Knox, Barbican, and Keywhiz have no published security vulnerabilities, while Vault and Conjur had few but they are fixed and patched already in newer versions. Knox currently has no open issues, and the ratio of open issues to total issues for Vault and Barbican is below the mean; Conjur and Keywhiz have more open issues than the average amongst the other KMS. The amount of commits made over the most recent month was below the mean ratio for Knox, Keywhiz and Barbican and above the average for Vault and Conjur.

Moving onto performance, the analysis showed that Barbican has a very high response time during when extracting the secrets from the storage, one order of magnitude higher than the other analysed KMSs. Vault, Knox and Keywhiz showed quite well response time values of few seconds and Conjur had a slightly higher response time but still below average. In terms of the generated traffic, the network usage analysis showed that Knox, Conjur and Vault key management tools send more data over the network than the average.

In terms of their features, there was some variation among the set. Knox, Vault support authentication using multiple different types of methods. Knox supports three auth methods: Mutual TLS, Github Access Tokens and SPIFFE but, during the setup process, only the Github Access is available. Vault supports Github credentials, tokens, certificates and credentials to cloud providers. Square Keywhiz supports authentication with password and certificates. Openstack Barbican supports using SAML, user credentials, tokens and certificates. Conjur can authenticate using account ID and API key, LDAP and AWS credentials. All compared KMSs, except Vault, are able to start automatically using a command at server boot up. Vault requires unlocking of the server using a set of keys. Conjur, Vault and Barbican support HSM as a storage backend, and Knox and Keywhiz do not support HSM.

Almost all KMSs have well-written documentation, with thorough explanations of the features, configurations and various functionalities. However, Knox lacks the technical details on how to use the provided API, and Keywhiz only explains how to use the tool in the development mode but lack guidelines for making it production ready. It has also broken external links. Barbican lacks a logical structure that makes it difficult to find a right section. Installation complexity analysis showed that during installation the Knox source code requires a lot of editing to finally operate correctly. Vault, Keywhiz, Barbican and Conjur are relatively easy to install, through configuration files and running commands. Pinterest Knox and Keywhiz do not provide any technical support while Vault and Barbican offer it through the open IRC channel. Finally, from the perspective of popularity, Barbican, Knox and Conjur scored lower than Vault and Keywhiz, which are significantly higher in terms of ranking amongst similar applications.

Altogether, the analysis showed that Hashicorp Vault has the highest final score, while Square Keywhiz got the lowest score among key management tools.

5   Discussion and Conclusions

Based on an extensive search, a comprehensive list of key management systems was identified as viable KMS alternatives for small business. Totally, out of 58 tools, 32 were open source and 26 were closed source. Open source KMSs varied in terms of complexity: from tools for in-house usage, like Pinterest Knox, to KMSs that are part of company business plans, like Hachicorp Vault. A similar variation of complexity can also be seen in the closed sourced KMSs, with some are available as a service, such as Amazon AWS KMS or Microsoft Azure Key Vault, and others being hosted locally, such as Thales Vormetric Data Security Manager.

Each organisation does have a specific set of KMS requirements, but in the paper we proposed a common set likely to be specific for all SMEs. First of all, the chosen level of logging favours traceability over performance and disk usage, to make sure that all actions can be traced back to a user. Secondly, the communication between clients and the KMS needs to be secure to prevent leakage due to snooping. Next, for usability, the preference is for the KMS were to start automatically on boot, since such a KMS would have a less negative impact on its clients during an unplanned reboot. Finally, the security policy also states that the keys and secrets should be on the premises because utilising key management as a service from third-parties requires trust in the service provider; this can bring usability advantages but may weaken the confidence.

For more detailed analysis of selected five key management tools the qualitative attributes were defined. Among them there were the quality of installation guides, popularity of tool among community, implementation and usage simplicity, availability of technical support, and the variety of authentication methods.

The evaluation concluded that Hachicorp Vault scored highest as it is equipped with well-written documentation and educational guides, and due to the wide range of authentication methods and storage backends that it includes, which makes it suitable for multiple different businesses. For best practice, Hachicorp Vault should be configured and installed with its own storage backend, named Consul, on physical machines with restricted access. Further, Hachicorp Vault should only communicate securely using TLS; the machines, Vault, and other running services should be actively updated to mitigate unauthorized access. Compared to the other KMSs, Vault sends more data than average during key exchange because it includes more metadata.

One major reason for the success of Vault was its business model. Hachicorp offers Vault based on a freemium business model, where the entry model of the version is free and additional tiers costs. This means that Vault can be extended in the paid version, for example, should HSM support be required.

The results of the paper can be used by small businesses as a guideline of how to perform an evaluation themselves. The results can also be used either partly or fully by a small company if their requirements of a KMS are partly or completely equal to the requirements outlined in this study.

As part of future work, commercial, closed-sourced KMSs should be investigated, in order to get a better understanding of the differences (if any) between paid and free of charge KMS, and thus deciding if they justify the cost. Another way of extended study is evaluating more systems that give a broader perspective of the use cases and limitations from various KMSs. It would also provide a better comparison for selected attributes. Moreover, the attributes applied could also be extended and include post installation comparison as how easy a system can be updated, backed up and restored.

Acknowledgement. This project has received funding from the European Union Horizon 2020 research and innovation programme under grant agreement no. 786698 and no. 833673. This work reflects authors view and Agency is not responsible for any use that may be made of the information it contains.

References

1. Global Encryption Trends Study. Ponemon Institute Research Report (2020)
2. Sinha, V.S., et al.: Detecting and mitigating secret-key leaks in source code repositories. In: 12th Working Conference on Mining Software Repositories (MSR), Florence, pp. 396–400. IEEE/ACM (2015)
3. Björkqvist, M., et al.: Design and implementation of a key-lifecycle management system. In: Sion, R. (ed.) FC 2010. LNCS, vol. 6052, pp. 160–174. Springer, Heidelberg (2010). https://doi.org/10.1007/978-3-642-14577-3_14
4. Selecting the right key management system. Cryptomathic White Paper (2019)
5. Attridge, J.: An Overview of Hardware Security Modules. SANS Institute. Information Security Reading Room (2002)
6. Biggs, A., Cooley, S.: Management Service Architecture, IETF Internet draft (2015)
7. Mogull, R: Understanding and Selecting a Key Management Solution. Securosis LLC. (2013)
8. Allen, C.: Exploring the Lifecycle of a Cryptographic Key (2018). https://www.cryptomathic.com/news-events/blog/exploring-the-lifecycle-of-a-cryptographic-key-. Accessed 17 Jun 2020
9. Cryptera. Understanding Remote Key Loading. https://www.cryptera.com/wp-content/uploads/2014/07/Cryptera_WP_Understanding-RKL_To-Launch.pdf. Accessed 10 Jun 2020
10. EMV Key Management. Cryptomathic White Paper (2017)
11. Kumar, V., Sharma, I.: Bring-your-own-encryption: how far are we? In: 11th International Conference on Industrial and Information Systems (ICIIS), Roorkee, pp. 672–677 (2016)
12. AlBelooshi, B., Damiani, E., Salah, K., Martin, T.: Securing cryptographic keys in the cloud: a survey. IEEE Cloud Comput. 3(4), 42–56 (2016)
13. Mogull, R.: Pragmatic Key Management for Data Encryption. Securosis LLC., Phoenix (2012)
14. Kuzminykh, I., Fliustikova, M.: Mechanisms of ensuring security in Keystone service. Probl. Telecommun. 2(25), 78–96 (2019)
15. Sitaram, D., Harwalkar, S., Simha, U., Iyer, S., Jha, S.: Standards based integration of advanced key management capabilities with openstack. In: IEEE International Conference on Cloud Computing in Emerging Markets (CCEM), pp. 98–103. IEEE, Bangalore (2015)
16. White, C., Edwards, S.: Server-client PKI for applied key management system and process. US Patent US10560440B2 (2020)
17. Kuzminykh, I., Yevdokymenko, M., Sokolov, V.: Encryption Algorithms in IoT: Security vs Lifetime. Data-Centric Business and Applications. LNDECT. Springer, Cham (2021, in press)
18. Kuzminykh, I., Carlsson, A.: Analysis of assets for threat risk model in avatar-oriented IoT architecture. In: Galinina, O., Andreev, S., Balandin, S., Koucheryavy, Y. (eds.) NEW2AN/ruSMART -2018. LNCS, vol. 11118, pp. 52–63. Springer, Cham (2018). https://doi.org/10.1007/978-3-030-01168-0_6
19. BenchmarkDotNet. Frequently asked questions. https://benchmarkdotnet.org/articles/faq.html. Accessed 10 Jun 2020
20. Dooley, R., Edmonds, A., Hancock, D.Y., et al.: Security best practices for academic cloud service providers. Technical report (2018)

21. Topper, J.: Compliance is not security. Comput. Fraud Secur. **2018**(3), 5–8 (2018)
22. Hashicorp. High Availability. https://www.vaultproject.io/docs/internals/high-availability.html. Accessed 17 Jun 2020
23. Hashicorp. Production hardening. https://learn.hashicorp.com/vault/operations/production-hardening. Accessed 17 Jun 2020
24. Openstack. Barbican Documentation. https://docs.openstack.org/barbican/latest/. Accessed 17 Jun 2020
25. Pinterest. Knox Wiki. https://github.com/pinterest/knox/wiki/. Accessed 17 Jun 2020
26. Square. Keywhiz. https://github.com/square/keywhiz. Accessed 17 Jun 2020
27. Cyberark conjur automatically secures secrets used by privileged users and machine identities. https://github.com/cyberark/conjur. Accessed 17 Jun 2020

Detection of Anonymised Traffic:
Tor as Case Study

Bruno Dantas[1], Paulo Carvalho[1(✉)], Solange Rito Lima[1],
and João Marco C. Silva[2]

[1] Centro Algoritmi, Universidade do Minho, 4710 057 Braga, Portugal
a74207@alunos.uminho.pt, {pmc,solange}@di.uminho.pt
[2] HASLab, INESC TEC, Universidade do Minho, Braga, Portugal
joao.marco@inesctec.pt

Abstract. This work studies Tor, an anonymous overlay network used
to browse the Internet. Apart from its main purpose, this open-source
project has gained popularity mainly because it does not hide its implementation. In this way, researchers and security experts can fully examine
and confirm its security requirements. Its ease of use has attracted all
kinds of people, including ordinary citizens who want to avoid being profiled for targeted advertisements or circumvent censorship, corporations
who do not want to reveal information to their competitors, and government intelligence agencies who need to do operations on the Internet
without being noticed. In opposition, an anonymous system like this represents a good testbed for attackers, because their actions are naturally
untraceable. In this work, the characteristics of Tor traffic are studied in
detail in order to devise an inspection methodology able to improve Tor
detection. In particular, this methodology considers as new inputs the
observer position in the network, the portion of traffic it can monitor, and
particularities of the Tor browser for helping in the detection process. In
addition, a set of Snort rules were developed as a proof-of-concept for
the proposed Tor detection approach.

1 Introduction

Privacy is a human right and online privacy should be no different. While communications and data need firm online protections, bureaucracy has been slow to
respond to the pace of technological changes. The lack of trust in the Information
Technology (IT) domain has led individuals to discover different ways of hiding
their online identities (online anonymity). The main argument against online
anonymity by governments is about users having a lack of accountability. In
other words, anonymity can harbour criminal activity by making the tracing of
online activities more difficult [1]. Further, anonymous traffic hardens the management and monitoring of network infrastructures because the traffic cannot
be easily associated with its original sources and/or destinations. Nevertheless,
detecting and blocking anonymous traffic may, in some cases, be crucial for the
good operation of the network.

© Springer Nature Switzerland AG 2020
O. Galinina et al. (Eds.): NEW2AN 2020/ruSMART 2020, LNCS 12526, pp. 95–109, 2020.
https://doi.org/10.1007/978-3-030-65729-1_9

This work studies Tor, a tool that allows its users to achieve online anonymity. By using Tor, users can access the public Internet without worrying about censors, governments, service providers, and so on. The motivation of this work is to take the area of anonymous traffic detection one step further in its continuous research. In particular, this paper starts by dissecting the main Tor architectural components and operation in order to establish an encompassing methodology for its detection. This involves a systematic coverage of relevant aspects to consider in the traffic inspection strategy, such as the observer's position in the network, the portion of traffic under analysis and Tor traffic characteristics at distinct network layers. As proof-of-concept, after exploring and identifying Tor behaviour and particularities, a set of Snort rules was created to detect Tor traffic.

This paper is organised as follows: a discussion on traffic characterisation, anonymity systems and other related works is carried out in Sect. 2; in Sect. 3, the methodology for detecting Tor traffic is discussed from different perspectives and protocolar levels. As proof-of-concept, the definition of Snort rules for Tor detection and the experimental results are provided and discussed in Sect. 4. Finally, the main conclusions of the study are included in Sect. 5.

2 State-of-the-Art

2.1 Traffic Classification

The discipline of traffic classification tries to associate traffic flows or packets with the applications, or application types, that generated them. In the context of computer networks, the five tuple (destination/source Internet Protocol (IP) address, destination/source port number, protocol field) is commonly used to (uniquely) identify different flows, and is used since the first-generation firewalls [2].

While in the early days of the Internet port-based approaches (checking packets' port numbers) was enough to achieve high accuracy classification results [3], over the last two decades, some developments make it difficult for operators and service providers to classify traffic flows: applications that have no IANA registered ports; the use of well-known ports to circumvent filtering; physical servers may offer services through the same public address but on different ports.

Operators were then forced to use another approach, commonly called Deep Packet Inspection (DPI), by looking at packets' content to discover the application being used [4]. This approach has two downsides. The use of pattern matching can become easily slow because each incoming packet has to be compared with thousands of different signatures. Also, end-to-end encryption is becoming ubiquitous, which makes DPI less effective [5]. Nevertheless, relevant information can be extracted from encrypted connections, typically from the session's initiation. The reason for this is that security protocols usually have an initialisation phase that is not encrypted.

With the increasing complexity of networks, the classification methods are usually supported with the help of protocols knowledge [5], coupling traffic classification with other approaches, such as machine learning, deep learning, and specific heuristics [3,5]. These approaches are mainly applied to specific network metrics depending on each application characteristics, at different granularity levels, being also referred as host behaviour and statistical classification. Despite this, if operators' techniques are publicly known, developers intentionally change the application's network metrics (e.g. packets' inter-arrival times, packets' length, using dynamic ports). By modifying them, it is possible to obfuscate the application generating the traffic.

2.2   Online Anonymity Systems

The main goal of anonymity systems is to avoid traffic analysis and network surveillance, and to block any tracking of users' identities in the Internet [6]. Why is it needed, if almost all applications' data is encrypted? First, service providers usually have logging systems to monitor their infrastructure. The recorded logs can have information that can be used to keep track of users' identities or activities. Secondly, secure communication protocols can reveal information or have implementation flaws. For example, the Client Hello message in the Transport Layer Security (TLS) handshake can carry the Server Name Indication in plain text (SNI extension). Thirdly, as already mentioned, traffic classification techniques are currently adopting statistical approaches to classify encrypted traffic, based on network and transport layers information, communication metrics and user behaviour. In other words, it is still possible to guess, with some level of certainty, what kind of services users are accessing, even if the communications are encrypted. These discussed points are the reasons why most of the anonymity systems use techniques in network or transport layers. The goal is to separate the application data from the lower level layers as a way to obfuscate who is accessing the service. Typically, this is achieved by bouncing the traffic to an intermediate entity before accessing the final service. That entity then uses some strategy to obfuscate the traffic (discussed next).

Depending on the architecture, anonymity systems can be used to circumvent geographically blocked content, dodge targeted marketing or test network attacks. Also, they are a troublesome for governments in censorship countries, as they allow citizens to access censored websites without being discovered. As a consequence, those countries' government agencies and particular service providers block traffic generated or sent to those tools. When an anonymity system starts to become more famous, the simplest approach is to block their public IP addresses [7]. In this way, citizens are forced to access the service without an anonymity system or to find other system less famous and not blocked yet. Without directly blocking anonymity systems, these agencies would have to apply other traffic classification techniques already discussed. If the traffic is classified as belonging to some anonymity system and is blocked, citizens are unable to access whatever they like through that system (even if, the content is legal).

Currently, there is no anonymity system capable of leaving all parties satisfied. These systems use techniques such as proxies, mix networks, tunnelling and overlay networks. Each one has its own design, which means that each one has its specific use case, advantages and disadvantages. This paper will focus on

Tor, an anonymity system that uses an overlay network to provide anonymous browsing to its users.

2.3   Tor Project

Tor (or Tor Project) is a continuously growing open-source project that provides anonymity at network/transport layers over the TCP/IP protocol stack. Its first release was in 2002 with the name The Onion Router (hence its actual abbreviated name). More specifically, Tor is a circuit-based low-latency anonymous communication service that provides perfect forward secrecy, congestion control, directory authorities, integrity checking, configurable exit policies, and a practical design for location-hidden services via rendezvous points [8].

The service is circuit-based because before sending any data, it creates a route of nodes through which the data will pass. Depending on the position in the circuit, each node can be called entry/guard, middle or exit node. Instead of nodes, these can also be called onion routers or relays. Tor provides a low-latency service because it was deployed to be used in interactive or non-linear environments, such as web browsing. Perfect forward secrecy means that once the session keys are deleted, subsequently compromised nodes cannot decrypt old traffic (unique session keys are created for different sessions). Tor uses an incremental path-building design, where the initiator negotiates session keys with each successive hop in the circuit, used for encrypting the message. Each onion router in the path then strips off a layer of encryption, until the exit node decrypts the last layer and becomes able to redirect the original message's request. Figure 1 illustrates this process with only two onion routers (in real operation there are at least three).

Fig. 1. Example of Tor encryption layers.

Congestion control is also implemented to prevent onion routers from getting congested. Directory authorities are trustworthy servers responsible for retrieving control information to clients (e.g., list of onion routers that will make up the circuit). Integrity checking is performed in two stages. First, onion routers use the TLS protocol to communicate with each other (see details in Sect. 3.1). Second, specific Tor messages called relay cells contain an end-to-end checksum for integrity checking. Configurable exit policies, as the name suggests, is a feature that enables users to circumvent problems with service usage (e.g., selecting the country of the last onion router in the circuit). Location-hidden services provide anonymous services to other users (users remain anonymous too), such as e-commerce, news or illegal activities [9].

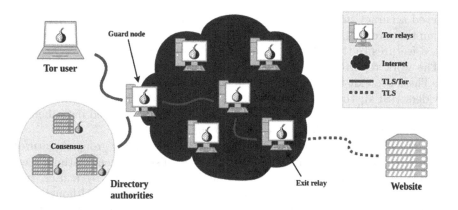

Fig. 2. Tor architecture review and related terminology.

A typical architecture of Tor is depicted in Fig. 2. At its core, Tor is simply a tool that can build paths given a set of routers [7]. One relay is chosen more frequently, the guard node, which is highlighted in the figure. On the one hand, this relay is a special trustworthy node that always acts as the entry relay, as long as it is not compromised or (periodically) rotated. On the other hand, middle relays and exit relays are chosen proportionally to their available bandwidth[1]. There are fewer exit relays than middle relays because Tor allows volunteers to run either as middle or exit relays. The reason is that exit relays do not know what websites are being accessed by users, and so they are more vulnerable to attacks if the websites are (intentionally) compromised [8].

The directory authorities are responsible for distributing control information across the (overlay) network. Basically, they agree on a consensus, a compressed document, so that each relay can check its validity. Communications within Tor use their own defined encryption techniques(over a TLS layer).

2.4   Related Work

In [11], machine learning techniques are used for traffic classification in three different anonymity tools: Tor, JonDonym and I2P. Using the *Anon17* dataset[2], the authors measure three different levels of granularity to distinguish between the anonymity tool, traffic type and application. The results showed high accuracy, progressively reduced for each granularity level, evaluated after receiving the flows' eighth packet (as the beginning of a flow contains the negotiation of parameters and requests between client/server or peers, with protocol-specific headers and message sequences [3]). Despite this, the authors show the maximum

---

[1] The bandwidth is constantly tested by directory authorities to prevent attacks where relays claim to have more bandwidth than they really have (to be more frequently chosen) [8,10].

[2] https://web.cs.dal.ca/~shahbar/data.html.

achieved accuracy and F-measure, along with the number of packets needed to sustain those results. The effects of feature importance (up to 74) and temporal-related features to the network are also investigated.

The work reported in [12] demonstrates the presence of *hot exit points* in Tor. These are exit-nodes agglomerations, controlled by some Internet Service Providers (ISPs), that are almost always used, despite the existence of other exit-nodes options. The results are based on 1.5 years of recorded data, being a threat to anonymity (as ISP can correlate traffic more easily).

A different Tor design is proposed in [13]. By introducing group signatures, a cryptographic technique, it is possible to distinguish between legitimate and illegitimate users. When some malicious action is performed by a user, it is possible to block or denounce him. This approach is not perfect. Although relay volunteers and ISPs increase trust in the overlay network, benign users have to trust the entity in charge of blocking or denouncing them (basically the same problem of mixing proxies).

The identification of TLS abnormalities in Tor is provided in [14]. The work begins by identifying TLS characteristics in Tor (e.g., certificate extensions). Then, Snort rules are created according to those characteristics, which could effectively identify the presence of Tor traffic. However, at the time of writing, Tor only supported TLS 1.0, resulting in outdated rules when considering the latest TLS 1.3 and 1.2 versions.

The work in [15] begins by identifying the most known attacks that could be used to deanonymise Tor circuits. The two outlined categories of attacks are traffic correlation and webpage fingerprinting. The vulnerable identified areas are the guard-node selection and rotation algorithm, the intercell transmission timings and other traffic metrics (cell order, amount, interval, size and direction). Then, the authors have focused on these areas to collect the proposed and already-implemented countermeasures that could enhance Tor resistance as regards the three mentioned vulnerabilities. Finally, the process of evaluation is accomplished by comparing each countermeasure with a set of (security) requirements previously defined (following the *MoSCoW* method).

A longitudinal study of Tor network is presented in [16]. The work is based on a passive analysis of TLS traffic over more than three years in four large universities. The results show that it is possible to identify Tor, specifically through some information present in X.509 certificates and other exchanged parameters within the TLS handshake. Despite this, it is assumed that Tor's detection will remain an arms race.

Although the mentioned studies address the problematic of Tor traffic classification and/or detection of malicious behaviours at some extend, important aspects of an encompassing methodology for Tor inspection and subsequent detection are not addressed as a whole. This motivates the present study and the methodological discussion presented below.

3   Inspecting Tor Traffic

This section is dedicated to discuss important Tor inspection methodology aspects namely, the observer's position in the network, the portion of traffic it can monitor, protocol layer issues and related metrics, and particularities of Tor browser.

3.1   Observer Position

As regards the observer position in the network, a Tor detector might be placed at three distinct points, i.e., between: (i) an onion proxy and a guard node; (ii) two onion routers (or a guard node and an onion router); and (iii) an exit node and the final destination.

(i) Onion proxy and guard node - an external observer monitoring any link between the onion proxy (or a Tor browser) and the guard node can infer relevant information. First, the (partial) location can be exposed through the inspection of the guard node's IP addresses involved in the connection. Second, it is possible to identify whether the client is using Tor. This detection is performed by inspecting the IP address and comparing it to known guard nodes[3], or inspecting the TLS handshake (assuming that the connection was not already established).

(ii) Two onion relays - this case and the previous one follow different traffic patterns. Although the TLS handshakes are slightly different, an external observer cannot distinguish them. In fact, one might think that it is easy to distinguish the two handshakes as in case (i) only one party authenticates himself (the guard node) and, in this case, both parties need to authenticate (to prevent impersonation attacks). As shown in Fig. 3, Tor handles this by performing a TLS handshake first, always as a server-only authentication handshake, and then performs an inner handshake to complete the authentication. To better illustrate this, consider two onion relays willing to communicate. At start, a normal client/server TLS handshake is performed, and only one of them (the next in the circuit) will authenticate itself using a local certificate. Only after this, inside the TLS session just created, the authentication will be completed in an inner handshake, specified by Tor (not a TLS handshake). In this inner handshake, the parties will agree in a common version, exchange certificates, and other parameters. To an external observer, the outer handshake is the same for those two cases.

After the handshake phase, traffic patterns can be slightly different. Only the first case (onion proxy and guard node) uses connection-level padding. Any other connection does not use it (a connection to a bridge is treated as the first case[4]). There are proposals for changing the circuit-level padding between onion

---

[3] Tor Bridges. In that case, the onion proxy connects to a bridge before the guard node and can obfuscate itself from his regional ISP, i.e., the regional provider can only conclude that the onion proxy was communicating with another peer.

[4] https://gitweb.torproject.org/torspec.git/tree/padding-spec.txt.

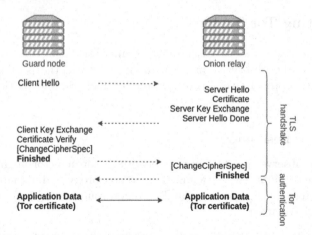

Fig. 3. Tor relays authentication

relays, however, they are not yet implemented. In connection-level padding, cells carry the same value as always, but new dummy cells are introduced to obfuscate traffic from external observers. Therefore, in theory, case (ii) leads to different traffic patterns from case (i).

(iii) Exit node and destination - from the exit node to the final destination, despite being a traditional HTTP/HTTPS connection, traffic can be analysed to possibly detect Tor presence. One way is to inspect the IP addresses involved in the connection and compare them to a list of known Tor (exit) nodes. Other possible way is to measure network metrics and infer that it is a Tor exit node if the delay of packets is higher than the normal. In this case, the packets' length is not fixed. In fact, the size of messages follows the normal operation of the HTTP protocol, but the exit node readjusts them to fit within the fixed required size (512 bytes) in the Tor network.

This knowledge might be helpful, for example, if a website administrator does not want Tor users to access his website. One possible reason for an administrator to want to block Tor under these conditions is that the information collected is no longer related to the original client's IP address, being now related to the exit node. Worse than that, a different client may use the same exit node, but they look the same to the website as both requests stem from the same IP address.

3.2   Observer Traffic Portion

In normal conditions, a passive observer can only monitor one link. However, monitoring more than one (overlay) link in Tor can be only achieved if that observer spans different countries. In fact, Tor assumes that does not have a defence against a global adversary [8]. By global adversary is meant a passive observer that can monitor more than one link, thus correlating flows and inferring the circuit that an onion proxy is using. Of course, one global adversary can be made of smaller adversaries working together. Either in real-time or from recorded logs, it is possible to aggregate that data and correlate it to know what website a client was accessing through Tor.

3.3 Traffic Characteristics

An external observer may inspect packets payload, however their encryption do not allow retrieving useful information (at least individually). Because of that, inspection can only occur at lower protocolar levels, such as network, transport and session layers. In addition, measuring network parameters can help detecting Tor traffic, where the most important metrics are the length and the delay of packets. The former is useful because Tor uses fixed-size messages of 512 bytes (connection establishment cells are variable-sized). The latter can suggest the presence of Tor because delay values will typically be higher than normal (packets have to traverse onion relays across different countries). If possible, these metrics should be used in conjunction with other indicators or rules for completeness (e.g., network congestion may produce a false positive).

At network layer, IP is the first protocol worth to be inspected. It is known that some ISPs are already blocking static IP addresses used by directory authorities, onion relays or guard nodes (fact that led to the introduction of Tor Bridges). In addition, the websites providing information regarding current active onion relays, their associated IP addresses, geographical location, and sometimes the volunteer's personal information (Twitter profile) are plentiful. Even with the introduction of bridges, it is assumed that there is no magic bullet for their discovery. Although it is more difficult to enumerate all the bridges IP addresses, their discovery is indeed possible [17].

At transport layer, the Tor Browser currently uses random ports to communicate with the guard node, while onion proxies use the port determined by guard nodes. The same applies to fetch network information through other relays (up to three connections). Each relay can optionally act as a directory authority to help in the distribution of the consensus document, but the ports are randomly chosen as well. Note that the randomness of ports at transport layer is useless from a signature-based Intrusion Detection System (IDS) point of view. However, an anomaly-based IDS could probably deduce information if some ports were used more than others.

At session layer, in the case of TLS, the followed approach is simple. The objective is trying to detect fields and parameters that are different from other TLS flows (web browsers). By comparing the Tor browser with other browsers, one can start ruling out other TLS sources until only the Tor browser is left. According to [16], there are several fields within TLS that can be used to detect Tor. The present work takes that list as a starting point to discuss which TLS fields are useful for creating Tor detection rules. In this context, the TLS messages `Client Hello` and `Server Hello` were identified as relevant elements for sensing Tor.

3.4 Tor Browser Particularities

As mentioned, Tor traffic characteristics can be derived from the Tor browser TLS handshaking phase.

Starting with the `Client Hello` message, the first parameter to inspect is the TLS version. As most browsers already support TLS 1.3, every website connection within the browser will use an extensive list of TLS extensions in `Client Hello` messages, when compared with the previous version. Although this extensions list may be useful, inspecting the TLS `version` field is useless as both versions (v1.2 and v1.3) use the value `0x0303` for backward compatibility. As regards the `Session ID` field, it can be helpful as Tor nodes do not resume sessions, conversely to common services. Regarding cipher suites information, a major differentiating parameter is the `Cipher Suites Length`. Despite this, if this value is the same for Tor and other browsers, a comparison can be established based on `Cipher Suites List` contents. Table 1 compares two of the discussed fields in the `Client Hello` message for Tor and the most used browsers according to *w3schools* [5].

Table 1. Client-side TLS parameters

Browser	Cipher suites	Extensions
Tor	14	6
Chrome	17	17
Safari	23	8
Edge	19	10
Firefox	18	14
Opera	17	17

The `Server Hello` handshake message also carries useful information, however, its scope is broader than in the client. Therefore, this message should only be inspected to complement the `Client Hello`, as the number of different servers is very large, and each server has to follow the client behaviour. Note that considering `Server Hello` messages implies a stateful detection system [2] due to a potentially high number of sessions being handled concurrently (which may affect the trade-off between accuracy and performance). The `extensions` field can be a major field in the detection process, as Tor nodes use shorter extension lists than common servers (usually with a length of 13 or 18).

4 Experimental Evaluation

Based on the specific characteristics of Tor traffic presented above, Snort rules were defined and evaluated under distinct test scenarios. These rules allow to

---

[5] https://www.w3schools.com/browsers/default.asp.

introduce simple and effective detection in existing network systems, e.g., IDS or firewalls. The configuration details and the obtained results are discussed in the following sections.

4.1 Snort Rules

To explore the detection of Tor traffic, Snort rules were created targeting specific characteristics of TLS messages as explained in Sect. 3.4. To do so, a first rule (presented as Listing 1) triggers for every TLS packet sent from the internal network $HOME_NET to any external network having the **Cipher Suites Length** field with the value 28 (14 cipher suites supported).

```
1   alert tcp $HOME_NET any -> any any \
2       (content:"|16|"; offset:0; depth:1; \
3       content: "|00 1c|"; offset:44; depth:47; \
4   flowbits:set,tor_browser; flowbits:noalert; sid:1000001)
```

Listing 1: Snort rule: setting initial state

Note that an alert will not be generated for each packet matching this rule. Instead, the **tor_browser** variable will be set with the **flowbits:set** rule option. The alert is only generated if the response packet matches one of the two rules following this one (which is the purpose of the rule option **flowbits:isset**). These two rules are illustrated in Listing 2.

```
1    alert tcp any any -> $HOME_NET any \
2        (msg: "TOR BROWSER DETECTED ! ! !"; \
3        content:"|16|"; offset:0; depth:1; \
4        content:"|00 0d|"; offset:47; depth:50; \
5        flowbits:isset,tor_browser; sid:1000002)
6    alert tcp any any -> $HOME_NET any \
7        (msg: "TOR BROWSER DETECTED ! ! !"; \
8        content:"|16|"; offset:0; depth:1; \
9        content:"|00 12|"; offset:47; depth:50; \
10       flowbits:isset,tor_browser; sid:1000003)
```

Listing 2: Snort rules: detecting Tor

Basically, these rules will match response (**Server Hello**) packets which have the **Extension Length** field with the values 13 or 18. Within the rules, these values are represented in hexadecimal. Note that, the assumption that only **Client Hello** or **Server Hello** messages can match the rules can be violated as the protocol over TCP can be other than TLS. However, it is unlikely that a different protocol exactly matches the **content** rule options specified.

For the specific case of Snort, these rules might be enhanced by resorting to the SSL preprocessor, which allows the IDS to recognise a TLS session using the built-in **ssl_state** rule which matches every packet with **ssl_state: client_hello** or **ssl_state: server_hello** values.

4.2   Test Scenarios

In order to assess the proposed rules, background traffic was generated along with Tor connections following two test approaches: a simpler one, based on control traffic generated from non-anonymous browsers; and a more realistic test, in which Tor connections were introduced in real traffic captured in a campus network.

Tor connections were generated resorting to a script executing multiple instances of the Tor Browser Bundle, and connecting them to the Tor network, each time to a different guard node. To prevent from always connecting with the same guard node, each Tor Browser instance was set with a different list of wanted `EntryNodes`. Such node variability provides a more relevant test scenario, as it can detect guard nodes using different handshake protocols. Both background traffic and Tor specific traffic were merged using `tcpdump` and then processed by Snort, which applied both the community and the proposed rules. Mixing the general rules with Tor detection specific rules allow to address eventual collision with intrusion detection processes in operational networks. Details regarding the two test scenarios are:

(i) Browsers Traffic: In this first scenario, through a Python script, multiple connections to the fifty more accessed websites in Portugal[6] were established, using five commercial non-anonymous browsers (mentioned in Table 1) in a local network. The purpose of using different browsers is to have `Client Hello` messages varying the cryptographic parameters. In this way, at least 250 handshakes are performed (some websites perform more than one).

(ii) Real Traffic: In this scenario, a `Sophos XG 105 Firewall` was deployed for sniffing all traffic generated by multiple users sharing a LAN during one hour. The traffic passing through the firewall does only include each user's laptop in that LAN. The corresponding network traffic trace includes various applications, such as *OpenVPN*, *CiscoVPN*, *Microsoft OneDrive*, *Microsoft Teams*, *Skype*, *Slack*, *Spotify*, *EMC Avamar*, *Tortoise SVN*, *NetBeans* or *Maven*, resulting from a normal user activity.

Although performed in an offline environment (to prevent connection variations or instabilities across multiples sessions), all tests assume a monitoring point placed between the onion proxy and guard node (see Sect. 3.1).

4.3   Evaluation Results

The accuracy of the rules created is measured evaluating whether the number of Snort alerts triggered by Tor traffic is equal to the number of connections established through the script. False positives and false negatives are identified by comparing all processed packets with the trace containing only the Tor traffic.

For test scenario (i), with traffic generated by five different non-anonymous browsers, the detection rules led to 100% accuracy. In fact, some alerts were

---

[6] https://www.similarweb.com/top-websites/portugal.

triggered only by executing the Tor browser, which demonstrates their effectiveness in identifying Tor activity even before the user request any resource. This is possible as the Directory authority activity (see Sect. 2.3) follows the same TLS pattern as the relay nodes.

Considering the second and more realistic scenario, the proposed rules were also able to identify all connections originated from a Tor browser. However, in this case, it was also identified a significant number of false positives, 25%. Although being high, all the false positives were related to the same traffic type, namely *Microsoft Teams* desktop application.

A deeper inspection of false positives revealed they were caused by the way Snort processes packets. Basically, the proposed rules have a specific offset because when analysing Tor traffic, no session identifiers were present. Without session identifier, the `Client Hello` message has only one field in this context, the `Session ID Length` with the value zero. When this identifier is present, the `Client Hello` message also includes the length field with the corresponding value. Hence, when creating the rules, the field following the `Session ID Length` was not its actual value, but the next field, i.e., the `Cipher Suites Length`. All connections erroneously classified as Tor traffic had a session identifier which was causing a no alert triggering. However, the alerts were generated, so it is assumed that Snort can ignore the identifier value or shift the offset accordingly. A strategy that might prevent this type of false positive is the introduction of additional parameters into the rules. For instance, the SNI extension in the `Client Hello` might be analysed and compared either to a list of trusted server names or to a list of previously enumerated services.

Figure 4 (left) illustrates the total number of packets of test scenarios (i) and (ii), and the number of packets that Snort analysed. Although the analysis was not performed in real-time, processing the real traffic scenario efficiently required significant resources (it was analysed in less than 3 s, which corresponds to approximately 8 Gbps). This ratifies the importance of establishing simple detection rules, as adding new fields to be matched and/or more chained rules applied to all packets might be computationally prohibitive. In Fig. 4 (right), the number of Tor alerts and logs are expressed. As shown, Snort could correctly log all the generated alerts, however, the network trace with real traffic lead to 25% of false positives in detecting Tor traffic.

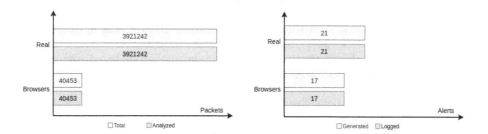

Fig. 4. Number of packets per test (left); Number of Tor alerts per test (right)

5 Conclusions

Within anonymisation systems, Tor has gained popularity as an anonymous overlay network used to browse the Internet. The present work has provided a comprehensive study exploring particular characteristics of Tor traffic in order to allow a simple and effective detection in production networks. The proposed Tor inspecting methodology considers new aspects to be considered for helping in the detection process, as the observer position in the network, the portion of traffic it can monitor, and the session-level particularities of the Tor browser. The proof-of-concept has involved the definition of a set of Snort rules tested in distinct traffic scenarios for Tor detection. In both scenarios, the results show the effectiveness of simple rules in detecting Tor traffic with high accuracy.

With respect to this area of research, it will remain a strong competition among the entities in search for online anonymity and the ones that search for surveillance and/or censorship. Currently, there is no one-fits-all solution to this problem. Different strategies have arisen due to the increasing interest in this area, but those only solve the problem to some extent. Most importantly, the anonymous systems research line must continue to evolve to allow users online privacy while allowing means of service providers and system administrators being able to control their infrastructures. This study represents a step forward in this direction.

Acknowledgements. This work is financed by National Funds through the Portuguese funding agency, FCT - Fundação para a Ciência e a Tecnologia within project UIDB /50014/2020, and by FCT – Fundação para a Ciência e Tecnologia – within the R&D Units Project Scope: UIDB/00319/2020.

References

1. Winkler, S., Zeadally, S.: An analysis of tools for online anonymity. Int. J. Pervasive Comput. Commun. **11**(4), 436–453 (2015)
2. Neupane, K., Haddad, R., Chen, L.: Next generation firewall for network security: a survey. In: Conference Proceedings - IEEE SOUTHEASTCON 2018, pp. 1–6 (April 2018)
3. Finsterbusch, M., Richter, C., Rocha, E., Müller, J.A., Hänßgen, K.: A survey of payload-based traffic classification approaches. IEEE Commun. Surv. Tutor. **16**(2), 1135–1156 (2014)
4. Dainotti, A., Pescapé, A., Claffy, K.C.: Issues and future directions in traffic classification. IEEE Netw. **26**(1), 35–40 (2012)
5. Adibi, S.: Traffic classification – packet-, flow-, and application-based approaches. Int. J. Adv. Comput. Sci. Appl. **1**, 6–15 (2010)
6. Haraty, R.A., Zantout, B.: The TOR data communication system: a survey. In: Proceedings - International Symposium on Computers and Communications Workshops, pp. 1–6 (2014)
7. Dingledine, R., Mathewson, N.: Design of a Blocking-resistant Anonymity System, pp. 1–24. svn.torproject.org (2006)

8. Dingledine, R., Mathewson, N., Syverson, P.: Tor: the second-generation onion router. In: Proceedings of the 13th Conference on USENIX Security Symposium, SSYM 2004, USA, vol. 13, p. 21. USENIX Association (2004)

9. Pistunovich, V.I.: Tor: the second-generation Onion router. Sov. At. Energy **46**(4), 337 (2005)

10. Bauer, K., McCoy, D., Grunwald, D., Kohno, T., Sicker, D.: Low-resource routing attacks against Tor, p. 11 (2007)

11. Montieri, A., Ciuonzo, D., Member, S., Aceto, G.: Anonymity services Tor, I2P, JonDonym: classifying in the dark (February 2018)

12. Koch, R., Golling, M., Rodosek, G.D.: How anonymous is the Tor network? A long-term black-box investigation. Computer **49**(3), 42–49 (2016)

13. Diaz, J., Arroyo, D., Rodriguez, F.B.: Fair and accountable anonymity for the Tor network. In: ICETE, vol. 4, pp. 560–565 (2017)

14. Granerud, A.O.: Identifying TLS Abnormalities in Tor. Information Security (2010)

15. Stone, J.A., Saxena, N., Dogan, H.: Systematic analysis: resistance to traffic analysis attacks in Tor system for critical infrastructures. In: Proceedings of the 2018 IEEE International Conference on Systems, Man, and Cybernetics, SMC 2018, pp. 2832–2837 (2019)

16. Amann, J., Sommer, R.: Exploring Tor's activity through long-term passive TLS traffic measurement. In: Karagiannis, T., Dimitropoulos, X. (eds.) PAM 2016. LNCS, vol. 9631, pp. 3–15. Springer, Cham (2016). https://doi.org/10.1007/978-3-319-30505-9_1

17. Ling, Z., Luo, J., Yu, W., Yang, M., Fu, X.: Tor bridge discovery: extensive analysis and large-scale empirical evaluation. IEEE Trans. Parallel Distrib. Syst. **26**(7), 1887–1899 (2015)

Polyhedra of Finite State Machines and Their Use in the Identification Problem

Sergey Yu. Melnikov[1]($\boxtimes$) and Konstantin E. Samouylov[1,2]

[1] Peoples' Friendship University of Russia (RUDN University), Moscow, Russia
melnikov@linfotech.ru, ksam@sci.pfu.edu.ru
[2] Federal Research Center "Computer Science and Control" of the Russian Academy of Sciences, Moscow, Russia

Abstract. The possible sets of joint distribution of the word occurrence frequencies in the finite state machine input and output sequences are considered. A geometric description of such sets as convex polyhedra in a real unit cube of suitable dimension is proposed. A method has been developed for comparison of unknown and reference automata by the observed input and output sequence fragments. The method does not require installation to the fixed initial state.

Keywords: FSM identification · Statistical properties of automata · Word occurrence statistics

1 Introduction

We will consider the problem of testing the hypothesis that an unknown automaton A (which input and output sequences are observed) coincides with the known automaton A_0. It is necessary to check whether such an initial state of the automaton A_0 exists, starting from which it transforms the observed input sequence into the observed output sequence. We believe that the unknown automaton A is selected from some finite class containing the automaton A_0. We assume that all automata from this class have the same alphabets and are pairwise nonequivalent.

This task is relevant in the theory of technical device testing and diagnostics, as well as in a number of cryptographic applications, in particular, when testing the hypothesis that the analyzed device implements some encryption algorithm with unknown key.

The formulated problem can be solved by installation of the automaton A_0 in each of the possible initial states, and application of the observable input sequence to its input. If for any initial state the resulting output sequence does not coincide with the observed one, then the hypothesis that A and A_0 coincide is rejected. If at least one of the variants shows a coincidence of sequences, it is concluded that the observed data do not contradict the tested hypothesis. The

O. Galinina et al. (Eds.): NEW2AN 2020/ruSMART 2020, LNCS 12526, pp. 110–121, 2020.
https://doi.org/10.1007/978-3-030-65729-1_10

complexity of this method is proportional to the nonequivalent state number of the automaton and is extremely high for automata modeling of the information processing equipment nodes.

The proposed approach uses the construction of a special polyhedron corresponding to the automaton A_0 inside a real unit cube of suitable dimension. In the observed input and output sequences of automaton A, the relative frequencies of certain word occurrences are calculated. These relative frequencies determine the coordinates of the points in the cube. The distance between the polyhedron of the automaton A_0 and these points is calculated. In the case when this distance exceeds a threshold depending on the observed sequence lengths, the hypothesis that A and A_0 coincide is rejected.

2   Related Works

Geometric representations are traditionally used to identify non-obvious statistical dependencies in the output sequence when analyzing pseudorandom sequence generators [1,2].

In [3], an approach is described related to the construction of automata geometric images, in which the automaton behavior is displayed in geometric figures, in particular, in curves on a plane.

When all possible words are fed to the automaton input, some output words do not appear (these words are "prohibitions" of the automaton [4]), but some output words appear repeatedly. The word frequencies in the output sequences in [5] are studied using the so-called histogram automaton function, which associates the word in the output alphabet with its frequency. The geometric constructions associated with the convex hull construction of point sets in n-dimensional space were used in [6] in the study of quantitative languages that assign a real number to each word.

In [7], a method was proposed for detection of covert channels in information systems by checking for the presence of forbidden fragments ("prohibitions") in transmitted sequences. Since the covert channel organizers do not know about this, then if such a fragment is found in the observed sequence, the controller determines that the covert channel is functioning. An analogy can be drawn between such an approach and the one considered in this paper: hypotheses about the absence of a covert channel or about the coinciding of an automaton with a reference one are rejected when a certain inequality holds for the certain event frequency in the observed sequences. The rejection criterion in both cases is deterministic, it has a zero error of the second kind.

The proposed approach can also be useful for checking the quality of pseudorandom sequence generators, which are widely used in modern traffic control technologies, such as Random-Access Channel [8] and device-to-device (D2D) communications [9,10].

3   Definition of a Polyhedron of an Automaton

Let B be a finite set (alphabet). By B^* we denote the set of all words in the alphabet B. We denote by Ω the set of all infinite sequences over B:

$$\Omega = \{\omega = w_1 w_2 \ldots | w_t \in B, t = 0, 1, \ldots\}. \tag{1}$$

For each word $\alpha \in B^*$, $\alpha = a_0 a_1 \ldots a_{m-1}$, where $a_i \in B$, $i = 0, 1, \ldots, m - 1$, $m = 1, 2, \ldots$ we define a cylinder

$$[\alpha] = [a_0 a_1 \ldots a_{m-1}] = \{\omega = w_0 w_1 \ldots | w_0 = a_0, w_1 = a_1, w_{m-1} = a_{m-1}\} \subset \Omega. \tag{2}$$

The characteristic function of an arbitrary subset $F \subset \Omega$ will be denoted by I_F:

$$I_F = \begin{cases} 1, & \text{if } \omega \in F \\ 0, & \text{if } \omega \notin F \end{cases}. \tag{3}$$

Instead of $I_{[\alpha]}$ we will simply write I_α.

Define a mapping T ("sequence shift") $T : \Omega \to \Omega$ by

$$T : \omega = w_0 w_1 \ldots \to \omega T = w_1 w_2 \ldots. \tag{4}$$

The equality

$$I_\alpha \left(\omega T^t \right) = 1 \tag{5}$$

means in such a way that

$$w_t = a_0, \; w_{t+1} = a_1, \ldots, \; w_{t+m-1} = a_{m-1}. \tag{6}$$

The number $\frac{1}{t} \sum_{j=0}^{t-1} I_\alpha \left(\omega T^{s+j} \right)$ is called the relative frequency of occurrence of the word α in the sequence ω on the segment from s to $s + t - 1$. We will use the notation

$$p_\alpha(\omega) = \lim_{t \to \infty} \frac{1}{t} \sum_{j=0}^{t-1} I_\alpha \left(\omega T^j \right), \tag{7}$$

if the limit on the right side exists. The value of $p_\alpha(\omega)$ can be interpreted as an average frequency of occurrence of the word α in the sequence ω [11].

Such limits exist, for example, for infinite periodic sequences (both purely periodic and periodic with an initial section), the set of which we denote by T_B. In this case, as can be seen from the formula (7), p_α is the ratio of the frequency of occurrence of the word α in the period (the number of places in the period from which the word α begins) to the length of the period. For example, in the case of sequence $010101 \ldots$ we have:

$$p_1 = 1/2, \; p_{01} = 1/2, \; p_{0101} = 1/2, \; p_{011} = 0. \tag{8}$$

Let $A = (X, Y, Q, h, f)$ be a strongly connected finite Moore machine with X and Y as input and output alphabets; Q as the set of states; $h : Q \times X \to Q$ as transition function; $f : Q \times X \to Y$ as output function.

Let us fix two sets of words

$$\{\alpha_i \in X^*, i = 1, 2, \ldots, t\} \text{ and } \{\beta_j \in Y^*, j = 1, 2, \ldots, k\}, t \geq 0, k \geq 1. \quad (9)$$

Let us suppose that an automaton A, starting to work from the state q_0, processes a sequence $\chi = (x_0, x_1, \ldots)$ into a sequence $\gamma = (y_0, y_1, \ldots)$. With sequence χ we associate the vector

$$z_{(A,q_0)}(\chi) = (p_{\alpha_1}(\chi), \ldots, p_{\alpha_t}(\chi), p_{\beta_1}(\gamma), \ldots, p_{\beta_k}(\gamma)), \quad (10)$$

if all quantities on the right-hand side exist.

The rule (10) defines a map

$$Z_{(A,q_0)} : T_X \rightarrow [0,1]^{t+k} \subset R^{t+k}. \quad (11)$$

The subject of our study is the closure (the set of all limit points) of the set $Z_{(A,q_0)}(T_X)$. This set will be denoted by R_A. The correctness of the accepted notation follows from the fact that if A is strongly connected, then $Z_{(A,q_0)}(T_X) = Z_{(A,q_0')}(T_X)$ for arbitrary two states q_0 and q_0'. It will be proved later (Theorem 1) that the set R_A is a convex polyhedron in the cube $[0,1]^{t+k}$. The set R_A will be called the polyhedron of the automaton A, corresponding to the sets of words $\{\alpha_i \in X^*, i = 1, 2, \ldots, t\}$ and $\{\beta_j \in Y^*, j = 1, 2, \ldots, k\}$.

The result of the Theorem 2 shows that if an automaton A processes a sufficiently long sequence χ with occurrences of words $\alpha_1, \ldots, \alpha_t$ close to $(p_{\alpha_1}(\chi), \ldots, p_{\alpha_t}(\chi))$ into a sequence γ with occurrences of words $\beta_1, \ldots, \beta_k$, close to $(p_{\beta_1}(\gamma), \ldots, p_{\beta_k}(\gamma))$, then point $(p_{\alpha_1}(\chi), \ldots, p_{\alpha_t}(\chi), p_{\beta_1}(\gamma), \ldots, p_{\beta_k}(\gamma))$ is located inside or near the automaton polyhedron.

4   The Automaton Polyhedron Structure

Let l be the maximum of the word lengths of the sets $\{\alpha_i \in X^*, i = 1, 2, \ldots, t\}$ and $\{\beta_j \in Y^*, i = 1, 2, \ldots, k\}$. We define the automaton $A^{(l)} = (X, Y, Q^{(l)}, h^{(l)}, f^{(l)})$, by setting
$\quad Q^{(l)} = \{((q^{(1)}, x^{(1)}), (q^{(2)}, x^{(2)}), \ldots, (q^{(l-1)}, x^{(l-1)}), q^{(l)}), \text{ where } h(q^{(i)}, x^{(i)}) = q^{(i+1)}, i = 1, 2, \ldots, l-1; q^{(j)} \in Q, j = 1, 2, \ldots, l, x^{(j)} \in X, j = 1, 2, \ldots, l-1\}$ is a set of states;

$h^{(l)} : Q^{(l)} \times X \rightarrow Q^{(l)}$ is a transition function;
$h^{(l)} (((q^{(1)}, x^{(1)}), (q^{(2)}, x^{(2)}), \ldots, (q^{(l-1)}, x^{(l-1)}), q^{(l)}), x)$
$= ((q^{(2)}, x^{(2)}), \ldots, (q^{(l-1)}, x^{(l-1)}), (q^{(l)}, x), h(q^{(l)}, x));$
$f^{(l)} : Q^{(l)} \times X \rightarrow Y$ is an output function;
$f^{(l)} (((q^{(1)}, x^{(1)}), (q^{(2)}, x^{(2)}), \ldots, (q^{(l-1)}, x^{(l-1)}), q^{(l)}), x) = f(q^{(l)}, x).$

By G_l we denote the transition graph of the automaton $A^{(l)}$, which arc $(q, h(l)(q, x))$ is labeled by the pair $(x, f(l)(q, x))$, $q \in Q(l)$. By an (oriented) cycle in a graph G_l we mean a cyclic sequence of pairwise distinct arcs in which the end of each arc coincides with the beginning of the next one. The set of all cycles in G_l is denoted by $C_l(A)$. With each cycle from $C_l(A)$ we associate the cyclic sequences consisting of the first and second coordinates of this cycle arcs labels. These sequences will be called the input and output markups, respectively, taking the notation $c^{(x)}$ and $c^{(y)}$ for them.

For $\xi = (\xi_0, \xi_1, \ldots \xi_m) \in B^*$ by $\langle \xi \rangle$ we denote the periodic sequence $\xi_0, \xi_1, \ldots \xi_m, \xi_0, \xi_1, \ldots \xi_m, \ldots$ with the period ξ.

For $c \in C_l(A)$ we introduce the notation:

$l(c)$ – cycle length,

$\nu_\alpha(c) = \frac{1}{l} \sum_{j=0}^{l(c)-1} I_\alpha \left(\langle c^{(x)} \rangle T^j \right)$ – the word α occurrence relative frequency in the input markup $c^{(x)}$,

$\nu_\beta(c) = \frac{1}{l} \sum_{j=0}^{l(c)-1} I_\beta \left(\langle c^{(y)} \rangle T^j \right)$ – the word β occurrence relative frequency in the input markup $c^{(y)}$,

$z(c) = (\nu_{\alpha_1}(c), \ldots, \nu_{\alpha_k}(c), \nu_{\beta_1}(c), \ldots, \nu_{\beta_t}(c))$ – the relative frequencies vector.

If E is some set of points from R^n, then $Conv E$ denotes the convex hull of E.

Theorem 1. *The equality*

$$R_A = Conv \{z(c), c \in C_l(A)\} \tag{12}$$

holds.

Proof. Obviously, $z(c) \in R_A$ holds for $c \in C_l(A)$. Let $C_l(A) = \{c_1, c_2, \ldots, c_\theta\}$. Let us show that

$$\sum_{j=1}^{\theta} p_j z(c_j) \in R_A, \text{ if } \sum_{j=1}^{\theta} p_j = 1, \ p_1, p_2, \ldots, p_\theta \geq 0. \tag{13}$$

Let us choose $q_0 \in Q$. Let us fix arbitrarily $\varepsilon > 0$. The proof consists in construction of a periodic sequence χ, for which

$$\left| z_{(A,q_0)}(\chi) - \sum_{j=1}^{\theta} p_j z(c_j) \right| < \varepsilon. \tag{14}$$

Let $\tilde{q}^{(0)}$ be an arbitrary state from a set $Q^{(l)}$ of the form $((q', x'), \ldots, (q'', x''), q_0)$. Let $\tilde{q}^{(i)} \in Q^{(l)}$ be an arbitrary state through which the cycle c_i passes, $i = 1, 2, \ldots, \theta$. Let $\chi^{(i)} = (x_0^{(i)}, \ldots, x_{l_i-1}^{(i)})$ be the input sequence under which the automaton $A^{(l)}$ passes the cycle c_i, starting from state $\tilde{q}^{(i)}$, l_i being the length of the cycle c_i, $i = 1, 2, \ldots, \theta$. By $\eta(\tilde{q}, \tilde{q}')$ we denote the shortest input sequence that transfers the automaton $A^{(l)}$ from state $\tilde{q}$ to state $\tilde{q}'$. We denote $\xi_i = \eta\left(\tilde{q}^{(i)}, \tilde{q}^{(i+1)}\right)$, $i = 0, 1, \ldots, \theta - 1$, $\xi_\theta = \eta\left(\tilde{q}^{(\theta)}, \tilde{q}^{(0)}\right)$.

For a natural M by χ_M we denote a periodic sequence which period has the form

$$\xi_0 \wedge \left(\chi^{(1)}\right)^{[Mp_1]} \wedge \xi_1 \wedge \left(\chi^{(2)}\right)^{[Mp_2]} \wedge \ldots \wedge \xi_{\theta-1} \wedge \left(\chi^{(\theta)}\right)^{[Mp_\theta]} \wedge \xi_\theta, \tag{15}$$

where $[Mp_i]$ is an integer part Mp_i, and the symbol $\wedge$ means the concatenation of sequences.

It is easy to see that

$$Z_{(A,q_0)}(\chi_M) = \sum_{j=1}^{\theta} p_j z(c_j) + O\left(\frac{1}{M}\right). \tag{16}$$

Therefore, if M is sufficiently large, then the sequence χ_M satisfies the condition (14).

So, we have proved the inclusion

$$R_A \supseteq Conv\left\{z(c), c \in C_l(A)\right\}. \tag{17}$$

Reverse inclusion. If a periodic sequence $x^{(i)}$, $i = 1, 2, \ldots$ arrives at the automaton input, then the sequence of vectors

$$\left(\left(q^{(i)}, x^{(i)}\right), \left(q^{(i+1)}, x^{(i+1)}\right), \ldots, \left(q^{(i+l-1)}, x^{(i+l-1)}\right)\right), \tag{18}$$

where $h\left(q^{(i)}, x^{(i)}\right) = q^{(i+1)}$, is also periodic. We denote its period by L. Consider the vector of relative frequencies

$$z(L) = \left(\nu_{\alpha_1}(L), \ldots, \nu_{\alpha_k}(L), \nu_{\beta_1}(L), \ldots, \nu_{\beta_t}(L)\right). \tag{19}$$

We show that

$$z(L) \in Conv\left\{z(c), c \in C_l(A)\right\}. \tag{20}$$

Induction by $|L|$.

1^0. $|L| = 1$. This case corresponds to a loop in the graph G_l. Obviously, the set $C_l(A)$ contains all the loops of the graph. Therefore $z(L) \in Conv\left\{z(c), c \in C_l(A)\right\}$.

2^0. Suppose that for $|L'| < |L|$ vector $z(L')$, formed by the selected words relative frequencies in the input and output markups of period L', belongs to the set $Conv\left\{z(c), c \in C_l(A)\right\}$. Now let the length of the period be equal to $|L|$. Two cases are possible:

a) All sections of length l are different. Then the period L of the sequence in G_l question is a cycle in and therefore $z(L) \in Conv\left\{z(c), c \in C_l(A)\right\}$.

b) Period L contains a pair of matching sections of the length l. Without loss of generality, we can assume that L has the following form:

$$\begin{bmatrix}((q_i, x_i), \ldots, (q_{i+l-1}, x_{i+l-1})), \ldots, (\ldots, (q', x')), \\ ((q_i, x_i), \ldots, (q_{i+l-1}, x_{i+l-1})), \ldots, (\ldots, (q'', x''))\end{bmatrix}. \tag{21}$$

Let us consider two periodic sequences: ζ_1 with the period

$$L_1 = [((q_i, x_i), \ldots, (q_{i+l-1}, x_{i+l-1})), \ldots, (\ldots, (q', x'))] \tag{22}$$

of the length $|L_1|$ and ζ_2 with the period

$$L_2 = [((q_i, x_i), \ldots, (q_{i+l-1}, x_{i+l-1})), \ldots, (\ldots, (q'', x''))] \tag{23}$$

of the length $|L_2|$. The vectors of relative frequencies $z(L_1)$ and $z(L_2)$ correspond to these two sequences.

Whereas

$$|L_1| + |L_2| = |L|, \tag{24}$$

and the word lengths of the sets $\{\alpha_i \in X^*, i = 1, 2, \ldots, t\}$ and $\{\beta_j \in Y^*, j = 1, 2, \ldots, k\}$ are limited by l, it is easy to see that

$$z(L) = z(\zeta_1)\frac{|L_1|}{|L_1| + |L_2|} + z(\zeta_2)\frac{|L_2|}{|L_1| + |L_2|}. \tag{25}$$

By the induction hypothesis

$$z(\zeta_i) \in Conv\left\{z(c), c \in C_l(A)\right\}, \tag{26}$$

so

$$z(L) \in Conv\left\{z(c), c \in C_l(A)\right\}. \tag{27}$$

Thus we have established that

$$Z_{(A,q)}(T_X) \subseteq Conv\left\{z(c), c \in C_l(A)\right\}. \tag{28}$$

Since the set on the right-hand side is closed, we obtain the set inclusion

$$R_A \subseteq Conv\left\{z(c), c \in C_l(A)\right\}. \tag{29}$$

The theorem is proved.

5   The Example of the Automaton Polyhedron

We give an example of construction of a polyhedron of the automaton with two states. Let $A = (X = Y = Q = \{0, 1\}, h, f)$ be the finite automaton, where $h(q, x) = q \oplus x$ is XOR, $f(q, x) = q$.

Let us choose $k = t = 1$, $\alpha_1 = \beta_1 = 1$. The automaton graph is shown in the Fig. 1, it contains exactly three elementary cycles: a loop at the "0" vertex with a label $(0, 0)$, a loop at the "1" vertex with a label $(0, 1)$, and a cycle of length 2 between vertices which arc labels are $(1, 0)$ and $(1, 1)$.

The vectors $z(c)$ of these cycles are $(0, 0)$, $(0, 1)$ and $(1, \frac{1}{2})$. Thus, $R_A = Conv\left\{(0, 0), (0, 1), (1, \frac{1}{2})\right\}$. The automaton polyhedron in this case is a flat polygon; it is shown in the Fig. 2. The abscissa and ordinates correspond to the relative frequencies of occurrence of the characters "1" in the input and output sequences.

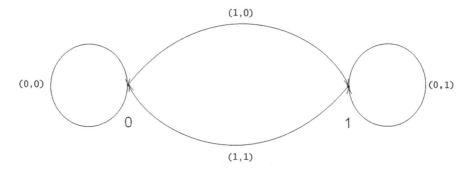

Fig. 1. The graph of the automaton A.

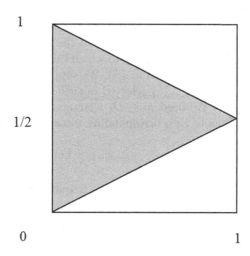

Fig. 2. The polygon of the automaton A.

6   The Case of Finite Sequences

The automaton A, starting to work from a certain initial state q_0, processes the input sequence $\chi^{(N)} = (x_0, x_1, \ldots, x_{N-1})$ into the output sequence $\gamma^{(N)} = (y_0, y_1, \ldots, y_{N-1})$. Let $p_{\alpha_1}^{(N)}, \ldots, p_{\alpha_t}^{(N)}$ be the relative frequencies of occurrence of words $\alpha_1, \ldots, \alpha_t$ in sequence $\chi^{(N)}$, and $p_{\beta_1}^{(N)}, \ldots, p_{\beta_k}^{(N)}$ be the relative frequencies of occurrence of words $\beta_1, \ldots, \beta_k$ in sequence $\gamma^{(N)}$:

$$
\begin{aligned}
p_{\alpha_s}^{(N)} &= \frac{\nu_{\alpha_s}^{(N)}}{N} = \frac{1}{N} \sum_{j=0}^{N-1} I_{\alpha_s}\left(\chi^{(N)} T^j\right), \quad s = 1, 2, \ldots, t; \\
p_{\beta_r}^{(N)} &= \frac{\nu_{\beta_r}^{(N)}}{N} = \frac{1}{N} \sum_{j=0}^{N-1} I_{\beta_r}\left(\chi^{(N)} T^j\right), \quad s = 1, 2, \ldots, k.
\end{aligned}
\tag{30}
$$

Let us find out how far the point

$$z^{(N)} = \left(p_{\alpha_1}^{(N)}, \ldots, p_{\alpha_t}^{(N)}, p_{\beta_1}^{(N)}, \ldots, p_{\beta_k}^{(N)} \right) \tag{31}$$

can be located from polyhedron R_A. By the distance between two points $u, v \in R^{t+k}$ we mean the maximum modulus of the difference of coordinates:

$$\rho(u, v) = |u - v| = \max \left| u^{(i)} - v^{(i)} \right|. \tag{32}$$

The distance between the two sets F and G, $F, G \subset R^{t+k}$ is defined as the exact lower bound of the distances between these sets points: $\rho(F, G) = \inf |u - v|$, where the infimum is taken for all pairs $u \in F$, $v \in G$.

Processing by the automaton A of the sequence $\chi^{(N)}$ corresponds to movement in the graph G_l along arcs which first coordinates of the labels are elements of this sequence. Let $\tilde{q}^{(0)}$ be an arbitrary state from a set $Q^{(l)}$ of the form $((q', x'), \ldots, (q'', x''), q_0)$. The vertex $\tilde{q}^{(0)}$ is one of the possible beginnings of the path in question. Let $\tilde{q}$ be the graph vertex to which this path will come after processing the sequence $\chi^{(N)}$, starting from $\tilde{q}^{(0)}$. We supplement the sequence $\chi^{(N)}$ with the characters $x_N, \ldots, x_{N+m-1}$ selected in such a way as to go from state $\tilde{q}$ to the initial state $\tilde{q}^{(0)}$. We need $m \le D_1$ characters, where D_1 is the diameter of the graph G_l. Denote the corresponding section of the output sequence $y_N, \ldots, y_{N+m-1}$.

Let $\chi = (x_0, x_1, \ldots, x_{N-1}, x_N, \ldots, x_{N+m-1})$. Let us estimate the distance between points $z(\chi)$ and $z^{(N)}$.

Let $\nu_{\alpha_s}^{(N)}$, $\nu_{\beta_r}^{(N)}$, $\nu_{\alpha_s}^{(N+m)}$, $\nu_{\beta_r}^{(N+m)}$ denote the frequencies of occurrence of the words α_s and β_r, $s = 1, 2, \ldots, t$, $r = 1, 2, \ldots, k$, in the sequences $\chi^{(N)}$ and χ and in the corresponding output sequences (in the periodic case – on the period).

Then, as it is easy to see,

$$0 \le \nu_{\alpha_s}^{(N+m)} - \nu_{\alpha_s}^{(N)}, \nu_{\beta_r}^{(N+m)} - \nu_{\beta_r}^{(N)} \le m + l - 1. \tag{33}$$

Therefore,

$$\left| z(\chi) - z^{(N)} \right|$$

$$\le \max_{s,r} \left\{ \left| \frac{(N+M)\nu_{\alpha_s}^{(N)} - N\nu_{\alpha_s}^{(N+m)}}{N(N+M)} \right|, \left| \frac{(N+M)\nu_{\beta_r}^{(N)} - N\nu_{\beta_r}^{(N+m)}}{N(N+M)} \right| \right\}$$

$$\le \max_{s,r} \left\{ \left| \frac{m\nu_{\alpha_s}^{(N)} - N(\nu_{\alpha_s}^{(N+m)} - \nu_{\alpha_s}^{(N)})}{N(N+M)} \right|, \left| \frac{m\nu_{\beta_r}^{(N)} - N(\nu_{\beta_r}^{(N+m)} - \nu_{\beta_r}^{(N)})}{N(N+M)} \right| \right\}$$

$$\le \frac{m+l-1}{N+m}. \tag{34}$$

Using the monotonicity of the function $\frac{x+A}{x+B}$ for $B > A > 0$, $x > 0$, we obtain

$$\left| z(\chi) - z^{(N)} \right| \le \frac{D_l + l - 1}{N + D_l}. \tag{35}$$

Let D denote the diameter of the transition graph of the automaton A. Using the inequality $D_l \leq D + l - 1$, we obtain the following statement.

Theorem 2. *Suppose that an automaton A processes a sequence $\chi^{(N)} = (x_0, x_1, \ldots, x_{N-1})$ into a sequence $\gamma^{(N)} = (y_0, y_1, \ldots, y_{N-1})$, $N = 1, 2, \ldots$. Let $z^{(N)} = \left(p_{\alpha_1}^{(N)}, \ldots, p_{\alpha_t}^{(N)}, p_{\beta_1}^{(N)}, \ldots, p_{\beta_k}^{(N)} \right)$ be the vector of relative frequencies of occurrence of words $\alpha_1, \ldots, \alpha_t$ (for $\chi^{(N)}$) and $\beta_1, \ldots, \beta_k$ (for $\gamma^{(N)}$). Let D be the diameter of the transition graph of the automaton A.*
Then the inequality

$$\rho(z^{(N)}, R_A) \leq \frac{D + 2(l-1)}{N + D + l - 1}, \tag{36}$$

holds, where $l = \max\{|\alpha_i|, |\beta_j|\}$.

7 The Use of Automaton Polyhedra in the Identification Problem

By the task of identification we understand the task of testing of the hypothesis that an unknown automaton (which input and output sequences are observed) coincides with a reference automaton.

Theorem 2 allows us to construct the following procedure for verifying that an unknown automaton A is identical to a given automaton A_0.

1. Sets $\alpha_1, \ldots, \alpha_t$ of words (for the input sequence) and $\beta_1, \ldots, \beta_k$ (for the output sequence) are selected and the polyhedron R_{A_0} of the automaton A_0 is constructed.
2. The word occurrence relative frequencies in the observed sequences are calculated. The distance ρ between the automaton polyhedron and the relative frequency vector is calculated. If the frequencies vector belongs to the polyhedron, then $\rho = 0$.
3. If $\rho > \frac{D + 2(l-1)}{N + D + l - 1}$, then the observed output sequence could not be obtained from the input one using an automaton A_0. If $\rho \leq \frac{D + 2(l-1)}{N + D + l - 1}$, then the observed frequencies of the selected words do not contradict the hypothesis that the unknown automaton is identical to the reference automaton. In the latter case it is reasonable either to move to another segment of the available sequences, or to change the word sets which frequencies are analyzed.

The described procedure is valid for arbitrary word sets $\{\alpha_1, \ldots, \alpha_t\}$ and $\{\beta_1, \ldots, \beta_k\}$. In particular, the set $\{\alpha_1, \ldots, \alpha_t\}$ may be empty. In this case, the analysis is based on word frequencies only in the output automaton sequence.

We emphasize that the described procedure, firstly, does not depend on the analyzed automaton initial state, and secondly, despite the fact that the certain event frequencies in the observed sequences are analyzed, it does not use any assumptions about the input sequence probabilistic nature.

Let us analyze the proposed procedure computational complexity if the number $|Q|$ of states of the automaton A_0 is large. It is determined by the contribution of two terms. Firstly, the preliminary polyhedron construction complexity, and secondly, the complexity of checking inequality (36).

The construction of a polyhedron by the Theorem 1 requires finding of all the cycles of the graph G_l and constructing of the convex hull of the set $\{z(c)\}$. Both of these problems are well studied; see, for example, [12–14].

The complexity of finding of all the cycles in our case can be limited by the number $O\left(2^{(|Q| \times |X|)^l}\right)$ of all subgraphs of G_l. The convex hull constructing complexity, in the case of a flat polygon or a three-dimensional polyhedron, can be estimated [14] as $O\left(|\{z(c)\}|\, Log\, |\{z(c)\}|\right)$. Note that analytical methods for construction of polyhedra are possible for some automaton classes.

If the polyhedron R_{A_0} is already constructed, then the inequality (36) checking complexity, as is easy to see, is not more than 2^{t+k} times the complexity of checking whether a given point belongs to a convex polyhedron R_{A_0}. The computational complexity of the last problem in the two-dimensional case ($t = k = 1$) can be estimated [14] by the value $O\left(Log\, v\right)$, where v is the polygon vertex number. Note that even faster algorithms [15] are proposed. To estimate v, we use the fact that all the polygon R_{A_0} vertices have the form $\left(\frac{p_1}{q_1}, \frac{p_2}{q_2}\right)$, $0 \le p_i \le q_i \le |Q^{(l)}|$, $i = 1, 2$. Counting the possible different vertex abscissa number, due to the polygon convexity, we get $v \le |Q|^{2l}$. Therefore, the inequality (36) check complexity in the case of a preliminarily constructed polygon is estimated as $O\left(Log|Q|\right)$.

Generally speaking, we can select several shorter continuous fragments of the observed sequences, and perform the procedure for each of them separately. If inequality (36) is violated for at least one fragment, the hypothesis about the coincidence of automata is rejected.

8   Conclusion

A method for verifying that an automaton which input and output sequences are observed coincides with the reference one is proposed. The method uses word occurrence frequencies in the input and output sequences. Specially selected input sequences are not required. Information on the analyzed machine initial state is not required.

If the polyhedron of an unknown automaton coincides with the reference automaton polyhedron for given sets of words in the input and output sequences, then the proposed procedure cannot distinguish between these automata. Therefore, the problem arises of classifying automata by their polyhedra.

It is intuitively clear that two automata, the polyhedra of which have an insignificant common part, are easily distinguishable. The important thing here is how likely it is that the point corresponding to a sequence fragment falls into the both polyhedral common part. It depends on the probability distribution on the input sequence set.

Acknowledgments. The publication has been prepared with the support of the RUDN University Program "5-100" (recipient K. Samouylov). The reported study was funded by RFBR, project numbers 19-07-00933 and 18-00-01555 (18-00-01685).

References

1. Marsaglia, G.: Random numbers fall mainly in the planes. Proc. Natl. Acad. Sci. **61**(1968), 5–28 (1968)
2. Haramoto, H., Matsumoto, M.: Again, random numbers fall mainly in the planes: xorshift128+, arxiv.org/abs/1908.10020. Accessed 30 Jun 2020
3. Tverdokhlebov, V.A.: Geometrical approach to technical diagnosing of automatons. In: Proceedings of the IEEE East-West Design & Test Symposium, EWDTS 2011, National University of Radioelectronics, Kharkov, pp. 240–243 (2011)
4. Babash, A.V.: Automaton barriers. Math. Notes **91**(5–6), 625–629 (2012)
5. Parkhomenko, D.V.: Automata generated p-languages. Discrete Math. Appl. **24**(4), 207–212 (2014)
6. Chatterjee, K., Doyen, L., Edelsbrunner, H., Henzinger, T.A., Rannou, P.: Mean-payoff automaton expressions. In: Gastin, P., Laroussinie, F. (eds.) CONCUR 2010. LNCS, vol. 6269, pp. 269–283. Springer, Heidelberg (2010). https://doi.org/10.1007/978-3-642-15375-4_19
7. Grusho, A.A., Timonina, E.E.: Prohibitions in discrete probabilistic statistical problems. Discrete Math. Appl. **21**(3), 275–281 (2011)
8. Gerasimenko, M., Petrov, V., Galinina, O., Andreev, S., Koucheryavy, Y.: Energy and delay analysis of LTE-Advanced RACH performance under MTC overload. In: 2012 IEEE Globecom Workshops, GC Wkshps 2012, pp. 1632–1637 (2012). Art. no. 6477830
9. Pyattaev, A., Johnsson, K., Surak, A., Florea, R., Andreev, S., Koucheryavy, Y.: Network-assisted D2D communications: implementing a technology prototype for cellular traffic offloading. In: IEEE Wireless Communications and Networking Conference, WCNC, pp. 3266–3271 (2014). Art. no. 6953070
10. Ometov, A., et al.: Toward trusted, social-aware D2D connectivity: bridging across the technology and sociality realms. IEEE Wirel. Commun. **23**(4), 103–111 (2016). Art. no. 7553033
11. Jacobs, K.: Turing-Maschinen und zufällige 0–1-Folgen. In: Jacobs, K. (ed.) Selecta Mathematica II Heidelberger Taschenbücher, vol. 67, pp. 141–167. Springer, Heidelberg (1970). https://doi.org/10.1007/978-3-642-88162-6_6
12. Johnson, D.B.: Finding all the elementary circuits of a directed graph. SIAM J. Comput. **4**(1), 77–84 (1975)
13. Liu, H., Wang, J.: A new way to enumerate cycles in graph. In: Proceedings of the Advanced International Conference on Telecommunications and International Conference on Internet and Web Applications and Services, AICT-ICIW 2006, Washington, DC, USA, pp. 57–59 (2006)
14. Preparata, F.P., Shamos, M.I.: Computational Geometry - An Introduction. Monographs in Computer Science. Springer, New York (1988). https://doi.org/10.1007/978-1-4612-1098-6
15. Skala, V.: Point-in-convex polygon and point-in-convex polyhedron algorithms with O(1) complexity using space subdivision. In: ICNAAM 2015, pp. 22–28. AIP Publishing LLC. (2015)

Probability Distributions of Instantaneous Amplitude Values of Random Optimal FTN Signal Sequences with Controlled ISI

Ilya Lavrenyuk[1]($\boxtimes$) (iD), Sergey B. Makarov[1] (iD), Boxiong Hu[1], Ge Dong[2] (iD),
and Tatyana Kudryashova[1]

[1] Peter the Great St. Petersburg Polytechnic University, St. Petersburg, Russian Federation
lavrenyuk_i@spbstu.ru
[2] Tsinghua University, Haidian District, Beijing, People's Republic of China

Abstract. An approaching to the transmission channel capacity with a limited frequency band ΔF is achieved by using signals with length Ts exceeding the duration of the symbol's transmission interval T. Such signals are transmitted under conditions of significant intersymbol interference. This leads to the fact that a random sequence of transmitted signals will have significant values of the peak to average power ratio (PAPR). To estimate the value of PAPR, it is necessary to determine the statistical characteristics of the random process emission. This will help to form the conditions for the permissible amplitude limitation of the output signal. In the work we find probability distributions of instantaneous amplitude values of the random optimal signal sequences with different durations ($T_s = 8T...16T$). The conditions for approximating the distribution histograms to the Gaussian process are found. As a information source, a Gaussian source with quantization of levels of sampled values was selected. It is shown that with the number of quantization levels exceeding 32, the histograms approach a truncated Gaussian distribution. Simulation results are given for the transmission speed of the channel alphabet symbols from $R = 1/T$ to $R = 10/T$, which corresponds to the faster-than-Nyquist transmission rate. Recommendations are given on the required dynamic range of operation for power amplifiers in transmitting devices in accordance with the obtained value of FTN signal sequences PAPR.

Keywords: Faster-Than-Nyquist · PAPR · Optimal pulses · Amplitude distributions

1 Introduction

Future wireless communication systems such as mobile communications and wireless personal networks involve the application of approaches to increase bandwidth efficiency and transmission rates. One of the methods to solve this problem is to use signals with an artificial ISI and higher symbol rate, which makes it possible to significantly increase the information transfer speed. This technique is called Faster-Than-Nyquist (FTN) [1–3]. Another promising approach is to use direct optimization of transmission pulse form

© Springer Nature Switzerland AG 2020
O. Galinina et al. (Eds.): NEW2AN 2020/ruSMART 2020, LNCS 12526, pp. 122–132, 2020.
https://doi.org/10.1007/978-3-030-65729-1_11

with increased pulse duration according to various criteria, for example, PSD out-of-band decay rate [4]. Concatenation of FTN signaling and pulse waveform optimization results in significant spectral efficiency increasement. One of the main disadvantages of this approach is the increase in peak-to-average power ratio which can lead to energy efficiency degradation. In [14] it was shown that the statistical analysis of FTN signaling amplitude distributions could be useful for selecting the operating mode of the amplifying stages.

An approaching to the transmission channel capacity with a limited frequency band ΔF and additive white Gaussian noise (AWGN) with an average power spectral density of N_0 is achieved by using signals of duration T_s which exceed the duration of the transmission interval T of the channel symbols. In [1], FTN signals are considered that allow to transmit messages above the Nyquist limit. They provide transmission without encoding at a rate of $R = 1/\xi T$ $(0 < \xi < 1)$ [2]. A random sequence consisting of N single signals $s(t)$ with energy E_s and duration $T_s = LT$, where $L = 2, 3, \ldots$, has significant intersymbol interference (ISI). If $T = 1$, then such a sequence can be written as:

$$y(t) = \sqrt{E_s} \sum_{n=-N/2}^{N/2} c_j^{(n)} s(t - n\xi T). \tag{1}$$

For FTN signals with the base of the channel symbols alphabet M, the symbol values $c_j^{(n)}$ in (1) are determined by the following expression:

$$c_j^{(n)} = \frac{M - 2j + 1}{M - 1}, j = 1 \ldots M. \tag{2}$$

For instance, with $M = 2$, the symbols will be $c_1^{(n)} = 1$; $c_2^{(n)} = -1$, and with M = 4, symbols will have following values $c_1^{(n)} = 1$; $c_2^{(n)} = 0.33$; $c_3^{(n)} = -0.33$; $c_4^{(n)} = -1$. The formation of single signals $s(t)$ can be done using low-pass filtering [3], which produces a random ISI, or by solving the problem of optimizing the shape of $s(t)$ [4], when the ISI could be controllable. Along with the spectral and energy characteristics of such signals, the probability distribution of instantaneous values of the levels of random sequences (1) is of interest. This is necessary for:

1) estimates of the peak to average power ration of the emitted oscillations, which makes it possible to rationally select the operation mode of powerful cascades of radio transmitters, providing maximum efficiency [5–10];
2) solving the problem of providing covert information transfer if it is possible to get close to the normal distribution;
3) to determine the statistical characteristics of the emissions of a random process, which will allow us to formulate the conditions for the permissible amplitude limitation of the output oscillation under different conditions [11–13].

The probability distribution of the instantaneous values of the levels of random sequences (1) in the general case depends on the distribution of values $c_j^{(n)}$, the transmission rate $R = 1/\xi T$, and the signal duration $T_s = LT$. It was shown in [14] that for the binary alphabet ($M = 2$), this probability distribution approaches the truncated Gaussian distribution only in the regions of transmission rates 10 higher than the Nyquist barrier.

The aim of the work is to determine the probability distribution form of instantaneous values of random sequences of optimal FTN signals with controlled ISI and to establish the dependence of the distribution form on the volume of the channel alphabet, signal duration and information transfer rate.

2 Simulation Modelling

In the work, baseband signals, the forms of which were obtained as a result of solving the optimization problem [15], were used as optimal FTN signals $s(t)$. The solution to the problem is sought in accordance with the criterion for ensuring the maximum decay rate of the energy spectrum level of a random sequence (1) under restrictions on the energy E_{opt}, duration T_s, correlation coefficient K_0, taking into account the level of controlled intersymbol interference ISI. The probability distributions of the instantaneous values of a random sequence of FTN signals were determined by simulation.

A source with a Gaussian distribution was used as a source of information (Fig. 1). At time instants that are multiples of T, selective values are taken from the Gaussian random process using the commutator.

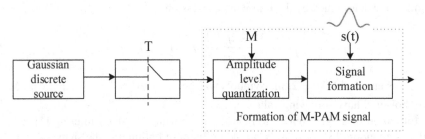

Fig. 1. A model flowchart for generating random sequences of optimal FTN signals.

In the modulation block, a preliminary amplitude quantization of the sample values occurs. This quantization is carried out at M levels in accordance with the base of the channel alphabet. Each quantized value is modulated by a signal $s(t)$ (1), of different durations $T_s = LT$. Depending on the symbol rate of the source R at the output of the device for generating M-level signals with amplitude-phase modulation, a random sequence of signals (1) will have a different level of intersymbol interference, which determines the distribution of the instantaneous values of the output oscillation. As an example, Fig. 2 shows the forms of a random sequence of signals (1) for $M = 2, N = 4$, and duration $T_s = 4T$.

In the figures, a sequence type (coefficients in (1)) of four symbols is selected: $+1, +1, -1, +1$. The bold line indicates the shape of the total baseband FTN signal. An increase in the duration s (t) leads to a reduction in the occupied frequency band ΔF. However, as can be seen from Fig. 2, significant intersymbol interference ISI arises in the signals. An increase in T_s leads to an increase in the number of interfering signals.

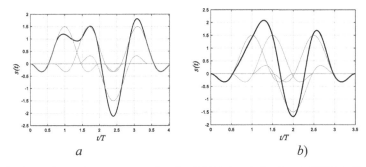

Fig. 2. The form of a random sequence of optimal FTN signals for $R = 1.42/T$ (*a*), $R = 2/T$ (*b*).

3 Analysis of Simulation Results

The search for optimal FTN waveforms $s(t)$ occurs by solving the optimization problem [4, 14, 15]. Such signals can increase the symbol rate of information transfer without loss of BER performance. A feature of such signals is the controlled level of ISI. The solution to the optimization problem is sought in numerical form. Assuming that $s(t)$ is an even function on the interval $[-T_s/2; T_s/2]$ we have:

$$s(t) = \frac{a_0}{2} + \sum_{k=1}^{m-1} a_k \cos\left(\frac{2\pi}{T}kt\right). \tag{3}$$

The solution of the optimization functional [6] is the coefficients a_k in (2) of the expansion in a limited Fourier series, where $k = 0, 1, 2 \dots m$. The number of members of the Fourier series m is determined by the accuracy of the solution of the optimization problem and, as a rule, it has the value $m = 10$–20. Table 1 shows the coefficients a_k in (2) for optimal FTN signals obtained as a result of solving the optimization problem in accordance with the criterion for ensuring a given rate of decay of the out-of-band emission level for the cross-correlation coefficient $K_0 = 0.01$.

The coefficients a_k presented in Table 1 were obtained by optimizing the waveform for the symbol rate $R = 1/T$. With increasing transmission rate R, intersymbol interference increases. This affects the shape of a random sequence of optimal FTN signals. Figure 3 shows the forms of the total sequence of optimal FTN signals for the pulse duration $T_s = 2T$ and provided that the message source is Gaussian (Fig. 1).

This figure shows the implementation (number of pulses $N = 10$) of the signal sequence for the different symbol transmission rates. As can be seen from a visual comparison of the waveforms in these figures, as the transmission speed increases, the level of intersymbol interference increases and the shape of the total signal degrades with a tendency to smooth out the amplitude emissions of the random process.

Consider the histograms of the distribution of random sequences of signals (1) for a different number of quantization levels of sample values of a Gaussian message source. In Figs. 4, 5, 6, 7, 8, 9, and 10 shows distribution histograms for the transmission rate of $2/T$ samples, signal durations $T_s = 2T$–$14T$ and a different number of quantization

Table 1. Fourier series expansion coefficients for optimal FTN pulses

T_s	$2T$	$4T$	$6T$	$8T$	$10T$	$12T$	$16T$
a_0	0.6358	0.3380	0.2307	0.1754	0.1399	0.1165	0.0838
a_1	0.7886	0.3726	0.2430	0.1814	0.1443	0.1187	0.0928
a_2	0.4178	0.3352	0.2302	0.1723	0.1397	0.1201	0.0866
a_3	−0.0342	0.3801	0.2440	0.1807	0.1445	0.1179	0.0893
a_4	0.0105	0.2161	0.2279	0.1760	0.1395	0.1151	0.0887
a_5	−0.0043	−0.0181	0.2487	0.1817	0.1449	0.1234	0.0896
a_6	0.0020	0.0079	0.1452	0.1720	0.1390	0.1152	0.0871
a_7	−0.0010	−0.0040	−0.0112	0.1797	0.1454	0.1192	0.0905
a_8	0.0005	0.0023	0.0056	0.1156	0.1376	0.1169	0.0879
a_9					0.1486	0.1221	0.0888
a_{10}					0.0002	0.1143	0.0887
a_{11}						0.1206	0.0897
a_{12}						0.0717	0.0870
a_{13}							0.0903
a_{14}							0.0884
a_{15}							0.0882
a_{16}							0.0524
a_{17}							−0.0034
a_{18}							0.0018
a_{19}							−0.0011

levels: for $M = 16$ (Figs. 4a, 5a, 6a, 7a, 8a, 9a, and 10a) and for $M = 32$ (Figs. 4b, 5b, 6b, 7b, 8b, 9b, and 10b). Table 2 shows the percentages of favorable outcomes when checking the approximation of the histogram to the Gaussian distribution of probabilities of reference levels from random sequences of optimal FTN signals with the chu-squared goodness of fit test.

As can be seen from Table 2, for a small number of quantization levels ($M = 16$), the probability distribution of the sample levels does not correspond to the Gaussian distribution. With an increase in the number of quantization levels to $M = 32$ in almost all tests, the sequence of readings has a normal distribution. The probabilities of such events for different signal durations are close within the statistical error.

Table 3 shows the percentages of favorable outcomes when checking the approximation of the histogram to the Gaussian distribution of probabilities of reference levels from random sequences of optimal FTN signals for $M = 8, 16, 32, 64, 128$ and 256 level numbers, $R = 1/T, 2/T, 2.5/T, 3.33/T, 5/T, 10/T$ symbol rates and for pulse duration $T_s = 8T$.

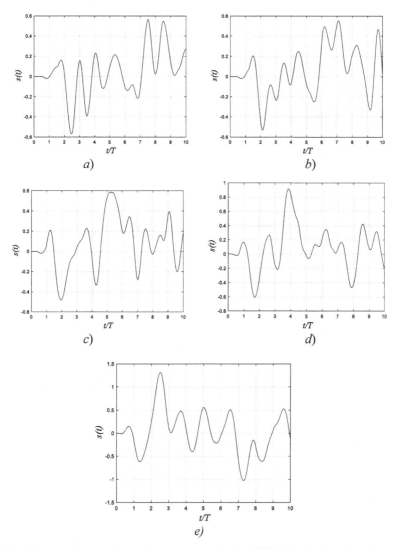

Fig. 3. Implementation type of a random sequence of optimal FTN signals for a Gaussian message source with following symbol rates: a) $R = 2/T$, b) $R = 2.5/T$, c) $R = 3.33/T$, d) $R = 5/T$, e) $R = 10/T$.

As can be seen from the analysis (Table 3) of the results of testing the histograms for normal distribution, with an increase in the transmission speed of messages with the number of quantization levels $M = 256$, the distribution of the levels of a random sequence of FTN signals begins to differ in a Gaussian law. With a small number of quantization levels, a significant difference between the histograms and the Gaussian distribution is observed.

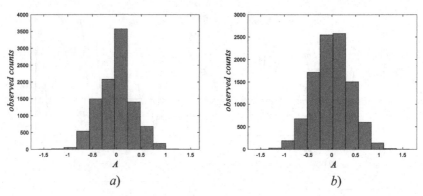

Fig. 4. Histogram for samples of optimal FTN sequence with $T_s = 2T$ for a) M = 16, b) M = 32.

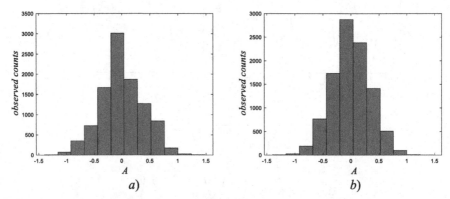

Fig. 5. Histogram for samples of optimal FTN sequence with $T_s = 4T$ for a) M = 16, b) M = 32.

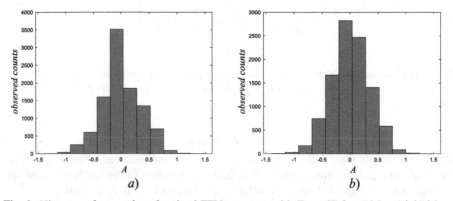

Fig. 6. Histogram for samples of optimal FTN sequence with $T_s = 6T$ for a) M = 16, b) M = 32.

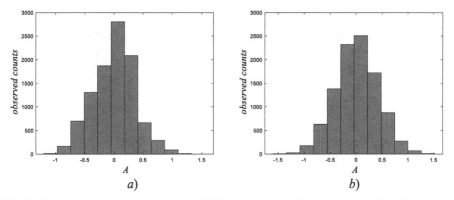

Fig. 7. Histogram for samples of optimal FTN sequence with $T_S = 8T$ for a) M = 16, b) M = 32.

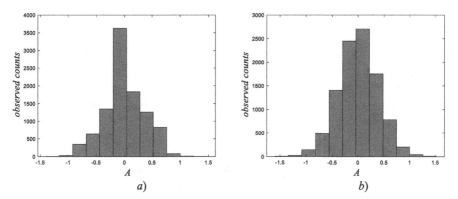

Fig. 8. Histogram for samples of optimal FTN sequence with $T_S = 10T$ for a) M = 16, b) M = 32.

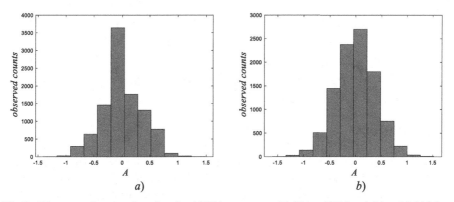

Fig. 9. Histogram for samples of optimal FTN sequence with $T_S = 12T$ for a) M = 16, b) M = 32.

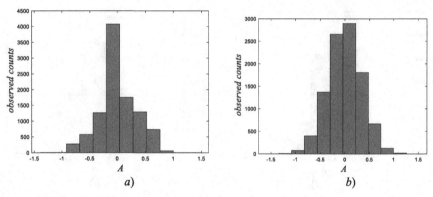

Fig. 10. Histogram for samples of optimal FTN sequence with $T_s = 14T$ for a) M = 16, b) M = 32.

Table 2. Chi-square normality test for samples of optimal FTN sequence

Pulse duration	$2T$	$4T$	$6T$	$8T$	$10T$	$12T$	$16T$
Normal distribution probability for $M = 16$	61.32%	48.72%	36.74%	47.40%	25.35%	25.70%	24.89%
Normal distribution probability for $M = 32$	99.85%	99.83%	99.79%	99.90%	98.63%	99.45%	98.39%

Table 3. Chi-square normality test for different M and R values and $T_s = 8T$.

M		8	16	32	64	128	256
Normal distribution probability	$R = 1/T$	0%	21.6%	91.9%	97.1%	99.7%	99.9%
	$R = 2/T$	0%	61.8%	100%	99.9%	99.7%	99.9%
	$R = 2.5/T$	96.0%	99.6%	99.9%	100%	99.8%	100%
	$R = 3.33/T$	100%	99.8%	99.8%	99.6%	99.9%	99.9%
	$R = 5/T$	99.1%	98.9%	99.7%	99.2%	99.0%	99.1%
	$R = 10/T$	87.6%	85.4%	87.6%	87.8%	86.3%	87.5%

4 Conclusions

The following conclusions can be drawn from the consideration of the statistical characteristics of random sequences of optimal FTN signals when using a source with a Gaussian distribution. First, as follows from the analysis of the probability distributions of the values of the levels of random sequences of optimal FTN signals, the approximation of these distributions to the truncated normal form occurs in the regions of quantization of signal levels above 32. Secondly, with an increase in the message transmission rate up to 10 times the Nyquist barrier with the number of quantization levels

$M = 256$, the distribution of the levels of a random sequence of FTN signals begins to differ in a Gaussian law. Thirdly, an increase in the duration of optimal FTN signals leads to a slight discrepancy between the histogram form and the normal law. However, this effect begins to manifest itself significantly with signal durations greater than $10T$.

Acknowledgment. This research work was supported by Peter the Great St. Petersburg Polytechnic University in the framework of the Program "5-100-2020" and used computational resources of Peter the Great Saint-Petersburg Polytechnic University Supercomputing Center (http://www.scc.spbstu.ru).

References

1. Mazo, J.E.: Faster-than-nyquist signaling. Bell Syst. Techn. J. **54**(8), 1451–1462 (1975). https://doi.org/10.1002/j.1538-7305.1975.tb02043.x
2. Anderson, J.B., Rusek, F., Öwall, V.: Faster-than-nyquist signaling. Proc. IEEE **101**(8), 1817–1830 (2013). https://doi.org/10.1109/JPROC.2012.2233451
3. Rusek, F., Anderson, J.B.: Constrained capacities for faster-than-nyquist signaling. IEEE Trans. Inf. Theor. **55**(2), 764–775 (2009). https://doi.org/10.1109/TIT.2008.2009832
4. Lavrenyuk, I.I., Ovsyannikova, A.S., Zavjalov, S.V., Volvenko, S.V., Makarov, S.B.: Improving energy efficiency of finite time FTN pulses detection by choosing optimal envelope shape. In: 2019 26th International Conference on Telecommunications (ICT), Hanoi, Vietnam, 2019, pp. 289–294 (2019). https://doi.org/10.1109/ict.2019.8798830
5. Kazimierczuk, M.K.: RF Power Amplifiers. Wiley, Chichester, UK (2014)
6. Grebennikov, A., Sokal, N.O.: Switchmode RF Power Amplifiers. Newnes, New York (2007)
7. Pergushev, A., Sorotsky, V., Ulanov, A.: Criteria for selection envelope tracking power supply parameters for high peak-to-average power ratio applications. In: 2019 IEEE International Conference on Electrical Engineering and Photonics (EExPolytech), St. Petersburg, Russia, 2019, pp. 13–16 (2019). https://doi.org/10.1109/eexpolytech.2019.8906793
8. Pergushev, A., Sorotsky, V., Ulanov, A.: Output voltage PWM conversion inaccuracies in envelope tracking power supply for high peak-to-average power ratio applications. In: 2019 IEEE International Conference on Electrical Engineering and Photonics (EExPolytech), St. Petersburg, Russia, 2019, pp. 9–12 (2019). https://doi.org/10.1109/eexpolytech.2019.8906854
9. Zudov, R.I.: Efficiency of a class DE power amplifier for RF signals with high peak-to-average power ratio. In: 2019 IEEE International Conference on Electrical Engineering and Photonics (EExPolytech), St. Petersburg, Russia, 2019, pp. 28–30 (2019). https://doi.org/10.1109/eexpolytech.2019.8906856
10. Pergushev, A., Sorotsky, V.: Signal distortion decreasing in envelope tracking power amplifiers. In: 2018 IEEE International Conference on Electrical Engineering and Photonics (EExPolytech), St. Petersburg, 2018, pp. 44–47 (2018). https://doi.org/10.1109/eexpolytech.2018.8564443
11. Thompson, S.C., Proakis, J.G., Zeidler, J.R.: The effectiveness of signal clipping for PAPR and total degradation reduction in OFDM systems. In: IEEE Global Telecommunications Conference, GLOBECOM 2005, St. Louis, MO, 2005, pp. 5 pp.-2811 (2005). https://doi.org/10.1109/glocom.2005.1578271
12. Nguyen, D.C., Zavjalov, S.V., Ovsyannikova, A.S.: The effectiveness of application of multi-frequency signals under conditions of amplitude limitation. In: Galinina, O., Andreev, S., Balandin, S., Koucheryavy, Y. (eds.) NEW2AN/ruSMART -2019. LNCS, vol. 11660, pp. 681–687. Springer, Cham (2019). https://doi.org/10.1007/978-3-030-30859-9_59

13. Rashich, A., Fadeev, D.: Optimal input power backoff of a nonlinear power amplifier for FFT-based trellis receiver for SEFDM signals. In: Galinina, O., Balandin, S., Koucheryavy, Y. (eds.) NEW2AN/ruSMART -2016. LNCS, vol. 9870, pp. 641–647. Springer, Cham (2016). https://doi.org/10.1007/978-3-319-46301-8_55

14. Makarov, S.B., Ovsyannikova, A.S., Lavrenyuk, I.I., Zavjalov, S.V., Volvenko, S.V.: Distributions of probability of power values for random sequences of optimal FTN signals. In: 2018 International Symposium on Consumer Technologies (ISCT), St. Petersburg, 2018, pp. 57–59 (2018). https://doi.org/10.1109/ISCE.2018.8408919

15. Makarov, S., Zavjalov, S., Ovsyannikova, A., Lavrenyuk, I., Xue, W.: Comparison of the spectral and energy efficiency of FTN signals based on RRC pulses and obtained by the optimization method. In: 2019 IEEE International Conference on Electrical Engineering and Photonics (EExPolytech), St. Petersburg, Russia, 2019, pp. 177–180 (2019). https://doi.org/10.1109/eexpolytech.2019.8906866

A Method of Finding Optimal Parameters of Speckle Noise Reduction Filters

Andrei A. Belov⬭, Vitalii A. Pavlov⬭, and Anna A. Tuzova$^{(\boxtimes)}$⬭

Institute of Physics, Nanotechnology and Telecommunications, Peter the Great St. Petersburg Polytechnic University, Saint Petersburg, Russia
{belov,pavlov_va}@spbstu.ru, tuzova.aa@edu.spbstu.ru

Abstract. The reduction of multiplicative speckle noise in synthetic aperture radar (SAR) images is an important problem. Many speckle noise reduction filters have been proposed. Most of them have several parameters that control their operation. Finding the optimal values of these parameters is often a non-trivial task. A method of automating the search for optimal parameters is proposed. The method uses two variants of a specially designed test image, original noise free image and the same image but with speckle noise added. Then the Structural Similarity Index (SSIM) metric is used for finding the parameters that make the filtered image as close to the original noise free image as possible. The application of the method is illustrated using the Frost filter applied to various images, but the method can be used for any filter type.

Keywords: Speckle noise · Radar image · Noise reduction · Image filtering · Frost filter · SSIM · Selection of filter parameters

1 Introduction

The radar image is an image obtained by remote sensing the earth's surface using a radar [1–4]. A widely used method of producing high-resolution radar images is the aperture synthesis [5–10]. Using a synthetic aperture radar (SAR), one can obtain images of areas and objects at a significant distance regardless of weather and lighting conditions [5–10].

The important feature of the SAR images is the granularity (unevenness) of the background caused by speckle noise [6, 11]. Speckle noise arises from the coherent addition of signals received from many elementary reflectors located within one element of the surface resolution. This type of noise is undesirable and can lead to false alarms or to missed detections. That is why it is necessary to filter noise of this type to enhance the quality of SAR images and to minimize the detection errors [12].

Speckle noise on SAR images is not additive and can be mathematically described using a model of multiplicative noise [13, 14]. A noisy image can be produced by multiplying the original image by a random signal. Then the noisy image $I'(x, y)$ is described by the equation [6]:

$$I'(x, y) = I(x, y)(1 + n(x.y)) \tag{1}$$

© Springer Nature Switzerland AG 2020
O. Galinina et al. (Eds.): NEW2AN 2020/ruSMART 2020, LNCS 12526, pp. 133–141, 2020.
https://doi.org/10.1007/978-3-030-65729-1_12

where $I(x, y)$ is the original image (noise free); $n(x, y)$ is a random process describing speckle noise.

The most commonly used speckle noise reduction filters are so called local filters. Image processing in such filters is carried out in a sliding 2-dimentional window, the dimensions of which are much smaller than the size of the entire image.

However, many speckle noise reduction filters have several parameters that control their operation [15, 16]. In articles devoted to application of such filters in image processing, the authors usually do not explain the method of choosing the values of such parameters [17–20]. Therefore, the aim of this work is to present a formal method of finding optimal parameters of speckle noise reduction filters in terms of the quality of the processed image.

2   Frost Filter

One of the many filters with variable parameters is the Frost filter [13]. The central pixel $\hat{I}_{ij}$ of the sliding window is estimated using the following formula:

$$\hat{I}_{ij} = \sum_{k=i-m}^{i+m} \sum_{l=j-m}^{j+m} W_{kl} I'_{kl} \bigg/ \sum_{k=i-m}^{i+m} \sum_{l=j-m}^{j+m} W_{kl} \tag{2}$$

where m is the size of the sliding window within which the estimate $\hat{I}_{ij}$ is evaluated; I_{kl} is the brightness value of a pixel of the noisy image; $W = exp(-BS)$ is a weight function; B is a coefficient, which is calculated using the formula:

$$B = D\left(\sigma_{I'}^2 \big/ \bar{I}'^2\right) \tag{3}$$

D is the damping coefficient that allows adjusting the smoothing properties of the filter; $\bar{I}'$ is the average value of the brightness of the SAR image in the processing window; $\sigma_{I'}^2$ is the brightness variance in the window; S is the matrix of distances from the central element in the processing window to the neighboring elements.

The variable parameters of the Frost filter are the size of the sliding window and the damping coefficient D.

3   Evaluation of Noise Filtering Quality

Image quality assessment (IQA) is one of the most important research topics in image processing [21, 22]. At the moment, there is no single universal method for assessing the quality of processed images.

There are two classes of image quality assessment methods: subjective (expert) assessments and formal mathematical methods (metrics). You can get high-quality assessments using the subjective method, but this method requires the availability of group of experts.

To speed up and simplify the process of image quality assessing, formal mathematical methods are used [23]. Comparison of metrics with subjective assessment, sometimes show that metrics may be not very close to human perception. Therefore, it is necessary to choose a metric that will give the most adequate assessment from a human point of view.

Of many available metrics, the structural similarity index (*SSIM*) is one of the most promising. It is widely believed that *SSIM* gives an image quality assessment that is close enough to human perception, and it also seems to perform well when applied to SAR images [24–27].

This metric determines the degree of similarity of the corresponding parts (sliding windows) of the compared images using three components: brightness, contrast, structure. The total value is the average of the values calculated in all windows. The closer the metric value is to one, the closer the estimated image to the original image.

The metric is calculated using the following formula:

$$SSIM\left(I, \hat{I}\right) = \left((2\mu_I\mu_{\hat{I}} + C_1)(2\sigma_{I\hat{I}} + C_2)\right) \Big/ \left(\left(\mu_I^2 + \mu_{\hat{I}}^2 + C_1\right)\left(\sigma_I^2 + \sigma_{\hat{I}}^2 + C_2\right)\right)$$

(4)

where μ_I and μ_f are the average values of the noisy image and the image after filtering, respectively; σ_f^2 and $\sigma_{\hat{I}}^2$ are the variances of the noisy image and the image after filtering, respectively; $\sigma_{f\hat{I}}$ is covariance of the noisy image and the image after filtering; $C_1 = (k_1L)^2$, $C_2 = (k_2L)^2$ are variables, where $L = 2^{\text{bits per pixel}} - 1$, $k_1 = 0.01$, $k_2 = 0.03$.

4 Speckle Noise Distribution

It is necessary to have the reference image without noise for evaluating the filter's operation. Speckle noise is superimposed on the reference image, then noisy image is filtered and the quality of the filtering is evaluated by comparing both images. To do this it is necessary to know the distribution and statistical parameters of the speckle noise.

For this eight real SAR images were used. Three to five uniform areas that did not contain any objects were selected in each image. For each of the selected fragments, histograms were constructed and statistical parameters were estimated assuming several different speckle noise distributions. Based on these results, it was concluded that the speckle noise in SAR images most often has a distribution close to the Rayleigh distribution [28–31], and the average value of the distribution scale parameter for all examined fragments is close to $\sigma = 0.2707$.

5 The Selection of Optimal Parameters

An iterative algorithm for finding the optimal parameters of speckle noise filters for use on SAR images is described in this section. The algorithm includes the following steps:

1. The selection of metrics (or one metric) for image quality assessment.
2. The selection or creation of a test image.
3. Superimposing the speckle noise with the selected distribution on the test image.
4. The calculation of the dependence of the values of the selected metrics on various values of the variable parameter for a fixed size of the filter sliding window, for example, 11×11.

4.1. If there are two variable parameters, except the size of filter window, then a family of dependencies of metric values on the values of the first parameter at various values of the second parameter is calculated.

4.2. If there are three variable parameters, then one of the parameters is fixed, and for the other two, a family of curves is calculated, as described in step 4.1. Next, the optimal values are selected for the two parameters, as described in step 5. The selected values are fixed and the dependence of the metric values on the various values of the third parameter is calculated. The optimal value of the third parameter is obtained, as described in step 5. The value of third parameter is fixed and the values of two other parameters are found.

5. The selection of the optimal filter parameter value from the calculated curve. The optimal parameter value is considered to be the value for which the selected metrics have their best value (for the *SSIM* metric, this is the maximum value).

6. The calculation of the dependence of the values of the selected metrics on the various sizes of the sliding window with fixed values of the filter parameters that were found as described in step 5.

7. The selection of the optimal value of the size of filter window from the obtained curve.

8. Fine tuning of the optimal value of the filter's parameters, similar to steps 4–5, using a new size of the filter window, found at step 7.

6 An Example of Selecting the Optimal Filter Parameters for the Frost Filter

As an example will use the synthetic image shown in Fig. 1 for selecting the optimal parameters of the Frost filter. The test image contains a sharp edge separating the dark and light regions, a large object (circle) and several small objects (triangles and stars).

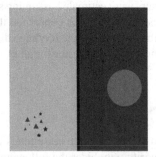   

Fig. 1. Test image with the size of 500 × 500 pixels.   **Fig. 2.** Test image with speckle noise with a Rayleigh distribution with scale parameter $\sigma = 0.2707$ superimposed.

Multiplicative speckle noise must be superimposed on the test image. It was determined above that the Rayleigh distribution can be used as the speckle noise distribution. The image with speckle noise superimposed is shown in Fig. 2.

Let us consider the search for the optimal Frost filter parameters using the *SSIM* metric. The initial size of the filter window is 11×11.

This filter has one variable parameter (damping coefficient D), if the size of the filter window is not taken into account. Therefore, we begin the search for the optimal value of the parameter D by calculating the dependence of the *SSIM* metric values on various values of the parameter D for a fixed size of the filter window 11×11 (Fig. 3a). From Fig. 3a) we find that the optimal value of the parameter D given by the maximum value of *SSIM* metric is 14.5. Now the dependence of the *SSIM* metric values on various sizes of the sliding window with a fixed value of $D = 14.5$ is plotted (Fig. 3b). The optimal filter window value is selected using the calculated curve and is 13×13. Finally, we fine tune the optimal value of the parameter D with a fixed size of the filter window 13×13 (Fig. 3c). As a result, we find that the optimal value of the parameter D of the Frost filter by the maximum of *SSIM* metric is 14 and the size of sliding window of 13×13. This iterative process can be repeated as many times as required.

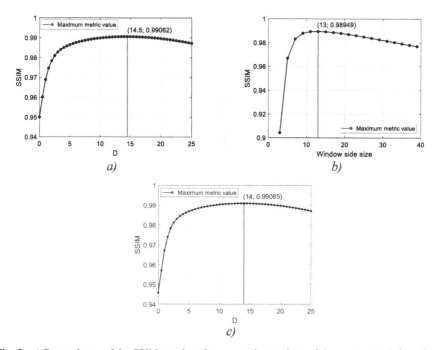

Fig. 3. a) Dependence of the *SSIM* metric values on various values of the parameter D for a fixed size of the filter sliding window 11×11; b) The dependence of the values of the *SSIM* metric on the various sizes of the sliding window for a fixed value of $D = 14.5$; c) Dependence of the *SSIM* metric values on various values of the parameter D for a fixed size of the filter sliding window 13×13.

The test image after applying the Frost filter with optimal parameters is shown in Fig. 4.

Fig. 4. Test image after applying the Frost filter with D = 14 and with the window size of 13 × 13.

One-dimensional slices of image can be used to visualize the effect of filtering (Fig. 5). In this case, we took a slightly modified test image so that the slice crosses all the important objects. The curves in Fig. 5b) are shifted vertically so that they do not overlap.

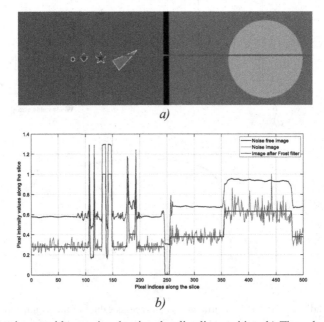

Fig. 5. a) Test image without noise showing the slice line position; b) The values of the pixel intensity along the slice line for the test image before and after filtering.

From the obtained slices, we can visually evaluate the filters, that is, how much the image slice after filtering coincides with the original noise-free slice. As can be seen from Fig. 5, the image after application of the Frost filter with optimal parameters is fairly close to the original image.

7 Applying the Frost Filter with Optimal Parameters

Let us give more examples of applying the Frost filter with selected optimal parameters using real aerial optical images (Fig. 6).

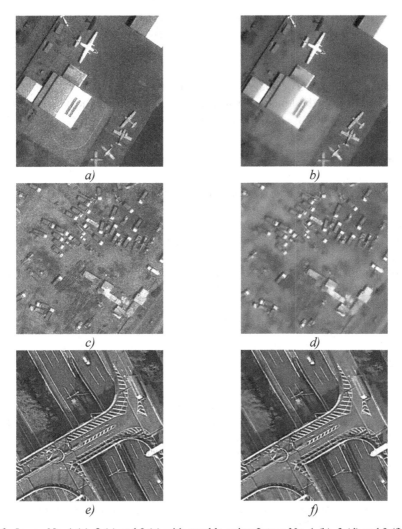

Fig. 6. Image No. 1 (a), 2 (c) and 3 (e) with speckle noise; Image No. 1 (b), 2 (d) and 3 (f) after the Frost filter, window size 13×13, $D = 14$.

Table 1 shows the *SSIM* metric values before and after processing by the Frost filter with optimal parameters. For comparison, the *SSIM* metric values for non-optimal Frost filter parameters are included in the table.

Table 1. Values of the *SSIM* metric before and after processing by the Frost filter with optimal (third column) and non-optimal parameters.

Image No.	Without a filter	$13 \times 13, D = 14$	$5 \times 5, D = 1$	$11 \times 11, D = 3$
1	0.6792	0.8124	0.7474	0.7019
2	0.4915	0.7113	0.6816	0.5864
3	0.8061	0.8482	0.5097	0.5067

As can be seen from the table, images obtained by filtering with optimal parameter values indeed have the best metrics. This confirms the validity of the proposed method and the possibility of its use in SAR image processing.

8 Conclusion

This paper presents a method for selecting the optimal parameters of speckle noise reduction filters. Using the Frost filter as an example, it is shown in detail how to obtain the optimal values of its two parameters (damping coefficient and window size) using the *SSIM* metric. Similar method can be used to select parameters of other speckle noise reduction filters.

The Frost filter was tested on real aerial optical images. Image processing was carried out using both the optimal and non-optimal parameter values. It was shown that, the filtering quality can be up to 20–40% better (by the *SSIM* metric) when using optimal parameter values compared with non-optimal ones.

References

1. Moroz, A.V., Davydov, V.V.: Fiber-optical system for transmitting heterodyne signals in active phased antenna arrays of radar stations. J. Phys. Conf. Ser. **1368**, 022024 (2019)
2. Filimonov, A.V., Zemlyakov, V.E., Egorkin, V.I., Maslevtsov, A.V., Wurz, M.C., Vainshtein, S.N.: Nanosecond miniature transmitters for pulsed optical radars. In: Galinina, O., Andreev, S., Balandin, S., Koucheryavy, Y. (eds.) NEW2AN/ruSMART/NsCC -2017. LNCS, vol. 10531, pp. 490–497. Springer, Cham (2017). https://doi.org/10.1007/978-3-319-67380-6_45
3. Tsikin, I.A., Poklonskaya, E.S.: Accuracy of secondary surveillance radar system remote analysis station. In: Galinina, O., Andreev, S., Balandin, S., Koucheryavy, Y. (eds.) NEW2AN/ruSMART/NsCC -2017. LNCS, vol. 10531, pp. 598–606. Springer, Cham (2017). https://doi.org/10.1007/978-3-319-67380-6_56
4. Tarasenko, M.Y., Lenets, V.A., Malanin, K.Y., Akulich, N.V., Davydov, V.V.: Features of use direct and external modulation in fiber optical simulators of a false target for testing radar station. J. Phys. Conf. Ser. **1038**, 012035 (2018)
5. Pavlov V.A., Belov A.A., Tuzova, A.A.: Implementation of synthetic aperture radar processing algorithms on the Jetson TX1 platform. In: IEEE International Conference on Electrical Engineering and Photonics (EExPolytech) 2019, St. Petersburg, Russia, pp. 90–93 (2019)
6. Özdemiir, C.: Inverse Synthetic Aperture Radar Imaging with MATLAB Algorithms, p. 387. Wiley, New Jersey (2012)
7. M. Skolnik: Radar handbook. McGraw-Hill, 2008

8. Brown, W.M., Porcello, L.J.: An introduction to synthetic-aperture radar. IEEE Spectr. **6**(9), 52–62 (1969)
9. Chan, Y.K., Koo, V.C.: An introduction to synthetic aperture radar (SAR). Progr. Electromagnet. Res. **62**, 27–60 (2008)
10. Oliver, C., Quegan, S.: Understanding Synthetic Aperture Radar Images. SciTech Publishing, Raleigh, NC (2004)
11. Goodman, J.: Some fundamental properties of speckle. J. Opt. Soc. Am. **66**(11), 1145–1150 (1976)
12. Fursov, V., Zherdev, D., Kazanskiy, N.: Support subspaces method for synthetic aperture radar automatic target recognition. Int. J. Adv. Robot. Syst. **13**(5) (2016)
13. Frost, S.: A model for radar images and its application to adaptive digital filtering of multiplicative noise. IEEE Trans. Pattern Anal. Mach. Intell. **4**(2), 157–166 (1982)
14. Goldfinger, A.D.: Estimation of spectra from speckled images. IEEE Trans. Aerosp. Electron. Syst. AES **18**(5), 675–681 (1982)
15. Dong, X., Zhang, D., Cui, K.: Spatial filtering strategies on deforestation detection using SAR image textures. In: CIE International Conference on Radar (RADAR), pp. 1–4 (2016)
16. Lee, J.-S., Wen, J.-H., Ainsworth, T.L.: Improved sigma filter for speckle filtering of SAR imagery. IEEE Trans. Geosci. Remote Sens. **47**(1), 202–213 (2009)
17. Prakash, K.B., Babu, R.V., Gopal, B.: Image independent filter for removal of speckle noise. Int. J. Comput. Sci. Issues **8**(5), 196–201 (2011). no. 3
18. Gifani, P., Behnam, H., Sani, Z.A.: Noise reduction of echocardiographic images based on temporal information. IEEE Trans. Ultrason. Ferroelectr. Freq. Control **61**(4), 620–630 (2014)
19. Sarode, V., Deshmukh, P.R.: Reduction of speckle noise and image enhancement of images using filtering technique. Int. J. Adv. Technol. **2011**, 30–38 (2011)
20. Lopera, O., Heremans, R., Pizurica, A., Dupont, Y.: Filtering speckle noise in SAS images to improve detection and identification of seafloor targets. Int. Water Side Secur. Conf. **2010**, 1–4 (2010)
21. Kuznetsova, O.B., Savchenko, E.A., Andryakov, A.A., Savchenko, E.Y., Musakulova, Z.A.: Image processing in total internal reflection fluorescence microscopy. J. Phys: Conf. Ser. **1236**(1), 1–6 (2019)
22. Korobeynikov, A.G., Grishentsev, A.Yu., Velichko, E.N., Korikov, C.C., Aleksanin, S.A., Fedosovskii, M.E., Bondarenko, I.B.: Calculation of regularization parameter in the problem of blur removal in digital image. Opt. Memory Neural Netw. **25**(3), 184–191 (2016). https://doi.org/10.3103/S1060992X16030036
23. Andryakov, A.A.: Image filtering for the nanosatellite vision system. J. Phys: Conf. Ser. **1326**(1), 1–7 (2019)
24. Swati A. Gandhi, C.V. Kulkarni: MSE Vs SSIM. International Journal of Scientific & Engineering Research, vol. 4, no. 7, pp. 930–934, July-2013
25. Wang, Z., Bovik, A.C., Sheikh, H.R.: Image Quality Assessment: From Error Visibility to Structural Similarity. IEEE Trans. Image Process. **13**(4), 1–14 (2004)
26. Singh, P., Shree, R.: A new SAR image despeckling using directional smoothing filter and method noise thresholding. Eng. Sci. Technol. Int. J. **21**, 589–610 (2018)
27. Jiao, S., Dong, W.: SAR image quality assessment based on SSIM using textural feature. In: Seventh International Conference on Image and Graphics, pp. 281–286 (2013)
28. Abramov, S., et al.: Methods for blind estimation of speckle variance in SAR images: simulation results and verification for real-life data. In: Awrejcewicz, J. (ed.) Computational and Numerical Simulations, pp. 303–327. Intech Open (2014)
29. Choi, H., Jeong, J.: Speckle noise reduction technique for SAR images using statistical characteristics of speckle noise and discrete wavelet transform. Remote Sens. **11**, 1184 (2019)
30. Xie, H., Pierce, L.E., Ulaby, F.T.: Statistical properties of logarithmically transformed speckle. IEEE Trans. Geosci. Remote Sens. **40**(3), 721–727 (2002)
31. Singh, P., Pandey, R.: Speckle noise: modelling and implementation. Int. J. Circ. Theor. Appl. **9**, 8717–8727 (2016)

Performance Optimization
of Communication System Cooperating
with the MIMO Radar

Jerzy Martyna[✉]

Institute of Computer Science, Faculty of Mathematics and Computer Science
Jagiellonian University, ul. Prof. S. Lojasiewicza 6, 30-348 Cracow, Poland
jerzy.martyna@uj.edu.pl

Abstract. The paper concerns research on the efficiency of the communication system and MIMO radar cooperating with each other. For this system a measure of efficiency was determined, which is the speed of radar estimation and the speed of data transfer. The combination of these measures made it possible to set a performance limit for this system. The original the solution is to optimize the efficiency of the communication system cooperating with MIMO radar. Using derivative-free optimization method has been maximized radar estimation speed and information transfer speed. This makes it possible to find optimal parameters for both systems, which is helpful in its design or analysis. Simulation tests confirmed the correctness of the analysis.

Keywords: MIMO radar · Communication system ·
Radar-communication system coexistence · Performance evaluation ·
Derivative-free methods

1 Introduction

Development of wireless communication systems enables emerging new applications already known radio devices. It is expected that the number of such government will reach millions. Applicable it is also radars, which will be found in wide use with the autonomy becoming more widespread cars [1]. Thanks to it, an autonomous car will be able to get information about obstacles off-road vehicles or other vehicles that will be possible further analyze using the on-board computer. Currently used radar applications operate in the band S (2–4 GHz) (so-called 10-centimeter radar systems) and the L (4–8 GHz) band (so-20 cm systems radar), which means that they share a frequency S used in DAB digital terrestrial radio systems or wireless computer networks (IEEE 802.11, IEEE 802.16).

Modern radar systems may have shared radio channel, which means they can performing data transmission, but after signal detection radar discontinue transmission and send only impulses radar. This technique was presented in

© Springer Nature Switzerland AG 2020
O. Galinina et al. (Eds.): NEW2AN 2020/ruSMART 2020, LNCS 12526, pp. 142–153, 2020.
https://doi.org/10.1007/978-3-030-65729-1_13

paper of Saruthirathanaworakun *et al.* [2]. At work Sodari *et al.* [3] NSP projection method was proposed (Null Space Projection) for simultaneous interaction MIMO radar and base station. In further research carried out, among others by Kluwera *et al.* [4], the effectiveness of object detection was examined using MIMO radar. In the paper by Mahal *et al.* [5] suggested method for combining MIMO radars and cellular systems using techniques MIMO.

Other studies have solved the problem of the coexistence of MIMO radar and communication with multiple users in MIMO systems by introducing a radar beam with incomplete information about the channel status (*imperfect channel state information*, CSI) [6]. In the next paper [7] a new one was proposed beam forming design that uses interference as a useful energy source. Thanks to this it was obtained significant energy savings. In addition, to improve the efficiency of such a system it was proposed to include spectrum division schemes based on the LSA (Licensed Shared Access) approach [8], which uses cognitive radio techniques.

Recently, information embedding into the radiation of MIMO radar has been stated in the paper by Hassanien *et al.* [9,10]. MIMO radars have a greater degree of freedom, but their construction requires more orthogonal waveforms necessary for their operation. Other papers noted that MIMO radar should use chirp-based waveforms. Among others, in the paper by Kim [11] an OFDM chirp waveform design scheme is proposed, which allows the generated waveforms to occupy common spectral support and thereby enables them to exploit the full bandwidth. The same technique was used by Nusenu *et al.* [12] to show that the communication operation does not interfere with the MIMO radar function. Then, the waveforms will remain orthogonal under arbitrary delays and Doppler shifts, while the impact of time delays and Doppler shifts are often ignored in existing MIMO radar waveform diversity design methods.

In turn, the new technique for communication information embedding into the emission of multiple-input multiple-output (MIMO) radar using sparse antenna array configurations has been proposed by Wang *et al.* [13]. In this MIMO radar obtained the association of independent waveforms with the transmit antennas can change over different pulse repetition periods without impacting the radar functionality. An improved signal-to-noise ratio for the radar operation in dual-function radar communication has been achieved by Ahmed *et al.* [14]. Has been used in this case a novel dual-function radar-communication strategy by exploiting directional power control and waveform diversity. Despite this, these works did not optimize data rates of both flows, one for MIMO radar and the other for the communication system.

To find the basic bounds of performance of the system connecting the wireless network and the radar remained presented by Guerci *et al.* [15] concept speed of radar information processing that allowed to compare the speed of both systems.Similar results were presented in [16] and [17], where a theoretical model based on distortion theory.

The main purpose of this work is to present the model communication system cooperating with the MIMO radar. For this model, the efficiency measure was

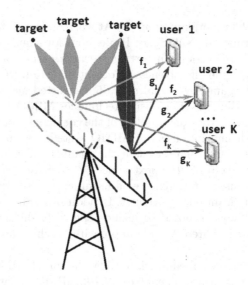

Fig. 1. System with separate antennas for radar and communication.

determined, what is the speed of radar estimation and speed data transfer. By treating these measures together you can set limits on the effectiveness of this system. the original the optimization proposal is the solution performance of the radar communication system. Allows it for the optimization of both systems: communication and radar at the same time, which is helpful with its design or analysis.

The remainder of the paper is organised as follows. Section 2 gives the system model with MIMO antennas, considering the possibility of separating the antennas for radar and communications and by treating antennas together for radar and communication. Section 3 presents the main ones measures of the effectiveness of such a system. Section 4 provides optimizing the performance of this system. In Sect. 5 shows the results of simulation tests. Summary conclusions of the work are included in Sect. 6.

2   System Model

Let there be a given radio and radar system equipped with MIMO (multiple input multiple output) enabling multi-antenna transmission both on the sending and receiving sides. System this one has N antennas that support K single-antenna users in the downlink when detecting different goals at the same time. Two scenarios are possible implementations of this system: (a) antenna separation for radar from communication system antennas, (b) joint use of anrenas for radar and communication.

2.1 System with Separate Antennas for Radar and Communication

As shown in Fig. 1, the antennas are divided into two groups: one radar and one for downlink communication. In this case the received signal of the i-user is given by [18]:

$$x_i[l] = \mathbf{g}_i^T \sum_{k=1}^{K} \mathbf{w}_k d_k[l] + \mathbf{f}_i^T \mathbf{s}_i + \omega_i[l], \quad \forall i \qquad (1)$$

where $\mathbf{g}_i \in \mathbb{C}^{N_C \times 1}$ and $\mathbf{f}_i \in \mathbb{C}^{N_R \times 1}$ are channel vectors for communication antennas and radar antennas, respectively. for i-th user, N_C and N_R are numbers dedicated antennas for communication and radar, $d_i[l]$ is the symbol of communication in the i-th time interval, $\omega_i[l] \sim \mathcal{CN}(0, N_0)$ is the received noise by the i-th user in the time interval l, $\mathbf{w}_i \in \mathbb{C}^{N_C \times 1}$ means vector shaping the i-th user relationship, $\mathbf{s}_l \in \mathbb{C}^{N_R \times 1}$ is the 1-tracker on radar antennas.

The power of communication transmission is obtained by calculating:

$$P_1 = \sum k = 1^K tr(\mathbf{W}_k) \qquad (2)$$

where $\mathbf{W}_k = \mathbf{w}_k \mathbf{w}_k^H$. The channel interference matrix, $\mathbf{H}$, is given as follows:

$$\mathbf{H} = [\mathbf{h}_1, \mathbf{h}_2, \ldots, \mathbf{h}_K] \qquad (3)$$

where $\mathbf{h}_l, \mathbf{g}_l \in \mathbb{C}^{N \times 1}$. Thus, using the Eq. (1) can be obtained the *signal-to-noise ratio* (SINR) given as follows:

$$
\begin{aligned}
SINR_i &= \frac{| \mathbf{g}_i * T \mathbf{w}_i |^2}{\sum_{k=1, k\neq i}^{K} | \mathbf{g}_i^T \mathbf{w}_k |^2 + \mathbf{f}_i^T \mathbf{R}_1 \mathbf{f}_i^* + N_0} \\
&= \frac{tr(\mathbf{g}_i^* \mathbf{g}_i^T \mathbf{W}_i)}{tr\left(\mathbf{g}_i^* \mathbf{g}_i^T \sum_{k=1, k\neq i}^{K} \mathbf{W}_k\right) + tr(\mathbf{f}_i^* \mathbf{f}_i^T \mathbf{R}_1) + N_0}
\end{aligned}
\qquad (4)
$$

where $\mathbf{R}_1 \in \mathbb{C}^{N_R \times N_R}$ is the covariation matrix of radio signal sample.

2.2 System with Common Antennas for Radar and Communication

As shown in Fig. 2, the antennas are common to both radar and downlink communication system. Received signal from i-th user is given as:

$$x_i[l] = \mathbf{b}_i^T \sum_{k=1}^{K} \mathbf{t}_k d_k[l] + n_i[l], \quad \forall i \qquad (5)$$

where $\mathbf{t}_i \in \mathbb{C}^{N \times 1}$ oraz $n_i[l] \sim \mathcal{CN}(0, N_0)$ represent the beam shaping vector and the received noise by i-th user, respectively. The following assumptions are made:

1) the system uses the communication signal as a so-called radar probe;
2) the channel interference matrix is given as above, but it is assumed to be perfect.

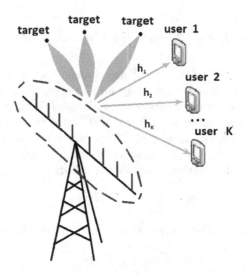

Fig. 2. System with common antennas for radar and communication.

The power of communication transmission is given as follows:

$$P_2 = \sum_{k=1}^{K} tr(\mathbf{T}_k) \tag{6}$$

where $\mathbf{T}_k = \mathbf{t}_k \mathbf{t}_k^H$. Thus, SINR for i-th user is given by:

$$
\begin{aligned}
SINR_i &= \frac{|\mathbf{h}_i * T\mathbf{t}_i|^2}{\sum_{k=1,k\neq i}^{K} |\mathbf{h}_i^T \mathbf{t}_k|^2 + N_0} \\
&= \frac{tr(\mathbf{h}_i^* \mathbf{h}_i^T \mathbf{T}_i)}{tr\left(\mathbf{h}_i^* \mathbf{h}_i^T \sum_{k=1,k\neq i}^{K} T_k\right) + N_0}
\end{aligned}
\tag{7}
$$

3   Performance Bounds for Communication System Cooperating with Radar

The basic measure of the efficiency of a radar system is the *radar estimation rate*. It determines the rate at which radars recognize targets, which is achieved by using a mean square error estimator, called the Rao-Craméra inequality [18]. Similarly for a communication system its a measure of effectiveness is the data

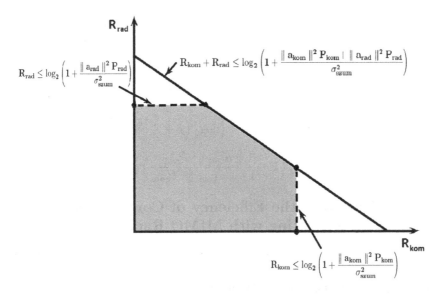

Fig. 3. The area of effective use of a communication system cooperating with radar.

transfer rate (*data information rate*). They determine their mutual relations the effectiveness of such a system.

Let the channel propagation gain for the communication system be given as a_{com}, while the propagation gain for the radar system is a_{rad}. It is assumed that the transmission power of the communication system is given by P_{com}. Let the radar system transmission power be P_{rad}. Assuming that the noise variance is equal to σ_{noise}^2, you can specify a basic speed limit for both systems [16]:

$$R_{com} \leq \log_2 \left(1 + \frac{\| a_{kom} \|^2 P_{kom}}{\sigma_{noise}^2}\right) \tag{8}$$

$$R_{rad} \leq \log_2 \left(1 + \frac{\| a_{rad} \|^2 P_{rad}}{\sigma_{noise}^2}\right) \tag{9}$$

where P_{com} oraz P_{rad} are transmission powers of communication and radar system, respectively.

Then there is a condition limiting the speed of both systems:

$$R_{com} + R_{rad} \leq$$
$$\log_2 \left(1 + \frac{\| a_{com} \|^2 P_{com} + \| a_{rad} \|^2 P_{rad}}{\sigma_{noise}^2}\right) \tag{10}$$

Figure 3 shows the area of effective use of a communication system cooperating with radar. The vertices of the resulting polygon are found by jointly solving the constraints given by Eqs. (8) and (9) and are:

$$\{R_{com}, R_{rad}\} = \Big\{ \log_2 \Big(1 + \frac{\parallel a_{com} \parallel^2 P_{com}}{1 + \parallel a_{rad} \parallel^2 P_{rad}}\Big),$$

$$\log_2 \Big(1 + \frac{\parallel a_{rad} \parallel^2 P_{rad}}{\sigma_{noise}^2}\Big)\Big\} \tag{11}$$

and

$$\{R_{com}, R_{rad}\} = \Big\{ \log_2 \Big(1 + \frac{\parallel a_{com} \parallel^2 P_{com}}{\sigma_{noise}^2}\Big),$$

$$\log_2 \Big(1 + \frac{\parallel a_{rad} \parallel^2 P_{rad}}{1 + \parallel a_{kom} \parallel^2 P_{com}}\Big)\Big\} \tag{12}$$

4   Optimization of the Efficiency of Communication System Cooperating with MIMO Radar

Optimization of the performance of the communication system cooperating with the radar belongs to the multi-criteria optimization and has an infinite number of solutions. Maximizing both functions, i.e. radar estimation speed and information transfer speed, requires their definition to take account of the weight of these objectives. So if both have the same meaning then the following function can be minimized.

$$f(P_{com}, P_{rad}) = (R_{com}(P_{com}, P_{rad}) - K)^2$$

$$+ (R_{rad}(P_{com}, P_{rad}) - F)^2 \tag{13}$$

where K and F are known maximum values for information transmission speed and radar estimation speed, respectively.

To find the maximum value of $f(P_{com}, P_{rad})$, you can use the value of the function f at a given point (P_{com}, P_{rad}). They can be found through the use of *derivative-free optimization* [19]. The concept of this method derives directly from the work of Spendley *et al.* [20] and publications of Nelder and R. Mead [21], regarding optimization algorithms based on the so-called downhill simplex. Methods of this type of optimization work well even for highly non-linear functions, however, they require a considerable amount of numerical work, especially with a large number of decision variables.

Derivative optimization uses approximate derivatives based on finite differences or derivatives of interpolating functions. A natural indicator of the quality of a model used for optimization is the degree to which the model locally approximates the function f and its derivatives. This allows you to create a local square model for the point $p^k = (P_{com}^k, P_{rad}^k)$, $k = 0, 1, 2, \ldots$, namely

$$m_k(p^k + d) = f(p^k) + (y^k)^T d + \frac{1}{2} d^T \mathcal{H}^k d \tag{14}$$

In the above equation, it is assumed that $p^{k+1} = p^k + d^k$. Then for small values ϵ, $\epsilon > 0$, is obtained by:

$$g^k = (g_1, g_2)^T, \quad g_i = \frac{f(p^k + \epsilon e_i) - f(p^k - \epsilon e_i)}{2\epsilon^2} \tag{15}$$

Algorithm 1. Derivative-free optimization model

1: **procedure** GENERAL ALGORITHM
2: **Initialisation:**
3:    Let $\epsilon > 0, d > 0, 0 < \gamma < 1, \eta \leftarrow \eta_{res}$;
4:    Choose initial point $p^0 \leftarrow (P^0_{com}, P^0_{rad})$
5:    **for** $k \leftarrow 0, K$ **do**
6:        Select a aubset of Y_k for model building
7:        Calculate $m_k(p^k)$ in Y_k
8:        **while** $\| \nabla m_k(p^k) \| < \epsilon$ **do**
9:            **if** m_k is accurate on $\mathcal{B}(p^k; \Delta_k)$ **then**
10:                $\Delta_k \leftarrow \gamma \Delta_k$
11:            **else**
12:                Make Y_k more accurate on $\mathcal{B}(p^k; \Delta_k)$
13:            **end if**
14:        **end while**
15:        Generate a direction $d^k \in \mathcal{B}(0; \Delta_k)$
16:            so that $p^k + d^k$ maximizes m_k
17:        Evaluate $m_k(p^k + d^k)$
18:        **if** m_k is inaccurate on $\mathcal{B}(p^k; \Delta_k)$ **then**
19:            Add model improving point to Y_k
20:        **end if**
21:        **if** $p^k > \eta$ **then**
22:            $p^{k+1} \leftarrow p^k + d^k$
23:        **else**
24:            $p^{k+1} \leftarrow p^k$
25:        **end if**
26:        $Y_{k+1} \leftarrow Y_k$
27:    **end for**
28: **end procedure**

where $e_1 = (1,0)^T$ and $e_2 = (0,1)^T$ are approximate gradients. Hessian matrix $\mathcal{H}^\mathbf{k}$ is given by

$$\mathcal{H}^k = \begin{pmatrix} \vartheta_{11} & \vartheta_{12} \\ \vartheta_{21} & \vartheta_{22} \end{pmatrix} \tag{16}$$

where ϑ_{ij} given by

$$\vartheta_{ij} = \frac{F(p^k + \epsilon e_i + \epsilon e_j) - F(p^k) - F(p^k + \epsilon e_j) + F(p^k)}{\epsilon^2} \tag{17}$$

is a Taylor approximation of the Hessian.

The pseudocode of the algorithm for placing packets in the sliding window is represented by Algorithm 1. The algorithm for derivative-free model works by managing the set of Y_k points used here to construct the m_k model. The points Y_k need not necessarily be elements of the set $\mathcal{B}$, which is interpolation set of the trust-region radius (i.e. $Y_k \subset \mathcal{B}(p^k; \Delta_k)$). By operating in the loop for subsequent iterations $k = 0, 1, \ldots, K$ within $\mathcal{B}(p^k, \Delta_k)$ the model m_k is improved. To increase accuracy, direction d_k is generated that maximizes model

Table 1. Main simulation parameters.

Parameter	Value
Number of transmit antennas (MIMO radar)	12
Number of receive antennas (MIMO radar)	12
Number of receive antennas (Comm. system)	10
Carrier frequency	3.5 GHz
Wavelength	8.5 cm
Radar power	100 W
Radar target range	10 km
Radar antenna gain	10 dBi
Communication power	100
Signal to Noise ratio	0 − 10 dB

m_k. If m_k does not improve, then it is added to the set Y_k and the iteration process is continued. In the end, used restrictions on Y_k determines whether m_k is an interpolation of maximum p^k.

It should be noted that the derivative-free method requires an additional test of model quality. But thanks to the fact that Taylor's theorem used here, it secures that accuracy of model for small value of Δ_k. Moreover, if $\Delta_k \to 0$, then this algorithm converges.

5   Performance Analysis

This section will present the results of simulation tests for a communication system cooperating with radar. The simulation was carried out using Matlab. It was assumed that the system consists of 12 antennas, spaced every half wavelength. The radar was assumed to operate in 500 MHz band with a carrier frequency of 8 GHz. For the communication system, it was assumed that the frame length is 20 radar pulses. The main simulation parameters are shown in Table 1.

To determine the efficiency bound, the average achievable sum rate for both systems treated together as a function of signal-to-noise power ratio was examined for different modulations. Figure 4 shows the average sum of this flow in the SNR function for modulation BPSK, QPSK, 16-QAM using an antenna system 8 × 4. It is evident that the increase in modulation speeds gives an increase in the system's carrying capacity.

Figure 5 shows the bound on data rate of communication system depending on the radar rate estimation. For comparison, the results of numerical calculations carried out include using derivative-free model were marked with a solid red line. The results of simulation study were presented on the dotted line.

Figure 6 presents the relationship between the communication and radar performance. As a measure this efficiency was adopted here the detection probability, P_D, which is calculated a. o. in [22]. For the adopted data, i.e. a fixed value of

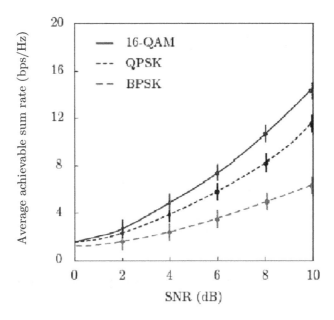

Fig. 4. The average achievable sum rate versus SINR.

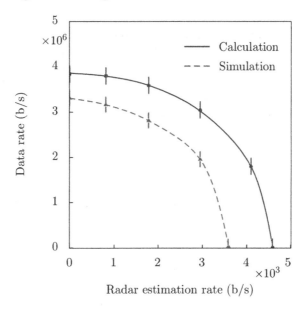

Fig. 5. The area of effective use of a communication system cooperating with radar.

SNR equal to -5 dB, given the false-alarm probability for radar, $P_{F,A} = 10^{-7}$ [23], and a fixed number of users was determined P_D depending on average achievable rate of system. From the drawing is visible, that the P_D value is higher for the optimization carried out using the proposed method than in its absence.

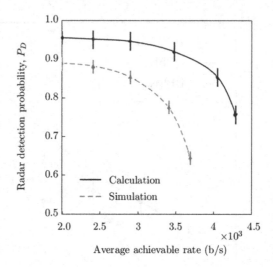

Fig. 6. The radar detection probability versus the average achievable rate for given SNR $= -5$ dB and $K = 5$.

6 Conclusion

The paper presents a model of a communication system cooperating with MIMO radar given performance bounds of such a system and proposed method of its optimization. Thanks to it it is possible selection of basic parameters of the communication system cooperating with the radar, which will allow for obtaining the required performance. This will also allow choosing the area of operation of such a system, already at the design stage.

References

1. DARPA. (2016) Shared spectrum access for radar and communications (SSPARC). [http://www.darpa.mil/program/shared-spectrum-access-for-radar-and-communications]
2. Saruthirathanaworakun, R., Peha, J.M., Correia, L.M.: Opportunistic sharing between rotating radar and cellular. IEEE J. Sel. Areas Comm. **30**(10), 1900–1910 (2012)
3. Sodagari, S., Khawar, A., Clancy, T.C., McGwier, R.: A projection based approach for radar and telecommunication systems coexistence. In: IEEE Global Communication Conference (GLOBECOM), pp. 5010–5014 (2012)
4. Khawar, A., Abdelhadi, A., Clancy, C.: Target detection performance of spectrum sharing MIMO radars. IEEE Sens. J. **15**(9), 4928–4940 (2015)
5. Mahal, J.A., Khawar, A., Abdelhadi, A., Clancy, T.C.: Spectral coexistence of MIMO radar and MIMO cellular system. IEEE Trans. Aerosp. Electron. Syst. **53**(2), 655–668 (2017)
6. Liu, F., Masouros, C., Li, A., Ratnarajah, T.: Robust MIMO beam forming for cellular and radar coexistence. IEEE Wirel. Comm. Lett. **6**(3), 374–377 (2017)

7. Liu, F., Masouros, C., Li, A.T., Ratnarajah, J.Z.: Interference exploitation for radar and cellular coexistence: the power-efficient approach (2017). arXiv:1704.08920

8. Yousif, E.H.G., Filippou, M.C., Khan, F., Ratnajah, T., Sellathurai, M.: A new LSA-based approach for spectral coexistence of MIMO radar and wireless communications systems. In: Proceedings of IEEE International Conference Communication (ICC), pp. 1–6 (2016)

9. Hassanien, A., Amin, M.G., Zhang, Y., Himed, B.: A dual-function MIMO radar communications system using PSK modulation. In: Proceedings of the European Signal Processing Conference (EUSIPCO), Budapest, Hungary (2016)

10. Hassanien, A., Himed, B., Rigling, B.D.: A dual-function MIMO radar-communications system using frequency-hopping waveforms. Proc. IEEE Radar Conf. **1721–1725**(May), 8–12 (2017)

11. Kim, J.H., Younis, M., Moreira, A., Wiesbeck, W.: A novel OFDM chirp waveform scheme for use of multiple transmitters in SAR. IEEE Geosci. Remote Sens. Let. **10**(3), 568–572 (2013)

12. Nusenu, ShY, Chen, H., Wen, Q.W.: Dual-function MIMO radar-communications employing frequency-hopping chirp waveforms. Prog. Electromagn. Res. M **64**, 135–146 (2018)

13. Wang, X., Hassanien, A., Amin, M.G.: Dual-function MIMO radar communications system design via sparse array optimization (2018). https://arxiv.org/pdf/1808.04940.pdf

14. Ahmed, A., Gu, Y., Silage, D., Zhang, Y.D.:n Power-efficient multi-user dual-function, radar-communications. In: Conference on IEEE 19th International Workshop on Signal Processing Advances in Wireless Communication (SPAWC) (2018)

15. Guerci, J.R., Guerci, R.M., Lackpour, A., Moskowitz, D.: Joint design and operation of shared spectrum access for radar and communications. IEEE Radar Conference (RadarCon), pp. 0761–0766 (2015)

16. Chiriyath, A.R., Paul, B., Jacyna, G.M., Bliss, D.W.: Inner bounds on performance of radar and communications co-existence. IEEE Trans. Signal Proc. **64**(2), 464–474 (2016)

17. Chiriyath, A.R., Paul, B., Bliss, D.W.: Radar-communications convergence: coexistence, cooperation, and co-design. IEEE Trans. Cogn. Comm. Netw. **3**(1), 1–12 (2017)

18. Li, J., Stoica, P.: MIMO Radar Signal Process. John Wiley Sons, Hoboken (2009)

19. Conn, A.R., Scheinberg, K., Vicente, L.N.: Introduction to Derivative-free Optimization. SIAM-MPS, Philadelphia (2009)

20. Spendley, W., Hext, G.R., Himsworth, F.R.: Sequential application for simplex designs in optimisation and evolutionary operation. Technometrics **4**, 441–461 (1962)

21. Nelder, J.A., Mead, R.: A simplex method for function minimization. Comput. J. **7**, 308–313 (1965)

22. Aqunallah, N., Khalfa, A.: Analysis study of radar probability of detection for fluctuating and non-fluctuating targets. Alg. J. Sig. Syst. (AJSS) **2**(1), 12–20 (2017)

23. Nguyen, V.T.P., Tang, L., Mukhopadhyay, S.C., Nguyen, D.M., Hasan, F.: Probabilities of false alarm for vital sign detection on the basis of a doppler radar system. Sensors **18**(3), 1–16 (2018)

Performance of 5G SU-MIMO Employing OFDM Bandwidth and Per-Subcarrier Precoding

Viacheslav Ivanov$^{(\boxtimes)}$ ⓘ, Artem Medvedev ⓘ, Irina Bondareva ⓘ,
and Vladimir Grigoriev

ITMO University, St. Petersburg 197101, Russia
ivanov@niuitmo.ru

Abstract. This paper presents the performance analysis of Single User Multiple Input Multiple Output (SU-MIMO) 5G cellular communication when combined with frequency-domain precoding technique in spatially correlated Tapped-delay-line (TDL) Rician channel. We investigated how calculation of precoder coefficients at individual resource blocks (RB) by performing singular value decomposition (SVD) of channel estimate would improve performance of multiple input multiple output (MIMO) system, compared to single coefficient per bandwidth-averaged channel estimate. We compared gains for systems with 1 and 2 transmission layers over channels with different delay spreads (DS), K-factors, spatial correlations and found such technique provides small but quantifiable gains in throughput, the highest gains being in spatially correlated NLOS channels.

Keywords: 5G · SU-MIMO · TDL · PDSCH · Spatial correlation · SVD · K-factor · LOS · NLOS

1 Introduction

In 5th generation cellular networks it is possible to perform physical downlink shared channel (PDSCH) spatial multiplexing by means of singular value decomposition (SVD) of averaged channel estimate. This channel estimation may be performed in two ways. First option is by the base station (BS) based on Sounding Reference Signal (SRS) transmitted from user equipment (UE) to BS by exploiting channel reciprocity when operating in time division duplex (TDD) mode with proper calibration. The second option is by UE, utilizing channel state information reference signal (CSI-RS) sent in downlink from BS to UE and report estimated CSI back from UE to BS via physical uplink control channel (PUCCH) for periodic reporting or via physical uplink shared channel (PUSCH) for aperiodic reporting.

There are several ways for single-user multi-antenna precoding at the transmitter. One way is channel inversion precoding like zero-forcing (ZF) precoding with total and per-antenna element power constrains, where transmitter tries to inverse channel estimate for precoding weights. Other precoding techniques are MMSE precoding, nonlinear

O. Galinina et al. (Eds.): NEW2AN 2020/ruSMART 2020, LNCS 12526, pp. 154–161, 2020.
https://doi.org/10.1007/978-3-030-65729-1_14

precoding [1], and codebook-based precoding. Most commonly used is SVD-precoding, which redistributes signal to multiple antennas so that diversity gain is maximized by multiplying signal from each layer by a corresponding columns of the right-hand (V) matrix.

Whatever the antenna precoding method is utilized, there is an option to do averaging of channel estimate over all subcarriers of transmission bandwidth [2], to reduce CSI transmission overhead. Another option is to treat multiple RB independently: in [7, Sect. 5.1.2.3] it is stated that in 5G the precoding granularity can be as low as just two consecutive resource blocks (RB).

Depending on type of the channel impulse response and overall bandwidth, the averaging of channel transfer function over the whole bandwidth might lead to precoding ineffectiveness as the singular values distribution of the channel estimate at some parts of the bandwidth will be too different from singular values of the average channel estimate. Non-averaging of channel transfer function, i.e. picking up precoder coefficients for each subcarrier individually on the other hand might lead to improvement, which might be understood as elimination of beam-squint effect in single-layer transmission. The effectiveness of per-subcarrier precoding would depend on number of layers and channel rank. Such approach has several drawbacks, namely complexity – the SVD operation should be performed multiple times, and if channel estimate comes from CSI feedback, the overhead of such feedback might be large.

In [3] the possibility of improving resource allocation for users was suggested based on channel estimate coherence bandwidth. In 5G the resources are likely going to be allocated based on industry verticals [4], and technique of user frequency allocation is inconvenient. In [5] the performance limitation of optimal frequency-flat precoders in frequency-selective channel is considered with beam-squint penalties. In [6], to reduce CSI feedback overhead, a decomposition of channel state information into subcarrier-dependent and subcarrier-independent parts was proposed, so per-subcarrier precoding is in principle realizable with no much overhead worsening. Also in [6] the simulation results are given for 2×2 multiple input multiple output (MIMO) 2-layers transmission with various channel correlation values in terms of BER and throughput, for Wi-Fi systems.

In this paper, we picked a number of system cases to analyze, namely 2 layers and 1 layer operation of 5G 2×2 MIMO signal comparing variations of SVD precoding approach – with whole bandwidth channel estimate averaging prior to SVD and per-RB channel estimate averaging. We show modeling results for different channel types. We consider realistic 5G signal with realistic numerology, LDPC and adaptive modulation-coding schemes to include correlation and bandwidth-selectivity impairments impact reduction in 5G.

2   System Model

The transmission system used for simulations is set up as shown in Fig. 1.

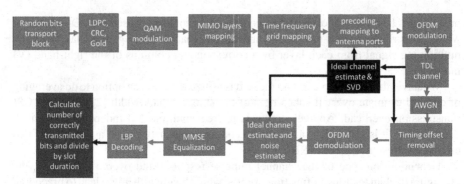

Fig. 1. Transmission model implemented in MATLAB. Blue blocks are PHY-layer functions and blue lines aid to visualize order of functions execution. Orange block describes procedure to obtain throughput. Ideal channel estimate data (black block) is passed to multiple digital signal processing blocks in transmitter and receiver. (Color figure online)

For each signal to noise ratio (SNR) point and Modulation coding schemes (MCS) set, the same pseudo-random transport block bit sequence is generated. Then this bit sequence is passed through PDSCH encoding procedure. This procedure consists of Cyclic Redundancy Check (CRC) sum attachment to transport block, code block segmentation, code block CRC attachment, Low density parity check (LDPC) encoding, rate matching with bit interleaving, code block concatenation, using channel coding procedures described in [8, Sect. 7.2]. The resulting single codeword per slot and all transmission layers is then scrambled using Gold Sequence prior to quadrature phase shift keying (QPSK) or QAM modulation; modulated symbols are mapped onto transmission layers, antenna ports and RB. These procedures are specified in [9, Sect. 7.3].

After this, the resource grids for each layer and antenna port are precoded using SVD of ideally known channel estimate. The decomposition is done either upon averaged channel estimate over the whole bandwidth, or per each subcarrier independently – two regimens compared in this work.

Finally, the obtained PDSCH resources are OFDM-modulated according to [9, Sect. 5.3].

The obtained PDSCH baseband time-domain signal is then consequently passed through the correlated tapped-delay line (TDL) channel and additive white Gaussian noise (AWGN):

At the receiver, perfect timing estimate and timing offset removal is performed, followed by OFDM-demodulation, ideal channel and noise estimation, minimum mean square error (MMSE) equalization, PDSCH decoding using LDPC layered belief propagation algorithm with maximum 6 iterations.

Throughput is calculated as a number of successfully received information bits per slot duration.

The modeled system is 2 transmit and 2 receive antennas and can be described as follows:

$$
\begin{pmatrix} y_1(f) \\ y_2(f) \end{pmatrix} = \begin{pmatrix} h_{11}(f) & h_{12}(f) \\ h_{21}(f) & h_{22}(f) \end{pmatrix} \cdot \begin{pmatrix} \tilde{x}_1(f) \\ \tilde{x}_2(f) \end{pmatrix} + \begin{pmatrix} n_1(f) \\ n_2(f) \end{pmatrix} \tag{1}
$$

Here f denotes frequency index, i.e. subcarrier, y_i is a symbol received at receiver antenna i, h_{ij} is channel transfer function between transmit antenna j and receive antenna i, $\tilde{x}_j$ is precoded signal for antenna j. The channel transfer function H is decomposed as follows:

$$H = USV^*$$ (2)

$$H = \begin{pmatrix} u_{11}(f) & u_{12}(f) \\ u_{21}(f) & u_{22}(f) \end{pmatrix} \begin{pmatrix} s_{11}(f) & 0 \\ 0 & s_{22}(f) \end{pmatrix} \begin{pmatrix} v_{11}(f) & v_{12}(f) \\ v_{21}(f) & v_{22}(f) \end{pmatrix}^*$$ (3)

In Eq. 2–3 S is diagonal matrix, V and U are unitary matrices. After decomposition, the signal mapped to transmission layers X is multiplied by V matrix. In single layer scenario the first column of V matrix is used, highlighted bold.

$$\tilde{X} = VX$$ (4)

After signal is precoded the streams for multiple antennas are orthogonalized and can be received independently, as outlined in Eq. (5)–(7).

$$UU^* = I = V^*V$$ (5)

$$Y = U^* \cdot (H \cdot V \cdot X + N)$$ (6)

$$y_i(f) = s_{ii}(f) \cdot x_i(f) + \hat{n}_i(f)$$ (7)

Instead of matrix U^*, the receiver applies MMSE equalization based on demodulation reference signal (DMRS), which is performance-equivalent.

3 Simulations

3.1 Simulation Parameters

For our simulation we assume conventional 5G New Radio (NR) Sub-6 GHz system, PDSCH, 15 kHz subcarrier spacing, 20 MHz bandwidth. We chose a range of wireless channel parameters, including delay spread (DS) of 50 ns and 500 ns, which approximately corresponds to delay spread data given in [11, Table 7.7.3-2] for Urban Micro (UMi) street-canyon scenarios between 2 GHz to 6 GHz with normal and long delay profiles.

The simulation parameters are given in Tables 1 and 2.

Table 1. Physical layer parameters

Heading level	Example
Modulation-coding scheme (MCS) set	A subset of standard table [7, Table 5.1.3.1-3]
Number of 1 ms subframes	Up to 1000
Channel estimation	Ideal channel knowledge
Bandwidth	20 MHz (106 RB)
Subcarrier spacing	15 kHz
Cyclic Prefix	Normal
Hybrid automatic repeat query (HARQ)	No HARQ
Number of transmission layers	1, 2
MIMO dimensionality MxN	2 x 2
LDPC decoding algorithm	Layered belief-propagation, with 6 iterations
PDSCH allocation	All 14 symbols

Table 2. Channel model parameters

Heading level	Example
Power delay profile	'TDL-D', 'TDL-E', [11, Table 7.7.2-4, 7.7.2-5]
Rician K-factor	−13 dB (NLOS), 0 dB (2 first taps equal), 13 dB (LOS)
Residual mean square delay spread	50 ns, 500 ns
Spatial Correlation	'Low' (identity matrix) or 'Medium' [10, Sect. B.5A.3]

3.2 Simulation Results

The throughput was simulated for the pure downlink transmission, without resource allocation for uplink, control and other channels. For a subset of MCS given in [7, Table 5.1.3.1-3], throughput is obtained via simulations in Matlab, and maximum throughput over each MCS is chosen for each SNR point. Examples of throughput curves for chosen set of MCS is shown in Fig. 1. As may be seen from a system case in Fig. 1, per-RB averaging allows a throughput gain compared to whole-bandwidth (BW) averaging, especially for 16QAM and 64QAM formats.

Comparing final throughput envelopes over all MCS curves, Fig. 2. shows how throughput is increased for various channel parameters and number of transmission layers when per-RB channel estimate averaging is applied instead of whole-BW averaging.

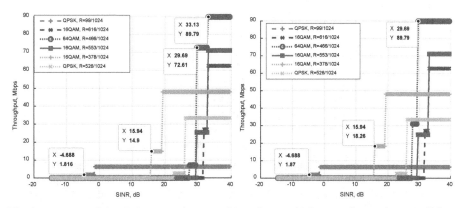

Fig. 2. Example of simulation over chosen MCS set for two SVD precoding regimes. Left: BW averaging of channel estimate; right: per-RB averaging of channel estimate.

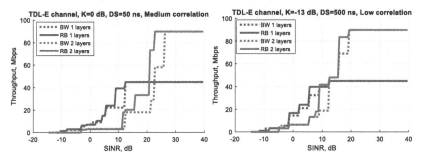

Fig. 3. Examples of throughput simulated over a set of MCSes for TDL-E channel and various channel parameters and number of transmission layers by using per-RB channel estimate averaging for SVD (solid lines) and BW channel estimate averaging (dashed lines).

Although in many cases such as in Fig. 2 there was a clear benefit in applying per-RB channel estimate averaging for SVD-precoding, in other cases the improvement was barely visible or even a degradation was observed. We analyzed differences in throughput over wide range of systems, and in Fig. 3 shown the histogram of unique differences in throughput. By unique we define unique differences between dashed and solid curves as examples in Fig. 2. The histogram in Fig. 3 is shown over 48 different systems composed of two delay profiles, three K-factors, two delay spreads, two MIMO spatial correlation matrices, as given in Table 2, and 1 or 2 layers transmission regimes.

We also investigated in what wireless channel types the per-RB channel estimate averaging leads to highest gains. In Fig. 4 a) we plotted mean unique throughput gains vs K-factor and DS. We conclude the largest gains are obtained for channels with high delay spread and low K-factor, or NLOS channels. For LOS scenarios with 13 dB K-factor throughout gain does not occur. In Fig. 4 b) shown similar data, but vs number of transmission layers and spatial correlation, from which it is evident that per-RB SVD effectiveness for two transmission layers is larger compared to one transmission layer,

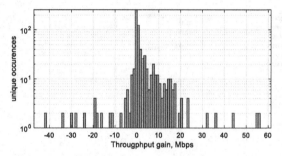

Fig. 4. Left: Histogram of throughput gains for 48 simulated systems. Throughput gain in Mbps is defined as difference between throughput achieved by per-RB averaged channel estimate precoding and throughput achieved with whole-BW averaged channel estimate precoding. The expected unique throughput gain is positive and of order ~5 Mbps.

especially in medium spatial correlation channel, while in low spatial correlation scenario the differences between 1 and 2 transmission layers are not so pronounced.

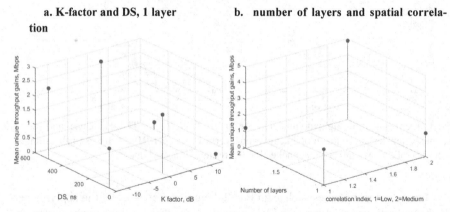

Fig. 5. Sum of unique gains from Fig. 3 for systems with given parameters in x and y axis. (a): vs DS and K-factor, one transmission layer; (c): vs number of transmission layers and spatial correlation.

4 Conclusions

In this paper we presented the performance analysis of Single User Multiple Input Multiple Output (SU-MIMO) 5G cellular communication system. We estimated throughput gains for spatially correlated Tapped-delay-line (TDL) Rician channel by applying per-RB precoding as opposed to whole BW channel transfer function estimate averaging. We found that for realistic 5G MIMO systems with spatial correlation, per-RB precoding gains are usually minor, but still some positive effect is observed, especially in NLOS large-delay spread, low K-factor rank = 2 channel.

Acknowledgments. Authors would like to acknowledge Eugeniy Pustovalov for very useful discussions and help during preparation of this paper.

References

1. Hasegawa, F., et al.: Non-linear precoding for 5G NR. In: 2018 IEEE Conference on Standards for Communications and Networking (CSCN), Paris, pp. 1–7 (2018). https://doi.org/10.1109/cscn.2018.8581859
2. Ren, Y., et al.: Channel reconstruction for SVD-ZF precoding in massive 3D-MIMO systems: low-complexity algorithm. In: 2016 IEEE 83rd Vehicular Technology Conference (VTC Spring). IEEE (2016)
3. Hang, L., et al.: Improved wideband precoding with arbitrary subcarrier grouping in MIMO-OFDM systems. ETRI J. **34**(1), 9–16 (2012)
4. De la Oliva, A., et al.: 5G-Transformer: slicing and orchestrating transport networks for industry verticals. IEEE Commun. Mag. **56**(8), 78–84 (2018)
5. Venugopal, K., González-Prelcic, N., Heath, R.W.: Optimal frequency-flat precoding for frequency-selective millimeter wave channels. IEEE Trans. Wirel. Commun. **18**(11), 5098–5112 (2019)
6. Kim, K.J., Pun, M.-O., Iltis, R.A.: QRD-based precoded MIMO-OFDM systems with reduced feedback. IEEE Trans. Commun. **58**(2), 394–398 (2010)
7. 3GPP TS 38.214. NR; Physical layer procedures for data. v16.1.0, Apr. 2020
8. 3GPP TS 38.212. NR; Multiplexing and channel coding. v16.1.0, Apr. 2020
9. 3GPP TS 38.211. NR; Physical channels and modulation. v16.1.0, Apr. 2020
10. 3GPP TS 36.104. Evolved Universal Terrestrial Radio Access (E-UTRA); Base Station (BS) radio transmission and reception. v16.5.0, Apr. 2020
11. 3GPP TR 38.901. Study on channel model for frequencies from 0.5 to 100 GHz. v16.1.0 Jan. 2020

Noncoherent Detection of Optimal FTN Signals with Differential Encoding

Sergey B. Makarov⬤, Ilnur R. Ishkaev, Ilya I. Lavrenyuk⬤,
Anna S. Ovsyannikova$^{(\boxtimes)}$, and Sergey V. Zavjalov⬤

Peter the Great St. Petersburg Polytechnic University, St. Petersburg, Russia
makarov@cee.spbstu.ru,ilnurishkaev@yandex.ru,
{lavrenyuk_i,ovsyannikova_as,zavyalov_sv}@spbstu.ru

Abstract. Noncoherent signal detection has a long history of application in the data transfer systems. Currently, this method is being considered for application in 6G communication standards. This article is devoted to the study of the possibility of joint use of noncoherent detection algorithm and optimal Faster than Nyquist (FTN) signals. The optimal FTN signals are obtained as a solution to the optimization problem in accordance with the criterion of the fixed reduction rate of out-of-band emissions. These signals are characterized by controlled interference in time, which allows you to get the desired level of bit error rate (BER) performance. The article presents the results of simulation modeling of data transmission in the channel with additive white Gaussian noise (AWGN) using the proposed optimal differential FTN (DFTN) signals and noncoherent symbol-by-symbol detection. A similar experimental study based on the software defined radio (SDR) platform was also conducted. The difference between the results of simulation and experiment is determined by the influence of symbol synchronization inaccuracy and is not more than 1 dB.

Keywords: Differential Faster than Nyquist signaling · Optimization problem · SDR platform

1 Introduction

In packet transmission, application of differential encoding gives the possibility not to use pilot subcarriers. It significantly simplifies implementation of the receiver since noncoherent algorithms may be used for signal processing. Noncoherent detection is mostly used in cases when it is difficult to provide high stability of frequency for reference generator at the transmitter and to provide the absence of phase jump of high-frequency oscillation in phase-locked loop at the receiver. For instance, such challenge takes place while developing the equipment for data transmission in low orbit small-sized telecommunication devices.

In paper [1] a thorough analysis of the sixty-year development of noncoherent detection methods is done. Special attention is paid to improvement of the

© Springer Nature Switzerland AG 2020
O. Galinina et al. (Eds.): NEW2AN 2020/ruSMART 2020, LNCS 12526, pp. 162–173, 2020.
https://doi.org/10.1007/978-3-030-65729-1_15

ideas for such signal processing in the context of 6G. Terahertz communication systems and space-air-ground integrated network are considered in detail as well as non-orthogonal multiple access (NOMA) technology. In this work, the possibility of exploiting extra resources of the energy spectrum due to optimization of transmission channel capacity and improving the energy efficiency of detection is discussed as one of 6G development strategies for the next 10–15 years.

Spectral requirements for the operation of highly efficient telecommunication systems are considered in [2] to a certain extent. It is shown that new systems must work under conditions of spectral efficiency equal to 3–8 bps/Hz. It may be achieved only by application of Faster than Nyquist (FTN) signals. The challenges of overcoming the "Nyquist barrier" with minimum energy losses when using optimal coherent detection in an additive white Gaussian noise (AWGN) channel are considered in numerous works [2–4]. In [5,6] the possibility of binary signal transmission at the symbol rate $R = 1/\xi T$ $(0 < \xi < 1)$ which is 25% above the "Nyquist barrier" is established. The mentioned increase in the symbol rate does not cause bit error rate (BER) performance degradation.

The method of differential Faster than Nyquist signaling which is applied in channels with fading and Doppler frequency shift is presented in [7]. It allows to achieve rather high values of the spectral efficiency up to 0.96 bps/Hz for packet length 2048 bits in case of using signals based on root raised cosine (RRC) pulses with the roll-off factor $\beta = 0.3$.

The attempts to find the optimal possibilities to increase the symbol rate in the occupied frequency bandwidth have been made in [8]. It shows that an increase in the capacity of smooth transmission channel may be obtained by the solving of the optimization problem using well-known water-filling algorithm [9]. Due to this solution, the resources of spectral efficiency improving in channels with AWGN and nonrectangular shape of amplitude-frequency characteristic can be estimated according to Shannon. However, the obtained solutions to this problem do not give instructions how to use any type of modulation or pulse shape in practice.

The objective of this work is the study of the possibility of applying differential encoding to FTN signals which shapes are obtained as a result of solving of the optimization problem conforming to the criterion of the maximum reduction rate of out-of-band emissions. We use packet communication protocol and noncoherent detection algorithm in AWGN channels.

The rest of the paper is organized as follows. Section 2 contains the method of constructing optimal FTN signals with differential encoding and a basic diagram of information transmission system. In Sect. 3, the simulation model of transmitting differentially encoded data over AWGN channels is proposed and the results of the simulation modeling are presented. In Sect. 4, the possibility of practical implementation of the information transmission system is discussed. Finally, Sect. 5 summarizes the results of applying differential encoding and concludes the work.

2   Optimal FTN Signals with Differential Encoding

The synthesis of optimal FTN signals has been the subject of several works [3,4,10–13]. Let us consider a packet consisting of N modulation symbols. Each modulation symbol is transmitted by a signal of duration $T_s = LT$ ($L \geq 1$) with an arbitrary pulse shape $a(t)$ and a maximum value A_0 at a carrier frequency f_0. Then the signal packet can be written in the following form (1):

$$s(t) = A_0 \sum_{k=0}^{N-1} a(t - kT)d^{(k)} \cos(2\pi f_0 t + \phi_0), \tag{1}$$

where $d^{(k)}$ is the value of the modulation symbol. For example, for binary phase shift keying (BPSK) $d^{(k)} = \pm 1$. It is assumed that the random initial phase ϕ_0 is uniformly distributed in the interval $[0, \pi]$.

The optimization problem is formulated as the search for the function $a(t)$ that provides the minimum of the functional J with the constraints on the signal energy (we take $A_0 = 1$), on the reduction rate of the out-of-band emissions (OOBE) and on the minimum level of intersymbol interference (ISI) [4,10]:

$$\arg\{\min_{a(t)} J\}, \ J = \int_{-\infty}^{\infty} g(f) \left| \int_{-\infty}^{\infty} a(t) \exp(-j2\pi f t) dt \right| df. \tag{2}$$

The weighting function $g(f) = f^{2n}$ in (2) determines the occupied frequency bandwidth and the reduction rate of OOBE. The coefficient n in (2) is specified as a constraint on the solution to the optimization problem. The occupied frequency bandwidth ΔF will be determined by the criterion of the level $|S(f)|^2$ relative to the maximum value of the energy spectrum. For example, $\Delta F_{-30\text{dB}}$ corresponds to the occupied frequency bandwidth defined according to the level of the energy spectrum −30 dB.

The constraints on the signal energy and the boundary conditions that determine the reduction rate of OOBE have the following form [4,10]:

$$\int_{-T_s/2}^{T_s/2} a^2(t) dt = 1; \ a^{(k)}(t)\Big|_{t=\pm T_s/2} = 0, \ k = 0...(n-1), \tag{3}$$

where $a^{(k)}(t)$ is the k-th derivative of function $a(t)$.

The constraints on the level of ISI can be expressed numerically by cross-correlation coefficient. This coefficient takes into account the main effect on the value of K_0 of one nearest signal. Under these conditions, the expression for K_0 has the next form [4,12]:

$$K_0 = \max_{k=1...(L-1)} \int_{-T_s/2+kT}^{T_s/2} a(t)a(t - kT) dt. \tag{4}$$

Another constraint is the constraint on the symbol rate R. It is included in (4) indirectly. When R is increased twice ($\xi = 0.5$, it means that the "Nyquist barrier" is exceeded by two times), the function $a(t - kT)$ in (4) is replaced by $a(t - kT/2)$.

Since $a(t)$ is symmetric with respect to zero or $T_s/2$, the original optimization problem (2) may be reduced to the problem of searching for the set of coefficients which minimizes the function of many variables [4]:

$$J(\{a_k\}_{k=1}^m) = \sum_{k=1}^m a_k^2 (2\pi k)^{2n}. \tag{5}$$

Note that the set of coefficients of the Fourier series in (5) is limited by m. The number m is chosen in accordance with the root mean square (RMS) error of $a(t)$ representation. In this work, m corresponds to the RMS error not more than 0.1%.

The optimization problem is solved for each set of constraints. The result of the solving is the Fourier series coefficients a_k in (5).

The methodology of the numerical solving of (5) is presented in [4]. The solutions for optimal FTN signals which will be used in the simulation modeling and experimental research are given below. The reduction rate of OOBE of the spectrum corresponding to optimal signal sequence is at least $1/f^6$ ($n = 2$ in (2)). Due to the cross-correlation coefficient $K_0 = 0.01$ the energy loss relative to the theoretical BER performance is limited by 0.3 dB.

Figure 1, a) shows the pulse shapes $a(t)$ for signal duration $T_s = 2T$, $8T$, $16T$ and the symbol rate $R = 1/T$. The values of $a(t)$ are normalized according to (3). In Fig. 1, b) the normalized energy spectra $|S_a(f)|^2/|S_a(0)|^2$ of random signal sequences are plotted.

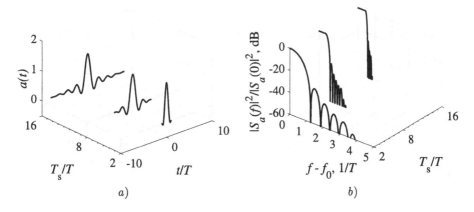

Fig. 1. Optimal pulses $a(t)$ (a) and corresponding normalized energy spectra (b).

To detect an FTN signal packet under conditions of an unknown initial phase ϕ_0, differential Faster than Nyquist signaling (DFTN) is used. In Fig. 2 the block diagram of data transmission using DFTN signals is presented. Information symbols generated in the block "Binary source" go to "BPSK mapper", where the original bits {0/1} are transformed into {+1, −1}. The transformed symbols of the channel alphabet undergo differential encoding. The block "Modulator of optimal FTN signals" forms optimal pulse shape $a(t)$ and modulates a carrier frequency. The signal packet on the output of this block is determined by $a(t)$ shape, signal duration T_s and by the symbol rate R. The formed signal is amplified and transmitted over AWGN channel.

The mixture of DFTN signal and noise is fed to a low-noise amplifier (LNA) and then to the block "Demodulator of optimal FTN signals". Here the signal is demodulated according to the pulse shape $a(t)$, its duration and the symbol rate R. The decisions {+1, −1} from the output of the demodulator go to the block "Differential Decoding" and then to "BPSK demapper". Finally, the sequence of detected information bits is formed.

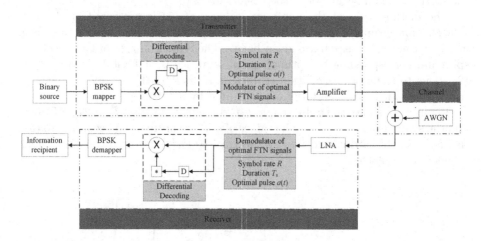

Fig. 2. Block diagram of data transmission using DFTN signals.

Let us analyze noncoherent detection of optimal FTN signals with the pulse shapes which are the solutions to the optimization problem conforming to the criterion of the maximum reduction rate of OOBE. This analysis is done with the help of simulation modeling and experimental research on the block diagram in Fig. 2.

3   The Simulation Model of Data Transmission Using Differential Encoding

The purpose of the simulation modeling is to estimate BER performance of noncoherent symbol-by-symbol detection for optimal binary FTN signals at the symbol rates from $R = 1/T$ to $R = 2.5/T$. In order to exclude symbol synchronization errors, we use the same pulse sequence at a clock rate to control the operation of the blocks "Modulator of optimal FTN signals" and "Demodulator of optimal FTN signals" (Fig. 2).

The simulation model is shown in Fig. 3. Information bits are generated in the block "Binary source". The bits are transformed into modulation symbols and differentially encoded. Then, modulation with the use of optimal FTN signals with the specified symbol rate R, the signal duration T_s and the required reduction rate of OOBE n is performed.

The formed signal goes to the block called "Calculating of energy spectrum". Here the occupied frequency bandwidth is determined for further estimation of the spectral efficiency. The signal sequence is transmitted through the "Channel", where AWGN is added. The value E_b/N_0 is set in the block of initialization of the simulation parameters. The signal energy E_b calculated by (3) is constant for all T_s. $N_0/2$ is average power spectral density of AWGN.

The mixture of DFTN signal and noise is fed to the input of the receiver where demodulation and decoding are carried out. The obtained estimations of the information bits are used for calculating of the error probability p. At least 10^6 information bits are transmitted to calculate each value of p.

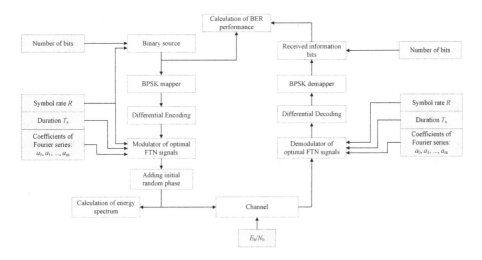

Fig. 3. Block diagram of simulation model of data transmission using DFTN signals.

The obtained spectral characteristics are given in Fig. 4. Optimal signals with $n = 2$, $K_0 = 0.01$, $T_s = 8T$ transmitted at the symbol rate $R = 1/T$ and $R = 2/T$ have been used. During simulation, the sample rate has been equal to 1 MHz, $T = 100\,\mu s$, $R = 1/T = 10$ kbits/s, $R = 2/T = 20$ kbits/s. As it is seen in Fig. 4, the occupied frequency bandwidth defined by the energy spectrum level -30 dB is equal to $\Delta F_{-30\,\mathrm{dB}} = 24.2$ kHz for $R = 2/T$ and $\Delta F_{-30\,\mathrm{dB}} = 15.2$ kHz for $R = 1/T$. The occupied frequency bandwidth defined by the energy spectrum level -50 dB is equal to $\Delta F_{-50\,dB} = 45$ kHz for $R = 2/T$ and $\Delta F_{-50\,dB} = 38$ kHz for $R = 1/T$.

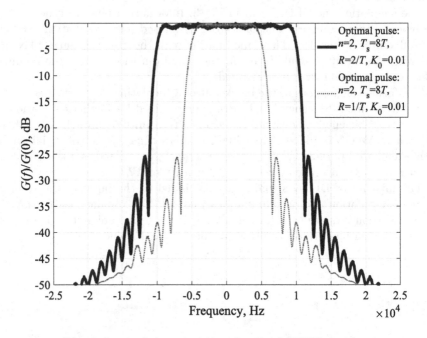

Fig. 4. Spectral characteristics of optimal DFTN signals.

The studied BER performance of noncoherent detection of optimal DFTN signals is presented in Fig. 5. Analyzing the dependencies plotted in Fig. 5, we can make the following conclusions.

First of all, BER performance of noncoherent detection for optimal DFTN signals obtained for the rate $R = 1/T$ and $R = 2/T$ almost equal to the one which conforms to the case of classical differential BPSK (DBPSK) signals with a rectangular pulse shape. The energy losses relative to these signals do not exceed 0.5 dB.

Secondly, noncoherent detection of optimal DFTN signals causes the energy losses about 1 dB compared to coherent detection of classical BPSK signals.

Thirdly, when optimal DFTN signals synthesized for $R = 2/T$ are transmitted at the rate $R = 2.5/T$ (2.5 times above the "Nyquist barrier"), the energy losses grow significantly. Thus, for $p = 4{\cdot}10^{-2}$ the energy losses reach 6 dB.

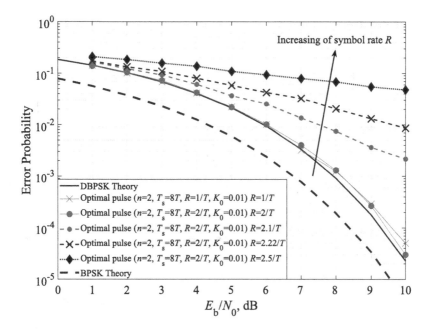

Fig. 5. BER performance of optimal DFTN signals during simulation modeling.

4   Experimental Research

The experimental research is done to estimate BER performance of noncoherent detection of binary optimal FTN signals at the rates $R = 1/T$ and $R = 2/T$ under real conditions with symbol synchronization. We use packet communication protocol and noncoherent detection algorithms in AWGN channel. The packet includes the preamble which represents 64-bit synchronization sequence, and 2048 information bits which correspond to the informational part of the packet. Optimal FTN signals are applied in the informational part of the packet.

The SDR platform NI USRP 2920 is used in the experimental research. The transmitting module consists of the soft modem and the SDR platform (Fig. 6). The soft modem forms the packet with adding the preamble to detect the beginning of the transmission at the receiver. Then the formed packet goes to the block "BPSK Mapper". Then, the resulting modulation symbols are differentially encoded and fed to the block "Modulator of optimal FTN signal". From the output of this block, the samples of quadrature components are transmitted to the SDR platform NI USRP 2920 via Ethernet for digital to-analog conversion (DAC) and for radiation at the carrier frequency.

The spectrum analyzer Agilent Technologies N9342C is used to monitor the spectrum. In the experiment, the carrier frequency is equal to 402 MHz, the sample rate is equal to 1 MHz, $T = 100\,\mu s$, $R = 1/T = 10\,\text{kbits/s}$, $R = 1/T = 20\,\text{kbits/s}$.

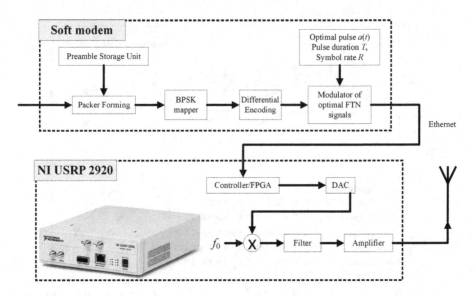

Fig. 6. Block diagram of the transmitter module of DFTN signals based on the SDR platform.

The results of the experiment for optimal FTN signals of duration $T_s = 8T$ with $K_0 = 0.01$ are given in Fig. 7. Figure 7, a) represents the spectrum of the signals with rectangular pulse shape used in the packet preamble. Figure 7, b) shows the energy spectrum of optimal FTN signals for the rate $R = 2/T = 20$ kbits/s. The occupied frequency bandwidth defined by the level -30 dB of the energy spectrum reaches 24.5 kHz for $R = 2/T$. These results correspond to the results of the simulation modeling (Fig. 4).

The block diagram of the receiver module for the case of DFTN signals is illustrated in Fig. 8. From the output of the receiving antenna the mixture of the signal and noise goes to the input of the SDR platform NI USRP 2920. At first, the signal with noise passes through a LNA. Then the signal is shifted to zero frequency and fed to analog-to-digital converter (ADC). At the final stage, the quadrature components are formed and transmitted to the soft modem via Ethernet.

During the first step of the reception the preamble must be found. If the preamble is found successfully, at the second step the samples of the quadrature components go to the demodulator of optimal FTN signals. The processing is carried out taking into account the symbol rate R and signal duration T_s. On the output of the demodulator the values of detected modulation symbols $\{\pm 1\}$ are formed. The sequence of detected modulation symbols must be differentially decoded and fed to "BPSK demapper". As a result, we obtain the sequence of detected information bits.

The detected information packet is compared with the transmitted one for calculation of BER. BER performance is estimated by variation of the signal-

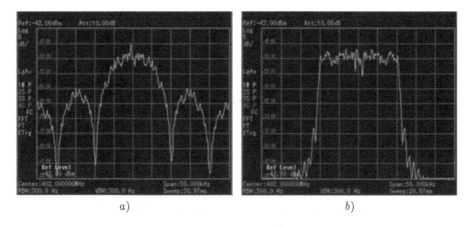

$a)$ $b)$

Fig. 7. Experimental spectral characteristics of optimal DFTN signals.

to-noise ratio. At each value of the signal-to-noise ratio at least 10^5 information bits are transmitted (the transmission of the information packets is repeated, if necessary).

The experimental results of BER performance estimation for optimal DFTN signals with $T_s = 8T$ and $K_0 = 0.01$ can be seen in Fig. 9. The transmission rate is $R = 1/T,\ 2/T,\ 2.22/T,\ 2.5/T$. The experiment has been carried out with the help of the model presented in Figs. 6 and 8 for an AWGN channel.

It can be noticed that the energy costs significantly grow with an increase in the transmission rate. Thus, if the "Nyquist barrier" is exceeded by 2.5 times,

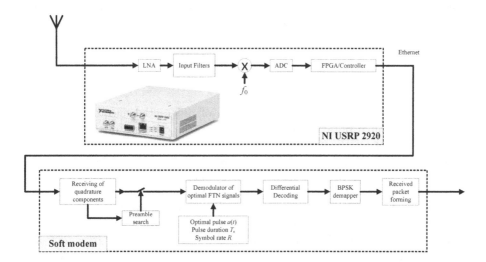

Fig. 8. Block diagram of the receiver module of DFTN signals based on the SDR platform.

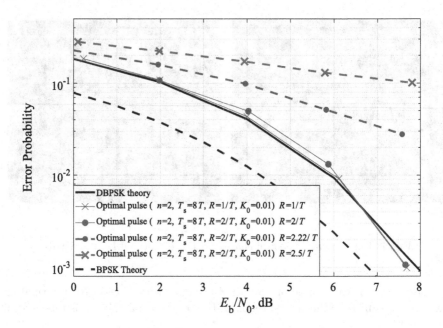

Fig. 9. Experimental BER performance of optimal DFTN signals.

the energy losses reach 5.8 dB at the error probability $p = 10^{-1}$. These values differ from the values obtained by the simulation modeling (Fig. 5) at most by 1 dB. Therefore, we can conclude that the influence of symbol synchronization inaccuracy with the preamble of 64 bits turns out to be insignificant for implementation of noncoherent symbol-by-symbol detection of optimal FTN signals with differential encoding, when the transmission rate is 2–2.5 times above the "Nyquist barrier".

5   Conclusions

In this work, the possibilities of application of differential encoding for FTN signals with optimal pulse shapes conforming to the criterion of the maximum reduction rate of OOBE are considered under conditions of packet communication protocol and noncoherent detection algorithm in channels with AWGN. It is shown that noncoherent detection of optimal DFTN signals obtained for the symbol rate $R = 1/T$ and $R = 2/T$ provides almost theoretical BER performance of classical DBPSK signals with rectangular pulse shape. The energy losses compared to these signals are not more than 0.5 dB.

When optimal DFTN signals obtained for the symbol rate $R = 2/T$ are transmitted at the rate increased up to $R = 2.5/T$ (2.5 times above the "Nyquist barrier"), the energy losses grow significantly. Thus, at the error probability $p = 4 \cdot 10^{-2}$ the energy losses are about 6 dB.

The results of the experimental research show that symbol synchronization inaccuracy is insignificant and leads to the energy losses at most 0.2 dB in case of packet transmission.

Acknowledgements. The results of the work were obtained under the grant of the President of the Russian Federation for state support of young Russian scientists (agreement MK-1571.2019.8 №075-15-2019-1155) and used computational resources of Peter the Great Saint-Petersburg Polytechnic University Supercomputing Center (http://www.scc.spbstu.ru).

References

1. Xu, C., et al.: Sixty years of coherent versus non-coherent tradeoffs and the road from 5G to wireless futures. IEEE Access **7**, 178246–178299 (2019)
2. Anderson, J.B., Rusek, F., Owall, V.: Faster-than-Nyquist signaling. Proc. IEEE **101**(8), 1817–1830 (2013)
3. Gelgor, A., Gorlov, A.: A performance of coded modulation based on optimal Faster-than-Nyquist signals. In: Proceedings of the IEEE International Black Sea Conference on Communications and Networking (BlackSeaCom 2017), pp. 1–5 (2017)
4. Zavjalov, S.V., Volvenko, S.V., Makarov, S.B.: A method for increasing the spectral and energy efficiency SEFDM signals. IEEE Commun. Lett. **20**(12), 2382–2385 (2016)
5. Mazo, J.E.: Faster-than-Nyquist signaling. Bell Syst. Tech. J. **54**(8), 1451–1462 (1975)
6. Liveris, A.D., Georghiades, C.N.: Exploiting faster-than-Nyquist signaling. IEEE Trans. Commun. **51**(9), 1502–1511 (2003)
7. Ishihara, T., Sugiura, S.: Differential faster-than-Nyquist signaling. IEEE Access **6**, 4199–4206 (2018)
8. Ganji, M., Zou, X., Jafarkhani, H.: On the capacity of faster than Nyquist signaling. IEEE Commun. Lett. **24**(6), 1197–1201 (2020)
9. Gallager, R.G., Gallager, R.R.: Information Theory and Reliable Communication. Wiley, New York (1968)
10. Rashich, A., Kislitsyn, A., Gorbunov, S.: Trellis demodulator for pulse shaped OFDM. In: Proceedings of the IEEE International Black Sea Conference on Communications and Networking (BlackSeaCom 2018), pp. 1–5 (2018)
11. Rashich, A., Urvantsev, A.: Pulse-shaped multicarrier signals with nonorthogonal frequency spacing. In: Proceedings of the IEEE International Black Sea Conference on Communications and Networking (BlackSeaCom 2018), pp. 1–5 (2018)
12. Gelgor, A., Gelgor, T.: New pulse shapes for partial response signaling to outperform faster-than-Nyquist signaling. In: Proceedings of the IEEE International Conference on Electrical Engineering and Photonics (EExPolytech 2019), pp. 144–148 (2019)
13. Anderson, J.B. (ed.): Bandwidth Efficient Coding. IEEE Series on Digital and Mobile Communication. IEEE Press and IEEE Xplore, Piscataway (2017)

On Application of Hard-Clipping and Soft-Clipping for SEFDM Signal with Optimal Envelope

Dac Cu Nguyen[1] (iD), Sergey V. Zavjalov[1] (iD), Anna S. Ovsyannikova[1(✉)] (iD),
Sergey V. Volvenko[1] (iD), Ekaterina Smirnova[1] (iD), and Canh Minh Nguyen[2]

[1] Peter the Great St. Petersburg Polytechnic University, St. Petersburg, Russia
daccu91.spb@gmail.com, {zavyalov_sv,ovsyannikova_as,
smirnova.en1}@spbstu.ru, volk@cee.spbstu.ru
[2] University of Transport and Communications, Hanoi, Vietnam
ncminh@utc.edu.vn

Abstract. Simulation modeling of information transmission using spectrally efficient multi-frequency signals with using peak-to-average power ratio (PAPR) reduction methods (hard-clipping and soft-clipping) on transmission was held. Simulation results show that for SEFDM with optimal envelope, using soft-clipping method for PAPR reduction will reduce out-of-band emission (OOBE) of the signal at 50 dB of energy spectrum compared to hard-clipping method, thereby increasing the spectral efficiency. Besides that, for SEFDM with optimal envelope, soft-clipping method also slightly reduces the probability of bit errors when the PAPR reduction value is between 2–6 dB. However, for SEFDM with rectangular envelope, soft-clipping method increases the probability of bit errors.

Keywords: Peak-to-average power ratio · PAPR reduction · Hard-clipping · Soft-clipping · PAPR · SEFDM

1 Introduction

Orthogonal frequency-division multiplexing (OFDM) is a popular technology for wideband digital communication, used in modern radio systems such as digital television and audio broadcasting, Wi-Fi, WiMAX and 4G/LTE. OFDM technology is a special case of multi-carrier modulation method, in which the subcarriers are orthogonal to each other, so that the signal spectrum in the subcarriers allows overlapping but the receiver can still restore the original signal. The signal spectral overlap provides much greater spectral efficiency of OFDM systems than conventional modulation techniques [1]. At the present time, development of communication networks, exemplified by 5th generation (5G) and future 6th generation (6G), requires further improvement of spectral efficiency, especially under conditions of limited frequency resources. The most promising alternative and development based on OFDM technology is the method of non-orthogonal frequency division multiplexing, also known as spectrally efficient frequency division

© Springer Nature Switzerland AG 2020
O. Galinina et al. (Eds.): NEW2AN 2020/ruSMART 2020, LNCS 12526, pp. 174–184, 2020.
https://doi.org/10.1007/978-3-030-65729-1_16

multiplexing (SEFDM) [2–6]. Compared with typical OFDM signals, SEFDM signals can increase spectral efficiency by 2–3 times [7, 8].

However, due to the large number of subcarriers, OFDM and SEFDM systems all have typical issues of multi-frequency signals. Firstly, these signals have a high Peak-to-Average Power Ratio (PAPR), which makes system performance very sensitive to the distortions caused by nonlinear devices such as high power amplifiers (HPA) [9]. Besides, a high PAPR leads to degradation of power amplifier performance [10–14]. The second issue for multicarrier systems is reduction of out-of-band emission (OOBE). Using optimal envelopes [4, 15–17] will help reduce OOBE, but it will also lead to higher PAPR, which means that the problem becomes more serious [18].

To reduce the PAPR, several techniques have been researched and developed, such as Tone Reservation, Clipping & Filtering, Active Constellation, Peak Windowing, Selected Mapping, PAPR Reduction Codes. Most of these methods cannot achieve a large PAPR reduction along with lower complexity. In [19, 20] we have considered the simplest method. It is the hard-clipping method, which can achieve a large reduction in PAPR by using amplifier and limiter to limit signal amplitude. However, this has led to an increase in OOBE. The using of soft-clipping method, which was proposed in [21] will partly reduce the increase in OOBE when reducing PAPR of signal.

Here, the main focus is on comparing the effectiveness of soft-clipping and hard-clipping methods in reducing PAPR of signal based on evaluation of bit error rate (BER) and OOBE.

The paper is structured as follows. Section 2 contains a brief description of the PAPR of SEFDM signals with optimal envelope. The description of PAPR reduction methods is given in Sect. 3. In Sect. 4, the simulation model with PAPR reduction part is presented. Section 5 describes the simulation results. In Sect. 6, conclusions are drawn.

2   PAPR of SEFDM Signals with Optimal Envelop

SEFDM technology was developed in 2003 based on Fast-OFDM [2]. A brief survey of the first 15 years of SEFDM was presented in [3]. In this work, we consider SEFDM symbols with a duration T of the following form [22]:

$$s(t) = \sum_{k=-\frac{N}{2}}^{\frac{N}{2}-1} C_k e^{j2\pi k \Delta f t}, t \in [0; T], \tag{1}$$

where N – number of used subcarriers, Δf – frequency separation between adjacent subcarriers, C_k – complex modulation symbol for k-th subcarrier. For SEFDM, $\Delta f = \alpha/T$, where $\alpha < 1$. For OFDM signals, $\alpha = 1$, that is, $\Delta f_{OFDM} = 1/T$. Because of $\alpha < 1$, SEFDM signals occupy a lower bandwidth and have higher spectral efficiency in comparison to OFDM signals.

The energy spectrum of SEFDM signals with a rectangular envelope has a low reduction rate of the OOBE. This leads to inefficient use of the frequency resources of systems with multi-frequency signals due to overlapping signal spectra. Therefore, the task is to optimize the envelope with a smoothed shape to minimize OOBE. To get the optimal envelope, we need to solve the optimization problem of minimizing the functional J:

$$\arg\left\{\min_{a(t)}(J)\right\}, \quad J = \int_{-\infty}^{+\infty} g(f) \left| \int_{-\infty}^{+\infty} a(t)e^{-j2\pi ft} dt \right|^2 df, \tag{2}$$

where $g(f) = f^{2n}$ – the weighting function, which determines the resulting spectral characteristics of the signals; $n = 1, 2,\ldots$ – the reduction rate of the OOBE. In [18], the optimization problem of minimizing the functional is solved by expanding the envelope $a(t)$ in terms of a finite Fourier series. The envelope $a(t)$ must meet the two constraints: the constraint on the energy and boundary conditions. The shapes of rectangular and smoothed optimal are presented in Fig. 1.

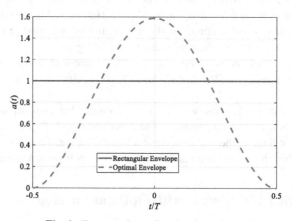

Fig. 1. Rectangular and optimal envelopes

The PAPR of the transmitted signal in (1) is defined as the maximum power P_{max} of discrete signal $s(t)$ divided by the average power P_{avg}:

$$PAPR = \frac{P_{max}}{P_{avg}} = \frac{\max\{s(t)^2\}}{E\{s(t)^2\}}, \tag{3}$$

where $E\{s(t)^2\}$ is expected value of SEFDM signal power.

Using the optimal envelope for the SEFDM signal will help increase the rate of OOBE reduction, but it also will increase the PAPR value of the signal. In Sect. 3, let us describe PAPR reduction methods, including hard-clipping and soft-clipping.

3   Description of PAPR Reduction Methods

Hard-clipping is one of the most popular clipping methods for PAPR reduction of signal. The procedure for hard-clipping technique is depicted in Fig. 2a). As long as input amplitude S_{in} does not exceed the value of clipping threshold A, the output amplitude S_{out} linearly depends on the input S_{in}. Starting with A, S_{out} stops changing. Relationship of the input and output amplitudes is expressed as:

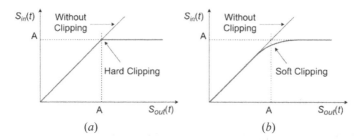

Fig. 2. Clipping methods for PAPR reduction

$$s_{out}(t) = \begin{cases} s_{in}(t), \ 0 \le s_{in}(t) < A \\ A, \ A \le s_{in}(t) \end{cases}. \tag{4}$$

Figure 2b) shows characteristics of soft-clipping technique. Unlike the typical hard-clipping, soft-clipping limits in a skew line, its slope is made suitable to solid state power amplifier (SSPA) characteristic. The SSPA has the transfer characteristic that is constant over the linear region, which is different form the TWTA (traveling wave tube amplifier).

The SSPA output is written according to the following formula [23]:

$$s_{out}(t) = \frac{v_k s_{in}(t)}{\left(1 + \left(\frac{v_k s_{in}(t)}{A}\right)^{2p_k}\right)^{1/2p_k}}, \tag{5}$$

where v_k - the small signal amplification, p_k - the model parameter and A - clipping threshold (the output amplitude at the saturation point).

The smoothness of the transition into the saturation region can be adjusted by the parameter p_k and v_k as indicated in Fig. 3. By changing the smoothness, the desired PAPR limit value can be achieved.

In the next section, we will consider the simulation model to evaluate the effectiveness of using the above PAPR reduction methods for SEFDM signal with optimal envelope.

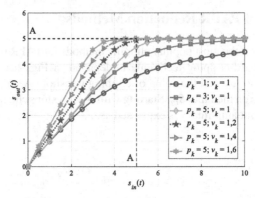

Fig. 3. Characteristics of the typical SSPA

4 Simulation Model

Figure 4 shows the simulation model of this research, which was built in the Matlab system. It includes an information source, a transmitter model, blocks for calculation of PAPR and spectral characteristics, a transmission channel with additive white Gaussian noise (AWGN) and a receiver model.

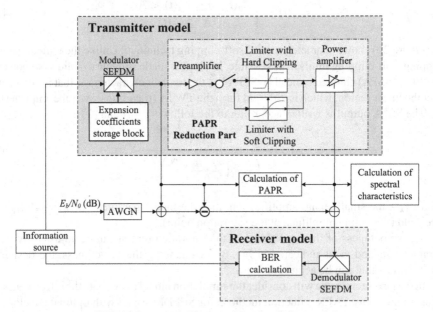

Fig. 4. Structural diagram of the simulation model

In the information source, a pseudo-random sequence of zeros and ones of a given volume is formed depending on the number of subcarriers and used symbols. Storage block of expansion coefficients $a(t)$ contains the coefficients of expansion of the envelope $a(t)$ obtained after the optimization problem solving. These coefficients are used to modulate the SEFDM signals.

The transmitter model includes an expansion coefficients storage block $a(t)$, an SEFDM modulator and a PAPR reduction part. Modulation type of BPSK is performed. Output signal form SEFDM modulator is sent to the PAPR reduction part. In this block, SEFDM signal amplitude is cut according to hard or soft-clipping algorithm by using limiter and amplifiers.

The clipping signal is transmitted to the calculation blocks of PAPR values and spectral characteristics. The ratio of the PAPR of the received signal at the output of the modulator ($PAPR_{orig}$) to the PAPR of the signal received at the output of the power amplifier ($PAPR_{red}$) is defined as the value of PAPR reduction (PR):

$$PR = PAPR_{orig}(dB) - PAPR_{red}(dB). \tag{6}$$

Then the signal is transmitted through the AWGN channel to the receiving device. In a communication channel, the noise is added at the same level as the SEFDM signal without PAPR reduction. The receiver model performs the procedures for detecting and restore SEFDM signals and BER caculation. The detection algorithm used here is the element-by-element algorithm.

In the modeling process, at least 75000 iterations are used per one fixed set of modeling parameters. The number of frequency subcarriers of the SEFDM signal $N = 16$ is chosen.

5 Simulation Results

In the beginning, we consider the case without PAPR reduction (PR $= 0$ dB). In this case, the signal has PAPR value more than 11 dB. The transmission of SEFDM signal with such high PAPR will be inefficient in terms of the use of power amplifiers. Therefore, measures should be taken to reduce PAPR. We can see the examples of normalized instantaneous power $p(t)/\max(p(t)$ for various values of the PR value in Fig. 5a) and b). Analyzing these figures, we can easily notice the difference between soft and hard-clipping methods that affect signal distortion.

Figure 6a) shows the energy spectrum $|S(f)|^2/|S(0)|^2$ of SEFDM signals with optimal envelope for two PAPR reduction methods at PAPR reduction value PR $= 4$ dB. Based on the analysis of the graphs in Fig. 6b), we can see that using soft-clipping method to reduce PAPR leads to a smaller level of OOBE compared to hard-clipping, which is clearly expressed at 50 dB.

Besides, compared to the energy spectrum results obtained in the case of SEFDM signal with rectangular envelope (Fig. 6b), it can be realized that the signal with the optimal envelope provides higher spectral efficiency. In Fig. 6b), the spectral efficiency benefits of using soft-clipping method over hard-clipping method are not obvious.

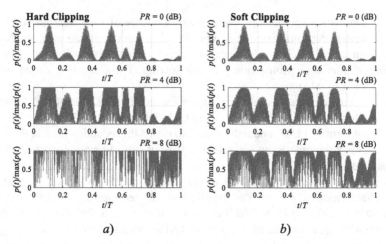

Fig. 5. Examples of normalized instantaneous signal power at different values of PR for hard-clipping (a) and soft-clipping (b) methods

According to the analysis above, for SEFDM signal with optimal envelope the use of soft-clipping increases the spectral efficiency compared to hard-clipping method. Along with that, Fig. 7a) shows that in case of using soft-clipping for PAPR reduction of SEFDM with optimal envelope, the error probability value is slightly smaller than in case of using hard-clipping between 2 and 6 dB. This difference reaches maximum at when the PR value is equal 4–5 dB.

Meanwhile, for SEFDM signal with rectangular envelope, the use of soft-clipping increases the probability of bit error compared to hard-clipping when the PR value is smaller than 6 dB. This is shown in Fig. 7,b).

In addition, when limiting the value of the PAPR, the average power of the emitted oscillations increases, which reduces the error probability value for fixed signal-to-noise ratio values. However, with a further increase in the level of limitation, the signals from neighboring subcarrier frequencies start mutually affecting each other, which ultimately leads to an increase in the probability of error. In [19] we have already found that, from the point of view of minimizing the probability of errors, the effective PR value is 4.5–5 dB for SEFDM signals with rectangular envelope in case of using hard-clipping method. In this work, Fig. 7b) illustrates that the use of soft-clipping provides the same result.

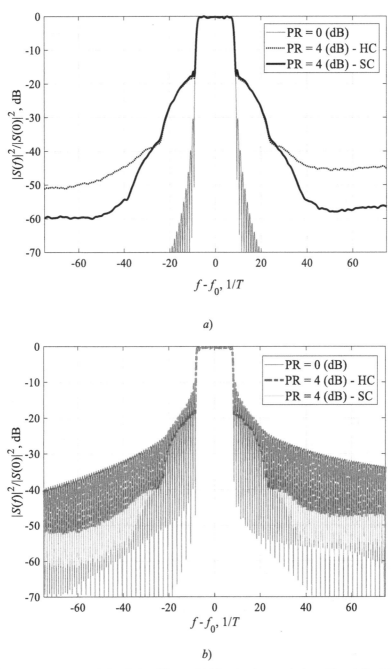

Fig. 6. Energy spectrum of signals for different PARP reduction methods at PR = 4 dB: (*a*) – with optimal envelope; (*b*) – with rectangular envelope. HC – Hard-clipping; SC – Soft-clipping

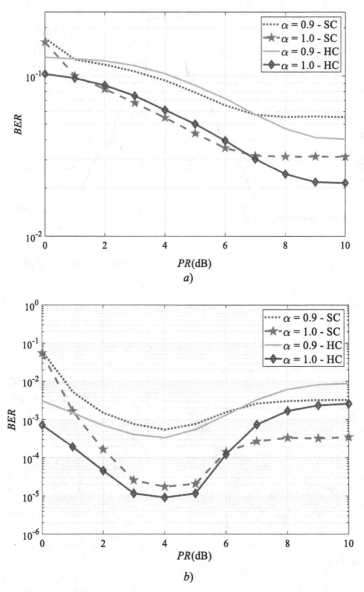

Fig. 7. Dependence of BER of receiving SEFDM signals on PR value: (*a*) – with optimal envelope; (*b*) – with rectangular envelope. HC – Hard-clipping; SC – Soft-clipping

6 Conclusions

In this paper, we have compared the effectiveness of using PAPR reduction methods, including hard-clipping and soft-clipping for SEFDM signals with optimal envelope. The simulation results show that the use of soft-clipping method increases the spectral efficiency at the level of energy spectrum to 50 dB, and reduces the probability of bit errors compared to hard-clipping method when the PR value is equal 2–6 dB. Meanwhile, applying soft-clipping method to SEFDM signals with rectangular envelope not only does not provide a more pronounced spectral effect than hard-clipping method but also increases the probability of bit errors.

In the further research we will consider other aspects of applying of clipping method to reduce PAPR of signals, so that we can benefit from this method.

Acknowledgments. This research work was supported by Peter the Great St. Petersburg Polytechnic University in the framework of the Program "5-100-2020" and used computational resources of Peter the Great Saint-Petersburg Polytechnic University Supercomputing Center (http://www.scc.spbstu.ru).

References

1. Nee, R.V., Prasad, R.: OFDM for wireless multimedia communications. Artech House, Inc. (2000)
2. Rodrigues, M., Darwazeh, I.: A spectrally efficient frequency division multiplexing based communications system. In: Proceedings of the 8th International OFDM Workshop, pp. 48–49 (2003)
3. Darwazeh, I., Ghannam, H., Xu, T.: The first 15 years of SEFDM: a brief survey, 2018 11th International Symposium on Communication Systems, Networks & Digital Signal Processing (CSNDSP), Budapest, pp. 1–7 (2018). https://doi.org/10.1109/csndsp.2018.8471886
4. Gelgor, A., Nguyen, V.P.: Outperforming conventional OFDM and SEFDM signals by means of using optimal spectral pulses and the M-BCJR algorithm. In: 2019 26th International Conference on Telecommunications (ICT), Hanoi, Vietnam, pp. 130–134 (2019). https://doi.org/10.1109/ict.2019.8798793
5. Rashich, A., Gorbunov, S.: Computational complexity analysis of SEFDM time and frequency domain equalizers. In: 2019 IEEE International Conference on Electrical Engineering and Photonics (EExPolytech), St. Petersburg, Russia, pp. 94–97 (2019). https://doi.org/10.1109/eexpolytech.2019.8906828
6. Gelgor, A., Gorlov, A., Nguyen, V.P.: Performance analysis of SEFDM with optimal subcarriers spectrum shapes. In: 2017 IEEE International Black Sea Conference on Communications and Networking (BlackSeaCom), Istanbul, pp. 1–5 (2017). https://doi.org/10.1109/blackseacom.2017.8277680
7. Yang, X., Ai, W., Shuai, T., Li, D.: A fast decoding algorithm for non-orthogonal frequency division multiplexing signals. In: International Conference on Communications and Networking in China (CHINACOM), pp. 595–598 (2007)
8. Kanaras, I., Chorti, A., Rodrigues, M., Darwazeh, I.: Analysis of Sub-optimum detection techniques for a bandwidth efficient multi-carrier communication system. In: Proceedings of the Cranfield Multi-Strand Conference, pp. 505–510. Cranfield University (2009)
9. Rapp, C.: Effects of HPA-non-linearity on a 4-DPSK/OFDM signal for digital sound broadcasting system. In: Proceedings of the Second Euro. Satellite Communication, pp. 179–184 (1991)
10. Pergushev, A.: The analytical model for calculating distortions in the envelope tracking power supply. In: 2019 IEEE International Conference on Electrical Engineering and Photonics (EExPolytech), St. Petersburg, Russia, pp. 72–75 (2019). https://doi.org/10.1109/eexpolytech.2019.8906813

11. Vizarreta, P.P., Montoro, G., Gilabert, P.L.: Hybrid envelope amplifier for envelope tracking power amplifier transmitters. In: 2012 42nd European Microwave Conference, Amsterdam, pp. 128–131 (2012). https://doi.org/10.23919/eumc.2012.6459324

12. Pergushev, A., Sorotsky, V., Ulanov, A.: Output voltage PWM conversion inaccuracies in envelope tracking power supply for high peak-to-average power ratio applications. In: 2019 IEEE International Conference on Electrical Engineering and Photonics (EExPolytech), St. Petersburg, Russia, pp. 9–12 (2019). https://doi.org/10.1109/eexpolytech.2019.8906854

13. Zudov, R.I.: Efficiency of a class DE power amplifier for RF signals with high peak-to-average power ratio. In: 2019 IEEE International Conference on Electrical Engineering and Photonics (EExPolytech), St. Petersburg, Russia, pp. 28–30 (2019). https://doi.org/10.1109/eexpolytech.2019.8906856

14. Pergushev, A., Sorotsky, V.: Signal distortion decreasing in envelope tracking power amplifiers. In: 2018 IEEE International Conference on Electrical Engineering and Photonics (EExPolytech), St. Petersburg, pp. 44–47 (2018). https://doi.org/10.1109/eexpolytech.2018.8564443

15. Makarov, S., Zavjalov, S., Ovsyannikova, A., Lavrenyuk, I., Xue, W.: Comparison of the spectral and energy efficiency of FTN signals based on RRC pulses and obtained by the optimization method. In: 2019 IEEE International Conference on Electrical Engineering and Photonics (EExPolytech), St. Petersburg, Russia, pp. 177–180 (2019). https://doi.org/10.1109/eexpolytech.2019.8906866

16. Sadovaya, Y., Gelgor, A.: Synthesis of signals with a low-level of out-of-band emission and peak-to-average power ratio. In: 2018 IEEE International Conference on Electrical Engineering and Photonics (EExPolytech), St. Petersburg, pp. 103–106 (2018). https://doi.org/10.1109/eexpolytech.2018.8564428

17. Rashich, A., Urvantsev, A.: Pulse-shaped multicarrier signals with nonorthogonal frequency spacing. In: 2018 IEEE International Black Sea Conference on Communications and Networking (BlackSeaCom), Batumi, pp. 1–5 (2018). https://doi.org/10.1109/blackseacom.2018.8433714

18. Nguyen, D.C., Zavjalov, S.V., Ovsyannikova, A.S., Nguyen, C.M.: The effectiveness of tone reservation method for peak-to-average power ratio reduction of SEFDM signals with optimal envelopes. In: 2019 IEEE International Conference on Electrical Engineering and Photonics (EExPolytech), St. Petersburg, Russia, pp. 165–168 (2019). https://doi.org/10.1109/eexpolytech.2019.8906819

19. Nguyen, D.C., Zavjalov, S.V., Ovsyannikova, A.S.: The effectiveness of application of multi-frequency signals under conditions of amplitude limitation. In: Galinina, O., Andreev, S., Balandin, S., Koucheryavy, Y. (eds.) Internet of Things, Smart Spaces, and Next Generation Networks and Systems. NEW2AN 2019. Lecture Notes in Computer Science, vol. 11660, pp. 681–687. Springer, Cham (2019)

20. Nguyen, D.C., Zavjalov, S.V., Ovsyannikova, A.S., Nguyen, C.M.: Improving the effectiveness of the multi-frequency signals application under conditions of amplitude limitation. J. Phys. Conf. Ser. **1326**(1), 012028 (2019). IOP Publishing

21. Ryu, H.G., Jin, B.I., Kim, I.B.: PAPR reduction using soft-clipping and ACI rejection in OFDM system. IEEE Trans. Consum. Electron. **48**(1), 17–22 (2002)

22. Rashich, A., Kislitsyn, A., Fadeev, D., Nguyen, T.N.: FFT-based trellis receiver for SEFDM signals. In: 2016 IEEE Global Communications Conference (GLOBECOM), Washington, DC, pp. 1–6 (2016)

23. Li, X., Cimini Jr., L.J.: Effects of clipping and filtering on the performance of OFDM. IEEE Commun. Lett. **2**(5), 131–133 (1998)

Evaluation of Packet Transmission Delay Variation in the G/G/1 System

Igor Kartashevskiy⬤, Marina Buranova$^{(\boxtimes)}$⬤, and Dinara Ergasheva⬤

Povolzhskiy State University of Telecommunications and Informatics, 23 L. Tolstoy,
443010 Samara, Russia
mburanova@yandex.ru

Abstract. Analyzing the performance parameters of IP-networks when processing multimedia streams is a very important task. There are many approaches to
evaluating the quality of service parameters in the G/G/1 system.

Changing the packet delay in the network is a very significant parameter
that determines the quality of traffic processing. It is particularly important for
multimedia streams. The delay variation is generally defined as a packet jitter.

However, the analysis of the delay variation is often based on assumptions
that do not allow the parameters to be determined with the required accuracy.
This paper presents a new approach to defining packet delay variation in the
G/G/1 system as delay variation. The presented approach is based on approximation of arbitrary distributions by hyperexponential distributions, i.e. modeling
the G/G/1 system by the $H_2/H_2/1$ system. The EM algorithm is used to estimate
the parameters of hyperexponential distributions. The paper presents the results
of simulation. The packet delay variation was evaluated when processing traffic
registered on a real network, CBR traffic, traffic with Pareto distribution of time
intervals between packets and packet lengths, and traffic with exponential distribution of time intervals between incoming packets. Due to the fact that CBR traffic
has explicit correlated properties, it can be noted that the presence of correlation
inherent in CBR traffic leads to a decrease in delay variation.

Keywords: Delay variation · EM-algorithm · Hyperexponential distribution

1 Introduction

When designing and organizing infocommunication networks, it is necessary to take into
account the heterogeneous nature of modern traffic. Algorithms for processing such traffic should account for the high requirements for various parameters when determining
the required level of quality of processing streams of different types (data, voice, multimedia streams, etc.). The main parameters considered when determining the quality of
service (QoS), are delay, delay variation (jitter variation) and loss probability. Research
on this topic focuses on the problem of delay retention at the required level [1–3].

It should be noted that certain types of traffic, for example, multimedia streams, are
highly critical not only to delay transmission, but also to the change in packet delay during

© Springer Nature Switzerland AG 2020
O. Galinina et al. (Eds.): NEW2AN 2020/ruSMART 2020, LNCS 12526, pp. 185–197, 2020.
https://doi.org/10.1007/978-3-030-65729-1_17

transmission. In [4–8], the problem of estimating change in packet delay is raised. They show that such an assessment involves a number of difficulties. Traditionally, the main mechanism to determine these parameters was the principal tool of queuing theory, which with high accuracy allows determining the parameters of network functioning only when processing simple flows. Systems processing such flows are described by the M/M/1 model [9]. At the same time, a feature of modern processed flows is the presence of self-similarity properties characterized by heavy tail distributions for random time intervals between packets and packet durations (model G/G/1). The effect of self-similarity is largely determined by the nature of user behavior, the organization of requests and the peculiarity of the TCP protocol. Statistical models based on heavy tail distributions such as Pareto and Weibull show more accurate estimates for the characteristics describing the rate of arrival of packets and their duration.

In this case, one should take into account the fact that the particular type of distribution underlying the mathematical model significantly depends on the specific traffic implementation and requires careful analysis. Another problem associated with the use of distributions with heavy tails is the complexity of their analysis and use. When using this type of distribution, it is required to obtain Laplace transformations of these distributions, at the same time, certain problems are caused by the lack of a convenient expression for the Laplace transforms of the Pareto and Weibull distributions.

Jitter estimation is associated with certain difficulties due to the lack of accurate estimation techniques, including the lack of adequate analytical models for jitter estimation in non-Poisson flows processing systems. Previously [4, 10], solved the problem of evaluating jitter in G/G/1 systems and ensuring packet jitter at a given level. Some assumptions make it possible to determine jitter with sufficient accuracy in systems such as M/M/1, G/M/1, but in the system where random time intervals between packets and packet lengths are described by arbitrary distributions, the jitter definition is associated with great computational difficulties. It was shown in [2, 3] that a sufficiently accurate approximation of the G/G/1 system allows one to use the approximation by the $H_l/H_k/1$ system. In this case, the problem is reduced to determining the parameters of hyperexponential distributions. To develop this topic, the paper proposes to use the $H_2/H_2/1$ approximation to model G/G/1 systems.

The $H_2/H_2/1$ model can be used in various approaches to describing systems. For example, [11] provides a technique for analyzing network performance when processing self-similar traffic using a hyperexponential distribution, where the first component of the distribution shows an exponential component and the rest describe the behavior of the heavy tail. But this approach is also labor-intensive enough to estimate network parameters and requires analysis of distributions with heavy tails. It is more convenient to take approaches using approximations by the sum of two exponentials [2, 3].

In this paper, we use an approximation of arbitrary distributions of G by hyperexponential distributions. The EM-algorithm is used to determine the parameters of hyperexponential distributions. This algorithm is a fairly convenient tool for implementing an iterative search procedure using numerical methods of extremum of the objective function in various optimization problems.

There are many works devoted to the description of the EM-algorithm procedures and possible ways of its application. The EM-algorithm is very effective for finding approximations of the observed realizations of both one-dimensional and multidimensional distributions. The EM-algorithm solves the problem of statistical estimation of mixture parameters. For example, [5–7] defines the procedure for implementing the EM-algorithm in the framework of cluster analysis, particularly in relation to problems of mixture separation.

The practice of using the EM-algorithm is usually associated with the separation of a mixture of normal distributions [17]. While in queuing theory, all distributions describing traffic behavior in a modern IP network refer to random variables that take non-negative values (for example, an exponential distribution is most often used). Therefore, the development of an EM algorithm for separating a mixture of exponential distributions is relevant when using the approximation of the G/G/1 system by the $H_2/H_2/1$ system.

2   Analysis of Delay Variation

The arbitrary probability density used in the G/G/1 system is denoted by $f(x)$. Then, the approximation $f(x)$ obtained using a mixture of exponential distributions will take the form:

$$f(x) = H_N(x) = \sum_{i=1}^{N} p_i h_i(x).$$ (1)

where $p_i \geq 0$ is probability of the i-th component of the mixture, $h_i(x)$,

$$\sum_{i=1}^{N} p_i = 1.$$

For the $H_2/H_2/1$ model, expression (1) is obtained in the form:

$$f(x) = p\alpha_1 e^{-\alpha_1 x} + (1-p)\alpha_2 e^{-\alpha_2 x}.$$ (2)

The change in packet transmission delay can be defined as a random variable defined as [12].

$$J_{i+1} = |T_{i+1} - T_i|,$$

where T_i is the delay time of the i-th packet in the network node, which is determined as $T_i = W_i + Q_i$. Here W_i is the waiting time of the i-th packet in the queue, Q_i is its service time, V_{i+1} is the time interval between the arrival of the $(i+1)$-th and i-th packets.

The general methodology for solving the problem of jitter determining according to this approach is shown in [4–8].

In this paper, the delay variation can be determined according to [13] as a variation of the packet delay. For variation of packet delay write

$$\sigma(X) = \sqrt{D(X)},$$

where $D(X)$ is dispersion of the delay of packets.

If we assume that random variables T_i, Q_i and V_i are independent of each other and independent in the structure of each sequence of a random quantity, the index i of the corresponding probability densities can be discarded and the notation: $f_T(x)$ is probability density of random variable T, $f_V(y)$ is probability density of random variable V and $f_Q(z)$ is probability density of random variable Q.

Given the independence of the considered time intervals, the G/G/1 system can be designated as GI/GI/1.

We use hyperexponential distributions to approximate the densities under consideration. For the probability density of time intervals between packets is $f_V(y)$:

$$f_V(\tau) = p_1 \gamma_1 e^{-\gamma_1 \tau} + p_2 \gamma_2 e^{-\gamma_2 \tau}, \tag{3}$$

for the service time is $f_Q(z)$, that is determined by the parameter μ:

$$f_Q(\tau) = q_1 \mu_1 e^{-\mu_1 \tau} + q_2 \mu_2 e^{-\mu_2 \tau}, \tag{4}$$

for transit time is $f_T(x)$, that is defined by δ:

$$f_W(\tau) = \Delta_1 \delta_1 e^{-\delta_1 \tau} + \Delta_2 \delta_2 e^{-\delta_2 \tau}. \tag{5}$$

Given that the packet delay is determined by the random value of T, the dispersion of the delay can be determined according to the expression:

$$D(X) = \int_0^\infty [x - M(X)]^2 f_T(x) dx = \int_0^\infty x^2 f_T(x) dx - \left(\int_0^\infty x f_T(x) dx \right)^2, \tag{6}$$

Since for the delay time T of the packet in the system is $T = W + Q$, the probability density $f_T(y)$ is determined by the convolution of the distributions of random variables W and Q (taking into account their independence):

$$f_T(y) = \int_0^\infty f_W(u) f_Q(y - u) du \tag{7}$$

Given (4) and (5), we obtain:

$$f_T(x) = D\mu_1 e^{-\mu_1 x} + C\mu_2 e^{-\mu_2 x} \tag{8}$$

where

$$C = (1 - q)\frac{g\delta_1}{\delta_1 - \mu_1} + (1 - \Delta)\frac{\delta_2}{\delta_2 - \mu_2},$$

$$D = (1 - \Delta)\frac{q\delta_2}{\delta_2 - \mu_2} + \Delta q \frac{\delta_1}{\delta_1 - \mu_1}.$$

As a result, for the packet delay variation taking into account (6) and (8), we can obtain:

$$\sigma = \sqrt{\frac{2D - D^2}{\mu_1^2} + \frac{2C - C^2}{\mu_2^2} - \frac{2DC}{\mu_1 \mu_2}}. \tag{9}$$

Thus, the solution to the problem of estimating changes in packet delay is reduced to determining the distribution parameters (3), (4) and (5) $(q, p, \Delta, \mu_1, \mu_2, \gamma_1, \gamma_1, \delta_1, \delta_2)$.

There are various approaches to determining the parameters of exponential distributions, for example, the method of determining parameters by two points (average, dispersion) of the initial distribution for independent random variables [8, 14]. Using this approach, it is possible to obtain analytical expressions of the initial moments of hyperexponential distributions up to the second order. The method is based on the use of the Laplace transform property.

If the researcher has a traffic implementation obtained in the experiment, then to determine the parameters of hyperexponential distributions, one can use an approach based on the use of the EM-algorithm (expectation-maximization) [14–19]. This method has proven itself and successfully provides reliable estimates of maximum likelihood for many applications, including estimating the density of a mixture.

The algorithm consists of two steps: E-step (expectation) and M-step (maximization). The initial data is the observed sequence $x_1, x_2, \ldots, x_N$ with a one-dimensional probability density $f(x, \theta_1, \ldots \theta_m)$ having m parameters. In this case, the implementation of the EM-algorithm will be associated with parameter estimation $\theta_1, \ldots \theta_m$.

If each element of the sample $x_1, x_2, \ldots, x_N$ can belong to the distribution of a mixture of K random variables with probability densities:

$$f^1\left(x, \theta_1^1, \ldots \theta_m^1\right), \ \ldots f^j\left(x, \theta_1^j, \ldots \theta_m^j\right), \ \ldots f^k\left(x, \theta_1^k, \ldots \theta_m^k\right),$$

the process will be associated with the assessment of the main distribution parameters of each of the indicated probability densities $(\theta_1^1, \ldots \theta_m^1, \theta_1^j, \ldots \theta_m^j, \theta_1^k, \ldots \theta_m^k)$, as well as the relative shares of observations of each random variable - $(\pi^1, \ldots \pi^k)$.

If the sequence in question $x_1, x_2, \ldots, x_N$ is a realization of a random variable with a probability density of distribution $f(x, \theta_1, \ldots \theta_m)$ having m parameters, then the likelihood function of the sample will take the form:

$$\mathcal{L}(\theta_1, \ldots \theta_m) = \prod_{i=1}^{N} f(x, \theta_1, \ldots \theta_m).$$

The likelihood function $\mathcal{L}$ represents the total density of individual observations for any given set of distribution parameters. The maximum likelihood score is the value of the distribution parameters that maximize $\mathcal{L}$:

$$\left(\hat{\theta}_1, \ldots \hat{\theta}_m\right) = \arg max(\mathcal{L}).$$

For Gaussian distributions, this approach gives quick and good results. Using in this case a mixture of exponential distributions $(f^j\left(x_i, \theta_1^j, \ldots \theta_m^j\right))$ complicates the problem and does not allow to use this approach in the form presented [15].

Obviously, if we cannot determine exactly which sample the observations belong to, we cannot determine which random variable generates each observation. This means that we do not know the relative distribution of observations belonging to each variable.

Therefore, the likelihood function of the sample will be:

$$L\left(\pi_1, \ldots \pi_k, \theta_1^1, \ldots \theta_m^1, \ldots \theta_1^k, \ldots \theta_m^k\right) = \prod_{i=1}^{N} \sum_{j=1}^{k} \pi_j f^j\left(x_i, \theta_1^j, \ldots \theta_m^j\right),$$

taking into account that $\sum_{j=1}^{K} \pi_j = 1$.

In this case, the estimate of the maximum likelihood of the distribution parameters of the mixture will be:

$$\left(\hat{\pi}_1, \ldots \hat{\pi}_k, \hat{\theta}_1^1, \ldots \hat{\theta}_m^1, \ldots \hat{\theta}_1^j, \ldots \hat{\theta}_m^j, \ldots \hat{\theta}_1^k, \ldots \theta_m^k\right) =$$

$$= \arg max\left\{L\left(\pi_1, \ldots \pi_k, \theta_1^1, \ldots \theta_m^1, \ldots \theta_1^k, \ldots \theta_m^k\right)\right\}$$

Taking into account the introduced notation, the likelihood functions will take the form:

$$g(x, p, \lambda_1, \lambda_2) = p\lambda_1 e^{-\lambda_1 x} + (1-p)\lambda_2 e^{-\lambda_2 x} = p_1\lambda_1 e^{-\lambda_1 x} + p_2\lambda_2 e^{-\lambda_2 x}$$

In this case, the distribution parameters:$\pi_j = \left(p_1^j, p_2^j\right), \theta^j = \left(\lambda_1^j, \lambda_2^j\right)$.

At each step of the algorithm (v), the mixture component will be used $f_j^{(v)}(x_i) = \lambda_j e^{-\lambda_j x_i}$.

Then the density of the mixture is $g^{(v)}(x_i) = \sum_{j=1}^{k} p_j \lambda_j e^{-\lambda_j x_i}$

Accordingly, for a two-component mixture

$$p_1 = p, \ p_2 = 1 - p$$

M-step of the algorithm—the values of the distribution parameters at the current step are specified

$$p^{(v+1)} = \frac{f_j^{(v)}(x_i)p_j^{(v)}}{\sum_{i=1}^{N} g^{(v)}(x_i)}/N \tag{10}$$

$$\lambda_j^{(v+1)} = \frac{\sum_{i+1}^{N} \frac{f_j^{(v)}(x_i)x_i}{g^{(v)}(x_i)}}{\sum_{i+1}^{N} \frac{f_j^{(v)}(x_i)}{g^{(v)}(x_i)}} \tag{11}$$

Schematically, the principle of the EM-algorithm is presented in Fig. 1.

It is advisable to take stabilization of the values of the estimated parameters as the calculation stop criterion. Using this approach to the implementation of the EM-algorithm, the parameters of the components of the hyperexponential distributions (3) and (4) can be obtained. By defining the parameters μ_1 and μ_2 and taking into account the contribution of each of them to the average value μ, it is possible to determine δ_1

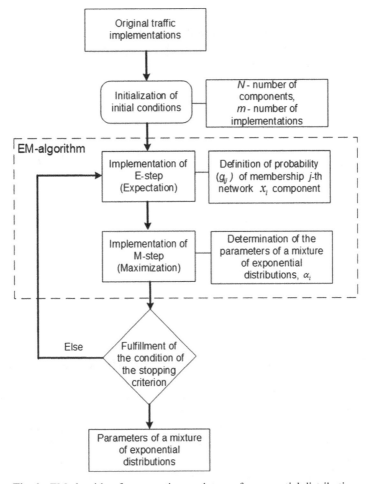

Fig. 1. EM algorithm for separating a mixture of exponential distributions

and δ_2 with shares corresponding to the contribution μ_1 and μ_2 to (4). At the same time, the need to determine the parameter value δ is obvious.

As shown in [9], the value can be determined from the equation:

$$\delta = \mu(1 - \xi), \tag{12}$$

where ξ is root of the equation $\xi = \Lambda_Q(\mu - \mu\xi)$, Λ_Q is Laplace transform of density $f_Q(\cdot)$, μ is average packet processing rate in the G/G/1 system. Given the above and taking into account (4), we obtain

$$\xi = \int_0^\infty e^{-s\tau} f_Q(\tau) d\tau$$

$$\begin{aligned}
\xi &= \int_0^\infty e^{-(\mu - \mu\xi)\tau} \left(p\mu_1 e^{-\mu_1\tau} + (1 - p)\mu_2 e^{-\mu_2\tau} \right) d\tau \\
&= p\mu_1 \frac{1}{s - \mu_1} + (1 - p)\mu_2 \frac{1}{s - \mu_2}.
\end{aligned} \tag{13}$$

Therefore, ξ can be defined as the root of Eq. (13).

To determine the parameter μ, consider that this is the inverse of the average packet processing time in the system—$\bar{\tau} = \frac{1}{\mu}$. The average packet processing time is determined according to the expression

$$\bar{\tau} = \int_0^\infty \tau f_Q(\tau) d\tau$$

Given (4) we get

$$\bar{\tau} = \int_0^\infty \left(q\tau\mu_1 e^{-\mu_1\tau} + (1-q)\tau\mu_2 e^{-\mu_2\tau} \right) d\tau = \frac{q}{\mu_1} + \frac{1-q}{\mu_2}$$

As a result, we have

$$\bar{\tau} = \frac{q\mu_2 + (1-q)\mu_1}{\mu_1\mu_2}$$

$$\bar{\mu} = \frac{\mu_1\mu_2}{q\mu_2 + (1-q)\mu_1}$$

$$\delta = \frac{\mu_1\mu_2}{q\mu_2 + (1-q)\mu_1}(1-\xi)$$

3   Analysis of Statistical Characteristics of Multimedia Traffic

For analysis, we used multimedia traffic, the statistical characteristics of which are given in [7]. Given the limitations on the independence of random variables within the sequence, it is obvious that verification of compliance with this condition is necessary.

Analysis of the distribution of random time intervals between packets showed that the Weibull distribution with parameters $\alpha = 0{,}32$, $\beta = 167$ is most accurate. For packet lengths the result was obtained in the form of Pareto distribution with the parameters: $\alpha = 0{,}3$, $\beta = 60$ (Fig. 2).

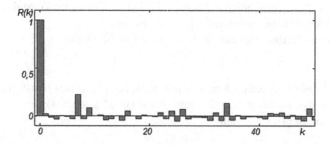

Fig. 2. Graph of correlation coefficients $R(k)$ of packet lengths

For the studied samples of the considered multimedia stream, the following dependence of the correlation coefficients was determined

The similar result was obtained for the time intervals between packets. An analysis of the dependency graphs of the correlation coefficients $R(k)$ for the considered samples shows that there are practically no correlations. This allows you to make an assumption on the independence of these random variables when analyzing the functioning parameters.

4 Results of Analytical and Simulation Modeling

4.1 Results of Analytical Modeling

When using the EM algorithm to analyze the parameters of hyperexponential distributions (3) and (4), according to the logic described above in Sect. 2, the following notation should be introduced:

- for (3), in the probability density of time intervals between packets, component weights—$\left(p_1^j, p_2^j\right) = \left(P_1^j, P_2^j\right)$, distribution parameters—$\left(\lambda_1^j, \lambda_2^j\right) = \left(\gamma_1^j, \gamma_2^j\right)$;
- for (4), in the probability density of packet processing durations, component weights $\left(p_1^j, p_2^j\right) = \left(q_1^j, q_2^j\right)$, distribution parameters—$\left(\lambda_1^j, \lambda_2^j\right) = \left(\mu_1^j, \mu_2^j\right)$.

To initialize the operation of the EM-algorithm, it is necessary to establish the initial parameters of the component weights $\left(P_1^0, P_2^0\right)$, $\left(q_1^0, q_2^0\right)$ and the parameters of the components of the mixture γ_1^0, μ^0. To establish these values, you can use standard methods [15–19], according to which it is assumed at the initial stage that in the case of a two-component mixture, the weight of each component $P_j^0 = 1/2$ and $q_j^0 = 1/2$. The average values of the sample are taken as the component parameters. To evaluate the distribution parameters (3) and (4), it should be taken into account that the distribution density of the sequences of time intervals between packets is characterized by the parameter $\bar{\gamma} = \frac{1}{\bar{t}}$, where $\bar{t}$ is the average value of the time intervals between packets, and the distribution density of the transmission duration of the packet is characterized by the parameter $\bar{\mu} = \frac{1}{\bar{\tau}}$, where $\bar{\tau}$ is the packet processing duration.

Taking into account the characteristics of the traffic investigated in Sect. 3, the following parameters can be used to initialize the algorithm:

$P_j^0 = 1/2$—for both components, similarly $q_j^0 = 1/2$;
$\gamma^0 = 0{,}000539$, s^{-1}—for time intervals between packets;
$\mu^0 = 0{,}2166$, s^{-1}—for packet transmission durations.

The parameters of hyperexponential distributions by the EM-algorithm were obtained according to expressions (9), (10) and (11). The results are presented in the Table 1.

Using the δ parameter values to calculate δ_1 and δ_2, we have $\delta = 0{,}002$ ms^{-1}.

The obtained values of the parameters for $f_V(y)$, show that the hyperexponential distribution degenerates into exponential with the parameter: $\gamma = 558$.

Based on the obtained parameter values and formula (9), the delay variation is determined—$\sigma = 0{,}005$ ms.

Table 1. Parameters of the hyperexponential distributions

Probability density of random variable	Parameters component of the mixture, ms^{-1}	Weight component of the mixture
$f_V(\tau)$	$\gamma_1 = 558{,}09, \gamma_2 = 558{,}06$	$P_1 = 0{,}96157, P_2 = 0{,}0{,}3843$
$f_Q(\tau)$	$\mu_1 = 1229{,}06, \mu_2 = 101{,}7$	$q_1 = 0{,}9989, q_2 = 0{,}0011$
$f_W(\tau)$	$\delta_1 = 0{,}0199, \delta_2 = 2{,}2 \times 10^{-6}$	$\Delta_1 = 0{,}9989, \Delta_2 = 0{,}9989$

It seems interesting to analyze the effect of network load depending on the load factor $\rho = \frac{\gamma}{\mu}$, the result of which is shown in Fig. 3. The load change in the model was realized by varying the time intervals between packets (which corresponds to the parameter γ, the parameter δ is recalculated accordingly) with a constant packet length (which corresponds to the parameter μ), while taking into account that the initial traffic implementation was obtained when the channel load was 0,4 (Fig. 4).

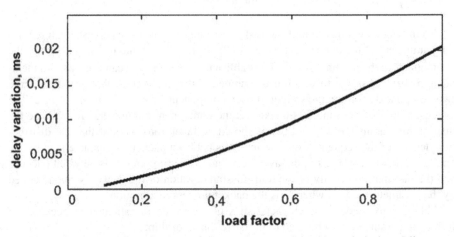

Fig. 3. The dependence of delay variation on the network load in analytical modeling

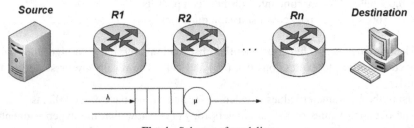

Fig. 4. Scheme of modeling

4.2   Results of Simulation Modeling

When choosing a modeling environment, there is a problem with the possible processing of different types of traffic; it is desirable to start streams that are registered on the real network. The ns2 software environment meets these requirements.

In the simulation environment, the following streams were processed:

- traffic that are registered on the real network, for which the results of analytical modeling were obtained;
- CBR-traffic;
- exponential stream;
- traffic with Pareto distribution of time intervals between packets and packet lengths.

The channel load in the model is set to 0.4.

For processing in a simulation environment, the flows were selected that are most characteristic for infocommunication networks [1, 7–9]. It is known that the exponential traffic processing system corresponds to the M/M/1 model. This stream is characterized by the absence of correlation within the sequence of the stream implementation.

On the contrary, CBR stream is characterized by strong correlations.

Based on the analysis of simulation results, the dependences of the delay variation on the network load were obtained (Fig. 5).

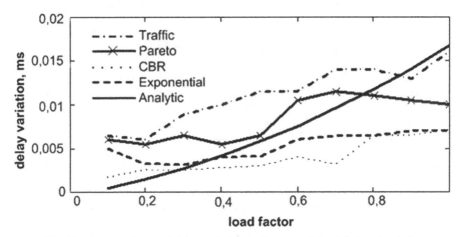

Fig. 5. The dependence of delay variation on the network load during simulation

From the results, it can be seen that for real traffic the delay variation is larger than for CBR and exponential flows. CBR traffic has delay variation values less than exponential. As you know, exponential flows are characterized by the absence of correlation. Considering the presence of correlations within the sequences of CBR traffic, as well as the absence of correlation for multimedia traffic established in the analysis, it can be stated that with an increase in the degree of correlation, the delay variation decreases.

5 Conclusion

1. Analytical evaluation of delay variation in the G/G/1 system simulated as $H_2/H_2/1$ is obtained. The obtained approach allows estimating the variation in packet delay during transmission, regardless of what actual distribution describes the waiting time of the packet in the queue.
2. The approach to determining the parameters of the hyperexponential distribution based on the EM-algorithm is proposed. Estimates are obtained of the variation in packet delay during network loading $\rho = 0,4$ as a result of analytical modeling—$\sigma = 0,005$ ms and simulation—$\sigma = 0,007$ ms. According to the results, the dependences of the delay variation on the network load were obtained, which showed that with an increase in the load, the delay variation increases.
3. Based on the analysis of the simulation results, it was found that with an increase in the degree of correlation, the variation of the delay decreases.

References

1. Kartashevskii, V.G., Kireeva, N.V, Buranova, M.A, Chupakhina, L.R.: Study of queuing system G/G/1 with an arbitrary distribution of time parameter system. In: 2nd International Scientific-Practical Conference Problems of Infocommunications Science and Technology, PIC S and T 2015, pp. 145–148. doi:http://doi.org/10.1109/INFOCOMMST.2015.7357297 (2015)
2. Keilson, J., Machihara, F.: Hyperexponential waiting time structure in hyperexponential $H_N/H_K/1$ system. J. Oper. Soc. Japan **28**(3), 242–250 (1985)
3. Tarasov, V.N., Kartashevskii, I.V.: Opredeleniye srednego vremeni ozhidaniya trebovaniy v upravlyayemoy sisteme massovogo obsluzhivaniya H2/H2/1 [Determination of the average waiting time for requirements in a managed queuing system H2/H2/1]. Control Syst. Inform. Technol. **3**(57), 92–96 (2014). (In Russian)
4. Dbira, H., Girard, A., Sanso, B.: Calculation of packet jitter for non-poisson traffic. In: Annals of telecommunications, vol. 71, issue 5–6, pp. 223–237 (2016)
5. Kartashevskiy, I., Buranova, M.: Calculation of packet jitter for correlated traffic. In: International Conference on « InInternet of Things, Smart Spaces, and Next Generation Networks and Systems. NEW2AN 2019 » , vol. 11660, pp. 610–620. (Lecture Notes in Computer Science, Springer, Cham). https://doi.org/10.1007/978-3-030-30859-9_53 (2019)
6. Dahmouni, H., Girard, A., Sanso, B.: An analytical model for jitter in IP networks. In: Annals of telecommunications-annales des telecommunications, pp. 81–90 (2012)
7. Kartashevskii, V.G., Buranova, M.A.: Modelirovaniye dzhittera paketov pri peredache po mul'tiservisnoy seti [Modeling packet jitter during transmission over a multiservice network]. Infocommun. Technol. **17**(1), 34–40 (2019). (In Russian)
8. Buranova, M.A., Kartashevskii, V.G., Latypov, R.T.: Ocenka dzhittera v sisteme G/M/1 na osnove ispol'zovaniya gipereksponencial'nyh raspredelenij [Jitter estimation in the G/M/1 system based on the use of hyperexponential distributions]. Infocommun. Technol. **18**(1), 13–20 (2020). (In Russian)
9. Kleinrock, L.: Queueing Systems: Volume I, Theory, p. 417. Wiley Interscience, New York (1975)

10. Kartashevskii, V.G., Buranova, M.A.: Analysis of packet jitter in multiservice network. In: 5th International Scientific-Practical Conference Problems of Infocommunications Science and Technology, PIC S and T 2018, pp. 797–802. https://doi.org/10.1109/infocommst.2018. 8632085 (2018)
11. Feldmann, A., Whitt, W.: fitting mixtures of exponentials to long-tail distributions to analyze network performance models. In: Proceedings IEEE INFOCOM'97, pp. 1096–1104. IEEE, Piscataway, NJ (1997)
12. Internet protocol data communication service IP packet transfer and availability performance parameters. ITU-T Recommendation Y.1540. https://www.itu.int/rec/T-REC-I.380-199902-S/en, last accessed 2020/02/10
13. Demichelis, C, Chimento, P.: IP packet delay variation metric for IP performance metrics (IPPM), institution IETF, RFC 33934, p. 21. https://doi.org/10.17487/rfc3393 (2000)
14. Tarasov, V.N., Gorelov, G.A., Ushakov, Y.A.: Vosstanovleniye momentnykh kharakter-istik raspredeleniya intervalov mezhdu paketami vkhodyashchego trafika [Recovery of moment characteristics of the distribution of intervals between packets of incoming traffic]. Infocommun. Technol. **2**, 40–44 (2014). (In Russian)
15. Baird, SR.: Estimating mixtures of exponential distributions using maximum likelihood and the EM algorithm to improve simulation of telecommunication networks. https://open.library. ubc.ca/collections/ubctheses/831/items/1.0090805 (2002)
16. Buranova, M.A., Ergasheva, D.R., Kartashevskiy, V.G.: Using the EM-algorithm to approxi-mate the distribution of a mixture by hyperexponents. In: International Conference on Engi-neering and Telecommunication, EnT 2019, pp. 1–4. doi:http://doi.org/10.1109/EnT47717. 2019.9030551 (2019)
17. Day, N.E.: Estimating the components of a mixture of normal distributions. Biometrika **56**(3), 463–474 (1969)
18. Korolyov, V. YU.: EM-algoritm, ego modifikacii i ih primenenie k zadache razdeleniya smesej veroyatnostnyh raspredelenij. Teoreticheskij obzor [The EM algorithm, its modifications, and their application to the problem of separating mixtures of probability distributions. Theoretical review]. M.: IPI RAN, p. 94 (2007). (In Russian)
19. Voroncov, K.V. Matematicheskie metody obucheniya po precedentam (teoriya obucheniya mashin) [Mathematical teaching methods on precedents (machine learning theory)]. http://www.machinelearning.ru/wiki/images/6/6d/Voron-ML-1.pdf, last accessed 2019/09/10

The Fourier Series Model for Predicting Sapflow Density Flux Based on TreeTalker Monitoring System

Dmitry Efrosinin[1,2], Irina Kochetkova[2,3(✉)], Natalia Stepanova[4],
Alexey Yarovslavtsev[2,5], Konstantin Samouylov[2,3], and Riccardo Valentini[2,6]

[1] Johannes Kepler University Linz, Altenbergerstrasse 69, 4040 Linz, Austria
dmitry.efrosinin@jku.at
[2] Peoples' Friendship University of Russia (RUDN University), 6 Miklukho-Maklaya St.,
Moscow 117198, Russian Federation
{gudkova-ia,yaroslavtsev-am,samuylov-ke}@rudn.ru
[3] Institute of Informatics Problems, Federal Research Center "Computer Science and Control"
of the Russian Academy of Sciences, 44-2 Vavilova St., Moscow 119333, Russian Federation
[4] V.A. Trapeznikov Institute of Control Sciences of RAS, Profsoyuznaya St., 65,
117997 Moscow, Russia
natalia0410@rambler.ru
[5] LAMP, Russian Timiryazev State Agrarian University, 49 Timiryazevskaya st.,
Moscow 127550, Russian Federation
[6] Tuscia University, Via S.M. in Gradi n.4, 01100 Viterbo, Italy
rik@unitus.it
http://www.jku.at, http://eng.rudn.ru

Abstract. The development and application of smart technologies in various fields is increasing every year. Different monitoring systems and sensors generate a large amount of data sets which allows to solve various tasks on data prediction and classification. This paper deals with data sets generated by a new tree monitoring system TreeTalker© which evaluates in particular the sap flow density flux describing water transport in trees. The main task consists in prediction of the values of this characteristic which reflects the tree life state based only on observable air temperature during the predictable time interval and subsequent classification of trees according to some prespecified classes. The Fourier series based model is used to fit the data sets with periodic patterns. The multivariate regression model defines the functional dependencies between sap flow density and temperature time series. The paper shows that Fourier coefficients can be successfully used as elements of the feature vectors required to solve different classification problems. Artificial multilayer neural networks are used as classifiers. The quality of the developed model for prediction and classification is verified by numerous numerical examples.

Keywords: Tree monitoring · Fourier series · Multivariate linear regression · Time series prediction and classification · Neural network

The work was supported by the Russian Science Foundation, project 19-77-30012 (recipients I. Kochetkova, A. Yarovslavtsev, R. Valentini). The publication has been prepared with the support of the "RUDN University Program 5-100" (recipients D. Efrosinin, K. Samouylov).

O. Galinina et al. (Eds.): NEW2AN 2020/ruSMART 2020, LNCS 12526, pp. 198–209, 2020.
https://doi.org/10.1007/978-3-030-65729-1_18

1 Introduction

The TreeTalker (TT) [19] is a new complex sensor for real-time ecological monitoring made with the concept of the Internet of Things (IoT) in mind from Nature 4.0 company. A TreeTalker device includes a low power chipset LoRa for data transmission to the gateway called TT-Cloud, which could collect data from up to 48 devices in one cluster (20 recommended) and re-transmit it to the webserver via 3G modem. In most cases, data is collected hourly, but in Russian conditions, 1.5 h are recommended. The performance of TreeTalkers is being tested at several sites all over Eurasia continent from Spain to China, with a wide variety of tree species, climate, topography, and land use with multiple tests of device reliability in terms of sensors operational limits of the sensors, data transmission, and battery effectiveness. The device is based on an ATMega 328 processor chip, which is responsible for collecting data from all sensors and transforming the analog signal to meaningful variables: sap flow density, temperature, and humidity of the air and wood, spectral characteristics of the canopy, radial growth of the trunk, and data from accelerometer about 3D position of trunk, since TreeTalker devices are fixed to trees with a tight belt. The power source of the device is a combination of solar panels and Lithium-ion batteries.

The sap flow density is calculated according to the Heat Balance Method developed by Granier [8] in the modification of Doe [5] (who showed that the reasonable results could be achieved without constant heating). For these two 20 mm long temperature probes, inserted into the xylem (Fig. 1). One probe is installed 10 cm higher along the trunk than the other and heated while the lower is not heated and used as a reference.

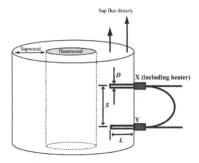

Fig. 1. Sup flux density in greenwood stem based on Granier method

The maximum temperature difference between probes should denote zero flux since the upward stream of sap in xylem should dissipate heat and lead to the minimum difference between probes. To calculate sap flux density according to Do [5], first, the thermal index K_1 was calculated which is based on the ratio between the maximum temperature increase, recorded under zero flow T_0, and the increase under the measured flow T_u:

$$K_1 = \frac{T_0 - T_u}{T_u}.$$

Next, for each investigated tree species, the empirical coefficient was calculated, which allowed the conversion of the thermal index into sap flux density:

$$J = a \cdot K_1 \quad [l \cdot s^{-1} \cdot m^{-2}]$$

The individual sap flow for each tree was calculated as a result of the multiplication of sap flux density and sap flux area, which was assessed with wood cores on species level:

$$F = J \cdot S_s \quad [l \cdot s^{-1}]$$

A thermo-hygrometer, embedded on the microcontroller, completes the set of sensors; air exchange through the device case is allowed by a 0.6 mm wide circular hole covered with a water vapor-permeable membrane (Table 1).

Table 1. TreeTalker parameters

Components and sensors	Description
Sap flow	Reference and heated temperature probes ($\pm 0.1\,°C$)
Stem humidity	Capacitive sensor MicroPCB ($20 \times 3 \times 2$) mm with copper plates
Canopy light transmission	Spectrometer-12 spectral bands (450, 500, 550, 570, 600, 610, 650, 680, 730, 760, 810, 860 nm) Full width half max: 20 nm (VIS); 40 nm (NIR) Manufacturer: AMS. Model: AS7262 (Visible range), AS7263 (Near Infrared range)
Tree trunk radial growth	Infra-red distance sensor (min $\pm 100\,\mu m$) Manufacturer: SHARP
Tree trunk axis movement	Accelerometer ($\pm 0.01°$)
Air temperature and humidity	Thermohygrometer ($\pm 0.1\,°C$, $\pm 2\%$).
Flash memory for data storage	16 Mbyte
LoRa module for data transmission	Transmission 600 m (in urban/rural environment). It can reach >3 km in case line of sight
4 Li-Ion batteries + solar panel	3.7 V

In May 2019, 60 TreeTalkers were installed on trees of six species in RUDN University campus: *Tilia cordata Mil.*, *Acer platanoides L.*, *Picea abies L*, *Populus tremula L.*, *Pinus silvestris L*, *Betula pendula Roth* (10 trees of each species). Data from all devices was collected till the end of November 2019 and stored on a remote web server.

All data for basic variables was 3 sigma filtered, despiked and gap filled with linear interpolation for gaps smaller than 4 measurements. Sapwood area data was combined with TreeTalkers data, and individual tree sap flux was calculated utilizing R software.

While there are several papers where modern modelling techniques implemented for predicting evapotranspiration of planted areas with environmental data [4, 10, 16], there are very limited amount of papers about individual tree sap flow modelling [18]. Taking into account growing trend of IoT devices used in environmental monitoring [2, 15, 20] modelling of one of the main physiological tree characteristics can be of great interest

In this paper we provide a prediction model for the sap flow density flux data based on its dependency on the air temperature. We expect that the characteristic of the sap flow density can be meaningful for life diagnostics, description and classification of trees. As we will see, the data for the sap flow density flux and, of course, for the temperature, follow periodic patterns. A lot of work has been done to analyze the periodic data. But normally the predicting is performed using a past history of data or time series consisting of a long term trend, a seasonal variation, a cyclic variation and random effects. In our case, the prediction should be made on the basis of the observed values of another series describing the temperature dynamics that correlates with the series of interest. The model based on Fourier series are a particularly promising approach to quantify analytically periodic variability by transforming periodic signals into frequencies driven by sums of sines and cosines [17]. Fourier series have been used for data fitting with complex periodic patterns in different applications, see e.g. [6] and [12] and references therein. In this paper we present a Fourier series model that incorporates Fourier series as explicit representation of the periodic data sets and multivariate regression model coupling the estimated Fourier coefficients of the temperature and flux into time series prediction and classification.

The rest of the paper is organized as follows. In Sect. 2, we describe the Fourier series model and give a brief presentation of the estimation method for unknown parameters. In Sect. 3, we verify the proposed prediction model and provide comparison analysis with a simple neural network regression model. In Sect. 4, we study the problem of trees classification within the same species based on feature vector estimated in previous section.

For use in sequel, let I_n denote the identity matrix of dimension n. The notation "$\prime$" appearing in a vector or matrix will stand respectively for the vector or matrix transpose. The notation $\otimes$ will stand for the Kronecker product of two matrices. The notation $y_{[a:b]} = (y_a, y_{a+1}, \ldots, y_b)$ specifies the selected data set from the interval $[a, b]$.

2 Model Development

As it is known, any periodic function $f(t)$ with a period T can be represented as a Fourier series

$$f(t) = \lim_{n \to \infty} s_n(t) = a_0 + \sum_{n=1}^{\infty} [a_n \cos(\omega_n t) + b_n \sin(\omega_n t)], \tag{1}$$

where a_n and b_n are Fourier coefficients defined as integrals of the periodic function $f(t)$, a_0 is the average value of the series, $\omega_n = n\frac{2\pi}{T}$ is a frequency. We have series with periodic patterns for the air temperature (*tair*) and for the sap flow density flux (*flux*). Each cycle includes mostly $N = 16$ measurements that are made at equally spaced time intervals $\Delta t = 1.5$ h. The total time within a cycle is $T = N\Delta t = 24$ h. A truncated Fourier series can be used to find approximations for periodic functions $f_{tair}(t)$ and $f_{flux}(t)$ with a fundamental period T that passes through all of the points,

$$f_{tair}(t) \approx a_0 + \sum_{n=1}^{m < \frac{N}{2}} \left[a_n \cos\left(\frac{2\pi nt}{T}\right) + b_n \sin\left(\frac{2\pi nt}{T}\right) \right], \tag{2}$$

$$f_{flux}(t) \approx \alpha_0 + \sum_{n=1}^{m < \frac{N}{2}} \left[\alpha_n \cos\left(\frac{2\pi nt}{T}\right) + \beta_n \sin\left(\frac{2\pi nt}{T}\right) \right]. \tag{3}$$

The coefficients a_n, b_n and α_n, β_n can not be explicitly derived since the functions $f_{tair}(t)$ and $f_{flux}(t)$ are not available in explicit form and hence they must be estimated. We have only data $\mathbf{y}_{tair} = (y_{tair,1}, y_{tair,2}, \ldots, y_{tair,n_s})'$ and $\mathbf{y}_{flux} = (y_{flux,1}, y_{flux,2}, \ldots, y_{flux,n_s})'$ generated by the sensors. The known periodic patterns of the approximated functions $f_{tair}(t)$ and $f_{flux}(t)$ are expressed through vectors of parameters $\mathbf{a} = (a_0, a_1, \ldots, a_m, b_1, \ldots, b_m)'$ and $\alpha = (\alpha_0, \alpha_1, \ldots, \alpha_m, \beta_1, \ldots, \beta_m)'$. These parameters are estimated using the method of the linear least squares

$$\sum_{t=(i-1)T}^{iT} (y_{tair,t} - f_{tair}(t))^2 \Rightarrow \min_a, \quad \sum_{t=(i-1)T}^{iT} (y_{flux,t} - f_{flux}(t))^2 \Rightarrow \min_\alpha, \ 1 \le i \le n_p,$$

where $n_p = \frac{n_s}{N}$ is a number of cycles of length T within the observations with a total sample size n_s. As it is known, the estimate vectors for $\mathbf{a}$ and α in each cycle i can be represented in form

$$\hat{\mathbf{a}}_i = (\Phi_i'\Phi_i)^{-1}\Phi_i'\mathbf{y}_{tair,[(i-1)T:iT]}, \ \hat{\alpha}_i = (\Phi_i'\Phi_i)^{-1}\Phi_i'\mathbf{y}_{flux,[(i-1)T:iT]}, \ 1 \le i \le n_p, \tag{4}$$

where in our model $\Phi_i = [\varphi_{t,j}]_{\substack{(i-1)T \le t \le iT \\ 0 \le j \le 2m}}$ and

$$\varphi_{t,0} = 1, \varphi_{t,n} = \begin{cases} \cos\left(\frac{2\pi nt}{T}\right) & 1 \le n \le m, \\ \sin\left(\frac{2\pi nt}{T}\right) & m+1 \le n \le 2m. \end{cases}$$

The corresponding estimators for $\hat{\mathbf{a}}_i$ and $\hat{\alpha}_i$ are normally distributed with the means $\mathbf{a}, \alpha$ and covariance matrices $\sigma^2_{tair,i}(\Phi_i'\Phi_i)^{-1}$ and $\sigma^2_{flux,i}(\Phi_i'\Phi_i)^{-1}$. With this research we want to show the possibility to evaluate a one day predictions of the sap flow density flux based only on observable during this period values of the air temperature y_{tair}. The choice of this parameter in the presence of others, such as humidity and the coefficient VPD, which combines the temperature and relative humidity signals, is explained by the fact that it is the factor temperature that has the highest stable value of the correlation with the data for the sap flow density flux. The analysed data sets $\mathbf{y}_{tair}$ and $\mathbf{y}_{flux}$ are high correlated, see e.g. data samples for two species *Larix sibirica* and *Acer platanoids* in Fig. 2. The correlations between two vectors $\mathbf{y}_{tair}$ and $\mathbf{y}_{flux}$ are equal respectively 0.64 and 0.53.

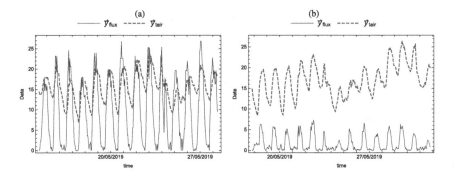

Fig. 2. Data y_{tair} and y_{flux} for *Larix sibirica* (a) and *Acer platanoids* (b)

The data preprocessing step includes the denoising by locally data smoothing. We use for that a low pass filter which passes signals with a frequency lower than a selected cutoff frequency $\omega_c = 0.9$. Smaller values of ω_c result in greater smoothing. To estimate the unknown parameters $\alpha = (\alpha_0, \alpha_1, \ldots, \alpha_m, \beta_1, \ldots, \beta_m)$ in approximation (3) based on a observations of temperature we assume the following linear relation between the elements of parameter vectors α and a,

$$\alpha_n = \theta_{0,n} + \theta_{1,n}a_0 + \sum_{j=1}^{m}[\theta_{j+1,n}a_j + \theta_{m+j+1,n}b_j], \; 0 \leq n \leq m, \tag{5}$$

$$\beta_n = \theta_{0,n+m} + \theta_{1,n+m}a_0 + \sum_{j=1}^{m}[\theta_{j+1,n+m}a_j + \theta_{m+j+1,n+m}b_j], \; 1 \leq n \leq m,$$

where $\theta_n = (\theta_{0,n}, \theta_{1,n}, \ldots, \theta_{2m+1,n})', 0 \leq n \leq 2m$, denotes the vector of unknown parameters. Assume that the elements of vectors $\hat{\alpha}_0 = (\hat{\alpha}_{1,0}, \hat{\alpha}_{2,0}, \ldots, \hat{\alpha}_{n_p,0})', \hat{\alpha}_n = (\hat{\alpha}_{1,n}, \hat{\alpha}_{2,n}, \ldots, \hat{\alpha}_{n_p,n})'$ and $\hat{\beta}_n = (\hat{\beta}_{1,n}, \hat{\beta}_{2,n}, \ldots, \hat{\beta}_{n_p,n})', 1 \leq n \leq m$ are realizations of the corresponding random variables A_0, A_n and $B_n, 1 \leq n \leq m$, which can be used to construct the linear regression model. Now we introduce the following column macro-vectors: $A = (A_0, A_1, \ldots, A_m, B_1, \ldots, B_m)'$, $\theta = (\theta_0, \theta_1, \ldots, \theta_{2m})'$, $\varepsilon = (\varepsilon_0, \varepsilon_1, \ldots, \varepsilon_{2m})$. The last vector denotes the vector of independent normal distributed random variables with mean 0 and variance σ_ε^2.

Proposition 1. *The liner regression model can be represented in the form*

$$A = (I_{2m+1} \otimes \Psi)\theta + \varepsilon, \tag{6}$$

where $\Psi = [\psi_{i,j}]_{\substack{1 \leq i \leq n_p \\ 0 \leq j \leq 2m+1}}$ *is a matrix with elements* $\psi_{i,0} = 1$ *and*

$$\psi_{i,j} = \begin{cases} \hat{a}_{i,j-1} & 1 \leq j \leq m+1, \\ \hat{b}_{i,j-m-1} & m+2 \leq j \leq 2m+1. \end{cases}$$

Proof. The proposition follows directly from the linear relation (5). By expressing this relation for the samples $\hat{\alpha}_0, \hat{\alpha}_n$ and $\hat{\beta}_n, 1 \leq n \leq m$, in matrix form we obtain the expression (6).

Corollary 1. *The estimates for elements of vector* θ *are of the form*

$$\hat{\theta}_n = (\Psi'\Psi)^{-1}\Psi'\hat{\alpha}_n, \ 0 \le n \le m,$$

$$\hat{\theta}_{n+m} = (\Psi'\Psi)^{-1}\Psi'\hat{\beta}_n, \ 1 \le n \le m.$$

Finally, the estimated vector θ together with a vector $\hat{a}$ of the Fourier coefficients of temperature data for a newly predictable cycle must be substituted to relations (6) and the obtained coefficients will produce with (3) a prediction function. To check the quality of the proposed Fouries series model (FSM) we have trained multi-layer neural networks (NNs) for the vector relations of the type $\{a_i \rightarrow \alpha_i : 1 \le i \le n_p\}$. However, different types of NNs have never produced a better result than the proposed multivariate regression model. We may assume that these two vectors exhibit mostly linear dependencies. Therefore, as alternative to our model, we took a simple neural network regression model (NNR) for the scalar relation $\{y_{\text{tair},t} \rightarrow y_{\text{flux},t} : 1 \le t \le n_s\}$. In general, it can provide much more prediction power compared to a traditional regression but as we will see the prediction accuracy will be not high enough comparing to the FSM. But as it is shown in Sect. 4, the neural network classifier is successfully used in trees classification problems.

3   Verification of the Prediction Model

Denote prediction error e_t as a difference between an observed value $y_{\text{flux},t}$ and its forecast $\hat{y}_{\text{flux},t}$, i.e. $e_t = y_{\text{flux},t} - \hat{y}_{\text{flux},t}$. The value e_t specifies the unpredictable part of an observation. We note that the usage of the percentage error

$$\text{Mean absolut percentage error:} \quad \text{MAPE} = \frac{1}{n_s} \sum_{t=1}^{n_s} \frac{100e_t}{y_{\text{flux},t}},$$

since for some t the observation $y_{\text{flux},t}$ can be very small or even equal to 0. Therefore we evaluate the following scale-dependent and scaled measures. The mostly used scale-dependent measures are calculated based on the absolute errors or squared errors:

$$\text{Mean absolute error:} \quad \text{MAE} = \frac{1}{n_s} \sum_{t=1}^{n_s} e_t, \tag{7}$$

$$\text{Root mean squared error:} \quad \text{RMSE} = \sqrt{\frac{1}{n_s} \sum_{t=1}^{n_s} e_t^2} \tag{8}$$

We calculate also scaled errors proposed in [9], which are used to compare prediction accuracy for series with different units. For ordinary and seasonal time series with period T the calculated metrics are of the form:

$$\text{Mean absolute scaled error:} \quad \text{MASE} = \frac{n_s - 1}{n_s \sum_{t=1}^{n_s} |y_{\text{flux},t} - y_{\text{flux},t-1}|} \sum_{j=1}^{n_s} e_j, \tag{9}$$

$$\text{Seasonal mean absolute scaled error:} \tag{10}$$

$$\text{SMASE} = \frac{n_s - T}{n_s \sum_{t=T+1}^{n_s} |y_{\text{flux},t} - y_{\text{flux},t-T}|} \sum_{j=1}^{n_s} e_j$$

Note that the expressions in numerator and denominator of (9) and (10) have the same scales, therefore these metrics are independent of the scale of original data. If MASE < 1 or SMASE < 1, then the prediction is better than the moving average forecast and vice versa. Two more metrics are used to check the accuracy of a proposed prediction model: a statistic

$$\text{Rsquared}: R^2 = 1 - \frac{\sum_{t=1}^{n_s}(y_{\text{flux},t} - \hat{y}_{\text{flux},t})^2}{\sum_{t=1}^{n_s}(y_{\text{flux},t} - \frac{1}{n_s}\sum_{j=1}^{n_s}y_{\text{flux},j})^2}, \tag{11}$$

where $0 \leq R^2 \leq 1$, which is a measure of how strongly the random vectors Y and $\hat{Y}$ correlate and

$$\text{Adjusted Rsquared}: R^2_{ad} = 1 - \frac{n_s - 1}{n_s - (2m + 1)}(1 - R^2), \tag{12}$$

which takes into account the influence of extra explanatory variables in different regression models.

Example 1. In this example we illustrate an application of the proposed in the previous section the sap flow prediction approach with real data consisting of arbitrary selected samples for *Acer platanoides* and *Larix sibirica*. The difference between the two methods is obvious. Applying the proposed formulas for accuracy calculation to the data y_{flux} we get results summarized in Table 2 and 3. The values of scaled for metrics by using the FSM are smaller than 1 and the R^2 statistics are very close to 1. This means good quality of a prediction (Fig. 3).

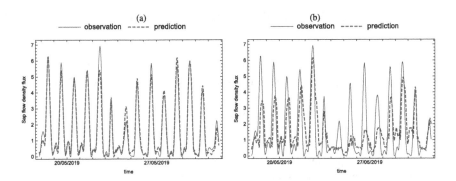

Fig. 3. 24 h prediction of the sap flow density flux measured over two weeks by FSM (a) and NNR (b) for *Acer platanoides*

As was expected, Fourier series are a promising approach to quantify periodic dynamics of the predictable underlying tree characteristic. For the coefficient estimation we have used the coefficients of the Fourier series fitted the observable air temperature data. As an alternative way we could propose instead the FSM the usage of linear stochastic processes in particular the Seasonal Autoregressive Integrated Moving Average, or SARIMA [3], with a known period. The parameters of this model can be also

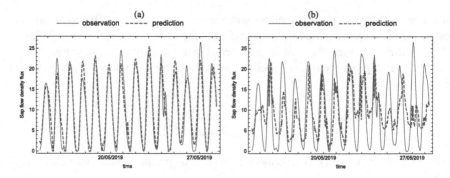

Fig. 4. 24 h prediction of the sap flow density flux measured over two weeks by FSM (a) and NNR (b) for *Larix sibirica*

Table 2. Prediction accuracy for *Larix sibirica*

Method	Metric					
	RMSE	MAE	MASE	SMASE	R^2	R^2_{ad}
FSM	2.1235	1.6368	0.9173	0.5128	0.9295	0.9271
NNR	6.1222	4.8322	2.7079	1.5139	0.3659	0.3444

estimated from parameters of the Fourier series or of the SARIMA process evaluated with the air temperature data. This model will be developed in framework of our next research (Fig. 4).

4   Trees Classification Based on Fourier Coefficients

Here we report shortly first experiments carried out on data sets extracted by the TT monitoring system and dedicated to classification. Artificial neural networks is a part of a supervised machine learning which is most popular in different problems of data classification, pattern recognition, regression, clustering, time series forecasting. We study the possibility to use NN to classify the trees of the same species but with different age groups and VTA scores. As classification features we use a predicted Fourier coefficients of the sap flow density flux approximation function. In the long term, this approach which incorporates data generated by the TT with the proposed FSM can be used to determine the anomalous state of a tree or generally monitor forest ecology.

Table 3. Prediction accuracy for *Acer platanoides*

Method	Metric					
	RMSE	MAE	MASE	SMASE	R^2	R^2_{ad}
FSM	0.3591	0.2379	0.5646	0.3182	0.9615	0.9602
NNR	1.4008	1.0064	2.3965	1.3459	0.4144	0.3945

Table 4. Classes of *Selix albe* (a) and *Acer platanoides* (b)

(a)			(b)		
Class N	Age group	VTA score	Class N	Age group	VTA score
1	IV	2	1	VI	1
2	IV	3	2	VI	2
3	III	2	3	VI	3
			4	VI	4

Example 2. Consider data sets for two species of trees: *Salix albe* and *Acer platanoides*. The data of the first and second groups of trees we divide respectively into three and four subgroups according to the Table 4. We prepare a data for classification in form of the set of the following relations,

$$S = \{(\hat{\alpha}_{i,0}, \hat{\alpha}_{i,1}, \ldots, \hat{\alpha}_{i,m}, \hat{\beta}_{i,1}, \ldots, \hat{\beta}_{i,m}) \rightarrow \text{Class } N : 1 \leq i \leq n_p\}.$$

70% of sample S is referred to as training data and the rest – as validation data. We train a multilayer (6-layer) NN using an adaptive moment estimation method [11] and the neural network toolbox in *Mathematica*© of the Wolfram Research. Then we verify the classifier which should be accurate enough to be used to predict new output from verification data. The algorithm was ran many times on samples and networks with different sizes. In all cases the results were quite positive and indicate the potential of machine learning methodology for trees classification problem based on the estimated Fourier coefficients.

The results of predictions are visualized in form of confusion matrices shown in Fig. 5. Each row of these matrices represents the instances in a predicted value while each column represents the instances in an actual value. Different statistical measures of the performance of a binary classification, such as the overall accuracy (ACC), sensitivity (true positive rate – TPR), specificity (true negative rate – TNR) as well as $F1$-scores which is the harmonic mean of precision and sensitivity, are given in Table 5. For more details about these measures, refer to [1]. We can see that the first data can be classified with higher accuracy as the second one.

It should be noticed that the main goal of the paper was not to classify subgroups of trees with the highest possible accuracy, but to check the overall expediency of using Fourier coefficients as characteristic parameters or features of different classes. As we can see, the accuracy of classification is encouraging. To improve it, firstly, we need to use more data, and secondly, we need to synchronize these data more precisely in time and in intervals of cycles. In the future, we expect to consider this topic in more detail as part of our joint research.

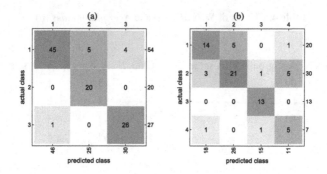

Fig. 5. Confusion matrices for classification of *Salix alba* (a) and *Acer platanoides* (b)

Table 5. Classification performance

Data	Metric			
	ACC	TPR	TNR	F1-scores
Salix albe	0.9009	1 → 0.8333	1 → 0.9787	1 → 0.9000
		2 → 1.000	2 → 0.9382	2 → 0.8889
		3 → 0.9629	3 → 0.9459	3 → 0.9123
Acer platanoides	0.7571	1 → 0.7000	1 → 0.9200	1 → 0.7368
		2 → 0.7000	2 → 0.8750	2 → 0.7500
		3 → 1.000	3 → 0.9649	3 → 0.9286
		4 → 0.7143	4 → 0.9048	4 → 0.5556

5   Conclusion

On the basis of the proposed experiments, it can be noticed that the temperature observations can be mapped to the values of the sap flow density flux through the corresponding Fourier coefficients which is resulting in high quality predictions. Moreover,
the estimated coefficients for the function approximating the sap flow density have good
potential to be used as feature vector in trees classification tasks even within the same
species. From here we can draw a conclusion about the perspective to use the TreeTalker
equipment together with the proposed methodology for solving problems of trees monitoring and anomaly state recognition.

References

1. Altman, D.G., Bland, J.M.: Diagnostic tests. 1: sensitivity and specificity. BMJ **308**(6943),
   1552–1570 (1994)
2. Boursianis, A., et al.: Internet of Things (IoT) and Agricultural Unmanned Aerial Vehicles
   (UAVs) in smart farming: a comprehensive review. IoT, 100187 (2020, in press)
3. Box, G.E.P., Jenkins, G.M., Reinsel, G.C., Ljung, G.M.: Time Series Analysis: Forecasting
   and Control. Wiley, Hoboken (2016)

4. Tang, D., Feng, Y., Gong, D., Hao, W., Cui, N.: Evaluation of artificial intelligence models for actual crop evapotranspiration modeling in mulched and non-mulched maize croplands. Comput. Electron. Agric. **152**, 375–384 (2018)

5. Do, F.C., Puangjumpa, N., Rocheteau, A., Duthoit, M., Nhean, S., Isarangkool Na Ayutthaya, S.: Towards reduced heating duration in the transient thermal dissipation system of sap flow measurements. ISHS Acta Horticulturae **1222**, 149–154 (2018)

6. Fidino, M., Magle, S.B.: Using Fourier series to estimate periodic patterns in dynamic occupancy models. Ecosphere **8**(9), e01944 (2017)

7. Galinina, O., et al.: Capturing spatial randomness of heterogeneous cellular/WLAN deployments with dynamic traffic. IEEE J. Sel. Areas Commun. **32**(6), 1083–1099 (2014). Art. no. 6824742

8. Granier, A.: A new method of sap flow measurement in tree stems. Annales des Sciences Forestières **42**, 193–200 (1985)

9. Hyndman, R.J., Koehler, A.B.: Another look at measures of forecast accuracy. Int. J. Forecast. **22**(2), 679–688 (2006)

10. Fan, J., et al.: Evaluation of SVM, ELM and four tree-based ensemble models for predicting daily reference evapotranspiration using limited meteorological data in different climates of China. Agric. For. Meteorol. **263**, 225–241 (2018)

11. Kingma, D.P., Adam, B.J.L.: A Method for stochastic optimization (2015). https://arxiv.org/abs/1412.6980

12. Lewisa, B.G., Herbertb, R.D., Bellc, R.D.: The application of Fourier analysis to forecasting the inbound call time series of a call centre (2003). http://citeseerx.ist.psu.edu/viewdoc/download?doi=10.1.1.497.2540&rep=rep1&type=pdf

13. Pyattaev, A., Johnsson, K., Surak, A., Florea, R., Andreev, S., Koucheryavy, Y.: Network-assisted D2D communications: implementing a technology prototype for cellular traffic offloading. In: IEEE Wireless Communications and Networking Conference, WCNC, pp. 3266–3271, (2014). Art. no. 6953070

14. Pyattaev, A., Johnsson, K., Andreev, S., Koucheryavy, Y.: Proximity-based data offloading via network assisted device-to-device communications. In: IEEE Vehicular Technology Conference (2013). Art. no. 6692723

15. Yamaç, S.S., Todorovic, M.: Estimation of daily potato crop evapotranspiration using three different machine learning algorithms and four scenarios of available meteorological data. Agric. Water Manag. **228**, 105875 (2020)

16. Mokrani, H., Lounas, R., Bennai, M.T., Salhi, D.E., Djerbi, R.: Air quality monitoring using IoT: a survey. In: 2019 IEEE International Conference on Smart Internet of Things (SmartIoT), pp. 127–134. IEEE (August 2019)

17. Shumway, R.H., Stoffer, D.S.: Time Series Analysis and Its Applications: With R Examples. Springer Texts in Statistics, vol. 4. Springer, New York (2017). https://doi.org/10.1007/978-3-319-52452-8

18. Siqueira, J.M., Paço, T.A., Silvestre, J.C., Santos, F.L., Falcão, A.O., Pereira, L.S.: Generating fuzzy rules by learning from olive tree transpiration measurement - an algorithm to automatize Granier sap flow data analysis. Comput. Electron. Agric. **101**, 1–10 (2014)

19. Valentini, R., et al.: New tree monitoring systems: from Industry 4.0 to Nature 4.0. Ann. Silvicultural Res. **43**(2), 84–88 (2019)

20. Xu, G., Shi, Y., Sun, X., Shen, W.: Internet of Things in marine environment monitoring: a review. Sensors **19**(7), 1711 (2019)

A Jamming Latency Game
with Incomplete Information on Network
Parameters

Andrey Garnaev$^{(\boxtimes)}$

WINLAB, Rutgers University, North Brunswick, USA
garnaev@yahoo.com

Abstract. We consider the communication between a source (user) and
a destination in the presence of a jammer with latency as the user's
communication utility and two-sided incomplete information on network
parameters. We study an impact of such incomplete information on equilibrium resource assignment strategies of the user and the jammer. The
equilibrium strategies are found as a fixed point of the superposition of
the best response strategies, and numerically illustrated. Uniqueness of
equilibrium is proven.

Keywords: Latency · Bayesian equilibrium · Nash equilibrium ·
Incomplete information

1 Introduction

The shared and open-access nature of the wireless medium makes wireless networks vulnerable to hostile interference or jamming that can disrupt the communication. A key characteristics of such problems is that they involve different
agents (e.g., a user and a jammer), each of them having its own objectives. Naturally, game theory has been widely employed to model and analyze such multi-
objective problems [18]. In jamming problems, SINR (signal-to-interference-plus-
noise ratio) [2,7,10,19,25,26,29,30] are the typical metrics considered for the
user's communication utility (UCU). In [3,4,6,9,15,16,20,22,24,27,28,31], the
UCU was throughput. In [21], the UCU was an age-of-information metric, modeled by an affine function of the inverse SINR to reflect latency in information
updating. Latency as UCU was also considered in [11] and [12], modeled as the
inverse SINR and the inverse throughput correspondingly. In [11,12] and [21], the
power control problems with latency as UCU were investigated with complete
information on network parameters. In this paper we consider a complimentary
aspect to [11,12] and [21], namely, we investigate an impact of incomplete information on the network parameters on optimal power control transmission with
latency as UCU. We reduce the problem to find an equilibrium strategy to design
a fixed point of one-variable function. The suggested algorithm to find this fixed
point can be considered as a *learning* algorithm since it allows to reduce the zone
of uncertainty for the equilibrium by a half per iteration.

© Springer Nature Switzerland AG 2020
O. Galinina et al. (Eds.): NEW2AN 2020/ruSMART 2020, LNCS 12526, pp. 210–221, 2020.
https://doi.org/10.1007/978-3-030-65729-1_19

2   Communication Model

Let us consider a network with two agents, namely, a *user* and an *adversary*. The adversary is a jammer, who intends to degrade the user's communication through interference. The communication occurs on a single carrier and the channel is assumed to be flat fading. The strategy for the user is its transmission power P, with $P \in \mathbb{R}_+$ and for the jammer, its jamming power J, with $J \in \mathbb{R}_+$. Then, throughput of the transmitted signal is

$$T(P, J) = \ln(1 + \mathrm{SINR}(P, J)), \tag{1}$$

where $\mathrm{SINR}(P, J) = hP/(N + gJ)$ is SINR at the receiver, h is the source-destination fading channel gain, g is the jammer-destination channel gain (or interference channel gain), N is the background noise variance.

Note that according to Little's Law of queueing theory, in a stable system, the average number of packets in a queue equals to the product of the packet arrival rate and the average time packets spent in the queue (latency). Thus, in steady state, for a fixed queue length, the latency is proportional to the inverse arrival rate, or to the inverse throughput, since the system is stable. Thus, the inverse of the throughput, i.e., $1/T(P, J)$ relates to latency. Then, the payoffs to the user and the jammer are given as follows:

$$v_U(P, J) = -\frac{1}{T(P, J)} - C_P P, \tag{2}$$

$$v_J(P, J) = \frac{1}{T(P, J)} - C_J J, \tag{3}$$

where C_P and C_J are the transmission and jamming costs per unit transmission and jamming power correspondingly. We assume that the user and the jammer know the fading channel gains h, g, the background noise variance, N, as well as the power costs C_P and C_J. Each of the players wants to maximize its payoff. Thus, here we deal with non-zero sum game and we look for Nash equilibrium (NE) [18]. Recall that (P, J) is a NE if and only if:

$$v_U(\tilde{P}, J) \leq v_U(P, J), \ v_J(P, \tilde{J}) \leq v_J(P, J), \ \forall(\tilde{P}, \tilde{J}). \tag{4}$$

Denote this game by Γ_C.

Theorem 1. *In the game Γ_C there exists the unique NE (P, J), and it is given as follows:*

(i) if

$$(gC_P + hC_J) \ln^2 \left(1 + \frac{h}{g} \frac{C_J}{C_P}\right) \geq \frac{hg}{N} \tag{5}$$

then $J = 0$ and P is the unique positive root of

$$(1 + hP/N) \ln^2(1 + hP/N) = h/(NC_P), \tag{6}$$

which can be presented in closed form as follows:[1]

$$P = \frac{N}{h} \left(\frac{h/(C_P N)}{4 \, Lambert W^2 \left(\sqrt{h/(4 \, NC_P)} \right)} - 1 \right), \qquad (7)$$

(ii) if

$$(gC_P + hC_J) \ln^2 \left(1 + \frac{h}{g} \frac{C_J}{C_P} \right) < \frac{hg}{N} \qquad (8)$$

then

$$P = \frac{hC_J}{C_P \left(hC_J + gC_P \right) \ln^2 \left(1 + hC_J/(gC_P) \right)}, \qquad (9)$$

$$J = \frac{h}{(gC_P + hC_J) \ln^2 \left(1 + hC_J/(gC_P) \right)} - \frac{N}{g}. \qquad (10)$$

The proof can be found in Appendix 6.1

3   Uncertainty on Network Parameters

In this section we consider that the players do not know exact state of the network parameters. Namely, the players only know that the network parameters can be in state (N_i, g_i, h_i) with probability γ_i, where $i \in \mathcal{M} = \{1, \dots, M\}$ and $\sum_{i \in \mathcal{M}} \gamma_i = 1$. Then, the expected payoffs to the user and the jammer are given by:

$$V_U(P, J) = - \sum_{i \in \mathcal{M}} \frac{\gamma_i}{T_i(P, J)} - C_P P, \qquad (11)$$

$$V_J(P, J) = \sum_{i \in \mathcal{M}} \frac{\gamma_i}{T_i(P, J)} - C_J J, \qquad (12)$$

where

$$T_i(P, J) \triangleq \ln \left(1 + \text{SINR}_i(P, J) \right), \qquad (13)$$

$$\text{SINR}_i(P, J) \triangleq \frac{h_i P}{N_i + g_i J}. \qquad (14)$$

Thus, this is non-zero sum game with two-sided incomplete information on the network parameters. Denote this game by Γ_U.

Moreover the case with at least one g_i equals to zero corresponds the scenario where in state (N_i, g_i, h_i) the jammer is not active, since, in this state, the jamming power does not impact on the UCU. In this case, the game can be considered also as a Bayesian game with incomplete information whether the jammer is active or non-active. As examples of using Bayesian games we refer to [8, 13, 14, 17, 19, 23, 28].

---

[1] LambertW(x) is the unique analytic function of x being solution of the equation $y \exp(y) = x$..

Theorem 2. *In the game Γ_U, there is at least one NE.*

The proof can be found in Appendix 6.2.

By (11) and (12), (P, J) is NE if and only if each of these strategies is the best response to the other, i.e., they are solution of the best response equations (BRE):

$$P = \mathrm{BR}_U(J) = \mathrm{argmax}\,\{V_U(P, J) : P \in \mathbb{R}_+\}, \tag{15}$$

$$J = \mathrm{BR}_J(P) = \mathrm{argmax}\,\{V_J(P, J) : J \in \mathbb{R}_+\}. \tag{16}$$

To prove uniqueness of the NE as well as to design NE we will use a constructive approach directly solving the BRE.

3.1 Auxiliary Notations and Results

In this section we introduce auxiliary notations and results used in the next section to derive the equilibrium. Let

$$M_{U,i}(P, J) \triangleq \frac{h_i}{(N_i + g_i J + h_i P)T_i^2(P, J)}, \tag{17}$$

$$M_{J,i}(P, J) \triangleq \frac{h_i g_i P}{(N_i + g_i J)(N_i + g_i J + h_i P)T_i^2(P, J)}, \tag{18}$$

$$M_U(P, J) \triangleq \sum_{i \in \mathcal{M}} \gamma_i M_{U,i}(P, J), \tag{19}$$

$$M_J(P, J) \triangleq \sum_{i \in \mathcal{M}} \gamma_i M_{J,i}(P, J). \tag{20}$$

In the following proposition we establish monotonous properties of $M_U(P, J)$.

Proposition 1. **(a)** *For a fixed $J \geq 0$, $M_U(P, J)$ decreases from infinity for $P \downarrow 0$ to zero for $P \uparrow \infty$.*
(b) *For a fixed $P > 0$, $M_U(P, J)$ increases from $M_U(P, 0)$ to infinity for $J \uparrow \infty$.*
(c) *For each $J \geq 0$ there exists the unique $\mathcal{P}(J)$ such that $M_U(\mathcal{P}(J), J) = C_P$.*
(d) *$\mathcal{P}(J)$ is continuous and strictly increases to infinity while $J \uparrow \infty$.*

The proof can be found in Appendix 6.3.

In the following proposition we establish monotonous properties of $M_J(P, J)$.

Proposition 2. **(a)** *For a fixed $J \geq 0$, $M_J(P, J)$ decreases from infinity for $P \downarrow 0$ to zero for $P \uparrow \infty$.*
(b) *For a fixed $P > 0$, $M_J(P, J)$ decreases from $M_J(P, 0)$ for $J = 0$ to $M_J(P, \infty) = \sum_{i \in \mathcal{M}} \gamma_i g_i/(h_i P)$ for $J \uparrow \infty$.*
(c) *There are the unique P_0 and P_∞ such that $M_J(P_0, 0) = C_J$ and $M_J(P_\infty, \infty) = C_J$. Moreover, $P_\infty < P_0$ and $P_\infty = \sum_{i \in \mathcal{M}} \gamma_i g_i/(h_i C_J)$.*
(d) *If $M_J(P, 0) < C_J$ then $M_J(P, J) < C_J$ for $J \geq 0$.*
(e) *If $M_J(P, \infty) > C_J$ then $M_J(P, J) > C_J$ for $J \geq 0$.*
(f) *If $M_J(P, \infty) < C_J < M_J(P, 0)$ then there is the unique $\mathcal{J}(P)$ such that $M_J(P, \mathcal{J}(P)) = C_J$.*
(g) *$\mathcal{J}(P)$ is continuous in $(P_\infty, P_0]$ and strictly decreases from infinity for $P \downarrow P_\infty$ to zero for $P = P_0$.*

The proof can be found in Appendix 6.4.

3.2 Best Response Strategies

In this Section based on the established monotonous properties of $M_U(P, J)$ and $M_J(P, J)$ we derive the best response strategies.

Proposition 3. (a) *The user's best response strategy is*

$$BR_U(J) = \mathcal{P}(J). \tag{21}$$

(**b**) *The jammer's best response strategy is*

$$BR_J(P) = \begin{cases} \infty, & P \leq P_\infty, \\ \mathcal{J}(P), & P_\infty < P < P_0, \\ 0, & P_0 \leq P. \end{cases} \tag{22}$$

The proof can be found in Appendix 6.5.

3.3 Uniqueness of Nash Equilibrium

In this section we prove uniqueness of NE as well as design NE. Moreover, user's equilibrium strategy will be found as fixed point of the superposition of the best response strategies.

Theorem 3. *In the game* Γ_U, *NE* (P, J) *is unique, and*

(a) *if* $P_0 \leq \mathcal{P}(0)$ *then* $(P, J) = (\mathcal{P}(0), 0)$,
(b) *if* $P_0 > \mathcal{P}(0)$ *then* $(P, J) = (P_\star, \mathcal{J}(P_\star))$, *where* $P_\star$ *is the unique root in* $(P_\infty, P_0]$ *of*

$$\varphi(P_\star) = 0, \tag{23}$$

where

$$\varphi(P) \triangleq \mathcal{P}(\mathcal{J}(P)) - P.$$

Moreover, due to $\varphi(P)$ *is strictly decreasing in* $(P_\infty, P_0]$ *from infinity for* $P \downarrow P_\infty$ *to* $\mathcal{P}(0) - P_0$ *for* $P = P_0$, *the* $P_\star$ *can be found via the bisection method.*

See, for example, [1, 5] as the other application of the bisection methods.
    The proof of Theorem 3 can be found in Appendix 6.6.

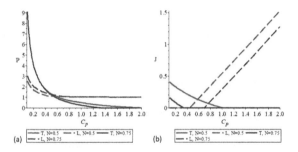

Fig. 1. (a) User's strategy and (b) jammer's strategy as functions on C_P for $N \in \{0.5, 0.7\}$ and $h = g == C_J = 1$.

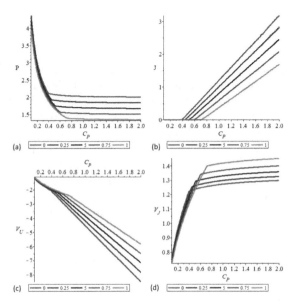

Fig. 2. (a) User's strategy, (b) jammer's strategy, (c) user's payoff and (d) jammer's payoff in game Γ_U as functions on C_P for $\gamma \in \{0, 0.25, 0.5, 0.75, 1\}$ $n = 2$, $(\gamma_1, \gamma_2) = (\gamma, 1 - \gamma)$, $N = (0.75, 5)$, $h = (1, 3)$, $g = (1, 6)$ and $C_J = 1$.

4   Discussion of the Results

One may wonder how the strategies of the user compare when 1/throughput is used as a metric instead of the well studied throughput metric. In this section we discuss some interesting differences. By [16, Corollary 2], it can be seen, when the metric is throughput and it holds that $C_P \geq h/N$, the user avoids to communicate, i.e. $P = 0$, and the delay is infinite. In particular, Fig. 1 illustrates that (a) if $N = 0.5$ then $P = 0$ for $C_P \geq 2$ and (b) if $N = 0.7$. then $P = 0$ for $C_P \geq 1.33$. While, if the metric is 1/throughput, Theorem 1 suggests that the user tries to communicate under any network conditions, i.e., $P > 0$. Moreover, for $C_P \uparrow \infty$, (8) always holds. Thus, the jammer also is active (i.e. $J > 0$) for enough large C_P, and, by (9), J is asymptotic equivalent to $gC_P/(hC_J^2)$, while P tends to $g/(hC_P)$ (Fig. 1). Thus, even under large transmission cost the user tries to communicate. *Thus, the latency metric used here might be better for emergency communications*, during which the user needs to have constant communication with the receiver. Figure 2 illustrates, for an example of the network when its communication parameters can be in two state (1-good and 2 - bad), that an increase in probability that the network parameters occur in bad state leads to an increase in the user's transmission power, what makes the jammer also to increase jamming power and the user's payoff decreases. Finally note that the suggested algorithm to find the user's equilibrium strategy as fixed point can be considered as a *learning* algorithm since it allows to reduce the zone of uncertainty for the equilibrium by a half per iteration.

5   Conclusions

A power control problem under jamming with latency metric (modeled by inverse to throughput) for user's communication has been studied in game-theoretical framework. We have reduced the problem to find an equilibrium strategy to design a fixed point of one-variable function. The suggested algorithm based on the bisection method to design this fixed point can be considered as a learning algorithm since it allows to reduce the zone of uncertainty for the equilibrium by a half per iteration. We have proven that independent on information on the network parameters the user communicates with the receiver under any network condition. Thus, such metric latency might be more appropriate for emergency communications, during which the user needs to use any chance to communicate with the receiver.

6   Appendix

6.1   Proof of Theorem 1

Note that P is the best response to J if and only if:

$$\frac{\partial v_U(P,J)}{\partial P} = \frac{h}{(N+gJ+hP)T^2(P,J)} - C_P$$
$$\begin{cases} = 0, & P > 0, \\ \leq 0, & P = 0. \end{cases} \tag{24}$$

Also, J is the best response to P if and only if:

$$\frac{\partial v_J(P,J)}{\partial J} = \frac{hgP}{(N+gJ)(N+gJ+hP)T^2(P,J)} - C_J$$
$$\begin{cases} = 0, & J > 0, \\ \leq 0, & J = 0. \end{cases} \tag{25}$$

By (24), $P > 0$. Then, by (24), we have that

$$\frac{h}{(N + gJ + hP)T^2(P, J)} = C_P \text{ for any } P. \tag{26}$$

Thus, we have separately consider only two cases: (I) $J = 0$ and (II) $J > 0$.

(I) Let $J = 0$. Substituting this $J = 0$ into (25) and (26) yield:

$$\frac{hgP}{N(N + hP)T^2(P, 0)} \le C_J, \tag{27}$$

$$\frac{h}{(N + hP)T^2(P, 0)} = C_P. \tag{28}$$

Eq. (28) is equivalent to (6). Dividing (27) by (28) and solving the obtained inequality on P implies $P \le NC_J/(gC_P)$. Substituting this upper-bound on P into left-side of (6) and taking into account that the left-side of (6) increases with P implies (5), and (a) follows.

(II) Let $J > 0$. Then, by (25),

$$\frac{hgP}{(N + gJ)(N + gJ + hP)T^2(P, J)} = C_J. \tag{29}$$

Dividing (29) by (26) implies

$$\text{SINR}(P, J) = hC_J/(gC_P). \tag{30}$$

While (29) can be present as follows:

$$\frac{\text{SINR}(P, J)}{1 + \text{SINR}(P, J)} \times \frac{g/(N + gJ)}{\ln^2(1 + \text{SINR}(P, J))} = C_J. \tag{31}$$

Substituting (30) into (31) and solving the obtained equation on J implies that J is given by (10). Substituting (10) into (30) and solving the obtained equation on P implies P is given by (9), and the result follows. ∎

6.2   Proof of Theorem 2

Note that

$$\frac{\partial^2 V_U(P, J)}{\partial P^2} = -\sum_{i \in \mathcal{M}} \frac{\gamma_i h_i^2 (2 + T_i(P, J))}{(N + g_i J + h_i P)^2 T_i^3(P, J)} \le 0.$$

Thus, $V_U(P, J)$ is concave in P. Also,

$$\frac{\partial^2 V_J(P, J)}{\partial J^2} = -\sum_{i \in \mathcal{M}} \frac{\gamma_i h_i g_i^2 P(2N_i + 2g_i J + h_i P)}{(N_i + g_i J + h_i P)^2}$$

$$\times \frac{\Phi(\text{SINR}_i(P, J))}{(N_i + g_i J)^2 T_i^3(P, J)}, \tag{32}$$

where $\Phi(x) \triangleq \ln(1+x) - 2x/(2+x)$. Note that

$$\Phi(x) > 0 \text{ for } x > 0, \tag{33}$$

since $\Phi(0) = 0$ and $\frac{d\Phi(x)}{dx} = \frac{x^2}{(1+x)(2+x)^2} > 0$ for $x > 0$. So, by (32), $\frac{\partial^2 V_J(P,J)}{\partial J^2} < 0$. Thus, $V_J(P, J)$ is concave on J. Thus, by Nash Theorem, at least one equilibrium exists. ∎

6.3   Proof of Proposition 1

(a) follows from (17) and (19). By (17), we have that

$$\frac{\partial M_{U,i}(P, J)}{\partial J} = \frac{h_i g_i F(\text{SINR}_i(P, J))}{T_i^3(P, J)(N_i + h_i P + g_i J)^2}, \tag{34}$$

where $F(x) \triangleq 2x - \ln(1+x)$. Note that

$$F(x) > 0 \text{ for } x > 0, \tag{35}$$

since $F(0) = 0$ and

$$\frac{dF(x)}{dx} = 2 - 1/(1+x) > 0 \text{ for } x \geq 0.$$

Thus, $\frac{\partial M_{U,i}(P,J)}{\partial J} > 0$, and, by (19), $\frac{\partial M_U(P,J)}{\partial J} > 0$, and (b) follows. (c) follows from (a), and (d) follows from (a)–(c). ∎

6.4   Proof of Proposition 2

Note that

$$\frac{\partial M_J(P, J)}{\partial J} = \frac{\partial^2 V_J(P, J)}{\partial J^2}.$$

By proof of Theorem 2,

$$\frac{\partial^2 V_J(P, J)}{\partial J^2} < 0.$$

Thus,

$$\frac{\partial M_J(P, J)}{\partial J} < 0.$$

Also,

$$\frac{\partial M_{J,i}(P, J)}{\partial P} = -\frac{h_i g_i F(\text{SINR}_i(P, J))}{T_i^3(P, J)(N_i + h_i P + g_i J)^2}. \tag{36}$$

This jointly with (33) and (35) imply that $\frac{\partial M_{J,i}(P,J)}{\partial P} < 0$. Also, since $\lim_{x \downarrow 0} \ln(1+x)/x = 1$ we have that

$$\lim_{J \uparrow \infty} M_{J,i}(P, J) = \lim_{J \uparrow \infty} \frac{h_i g_i P}{(N_i + g_i J)^2 \ln^2\left(1 + \frac{h_i P}{N_i + g_i J}\right)}$$

$$\times \lim_{J \uparrow \infty} \frac{1}{1 + h_i P/(N_i + g_i J)} = \frac{g_i}{h_i P}. \tag{37}$$

This and (36) imply (a) and (b). (c)–(f) follow from (a) and (b). While (g) follows from (a)–(f). ∎

6.5   Proof of Proposition 3

Note that

$$\frac{\partial V_U(P,J)}{\partial P} = M_U(P,J) - C_P \text{ and } \frac{\partial V_J(P,J)}{\partial J} = M_J(P,J) - C_J,$$

and the result straightforward follows from Proposition 1 and Proposition 2. ∎

6.6   Proof of Theorem 3

Let (P,J) be solution of Eqs. (15) and (16). Let $J = \infty$. Then, by (21) and Proposition 1(d), $P = \infty$. While, by (22), $P < P_\infty$. This contradiction implies that $J \in \mathbb{R}_+$. Let $P = 0$. Then, by (21), $J = \infty$. This cannot hold by the above discussion, Thus, $P > 0$, and we have to consider separately only two cases: (I) $J = 0$ and (II) $J > 0$.

(I) Let $J = 0$. Then, by (21), $P = \mathcal{P}(0)$. This jointly with (22) imply that $P = \mathcal{P}(0) \geq P_0$, and (a) follows.

(II) Let $J > 0$. Then, by (22), $P_\infty < P < P_0$. Also, by (21) and (22), $\varphi(P) = \mathcal{P}(\mathcal{J}(P)) - P = 0$. By Proposition 1(d) and Proposition 1(g), $\varphi(P)$ is decreasing in $(P_\infty, P_0]$ from infinity for $P \downarrow P_\infty$ to $\mathcal{P}(0) - P_0$ for $P = P_0$. Thus, Eq. (23) has the inner root and it is unique if and only if $\mathcal{P}(0) < P_0$, and (b) follows. ∎

References

1. Altman, E., Avrachenkov, K., Garnaev, A.: Closed form solutions for symmetric water filling games. In: Proceedings of the 27th Conference on Computer Communications (INFOCOM), pp. 673–681 (2008)
2. Altman, E., Avrachenkov, K., Garnaev, A.: Transmission power control game with SINR as objective function. In: Altman, E., Chaintreau, A. (eds.) NET-COOP 2008. LNCS, vol. 5425, pp. 112–120. Springer, Heidelberg (2009). https://doi.org/10.1007/978-3-642-00393-6_14
3. Aziz, F., Shamma, J., Stuber, G.L.: Jammer type estimation in LTE with a smart jammer repeated game. IEEE Trans. Veh. Technol. **66**, 7422–7431 (2017)
4. Aziz, F.M., Shamma, J.S., Stuber, G.L.: Resilience of LTE networks against smart jamming attacks. In: Proceedings of the IEEE Global Communications Conference (GLOBECOM), pp. 734–739 (2014)
5. Baston, V., Garnaev, A.: A search game with a protector. Nav. Res. Logist. **47**, 85–96 (2000)
6. El-Bardan, R., Brahma, S., Varshney, P.K.: Strategic power allocation with incomplete information in the presence of a jammer. IEEE Trans. Commun. **64**, 3467–3479 (2016)

7. Feng, Z., et al.: Power control in relay-assisted anti-jamming systems: a Bayesian three-layer Stackelberg game approach. IEEE Access **7**, 14623–14636 (2019)
8. Garnaev, A.: A remark on a helicopter and submarine game. Nav. Res. Logist. **40**, 745–753 (1993)
9. Garnaev, A., Hayel, Y., Altman, E., Avrachenkov, K.: Jamming game in a dynamic slotted ALOHA network. In: Jain, R., Kannan, R. (eds.) GameNets 2011. LNICST, vol. 75, pp. 429–443. Springer, Heidelberg (2012). https://doi.org/10.1007/978-3-642-30373-9_30. https://link.springer.com/chapter/10.1007%2F978-3-642-30373-9_30
10. Garnaev, A., Petropulu, A., Trappe, W., Poor, H.V.: A power control game with uncertainty on the type of the jammer. In: Proceedings of the IEEE Global Conference on Signal and Information Processing (GlobalSIP) (2019)
11. Garnaev, A., Petropulu, A., Trappe, W., Poor, H.V.: A multi-jammer game with latency as the user's communication utility. IEEE Commun. Lett. **24**, 1899–1903 (2020). https://doi.org/10.1109/LCOMM.2020.2995661
12. Garnaev, A., Petropulu, A., Trappe, W., Poor, H.V.: A switching transmission game with latency as the user's communication utility. In: Proceedings of the IEEE International Conference on Acoustics, Speech and Signal Processing (ICASSP), pp. 2912–2916 (2020)
13. Garnaev, A., Trappe, W.: Secret communication when the eavesdropper might be an active adversary. In: Jonsson, M., Vinel, A., Bellalta, B., Belyaev, E. (eds.) MACOM 2014. LNCS, vol. 8715, pp. 121–136. Springer, Cham (2014). https://doi.org/10.1007/978-3-319-10262-7_12
14. Garnaev, A., Trappe, W.: One-time spectrum coexistence in dynamic spectrum access when the secondary user may be malicious. IEEE Trans. Inf. Forensics Secur. **10**, 1064–1075 (2015)
15. Garnaev, A., Trappe, W.: Bargaining over the fair trade-off between secrecy and throughput in OFDM communications. IEEE Trans. Inf. Forensics Secur. **12**, 242–251 (2017)
16. Garnaev, A., Trappe, W.: The rival might be not smart: revising a CDMA jamming game. In: Proceedings of the IEEE Wireless Communications and Networking Conference (WCNC) (2018)
17. Garnaev, A., Trappe, W., Kung, C.-T.: Optimizing scanning strategies: selecting scanning bandwidth in adversarial RF environments. In: Proceedings of the 8th International Conference on Cognitive Radio Oriented Wireless Networks (CROWNCOM), pp. 148–153 (2013)
18. Han, Z., Niyato, D., Saad, W., Basar, T., Hjrungnes, A.: Game Theory in Wireless and Communication Networks: Theory, Models, and Applications. Cambridge University Press, Cambridge (2012)
19. Jia, L., Yao, F., Sun, Y., Niu, Y., Zhu, Y.: Bayesian Stackelberg game for antijamming transmission with incomplete information. IEEE Comm. Lett. **20**, 1991–1994 (2016)
20. Li, T., Song, T., Liang, Y.: Multiband transmission under jamming: a game theoretic perspective. In: Wireless Communications under Hostile Jamming: Security and Efficiency, pp. 155–187. Springer, Singapore (2018). https://doi.org/10.1007/978-981-13-0821-5_6
21. Nguyen, G., Kompella, S., Kam, C., Wieselthier, J., Ephremides, A.: Impact of hostile interference on information freshness: a game approach. In: Proceedings of the 15th International Symposium on Modeling and Optimization in Mobile, Ad Hoc, and Wireless Networks (WiOpt) (2017)

22. Sagduyu, Y. E., Berry, R., Ephremides, A.: MAC games for distributed wireless network security with incomplete information of selfish and malicious user types. In: Proceedings of the International Conference on Game Theory for Networks (2009)
23. Sagduyu, Y.E., Berry, R.A., Ephremides, A.: Jamming games in wireless networks with incomplete information. IEEE Commun. Mag. **49**, 112–118 (2011)
24. Tang, X., Ren, P., Wang, Y., Du, Q., Sun, L.: Securing wireless transmission against reactive jamming: a Stackelberg game framework. In: Proceedings of the IEEE Global Communications Conference (GLOBECOM) (2015)
25. Wang, K., Yuan, L., Miyazaki, T., Chen, Y., Zhang, Y.: Jamming and eavesdropping defense in green cyber-physical transportation systems using a Stackelberg game. IEEE Trans. Ind. Inform. **14**, 4232–4242 (2018)
26. Xiao, L., Chen, T., Liu, J., Dai, H.: Anti-jamming transmission Stackelberg game with observation errors. IEEE Comm. Lett. **19**, 949–952 (2015)
27. Xiao, L., Xie, C., Chen, T., Dai, H., Poor, H.V.: A mobile offloading game against smart attacks. IEEE Access **4**, 2281–2291 (2016)
28. Xu, Y., et al.: A one-leader multi-follower Bayesian-Stackelberg game for anti-jamming transmission in UAV communication networks. IEEE Access **6**, 21697–21709 (2018)
29. Yang, D., Xue, G., Zhang, J., Richa, A., Fang, X.: Coping with a smart jammer in wireless networks: a Stackelberg game approach. IEEE Trans. Wirel. Commun. **12**, 4038–4047 (2013)
30. Yang, D., Zhang, J., Fang, X., Richa, A., Xue, G.: Optimal transmission power control in the presence of a smart jammer. In: Proceedings of the IEEE Global Communications Conference (GLOBECOM), pp. 5506–5511 (2012)
31. Zhu, Q., Saad, W., Han, Z., Poor, H. V., Basar, T.: Eavesdropping and jamming in next-generation wireless networks: a game-theoretic approach. In: Proceedings of the IEEE Military Communications Conference (MILCOM), pp. 119–124 (2011)

Analytical Model of Early HARQ
Feedback Prediction

Tatiana Rykova[✉][ID], Barış Göktepe[ID], Thomas Schierl[ID],
and Cornelius Hellge[ID]

Fraunhofer Heinrich-Hertz-Institute, Einsteinufer 37, 10587 Berlin, Germany
{tatiana.rykova,baris.goektepe,thomas.schierl,
cornelius.hellge}@hhi.fraunhofer.de
https://www.hhi.fraunhofer.de

Abstract. We propose analytical model that investigates early Hybrid
Automatic Repeat reQuest (HARQ) prediction scheme as a path towards
Ultra-Reliable Low Latency Communication (URLLC). By incorporat-
ing early-HARQ (e-HARQ) and HARQ functionalities in terms of two
phases in a model, we can evaluate the performance of their parallel
processing. Moreover, we perform comparative analysis of the e-HARQ
model with a random predictor model and a model that covers a traditional HARQ approach. We show a benefit of e-HARQ model in terms
of various performance measures. We employ realistic data for transition
probabilities obtained by means of 5G link-level simulations into e-HARQ
model to get the evaluations of the main performance measures, such as
false-negative and false-positive probabilities, in a fast and accurate way.
The proposed model can be used as an efficient tool to get a quick estimate of the performance measures when selecting a classification-based
parameter in an e-HARQ mechanism.

Keywords: Analytical model · Stationary distribution · Performance
measures · 5G mobile communication · Low latency communication ·
HARQ · Early HARQ · Link-level simulation

1 Introduction

The achievable latency and reliability performance of the current Rel. 15 and
Rel. 16 Fifth Generation (5G) specifications, has driven the 3rd Generation
Partnership Project (3GPP) to set the objectives for enhancing use cases with
tight requirements, e.g.. Industrial Internet of Things (IIOT) services [16] and
URLLC with a target error rate of less than 10^{-5} and 1 ms end-to-end latency [4].
Among the research directions listed in [16] that aim to meet stringent URLLC
latency requirements is the User Equipment (UE) feedback HARQ enhancement.
In the past of mobile networks, HARQ has proven to be a reliable trade-off
mechanism between latency and spectral efficiency [6]. It operates on a physical
level by providing the transmitter the feedback data: ACK in case of successful

© Springer Nature Switzerland AG 2020
O. Galinina et al. (Eds.): NEW2AN 2020/ruSMART 2020, LNCS 12526, pp. 222–239, 2020.
https://doi.org/10.1007/978-3-030-65729-1_20

decode and NACK in case of an error that launches a retransmission process at higher target Block Error Rates (BLERs). However, it poses a bottleneck on a URLLC transmission, which is known as Round Trip Time (RTT) - a time interval between the initial transmission and the retransmission process.

In [12], an RTT reduction is achieved by shortening the actual transmission length to one Orthogonal Frequency Division Multiplexing (OFDM) symbol. However, it imposes higher requirements on both the receiver's instantaneous processing bandwidth and the transmitter's power constraint. Furthermore, even performing the transmissions on small multiples of OFDM symbols can reduce the latency only to a certain limit defined by HARQ RTT. Another approach approved in Rel. 16 comprises autonomous transmission of a number of redundant versions of data that is required to achieve reliability target until the first ACK is received [11]. Nevertheless, it obviously degrades the spectral efficiency in a way that more transmissions than required may be sent due to the processing and feedback delays. The processing time is recognized as the major part of RTT latency, and is mainly dominated by the decoding procedure at the receiver [8]. Therefore, predicting the decoder's outcome prior to actual decoding allows generating an early feedback ACK/NACK respond, which leads to overall HARQ latency reduction. Significant research effort has been done on the prediction of the instantaneous decoder outcome, also known as e-HARQ prediction. Most of the e-HARQ approaches are based on the estimation of Bit Error Rate (BER) found from the Log-Likelihood Ratios (LLRs) of bits as the input to the decoder and hard thresholding as classification algorithms [2,3,7,10]. In [10], the predictions are based on a Gaussian approximation of the likelihood ratios, which leads to a performance degradation when their distributions deviate from approximation. In [2,3], techniques based on LLRs for predicting the outcome of turbo decoder are proposed and e-HARQ performance in terms of misprediction rates is studied. In [3], the prediction is performed based on a small number of decoding operations on the received subcodes. Moreover, the machine learning techniques that predict the decoding outcome in compliance with subcodes are studied in [17]. The authors expand this approach in [18] and present a system model that incorporates scheduling effects for the system evaluation of e-HARQ. Other research papers, such as [5,9,13,15], study feedback prediction methods based on channel state estimation.

In this paper we propose analytical models that evaluate the behavior of e-HARQ prediction. To the best of our knowledge, this is the first time an analytical model using e-HARQ principle has been devised that covers the parallel processing of e-HARQ and HARQ mechanisms. In the experimental part, the analysis of the main performance measures found from the stationary distribution is conducted. Although simulation studies are among the widely used performance evaluation techniques, analytical modelling has its own benefits. A closed-form description of a networking architecture paves the way for network designers to have a quick estimate of the performance of their design, without the need to spend considerable time for simulation studies or expensive experimental setup.

The paper is organized as follows: in Sect. 2 we introduce the main aspects of e-HARQ and HARQ mechanisms. In Sect. 2.1 we describe a system model with a random predictor, derive its steady-state probability distribution. We also introduce a special case of the given model - a traditional HARQ scheme. A system model with an incorporated e-HARQ and HARQ schemes is introduced in Sect. 2.2, along with the stationary probability distribution and performance measures. Section 3 presents numerical results and comparative analysis of three schemes. Finally, Sect. 4 concludes the paper.

2 Introduction to e-HARQ and HARQ

As in LTE, 5G has adopted Orthogonal Frequency Division Multiplexing Access (OFDMA) due its scheduling flexibility, and therefore, a resource here means a part of channel bandwidth both in frequency (a number of subcarriers) and time (a number of OFDM symbols). Both regular HARQ and e-HARQ mechanisms can identify packet failure at the UE and request for a retransmission, which is provided after T_{RTT} from the actual transmission start, where RTT – is the Round-Trip Time. The main difference between two schemes is that the e-HARQ has a distinctive ability to predict packet's decodability and transmit ACK/NACK respond to gNB earlier, and therefore, reduce RTT. We assume n_0 to be a number of propagation time slots between the gNB and the UE. The e-HARQ prediction algorithm starts processing the data as soon as n_1 OFDM symbols are received at the UE and continues processing for n_2 time slots. Therefore, the ACK/NACK respond generated by the e-HARQ scheme reaches the gNB in $2n_0 + n_1 + n_2$ time slots from the beginning of the transmission, and then a retransmission may take place. To preserve the general terms, we assume that transmission length takes n_3 time slots, whereas the regular HARQ processing lasts for n_4 time slots. Given the notations, gNB can start retransmission based on the regular HARQ mechanism in $2n_0 + n_3 + n_4$ time slots, as shown in Fig. 1.

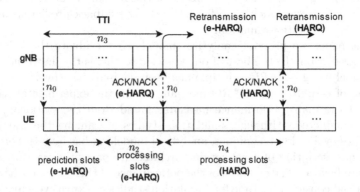

Fig. 1. Comparison of HARQ and eHARQ schemes in terms of timing.

The HARQ time line is mainly comprised by the processing time, which may scale with the TTI length [1], and the propagation time, which is independent of the TTI length. In the model, we take into account the scalability of the processing time, by equating $n_1 = n_2$ and $n_3 = n_4$. Since we are mostly interested in URLLC applications (tactile internet, industrial automation), where UEs are mainly located close to gNB, the propagation time can be considered insignificant and is supposed in the model to be zero. Furthermore, we assume that $n_1 + n_2 = n_3$, which means that at time moment n_3 we already have the e-HARQ FeedBack (e-FB) message at gNB, and may start the retransmission process. With all retransmissions needed for the successful transmission the request has to be transmitted to the UE in T_c time slots, otherwise we assume that the delay constraint is not sustained, and the packet is lost.

2.1 System Model with Random Predictor and HARQ

Let us perform analysis of one UE in a 5G network that receives a packet from a gNB, performs feedback generation based on a random predictor at the first phase, and then process it with a HARQ scheme at the second phase. We assume packets to be of the same length equal to an actual transmission length. The packet may be retransmitted until its successful reception or loss, in case a packet delay constraint T_c is not fulfilled. The structure of the proposed analytical model with two phases that constitute to random predictor and HARQ, respectively, is shown in Fig. 2.

The functioning of the system is given in discrete time with the length $n = n_3$, during which we have to receive and process a packet in order to generate a feedback response. So we assume that all the changes in the system occur at time moments $nh, h = 1, 2, \ldots$. A packet arrives at the first phase with the probability $a, 0 < a \leq 1$. If an early FeedBack (e-FB), generated by a random predictor, is ACK, then the packet continues its operation at the second phase with the probability $b_1(l)$, where l is a number of times the packet is being delivered to the UE. Otherwise, when the e-FB is NACK, the packet is to be retransmitted with the probability $\bar{b}_1(l)$. However, the processing of the previous negatively

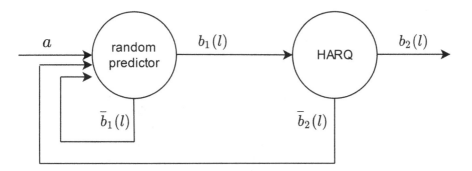

Fig. 2. The structure of the two-phase model with a random predictor and HARQ.

acknowledged packet based on a random predictor is still being done at the second phase with a deterministic probability equal to 1. The found Regular HARQ FeedBack (r-FB) allows leaving the system in case of ACK with the probability $b_2(l)$ or continuing the retransmission process in case of NACK with the probability $\bar{b}_2(l)$. If the packet reaches its delay constraint T_c, it is assumed to be lost. Note that a new packet arrives only at an empty system or in case the previous one was successfully delivered.

The functioning of the system is described by the homogeneous Markov chain ξ_n at time moments $nh, h = 1, 2 \ldots$ with the state space:

$$X = \{(0,0,0), (1,1,1), (s,l,v) : s \in \{1,2,3\},$$
$$l \in \mathbb{N}^{[\lceil \frac{v}{2} \rceil + u(s,v), v-1]}, v \in \mathbb{N}^{[2,T_c]}\}, \quad (1)$$

where v is a time slot number. Here and further, $\mathbb{N}^{[m,k]} := \{m, m+1, ..., k\}$ with $m, k \in \mathbb{N}, k > m$ is an interval of natural numbers between m and k, and

$$u(s,v) = \begin{cases} 1, & \text{if } \{s = 1\} \cap \{v = 2n, n = 2, 3, ...\}. \\ 0, & \text{otherwise.} \end{cases} \quad (2)$$

Here s demonstrates the processing at the phases and can be rewritten in a binary case for better understanding, which is presented in Table 1.

If $a, 0 < a \le 1$ the Markov chain ξ_n is aperiodic, and there exists a stationary probability distribution $[s,l,v], (s,l,v) \in X$ which is found from the balance equations:

$$a[0,0,0] = \bar{a}(\sum_{s=2}^{3} \sum_{v=2}^{T_c-1} \sum_{l=\lceil \frac{v}{2} \rceil}^{v-1} b_2(l)[s,l,v] +$$

$$+ \sum_{s=1}^{3} \sum_{l=\lceil \frac{T_c}{2} \rceil}^{T_c-1} [s,l,T_c]), \quad (3)$$

Table 1. Description of the phase states.

s	Phases State	Description
0	00	The system is empty
1	10	The packet is being received and processed at the first phase
2	01	The packet is being processed at the second phase due to ACK at the first phase
3	11	The packet is being retransmitted at the first phase because of NACK, and the negatively acknowledged packet is being processed at the second phase

$$[1,1,1] = a([0,0,0] +$$

$$+ \sum_{s=2}^{3} \sum_{v=2}^{T_c-1} \sum_{l=\lceil \frac{v}{2} \rceil}^{v-1} b_2(l)[s,l,v] + \sum_{s=1}^{3} \sum_{l=\lceil \frac{T_c}{2} \rceil}^{T_c-1} [s,l,T_c]), \quad (4)$$

$$[1,l,v] = \bar{b}_2(l-1)[2,l-1,v-1] \quad v = \overline{3,T_c}, \quad (5)$$

$$[2,l,v] = b_1(l) \left(\gamma(l,v)[1,l,v-1] + \bar{b}_2(l-1)\delta(l,v)[3,l-1,v-1] \right), \quad (6)$$

$$[3,l,v] = \bar{b}_1(l) \left(\gamma(l,v)[1,l,v-1] + \bar{b}_2(l-1)\delta(l,v)[3,l-1,v-1] \right), \quad (7)$$

where $l \in \{\lceil \frac{v}{2} \rceil + u(s,v), \lceil \frac{v}{2} \rceil + u(s,v) + 1, ..., v - 1\}, v \in \{2, ..., T_c\}$. Here,

$$\gamma(l,v) = \begin{cases} 1, & \text{if } l < v - 1\} \cup \{v = 2\}. \\ 0, & \text{otherwise.} \end{cases} \quad (8)$$

$$\delta(l,v) = \begin{cases} 1, & \text{if } \{l > \lceil \frac{v}{2} \rceil, v = 2n\} \cup \{v = 2n + 1\}, n = 1, 2, ... \\ 0, & \text{otherwise.} \end{cases} \quad (9)$$

The normalizing equation is defined as

$$\sum_{(s,l,v) \in X} [s,l,v] = 1, \quad (10)$$

Main performance measures. The balance equations along with the normalising condition allows finding the stationary probability distribution $[s,l,v]$, $(s,l,v) \in X$ and get the main performance measures. Let us designate X_{quit} as the set of states in which a packet can quit the system either successfully or unsuccessfully. Hence, it is defined as

$$X_{\text{quit}} := \{(s,l,v) : s \in \{2,3\}, l \in \mathbb{N}^{[\lceil \frac{v}{2} \rceil, v-1]}, v \in \mathbb{N}^{[2,T_c]}\}$$

$$\cup \{(1,l,T_c) : l \in \mathbb{N}^{[\lceil \frac{T_c}{2} \rceil + u(1,T_c), T_c - 1]}\}. \quad (11)$$

Then the probability of a packet not being serviced aka blocking probability, is given as

$$\pi = \sum_{x \in X_{\text{quit}}} P_{\text{quit}}(x)(1 - B(x)) \quad (12)$$

where $B(x), x \in X_{\text{quit}}$ is defined as

$$B(x) := \begin{cases} 0, & \text{if } s_x = 1 \\ b_2(l_x), & \text{if } (s_x = 2 \text{ or } s_x = 3) \text{ and } v_x = T_c, \\ 1, & \text{otherwise} \end{cases} \quad (13)$$

and $P_{quit} : X_{quit} \rightarrow [0, 1]$ is a conditional probability that a packet no matter how, successfully or not, quits the system at state $x, x \in X_{quit}$:

$$P_{quit}(x) := \frac{b_{quit}(x)[x]}{\sum_{x \in X_{quit}} b_{quit}(x)[x]}, \tag{14}$$

where

$$b_{quit}(x) := \begin{cases} b_2(l_x), & \text{if } (s_x = 2 \text{ or } s_x = 3) \text{ and } v_x < T_c \\ 1, & \text{otherwise} \end{cases} . \tag{15}$$

The mean number of deliveries is calculated analogously

$$M = \sum_{x \in X_{quit}} P_{quit}(x)L(x) \tag{16}$$

where $L(x)$ the number of deliveries at state x is defined as

$$L(x) := \begin{cases} l_x - 1 & \text{if } s_x = 1 \\ l_x & \text{if } s_x = 2 \text{ or } s_x = 3 \end{cases} . \tag{17}$$

The mean spending time of a packet in the system, which has been successfully transmitted, is calculated as

$$T = \sum_{x \in X_{quit}} P_{success}(x)v_x, \tag{18}$$

where $P_{success}(x) : X_{quit} \rightarrow [0, 1]$ is defined as $P_{quit}(x)$ with b_{quit} being replaced by $b_{success}$:

$$b_{success}(x) := \begin{cases} b_2(l_x), & \text{if } s_x = 2 \text{ or } s_x = 3 \\ 0, & \text{otherwise} \end{cases} . \tag{19}$$

The probability of the system being idle is:

$$P_0 = [0, 0, 0] . \tag{20}$$

In general, the errors of the e-HARQ scheme are classified into false negative errors (e-HARQ predicts NACK, whereas HARQ sends ACK), and false positive ones (e-HARQ predicts ACK, whereas HARQ sends NACK respond). False negative predictions result in unnecessary transmissions, which degrade spectral efficiency of the HARQ scheme but have no impact on latency and reliability, i.e. BLER. Therefore, false negative errors can be tolerated up to a certain limit. False positive errors correspond to a predictor's failure since it was not able to get a corresponding transmission. Most of the defined e-HARQ predictors use a predefined threshold value in their algorithms as a classification mechanism between ACK and NACK. Therefore, the selection of a threshold value is critical for the performance value of e-HARQ. The false negative probability of a random predictor is computed as

$$P_{FN} = \sum_{v=2}^{T_c} \sum_{l=\lceil \frac{v}{2} \rceil}^{v-1} b_2(l)[3, l, v], \tag{21}$$

whereas the false positive probability of a random predictor is computed as

$$P_{FP} = \sum_{v=2}^{T_c} \sum_{l=\lceil \frac{v}{2} \rceil}^{v-1} \overline{b}_2(l)[2, l, v].$$ (22)

Note that in case $b_1(l)$ is equal to 1, we arrive at a specific case of traditional HARQ operation, i.e. all of the states obtained due to a retransmission attempt at the first phase have steady-state probabilities equal to 0. We will show this behavior in a comparative analysis demonstrated in Sect. 3.

2.2 System Model with e-HARQ Predictor and HARQ

The randomness of the predictor in the model described in the previous subsection can be partly overcome by adding a transition probability $b_3(l)$ at the second phase. Here, the transition probability $b_1(l)$ does not differ from the previously defined in Sect. 2.1, however we have to clarify the difference between $b_2(l)$ and $b_3(l)$ that can be expressed in terms of the feedback (RVs) $p, d \in \{\text{ACK}, \text{NACK}\}$ as

$$b_2(l) := P(d_l = \text{ACK}|p_l = \text{ACK}) \text{ and}$$ (23)
$$b_3(l) := P(d_l = \text{ACK}|p_l = \text{NACK}),$$ (24)

where p and d represent the eHARQ and HARQ feedback, respectively. By adding a $b_3(l)$ transition probability and setting the dependence between the feedback generated at the first phase and HARQ's decision at the second phase in terms of transition probabilities, we achieve a system model that can be used for analysis of existing e-HARQ prediction schemes. Figure 3 demonstrates

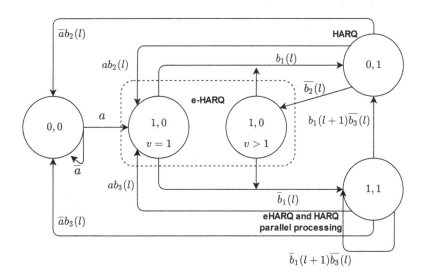

Fig. 3. Transition probabilities of e-HARQ model in terms of s phase states.

a graph of transition probabilities with a $b_3(l)$ parameter for various s phase states. Note that the binary representation of the phase states may be seen as follows: the position of one stems for the phase operation.

The introduced $b_3(l)$ transition probability slightly changes the balance equations defined in Sect. 2.1 by modifying index from $b_2(l)$ to $b_s(l)$ in (3), (4), and from $\bar{b}_2(l)$ to $\bar{b}_3(l)$ in (6) and (7). Based on the balance equations and normalising condition the stationary probability distribution $[s, l, v], (s, l, v) \in X$ is obtained, and the main performance measures similar to the ones in Sect. 2.1 are derived, taking into account modified Eqs. (13), (15) and (19):

$$B(x) := \begin{cases} 0, & \text{if } s_x = 1 \\ b_2(l_x), & \text{if } s_x = 2 \text{ and } v_x = T_c \\ b_3(l_x), & \text{if } s_x = 3 \text{ and } v_x = T_c \\ 1, & \text{otherwise} \end{cases} \quad (25)$$

$$b_{\text{quit}}(x) := \begin{cases} b_2(l_x), & \text{if } s_x = 2 \text{ and } v_x < T_c \\ b_3(l_x), & \text{if } s_x = 3 \text{ and } v_x < T_c \\ 1, & \text{otherwise} \end{cases} \quad (26)$$

$$b_{\text{success}}(x) := \begin{cases} b_2(l_x), & \text{if } s_x = 2 \\ b_3(l_x), & \text{if } s_x = 3 \\ 0, & \text{otherwise} \end{cases} \quad (27)$$

3   Experimental Results

3.1   Link-Level Simulation Setup

To evaluate the previously described models, we extracted the required transition probabilities, i.e. $b_1(l)$, $b_2(l)$ and $b_3(l)$, from 5G-complaint link-level simulations (refer to Table 2 for simulation parameters). A slot in our analytical model equals to two OFDM symbols of our simulation where e-HARQ processes the first OFDM symbol only and HARQ processes both OFDM symbols. A packet of 360 bits have been encoded using 5G-complaint LDPC codes and mapped to an 1.08 MHz OFDM transmission using a 16-QAM modulation. The encoded signal has been transmitted over a TDL-C fading channel and processed at the receiver using frequency domain MMSE and an LDPC min-sum decoder. Furthermore, a logistic regressions (LR), as described in [18], has been used to predict the decoding outcome in the first stage. Monte-Carlo simulations with 1.7M iterations have been performed to estimate the probabilities, as described in the subsections below.

Table 2. Link-level simulation assumptions for training and test set generation.

Number of Transport Blocks (TBs)	1.7 M (0.85 M train, 0.85 M test)
TB size in bits (N_{Bits})	360
Slot duration	2 OFDM symbols
Transmission bandwidth	1.08 MHz (6 RBs)
Channel code	Rate-1/5 LDPC (see [14])
Modulation order and algorithm	16-QAM, Approximated LLR
Power allocation	Constant E_b/N_0
Waveform	3GPP OFDM, normal cyclic-prefix, 15 kHz subcarrier spacing
Channel type	1 Tx 1 Rx, TDL-C 100 ns, 2.9 GHz, 3.0 km/h
Equalizer	Frequency domain MMSE
Decoder type	Min-Sum (50 iterations)

3.2 Experimental Analysis of Random Predictor Model and HARQ

The model described in Sect. 2.1 incorporates two transition probabilities $b_1(l)$ and $b_2(l)$, where $b_1(l)$ can be chosen arbitrarily. The values for $b_2(l)$ are obtained from the link-level simulations as following:

$$b_2(l) = P(d_l = \text{ACK}|d_{l-1} = \text{NACK}). \tag{28}$$

We start experimental analysis, by comparing a random predictor model with a traditional HARQ operation in terms of the main performance measures defined in Sect. 2.1. We obtain results for the HARQ operation by considering $b_1(l)$ equal to 1 in the model with a random predictor. Moreover, to verify the model's performance we have conducted an event-based imitation analysis, in which we have went through the states of the model during 1 million of time slots. The given imitation model allows obtaining the probability distribution along with the performance measures based on the collected statistical data. For clearer visualisation of results we vary $b_1(l)$ from 0.1 to 1 for a random-predictor case, and do not differentiate the transition probabilities in terms of l number of deliveries. Moreover, we consider various constraint values T_c for both models. The values for $b_2(l)$ are taken from the link-level simulations, the assumptions of which are summarized in Table 2. The arrival rate is considered to be 0.9 for all of the simulation scenarios, which correspond to use cases that experience a transmission flow of packets.

Figure 4 shows comparison of two schemes in terms of a blocking probability along with the imitation analysis results. The small values of $b_1(l)$ correspond to frequent retransmissions, which result in a smaller blocking probability in comparison with HARQ case. By increasing $b_1(l)$ up to 1 the HARQ scenario is approached. It can be also seen that at higher T_c values, the blocking probability is getting even smaller due to the ability to conduct more retransmissions

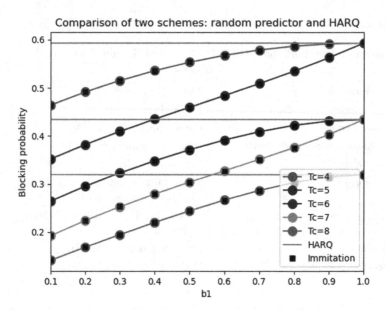

Fig. 4. Blocking probability comparison of random predictor and HARQ models.

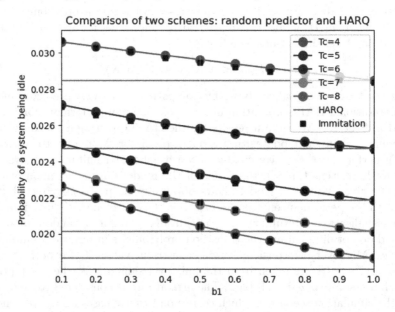

Fig. 5. Probability of a system being idle for random predictor and HARQ models.

during the given time interval. The imitation model shows very similar results to random-predictor model, which verifies the correctness of the found performance measures based on the analytical modeling. The probability of a system being idle for two schemes is demonstrated in Fig. 5, in which we obviously see the

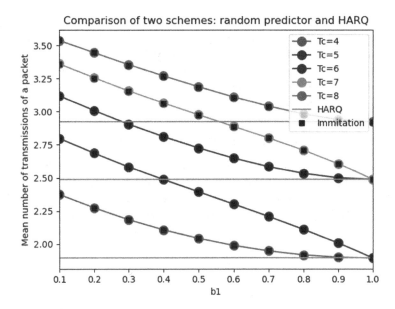

Fig. 6. Mean number of transmissions for random predictor and HARQ models.

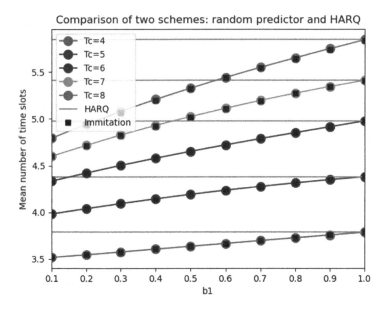

Fig. 7. Mean spending time of a packet for random predictor and HARQ models.

benefit of an incorporated random predictor compared to a traditional HARQ operation throughout all of the T_c values. Figures (6 and 7) demonstrate a mean number of deliveries and a mean spending time of a packet for various T_c values.

Please note that in Figs. (4, 6) at $b_1 = 1$ the values coincide for consequent odd and even T_c values. This is due to the fact that in odd T_c at the last time slot the packet has no ability to be successfully delivered, which result in the identical values for blocking probability and mean number of deliveries. Figure 7 demonstrates that the random-predictor scheme spends in average up to 1 time slot less in comparison with HARQ scheme for small b_1 values.

3.3   Experimental Analysis of LR e-HARQ Model

We now perform experimental analysis of the three schemes, including the random-dom predictor model, HARQ and an e-HARQ LR predictor model. Note that the performance of the LR e-HARQ predictor heavily depends on the chosen $b_1(l)$. At smaller $b_1(l)$ it operates more conservatively with sending ACKs whereas at high $b_1(l)$ it tends to send more ACKs than actually needed. Hence, the LR predictor has been tuned such that it achieves a certain $b_1(l)$ and then the other two transition probability functions $b_2(l)$ and $b_3(l)$ have been derived.

To keep the simulation and processing effort tractable the transition probabilities have been approximated as

$$b_2(l) = P(d_l = \text{ACK}|p_l = \text{ACK}, d_{l-1} = \text{NACK})$$
$$\approx 1 - \frac{P(d_l = \text{NACK}|p_l = \text{ACK})}{P(d_{l-1} = \text{NACK}|p_{l-1} = \text{ACK})} \text{ and} \quad (29)$$

$$b_3(l) = P(d_l = \text{ACK}|p_l = \text{NACK}, d_{l-1} = \text{NACK})$$
$$\approx 1 - \frac{P(d_l = \text{NACK}|p_l = \text{NACK})}{P(d_{l-1} = \text{NACK}|p_{l-1} = \text{NACK})}. \quad (30)$$

For the sake of simplicity, the threshold optimization problem has been reduced to a one-dimensional optimization problem. The $b_1(l)$ values have been initialized to the corresponding decoding probabilities $b_1(l) := P(d_l = \text{ACK}|d_{l-1} = \text{NACK})$ for threshold 1 and have been increased by a step size of 0.1 for each l, respectively. Furthermore, the transition probabilities $b_1(l)$ have been capped at 1. Hence, resulting to $b_1(l) = 1$ for all l values at threshold 10.

Figures 8 and 9 show the performance behavior of three models in terms of a blocking probability and a mean number of transmissions, respectively. All of the values for $b_i(l), i = \overline{1,3}$ are taken from the link-level simulations, and the time constraint T_c is set to be 8. The behaviour of the curves on these plots shows the obvious advantage of e-HARQ operation in comparison to a random predictor case and traditional HARQ. In terms of mean number of deliveries of a packet, the e-HARQ LR predictor achieves around 35% increase in comparison with HARQ scheme and about 26% increase compared to a random predictor for small threshold values. This increased number of deliveries in turn achieve a lower blocking probability compared to HARQ and the random predictor case.

Especially in the threshold regime of 2 and 3, e-HARQ lowers the blocking probability by approximately 13% compared to the random predictor.

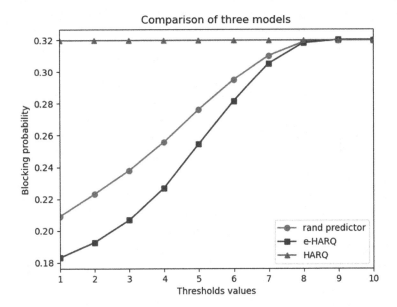

Fig. 8. Blocking probability comparison for three models.

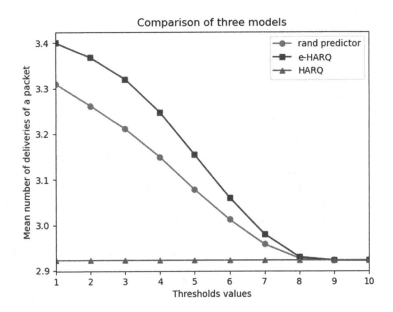

Fig. 9. Mean number of deliveries of a packet.

A similar behavior is also observable for the probability of the system being in idle state, as shown in Fig. 10. The probability of the system being in idle state is increased for the random predictor and the e-HARQ compared to the HARQ system, especially for low b_1 values.

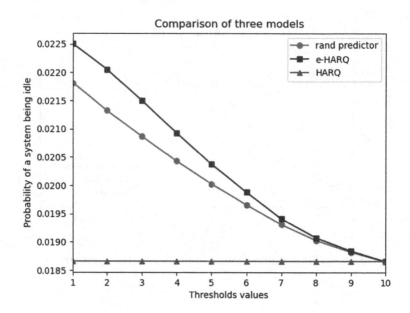

Fig. 10. Probability of a system being in idle state.

We further analyse the errors of the two models with predictors in terms of false negative and false positive probabilities demonstrated in Figs. 11 and 12. Here lies the explanation for the better performance of the e-HARQ scheme compared to the random predictor, as observed in the previous performance metrics. The e-HARQ prediction scheme clearly outperforms the one with the random predictor for both types of errors. Only at very high thresholds, corresponding to b_1 very close to 1, the performance of the two schemes start matching each other. This is an expected result since at threshold 10 ($b_1 = 1$), there is no prediction anymore since the e-HARQ predictor is always outputting ACKs. Hence, the e-HARQ and random predictor system reduces to an ordinary HARQ system.

The given behavior of various performance measures of the e-HARQ LR predictor scheme gives us a clear picture of its operation for various threshold values and can be used to select an optimal threshold for operation in a link-level system.

At last we study the mean spending time of a successful transmission, as shown in Fig. 13. The behavior of the mean spending time of a successful packet is lower at low b_1 values for the random predictor and even slightly smaller for the e-HARQ system. Hence, both random- predictor and e-HARQ schemes deliver packets faster in average compared to the HARQ system and thus both

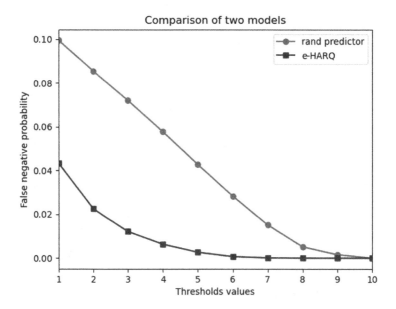

Fig. 11. False negative probability comparison for two models.

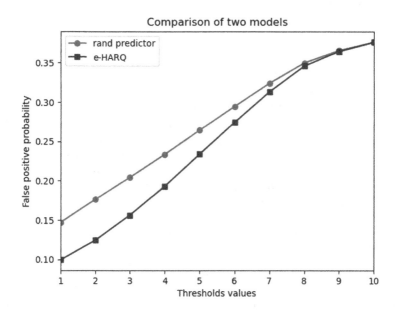

Fig. 12. False positive probability comparison for two models.

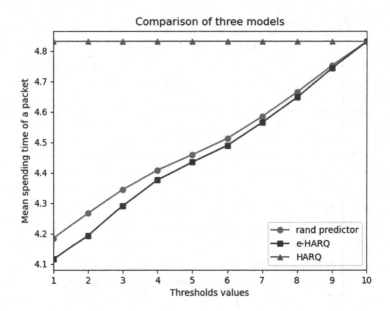

Fig. 13. Mean spending time for three models.

spend more time in idle state. Here, the e-HARQ prediction shows its advantage over the random predictor since e-HARQ can deliver more packets successfully within the same delay budget with a slightly smaller average latency.

4   Conclusion

In this paper we proposed an efficient analytical model that evaluates the behavior of the e-HARQ prediction of the HARQ decoded output. The model covers parallel processes of e-HARQ and HARQ operation, and clearly demonstrates the benefit of used e-HARQ mechanism in comparison with a traditional HARQ system in terms of main performance measures, e.g.. mean number of packet's transmissions. The proposed model can be used for network designers and architects to get a quick estimate of the threshold value when designing an e-HARQ mechanism without the need to spend considerable time for simulation studies or expensive experimental setup.

References

1. 3GPP: TR 36.881 Study on latency reduction techniques for LTE. Technical report, 3GPP (2016)
2. Berardinelli, G., Khosravirad, S.R., Pedersen, K.I., Frederiksen, F., Mogensen, P.: Enabling early HARQ feedback in 5G networks. In: 83rd IEEE Vehicular Technology Conference (VTC Spring), pp. 1–5 (2016). https://doi.org/10.1109/VTCSpring.2016.7504213

3. Berardinelli, G., Khosravirad, S.R., Pedersen, K.I., Frederiksen, F., Mogensen, P.: On the benefits of early HARQ feedback with non-ideal prediction in 5G networks. In: International Symposium on Wireless Communication Systems (ISWCS), pp. 11–15 (2016). https://doi.org/10.1109/ISWCS.2016.7600846
4. Bertenyi, B., et al.: 5G NR radio interface. J. ICT Stand. **6**(3), 31–58 (2018). https://doi.org/10.13052/jicts2245-800X.613
5. Chaitanya, T.V.K.: HARQ systems: resource allocation, feedback error protection, and bits-to-symbol mappings. Ph.D. thesis, Linköping University Electronic Presss, Linköping (2013)
6. Frederiksen, F., Kolding, T.E.: Performance and modeling of WCDMA/HSDPA transmission/H-ARQ schemes. In: Proceedings IEEE 56th Vehicular Technology Conference, vol. 1, pp. 472–476 (2002). https://doi.org/10.1109/VETECF.2002.1040388
7. Göktepe, B., Fähse, S., Thiele, L., Schierl, T., Hellge, C.: Subcode-based early HARQ for 5G. In: IEEE International Conference on Communications (ICC) Workshops (2018). https://doi.org/10.1109/ICCW.2018.8403491
8. Holma, H., Toskala, A.: LTE for UMTS: OFDMA and SC-FDMA Based Radio Access. Wiley (2009)
9. Hou, Z., She, C., Li, Y., Zhuo, L., Vucetic, B.: Prediction and communication co-design for ultra-reliable and low-latency communications. IEEE Trans. Wireless Commun. **19**(2), 1196–1209 (2020)
10. Letzepis, N., Grant, A.: Bit error estimation for turbo decoding. In: IEEE International Symposium on Information Theory, pp. 437 (2003). https://doi.org/10.1109/ISIT.2003.1228454
11. Liu, Y., Deng, Y., Elkashlan, M., Nallanathan, A., Karagiannidis, G.K.: Analyzing grant-free access for URLLC service (2020)
12. Mahmood, N.H., Abreu, R., Böhnke, R., Schubert, M., Berardinelli, G., Jacobsen, T.H.: Uplink grant-free access solutions for URLLC services in 5G new radio. In: 2019 16th International Symposium on Wireless Communication Systems (ISWCS), pp. 607–612 (2019). https://doi.org/10.1109/ISWCS.2019.8877253
13. Makki, B., Svensson, T., Caire, G., Zorzi, M.: Fast harq over finite blocklength codes: a technique for low-latency reliable communication. IEEE Trans. Wireless Commun. **18**(1), 194–209 (2019). https://doi.org/10.1109/TWC.2018.2878713
14. MCC Support: 3GPP TS 38.212 v16.0.0. Technical report, 3GPP, pp. 19–30 (2020)
15. Nadas, J., Klaine, P., Zhang, L., Zhao, G., Imran, M., Souza, R.: Performance analysis of early-harq for finite block-length packet transmission. In: 2019 IEEE International Conference on Industrial Cyber Physical Systems (ICPS), pp. 391–396 (2019). https://doi.org/10.1109/ICPHYS.2019.8780207
16. Nokia, N.S.B.: Enhanced Industrial Internet of Things (IoT) and URLLC support. Technical report RP-193233, 3GPP (2019)
17. Strodthoff, N., Göktepe, B., Schierl, T., Samek, W., Hellge, C.: Machine learning for early HARQ feedback prediction in 5G. In: IEEE Globecom (GC) Workshops. pp. 1–6 (2018). https://doi.org/10.1109/GLOCOMW.2018.8644343
18. Strodthoff, N., Göktepe, B., Schierl, T., Hellge, C., Samek, W.: Enhanced machine learning techniques for early HARQ feedback prediction in 5G. IEEE J. Sel. Areas Commun. **37**(11), 2573–2587 (2019). https://doi.org/10.1109/JSAC.2019.2934001

Analytical Model for CSMA-Based MAC Protocol for Industrial IoT Applications

Alexey Tsarev[1] (ID), Emil Khayrov[1] (ID), Ekaterina Medvedeva[1,2]([⊠]) (ID),
Yuliya Gaidamaka[1,2] (ID), and Chiara Buratti[3] (ID)

[1] Peoples' Friendship University of Russia (RUDN University), Moscow, Russia
egmedvedeva@gmail.com
[2] Federal Research Center "Computer Science and Control" of the Russian
Academy of Sciences, Moscow, Russia
[3] Wi-Lab, CNIT/DEI, University of Bologna, Bologna, Italy

Abstract. The paper provides a method for calculating characteristics of a Carrier Sense Multiple Access with Collision Avoidance (CSMA/CA) protocol to be used at the Medium Access Control (MAC) layer in an Industrial Internet of Things (IIoT) network. In particular, we consider a set of nodes equipped with sensors, deployed into an industrial machine, and having to transmit measured data to a final gateway. The gateway is equipped with multiple antennas and sweeps the entire area to gather data from the different nodes. A CSMA/CA protocol is used to limit interference among nodes. The mathematical model is based on an absorbing Discrete Time Markov Chain (DTMC) and the approach allows to estimate the average delay, the collision probability and the transmission probability by solving the system of transcendental equations. In addition, a queueing network method is also proposed for the modelling and compared to the absorbing DTMC solution. High accuracy of the absorbing DTMC method has been validated in numerical results by comparison with simulation results and with the queueing network method. The model obeys optimizing system parameters, such as the back-off time duration and other parameters of the CSMA/CA protocol.

Keywords: Industrial Internet of Things · Carrier sense multiple access with collision avoidance · Collision probability · Average delay

1 Introduction

The inclusion of ICT (Information and Communication Technology) in manufacturing processes is expected to revolutionize the industrial scenario. The Internet of Things (IoT) is one of the main enablers of this revolution; its application to industry plants is known as the Industrial IoT (IIoT). In this paper we consider a scenario where nodes, embedding sensor devices, are deployed over a machinery and provide data to a centralized control unit, denoted as Gateway (GW), through wireless links.

From the communication viewpoint, this scenario is extremely challenging: density of nodes and offered overall throughput might be extremely high; control in automation

© Springer Nature Switzerland AG 2020
O. Galinina et al. (Eds.): NEW2AN 2020/ruSMART 2020, LNCS 12526, pp. 240–258, 2020.
https://doi.org/10.1007/978-3-030-65729-1_21

processes sets very stringent requirements in terms of delays; finally, nodes miniaturization is fundamental. All these requirements cannot be fulfilled by current wireless technologies, and calls for the use of future technologies supporting Terabits per second links (Tbps) with high throughput and negligible latency [1, 2]. One of enablers for such communications in 5G+/6G networks is the terahertz (THz) band, which integration into the full communication stack is fraught with overcoming problems on a MAC, network and transport layer [3, 4]. In particular, [5] identifies challenges in building new MAC protocol design to take full advantage of THz potential benefits, including efficient channel access, control messaging, channel establishment, mobility management, and line-of-sight blocking mitigation.

In this paper, constructing the version of CSMA-based MAC protocol for IIoT we take into account the peculiarities of highly directional transmission, which is characteristic of the sub-THz or THz transmission. We assume nodes have only one antenna element, while the GW can have many, generating highly directive beams. As a result, transmission ranges are compatible with the machine level scenario addressed (one or two meters). In order to gather data from all nodes in the machine, the GW periodically sweeps the entire machine volume and in each beam direction waits for possible data to be generated and sent by nodes. Nodes belonging to the same beam compete for the access to the channel, implementing a Carrier Sense Multiple access protocol with Collision Avoidance, with Request-to-Send (RTS) and Clear-to-Send (CTS) packets transmissions [6].

The paper provides a method for calculating one the main characteristic of this CSMA/CA protocol, namely, the collision probability of RTS signaling messages during CSMA/CA session initiation procedure between the gateway and a node. The method is based on the developed baseline model for calculating the average delay in the form of absorbing discrete time Markov chain and the approach with estimating the collision probability by solving the system of transcendental equations [7–9]. The framework format allows us not to take into account technical parameters, like SNR, power values, antenna description [3, 4], a more detailed analysis will be carried out with further research.

The goal of the work is to build the tractable analytical model of the CSMA/CA protocol, which will allow optimizing the session initiation procedure [1]. The model is detailed enough to take into account parameters of the protocol in order to formulate and solve the optimization problems regarding the main performance measures of the system such as a CSMA/CA session delay and the network throughput. The novelty of the work is that the developed analytical model includes parameters allowing investigation of the potential effects of MAC layer parameters on the performance measures. In particular, the signal propagation time was included in developed both analytical and simulation models, which in further analysis can be modeled as a function of nodes' spatial positions. The discrete time Markov chain also includes the states for time-out and back-off periods for the analysis of their impact to the protocol performance metrics in case of any protocol modifications, where the durations of these periods can be parameters for optimization. Finally, it is assumed that the model will become the basis for the study of protocol enhancements like introducing carrier sensing during back-off to avoid collision.

The paper is organized as follows. System model and a CSMA/CA protocol are described in Sect. 1.1 and 1.2 correspondingly. The target performance metrics are indicated in Sect. 1.3. In Sect. 2 the CSMA/CA session initiation procedure of a node /a gateway handshaking is described using two mathematical models - in the form of an absorbing Discrete Time Markov Chain in Sect. 2.1, in the form of a queueing network in Sect. 2.2. The method for the collision's probability estimation, as well as some other CSMA/CA protocol important performance metrics are described in Sect. 2.3. Section 3 is devoted to the numerical experiment for estimation the accuracy of the analytical solution. Section 3.1 shows the architecture of the simulator developed for modelling the process of exchanging messages between a node and the GW and initial data close to the reality. Section 3.2 gives an example of a numerical experiment and a comparison of the results of the analytical approach and simulation. Further research is identified in Sect. 4.

1.1 System Model

The reference scenario is modeled via a 3D sphere of radius R, having the GW in its center. Nodes are randomly and uniformly deployed inside the sphere (see Fig. 1).

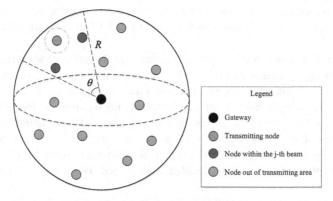

Fig. 1. Sphere of gateway's antenna signal

We assume the GW is equipped with multiple antenna elements that form the beam of width θ. The GW will sweep the beams in order to communicate with all nodes, according to a time division approach.

We assume time is organized into frames of duration T_{frame} and frames are divided into sub-frames, each dedicated to the exploration of one beam. Indeed, during each frame the GW sweeps all the beams present in the sphere and remains in the j-th direction for a time $T_{beam j}$ (sub-frame duration). We assume the time needed to change the beam is negligible. During the j-th sub-frame a beacon packet is sent by the GW to notify to nodes in the beam it is ready to receive data.

On the other hand, every node is equipped with a single omnidirectional antenna; thus, it is able to receive data from the GW, but not from the other nodes in the beam, since the transmission range, when no multiple antennas are used, is in the order of few centimeters.

The node doesn't have information either about other nodes' distribution among the space or their transmission schedule. Moreover, every node could generate data for transmission with some probability p_a. The only way for the node to ensure there will be no collisions during the data transmission is to synchronize the data transmission with the gateway. In order to do that, CSMA/CA is anticipated by an initiation phase where RTS and CTS control packets are exchanged between the node and the GW (see Sect. 1.2).

1.2 Protocol Description

As soon as a node in a beam receives the beacon and it has a packet to be transmitted in the queue, it will send an RTS packet to the GW. RTS transmission is performed without sensing since, as stated above, nodes are equipped with a single antenna and their reception range is too small to receive data packets from other nodes in the beam. Therefore, in order to limit collisions among RTS packets a randomly and uniformly distributed back-off delay τ_ω is performed, before the transmission of the RTS. The protocol is shown in Fig. 2.

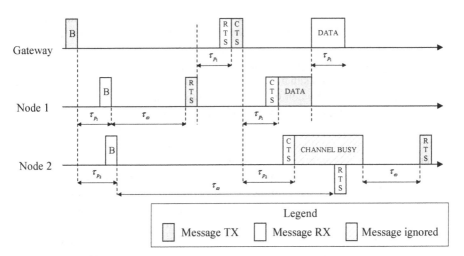

Fig. 2. Message sequence diagram with success RTS transmission

A propagation time τ_p depends on the distance between a node and a gateway and RAN technology. Having transmitted RTS message the node listens the channel for Clear-to-Send (CTS) message response from the gateway during τ_{out}. Receiving of CTS message means the channel is free, thus, there will be no data collision. The fact there is no response within specified timeout implies either the collision of sent RTS message with another RTS message or existing active data transmission. Correspondingly, in case of absent CTS response the node starts session initiation retry with doubled back-off delay (Fig. 3). Once retransmission limit is exceeded, the data transmission is considered as failed. As a result of successful data transmission, the gateway sends acknowledgment message to the node.

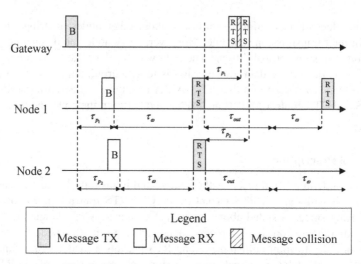

Fig. 3. Message sequence diagram with collision

Further, we mean by a session the procedure of the attempt to transmit data by a node within $(N + 1)$ RTS transmissions in condition of presence a data packet on a node.

Assume we have n_{θ_j} nodes that send data packets to the gateway within the j-th beam with beam width θ_j via CSMA/CA protocol according to diagram in the Fig. 2 and 3.

We define a collision as a situation, when a RTS message from a node arrives to the gateway during the interval when the gateway is busy with receiving a RTS message from another node, that has arrived ahead. We also consider a collision when gateway ignores a RTS message from a node because the gateway is busy after recent successful RTS message receiving from another node, i.e. the gateway is busy with active DATA receiving, including a data packet, CTS, ACK transmissions and propagation time. The collision entails the retransmission of all collided RTS messages, which lengthens the duration of the CSMA/CA session initiation procedure and decreases the probability of successful data transmission from a node to a gateway. The collision probability is metric influencing most performance measures of the system on MAC layer. It has a complex dependency on the beam width, the number and the spatial distribution of nodes in the beam, probability for a node to have a data packer for transmission, internal protocol parameters, etc. Since collisions make an integral part of multiple access, the collision probability is one of the key characteristics of the protocol, which allows one to judge its effectiveness. Assessing the collision probability is the main task that we solve further in the work.

The CSMA/CA procedure [6] will be shown in more detail in Sect. 2.2, where a method for analyzing the performance metric using the absorbing DTMC is described. This approach is used in multiple access technologies for plenty of applications from RF charging to D2D communications [10–12].

1.3 Performance Metrics

Since the collision probability in RTS /CTS procedure is a complex function of several arguments, primarily on the number of nodes in a beam, as well as on the spatial distribution of nodes and internal protocol parameters, for example, back-off and timeout duration, a compact analytical expression for collision probability is available only in special cases, useless from the point of view of real applications. To find the collision probability in the general case, we use approach [7] in combination with the methods of average session delay estimation developed in Sect. 2. We also verify the analytical approach with simulation in Sect. 3 from the point of view of main characteristics of the CSMA/CA protocol.

The main metrics studied are the following:

- $D(p)$ – average session delay;
- $\tau(p)$ – probability for a node of being in RTS transmission;
- $p\big(n_{\theta_j}\big)$ – collision probability, depending on n_{θ_j}.

2 Analytical Model

Section 2 proposes a method for calculating the collision probability. The method is based on the proposed models for average session delay calculation as an average time $D_{MC}(p)$ to reach one of the absorbing states in the absorbing discrete time Markov Chain (MC) model (Sect. 2.1) [9], as an average cycle time $D_{QN}(p)$ for IDLE state in the queueing network (QN) model (Sect. 2.2) [13] and the approach [7, 8] with estimating the collision probability solving the system of transcendental equations (Sect. 2.3).

2.1 Absorbing Markov Chain

According to the first approach we build a mathematical model of the process of session initiation with start in the IDLE state and finish in success (successful data packet transmission within $(N + 1)$ attempts) or failure (failure of a data packet transmission after $(N + 1)$ attempts) in term of absorbing Discrete Time Markov Chain with finite state space $\mathbf{X}_{MC}$ to describe state of a node within one time slot (time unit). According to [9] in each time slot a node can be in one state of the state space

$$\mathbf{X}_{MC}=\Big\{idle, BO_1^{(1)}, BO_2^{(1)}, \ldots, BO_{T\max -1}^{(1)}, Tx_{RTS}^{(1)}, T_{out}^{(1)}, \ldots, T_{out}^{(N+1)}, Tx_{DATA}, s, f\Big\},$$

where "idle" state corresponds to the node's state with no data packet for transmission to the gateway; "$T_{RTS}^{(i)}$" state – to the i-th RTS transmission, $i = 1, \ldots, N + 1$; "$T_{out}^{(i)}$" state – to the i-th time-out, $i = 1, \ldots, N + 1$; "Tx_{DATA}" – the DATA transmission, including a data packet, CTS, ACK transmissions; "s" - a session success (no collision in RTS transmissions within allowed $N + 1$ attempts); "f" - a session failure (collision in each on $N + 1$ RTS transmissions), where N - the number of allowed RTS retransmissions, so the maximum number of RTS transmissions equals to $N + 1$. The groups of "BO" states model the back-off periods of a random duration in the following way: the duration of τ_ω^i of the i-th back-off in time units is a random variable uniformly distributed with parameter T_{max}, so that

$$\tau_\omega^i \sim Uni[0, i \cdot T_{max}]. \qquad (2.1)$$

To avoid the cumbersomeness we didn't include the propagation time in the state space of DTMC (Fig. 4), but we will take it into account in detailed analysis of constituents of session delay below. The transition probabilities for $\mathbf{X}_{MC}$ shown in Fig. 4 correspond to the non-zero elements of transition matrix $\mathbf{\Phi}_{MC}$ of DTMC.

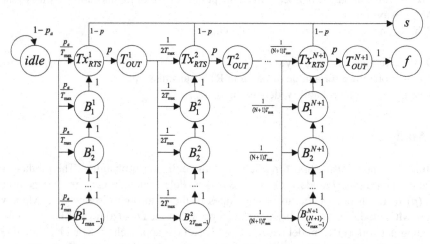

Fig. 4. State transitions diagram for the absorbing Discrete Time Markov Chain

The apparatus of absorbing Markov Chains is traditionally used in problems of finding the expected number of steps before being absorbed when starting in a certain transient state. We will use this absorbing Markov Chain to determine the average time to reach one of the absorbing states, namely "s" and "f", as it was done in [9] for RACH procedure.

The method for estimation of session delay is based on time sequence diagram for the message flow between a node and the gateway shown in details in Fig. 5.

Since we define a session as the procedure of an attempt to transmit data by a node within $(N + 1)$ RTS transmissions in condition of presence a data packet on a node, we don't take into account the time interval for beacon transmission in the average session delay estimation.

First, we denote the time intervals Δ_{rts}^i for i RTS transmissions (either till the start of successful DATA transmission or till the start of the i-th time-out) and Δ_{DATA} for DATA transmission after RTS message successfully receiving by the gateway:

$$\Delta_{RTS}^i = (i - 1)\tau_{out} + \sum_{n=1}^{i} \tau_\omega^i \cdot T_{unit} + i \cdot \tau_g^{RTS}, \quad i = 1, \ldots, N + 1; \qquad (2.2)$$

$$\Delta_{DATA} = \tau_p + \tau_g^{CTS} + \tau_p + \tau_p + \tau_g^{data} + \tau_g^{ACK} + \tau_p. \qquad (2.3)$$

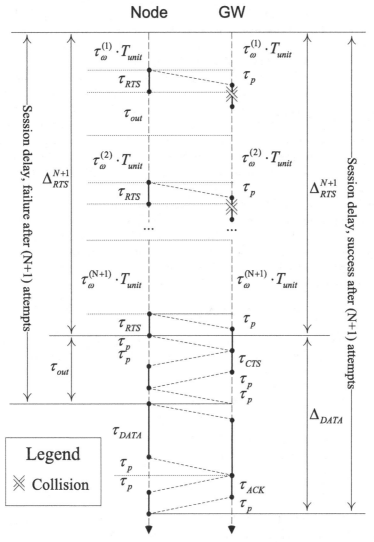

Fig. 5. Time sequence diagram in case of failure after the (N + 1) RTS transmissions (left) or success in the (N + 1)-th RTS transmission (right)

According to the notation (2.3) we will use capital letters DATA below meaning the time interval of duration $\left(\tau_p + \tau_g^{CTS} + \tau_p + \tau_p + \tau_g^{data} + \tau_g^{ACK} + \tau_p\right)$. Here $\tau_{out}, \tau_\omega^i, \tau_g^{RTS}, \tau_g^{CTS}, \tau_g^{data}, \tau_g^{ACK}$ - random variables with given distributions. We assume that $\tau_{out}, \tau_g^{RTS}, \tau_g^{CTS}, \tau_g^{data}, \tau_g^{ACK}$ are constants with values $T_{out}, T_{RTS}, T_{CTS}, T_{data}, T_{ACK}$. The duration τ_ω^i of the i-th back-off in time units is a random variable uniformly distributed with parameter T_{max} according to (2.1). Note, that the random duration τ_ω^i is the subject of optimization. We also include the propagation time τ_p in $D_{MC}(p)$ estimation as a blank for future research. We plan to define the random variable of τ_p as a function of nodes' spatial positions, namely, the distance between the node and the gateway, and RAN technology.

The session delay differs in case of failure and in case of success of a data packet transmission. Time sequence diagrams for success with N collisions and for failure are illustrated in right and left parts of Fig. 5 correspondingly. In both cases a session starts from the beginning of the first time-out after the last bit of beacon message receiving on the node. In case of a session failure the session delay $D_{failure}$ is a time elapsed till the end of the last $(N + 1)$-th time-out on the node after the last $(N + 1)$-th RTS transmission. In case of a session success the session delay $D_{success}$ is a time elapsed till the last bit of ACK message received by a node.

We also define $D_s(i)$ as the time for session initiation finished by successful DATA transmission with exactly i RTS transmissions before success, $i = 1, \ldots, N + 1$. So $D_s(i)$ is the time interval since the beginning of the first time-out till the last bit of ACK message received by a node in case of success with i RTS transmission attempts.

So, for DATA transmission after RTS success transmission after exactly $(i - 1)$ collisions we have for entire session:

$$D_s(i) = \Delta_{RTS}^i + \Delta_{DATA}, \quad i = 1, \ldots, N + 1. \tag{2.4}$$

In case of failure for DATA transmission (collision in each on $N + 1$ RTS transmissions) the expression for $D_{failure}$ has the following form (time sequence diagram in Fig. 5, left):

$$D_f = \Delta_{RTS}^{N+1} + \tau_{out}. \tag{2.5}$$

Note, that

$$P_s(i) = p^{i-1}(1 - p), \quad i = 1, \ldots, N + 1, \tag{2.6}$$

$$P_f = p^{N+1}, \tag{2.7}$$

where $P_s(i)$ – probability for DATA transmission after RTS success transmission with exactly $(i - 1)$ collisions, P_f – probability of failure for DATA transmission.

Let $D_{non-idle}(p)$ be an average session delay in condition of presence a data packet for transmission, i.e. average time interval for one DATA transmission attempt no matter success or failure in session initiation, where p is the collision probability. Then from (2.4)–(2.7) substituting (2.1)–(2.3) in case of $\tau_p = 0$ we obtain

$$D_{non-idle}(p) = \sum_{i=1}^{N+1} D_s(i) \cdot P_s(i) + D_f \cdot P_f$$

$$= \sum_{i=1}^{N+1} \left(\Delta_{RTS}^i + \Delta_{DATA} \right)(1 - p)p^{i-1} + \left(\Delta_{RTS}^{N+1} + \tau_{out} \right)p^{N+1}$$

$$= \sum_{i=1}^{N+1} \left(\left[(i-1)T_{out} + \sum_{n=1}^{i} \frac{n \cdot T_{max} - 1}{2} \cdot T_{unit} + i \cdot T_{RTS} \right] + [T_{CTS} + T_{data} + T_{ACK}] \right)(1 - p)p^{i-1}$$

$$+ \left((N + 1)T_{out} + \sum_{i=1}^{N+1} \frac{i \cdot T_{\max} - 1}{2} \cdot T_{unit} + (N + 1) \cdot T_{RTS} \right) p^{N+1}. \tag{2.8}$$

Note, that according to the CSMA/CA protocol after receiving a beacon from the gateway a node checks the presence of a data packet for transmission and starts CSMA/CA session initiation procedure only if there is a data packet for transmission on a node. The probability that a node has a data packet is denoted by p_a. If a node doesn't have a data packet (with complementary probability $(1 - p_a)$), then the interval for the next checking for the presence of a data packet is T_{idle}.

Therefore, the average session delay $D_{MC}(p)$ for CSMA/CA procedure can be defined as following:

$$D_{MC}(p) = (1 - p_a) \cdot T_{idle} + p_a \cdot D_{non-idle}(p). \tag{2.9}$$

The approach [7] also gives the estimation of the average time the lumped state "RTS transmission" as

$$D_{MC,RTS}(p) = \sum_{i=1}^{N+1} T_{rts} \cdot p_a \cdot p^{i-1}. \tag{2.10}$$

The formulas (2.9) and (2.10) for Markov Chain model are used in Sect. 3 for defining performance metrics of CSMA/CA procedure.

2.2 Closed Queueing Network

We also consider the third approach to the estimation of average session delay with the help of average cycle duration in the mathematical model in terms of a closed queueing network (Gordon-Newell network) [13]. The network consists of $3(N + 1) + 2$ nodes (Fig. 6)

$$X_{QN} = \left\{ \text{IDLE}, \text{BO}^1, \text{RTS}^1, \text{OUT}^1, \ldots, \text{BO}^{N+1}, \text{RTS}^{N+1}, \text{OUT}^{N+1}, \text{DATA} \right\}$$

with Infinite Servers discipline and finite number of customers n_{θ_j}, circulated through the nodes in the network. Note that the term "a network's node" corresponds to the state of a node in CSMA/CA session initiation procedure, the term "a customer" corresponds to the node in CSMA/CA session initiation procedure. The transition probabilities between states of X_{QN} shown in Fig. 6 corresponds to the non-zero elements of DTMC's transition matrix $\Phi_{QN} = [\varphi_{m1,m2}]$, $m1, m2 \in X_{QN}$.

The service times in the network's nodes correspond to the random variables $\tau_{idle}, \tau_g^{RTS}, \Delta_{DATA}, \tau_{out}, \tau_\omega^i$ with the following values:

$$\mu_{idle}^{-1} = T_{idle}, \ \mu_{RTS}^{-1} = T_{RTS}, \ \mu_{DATA}^{-1} = T_{CTS} + T_{data} + T_{ACK},$$

$$\mu_{OUT\,i}^{-1} = iT_{out}, \ \mu_{BO\,i}^{-1} = \frac{i \cdot T_{\max} - 1}{2} \cdot T_{unit}, \ i = 1, \ldots, N + 1.$$

The task here is to find the average time interval $Ec*_{IDLE}$ between adjacent visits of the IDLE network's node.

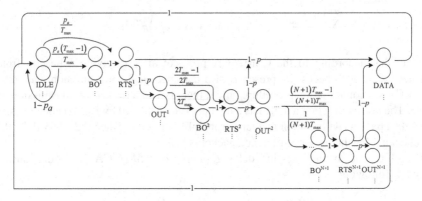

Fig. 6. A scheme of the closed queueing network for CSMA/CA procedure

Using the approach [13] we obtain $D_{QN}(p)$ in the form of

$$D_{QN}(p) = Ec^*{}_{IDLE} = n_{\theta_j} \cdot \frac{d_{IDLE}}{\rho_{IDLE}(n_{\theta_j})}, \tag{2.11}$$

where $\rho_{IDLE}(n_{\theta_j}) = \lambda_{IDLE}(n_{\theta_j})/\mu_{IDLE}$, $\lambda_{IDLE}(n_{\theta_j})$ is calculated using Buzen's convolution algorithm [14].

Formula (2.11) for queueing network model is used in Sect. 3 for comparing with other estimations of average session delay of CSMA/CA procedure.

2.3 Performance Metrics

In Sect. 2.3 we provide analytical expressions for here main metrics studied, i.e. average session delay, probability for a node of being in RTS transmission, and the target metric – the collision probability.

The average session delay is the important metric for the collision probability analysis since it is the part of transcendental equation according to [7] approach. According to [7, 8] the collision probability p can be estimated as a solution of the transcendental equation:

$$p = 1 - (1 - \tau(p))^{n_\theta - 1}, \tag{2.12}$$

where $\tau(p)$ is the probability for a node to be in RTS transmission.

The natural approach is to use for $\tau(p)$ estimation the fraction of the session delay during which a node has been in RTS transmission state. Regarding this approach, we can express $\tau(p)$ in terms of an absorbing Markov Chain using (2.9), (2.10):

$$\tau(p) = \frac{D_{MC,RTS}(p)}{D_{MC}(p)} = \sum_{i=1}^{N+1} \frac{T_{rts} \cdot p_a \cdot p^{i-1}}{D_{MC}(p)}, \tag{2.13}$$

where p_a is the probability that a node has a data packet for transmission.

The accuracy of the calculations using analytical formulas is estimated in Sect. 3 using a comparison with simulation results.

3 Simulations

3.1 Simulator Architecture

We designed and implemented CSMA/CA protocol simulator considering RTS/CTS session initiation. Our simulator is intended for modelling on access point and a set of data transceivers. It is possible to define nodes distribution within a sphere of a radius R. In addition, the simulator supports cyclic and non-cyclic modes.

Simulator state machine for Gateway is represented on the Fig. 7.

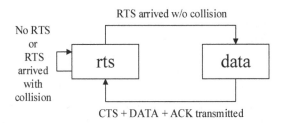

Fig. 7. Gateway state machine

Gateway can belong to the one of two possible states: receiving RTS messages from nodes (both useful receiving time and RTS waiting) or performing data transfer that includes sending CTS, transmitting data and sending ACK message. Simulator state machine for Node demonstrated in Fig. 8 is a little more complicated.

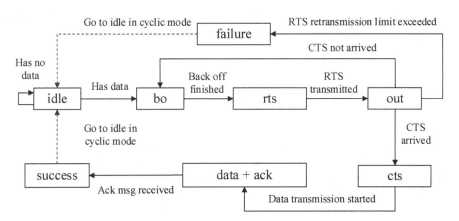

Fig. 8. Node state machine

Node starts the simulation in IDLE state. At the end of IDLE state, the node checks if there is RTS message to transmit by a generation of random variable between zero and unity. In case the generated value is less than p_a the node keeps being idle, otherwise the node starts back off delay. Having transmitted RTS message the node starts to wait CTS response in OUT state. In case of absent CTS response, the node goes to new back off if retransmissions limit is not exceeded. Otherwise the node moves to FAILURE state.

The node could go from FAILURE state to IDLE state only if cyclic mode is active. When the node receives CTS response in OUT state, the node moves to CTS state. At the end of data transmission, the node receives ACK message from Gateway and goes to SUCCESS state. The node could go from SUCCESS state to IDLE state only if cyclic mode is active.

3.2 Numerical Experiment for Estimation of Analytical Solution

The input data for the experiment is close to the reality and corresponds to IoT applications. We model the CSMA/CA session initiation procedure for $n_{\theta_j} = \overline{1, 50}$ nodes in a beam for the sphere of radius $R = 2$ m. The number of allowed RTS retransmissions $N = 3$. The probability of presence data for transmission on a node $p_a \in \{0.25, 0.5, 1.0\}$. We assume 20 bytes for RTS, CTS and ACK messages and 100 bytes for a data packet, then with 50 Gbps channel $T_{RTS} = T_{CTS} = T_{ACK} = 3.2 \cdot 10^{-9}s = 3.2\,ns$, $T_{data} = 1.6 \cdot 10^{-8}s = 16.0\,ns$. For numerical study below we consider zero propagation time, but the model assumes taking into account the propagation time in future research. We take $T_{\max} = 12$ with $T_{unit} = T_{RTS}$.

The goal of the conducted numerical experiment was to evaluate the accuracy of the developed analytical approach for the average session delay (Sect. 3.2.1), the probability of being in RTS transmission (Sect. 3.2.2), the collision probability (Sect. 3.2.3) in comparison with the corresponding metrics collected from the simulations.

3.2.1 Average Session Delay

Average session delay is the easiest to interpret metric that can be taken from simulations according to a session definition from Sect. 1.2. To get the average session delay we use the following formula:

$$D_{sim} = \frac{1}{n_{\theta_j}} \sum_{n=1}^{n_{\theta_j}} \left[\frac{1}{S(n)} \sum_{s=1}^{S(n)} T_{cycle}(n, s) \right], \tag{3.1}$$

where

$T_{cycle}(n, s)$ - the s-th session delay of the n-th node, $T_{cycle}(n, s) \in \{T_{idle}, D_s(1), \ldots, D_s(N + 1), D_f\}$; $S(n)$ - the number of attempts to start a session initiation procedure within T_{beam} for the n-th node irrelevant to the presence of a data packet on the node, $S(n) = S_{idle}(n) + S_{data}(n)$, $S_{idle}(n)$ - the number of attempts to start a session initiation procedure within T_{beam} for the n-th node, in condition that the node has no data packet for transmission; $S_{data}(n)$ - the number of attempts to start a session initiation procedure within T_{beam} for the n-th node, in condition that the node has a data packet for transmission.

The average session delay from (2.9) blue curve, (2.11) brown curve and from simulations (3.1) black curve, depending on the number of nodes in a beam is presented in Fig. 9 for three values of p_a, namely $p_a = 0.25$ (dotted), $p_a = 0.5$ (dashed), $p_a = 1.0$ (solid).

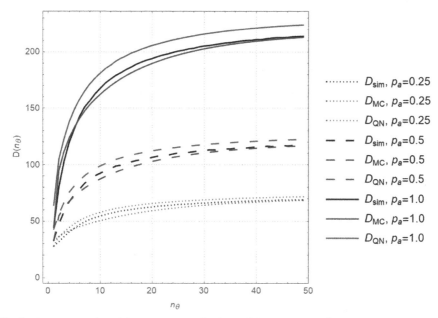

Fig. 9. Average session delay (*nanoseconds*) from (2.9), (2.11) and from simulations (3.1) vs number of nodes in a beam (Color figure online)

The MC model (2.9) demonstrates a more accurate result vs simulation then the queueing network model (2.11). The relative error for MC model decreases with a growth in the number n_{θ_j} of node, lies in the 5% limit for $n_{\theta_j} > 20$ for all values of p_a and drops to tenths of a percent at $n_{\theta_j} = 50$ nodes. The relative error for QN model also decreases with a growth in the number n_{θ_j} of node, but it lies in the 4–6% interval up to $n_{\theta_j} = 50$ nodes. The poorer accuracy for the QN model is expected since in Sect. 2.2 we don't model the CSMA/CA protocol exactly - in the queueing network model, we can have several customers in the DATA node. This situation corresponds to the simultaneous DATA transmission by several nodes, which is impossible according to CSMA/CA protocol. But the queueing network model approach has the advantage of low-cost implementation due to plenty of free soft for closed queueing network calculating. We used it only for cross-verifying results of several approaches to the average session delay estimation and will not to take it into account for further analysis.

It is interesting that with a growth in p_a the two models behave the opposite way: MC model increases while QN model decreases the accuracy vs simulation.

3.2.2 Probability of Being in RTS Transmission

Regarding the metric, that lies in the base of analytical approach for collision probability estimation [7], i.e., probability for a node of being in RTS transmission (Fig. 10), we get very high accuracy.

The values $\tau_{MC}(p)$ for analytical solution of the system (2.12)–(2.13) are shown in Fig. 10 by blue curves.

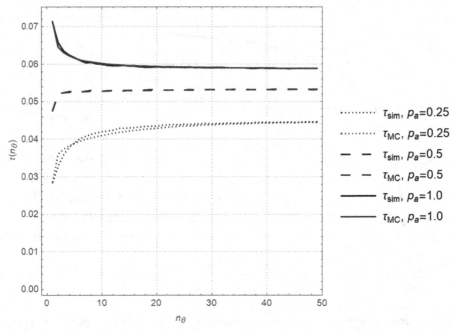

Fig. 10. Probability for a node of being in RTS transmission from (2.13) and from simulations (3.2) vs number of nodes in a beam (Color figure online)

To obtain the probability of being in RTS transmission τ_{sim} form simulations (black curve in Fig. 10) we use the following formula:

$$\tau_{sim} = \frac{1}{n_{\theta_j} \cdot T_{beam}} \sum_{n=1}^{n_{\theta_j}} \sum_{s=1}^{S(n)} T_{rts}(n, s), \tag{3.2}$$

where $T_{rts}(n, s)$ - total time of RTS transmission for the s-th session of the n-th node; $S(n)$ - the number of attempts to start a session initiation procedure within T_{beam} for the n-th node irrelevant to the presence of a data packet on the node.

The relative error for analytical approach and simulation in Fig. 10 is less than 1% for almost all number of nodes in a beam. This testifies to the high accuracy of the approach proposed in [7]. It also speaks in favor of the method of an average session delay estimation proposed in Sect. 2.1.

3.2.3 Collision Probability

Regarding estimating collision probability p from simulation we use two approaches for cross-verifying results.

According to the first one, we estimate the probability P_f of failure in session initiation in condition of presence a data packet on a node from the point of view of a node. First, we collect the average number of nodes having a data packet, that finished the cycle with failure to transmit a data packet after $(N + 1)$ RTS transmissions. This metric corresponds to the probability P_f of failure for DATA transmission:

$$P_f = \frac{1}{n_{\theta_j}} \sum_{n=1}^{n_{\theta_j}} \left[\frac{1}{S_{data}(n)} \sum_{s=1}^{S_{data}(n)} I \left\{ \begin{array}{l} \text{failure of the } n\text{ - th node with data} \\ \text{in the } s\text{ - th attempt of session initiation} \end{array} \right\} \right], \quad (3.3)$$

where $S_{data}(n)$ - the number of attempts to start a session initiation procedure within T_{beam} for the n-th node, in condition that the node has a data packet for transmission;

$I\{A\}$ - indicator function, $I\{A\} = \begin{cases} 1, & A \text{ is true;} \\ 0, & \text{otherwise.} \end{cases}$

In Fig. 11. the analytical solutions of the system of transcendental Eqs. (2.12)–(2.13) blue curve and simulation (3.3) black curve are shown for three values of p_a, namely $p_a = 0.25$ (dotted), $p_a = 0.5$ (dashed), $p_a = 1.0$ (solid).

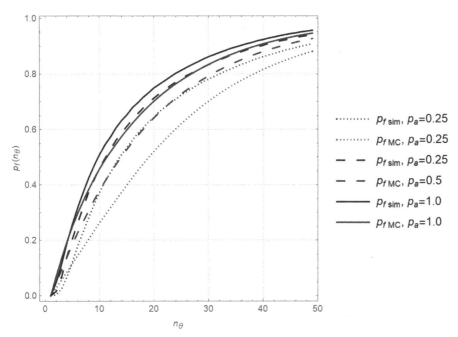

Fig. 11. Analytical solution of (2.12)–(2.13) and P_f from simulations (3.3) vs number of nodes in a beam (Color figure online)

Formula (2.13) shows acceptable accuracy for $p_a = 0.5$ and $p_a = 1.0$ - the relative error lies in the 5% limit for $n_{\theta_j} > 30$ for all values of p_a and decreases with a growth of the number of nodes. Rather high (up to 10% for $n_{\theta_j} > 30$) values of the relative error for accuracy for $p_a = 0.25$ appears due to the rare success in session initiation.

Continuing with the first approach, we estimate $p_{sim,node}$ from the point of view of a node using (2.7) and (3.3)

$$p_{sim,node} = P_f^{1/(N+1)}. \quad (3.4)$$

According to the second approach, we estimate $p_{sim,GW}$ from the point of view of a gateway as a fraction of unsuccessfully RTS to the

$$p_{sim,GW} = \frac{n_{collided\ RTS} + n_{ignored\ RTS}}{n_{arrived\ RTS}}, \tag{3.5}$$

where $n_{collided\ RTS}$, $n_{ignored\ RTS}$, $n_{arrived\ RTS}$ - the corresponding number of RTS on the gateway within T_{beam}; $n_{arrived\ RTS}(s) = n_{collided\ RTS}(s) + n_{ignored\ RTS}(s) + n_{successful\ RTS}(s)$.

The collision probabilities $p_{sim,node}$ from (3.4) and $p_{sim,GW}$ from (3.5) are in line with the relative error is less than 1%, so only $p_{sim,GW}$ (3.5) black curve is shown in Fig. 12 in comparison with the collision probability p_{MC} from (2.12)-(2.13) blue curve for three values of p_a, namely $p_a = 0.25$ (dotted), $p_a = 0.5$ (dashed), $p_a = 1.0$ (solid).

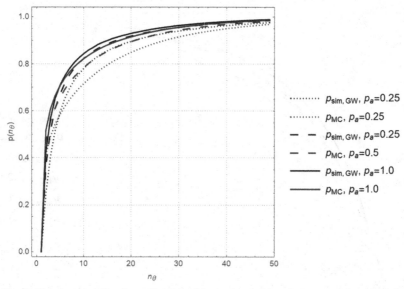

Fig. 12. Collision probability from (2.13) and from simulations (3.5) vs number of nodes in a beam (Color figure online)

The relative error for analytical approach (2.12)–(2.13) based on MC model (2.9) vs simulation (3.5) in Fig. 12 lies in the 8% limit even for the worst case $p_a = 0.25$ for all number of nodes in a beam and is less than 1% at $n_{\theta_j} = 50$ nodes. For the best case $p_a = 1.0$ the relative error is less than 2% starting with $n_{\theta_j} = 15$ nodes and decreasing up to tenths of a percent with a growth of the number of nodes.

Collision probability is the key parameter influencing other performance metrics. High values of the collision probability, even for a small number of nodes, indicate the need to use special mechanisms for collisions avoidance, for example, carrier sensing.

4 Conclusion and Future Work

The work proposes a method for estimating performance metrics of CSMA/CA protocol on the MAC layer. Further this method should be combined with those at the physical layer, which in the case of a wireless channel is dependent essentially on radio access technology. Taking into account the features of both MAC and physical layers will allow to study the network performance metrics, i.e., network throughput and session delay. In addition, an interesting task for further research is to modify the session initiation procedure to reduce the collision probability, which can be done, for example, by varying the duration of the back-off period. Moreover, the high values of the collision probability even for a small number of nodes indicate the need for modification of CSMA/CA session initiation procedure, for example, listening to the carrier during a back-off, as suggested in [15]. The proposed model was built to analyze such a possible modification.

Acknowledgements. The publication has been prepared with the support of the RUDN University Program "5-100" (E. Khayrov). The reported study was funded by RFBR, project numbers 18-07-00576 (Yu. Gaidamaka) and 20-07-01064 (E. Medvedeva).

References

1. Buratti, C., Mesini, L., Verdone, R.: Comparing MAC protocols for industrial IoT using Terahertz communications. In: IEEE PIMRC, August 2020
2. Elayan, H., Amin, O., Shubair, R.M., Alouini, M.: Terahertz communication: the opportunities of wireless technology beyond 5G. In: CommNet, April 2018, pp. 1–5. IEEE (2018). https://doi.org/10.1109/commnet.2018.8360286
3. Polese, M., Jornet, J., Melodia, T., Zorzi, M.: Toward end-to-end, full-stack 6G terahertz networks. IEEE Commun. Mag. arXiv:2005.07989v1 [cs.NI]
4. Tekbıyık, K., Ekti, A.R., Kurt, G.K., Gorcin, A.: Terahertz band communication systems: challenges, novelties and standardization efforts. Phys. Commun. **35**, 100700. https://doi.org/10.1016/j.phycom.2019.04.014
5. Ghafoor, S., Boujnah, N., Rehmani, M.H., Davy, A.: MAC protocols for terahertz communication: a comprehensive survey. arXiv:1904.11441v3 [cs.NI]
6. Recommendation ITU-R M.1450-5 (02/2014): Characteristics of broadband radio local area networks, ITU-R, February 2014
7. Bianchi, G.: IEEE 802.11-saturation throughput analysis. IEEE Commun. Lett. **2**(12), 318–320 (1998). https://doi.org/10.1109/4234.736171
8. Bianchi, G., Tinnirello, I.: Remarks on IEEE 802.11 DCF performance analysis. IEEE Commun. Lett. **9**(8), 765–767 (2005). https://doi.org/10.1109/lcomm.2005.1496609
9. Samouylov, K.E., Gaidamaka, Y.V., Gudkova, I.A., Zaripova, E.R., Shorgin, S.Y.: Baseline analytical model for machine-type communications over 3GPP RACH in LTE-advanced networks. In: Czachórski, T., Gelenbe, E., Grochla, K., Lent, R. (eds.) ISCIS 2016. CCIS, vol. 659, pp. 203–213. Springer, Cham (2016). https://doi.org/10.1007/978-3-319-47217-1_22
10. Pyattaev, A., Johnsson, K., Surak, A., Florea, R., Andreev, S., Koucheryavy, Y.: Network-assisted D2D communications: Implementing a technology prototype for cellular traffic offloading. WCNC, art. **6953070**, 3266–3271 (2014)
11. Galinina, O., Tabassum, H., Mikhaylov, K., Andreev, S., Hossain, E., Koucheryavy, Y.: On feasibility of 5G-grade dedicated RF charging technology for wireless-powered wearables. IEEE Wirel. Commun. **23**(2), 7462482, 28–37 (2016)

12. Ometov, A., et al.: Toward trusted, social-aware D2D connectivity: Bridging across the technology and sociality realms. IEEE Wirel. Commun. **23**(4), 7553033, 103–111 (2016)
13. Gordon, W.J., Newell, G.F.: Closed queuing systems with exponential servers. Oper. Res. **15**(2), 185–370 (1967). https://doi.org/10.1287/opre.15.2.254.JSTOR168557
14. Buzen, J.P.: Computational algorithms for closed queueing networks with exponential servers. Commun. ACM **16**(9), 527–531 (1973). https://doi.org/10.1145/362342.362345
15. Zhu, M., Chang, L., Wang, N., You, I.: A smart collaborative routing protocol for delay sensitive applications in industrial IoT. IEEE Access **8**, 20413–20427 (2020). https://doi.org/10.1109/ACCESS.2019.2963723

Cesaro Sequences and Cesaro Hereditary Automata

Sergey Yu. Melnikov[1]([✉]) and Konstantin E. Samouylov[1,2][iD]

[1] Peoples' Friendship University of Russia (RUDN University), Moscow, Russia
melnikov@linfotech.ru, ksam@sci.pfu.edu.ru
[2] Federal Research Center "Computer Science and Control" of the Russian Academy
of Sciences, Moscow, Russia

Abstract. We consider a class of so-called cesaro sequences over a finite alphabet, which possess the property of stability of the relative frequencies of occurrence of an arbitrary word in growing initial segments. This class includes a class of periodic sequences. A finite state automaton is called cesaro-hereditary if it processes cesaro sequences in the input alphabet into cesaro sequences in the output alphabet. Examples of automata that possess and do not possess the property of cesaro-heredity are given. The conditions are proposed so that the automaton possesses and does not possess the property of cesaro-heredity.

Keywords: Statistical properties of automata · Word occurrence statistics · Cesaro sequences

1 Cesaro Sequences

Various randomness models are used to study the statistical properties of sequences generated by pseudo-random sequence generators. One of the possible models is the so-called cesaro sequences.

Let B be a finite set (alphabet). By B^* we denote the set of all words in the alphabet B. We denote by Ω the set of all infinite sequences over B:

$$\Omega = \{\omega = w_1 w_2 ... | w_t \in B, \, t = 0, 1, ...\}. \tag{1}$$

For each word $\alpha \in B^*$, $\alpha = a_0 a_1 ... a_{m-1}$, where $a_i \in B$, $i = 0, 1, ..., m - 1$, $m = 1, 2, ...$ we define a cylinder

$$[\alpha] = [a_0 a_1 ... a_{m-1}] = \{\omega = w_0 w_1 ... | w_0 = a_0, w_1 = a_1, w_{m-1} = a_{m-1}\} \subset \Omega. \tag{2}$$

The characteristic function of an arbitrary subset $F \subset \Omega$ will be denoted by I_F:

$$I_F = \begin{cases} 1, & \text{if} \quad \omega \in F \\ 0, & \text{if} \quad \omega \notin F \end{cases}. \tag{3}$$

O. Galinina et al. (Eds.): NEW2AN 2020/ruSMART 2020, LNCS 12526, pp. 259–269, 2020.
https://doi.org/10.1007/978-3-030-65729-1_22

Instead of $I_{[\alpha]}$ we will simply write I_α.

Define a mapping T ("sequence shift") $T : \Omega \to \Omega$ by

$$T : \omega = w_0 w_1 \ldots \to \omega T = w_1 w_2 \ldots . \tag{4}$$

The equality

$$I_\alpha \left(\omega T^t \right) = 1 \tag{5}$$

means in such a way that

$$w_t = a_0, \ w_{t+1} = a_1, \ldots, \ w_{t+m-1} = a_{m-1}. \tag{6}$$

The number $\frac{1}{t} \sum_{j=0}^{t-1} I_\alpha \left(\omega T^{s+j} \right)$ is called the relative frequency of occurrence of the word α in the sequence ω on the segment from s to $s + t - 1$.

We say that the sequence ω is cesaro relative to the word α, if the limit $\lim_{t \to \infty} \frac{1}{t} \sum_{j=0}^{t-1} I_\alpha \left(\omega T^j \right)$ exists. In this case the value of this limit

$$p_\alpha(\omega) = \lim_{t \to \infty} \frac{1}{t} \sum_{j=0}^{t-1} I_\alpha \left(\omega T^j \right), \tag{7}$$

can be interpreted as an average frequency of occurrence of the word α in the sequence ω [1, 2].

A sequence ω we will call l-cesaro if ω is cesaro relative to all words from B^* of length less than or equal to l, $l = 1, 2, \ldots$. We denote the class of l-cesaro sequences as $\Sigma_B^{(l)}$. A sequence ω we will call cesaro if ω is cesaro relative to the arbitrary word from B^*. We denote the class of cesaro sequences by Σ_B.

Obviously, the following inclusions are valid:

$$\Sigma_B^{(1)} \supseteq \Sigma_B^{(2)} \supseteq \ldots \supseteq \Sigma_B. \tag{8}$$

Examples of sequences from the set Σ_B are infinite periodic sequences (both purely periodic and periodic with an initial section), the set of which we denote by T_B. In this case, as can be seen from the formula (7), p_α is the ratio of the frequency of occurrence of the word α in the period (the number of places in the period from which the word α begins) to the length of the period. For example, in the case of binary alphabet and sequence $001001001\ldots \in T_{\{0,1\}}$ we have:

$$p_1 = 1/3, \ p_{01} = 1/3, \ p_{11} = 0, \ p_{011} = 0. \tag{9}$$

So, the inclusion $\Sigma_B \supseteq T_B$ of sets is valid.

The set of cesaro sequences Σ_B is much wider than the set T_B of periodic sequences. Since the set of possible periods is countable, the set of possible initial sections is countable, then the set of periodic sequences is also countable. In contrast, the set of cesaro sequences, according to the Theorem 1 below, is uncountable.

In [3] (see also the review in [4]), methods for construction of l-cesaro non-periodic sequences were investigated. Classic examples of such sequences in the binary case are the Thue-Morse sequence (number A010060 in The On-Line

Encyclopedia of Integer Sequences [5]), the initial segments of which are the table vector of the Boolean function for the lexicographic order of the arguments, and the Keene sequence [6] obtained by starting with 0 and iterating the morphism $0 \to 001$, $1 \to 110$, (number A064990 in The On-Line Encyclopedia of Integer Sequences), called by the author a "waltz of infinite order" or "Mephisto Waltz infinite word":

$$\omega_{Thue\ Morse} = 011010011001\ 01101001\ 011001101...$$
$$\omega_{Keane} = 001\ 001\ 110\ 001\ 001\ 110\ 110\ 110\ 001....$$

It can be shown that in the case $\alpha = 1$ the equalities:

$$p_1\left(\omega_{Thue\ Morse}\right) = p_1\left(\omega_{Keane}\right) = \frac{1}{2} \tag{10}$$

are valid.

Let us show that the set Σ_B contains in a certain sense "almost all" sequences over the alphabet B. Let $|B|$ be the number of elements in the set B.

Theorem 1. *Let $(w_0, w_1, ...)$ be a representation of the real number $x \in (0,1)$ in the form of a $|B|$-fraction. (In the case of an ambiguous representation, we choose a sequence with an infinite number of zeros). The Lebesgue measure of the set of such $x \in (0,1)$ for which $(w_0, w_1, ...)$ is cesaro sequence is equal to 1.*

Proof. Note that the Lebesgue measure of intersection of a countable number of such subsets of the interval $(0,1)$, each of which has measure 1, is equal to 1. Therefore it is sufficient to prove that the measure of the set of points of the interval for which the limit (7) exists for an arbitrary $\alpha \in B^*$ is 1.

Let us consider the probability space formed by the interval $(0,1)$, the σ-algebra of Lebesgue measurable sets, and the Lebesgue measure *mes* chosen as probability.

Firstly, we note that the random variables $w_0, w_1, ...$ are independent. In fact, for fixed $i_0, i_1, ..., i_{s-1}$, $i_j \in B$, $j = 0, 1, ..., s - 1$, $s = 1, 2, ...$ the equalities

$$mes\left\{x : w_0 = i_0, w_1 = i_1, ..., w_{s-1} = i_{s-1}\right\} = \frac{1}{|B|^s} = \prod_{k=0}^{s-1} mes\left\{x : w_k = i_k\right\} \tag{11}$$

are satisfied.

Secondly, the sequence $I_\alpha\left(\omega T^j\right)$, $j = 0, 1, ...$ is the sequence of m-dependent random variables [7]. Indeed, for $t = m + 1, m + 2, ...$, the random variables $I_\alpha\left(\omega T^j\right)$ and $I_\alpha\left(\omega T^{j+t}\right)$ are independent, because the equalities

$$mes\left\{x : I_\alpha\left(\omega T^j\right) = a \text{ and } I_\alpha\left(\omega T^{j+t}\right) = b\right\}$$
$$= mes\left\{x : I_\alpha\left(\omega T^j\right) = a\right\} \times mes\left\{I_\alpha\left(\omega T^{j+t}\right) = b\right\}, \tag{12}$$

where $a, b = 0, 1$, $j = 0, 1, ...$, are satisfied.

Therefore, the strong law of large numbers is valid [7] for the sequence $I_\alpha \left(\omega T^j \right)$, $j = 0, 1, \ldots$. It means, in particular, the existence of limit (7) for a fixed α almost everywhere. Therefore the measure of the set of such $x \in (0, 1)$ for which $(w_0, w_1, \ldots)$ is cesaro sequence is equal to 1.

2   Cesaro-Hereditary Automata

Let $A = (X, Y, Q, h, f)$ be a strongly connected finite Moore machine with X and Y as input and output alphabets; Q as the set of states; $h : Q \times X \to Q$ as transition function; $f : Q \times X \to Y$ as output function.

We call an automaton A cesaro-hereditary if, starting to work from an arbitrary initial state $q \in Q$, it transforms an arbitrary sequence $\chi \in \Sigma_X$ into a sequence γ, wherein $\gamma \in \Sigma_\gamma$.

Theorem 2. *If an automaton A has the property that for any of its initial state and an arbitrary input word, the last letter of the output word depends only on the last k characters of the input word, then A is a cesaro-hereditary one.*

Proof. The presence of a specific l-gram in the output sequence depends only on the $(l + k)$-gram in the input sequence. Therefore, the existence of limits (7) for all $(l + k)$-grams in the input sequence provides their existence for an arbitrary l-gram in the output sequence.

Example 1 (The shift register is a cesaro-hereditary automaton). Let V_n be the space of n-dimensional binary vectors, F_n be the set of all Boolean functions of n arguments, $n = 1, 2, \ldots$. Let $A_f = (X = \{0, 1\}, V_n, Y = \{0, 1\}, h, f)$ be the Moore machine (n-bit shift register [8]) with the states V_n, the transition function $h((a_1, \ldots, a_n), x) = (a_2, \ldots, a_n, x)$, $x, a_i \in \{0, 1\}$, $i = 1, 2, \ldots, n$, the output function $f(x_1, x_2, \ldots, x_n) \in F_n$. According to the Theorem 2, A_f is a cesaro-hereditary automaton.

Example 2 (The trigger is not a cesaro-hereditary automaton). Let $A = (X = Y = Q = \{0, 1\}, h, f)$, where $h(q, x) = q \oplus x$ be XOR, $f(q, x) = q$. Let us show that there exists a binary cesaro sequence $\chi = (x_0, x_1, \ldots)$ that is transformed by the automaton A into a binary sequence $\gamma = (y_0, y_1, \ldots)$ that is not a cesaro one.

The machine A is a trigger. It can be in one of the two states. Upon receipt of "0" at the input, the automaton maintains its state; upon receipt of "1", it changes.

As an input sequence, we choose the sequence of the following form:

$$\chi = 0\,10\,1000\,10000000\,100\ldots,$$

in which the symbols "1" are located in the places with numbers 2^i, $i = 1, 2, \ldots$. If the initial state of the automaton was $q = 0$, then the sequence of states (and outputs) has the form

$$\gamma = 0\,0\,11\,0000\,11111111\,000\ldots.$$

The sequence γ is formed (starting from the second character) by alternating of series of zeros and ones, the length of which doubles from series to series.

To prove that χ is the cesaro sequence, it is sufficient to analyze the relative frequency of "1" in the growing initial segments. From the one hand, the limit of the relative frequency of occurrence of an arbitrary word α other than 0^k, $k = 0, 1, ...$, exists and is equal to 0:

$$0 \leq \frac{1}{t} \sum_{j=0}^{t-1} I_\alpha \left(\chi T^j \right) \leq \frac{1}{t} \sum_{j=0}^{t-1} x_j = O\left(\frac{\mathrm{Log} t}{t} \right);$$ (13)

from the other hand, for words of the form 0^k, $k = 0, 1, ...$, the corresponding limits also exist and are equal to 1:

$$O\left(\frac{t - \mathrm{Log} t}{t} \right) \leq \frac{1}{t} \sum_{j=0}^{t-1} I_{0^k} \left(\chi T^j \right) \leq 1.$$ (14)

Hence, $\chi \in \Sigma_{\{0,1\}}$.

To prove that γ is not a cesaro sequence, we will show that the sequence γ is not cesaro relative to the word $\alpha = 1$. Let us consider the partial limits of the sequence $\frac{1}{t} \sum_{j=0}^{t-1} y_j$ corresponding to two subsequences with the indices $2^k - 1$, $k = 0, 1, ...$ for even and odd k. Applying the formula for the sum of geometric progression, it is easy to see that the values of these limits are $\frac{2}{3}$ and $\frac{1}{3}$, respectively. Therefore, the limit of the sequence $\frac{1}{t} \sum_{j=0}^{t-1} y_j$ does not exist.

Hence, $\chi \notin \Sigma_{\{0,1\}}$.

Therefore, A is not a cesaro-hereditary automaton.

3   Polyhedra of the Cesaro-Hereditary Automata

Let $A = (X, Y, Q, h, f)$ be a strongly connected finite Moore machine with X and Y as input and output alphabets; Q as the set of states; $h : Q \times X \to Q$ as transition function; $f : Q \times X \to Y$ as output function.

Following [9], we fix two sets of words

$$\{\alpha_i \in X^*, i = 1, 2, ..., t\} \text{ and } \{\beta_j \in Y^*, j = 1, 2, ..., k\}, t \geq 0, k \geq 1.$$ (15)

Let us suppose that an automaton A, starting to work from the state q_0, processes a sequence $\chi = (x_0, x_1, ...)$ into a sequence $\gamma = (y_0, y_1, ...)$. With sequence chi we associate the vector

$$z_{(A,q_0)}(\chi) = \left(p_{\alpha_1}(\chi), ..., p_{\alpha_t}(\chi), p_{\beta_1}(\gamma), ..., p_{\beta_k}(\gamma) \right),$$ (16)

if all quantities on the right-hand side exist.

The rule (16) defines a map

$$Z_{(A,q_0)} : T_X \to [0, 1]^{t+k} \subset R^{t+k}.$$ (17)

It was shown in [9] that the closure (the set of all limit points) of the set $Z_{(A,q_0)}(T_X)$ is a convex polyhedron in $[0,1]^{t+k}$. This set will be denoted by R_A.

Let us set:

$$R_A^\Sigma = Z_{(A,q_0)}(\Sigma_X) \subseteq [0,1]^{t+k},$$
$$R_A^T = Z_{(A,q_0)}(T_X) \subseteq [0,1]^{t+k}. \tag{18}$$

We emphasize that the first set is defined only for the cesaro-hereditary, and the second – for the arbitrary strongly connected finite automaton A. The correctness of the accepted denotations follows from the fact that if the automaton A is strongly connected, then $Z_{(A,q_0)}(T_X) = Z_{(A,q_0')}(T_X)$ and $Z_{(A,q_0)}(\Sigma_X) = Z_{(A,q_0')}(\Sigma_X)$ for two arbitrary states q_0 and q_0'.

It is easy to see that the set R_A^T is not more than countable, and the set R_A^Σ at $t > 0$ is uncountable. The following statement shows that in the case of a cesaro-hereditary automaton, for each point of its polyhedron there is a cesaro input sequence that provides limiting relative frequencies of occurrence of words at the input and output of the automaton that are exactly equal to the coordinates of this point.

Theorem 3. *For the cesaro-hereditary automaton A the set R_A^T is dense in R_A^Σ. The following equality is true $R_A^\Sigma = R_A$.*

Proof. Let us consider the arbitrary point $z \in R_A^\Sigma$. According to the definition of a dense set [10], we need to present a sequence of points from R_A^T, that would converge to z.

For the suitable sequence $\chi = (x_0, x_1, ...) \in \Sigma$ we have

$$z = z_{(A,q_0)}(\chi) = (p_{\alpha_1}(\chi), ..., p_{\alpha_t}(\chi), p_{\beta_1}(\gamma), ..., p_{\beta_k}(\gamma)), \tag{19}$$

where $\gamma = Ext_{(A,q_0)}(\chi)$. By χ_k we denote by a periodic sequence with the period $(x_0, x_1, ..., x_{k-1})$. Let $z_k = z_{(A,q_0)}(\chi_k)$. It is easy to verify that the corresponding coordinates of the vectors z and z_k differ by $o(1)$. Therefore

$$z_k \to z, \text{ if } k \to \infty. \tag{20}$$

Considering that $z_k \in R_A^T$, we obtain the equality of the closure of the set R_A^T and the set R_A^Σ. The theorem is proved.

4 Geometric Features of Polyhedra and Cesaro-Heredity

We give examples of images of polyhedra of automata in the flat case. If $k = t = 1$, $\alpha_1 = \beta_1 = 1$, then the automaton polyhedron is a flat polygon in the square $[0,1] \times [0,1]$. The abscissa axis corresponds to the relative frequencies of occurrence of the symbol "1" in the input sequence, the ordinate axis in the output one.

Let us consider the automaton A_f, defined above in the Example 1, in the case $f(x_1, x_2) = x_1 x_2$. The transition graph of this automaton is the de Bruijn binary graph of degree 2 [8]. It has 4 vertices (00), (01), (11), (10) and the following 6 cycles:

1. the loop at the vertex (00) with marking $(0,0)$,
2. the loop at the vertex (11) with marking $(1,1)$,
3. the cycle of the length 2 with the vertices (01) and (10) and marking (01, 00),
4. the cycle of the length 3 with the vertices (00), (01), (10) and marking (100, 000),
5. the cycle of the length 3 with the vertices (01), (11), (10) and marking (101, 010),
6. the cycle of the length 4 with the vertices (00), (01), (11), (10) and marking (1100, 0010).

The transition graph of the automaton A_f is shown in the Fig. 1.

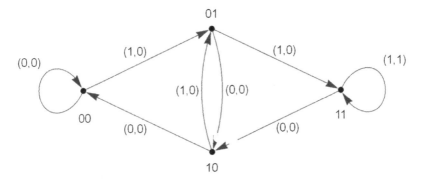

Fig. 1. The transition graph of the automaton A_f.

According to the Theorem 1 of [9], the following equality is correct

$$R_A = Conv\left\{(0,0),(1,1),\left(\frac{1}{2},0\right),\left(\frac{1}{3},0\right),\left(\frac{2}{3},\frac{1}{3}\right),\left(\frac{2}{4},\frac{1}{4}\right)\right\}$$

$$= Conv\left\{(0,0),(1,1),\left(\frac{1}{2},0\right)\right\}. \tag{21}$$

The polygon of this automaton is shown in the Fig. 2.

The polygon of the automaton from Example 2 above, as shown in [9], is also a triangle. It is shown in the Fig. 3.

In the above example in the Fig. 3 the polygon of the automaton contains a side parallel to the ordinate axis.

Theorem 4. *Let $A = (X = Y = \{0,1\}, Q, h, f)$ be strongly connected automaton, $k = t = 1$, $\alpha_1 = \beta_1 = 1$. If the automaton A is cesaro-hereditary, then its polygon does not contain sides parallel to the ordinate axis.*

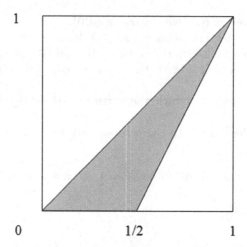

Fig. 2. The polygon of the automaton A_f, A_f is cesaro-hereditary.

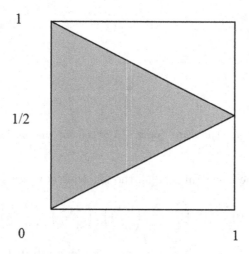

Fig. 3. The polygon of the automaton A, A is not cesaro-hereditary.

Proof. Since sequences consisting of only zeros and only ones can come to the input of the automaton, it is obvious that the polygon R_A should have points with abscissas 0 and 1. Let us suppose the contrary to what is being proved. If R_A contains a side parallel to the ordinate axis, then due to its convexity, the points on this side have abscissas 0 or 1 (see the Fig. 4).

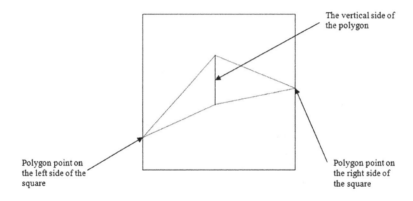

Fig. 4. The polygon R_A by virtue of convexity, has no vertical sides in the inner area of the square.

Without loss of generality we consider that the side under consideration lies on the straight line $z_1 = 0$. The vertices of the polygon R_A, that the side under consideration pulls together in the transition graph of the automaton correspond to the two different cycles c_1 and c_2, such that

$$z_1(c_1) = z_1(c_2) = 0, \quad z_2(c_1) \neq z_2(c_2). \tag{22}$$

Let the set of states of the cycle c_i be $\left\{ q_1^{(i)}, ..., q_{l_i}^{(i)} \right\}$, l_i is the length of the cycle c_i, $i = 1, 2$. Let $\chi^{(i)} = 0^{l_i}$ be the input sequence under which the automaton A goes through the cycle c_i, starting from the state $q_1^{(i)}$, $i = 1, 2$. By $\xi_{12}(\xi_{21})$ we denote the shortest sequence that transfers the automaton A from the state $q_1^{(1)}$ to the state $q_1^{(2)}$ (from the state $q_1^{(2)}$ to the state $q_1^{(1)}$) (see the Fig. 5).

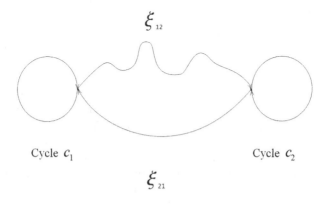

Fig. 5. Structure of the sequences ξ_{12} and ξ_{21}.

Let us consider the sequence

$$\chi = \left(\chi^{(1)}\right)^{k_1} \wedge \xi_{12} \wedge \left(\chi^{(2)}\right)^{k_2} \wedge \xi_{21} \wedge \left(\chi^{(1)}\right)^{k_3} \wedge \xi_{12} \wedge \left(\chi^{(2)}\right)^{k_4} ..., \qquad (23)$$

where the symbol $\wedge$ means concatenation of sequences.

It is easy to see that at $k_i = 2^{2^i}$ the following takes place $\chi \in \Sigma$. Let $\gamma = Ext_{(A,q_0)}(\chi)$ be the output sequence. Let us consider the initial segment of the sequence γ of the length $k_1 + |\xi_{12}| + k_2 + |\xi_{21}| + ... + k_N$. Since $|\xi_{12}|$ and $|\xi_{21}|$ do not exceed the diameter of the graph of the automaton, it is easy to show that the relative frequency of occurrence of units on this segment is equal to $z_2(c_1)\left(1 + O\left(N2^{-2^N}\right)\right)$ at odd N and $z_2(c_2)\left(1 + O\left(N2^{-2^N}\right)\right)$ at even N. This means that relative frequencies sequence has no limit and, therefore, $\gamma \notin \Sigma$, that contradicts the cesaro-heredity condition of the automaton A.

5   Comment

The so-called principle of statistical stabilization of relative frequencies in various topologies is developed, in particular, in [11,12] and other papers. By virtue of this principle statistical stabilization of the relative frequencies of certain events (these frequencies are rational numbers) can be considered not only in the real topology on the field of rational numbers, but in other topologies on the set of rational numbers, in particular, in p-adic ones. The limits of relative frequencies under this consideration belong to the expansion of the field of rational numbers relative to the topology of statistical stabilization. The sequences of relative frequencies of such events for which there is no statistical stabilization in the field of real numbers, but it is present in one of the fields of p-adic numbers are of particular interest. The mentioned papers cite several examples of statistical models in which relative frequencies oscillate (i.e., have no limit) in the field of real numbers, but stabilize (i.e. have a limit) in one of the fields of p-adic numbers.

Such a situation is also possible for the problem considered in the paper. In particular, in proving that one or another automaton is not cesaro-hereditary, we construct special input sequences that lead to the appearance of a non-cesaro sequence at the output of the automaton. This output sequence is an alternation of series of cyclically repeating fragments connected with each other by short "inserts". The lengths of the series in such a sequence are chosen so as to prove the non-existence of the limit (in the field of real numbers) of the relative frequency of the symbol. However, such a limit may exist in the field of p-adic numbers. We recall that the polyhedron of an automaton in [9] is defined as the set of all limit points of a certain set of points with rational coordinates. The extension of this definition to a p-adic topology is interesting and promising.

6   Conclusion

We study cesaro sequences over a finite alphabet, which possess the property of stability of the relative frequencies of occurrence of an arbitrary word in growing initial segments. A finite state automaton is called cesaro-hereditary if it processes cesaro sequences in the input alphabet into cesaro sequences in the output alphabet. It is shown that the shift register is a cesaro-hereditary automaton, and the trigger is not. The proposed sufficient conditions so that the automaton does not possess the property of cesaro-heredity are connected with the presence of special cycles in the transition graph of the automaton.

Acknowledgments. The publication has been prepared with the support of the RUDN University Program "5–100" (recipient K. Samouylov). The reported study was funded by RFBR, project numbers 19-07-00933 and 18-00-01555 (18-00-01685).

References

1. Jacobs, K.: Turing-Maschinen und zufallige 0-1-Folgen. In: Jacobs, K. (eds.) Selecta Mathematica II, Heidelberger Taschenbucher, vol. 67, pp. 141–167. Springer, Berlin (1970). https://doi.org/10.1007/978-3-642-88162-6_6
2. Muchnik, A., Pritykin, Y., Semenov, A.: Sequences close to periodic. Russ. Math. Surv. **64**(5), 805–871 (2009)
3. Allouche, J.-P., Shallit, J.: Automatic Sequences. Theory, Applications, Generalizations. Cambridge University Press, Cambridge (2003)
4. Cusick, T.W., Fredricksen, H., Stanica, P.: On the delta sequence of the Thue-Morse sequence // Australas. J. Comb. **39**, 293–300 (2007)
5. The On-Line Encyclopedia of Integer Sequences. https://oeis.org. Accessed 30 June 2020
6. Keane, M.: Generalized Morse sequences. Z. Wahrscheinlichkeitstheorie verw. Geb. **10**, 335–353 (1968)
7. Doob, J. L.: Stochastic Processes. Wiley, New York; Chapman & Hall, London (1953)
8. Golomb, S.W.: Shift Register Sequences. Aegean Park Press. Laguna Hills, Calif. (1981)
9. Melnikov, S.Yu., Samouylov, K.E.: Polyhedra of Finite State Machines and their Use in the Identification Problem (2020, to appear)
10. Kolmogorov, A.N., Fomin, S.V.: Elements of the Theory of Functions and Functional Analysis. Vol I&II. - Eastford, CT 06242, USA: Martino Fine Books (2012)
11. Anashin, V.S., Khrennikov, A.U.: Applied Algebraic Dynamics. de Gruyter Expositions in Mathematics, Berlin (2009)
12. Khrennikov, A.Yu.: Interpretations of Probability and Their p-Adic Extensions. Theory Probab. Appl. **46**(2), 256–273 (2002)

Development of Risk Controlling Mechanism and Tools for Agile Projects in Telecommunications

Sergei Grishunin[1]([✉]) [iD], Svetlana Suloeva[2]([✉]) [iD], Tatyana Nekrasova[2]([✉]) [iD], and Ekaterina Burova[2]([✉]) [iD]

[1] National Research University Higher School of Economics, Moscow, Russia
sgrishunin@hse.ru
[2] Peter the Great St. Petersburg Polytechnic University, St. Petersburg, Russia
{suloeva_sb,burova_ev}@spbstu.ru, nekrasova_tp@sbpstu.ru

Abstract. We developed the mechanism and tools of risk controlling in agile projects for companies in information and communication (ICT) industry. The relevance of this topic is underpinned by (1) the growing number of failures of agile projects due to realization of unique set of risks; and (2) the fact that standard agile practices neglect important risk management steps. The paper fills the research gaps in this area and addresses inefficiencies in explicit agile risk management frameworks. The results include the development of the mechanism's concept and the block diagram for scrum framework. They also include risk controlling tools: risk-based release planning, system of key risk indicators and agile risk controlling effectiveness evaluation tree. Unlike peers mentioned in existing studies the mechanism provides holistic approach to the agile risk management while keeps the spirit of agile. It addresses risk governance issues, ensures integration and coordination of risk management activities both inside the team and across the company and provides for lightweight but efficient tools. The mechanism can be adapted for other agile frameworks and can be applied by scrum masters and project managers in ICT industry as well as by the researches who are interested in further enhancement in agile risk management practices.

Keywords: Risk management · Risk controlling · Agile · Project management · Information and communication · Software development

1 Introduction

Recently, companies in information and communication (ICT) industry have started implementing agile project management (APM) to pursue breakthrough innovations. However, the surveys indicated: many of them failed in implementing APM [1, 7]. That was underpinned by the overlooking of unique set of risks brought about by agile while the its standard practices neglected important risk management (RM) steps. The pitfalls included declining communication across the company; poor version and configuration management; inefficient forecasting, or delivery risks [1, 7]. The realization of risks

© Springer Nature Switzerland AG 2020
O. Galinina et al. (Eds.): NEW2AN 2020/ruSMART 2020, LNCS 12526, pp. 270–284, 2020.
https://doi.org/10.1007/978-3-030-65729-1_23

resulted in losses caused by cost overruns, decrease of speed to market or increase in number of defects and reworks [15]. To cure these problems RM practices must be integrated into the APM to explicitly address risks while maintaining the spirit of agile.

Literature has suggested a number of frameworks for such integration [1–3, 6, 15]. However, many of these studies have gaps making the frameworks inefficient in the current ever-changing environment. They are reactive in nature, not fully address risk governance issues, miss linkages between risks and project goals and provide fragmented sets of tools rather than the comprehensive RM systems.

We closed those gaps in the studies and developed RM mechanism and the related tools for agile research and development (R&D) projects in ICT. The mechanism is based on risk controlling principles and adapted for scrum framework. The novelty of the paper is driven by the advantages of the mechanism over its peers. It provides holistic and proactive approach to RM and ensures that critical project risks are timely identified and managed. It addresses the risk governance and provides for integration and coordination of processes, roles and responsibilities both inside agile teams and across the company. We also developed the related tooling: the framework of risk-adjusted project planning, the key performance indicators and the criteria for assessing the effectiveness of RM in APM. The mechanism can be used by the practitioners and researches who are interested in enhancement of risk management in agile.

The rest of the paper is organized as follows. Section 2 explores outlook and challenges of APM in telecommunication. Literature review and gaps in the studies are outlined in Sect. 3. Section 4 explains the application of risk controlling in APM. Section 5 provides the mechanism and its tools. Section 6 formulates the conclusions.

2 Agile Project Management in Telecommunication: Outlook and Challenges

Current ever-changing environment destroys the boundaries between telecommunication and informational industries; they have been merging into a single information and communication (ICT) space [18]. In 2020–2024, disruptions will continue to drive the industry. We expect fierce competition in the emerging technologies such as 5G fixed wireless and satellite internet, the next generation fixed broadband, edge computing and various 5G applications in healthcare, education, manufacturing, retail and transportation industries. In this environment, waterfall project management, which values fixed customer requirements, low technological and product risks, extensive planning and preproduction, has become inefficient. [3, 19, 20]. Contrary to waterfall approach, APM is an interactive method delivering a project throughout its life cycle. It implies delivering rapid product development though incremental updates based on the frequent feedbacks from customers [19]. Thus, APM addresses the key issues of R&D project management in ICT industry (Table 1).

Table 1. Key issues of project management in ICT and how APM addresses these issues

Key issues of project management in ICT	How APM addresses these issues
1. Developing complex scalable systems consisting of multiple components	1. Flexible, adaptive method applicable for uncertain environment
2. Dealing with uncertain and unstable customer requirements	2. Fosters creativity and innovations
3. Limited R&D budgets, high cost of errors and reworks	3. Encourage changes through frequent iterations
4. Minimal cost of change, flexible operations	4. Each iteration results in release of workable product or its prototype
5. Demand for frequent and fast innovations	5. Reduced time to market
6. Uncertain, risky technologies	6. Cost reduction from decreasing overheads and higher team performance
7. Emphasis on teamwork, transparency, revolutionary ideas and continuous improvement	7. Focus on quality and reduction of waste
	8. Increased customer centricity
	9. Faster return on investment
	10. Faster feedback – safe innovation

Sources: [18–20]

There is a growing number of implementations of APM in R&D not only in start-ups but also in the ICT giants such as Ericsson, ZTE, Telecom Australia or Vodafone [19]. Mostly, APM is used for the software development but there is a trend of spreading the APM into maintenance of legacy systems and development of hardware. Scrum is the most widespread method in APM [19]. In scrum, minimal viable product (MVP) is delivered in increments (sprints, usually 2–4 weeks iterations) [5, 21, 22]. The second widespread method is Dynamic System Development (DSDM). It is used for the development projects of IT systems which require tough timing and budgets [1]. Extreme programming (XP) is the least frequent method. Its limitations include focusing on programming code rather than design, lack of documentation and quality control. Given the widespread of scrum we adjusted our mechanism for this method.

Still, many ICT companies have been slow in adopting APM in their R&D practices [3, 21]. The key hurdles included (1) attempts to mix traditional waterfall and agile methods in one project; (2) lack of team's knowledge, resources, tooling or methodologies; (3) communication problems with the rest of the company; (4) poor segregation of duties within the teams; (5) lack of documentation and track records of the past projects [16]. There is yet another critical failure factor – the neglect of RM. Teams are concentrated on processes and organizational issues rather than on risk analysis and development of risk mitigation strategies. This neglect will likely result in projects' failures. The challenges include missing time or cost targets, inferior quality of the final products. These challenges require agile project managers to reconsider their approaches to RM and explicitly integrate RM into the APM.

3   Risk Management in Agile Projects: A Literature Review

The literature explored various approaches to RM in agile projects. We divided them into (1) the implicit approach to RM; (2) the explicit "conventional" approach to RM; and (3) the "lightweight" agile RM approach. The implicit approach states that the risk mitigation activities are already embedded in the APM and limited RM processes are required [13–15]. For example, Nyfjord and Kajko-Mattsson [13] argued that risks in APM were managed via (1) incremental MVP developments; (2) prioritization of tasks at the start of each sprint; (3) accounting for relative task difficulties in sprint planning; (4) frequent feedback from the customer. The weakness of this approach is the following: even though APM can partially mitigate risks related to scope creep, going off schedule and budget, technology and security breakdowns, it creates new specific risks [1]. They include: (1) lack of cross-functional collaboration; (2) flaws in design stage; (3) lack and fragmentation of tooling to keep the process efficient; (4) poor version and configuration management; (5) weak documentation and knowledge retention management; (6) inefficiencies in relationships with client; or (7) excessive haste resulted in low quality [7, 16]. The threats include reduction in productivity margins, dissatisfaction of clients; increase of product development time, higher number of defects and loss of profit [3, 16].

The explicit approach assumes implementation of "conventional" RM processes as those described in PMBOK, COSO or SEI [1, 3, 8, 9] with minimal adjustments to agile. They include (1) risk assessment (including risk identification, analysis and prioritization); and (2) risk control (including risk management planning, resolution and monitoring). The weakness of this approach is the "heavy weight" of RM tools. They are slow and centered around documentation and reporting. They weigh up to 30% of team's time which questions the team's ability to meet the time, quality and cost targets [14]. The opportunity is to reduce the burdens of RM by "simplifying" its tooling [15].

Such "simplification" reflected in agile RM (ARM) [1, 2, 15, 21–24]. It assumes application of the "lightweight" tools such as planning poker, risk boards and risk notes; risk checklists or logs of controls [15, 21]. They are complimented with organizational steps such as assignment of the risk champion, sprint planning sessions and risk discussion in scrum meetings. Despite adding some overheads, explicit approach provides the continuous risk management and ensures timely mitigation actions. The weakness of this approach is the absence of a holistic mechanism which integrates and coordinates all tooling and organizational steps together. Its absence results in poor risk communication across the organizational silos. Other limitations include (1) focusing on the individual risks and overlooking correlations among them; (2) recognizing only compliance, security, and financial risks; (3) weighting only deviations from standard controls [10–12]. These make ARM obsolete in the business environment characterized by disruptions and volatility. These weaknesses can be overcome by implementation of risk controlling system [10].

4   Risk Controlling: A New Philosophy of Risk Management in Agile Practices

Risk controlling (RC) is a goal-oriented system of integrated RM in the firm, including project work. It puts in the forefront the following six principles: (1) creation of value for stakeholders; (2) coordination of RM activities across the firm; (3) integration of risk management into the decision making; (4) maintaining a stable and continuous operations; (5) continuous monitoring and tracking of risks; (6) focusing on risk prevention; and (7) instilling the risk culture [10–12]. RC provides the architecture (methods, processes, and tooling) or risk management while the project managers apply it to make risk-informed decisions [10]. RC's principles match the key value of Agile Manifesto [12]. Therefore, RC in lightweight version (agile risk controlling (ARC)) is suitable for APM. It solves three main tasks: (1) ensuring product release with the minimal variances from the plan; (2) achieving the proper balance between value creation, risks and resources; (3) coordination of RM practices with the rest of the company. Implementation of ARC reduces the variances from the project's plan by 10%–30% [10].

In ARC, the team performance is measured with the application of earned value management (EVM) metrics [24, 27]. EVM allows to effectively evaluate work performed and helps to form client fee payment structure [24]. The key two metrics are (1) release performance index (RPI); and (2) expected project return on investments (ROI). The latter is compared with the planned ROI set at the inception of the project.

$$RPI = \frac{n_a + SP_r/v_a}{SP_p/v_p} \tag{1}$$

Where n_a – actual number of sprints completed up to date of analysis, SP_r – story points remained in the project, v_a – actual team's velocity, SP_p – originally planned story points in release, v_p - planned team velocity

$$ROI = \frac{\sum_{s=1}^{n_a + \frac{SP_r}{v_a}} \left[\frac{BPI_s - DC_s - O_s - F_s)}{(1 + WACC)^S} \right]}{CE} \tag{2}$$

Where BPI_s – the revenue from project backlog items realized in s-th sprint; DC_s, O_s – direct and indirect cost incurred by the team in s-th sprint, F_s – losses of revenue in s-th sprint due to inefficiency and quality problems, WACC – cost of project capital adjusted to sprint's length, CE- capital employed in the project.

For the management purpose these metrics are split into subfactors such as the cost and schedule variances and estimates to complete [27]. The scrum master tasks, though, are to reduce the variances of these subfactors from the plan and to bring estimates to complete to plan values by managing of project's risks.

5   Development of Risk Controlling Mechanism for Agile Projects in Telecommunications

5.1   Development of the Block Diagram of the Mechanism

The suggested risk controlling mechanism for agile projects is presented in Fig. 1.

Fig. 1. The block diagram of agile risk controlling mechanism for scrum

5.2 Buying into the APM and Setting the Project Risk Governance Structure

The *step A (Fig.* 1*)* in the mechanism is for project stakeholders to identify whether (1) APM suits for the particular project; and, if yes, (2) what agile method to choose [24]. These can be assessed by the internal rating [24, 25]. The scoring factors include: (1) the company's maturity for agile; (2) the scope and scale of the project; (3) the spread of development efforts (distributed or co-located teams); (4) stability and uncertainty of requirements; (5) criticality of the project and its tolerance for failures; (6) education and experience of developers; (7) maturity of development culture; and (8) the level of customer participation and frequency feedback. If the decision has been made to go ahead with the agile, the structure of the development contract should be set. The issues include (1) the minimal set of documentation; (2) the method, timing and structure of compensation; (3) cost sharing of risk realization; (4) means and frequency of client participation and feedback; and (5) the governance framework [24].

The *step B (Fig.* 1) of the mechanism is setting APM risk governance to ensure integration and co-ordination (1) within the team; (2) across the company; and (3) between the team and the customer. It is aimed at reduction of risks caused by the lack of organizational, environmental and executive sponsorships. Three-line of defense model, based on COSO framework [8, 15] is applied (Table 2):

Table 2. Risk governance structure in ARC

Lines of defense	Description
First line	The scrum master (SM) and the team. Perform the project within set risk-taking limits. Own the risk and responsible for effectiveness of risk planning, risk mitigation strategies, controls and decision making
Second line	Risk subject matter expert (RSME) serving as business partner. The RSME assists the scrum master in (1) providing risk guidance, methodological support to the team; (2) suggesting tools and risk mitigation strategies; (3) setting and maintaining of key risk indicators (KRIs); (4) bearing responsibility for risk and control documentation and repository; (5) challenging of the decisions to be made; and (6) making and support risk monitoring. The RSME serves as the risk liaison between the team, customer and the rest of the company. Complex, uncertain projects may include several RSME addressing risk controlling, security, compliance or human resources issues
Third line	Monitor the efficiency and effectiveness of ARC and provide assurance to stakeholders. This role is assigned to the company's internal audit (IA)

5.3   From Project Due Diligence to Risk-Based Release Planning

At *step C (Fig.* 1) of the mechanism the project due diligence is performed. The team and customer work together to (1) specify the product to be released; and (2) understand the customer's goals. This work will (1) crystalize the project scope and important dates; (2) specify the human and technical resources which both sides are ready to provide; and (3) agree, prioritized and document minimal functional requirements [24].

The *step D (Fig.* 1) of the mechanism is identification of risks. To make this process "lightweight" SM and RSME should (1) establish the strict timeframe for the process, for example, one working day [15]; (2) supply and educate the team on ARC's methodologies and tools; and (3) provide teams with "standard" templates, models and ready-made goal and risk statements. The latter can be done on the base of previously completed projects. This step consists of (1) analysis of project internal and external environment to identify the risk areas; (2) establishing the minimal objectives that need to be achieved at the project's end; (3) identification of risks related to these objectives; (4) risks analysis and modelling; (5) setting the risk appetites; and (6) risk-based release planning.

First task is performed with the "lightweight" version of SWOT – SNW (strength, neutral, weaknesses) analysis [12]. The second task is achieved with TOS (threshold of success) method, which set the minimum objectives that must be fulfilled to consider project as successful [15]. The number of objectives should not be large, no more than 10–15 and directly related to RPI and ROI. The objectives must be specific, measurable, achievable, relevant and time bound.

In the third task, risks are identified against the set of the minimum objectives and in the areas identified by the SNW [15]. The "lightweight" risk identification methods include review of "lessons learned" from retrospective projects, risk prompt lists prepared by RSME, risk checklists and risk brainstorming.

In the *step E* (Fig. 1). the identified risks are analyzed with the application of "bowtie" tree diagram (Fig. 2). Its goal is to split risks into their key risk factors (F_i) and triggers [10]. Risk-factors are linked to each another and to the objectives with the casual relationships. The leftmost nodes are the initial risk factors which can be controlled by the team. The central node is the final risk. Identified risks with risk factors must be documented in the risk register in team wiki and reflected on the risk board.

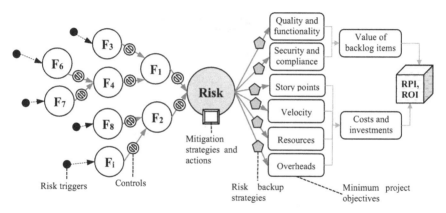

Fig. 2. Bowtie tree for risk analysis in agile projects

After risk analysis the risk assessment and release planning is performed. The bowtie trees are aggregated and converted into the probabalistic model. It can be done, for example, with ModelRisk[1]© add-in to MS Excel. This add-in replaces uncertain values of risk-factors with quantitative probability distribution functions and applies Monte Carlo simulation to automatically generate thousands of possible scenarios. To save time on risk planning meeting the template models should be prepared by the RSME in advance. To keep the system "lightweight" we recommend using only PERT distribution for inputs (frequency, impact, recovery rate) to all risk factors [10]. PERT has parameters (a,m,b) where a is the best-case estimate, m is the most likely outcome and b is the worst-case estimate. They are identified either (1) from actual team performance and risks realization in retrospective projects; or (2) from the outcome of team's "planning

---

[1] https://www.vosesoftware.com/products/modelrisk/

poker" [21]. Other inputs in the model are the correlations among risks. These are also inferred from results of retrospective projects, planning poker or team brainstorming.

Before performing the risk assessment, the team should set the limit parameters for ROI and RPI -the risk appetite and the risk tolerance. This is usually performed as part of step C. The risk appetite establishes the maximum variance of ROI or RPI's from objectives. The risk tolerance sets the minimum variances of ROI or RPI which consider not material. These values should be set in close co-operation with the stakeholders.

The third task is to run the Monte-Carlo simulation to get expected values of ROI and RPI given risks [10]. The first output of the simulation is the Tornado chart [10]. It provides the analysis of impact of each risk on the key project metrics. Tornado chart helps the team to identify top-5 risks for future management. The second output (Fig. 3) is the probabalistic histograms of key EVM metrics (ROI and RPI). They form the confidence intervals for these metrics given risk and show the most likely outcome for ROI and RPI. The team can estimate the expected value of ROI or RPI with the given probability and understand if metrics are within the risk-appetite limits or will exceed these limits.

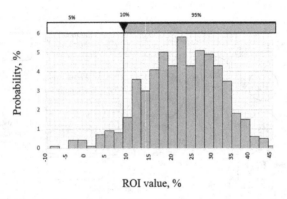

Fig. 3. The confidence interval of key EVM metrics (example for ROI)

5.4   Risks Mitigation and Controls

The *step F (Fig.* 1) of the mechanism is the development of risk mitigation strategies and action plans for the top-5 risks (including control procedures) [15]. If the risk simulation results in ROI and RPI within the risk tolerance limits than risk management actions are unnecessary. Conversely, mitigation of risks which resulted in key metrics going above risk appetite should be prioritized. The efficiency of each strategy are compared on the "cost-impact" basis. The top-5 risks and related mitigation strategies are discussed with customer and other stakeholders for making mutual decisions.

SM, RSME and the team develops the mitigation strategies into the specific risk management tasks. These tasks are assigned to individual team members and distributed among sprints [15]. The RSME is responsible to documenting these tasks into the respective sprint backlogs and risk register, performing the regular control of their fulfillment and monitoring of their progress with the burndown charts. The last step is to formulate the control objectives, design the specific control procedures and assign them to the individual team members [8, 12, 26]. The bowtie charts (Fig. 2) are used to determine the locations of controls in the processes.

5.5 Information, Communication and Monitoring

Regular risk monitoring in ARC (*step G* in Fig. 1) is performed with the system of key risk indicators (KRIs, Table 3). They (1) translate risk mitigation strategies into the clear goals and actions; (2) set responsibilities and measure the efforts of team members; (3) ensure feedback to develop the risk response strategies; and (4) serve as a communication tool within the team and between the team and the project's stakeholders. KRIs should meet the following criteria: (1) be the leading indicators; (2) provide the direct linkage to the risk factors; (3) be expressed quantitatively to measure and control the outcome of mitigation strategies; (5) be accessible and easy to understand; and (6) be linked to the certain time periods and provide comparability [12]. KRIs are posted visibly in burndown chart and reflected in wiki.

Table 3. Example of KIRs in ARC

Risk area	Indicator name	How to calculate
Scope	Scope volatility (SV)	$SV = \frac{CSP - ISP}{ISP} * 100\%$ (3) CSP -current must-have scope (in story points), ISP – initial scope (in story points)
Schedule	Release slippage (RSRI)	$RSRI = \frac{ASP/AP}{RSP/RP}$ (4) ASP, RSP – completed and required points in sprint, AP, RP – actual and required # person sprint hours
	Release Burn Down Performance (RBPI)	$RBPI = ASP/CSP * 100\%$ (5)
	Sprint Burn Down Performance (SPBI)	$SBPI = IRSP/ARSP$ (6) IRSP, ARSP – ideal and actual remaining points
Testing	Test coverage (TC)	$TC = TUS/CUS * 100\%$ (7) TUS, CUS – completed user stories which passed all tests and total number of completed stories
	Automated test coverage (CAT)	$CAT = NAT/TT$ (8) NAT, TT - # of automated tests in sprint, total tests

(continued)

Table 3. (*continued*)

Risk area	Indicator name	How to calculate
Quality	Rework Ratio (RR)	$RR = DDOD/SDOD * 100\%$ (9) DOOD, SDOD – # of defects in "done" stories, total # of "done" stories
	Number of failed tests (NFT)	$NFT = FTR/TTR * 100\%$ (10) FTR, TTR – # of failed test and total tests in release
Team performance	Number of productive hours (NPH)	$NPH = TPH/TH * 100\%$ (11) TPH –productive hours of team in sprint, TH – total working hours in sprint
Customer	Total customer conversations (TCC)	$TCC = TCH/TH * 100\%$ (12) TCH – total hours of conversation with customer
	Net promoter score (NPS)	$NPS = NSS - NSU$ (13) NSS, NSU – share of release's stories marked as "satisfied" (8–10 out of 10) and "unsatisfied" (1–3)

Source: developed by the authors

To keep the system "lightweight" the number of KRIs should not be large: 1-2 per each risk. RSME and team members review the values of KRIs at the daily scrum meetings and discuss corrective actions if KRI values go above signal or critical limits.

At the start of each sprint SM together with RSME and the customer discuss the sprint goals, risk register and update the register if new or emerging risks are identified (*step H* in Fig. 1). This discussion should be short and focused, with optimal length of 30 min. The agenda includes the discussion of (1) each risk's values; (2) effectiveness of mitigation strategies;(3) risks prioritization (4) setting limits for KRIs and; (5) the discovering of new and emerging risks. If the new risks have been discovered, RSME adds the new task to sprint backlog to develop the mitigation strategies and sets KRIs and controls for these risks. For identified risks the progress of fulfillment of risk management tasks is updated in the burndown chart. The team and RSME may decide to re-plan the project (go to the steps *D and E*) in case of the drastic changes in the risk register. At the end-sprint review meetings (*step I* in Fig. 1) the team spends up to 30 min for discussion of risk updates in the burn down charts, the overall project risk level and what risks have been realized in the sprint's timeframe. The talk also includes the review of mitigation plan status. If any risks have realized than the team discusses the causes of this event, informs the customer, decides on next backup steps such as reduction in work scope and complexity. The team also closes the realized risk in the register and in burn down charts.

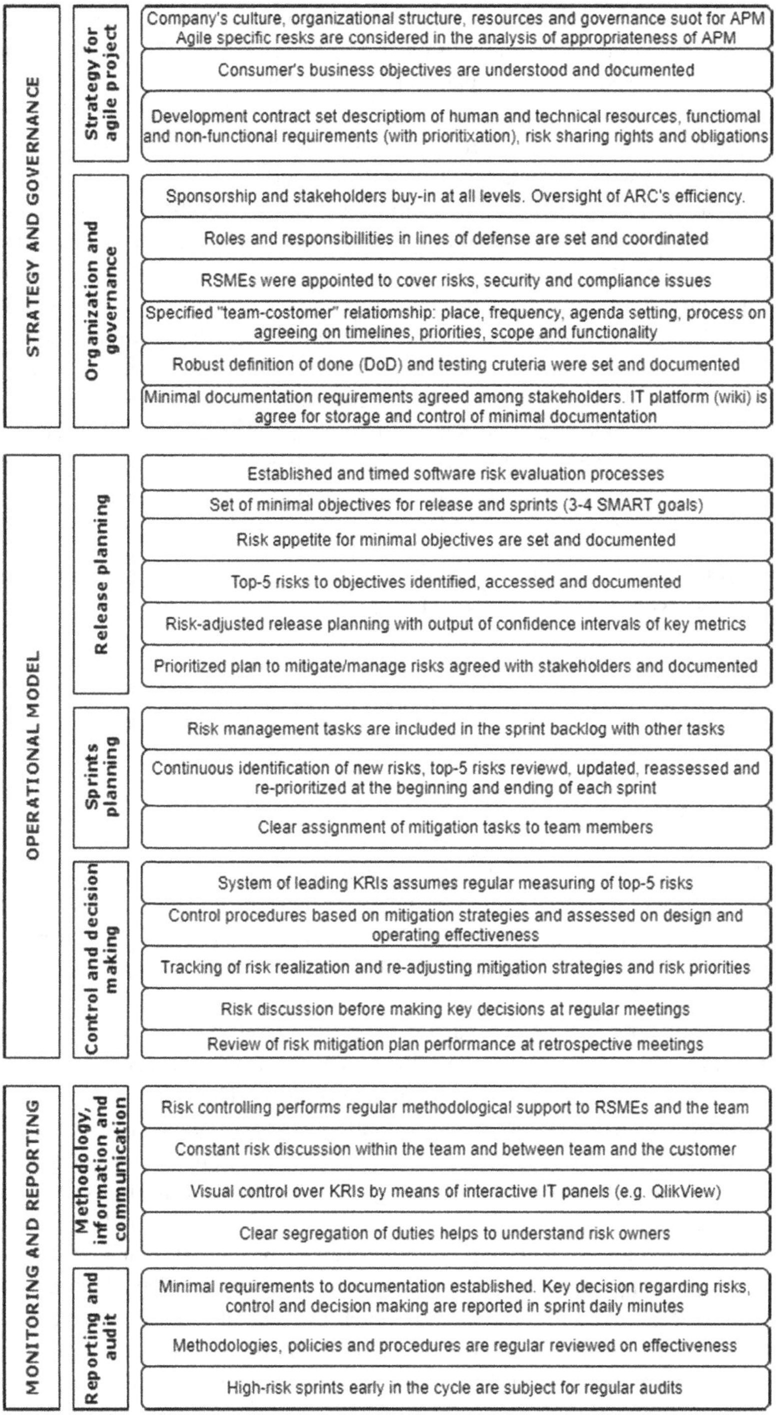

STRATEGY AND GOVERNANCE	Strategy for agile project	Company's culture, organizational structure, resources and governance suot for APM Agile specific resks are considered in the analysis of appropriateness of APM
		Consumer's business objectives are understood and documented
		Development contract set descriptiom of human and technical resources, functiomal and non-functional requirements (with prioritixation), risk sharing rights and obligations
	Organization and governance	Sponsorship and stakeholders buy-in at all levels. Oversight of ARC's efficiency.
		Roles and responsibillities in lines of defense are set and coordinated
		RSMEs were appointed to cover risks, security and compliance issues
		Specified "team-costomer" relatiomship: place, frequency, agenda setting, process on agreeing on timelines, priorities, scope and functionality
		Robust definition of done (DoD) and testing cruteria were set and documented
		Minimal documentation requirements agreed among stakeholders. IT platform (wiki) is agree for storage and control of minimal documentation
OPERATIONAL MODEL	Release planning	Established and timed software risk evaluation processes
		Set of minimal objectives for release and sprints (3-4 SMART goals)
		Risk appetite for minimal objectives are set and documented
		Top-5 risks to objectives identified, accessed and documented
		Risk-adjusted release planning with output of confidence intervals of key metrics
		Prioritized plan to mitigate/manage risks agreed with stakeholders and documented
	Sprints planning	Risk management tasks are included in the sprint backlog with other tasks
		Continuous identification of new risks, top-5 risks reviewd, updated, reassessed and re-prioritized at the beginning and ending of each sprint
		Clear assignment of mitigation tasks to team members
	Control and decision making	System of leading KRIs assumes regular measuring of top-5 risks
		Control procedures based on mitigation strategies and assessed on design and operating effectiveness
		Tracking of risk realization and re-adjusting mitigation strategies and risk priorities
		Risk discussion before making key decisions at regular meetings
		Review of risk mitigation plan performance at retrospective meetings
MONITORING AND REPORTING	Methodology, information and communication	Risk controlling performs regular methodological support to RSMEs and the team
		Constant risk discussion within the team and between team and the customer
		Visual control over KRIs by means of interactive IT panels (e.g. QlikView)
		Clear segregation of duties helps to understand risk owners
	Reporting and audit	Minimal requirements to documentation established. Key decision regarding risks, control and decision making are reported in sprint daily minutes
		Methodologies, policies and procedures are regular reviewed on effectiveness
		High-risk sprints early in the cycle are subject for regular audits

Fig. 4. Agile risk controlling effectiveness evaluation tree

After each sprint RSME and the team must perform the self-assessment to ensure that ARC system is effective. In addition to the team self-assessment, the project is independently reviewed by the company's internal audit (IA). This is *step K* (Fig. 1) of the mechanism. It assumes performing these reviews at early sprints with the focus on the several high-risk sprints. To identify high-risk sprints IA may develop a sprint risk rating [25]. To assess the effectiveness of ARC, IA does the end-project review with the ARC evaluation tree (see the next section). It is a responsibility of RSME to ensure that at least minimal documentation on key risks, controls and decision exists and stored which render the sprints auditable (*step J* in Fig. 1). The key documents for sprint are the meeting minutes. They contain an analysis of top-5 risks, a prioritized plan to mitigate and manage risks, the description of control procedures and KRIs with the warning and critical values. To ensure security and version control, the minutes should be recorded in electronic form (in team's wiki). Other documents include electronic snapshots of product and sprint backlogs and burndown chart, risk and control register and analysis or risk register. An appropriate audit step is also to collaborate with the stakeholders and customer to get the project feedback and recommendations (*step J.* in Fig. 1).

5.6   Post-release Review. ARC Evaluation Tree for Assessing Completeness and Effectiveness of Agile Risk Management

For the mechanism we summarized the key factors of ARC effectiveness and construct the ARC assessment tree for end-project assessment (Fig. 4). This assessment should result in recommendations for improvements in ARC for the next agile projects.

6   Conclusion

New industrial revolution in ICT industry expands the application of agile methods of project management in R&D. However, many of these projects failed due to neglection of important risk management steps. To address this challenge, we developed the lightweight risk management mechanism for scrum projects. It is based on risk controlling principles. The advantages of the mechanism over existing peers include: (1) rendering holistic approach to risk management; (2) addressing risk governance issues; and (3) providing for integration and coordination of processes, roles and responsibilities both inside the agile teams and across the entire company. The mechanism contains the variety of tooling such as risk-based release planning, system of leading key risk indicators and risk management effectiveness evaluation tree. They provide for (1) quantitative assessment of aggregate project exposures; (2) establishing the clear links between factors of uncertainty and key project metrics (e.g. ROI); (3) tracking risk developments over the project cycle; (3) assessing the effectiveness of the risk management actions after the project competition. The future research directions include adaptation of this mechanism for other type of agile methods such as Kanban or DDM, development of missing and enhancing of existing tooling. Other direction includes development series of case studies of implementation of the mechanism in the various agile projects in ICT.

References

1. Albadarneh, A., Albadarneh, I., Qusef, A.: Risk management in agile software development: a comparative study. In: Proceedings of 2015 IEEE Jordan Conference on Applied Electrical Engineering and Computing Technologies, AEECT 2015, IEEE, Amman, Jordan (2015)
2. Chuna, R., Pereira, C.S., Pinto, J.A.: Agile software project: proposal of a model to manage risks. In: Proceedings of 8th Iberian Conference on Information Systems and Technologies, CISTI, Lisbon, Portugal (2013)
3. Beaumont, M., Thuriaux-Aleman, B., Prasad, P., Hatton, C.: Using agile approaches for breakthrough product innovation. Strategy Leadersh. **45**(6), 19–25 (2017)
4. Kaczorowska, A.: Traditional and agile project management in public sector and ICT. In: Proceedings of 2015 Federated Conference on Computer Science and Information Systems, FedCSIS, Lodz, Poland, pp. 1521–1531 (2015)
5. Hossin, E., Ali Babar, M., Paik, H.-Y.: Using scrum in global software development: a systematic literature review. In: Proceedings of 4th IEEE International Conference on Global Software Engineering, ICGSE 2009; IEEE, Ireland, pp. 175–184 (2009)
6. Boehm, B.: Get ready for agile method with care. Computer **35**(1), 64–69 (2002)
7. Elbanna, A., Sarker, S.: The risks of agile software development: learning from adopters. IEEE Softw. **33**(5), 72–79 (2016)
8. Enterprise Risk Management. Integrating with Strategy and Performance. Committee of Sponsorship Organizations of the Treadway Commission, https://www.coso.org/Pages/def ault.aspx (2017)
9. A Guide to The Project Management Body of Knowledge (PMBOK Guides, Sixth Edition). Project Management Institute (2017)
10. Grishunin, S., Suloeva, S., Nekrasova, T.: Development of the mechanism of risk-adjusted scheduling and cost budgeting of R&D projects in telecommunications. In: Galinina, O., Andreev, S., Balandin, S., Koucheryavy, Y. (eds.) NEW2AN/ruSMART -2018. LNCS, vol. 11118, pp. 456–470. Springer, Cham (2018). https://doi.org/10.1007/978-3-030-01168-0_41
11. Grishunin, S., Mukhanova, N., Suloeva, S.: Development of concept of risk controlling for industrial enterprise. Organizer Prod. **26**(1), 45–46 (2018)
12. Funston, F., Wagner, S.: Surviving and Thriving in Uncertainty: Creating the Risk Intelligent Enterprise. Wiley, New York (2010)
13. Nyfjord, J., Kajko-Mattsson M.: Commonalities in risk management and agile process models, In: Proceedings of International Conference on Software Engineering Advances (ICSEA 2007), pp. 18–21. Cap Esterel, France (2007)
14. Paulk, M.: Agile methodologies and process discipline, crossTalk. J. Softw. Defense Eng. 15–18 (2002)
15. Nelson, Christopher R., Taran, G., de Lascurain Hinojosa, L.: Explicit risk management in agile processes. In: Abrahamsson, P., Baskerville, R., Conboy, K., Fitzgerald, B., Morgan, L., Wang, X. (eds.) XP 2008. LNBIP, vol. 9, pp. 190–201. Springer, Heidelberg (2008). https://doi.org/10.1007/978-3-540-68255-4_20
16. Dhir, S., Kumar, D., Singh, V.B.: Success and failure factors that impact on project implementation using agile software development methodology. In: Hoda, M.N., Chauhan, N., Quadri, S.M.K., Srivastava, P.R. (eds.) Software Engineering. AISC, vol. 731, pp. 647–654. Springer, Singapore (2019). https://doi.org/10.1007/978-981-10-8848-3_62
17. Alberts, C., Dorofee, A.: Risk Management Framework. Technical report CMU/SEI-2010-TR-017 ESC-TR-2010-017 (2010). https://resources.sei.cmu.edu/asset_files/TechnicalRep ort/2010_005_001_15245.pdf
18. Glukhov, V., Balashova, E.: Economics and Management in Info-communication: Tutorial. Piter, Saint Petersburg (2012)

19. Balashova, E., Gromova, E.: Agile Project management in telecommunication industry. Espacios **38**(41), 24–30 (2017)
20. Esbensen, K., Hjartar, K., Pralong, D., Salo, O.: A Tale of Two Agile Path: How a Pair of Operators Set Up Their Organizational Transformation. McKinsey and Company, https://www.mckinsey.com/industries/technology-media-and-telecommunications/our-insights/a-tale-of-two-agile-paths-how-a-pair-of-operators-set-up-their-organizational-transformations (2019)
21. Cohn, M.: Agile Estimating and Planning. Prentice Hall, New Jersey (2006)
22. Sutherland, J., Sutherland, J.J.: Scrum: The Art of Doing Twice the Work in Half the Time, 1st edn. Crown Business, New York (2014)
23. Odzaly, E., Greer, D., Stewart, D.: Lightweight risk management in agile projects. In: Proceedings of 1st EAI International Conference on Computer Science and Engineering, pp 324–345. EAI, Penang, Malaysia (2017)
24. Beardwood, J.: Shour, M: Risk Management and Agile Software: Optimizing Contractual Design. Comput. Law Rev. Int. **6**, 161–170 (2010)
25. Grishunin, S., Suloeva, S.: Development of project risk rating for Telecommunication company. In: Galinina, O., Balandin, S., Koucheryavy, Y. (eds.) NEW2AN/ruSMART -2016. LNCS, vol. 9870, pp. 752–765. Springer, Cham (2016). https://doi.org/10.1007/978-3-319-46301-8_66
26. COBIT framework. https://www.isaca.org/resources/cobit
27. Sulaiman, T., Barton, B., Blackburn, T.: Agile EVM – earned value management in scrum projects. In: Proceedings of AGILE 2006 Conference, pp. 7–16. Minneapolis, Minnesota, USA (2006)

Investment Attractiveness
of the Telecommunications Economic Sector
During the CoronaVirus Pandemic

Valery Leventsov[✉], Vladimir Gluhov[✉], and Alexandr Leventcov[✉]

Peter the Great St. Petersburg Polytechnic University, Saint-Petersburg, Russia
{vleventsov,vicerector.me}@spbstu.ru, drlev@mail.ru

Abstract. Investing in the financial market is an effective way to save and increase any free money an investor might have. The success of the investments is based on knowing the fundamentals of the financial and technical analysis of securities. The current uncertainty around the negative effect of the coronavirus COVID-19 on the world economy and its possible negative outcome contribute to their mass sell-out. The situation has been aggravated as well by the price war on the oil market, which has led to a significant drop in oil prices. A number of analysts believe that, despite the current market situation being near a panic, several of the falling stocks present a certain interest for investment, including stocks of metallurgical, energy, and telecommunications companies. In order to answer the question, which securities in which economic sectors free money can be invested in with minimum risk, it is necessary to identify the sectors of the economy which have the biggest investment potential. Many analysts point to the telecommunications sector as one of these economic sectors. Due to the continuous daily demand for telecommunications services, as well as their fairly stable growth, the stocks of telecommunications companies, the main ones of which are VimpelCom, Mega-Fon, MTS, Rostelecom and T2 RTK Holding, are highly attractive for investment. Furthermore, specialists from the company International Data Corporation (IDC) concluded that the outbreak of the coronavirus in China is able to have a positive impact on the development of the ICT-sector, opening up new opportunities for developing digital platforms and Big Data solutions. As a result of the threat of the coronavirus spreading, an extra push to develop the telecommunications sector of our country's economy is given by the transition of school-age and university students to distance learning, starting in mid-March 2020, as well as the transition to working from home, when possible. A fundamental analysis of the main companies of the telecommunications economic sector in our country has shown that, starting from 2015, they can be tentatively divided into groups of high performance companies and companies with lower performance. The first group includes MTS and MegaFon, while the second includes VimpelCom and Rostelecom. In this regard, the stocks of the companies from the first group are more attractive in terms of investment when compared to the second. In order to determine which stocks are the most attractive for investments, a fundamental analysis of the shares of the first group should be conducted. The analysis conducted showed a great investment attractiveness for shares of MTS.

© Springer Nature Switzerland AG 2020
O. Galinina et al. (Eds.): NEW2AN 2020/ruSMART 2020, LNCS 12526, pp. 285–296, 2020.
https://doi.org/10.1007/978-3-030-65729-1_24

Keywords: Investment · Telecommunications sector · Stocks · Investment attractiveness · Pandemic · Coronavirus

1   Introduction

When an individual or legal entity has free financial means (savings), especially in times of an economic crisis, then the natural question arises: how can they be saved, or better yet, multiplied?

The most effective way to save and multiply free money, in our view, is to invest it in the financial market, which can generate an income of several tens or hundreds percent in a year [1].

However, to truly be successful in increasing one's capital, it is necessary to understand the basics of how the financial market works, as well as methods for making investment decisions, i.e., knowing the fundamentals of financial and technical analysis.

One of the main methods for analyzing the movement and predicting the value of any shares is the fundamental analysis, the idea of which is to assess the influence of internal and external factors on the value in order to determine the future profitability of these financial instruments.

Technical analysis is understood as a set of tools and methods for predicting the value of financial instruments by using an in-depth analysis of their changes over the previous periods. By using this, the tendencies (trends) in changes in the value of these instruments and the right moment for buying and selling them can be determined [1].

The world markets are currently being negatively impacted by the coronavirus COVID-19, which was first reported on 31.12.2019 in the city of Wuhan, China. The existing uncertainty around its possible effects and the scale of it contributes to continued mass sell-outs, while renewed fears concerning the negative impact of COVID-19 on the global economy contribute to the growing bearishness on the global trading floors [2].

The decrease in production volumes has caused a price reduction on energy resources and, primarily, on oil, whose prices plummeted after the failed negotiations on the fate of dealings of OPEC+ on 06.03.2020 thanks to the position of our country refusing to reduce additional oil production. Moreover, the position of Saudi Arabia, who stated that it would increase oil production and slashed its selling price, led to a sharp collapse of oil prices to $31.27 (down more than 30%) on Monday 09.03.2020.

Analysts from the bank Goldman Sachs believe that "OPEC and Russia started a price war this weekend after Saudi Arabia aggressively reduced the relative price at which they sell their oil" [3]. This conclusion is well founded when taking into account that the representative from Russia who took part in the negotiations with the OPEC countries must have understood the effects of his refusal to reduce oil production. Furthermore, it should be remembered that our country's budget for 2020 established the price of Urals oil at $42.4 a barrel, although the price is now at around $30, i.e., significantly lower, thus confirming our earlier conclusion about the awareness among decision of Russia.

Therefore, it is hard not to agree with the opinion of experts who consider the "big game" to have only begun, and that Russia has made the first power move which has taken her potential opponents by surprise [4, 29].

In addition to this, the situation in the global economy has been aggravated by WHO's (World Health Organization) acknowledgement of the outbreak of the coronavirus pandemic [5], despite the fact that the spread of the coronavirus in China is currently on a steady decline [6]. The organization is currently being influenced by two factors: the coronavirus or the collapsing oil prices, which could, in the end, lead to a recession in the global economy or, even worse, to a global economic crisis. For investors in our country everything has been aggravated even more with the significant depreciation of the rouble.

The gravity of the situation in the global economy is also confirmed by the US Federal Reserve's urgent reduction of the target rate on 15.03.2020 to 0–0.25% [7], making the national currency cheaper and its goods more competitive.

Some experts believe that the panic on the market will continue and the price of oil will go lower and lower, leading to a further depreciation of the rouble against currencies [8]. On the other hand, analysts from the company Bloomberg believe that Russian oil companies are protected by the government thanks to the tax policy of Russia, providing them a shield against the volatility of oil prices as well as low production costs: around $20 a barrel. Therefore, Russians have little cause to panic [9], although the price of Russian oil from the brand Urals already fell below $19 a barrel on 18.03.2020 [10].

In turn, investor Warren Buffet, known throughout the whole world, considers the current market situation to be less terrible in comparison with 1987 and 2008 [11].

On the other hand, the inevitability of a wide-scale economic crisis is talked about by specialists from Bank of America, Goldman Sachs and Morgan Stanley. Those at Bank of America believe that the coming crisis will be one of the strongest in American history [12].

Kristalina Georgieva, Managing Director of the IMF, stated that a recession even worse than the Great Recession is awaiting the global economy in 2020 [13].

Asset Manager of SR Solutions Roman Andreev states that while although the current situation on the market is nearing a panic, several of the falling shares present an investment opportunity. In his opinion, the most interesting for investment are stocks in metallurgical, energy, and telecommunications companies [14].

Analysts from the investment company Rikom-Trast suggest at the moment to buy shares of gold mining companies and not in the oil export and telecommunications sector [15].

In connection with this, people with free monetary means are facing the question of which sectors of the economy and which securities they can invest in with minimum risk. In order to answer this question, the economic sectors with the most investment potential should be identified.

Analysts from the investment company Aton make a sound guess that "the outbreak of the coronavirus in China is fraught with more serious residual risks for the global and Russian economy." In their opinion, in the next few months shares in sectors such as the electric power industry, telecommunications, gold mining, as well as domestic consumer retailing, will have the tactical advantage [16].

As can be seen, all of the above mentioned analysts point to the telecommunications sector, made up of companies facilitating communications by way of the telephone or the internet, as one of the economic sectors of investment interest. In order to determine its investment potential, we will analyze the development prospects of the given sector and choose the most attractive company for investments.

2   Analysis of the Telecommunications Economic Sector During the Coronavirus Pandemic

The history of cellular and mobile communications begins in our country in 1992, although only a very few could afford its services at the time since the telephones themselves cost at least $1,000 with a price per minute of up to $5.

After the default of 1998, service providers were forced to reduce the cost of minutes to $0.15–0.18 at the end of 1999, thus gradually making cellular communication wide-scale.

Later the company Beeline on account of releasing a new type of product onto the market practically started a price war, causing a significant growth in the number of cellular users. The number of network subscribers began to rise even faster with the appearance of cheap GSM-standard phones from the companies Siemens, Phillips, Motorola and Nokia.

In the early 2000s the number of cellular network subscribers practically doubled in a year due to the expansion of federal providers to the regions, thus gradually taking over regional providers.

The financial and economic crisis of 2008–2009 did not impact subscribers very strongly since communication was already cheap. However, it limited the financial opportunities of network providers, slowing down the growth of their revenue, which declined for the first time in history in 2014. This showed that the expansive growth through increasing the number of subscribers had run its course.

In autumn 2006, the State Commission for Radio Frequencies (GKRC) allocated frequencies for third generation (3G) networks. It took about a year and a half for this standard of mobile communication to become widespread. During this time, smartphones came to the Russian market thanks to the gained popularity of Wi-Fi. Communication began moving towards mobile internet and information services. This tendency became even more noticeable with the appearance of the first fourth generation networks in 2011.

The development of the telecommunications market in the whole world is connected to fifth generation networks, the introduction of which is still facing problems in our country. By 2020 5G networks were supposed to have been extended to all cities with a population of over 1 million people. This, however, has yet to be reached [17]. At the same time, analysts predict an almost 90% growth of investment in the 5G sector [18].

In our country, a tendency has been noticed of a decreasing number of subscribers of landlines and a stagnation or small increase in the remaining sectors of the telecommunications market.

After 2020 an accelerated growth of the subscriber base in the machine-to-machine and internet segments is possible, gradually transitioning to a standard 5G network.

Meanwhile, thanks to the increasing speed of mobile internet access, a decline in the number of fixed broadband users is possible in its favor.

In the corporate sector, it is possible to expect more significant changes from fifth generation network use if they are, in fact, as good as they are said to be. Business will always find a use for them as much as makes economic sense [19, 30].

In connection with the constant daily demand for telecommunications services, as well as with their fairly stable growth, the securities of telecommunications companies, the main ones of which are VimpelCom, MegaFon, MTS, Rostelecom and T2 RTK Holding, are very attractive in terms of investment. Analysts from Aton generally believe that in the telecommunications sector of the economy, companies currently will have a steady cash flow and are not suffering from the coronavirus pandemic, pointing to MTS as the most attractive of these companies [20].

As a follow-up to this, specialists from the American analytic company International Data Corporation (IDC), specializing in IT-market research, concluded that the outbreak of the coronavirus in China may have a positive impact on the development of the ICT-sector, opening up new possibilities in the development of digital platforms and Big Data solutions [21].

An additional push for the development of the telecommunications sector of the economy in our country was given by the transition of Russian institutes, as well as a number of schools, to distance learning starting from the middle of March 2020 due to the threat of the coronavirus spreading. Education is conducted by means of special distance education learning systems as well as other forms of interaction between the teachers and students, both offline and in real time using Skype, video conferences, and so on. As of 17 March of this year, 65% of universities had already switched to online education [22].

In addition to this, due to the coronavirus, the Federal Service for Surveillance on Consumer Rights Protection and Human Wellbeing and the Russian Ministry of Health recommend, where possible, to transition to working from home, which will likewise lead to a growth in demand for telecommunications services.

At the same time, no one has canceled the implementation of the program "Digital Economy of the Russian Federation", which provides for the implementation of an integrated digital transformation of the economy and social sphere of our country by 2024 [23].

Thus, the telecommunications sector of the Russian economy has a great growth potential and, accordingly, a great investment attractiveness.

The specific factors of the telecommunications market are its government regulation and its dependence on the appearance of new technology and the income of the population.

A fundamental analysis of the main companies from the telecommunications sector of our country's economy shows that starting from 2015, they can be tentatively divided into groups of high performance companies, focused on increasing their value, and companies with low performance. The first group includes MTS and MegaFon, while the second includes VimpleCom and Rostelecom. Accordingly, the securities of companies of the first group are to be recommended for acquisition by investors, while those of the second are not recommended.

Since 2018 the virtually sole leader of the telecommunications market has been MTS.

Nevertheless, in order to confirm the conclusion made, a fundamental analysis of the shares of the first group of high performance companies needs to be conducted with the goal of using it to identify the most attractive in terms of investment.

Generally, when analyzing shares, they are compared in terms of the present value (PV), which is the closest in substance to the intrinsic value of the company. The formula for determining the PV looks as follows:

$$PV = \frac{C_1}{1+r} + \frac{C_2}{(1+r)^2} + \cdots + \frac{C_t}{(1+r)^t} \tag{1}$$

where: C_i is the size of the future income in the i-st period ($i = 1, 2, \ldots t$); r is the alternative (internal) rate of return [1].

In our case, we will limit ourselves to the specific indicators widely used in fundamental analysis for assessing the investment attractiveness of shares:

earnings per share (EPS);

the ratio of price to earnings per share (price/earnings, P/E), which are the most important indicators of the future value of shares [1].

The earnings per share is calculated as follows:

$$EPS = \frac{NI - PD}{CSO} \tag{2}$$

where: NI is the net profit; PD is the dividends on the preferred shares; CSO is the number of common shares outstanding.

The P/E coefficient is calculated as the ratio of market price to earnings per share (EPS):

$$P/E = P/EPS \tag{3}$$

A high value of the P/E indicator is usually considered a sign of the overvaluation of shares. Therefore, all other things being equal, investors, as a rule, give preference to companies with a lower P/E value.

Table 1 presents the main indicators of the analyzed companies for the period from 2015 to 2019.

It shows that the net profit of MTS is practically two times and the revenue practically 1.5 times higher than that of MegaFon. The much higher value of the P/E indicator speaks to the overvaluation of MegaFon shares.

Furthermore, MTS is a recognized leader of the Russian market with a cost-effective and well-managed business with an effective dividend policy and a stably growing network of stores, compared to the company MegaFon, whose growth phase has finished, costs of attracting and retaining subscribers are growing, and tariffs are being reduced. In addition to this, since late 2018 MegaFon shares have been transferred from the first quotation list to the third.

Table 1. Main indicators for the analyzed companies

Issuer	Indicator	Years				
		2015	2016	2017	2018	2019
MegaFon	Revenue, billion rub.	313.4	316.3	373.3	335.5	255.8*
	Net profit, billion rub.	39.0	25.5	4.5	35.2	8.5*
	EPS, rub.	62.9	41.1	7.34	56.7	13.7*
	P/E	13.5	14.1	69.9	–	–
MTS	Revenue, billion rub.	431.2	435.7	442.9	451.5	476.1
	Net profit, billion rub.	49.5	48.5	56.0	65.9	54.2
	EPS, rub.	24.0	23.5	28.0	33.0	27.1
	P/E	8.77	11.0	9.85	7.22	10.2

Everything mentioned above indicates the great investment attractiveness of MTS shares. After choosing to invest in the shares of this company, it is recommended to select the moment for their acquisition with consideration of the technical analysis signals.

As is known, the methods of technical analysis are subdivided into graphic and mathematical analysis. Both methods can be used when making investment decisions, for example, through the free service "Tekhanaliz" of the investment company Finam Holdings [24].

The index dynamics of MICEX – Telecommunications (MOEXTL) for May 2018 – March 2020 are presented at weekly intervals in Fig. 1. From it we can see that over four weeks the telecommunications market of Russia fell, practically reaching values of 1720 points on 19.03.2020, which is a serious support level from which, in our view, a trend reversal is to be expected.

This conclusion is confirmed by the daily graph of price changes for shares of MTS as of 23.03.2020, especially the change in the histogram of the oscillator MACD, showing the signal for buying the stock (see Fig. 2) [26].

However, it is not recommended to make investment decisions based on the signals of only one indicator or oscillator. Therefore, an intersection of simple moving averages with periods 5 and 10, for example, is to be applied (see Fig. 3) [27].

Fig. 1. Index dynamics of MICEX – Telecommunications [25]

From the graph in Fig. 3 it can be seen that the moment is approaching when the moving average with period 5 crosses the MA from top to bottom with the longer period 10, which will be the signal to acquire MTS shares. If the current tendency should continue as such then this could happen no later than by the end of this week.

Benjamin Graham, famous American economist and investor, rightly argued that the direction in which share prices will move cannot be predicted accurately in a short time period. Even securities undervalued at the time of acquisition can lose even more value [28]. In other words, an investor should be able to be patient and be psychologically stable.

Thus, the most important component of a successful investment is the psychology, the main principles of which are a rational individual psychology and a sound money management plan [1].

Fig. 2. Daily graph showing changes in share prices of MTS

Fig. 3. Daily graph showing changes in the share prices of MTS using the indicators of *Moving Average*

3 Conclusion

Thus, this paper has justified the investment attractiveness of the telecommunications sector of the economy during the economic crisis caused by the coronavirus pandemic and the price war on the oil market.

The results of the fundamental analysis of securities of high performance companies of this sector revealed that the shares of MTS are the most attractive for investment.

It is recommended to determine the right moment for buying these securities based on the signals of the technical analysis, while at the same time not forgetting about the individual psychology.

Acknowledgments. This research work was supported by the Academic Excellence Project 5-100 proposed by Peter the Great St. Petersburg Polytechnic University.

References

1. Leventsov V.A., Leventsov, A.N., Kryukov, I.N.: Finances and Engineering: theory and practice [Finansy i inzhiniring: teoriya i praktika] / SPb.: Polytechnic University, 334 p. (2014)
2. The virus is drowning world markets. Internet resource. https://www.finam.ru/analysis/new sitem/mirovye-rynki-tonut-v-virusnom-fone-20200227-093057/?utm_source=morning_r evi&utm_medium=new&utm_content=27.02.2020&utm_campaign=all_morning. Accessed 27 Feb 2020
3. Oil prices plummet 30%. Internet resource. https://www.rbc.ru/economics/09/03/2020/5e6 56d349a79474203e30da2. Accessed 09 Mar 2020
4. Russia starts a big game with a power move: foreign experts on the effects of Russia leaving OPEC + . Internet resource. http://actualcomment.ru/rossiya-nachinaet-bolshuyu-igru-del aya-silnyy-khod-zarubezhnye-eksperty-o-posledstviyakh-vykhoda-rf--2003091026.html. Accessed 09 Mar 2020
5. WHO announces the coronavirus pandemic in the world. Internet resource. https://www. finam.ru/analysis/newsitem/voz-ob-yavila-pandemiyu-koronavirusa-v-mire-20200311-200 943/?utm_source=morning_revi&utm_medium=new&utm_content=12.03.2020&utm_cam paign=all_morning Accessed 12 Mar 2020
6. Expert from China names an end date for the coronavirus epidemic. Internet resource. https://sovetov.su/news/109_Ekspert_iz_KNR_nazval_sroki_okonchaniya_epi demii_koronavirusa.html. Accessed 12 Mar 2020
7. Federal Reserve reduces base target rate to zero. Internet resource. https://www.finam.ru/ analysis/newsitem/frs-snizila-osnovnuyu-procentnuyu-stavku-do-nulya-20200316-014934/. Accessed 16 Mar 2020
8. Experts predict a further drop in the rouble and oil. Internet resource. URL: https://quote.rbc. ru/news/article/5e660bf09a79476d130d65a7. Accessed 13 Mar 2020
9. How much does oil really cost and what are the prospects of Russia in the oil war. Internet resource. http://krizis-kopilka.ru/archives/73982. Accessed 13 Mar 2020
10. Russian oil has dropped to $19 a barrel. Internet resource. https://www.rbc.ru/economics/19/ 03/2020/5e7344249a7947add13aeb78. Accessed 19 Mar 2020
11. Buffet: the situation on the market is not comparable to the crisis of 2008. Internet resource. https://investfuture.ru/news/id/baffet-situaciya-na-rynkah-ne-sravnima-s-kri zisom-2008-goda?utm_referrer=https%3A%2F%2Fpulse.mail.ru&utm_source=pulse_ mail_ru. Accessed 13 Mar 2020

12. Bank of America: an economic crisis has begun in the USA. Internet resource. https://sensay. mirtesen.ru/blog/43824663633/Bank-of-America-v-SSHA-nachalsya-ekonomicheskiy-kri zis?utm_referrer=mirtesen.ru&utm_campaign=transit&utm_source=main&utm_medium= page_0&domain=mirtesen.ru&paid=1&pad=1. Accessed 23 Mar 2020
13. IMF predicts a worse recession in 2020 than that of 2008. Internet resource. https://www. finam.ru/analysis/newsitem/mvf-prognoziruet-v-2020-godu-xudshuyu-recessiyu-chem-vo-vremya-mirovogo-finansovogo-krizisa-20200324-092835/?utm_source=morning_revi& utm_medium=new&utm_content=24.03.2020&utm_campaign=all_morning. Accessed 24 Mar 2020
14. Andreev R.: What to do with shares during a market panic. Internet resource. https://fomag. ru/news/chto-delat-s-aktsiyami-kogda-na-rynkakh-panika/?utm_referrer=https%3A%2F% 2Fpulse.mail.ru&utm_source=pulse_mail_ru. Accessed 13 Mar 2020
15. Top-11 shares on the Russian market to buy in a crisis. Internet resource. https://2stocks.ru/ 2.0/russian/stocks/news/top-11-akciy-na-rossiyskom-rynke-dlya-pokupki-v-krizis?utm_ref errer=https%3A%2F%2Fpulse.mail.ru&utm_source=pulse_mail_ru. Accessed 13 Mar 2020
16. The risks caused by the coronavirus are currently higher than any other time given the size of China's economy. Internet resource. URL: http://www.finmarket.ru/shares/analytics/516 3156. Accessed 22 Feb 2020
17. How telecommunications in Russia made a revolution in 20 years. Internet resource. https://www.vedomosti.ru/technology/articles/2019/12/02/817681-telekommunik atsii-rossii. 10 Feb 2020
18. Investments in 5G-infrastructure will double in 2020. Internet resource. http://www.dailyc omm.ru/m/48356/. Accessed 19 Mar 2020
19. Gapotchenko D.: Russian telecommunications market grows three times higher than pre-dicted. Internet resource. https://www.cnews.ru/reviews/telekom_2019/articles/rossijskij_r ynok_vyros_vtroe_vyshe. Accessed 10 Feb 2020
20. Best shares on the Russian market during a pandemic. Internet resource. https://investfuture. ru/articles/id/luchshie-akcii-rossiyskogo-rynka-v-period-pandemii?utm_referrer=https% 3A%2F%2Fpulse.mail.ru&utm_source=pulse_mail_ru. Accessed 22 Feb 2020
21. IDC: How the coronavirus will help the ICT-sector 2020. Internet resource. http://www.tad viser.ru/index.php/%D0%A1%D1%82%D0%B0%D1%82%D1%8C%D1%8F:%D0%98% D0%9A%D0%. Accessed 17 Feb 2020
22. Two-thirds of institutes move to distance learning. Internet resource. https://doxajournal.ru/ uni/uni_vs_coronavirus. Accessed 20 Feb 2020
23. Program "Digital Economy of the Russian Federation". Internet resource. https://data-eco nomy.ru/#rec38557658. Accessed 20 Feb 2020
24. Investment company Finam. Internet resource. https://www.finam.ru/. Accessed 23 Feb 2020
25. Russian indexes MOEXTL. Internet resource. https://www.finam.ru/profile/moex-indeksy/ micex-tlc/tehanalys-light/?market=91&freq=6&type=3&autoupdate=5&ma=1&maval= 100&uf=1&indval=7&lvl1=10&lv1val=7&lvl2=1&lv2val=&lvl3=1&lv3val=&Apply=% CE%E1%ED%EE%E2%E8%F2%FC. Accessed 19 Feb 2020
26. Daily graph of changes in share prices of MTS. Internet resource. https://www.finam.ru/pro file/moex-akcii/mts/tehanalys-light/?market=1. Accessed 23 Mar 2020
27. Daily graph of changes in share prices of MTS using the indicators Moving Average. Internet resource. https://www.finam.ru/profile/moex-akcii/mts/tehanalys-light/?market=1&freq=5& type=3&autoupdate=5&ma=3&maval=5&uf=1&indval=12&lvl1=1&lv1val=7&lvl2=1& lv2val=&lvl3=1&lv3val=&Apply=%CE%E1%ED%EE%E2%E8%F2%FC. Accessed 23 Mar 2020
28. Graham B.: The Intelligent Investor. A complete Guide to Value Investing. M.: Alpina Publisher, 568 p. (2020)

29. Glukhov, V.V., Ilin, I.V., Lepekhin, A.A.: Towards business optimization and development of telecommunication companies: tools analysis and their adaptation opportunities. In: Galinina, O., Andreev, S., Balandin, S., Koucheryavy, Y. (eds.) NEW2AN/ruSMART -2018. LNCS, vol. 11118, pp. 471–482. Springer, Cham (2018). https://doi.org/10.1007/978-3-030-01168-0_42

30. Eliakina, P.D., Evseeva, O.A., Evseeva, S.A., Ilyin, I.V.: Development of the national innovation system on the base of blockchain technology (case of the Russian Federation) In: Proceedings of the 32nd International Business Information Management Association Conference, IBIMA 2018 - Vision 2020: Sustainable Economic Development and Application of Innovation Management from Regional expansion to Global Growth, pp. 7773–7784 (2018)

Modern Digital Technologies and Telecommunications Mechanisms in the Implementation of Socio-Economic Policy at the Local and Regional Level

Tatyana Nekrasova[1]($\boxtimes$), Natalya Mukhanova[1]($\boxtimes$), Sergey Kretsy[2]($\boxtimes$), and Natalja Polyjanova[3]($\boxtimes$)

[1] Peter the Great St. Petersburg Polytechnic University, Saint Petersburg, Russia
dean@fem.spbstu.ru, nmukhanova@spbstu.ru
[2] Kuban State Technological University, Krasnodar, Russia
kretshu@mail.ru
[3] Belgorod National Research University, Belgorod, Russia
nvp-nir@ya.ru

Abstract. The current level of management of the functioning and development of economic processes in Russian regions is characterized by the predominance of analog methodology in the collection, processing and issuance of important information and products that largely determine the relevance, direction and effectiveness of the implementation of functions and mechanisms of state regional management. The purpose of the work is to modernize the organizational and economic support of the regional economy management processes based on digital technologies. The system of scientific research methods that provided the author's scientific results was formed on the basis of traditional and innovative methodological developments that provide the possibility of combining analog and digital assessments of the functioning of regional economic systems, applying qualitative and quantitative research procedures for the formation and transformation of research information arrays, developing promising directions for the introduction of digital telecommunications technologies as part of the functions and mechanisms for managing the economy of modern regions. Results: characteristics of the key features of the modern region as a subject of the digital economy, the specifics of electronic document management as the basis for rationalization of process management in the digital economy of the region, the organization of electronic document management on a regional scale based on the digital information node "Bank-business entity" and modern telecommunications technologies, localized banking structures as nodes of the regional digital infrastructure: resources, goals, functions, results, architecture and information and management flows of the digital node "Bank – economic entity" in the regional economic management system. Conclusions: the conclusion is made about the possibility and need for a qualitative increase in the scale and effectiveness of the use of digital telecommunications technologies in the implementation of the function of state management of the economy of regions, which will dramatically increase the effectiveness of its implementation.

© Springer Nature Switzerland AG 2020
O. Galinina et al. (Eds.): NEW2AN 2020/ruSMART 2020, LNCS 12526, pp. 297–307, 2020.
https://doi.org/10.1007/978-3-030-65729-1_25

Keywords: Telecommunications · Management · Socio-economic policy ·
Information resources · Regional economic potential · Digital services

1 Introduction

The global trend of digitalization of economic activity, which has proved its effectiveness in terms of transparency, predictability, security and manageability of economic processes, has not affected the regional level of economic management in the Russian Federation in any way, although the available examples of corporate information systems and services on a national scale clearly confirm the need for rapid mass implementation of digital technologies in the relevant functions, procedures and mechanisms.

It is the digital format of mechanisms and forms of interaction at all levels and branches of local, regional, sub-Federal, and national levels that is the basis for promising effective, systematic and integrated interaction of all economic entities in the region, as well as structures and institutions of the regional community that have their own, often unused, potential to accelerate regional economic processes. However, the real "digital revolution" of a regional scale in the Russian Federation is actually in a state of scientific search and fragmentary initiatives of individual territories, although it can be unified, scaled and integrated into a single digital standard for implementing the state function of managing modern Russian regions [5, 10].

The existing theoretical approaches to implementing the technological foundations of the "digital revolution" at the regional management level are as follows [1–3, 6]:

- new opportunities in the organization of regional socio-economic processes and management associated with quality growth implementation of functional and systematic digital technologies mean in the short and medium term a major breakthrough in the implementation of state management functions to the regional economy associated with a sharp increase in the availability of factual information on the status and activities of subjects and objects of economic management, speed of collection, verification, scale accumulation and primary processing in real-time;
- the best regional practices for implementing modern digital technologies have a significant potential for scaling and can be widely applied in the management of modern Russian regions at the regional, macroregion, and Federal district levels;
- for the applied implementation of the "regional" digital revolution and the implementation of the existing fundamental groundwork in specific management technologies, functions and mechanisms, an up-to-date digital infrastructure is needed, adapted to the specifics and content of the processes of regional socio-economic management and providing a real increase in its functionality, quality and efficiency.

2 Method of Research

The author's approach to the modernization of organizational and economic support of regional economic management processes based on digital technologies includes the following key innovations [15, 18, 21, 23]:

- characteristics of the region as a promising subject of the digital economy;
- specifics of electronic document management as the basis for rationalization of process management in the digital economy of the region;
- features of the organization of electronic document flow on a regional scale based on the digital information node "Bank-business entity»;
- main possibilities of using localized banking structures as nodes of regional digital infrastructure;
- architecture and information and management flows of the digital node "Bank-business entity" in the regional economic management system.

The characteristics of the key opportunities for converting the economy of a particular region to a digital format and the main directions for using digital technologies in regional management are as follows. We believe that the main directions of implementing digital telecommunications technologies in the region's economic management system are [4, 7, 12]:

- creation of systems for objective monitoring of the state and activity of all economic entities operating in the region (both endogenous residents and representatives of exogenous structures located within the Regional Economic System (RES));
- organization of digital monitoring of key socio-economic processes, differentiated by us depending on the source of origin and significance for the results of the RES operation;
- tracking the composition, intensity and effectiveness of management impacts at the local (local), regional, sub-Federal, and Federal levels based on a specific set of quantitative indicators that are generated and verified in digital format.

The implementation of these directions is designed to improve the efficiency, reliability and coverage of integrated electronic document management and archiving systems, the formation of regional socio-economic models and quantitative forecasts, and the formation of a factual base of strategic program documents [11, 16].

Characteristics of regional opportunities and features of the organization of system electronic document management as a system for ensuring the functioning and management of the digital economy of the region implies [8, 9, 14]:

- consideration of THE entire population of the territory (residents and mi-grants), economic entities (infrastructure and users differentiated by residency), institutions that ensure the functioning and functionality of the regional economic system (intra-level, inter-level, including from outside the RES), and regional economic management entities (municipal, regional, sub-Federal, Federal);
- inclusion in the tasks of organizing regional electronic document management: creation and updating of digital identification systems for RES subjects, creation of automated systems for recording and objective control of regional economic processes, implementation of automated procedures for primary and secondary processing of economic and managerial information (potential, activity, expectations and plans of RES subjects), logging and optimization of economic and management processes

at the regional level, infrastructure support for the functioning of the digitized segment of RES, aggregation of information resources of different economic actors and integration with existing digital systems (Rosstat, Central Bank, FNS, FMS, etc.) no creating and ensuring the functionality of the functional regional telecommunication systems electronic document management systems advanced information storage, accumulation and processing of the data streaming system of socio-economic information, system knowledge and support scenario forecasts, systems and services joint activities.

The activities of all entities that carry out economic activities within the region, as well as institutions that provide intra-and inter-level interaction of RES entities, can be transferred to an electronic format, taking into account the specifics of their functions and features of the formation and dynamics of the economic base. At the same time, the advantages of regional scale and significance available in the implementation of these efforts can be [13, 17, 19, 20]:

- systematic increase in transparency of regional economic processes based on reliable authorization of the entities involved in them;
- visualization and rapid tracking in digital format of key socio-economic processes at the local and regional levels with a perspective of their integration at the level of the country as a whole;
- double saving of all types of non-productive resources of all RES entities that accompany paper document flow: cost savings of the entities themselves and cost savings associated with the operation of certain types of activities within the RES (archives, notaries, offices, etc.);
- increased reliability of storage, if necessary – recovery of credentials on the basis of a complete transaction history, available when using "block-chain" technologies»;
- increasing openness of data on the actual activities of economic entities in the region, which allows automated generation of integrated accounting, statistical and other types of reports.

We also note that currently there are a significant number of large national ("state Services" resource) and corporate information and digital systems (for example, the information system of Sberbank PJSC, which covers almost the entire population of specific territories), in which, in fact, regional information research and monitoring tasks have already been solved, which requires integration with regional information resources and eliminates the need for duplication of costs for their formation [22].

Solving the problem of digitalization of regional document flow will allow using modern information systems for accumulation, processing and analysis of regional-scale data with the possibility of applying streaming principles for monitoring socio-economic information, implementing high-level economic and mathematical models and forecasts, organizing joint monitoring, research and management activities, including remote collaboration.

The author's key innovation of the regional electronic document management at the micro level of RES is to validate the feasibility of the transfer of the accounting function and reporting of corporate information resources for information resources of commercial banks, in fact, serving all regional transactions and their totality, Poreba thus for regional economic and social processes (Fig. 1).

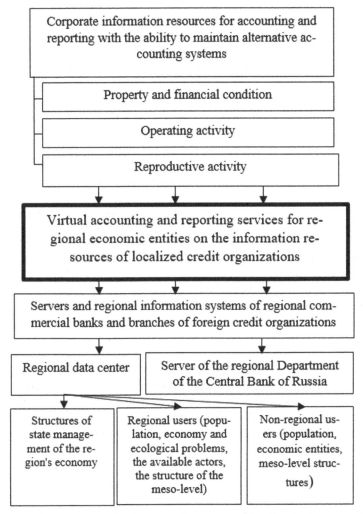

Fig. 1. Organization of electronic document flow on a regional scale based on the digital information node "Bank-business entity" (author's development)

This idea does not mean the abolition of corporate accounting and reporting, which can be conducted by business entities independently and in a format that meets the goals and objectives of corporate governance [24]. However, transferring the function of synthetic accounting and reporting to the information resources of commercial banks that serve the activities of regional economic entities can provide the following positive effects:

- overcoming the problems of fraud with corporate reporting at the system level;
- implementation of a unified accounting and reporting standard that allows effective integration of local and regional information resources of the appropriate orientation;
- outsourcing the function of synthetic accounting and reporting with a corresponding reduction in the cost and increase in the quality of these procedures (in the reliability and transparency of which are primarily interested in the service itself, economic entities and commercial banks);
- elimination of analog procedures for converting accounting and reporting information into statistical and managerial information necessary for the development and implementation of management decisions at the regional level;
- the ability to implement the necessary number and quality of virtual information procedures required in the activities of functional structures of state (municipal and regional management), regional and non-regional users.

It is also necessary to emphasize the need to create a full-fledged regional information hub of the regional economy – a regional data processing center, whose main function is to integrate information flows of localized credit organizations into a single regional information flow, followed by redirecting information to users of regional and supra-regional directions. Current situation when regional administration is repelled by analog possibilities of territorial structures of Federal state statistics service fundamentally unacceptable, for example, in the formation of the results of the economy of the region (in 2019 in the public domain do not exist relevant assessment 2017 in part of the region's GRP, significantly reducing the informational efficiency of such existing evidence base).

The features of using the capabilities of localized banking structures as nodes of the regional digital infrastructure are described in Table 1.

In the author's approach localized banking institutions have the potential of realization of services of a virtual digital service that provides support for electronic document accepted economic entities and their accounting and reporting functions of corporate governance, which provide local and regional integration of information flows and to achieve system growth information efficiency of the regional functions of public administration (Fig. 2).

This visualization shows the linear logic and clear sequence of the regional information process [23]:

- when the subjects and institutions of the RES interact with localized banking structures that can perform the function of nodes of the regional digital infrastructure, economic information flows are generated that characterize the property and financial position and economic activity of the Respondent organizations in an impersonal mode based on cloud information and computing services technologies;
- localized banking structures are able to integrate and issue a unified flow of economic information in the direction of the subject "Regional information flow Manager»;
- the regional information flow Manager integrates the flows of localized banking structures and transmits the generated flows to the regional data center, data Centers of functional management structures, as well as other users;

Table 1. Localized banking structures as nodes of regional digital telecommunications infrastructure: resources, goals, functions, results (author's development)

Characteristics	Description
1. Resources	Banking services as an integrated telecommunications and digital service that provides: - outsourcing and professional implementation of corporate accounting and reporting functions (with the effect of saving resources for its implementation at the corporate level); - the ability to integrate accounting data into local and regional information arrays in the context of territories, types of economic activity, essential characteristics of participants (residents, non-residents) and generate reports on the results of economic activity of RES subjects in real time; – increased security of information exchange based on certified cryptography and authorization technologies – - system cost savings for regional document management and increased information efficiency of the regional public administration function
2. Goals	2.1. Centralization and uniform format of accounting and reporting information as the basis for implementing the regional function of economic management. 2.2. Suppression of non-transparent economic processes and transactions in the region's economy. 2.3. Creating an up-to-date, complete and reliable quantitative information base that provides the ability to develop and record the results of management actions at the local and regional levels
3. Functions	3.1. Providing a single standard for the accounting and reporting function of corporate governance in relation to entities engaged in banking services. 3.2. Formation of statistical models and quantitative forecasts of the financial condition, creditworthiness, solvency and bankruptcy risk of regional mesostructures (strategic groups, technoparks, clusters, etc.). 3.3. Ensuring a single standard for issuing integrated/specialized accounting and reporting information to information systems at a higher level (regional data center and higher). 3.4. Secure electronic document management covering all essential processes and elements of economic activity of regional economic entities
4. Expected results	4.1. Transfer of the region's information system from analog to digital format. 4.2. The possibility of reasonable clarification of analog data (territorial bodies of Rosstat, FTS, FMS, etc.). 4.3. Formation and updating of relevant big Data arrays that provide operational monitoring, verification and operational processing of primary information about the facts of economic life within the RES

– the regional portal of information applications and services becomes an independent level of the regional information infrastructure, which allows users to implement any virtual procedures for accumulation, verification, primary and secondary processing, analysis, evaluation and issuance of statistical and managerial information.

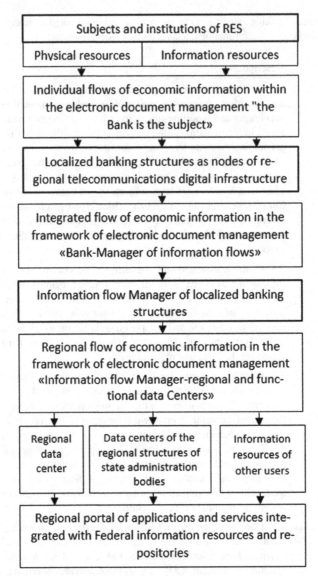

Fig. 2. Architecture and information and management telecommunications flows of the digital node "Bank-business entity" in the regional economic management system (author's development)

We emphasize that the proposed architecture of subjects and information processes necessary for the relevant monitoring of regional socio-economic dynamics does not imply the rejection of the current system of statistical and functional observation implemented by authorized structures of state administration, but is aimed at a qualitatively different level of recording, processing and interpretation of the content of the facts of economic activity within the economy of a particular region.

The implementation of the author's approach to the modernization of organizational and economic support of the regional economy management processes based on digital technologies will ensure the solution of the following national economic tasks at the regional level:

- formation of a relevant information base for regional management based on innovative digital interaction formats in the "Bank – business entity" nodes integrated into the regional information and economic system;
- systematic saving of non-productive costs of all types (temporary, material, monetary, other) that accompany the implementation of the document management function of economic entities, institutions, and state management structures of the region's economy;
- fixing quantitative responses and dynamics of regional socio-economic processes to changes in the factors of the macroeconomic order and institutional innovations;
- modernization of tools for forecasting the stability and development prospects of spatially localized economic systems with the transition to quantitative models of foresight, planning, and targeted regional management.

The implementation of the proposed author's innovation will actually ensure the achievement of the following regional economic results:

- full digitalization of regional economic potential, objective control of its dynamics and problematic aspects of formation, use and reproduction;
- total coverage of regional economic processes, effective counteraction to the regional "shadow" economy;
- application of quantitative tools for monitoring and controlling regional trends in corporate and socio-economic development;
- identification and unambiguous quantitative interpretation of the real effectiveness of municipal/regional management impacts with the possibility of adjustment.

3   Conclusion

Summing up, we emphasize the irreversibility of the processes of digitalization of the economy of modern Russian regions and note the significant economic efficiency associated with the transfer of certain management functions of the corporate sector and certain types of economic activity, as well as the entire function of state management of the region's economy to a digital format based on the use of advanced telecommunications technologies. The applied implementation of the author's innovations will allow a particular region to further strengthen its leadership within the economy of Federal districts and macro-regions in the near and medium term on the basis of qualitative growth of efficiency and reduction of resource intensity of management processes, increase regional competitiveness, and reduce existing barriers that significantly hinder the implementation of regional economic potential.

Acknowledgments. This research work was supported by the Academic Excellence Project 5-100 proposed by Peter the Great St. Petersburg Polytechnic University.

References

1. Gasparyan, A.Yu., Yessirkepov, M., Voronov, A.A., Koroleva, A.M., Kitas, G.D.: Updated editorial guidance for quality and reliability of research output. J. Korean Med. Sci. **33**(35), e247 (2018)
2. Gasparyan, A.Yu., Yessirkepov, M., Voronov, A.A., Koroleva, A.M., Kitas, G.D.: Comprehensive approach to open access publishing: platforms and tools. J. Korean Med. Sci. **34**(27), e184 (2019)
3. Mitrofanova, S.V., Demjanchenko, N.V., Novikov, S.V., Rudakova, O.V., Shmanev, S.V.: The role and characteristics of the enterprises' working conditions before and after the transition to market relations: a view from macroeconomic perspective. Int. J. Appl. Bus. Econ. Res. **15**(13), 63–72 (2017)
4. Blagova, E.A., Bugaeva, I.A., Dubrovsky, A.V.: On the issue of creating an information model of urban agglomeration. In: INTEREXPO GEO SIBERIA, no. 1, pp. 62–67 (2018)
5. Egorychev, S.A.: Organizational and economic modeling of the regional development management system in the conditions of the post-industrial economy formation. OSU Bull. **8**, 43–49 (2009)
6. Ivanyuk, V.A.: Simulation for managing innovation processes in the economy of regions. In: Proceedings of the 6th International Scientific and Practical Conference "Innovation Management", Moscow, IPU RAS, pp. 342–344 (2011)
7. Abdrakhma-Nova, G.I., Vishnevsky, K.O., Volkova, G.L., Gokhberg, L.M., et al.: Indicators of the digital economy: 2018. Statistical collection. In: HSE (2018). 268 p.
8. Klochkov, Y., Gazizulina, A., Muralidharan, K.: Lean six sigma for sustainable business practices: a case study and standardization. Int. J. Qual. Res. **13**(1), 47–74 (2019)
9. Klochkova, E., Evdokimov, K., Klochkov, Y., Samorukov, V.: Methodology for reducing risk of underperformance of personnel functions. Eng. Rural Dev. **17**, 1213–1222 (2018)
10. Kobyashev, V.G., Yurochkin, A.G.: Strategy for improving administrative management of the region on the basis of correlation relations of economic development and information technologies. Inf. Secur. **1**, 25–35 (2006)
11. Krasyuk, I., Kirillova, T., Bakharev, V., Lyamin, B.: Life cycle management in network retail enterprise based on introduction of innovations. IOP Conf. Ser.: Mater. Sci. Eng. **497**(1), 012125 (2019)
12. Krasyuk, I.A., Kobeleva, A.A., Mikhailushkin, P.V., Terskay, G.A., Chuvakhina, A.G.: Economic interests focusing as a basis of the formation of investment policy. Espacios **39**(31), 518–531 (2018)
13. Krasyuk, I., Medvedeva, Y.: Resource support in business analytics of innovative development of trade and technological systems. In: 2019 Proceedings of the 33rd International Business Information Management Association Conference, IBIMA 2019: Education Excellence and Innovation Management through Vision 2020, pp. 8807–8817 (2020)
14. Krymov, S., Kolgan, M., Suvorova, S., Martynenko, O.: Digital technologies and transformation of modern retail. IOP Conf. Ser.: Mater. Sci. Eng. **497**(1), 012126 (2019)
15. Krymov, S.M., Kolgan, M.V.: On the transformation the distribution channel structure in the digital business environment. In: 2019 Proceedings of the 33rd International Business Information Management Association Conference, IBIMA 2019: Education Excellence and Innovation Management through Vision 2020, pp. 2222–2226 (2020)
16. Machonin, Y.K., Makunin, I.A.: The simulation of the development and organization of management of region economy in market conditions. Reg. Econ.: Theory Pract. **7**, 2–9 (2010)
17. Mishin, V.V.: Improving the management of the economy of the Caucasus mineral waters region based on the introduction of information technologies. Econ. Bull. Rostov State Univ. **3**(4(Part 3)), 270–274 (2007)

18. Nekrasova, T., Leventsov, V., Gluhov, V.: Development of infocommunications services in Russia. In: Galinina, O., Andreev, S., Balandin, S., Koucheryavy, Y. (eds.) NEW2AN/ruSMART-2019. LNCS, vol. 11660, pp. 505–514. Springer, Cham (2019). https://doi.org/10.1007/978-3-030-30859-9_43

19. Ozerov, E.S., Pupentsova, S.V., Leventsov, V.A., Dyachkov, M.S.: Selecting the best use option for assets in a corporate management system. In: 2017 6th International Conference on Reliability, Infocom Technologies and Optimization: Trends and Future Directions, ICRITO 2017, 2018-January, pp. 162–170 (2018)

20. Pupentsova, S., Leventsov, V., Livintsova, M., Alexeeva, N., Vodianova, S.: Assessment of the internet of things projects on the real estate market. IOP Conf. Ser.: Mater. Sci. Eng. **618**(1) (2019). Paper № 012041

21. Sokolov, A.F.: Topical issues of improving regional management in the context of the formation of the information economy. Fundam. Res. №4 (2009)

22. Sokolov, B.V., Yusupov, R.M., Okhtilev, M.Y., Zjuban, A.V.: The methodology of situational and competence centers development in order to increase the national economic and social stability. In: Proceedings of 2017 IEEE 2nd International Conference on Control in Technical Systems, CTS 2017, pp. 3–4 (2017). Paper № 8109472

23. Tyukavkin, I.N.: Goals, principles and methods of management of Informatization of the economy of the region. Bull. SamGU **10**, 196–200 (2012)

24. Turovets, Y., Vishnevskiy, K., Tokareva, M., Kukushkin, K.: Technology foresight for digital manufacturing: Russian case. IOP Conf. Ser.: Mater. Sci. Eng. **497**(1), 1–7 (2019). Paper № 012062

The Concept of "Smart Cities": Prospects for the Telecommunications Business and the Current Trend in the Development of Modern Society

Pavel Arkin[1](✉), Ekaterina Abushova[1](✉), Viktoria Bondarenko[2](✉), and Nataliya Przdetskaya[2](✉)

[1] Peter the Great St. Petersburg Polytechnic University, Saint Petersburg, Russia
{arkin_pa,abushova_ee}@spbstu.ru
[2] Rostov State University of Economics (RINH), Rostov-on-Don, Russia
b14v@yandex.ru, nvpr@bk.ru

Abstract. The authors research the direction of the active development of information and communication techniques (ICT) in the world, which exceeds the growth of traditional sectors in the economy. It is reasonable for Russia, in relation to all the federal districts, to note the growing number of companies with telecommunications infrastructure, increased costs on the use of modern telecommunications techniques and creating "smart cities". Nowadays this practice is widely acknowledged and successful in federal megacities, for example, Moscow is one of the TOP-5 megacities in the world with high digital readiness of urban infrastructure. It is necessary for other cities in Russia to involve the telecommunications business in this area, which actualizes the study of the conceptual basis of the "smart cities" idea as the prospect for the telecommunications sector and the current trend in the development of modern society based on modern telecommunications techniques. It is necessary for identifying prospects of telecommunications business in the development of "smart cities" and understanding this trend in modern society on the basis of modern telecommunication techniques: 1) to evaluate current promising trends in the telecommunications business; 2) to understand the "smart city" conception and its relevance in Russian conditions. Promising trends determining the telecommunications sector development include the transformation of the operating model under the influence of digitalization, the massive introduction of business intelligence techniques based on the Big Data analysis using artificial intelligence methods, the construction of business ecosystems with business partners, as well as the entry of telecommunications business into related market niches, connected with technological solutions, financial services and IT. This involves adjusting the organizational environment of the telecommunications business and requesting competencies for staff and society members. The ecosystem approach is fully manifested in the "smart cities" conception forming a promising market for telecommunications business, and it allows to focus the economy of urban agglomerations on positive evolution and contributes to the life standard of the population in the regions of Russia.

© Springer Nature Switzerland AG 2020
O. Galinina et al. (Eds.): NEW2AN 2020/ruSMART 2020, LNCS 12526, pp. 308–317, 2020.
https://doi.org/10.1007/978-3-030-65729-1_26

Keywords: Telecommunications · Trend evaluation · Promising market · Partner ecosystems · Smart cities

1 Introduction

Information and communication techniques (ICTs) is a modern direction actively developing, forming new markets, on the one hand, and on the other, ICTs can improve the efficiency of economic systems and the competitiveness of economies [1].

The telecommunications industry, which forms its own infrastructure and provides other sectors of the economy has an impact on the growth of competitiveness of innovative products and services offered to the markets. Globally the ICT industry exceeds the traditional industrial sectors in terms of potential growth opportunities. Thus, the components of the traditional economy every year increase by 3%, while ICTs in the global cross-section show the growth up to 10%, involving up to 70% of the working population in their fairway [2, 3, 6]. Such changes contribute to changing the appearance of modern megacities, turning them into "smart cities" [4].

The Russian reality is also aimed at the development of ICT techniques and the active involvement of telecommunications companies in the positive evolution of the Russian regions' economy. The development of this sector and its potential are presented, in particular, by the growth dynamics of organizations that use the Internet for work, including broadband access, shown in Fig. 1.

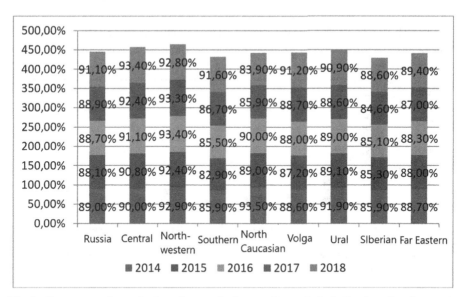

Fig. 1. Percentage of organizations that use the Internet for work, including broadband access in the federal districts of Russia in 2014–2018, % [7]

According to the data, the increase in this indicator is noticeable both in Russia as a whole and in some federal districts in particular. It is naturally that the Central Federal

District and the North-Western Federal District take leading places, representing megacities of federal significance, for example, demonstrating the best positions in building a "smart city". In 2018, investments in the development of the ICT component were significant in all the federal districts of Russia. For example, Fig. 2 presents information about costs on information and communication techniques in the federal districts of Russia in 2018.

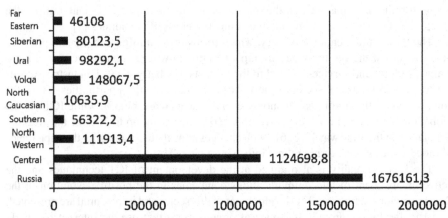

Fig. 2. Costs on information and communication techniques in the federal districts of Russia in 2018, million rubles [7]

Central Federal District also takes leading place, which is determined by the indicator of the number of subscribers of fixed broadband Internet access. It is shown in Fig. 3.

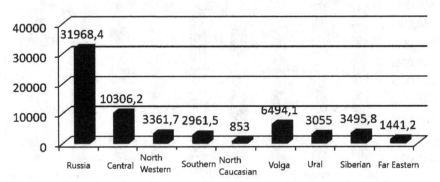

Fig. 3. The number of active subscribers of fixed broadband Internet access in the federal districts of Russia in 2018, thousand [7]

According to the number of active mobile subscribers using Internet access conditions, the Central Federal District, the Volga Federal District, and the North-Western Federal District take leading places, but the greatest results of their growth are evident in other federal districts. Information about the number of active mobile subscribers using Internet access in the federal districts of Russia is shown in Fig. 4.

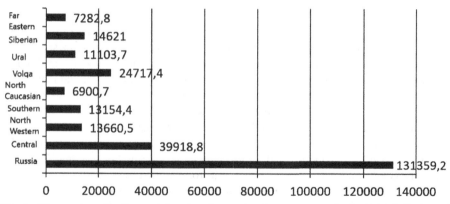

Fig. 4. The number of active mobile subscribers using Internet access in the federal districts of Russia in 2018, thousand. [7]

These facts demonstrate the readiness of the Russian telecommunications market to take an active part in the transformation of the economy of Russian regions, which fits into the direction of the development of this business to form "smart "cities" focusing the national economic system, as a whole, on the innovative development. These circumstances contribute to study the very conceptual basis of the "smart cities" idea as a perspective for the telecommunications business and a possible trend in the development of modern society based on modern telecommunications techniques.

2   Research Method

Identifying the prospects for the telecommunications business in the framework of the development of "smart cities" and understanding this trend in modern society based on modern telecommunications techniques need:

- the evaluation of current promising trends in the telecommunications business;
- understanding the "smart city" conception and its relevance in Russia.

2.1   The Evaluation of Current Promising Trends in the Telecommunications Business

Describing the main trends in the telecommunications sector in Russia, it is important to note that it has the same features as telecommunications systems in other countries. According to expert opinion, there are four basic dominant trends in telecommunications, such as the digitalization impact, which is expressed in the operating model change; the possibility of in-depth business analytics by operating with Big Data, building long-term mutually beneficial relationships, as ideal situation creating partner ecosystems [5], and searching for new promising markets for telecommunications companies [8]. These transformations are aimed at increasing business profitability and efficiency by operating in related markets within the framework of partner ecosystems.

The transformation of the operating model under the influence of digitalization is manifested in the ability to rationalize costs on interaction with consumers (up to 25% in comparison with the previous traditional model), fast response to their requests and, as a result, increased customer satisfaction (up to 30% in comparison with the traditional format of service) [9]. Digital techniques allow to make a product offer and marketing efforts as personalized as possible, which also contributes to a sharp increase in return on investment (according to expert data, the growth is up to 140%) [8].

In addition, the digitalization in telecommunications makes it possible to optimize various processes and routine operations. Also, it significantly reduces the customer path, which is the key to satisfaction and, in ideal situation, loyalty. For example, Telecom operator markets in Southeast Asia, which transformed the processes of attracting and physically connecting new customers, optimizing costs and reducing the time spent on connection by 60% [9].

Business analytics based on Big Data makes it possible for telecommunications companies to personalize their offer, taking into account the maximum value settings and predicted customer requests of subscribers.

This approach has reduced the outflow of customers and increased their interest in service offerings as part of a marketing campaign run by the telecommunications business. Based on Big Data and artificial intelligence, it is possible to track the value of consumers, to clarify their segmentation characteristics, to consolidate all the necessary data, to propose products and services from the core business and related offers of partners in the business ecosystem.

Participation in ecosystem partnerships allows telecommunications companies to actively work in new markets, implementing promising projects and occupying new niches. Such transformations allow to count on the growth of profitability of businesses developed within the framework of ecosystem interaction. According to expert data, the features of partner interaction between leading telecommunications companies and various partners in a number of areas are shown in Table 1.

Table 1. Partner projects implemented by telecommunications operators in Russia in 2012–2016 [7]

	The media business	Financial services	IT services	Techniques
Partnership	48	82	37	61
Creation and financing of a new enterprise	4	–	14	8
Organic growth	36	15	35	27
Acquisition of assets	11	1	14	3
Joint venture	1	2	1	1
Number of completed projects	337	254	223	126

As we can see, partnership and attracting co-investors are current trends, which allow to implement innovative projects in ICT. Nowadays in Russia, operators are involved in implementing projects to virtualize digital infrastructure and cloud services. This activity is of great interest in terms of opportunities to optimize processes of managing territories, providing services to the population and improving the life standard by implementing solutions for building "smart cities" and "digital twins" of various systems.

Experts note that this practice needs a certain level of the industry development and the telecommunications companies represented in it, and as a result a request for the competence characteristics of specialists, the infrastructure support and the activation of cooperation with co-investors (Table 2).

Table 2. The desired level of a number of components for the development of "smart services» [7]

	Digitalization in improving an operational model	Business analytics based on big data massives	Digital partner business ecosystems	Activity in the related markets	Directions of development
Required competencies	−	−	−	+	Knowledge of new industries
	−	−	±	+	Partnership skills
	−	±	−	±	Analytics
	+	+	+	+	Communication skills
Organizational culture	+	+	+	+	Agile techniques
	+	+	+	+	Cross-functional interaction
	+	+	+	+	Innovations
	±	±	±	±	Centralization
Infrastructure	±	±	±	±	IT-systems
	+	+	+	+	Open architecture
Partners, co-owners, co-investors	−	−	+	+	Readiness for "long" investments

These facts suppose the need for companies to evolve in terms of organizational culture, approaches to cooperation and the development of a number of competencies.

2.2   Clarification of the "Smart City" Conception and Its Relevance in Russian Conditions

Taking into account the importance of telecommunications companies in the development of "smart cities", we note that they are highly relevant, since more than a half of the population in the world live in urban agglomerations [10]. According to forecasts, by 2050 the population of large cities will be about 70% of the world's population [10]. Researchers investigate the very problem of "smart cities" within the framework of various components such as smart: economy, personnel mobility, urban environment, population, social life and general management of urban agglomeration [9]. These solutions and capabilities are based on the applied telecommunications techniques and relevant competencies.

Speaking about effective city management, according to the opinion of M. Kohno the modern "smart city" is initially based on new ICTs, and then the "smart city" itself produces a digital society that gives opportunities for the development in the new telecommunications space [16]. The main techniques of "smart cities" include infrastructure support for the transfer of information between all the elements in the urban environment, the Big Data analysis system, the system for ordering streaming information, and the Internet of things, which makes it possible to aggregate the data about certain objects and receive real-time feedback necessary for a rapid response to a changing situation [17].

Initiatives for the "smart cities" development can be implemented on the basis of cooperation between telecommunications operators, regional authorities and IT companies engaged in optimizing software that covers all the areas of urban agglomerations. Partnership relationships and business ecosystems create opportunities for the full implementation of "digital twins" in city management as well as making management decisions through complete analysis of available resources and capabilities in real time.

Describing the European experience of "smart cities", it is important to note that they are focused not only on ICTs, but also naturally include the problems of planning, tracking and managing transport systems and urban logistics, as well as focusing on the urban economy greening [18]. The environmental development initiatives are implemented in European countries on the basis of specialized services and ICTs that help to unite the efforts of the population, government and business located in the urban agglomeration [19].

In implementing "smart city" projects in Russia, the "digital twin" is based on a single information system, which allows to make the current operational analysis as well as to make the forecast of all the technological solutions and areas of the city's life, to improve the efficiency of urban infrastructure facilities, also it has a positive impact on the city's economy and the life standard of the population. Issues that determine the level of development of infrastructure subjects were considered in the works [11–15, 22], this allows us to create conditions and factors for the implementation of Smart city projects. The national project "Housing and urban environment" [21] and the national program "The digital economy of the Russian Federation" [23] are positive institutional solutions.

In Russia, an operational rating of cities focused on the formation of "smart" services and a "digital twin" in the management of urban agglomeration is currently formed, the leaders of which are located as follows:

1. Moscow;
2. Saint-Petersburg;
3. Novosibirsk;
4. Yekaterinburg;
5. Nizhny Novgorod;
6. Kazan;
7. Chelyabinsk;
8. Omsk;
9. Samara;
10. Rostov-on-Don;
11. Ufa;
12. Krasnoyarsk;
13. Perm;
14. Voronezh;
15. Volgograd;
16. Krasnodar;
17. Saratov;
18. Tyumen» [24].

In general, Russian cities and regions should actively integrate into this scheme of the development, which will facilitate the participation of telecommunications companies combining their efforts with regional authorities and co-investors from related industries.

According to international rankings on the readiness of megacities to transition to a "digital future" on the basis of modern telecommunications techniques, Moscow is in the TOP-5, occupying the same position as New York [25]. We believe that "smart cities" as a sphere of activity is a promising business for ICT companies and, at the same time, a socially significant project aimed at improving the life standard of the population and building the innovative economy. This direction is promising for the further development in the regions of Russia within the framework of global trends, it will contribute to the harmonious development of regional economies through the efforts of the government, the population, business and ICT companies.

3 Conclusion

The development of information and communication techniques in Russia, including their development in the federal districts, allows to understand that in the current situation, this area is in the pool of global trends and the national economic system is aimed at evolving on the basis of digitalization and modern telecommunications techniques.

Trends that determine the telecommunications sector development change the operating model under the influence of digitalization, the active implementation of business analytics techniques based on the Big Data analysis by methods of artificial intelligence, aimed at long-term cooperation with business partners in building a business ecosystem and entering telecommunications business into related market niches connected with technological solutions, financial services and IT.

In the current conditions, the "smart cities" conception is a promising directions for the development of telecommunications business and digital techniques, this conception is typical for developed foreign countries and it is being actively implemented in Russia.

The "smart cities" conception is a promising direction, since, in addition to the development of the ICT sector for the benefit of telecommunication business focuses the economy of urban agglomerations on the positive evolution and innovation, increasing the life standard of the population in the regions of Russia.

Acknowledgments. This research work was supported by the Academic Excellence Project 5-100 proposed by Peter the Great St. Petersburg Polytechnic University.

References

1. Potekhina, I.P.: The development of information and communication techniques in the context of globalization. Bull. Saratov State Socio-Econ. Univ. **2** (2012)
2. Manokhin, V.A.: The development of the information resources market in Russia. Bulletin S; GSEU **2**(26) (2009)
3. Nikitenkova, M.A.: Influence of the information and communication techniques development on the innovative economy infrastructure formation. Russia and America in the XX Century, No. 1 (2010)
4. Belyaeva, N.B., Mingaleeva, E.D.: "Smart city" conception and its implementation in Northern Europe and Russia. Proc. St. Petersburg State Univ. Econ. **5–1**(119), 95–98 (2019)
5. Bondarenko, V.A., Semernikova, E.A.: Marketing of relationships and consumer loyalty in the banking sector: the feasibility of forming an "ecosystem". Bull. Rostov State Univ. Econ. (RINH) **2**(54), 17–22 (2016)
6. Gluhov, V., Leventsov, V., Radaev, A., Nikolaevskiy, N.: Analytical modeling of development and implementation of telecommunication technologies. In: Galinina, O., Andreev, S., Balandin, S., Koucheryavy, Y. (eds.) NEW2AN/ruSMART -2018. LNCS, vol. 11118, pp. 428–440. Springer, Cham (2018). https://doi.org/10.1007/978-3-030-01168-0_39
7. Digital Russia: a new reality. The report of the experts of the McKinsey company. http://www.mckinsey.com/global-locations/europe-andmiddleeast/russia/ru/our-work/mckinsey-digital. Accessed 02 May 2020
8. Drozhzhinov, V.I., Kupriyanovsky, V.P., Namiot, D.E., Sinyagov, S.A., Kharitonov, A.A.: Smart cities: models, tools, rankings and standards. Int. J. Open Inf. Tech. **5**(3), 19–48 (2017)
9. Regions of Russia. Socio-economic indicators. Coll. of articles, vol. 1204, pp. 956–957. Rosstat, Moscow (2019)
10. Kononova, O.V., Pavlovskaya, M.A.: Digital economy techniques in "smart city" projects: participants and prospects. Mod. Inf. Tech. IT-Educ. **14**(3), 692–706 (2018)
11. Krasyuk, I., Kirillova, T., Bakharev, V., Lyamin, B.: Life cycle management in network retail enterprise based on introduction of innovations. IOP Conf. Ser.: Mater. Sci. Eng. **497**(1), 012125 (2019)
12. Krasyuk, I.A., Kobeleva, A.A., Mikhailushkin, P.V., Terskay, G.A., Chuvakhina, A.G.: Economic interests focusing as a basis of the formation of investment policy. Espacios **39**(31), 518–531 (2018)

13. Krasyuk, I., Medvedeva, Y.: Resource support in business analytics of innovative development of trade and technological systems. In: 2019 Proceedings of the 33rd International Business Information Management Association Conference, IBIMA 2019: Education Excellence and Innovation Management through Vision 2020, pp. 8807–8817 (2020)

14. Krymov, S., Kolgan, M., Suvorova, S., Martynenko, O.: Digital technologies and transformation of modern retail. IOP Conf. Ser.: Mater. Sci. Eng. **497**(1), 012126 (2019)

15. Krymov, S.M., Kolgan, M.V.: On the transformation the distribution channel structure in the digital business environment. In: 2019 Proceedings of the 33rd International Business Information Management Association Conference, IBIMA 2019: Education Excellence and Innovation Management through Vision 2020, pp. 2222–2226 (2020)

16. Lebedev, V.: Demographic problem. "Thesis about the "last generation". http://www.ukrupn enie.com/2050/2009/12/last-generation/. Accessed 02 May 2020

17. Maximov, S.N.: "Smart city": to the question of the concept and conception. PSE **1**(61) (2017). https://cyberleninka.ru/article/n/umnyy-gorod-k-voprosu-o-ponyatii-i-kontseptsii. Accessed 04 May 2020

18. Muravleva, T.V.: "Digital city" Project as a vector of the digital economy development in the region. Econ. Secur. Qual. **3**(32), 8–11 (2018)

19. National program "The Digital Economy of the Russian Federation". http://government.ru/rugovclassifier/614/events/. Accessed 03 May 2020

20. Nekrasova, T., Leventsov, V., Gluhov, V.: Development of infocommunications services in Russia. In: Galinina, O., Andreev, S., Balandin, S., Koucheryavy, Y. (eds.) NEW2AN/ruSMART -2019. LNCS, vol. 11660, pp. 505–514. Springer, Cham (2019). https://doi.org/10.1007/978-3-030-30859-9_43

21. Official website of the joint project "Internet + city" of the Institute for the Internet Development, the National Association of industrial Internet market participants, Rostelecom. http://xn--c1acnlfiapv6f.xn--h1aax.xn--p1ai. Accessed 03 May 2020

22. Pupentsova, S., Leventsov, V., Livintsova, M., Alexeeva, N., Vodianova, S.: Assessment of the internet of things projects on the real estate market. IOP Conf. Ser.: Mater. Sci. Eng. **618**(1), 1–14 (2019). Art. no. 012041

23. Rakhmanova, V.: Techniques of "smart" cities and forecasts of their development. https://vc.ru/26713-smart-city. Accessed 20 Apr 2020

24. The Passport of the National Project "Housing and Urban Environment" has been Published. http://government.ru/projects/selection/735/35560/. Accessed 03 May 2020

25. World's Population Increasingly Urban with More than Half Living in Urban Areas. United Nations, New York, 10 July 2014. http://www.un.org/en/development/desa/news/population/worldurbanizationprospects-2014.html. Accessed 02 May 2020

Telecommunications Techniques in the Healthcare Development: Foreign Experience and Russian Realities

Viktoria Bondarenko[1]([✉]), Dmitri Kostoglodov[1]([✉]), and Tatyana Nekrasova[2]([✉])

[1] Rostov State University of Economics, Rostov-on-Don, Russia
b14v@yandex.ru, d.d.kostoglodov@yandex.ru
[2] Peter the Great St. Petersburg Polytechnic University, Saint-Petersburg, Russia
nekrasova_tp@spbstu.ru

Abstract. The article analyses the of telecommunications techniques in the transformation of the Russian economy, focus on supporting this direction in the Russia's development. Telecommunications techniques create new opportunities for the health sector. There is a positive experience of some developed countries in the world actively implementing telecommunication techniques in health care practice for the social effect, the provision of quality medical services to people in the remote country's regions, the transfer of the medical experience to the staff and also the increase of the medical care systems economic efficiency. In Russia also there are initiatives for the health system digitalization and the modern telecommunications techniques use. However, there are some difficulties and obstacles in the implementation, confirmed by expert opinions. It is important for the study of the role of telecommunications, information and communication techniques in the health care development at the present stage, the increase of medical care quality and the industry efficiency to evaluate the professional community's perception of the healthcare digitalization; the foreign experience of the telecommunications techniques use in the health care development according to their economic efficiency; current prospects for the modern telecommunications techniques introduction taking into account the foreign experience. The foreign experience in patients' remote diagnostics and medical professionals training, as well as regular evaluation of the processes economic efficiency, can and should be actively implemented in Russia's practice. Such trends have been fully manifested only in Moscow, Moscow region, Saint-Petersburg, and Tatarstan. Other territories are significantly behind in providing telecommunications services to the healthcare sector. In Russia, the medical professional community realizes the importance of the health care digitalization, authorities supported and fixed the digitalization use at the institutional level, and the obstacles must be overcome on the basis of the expert community opinion and the international experience.

Keywords: Telecommunications · Health care · Telemedicine · Economic efficiency · Obstacles · Expert opinion · Foreign experience

© Springer Nature Switzerland AG 2020
O. Galinina et al. (Eds.): NEW2AN 2020/ruSMART 2020, LNCS 12526, pp. 318–327, 2020.
https://doi.org/10.1007/978-3-030-65729-1_27

1 Introduction

Currently, telecommunications techniques lead to the renewal of processes in the economic systems, change the conditions for functioning in various industries and areas, create new opportunities to improve the customer service quality, increase the audience coverage, and access to services that previously were unavailable due to the remoteness and the lack of the telecommunications infrastructure development. Experts, describing these processes and prolonging the situation for the future, predict serious changes, which they call the "new industrial revolution", consisting in the automation of more than 50% of all the work operations [1].

This situation is typical for most developed countries and corresponds to the processes initiated by the authorities and supported by business in Russia in terms of the economy digitalization and the digital transformation of its industries. Thus, in Russia, the digital economy ecosystem concept is fixed as "partner organizations ensuring the constant interaction of applied technology platforms, state information resources, Internet services and channels, and information systems of various departmental affiliation" [2]. The country has a target program "The digital economy of the Russian Federation", which promotes the creation of industry-specific digital platforms for the national economy various sectors [3].

Despite the trend to develop the digital economy on the platform of telecommunications techniques, the current contribution of the digital economy in Russia to GDP, as well as the volume of investment and the household participation, the digitalization are inferior to such indicators in a number of other countries (Fig. 1).

However, in relation to the Russia's economy, the situation is expected to change by 2025, including indicators of GDP growth based on innovations in information and communication techniques and the digital platforms introduction (Fig. 2).

The mentioned realities are fully related to the healthcare sphere, aimed at the task of increasing the efficiency (both the processes and financial results), changing under the influence of information and communication techniques. It should be noted that back in 2005, the countries-members of the World Health Organization (WHO) set goals to introduce electronic (digital) medicine, aimed at providing the maximum possible number of citizens, ideally, all the population with quality medical services through the telecommunications component development [4]. At the same time, specific tasks were set for servicing residents of remote territories, using telemedicine, creating electronic medical records, and staff training. These targets were to be combined with improving the financial efficiency of the digital health system [5].

A number of developed world economies demonstrate significant progress in the modern telecommunications techniques use in healthcare. For Russia, their experience is very important as issues such as improving work efficiency and maximum coverage of the population taking into account the remote rural regions with the objective lack of qualified and timely medical care [6], as well as quick personnel training in remote format are extremely urgent.

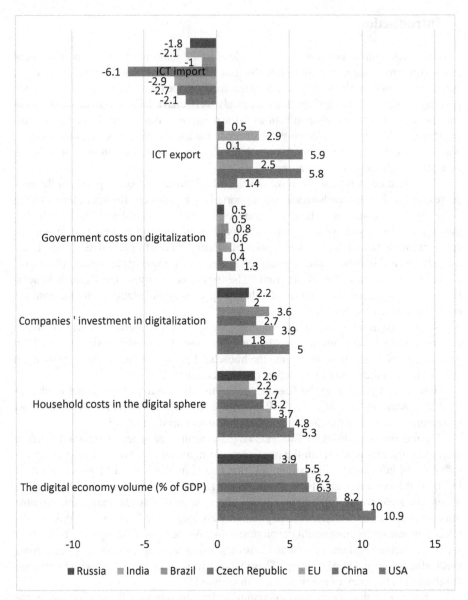

Fig. 1. The expert evaluation of the digital economy's contribution to GDP in a number of other countries, % [1]

This research aims to analyze the experience of the healthcare system development in a number of foreign countries based on telecommunications techniques, evaluating the economic efficiency of these innovations, as well as understanding the current stage in the information and communication techniques development in the healthcare sector in Russia and the possibilities of adapting solutions existing in the world practice.

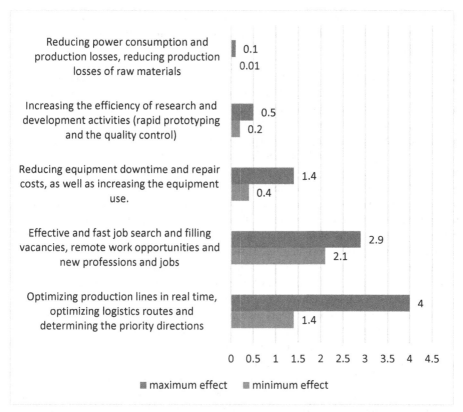

Fig. 2. Projected sources of GDP growth in Russia by 2025 due to ICT and the business processes digitalization, trillion US dollars [1]

2 Research Method

The study of the role and importance of telecommunications, information and communication technologies in the development of healthcare at the present stage in terms of improving the quality of patient care and improving the effectiveness of the industry allows us to conclude its importance.

It is important for the study of the role of telecommunications, information and communication techniques in the health care development at the present stage, the increase of medical care quality and the industry efficiency to evaluate:

– the foreign experience of the telecommunications techniques use in the health care development according to their economic efficiency;
– the professional community's perception of the healthcare digitalization;
– current prospects for the modern telecommunications techniques introduction taking into account the foreign experience.

2.1 The Evaluation of the Foreign Experience in the Telecommunications Techniques Use in Healthcare, Taking into Account Their Economic Efficiency

The telecommunications techniques use in healthcare, the industry digitalization and the operational processes automation in medical institutions free up doctors' time for professional communication with patients.

We automated collecting information about patients that is necessary for making decisions about treatment regimens and providing assistance in conditions of information certainty. The approach used for a preliminary (before an appointment with a doctor) independent self-survey of the patient seeking medical care, the results of which are processed and made available to the doctor.

The result of such self-surveys is the formation of pre-medical diagnostic questionnaires that function through a mobile app, thanks to which the doctor is able to understand the current health status of the patient in a complex, even wider than the spectrum of his/her direct professional orientation. This approach reduces the risk of misdiagnosis.

Telemedicine helps to solve the problem of the qualified medical personnel lack in a certain territory. So, tin order or solves this problem some countries create professional medical call centres, which makes it possible to reduce the burden on medical personnel and provide services to those patients who are not fully available in offline mode. Such solutions have been already implemented in India, Mexico, and the United Kingdom of Great Britain. In India, according to expert data, the medical care availability for the remote regions has increased fivefold [1].

In addition to teleconsultations of patients in the remote regions, telemedicine uses telemonitoring, which includes a system for notifying patients, monitoring and diagnostics of their health status by medical personnel. In the Netherlands, such programs are implemented for systematic remote monitoring of health status of patients with cardiovascular diseases. In the US, thanks to remote monitoring of veterans' health status (44 thousand people) the number of people admitted to the hospital decreased by 20%, which also reduced the cost of care by almost 8%. The number of primary medical care requests in the United States in 30% of cases is carried out with telemedicine use [7], which makes it possible to identify the problem at early stage and find a solution that helps preserve health [8].

Telemedicine is very promising in the tele-consultations and doctors' training. This is an opportunity to organize quick specialized consultations with narrow specialists, which helps in making a diagnosis and choosing the right treatment regimen [9]. It is also possible for doctors to get the necessary competencies online, ideally on-the-job or partially off-the-job.

Telemedicine is currently integrated into the national health care system in the United States, since the existing Medicare insurance program is involved in covering the costs of such a monitoring and diagnostics. For the current period, the amount of coverage was about 58.7 US dollars per month per patient [10].

In Japan, telecommunications techniques are also actively used in telemedicine for pregnant women, teleradiology, home-based tele-monitoring, etc. [11].

The telecommunications market has a pronounced customer-oriented character. The issues of customer orientation were discussed in [12–17], since it is not enough to have good financial results, if you set long-term goals, you need to ensure customer satisfaction.

In terms of the economic efficiency together with the patient care quality increase in the framework of the healthcare digitalization and the telecommunications techniques development in the United States, a comprehensive study obtained data describing positive results (Table 1) [18].

Table 1. Evaluating the cost-effectiveness of implementing digital telecommunications technologies in healthcare in the United States [18]

Technology	Results
Postoperative remote monitoring of the patient via video link	The savings were about 357 doll. per patient (since there is no transportation)
Remote patient consultations in real time	Savings in several times (with standard techniques-thousands of dollars; with new technology - hundreds of dollars)
Remote examination of the retina	Savings of about $30 per patient compared to traditional care
Remote consultation for primary health care	Savings of about $32 per patient compared to traditional care
Remote consultation with a psychiatrist	Savings of about $400 per patient compared to traditional care
Remote monitoring of cardiac failure	На 4 тыс. долл. дороже при 6 мес. использования в расчете на пациента по сравнению с традиционным обслуживанием
Remote consultation on stroke diagnostics	4 thousand dollars more expensive for the 6 months use per patient compared to traditional service

According to the data, it can be noted that the diagnosis and remote monitoring of heart diseases in the United States based on new techniques is now more expensive than with the traditional approach use. However, they help identify problems in early stages, helping to reduce possible risks. For the rest of the medical care options, telecommunications techniques, in addition to social benefits, provide a tangible economic impact. In Japan, the most significant economic effect of the telemedicine introduction can be seen in the monitoring of people with chronic diseases ($212–370 per year per patient), the remote consultation of dermatologists ($330 per week per patient), remote consultations of a specialist in palliative care ($5000 per year per patient) [19]. Thus, the telecommunications techniques use based on the foreign experience is reasonable, both socially and economically.

2.2 The Clarification of the Healthcare Digitalization Perception by the Professional Community in Russia and the Current Prospects Evaluation

We are wholly agree with the experts when they point out that it is necessary to create an effective digital platform in healthcare on the basis of the existing regulatory framework, ongoing programs and initiatives for attracting investment [20].

According to R. Khabriev, digital techniques and telecommunications in healthcare contribute to the high-quality medical care to the population, taking into account the general limited resources [23]. We believe that telecommunications techniques will help to increase the number of requests from citizens to medical institutions on early stages of a health problem. Currently, according to practitioners, "in Russia, 17% of the people never go to a doctor. 54% of the Russian population applies only in cases of extreme necessity" [24].

We believe that digital telecommunications solutions can change this situation to some extent, especially because Russia already has a large number of Internet users, including those who have full access to various services and applications from smartphones [25].

Today Russia develops systems for electronic patient diagnostics, recording the treatment protocol, centralized analytics, and online applications for the staff and patients. The healthcare digitalization has been shown to the maximum extent in Moscow, Saint Petersburg, the Republics of Tatarstan and Bashkortostan. The country implements pilot telemedicine projects related to monitoring patients living in remote regions and who has difficulties in organizing regular visits to a specialist. However, today, for example, such a technology electronic medical records, the introduction of which was announced quite a long time ago, is used only in 10% of Russian regions, and about 30–40% of the working time of average medical personnel and doctors is spent on maintaining various paper documentation [1].

However, today, for example, such a technique as electronic medical records, its introduction was announced quite a long time ago, is used only in 10% of Russia's regions, and about 30–40% of the working time of nursing staff and doctors is spent on filling out various paper documents [1]. Difficulties connected with the digitalization and the development of telecommunications techniques in the health sector is confirmed by the introduction of "top-down" programs "Digital pumping of the health sector" (supported by regional governments) in the Russia's regions.

The expert community, in the framework of professional sessions on the healthcare digitalization in the regions, formulated constraints, such as: the difficulty to create a full-fledged regional regulatory framework; the difficulty to integrate related reporting systems used in the functioning of medical institutions; the low percentage of digitized data and low IT qualifications of doctors and nurses; weak involvement of patients in remote diagnostics processes (data were obtained during the expert session on the healthcare digitalization in Rostov region in March 2020). We believe that these difficulties are the same for medical institutions almost in all the regions of the country. These difficulties can be solved jointly by the government, business involved in the supply of telecommunications equipment and techniques, and the healthcare sector representatives.

It should be noted that Russia also used pilot projects to the effectiveness of telecommunications techniques used in medicine. Thus, in 2003, the results of implementing telemedicine techniques in Irkutsk were evaluated when providing surgical care to patients with tuberculosis of the joints. The conclusions reached by the experts showed that the most effective in terms of treatment effectiveness and economic indicators was the option of using telemedicine (compared to the traditional option) and inviting specialists from other regions [26]. In 2014 in the Khanty-Mansi Autonomous district, the economic efficiency was also evaluated in terms of costs and benefits from the medical examinations of the population through telemedicine. The telecommunications use results have shown their effectiveness in comparison with the traditional approach [27].

We believe that the active introduction of telecommunications techniques in Russia's healthcare will go on. At the same time, it is necessary to make the evaluation of projects for the introduction of information and communication techniques regular.

3   Conclusion

1. The development of information and communication techniques changes business conditions in various industries and areas, creating additional opportunities relevant for the health sector, too. Some foreign countries have the positive experience demonstrating economic efficiency in the healthcare sector development based on telecommunications techniques. It is important to evaluate the economic efficiency of such projects in the Russian context.

2. Russia has prospects for the telecommunications techniques introduction in the health sector at the present stage, but also there are some constraints, connected with the lack of the complete mechanism for improving the institutional and infrastructure base for the information and communication techniques use.

3. In addition to institutional and infrastructure support, permanent training of medical human resources to work in new conditions adapting them to the digital environment and indirect contacts with patients through existing programs are very important [20].

4. It is important to involve patients to obtain remote medical services remotely within the early diagnosis, health monitoring, the formation of pre-diagnostic questionnaires as well as training and demonstrating simple online instructions for the certain services use. This direction becomes very popular due to the recognition by the majority of Russians (up to 95%) of the significance of the amendment to the Constitution on affordable and high-quality medicine [28].

5. In Russia, the medical professional community realizes the importance of the health care digitalization, authorities supported and fixed the digitalization use at the institutional level, and the obstacles must be overcome on the basis of the expert community opinion and the international experience.

Acknowledgments. This research work was supported by the Academic Excellence Project 5-100 proposed by Peter the Great St. Petersburg Polytechnic University.

References

1. Akiyama, M., Yoo, B.K.: A systematic review of the economic evaluation of telemedicine in Japan. J. Prev. Med. Public Health **49**(4), 83–96 (2016). https://doi.org/10.3961/jpmph. 16.043
2. American Telemedicine Association Advocacy Initiatives Result in New Medicare Coverage for Chronic Condition Monitoring (2018). https://thesource.americantelemed.org/blogs/jes sica-washington/2017/11/06/american-telemedicine-association-advocacy-initiatives-result-in-new-medicare-coverage-for-chronic-condition-monitoring. Accessed 06 Mar 2020
3. Bondarenko, V.A., Efremenko, I.N., Sagoyan, A.S.: The healthcare digitalization in reducing socio-economic inequality according to the criterion of medical services availability. Eurasian Legal J. **4**(143) (2020)
4. Decree of the President of the Russian Federation No. 203 from 09.05.2017 "On the strategy for the information society development in the Russian Federation for 2017–2030» (2017). http://www.kremlin.ru/acts/bank/41919. Accessed 14 May 2020
5. Digital Russia: a new reality. Report of the group's experts. Digital/McKinley (2017). https://roscongress.org/materials/tsifrovaya-rossiya-novaya-realnost/. Accessed 12 Mar 2020
6. Fedyaev, D.V., Fedyaeva, V.K., Omelyanovsky, V.V.: Economic substantiation for the use of telemedicine techniques for medical examinations of the population in remote regions. Pharmacoecon. Mod. Pharmacoecon. Pharmacoepidemiol. **7**(3), 30–35 (2014)
7. Gribanov, Y.: The main models for creating industry-specific digital platforms. Issues Innov. Econ. **8**(2), 223–234 (2018)
8. Global diffusion of eHealth: Making universal health coverage achievable. Report of the third global survey on eHealth. Global Observatory for eHealth (2016). http://apps.who.int/iris/bit stream/10665/252529/1/9789241511780-eng.pdf?ua=1. Accessed 04 May 2020
9. Health care availability was recognized by the Russians as the most important amendment (2020). https://wciom.ru/index.php?id=236&uid=10209&utm_source=yxnews&utm_medium=desktop&utm_referrer=https%3A%2F%2Fyandex.ru%2Fnews. Accessed 25 Mar 2020
10. Internet of Things Gartner IT glossary. Gartner (2012). https://www.gartner.com/en/inform ation-technology/glossary/internet-of-things. Accessed 25 Mar 2020
11. Khabriev, R.U., Yagudina, R.I., Pravdyuk, N.G.: The healthcare techniques evaluation. Monograph, p. 416. Moscow News Agency, Moscow (2013)
12. Krasyuk, I., Kirillova, T., Bakharev, V., Lyamin, B.: Life cycle management in network retail enterprise based on introduction of innovations. IOP Conf. Ser.: Mater. Sci. Eng. **497**(1), 012125 (2019)
13. Krasyuk, I., Medvedeva, Y., Baharev, V., Chargaziya, G.: Evolution of strategies of retail and technological systems under broad digitalization conditions. IOP Conf. Ser.: Mater. Sci. Eng. **497**(1), 012124 (2019)

14. Krasyuk, I.A., Kobeleva, A.A., Mikhailushkin, P.V., Terskay, G.A., Chuvakhina, A.G.: Economic interests focusing as a basis of the formation of investment policy. Espacios **39**(31), 518–531 (2018)
15. Krasyuk, I., Medvedeva, Y.: Resource support in business analytics of innovative development of trade and technological systems. In: 2019 Proceedings of the 33rd International Business Information Management Association Conference, IBIMA 2019: Education Excellence and Innovation Management through Vision 2020, pp. 8807–8817 (2020)
16. Krymov, S., Kolgan, M., Suvorova, S., Martynenko, O.: Digital technologies and transformation of modern retail. IOP Conf. Ser.: Mater. Sci. Eng. **497**(1), 012126 (2019)
17. Krymov, S.M., Kolgan, M.V.: On the transformation the distribution channel structure in the digital business environment. In: 2019 Proceedings of the 33rd International Business Information Management Association Conference, IBIMA 2019: Education Excellence and Innovation Management through Vision 2020, pp. 2222–2226 (2020)
18. Lemeshko, V.A., Teptsova, T.S.: Telemedicine: healthcare takes a step into the future. Med. Tech. Eval. Sel. **4**(30), 30–38 (2017)
19. Ozerov, E.S., Pupentsova, S.V., Leventsov, V.A., Dyachkov, M.S.: Selecting the best use option for assets in a corporate management system. In: 2017 6th International Conference on Reliability, Infocom Technologies and Optimization: Trends and Future Directions, ICRITO 2017, 2018-January, pp. 162–170 (2018)
20. Piven, D.V., Kozyakova, E.S., Tsoktoev, D.B.: The telemedicine economic efficiency evaluation in providing surgical care to patients with tuberculosis of bones and joints. (Irkutsk) **5**, 79–82 (2003)
21. Przelecki, Yu.V., Przeleckaya, N.V., Przeleckaya, V.Yu., Bondarenko, V.A.: The role of media education in medical personnel training and improving the medical services quality. Media Educ. **4**, 26–36 (2017)
22. Pupentsova, S., Leventsov, V., Livintsova, M., Alexeeva, N., Vodianova, S.: Assessment of the internet of things projects on the real estate market. IOP Conf. Ser.: Mater. Sci. Eng. **618**(1), 1–14 (2019). Art. no. 012041
23. Skryl, T.V., Paramonov, A.S.: The healthcare sector digital transformation: Russian and foreign specifics Karelian Sci. J. 6(3(20)), 137–140 (2017)
24. Tele-Avc: The tele-expertise and tele-consultation solution in an emergency medical situation/Europe en France (2011). http://en.europe-en-france.gouv.fr/just-realize-!/focus-on-best-projects/tele-avc-the-tele-expertise-and-tele-consultation-solution-in-anemergency-medical-situation. Accessed 12 Mar 2020
25. Telemedicine in Japan. JTTA (2013). http://jtta.umin.jp/pdf/telemedicine/telemedicine_in_japan_20131015-2_en.pdf. Accessed 06 Mar 2020
26. The healthcare digitalization: from investments to saved lives. https://roscongress.org/news/tsifrovizatsija-zdravoohranenija-ot-vlozhenij-k-spasennym-zhiznjam/. Accessed 25 Mar 2020
27. The Russian Federation's population use to the Internet according to the type of settlement and sex (October–November, 2018)/Federal state statistics service. http://www.gks.ru/free_doc/new_site/business/it/fed_nablcroc/publishdata/reports/files/2018/. Accessed 12 Feb 2020
28. Wilson, L., Kim, A., Szeto, D.: The evidence for the economic value of ehealth in the United States today: a systematic review. J. Int. Soc. Telemed. eHealth **4**, 1–20 (2016)

Building a Platform-Type Business Model to Form an Omnichannel Integration in the Telecommunications Industry

Irina Krasyuk[1]($\boxtimes$), Valery Leventsov[1]($\boxtimes$), Maria Kolgan[2]($\boxtimes$), and Yulia Medvedeva[2]($\boxtimes$)

[1] Peter the Great St. Petersburg Polytechnic University, Saint Petersburg, Russia
`iri-krasjuk@yandex.ru`, `vleventsov@spbstu.ru`
[2] Don State Technical University, Rostov-on-Don, Russia
`{mkolgan,ymedvedeva}@donstu.ru`

Abstract. The purpose of this article is to describe, using a research case, how the leading mobile operator in Russia, MTS, was able to create an original and unique innovative business model in the ICT sector. This model leads to higher rates of successful product innovation, continuous updating of the product range in accordance with the constantly changing needs of consumers, and outstanding results in terms of reputation and customer loyalty. MTS' platform-oriented business model is a good choice, as the company can build a solid foundation that integrates a wide range of products and services, sets rules, and provides opportunities to its customers. In addition, the company contributes to the creation of "traffic and attraction", which can be determined by the size and activity of the user base and the potential ecosystem surrounding it. The advantage of the platform business model is the economy of scale and volume, based on the network effect and the integrity of offers, which makes the consumer's choice of the platform long-term. The disadvantages of platforms include the fact that platforms have a longer lifecycle as compared to the offers that comprise it, in order to become the actual standard in the market.

Keywords: Infocommunications · Digital services · Business model · Omnichannel · Platform

1 Introduction

Business modeling is actively studied by scientists and business practitioners. The Osterwalder-Pigneur model, in our opinion, can be considered one of the notable publications in the field of building a business model [1]. The Osterwalder-Pigneur model is built on the basis of key blocks that form a conceptual view of the value of the offer, interaction with customers, the infrastructure that ensures the production of a product or service, and operational indicators. This universal and easy-to-use product-oriented model is suitable for many types of activities, but it allows you to illustrate only the

© Springer Nature Switzerland AG 2020
O. Galinina et al. (Eds.): NEW2AN 2020/ruSMART 2020, LNCS 12526, pp. 328–337, 2020.
https://doi.org/10.1007/978-3-030-65729-1_28

general mechanics of the business, without any reference to the specifics of the market, industry, or development tasks.

In contrast to a product-oriented system where various components seamlessly connect to each other, a platform serves as a foundation that integrates a complete set of products and services, defines the rules and conditions for interaction—e.g., management, workflows and processes—and, by offering features and tools for sharing, creates opportunities for its cutomers. Platforms organize market interaction in a new, technological way [2]. Markets have existed for centuries, connecting consumers and merchants, but Information and Communication Technologies have significantly reduced the need for physical infrastructure and assets [3]. Today, there are many types of platforms, but they all have an ecosystem with the same four elements.

1. Owners control their intellectual property management of the platform, deciding who and how can participate in its operation.
2. Providers offer a platform interface for interacting with consumers. Smartphones are similar providers for some businesses.
3. Suppliers of related products and services are strategic partners that create and produce various offers on the platform, such as various applications. In this case, interaction between providers of related services and users takes place using a smartphone (as a provider).
4. Users are consumers of the offer, but can also be sellers and buyers.

Such a market intermediary platform can only exist if all parties receive long-term benefits from trading on it. The benefits may not be evenly distributed, but all participants should be satisfied [4].

Now we will distinguish between three types of platform-oriented business models and describe the evolution of this business model type [5]. Platforms that facilitate interaction between two or more different but interdependent types of users and provide each other with advantages are called multi-party, and the term "multi-party networks" is also used. These platforms have different groups of clients or partners that they need to attract and retain in order to succeed [6]. The platforms run a variety of businesses, from dating (men and women) to games (developers and users).

The more users join the platform, the more applications and other offers they create, the higher the value of each one is: e.g., between manufacturers and consumers, suppliers and customers, senders and recipients, where it is potentially increased. The exponential growth of Facebook attracts new users because they believe that their friends also use the platform; the same logic was used by the company when it bought WhatsApp, which had 600 million users in 2014 [7]. In addition to network advantages, the breadth and volume of an integrated portfolio of products and services, premium services (such as personalized recommendations, free shipping), and a subscription-based monetization model can increase the likelihood that a consumer will continue to have a relationship with the platform provider, and often this leads to a chain of transactions.

Multi-party platforms can be either a store where consumers buy a seller-defined range of products (e.g., hm.com for H&M, Amazon in the early stages of its development and aggregators like Booking.com), or a marketplace where a portfolio of offers is formed as a result of user interaction, and the platform provider facilitates interaction and manages the process (e.g., Amazon Marketplace, Wikipedia, Uber) [7]. If the platform-oriented business model is open to third parties, providers can use data related to the sales of partners on the marketplace to create an offer for their products that have the highest sales.

To further promote standardization and reach, a new, third type of a platform-oriented business model has been introduced in the past decade [8, 9]. It provides a platform on which to develop other platforms, in other words, "an evolving system consisting of inter-dependent parts on which to create innovations." In this case, the platform provider offers a foundation for participants' innovation and development and often creates an ecosystem of providers offering related products and services, e.g., to consumers, other companies, and/or partners. These meta platforms do not provide this functionality (like the one-way or two-way platforms described above), but provide platform capabilities that can be used when developing new offers (e.g., the Android operating system for Google smart-phones and Amazon Web Services for creating extensible, high-performance websites) [10]. Therefore, we are talking not only about the compatibility of offers, but also about the compatibility of the platform. The growing ecosystem of related service providers leads to an increase in the number of value-adding offers, and therefore to the reach of the offer portfolio. For providers of related services, the platform is also strategic, as it requires investment in platform-specific capabilities and means betting on the future development of the platform.

2   Method of Research

To monitor the dynamic development of the infocommunication market, as well as business initiatives implemented within the framework of platform structures, this article uses a research case study as a research methodology. The academic literature suggests that the choice of methodology is determined by the problems and questions studied, as well as the development of the field of knowledge [11–13].

2.1   Omnichannel as a Tool for the Information and Communication Industry Development

Many market sectors have launched large-scale omnichannel transformations to ensure interaction with their consumers [14–17]. The banking sector, for example, is witnessing a widespread introduction of digital service channels. (In the USA, consumers now use mobile banking on average 76 times a year.) The telecommunications industry has undergone a similar disruptive change; the digital channel is now the main service channel (44% of all consumer requests are processed through digital channels, including the Internet and applications) [18]. In banking, telecommunications, and other industries, chatbots and other artificial intelligence (AI) assistants are now systematically used to support consumers in their digital movements. While companies in these industries still offer consumers traditional channels and contact points with service personnel, most consumers enjoy the convenience offered by these digital technologies.

We are witnessing the emergence and expansion of the presence of an omnichannel consumer who is constantly online, has multiple communication devices, and is most susceptible to targeted advertising. A distinctive feature of omnichannel consumers is their high digital activity [19]. Thanks to these users, the traditional way to purchase is undergoing significant changes.

According to the definition, "omnichannel is management of complex personalized sales in real time (an omnichannel platform)" [19, 20]. In other words, there are two key points here: complexity and personalization. The main goal of the omnichannel strategy is to create a so-called seamless client experience, connecting all communications (calls, text messages, messages in messengers, dialogs in chats, requests via social networks, etc.) in a single database, a single profile, to recognize the client at any point of contact. The key directions of omnichannel sales development directions are studied by both foreign and Russian scientists. Content analysis of publications devoted to the topic of retail omnichannel has confirmed the relevance of scientific developments in this area. Since 2015, there has been a growing interest in the definition with a multi-aspect view of its essence. Cao, Li (2015) presents a conceptual framework that explains the conditions for the impact of cross-channel integration on the company's sales growth [20].

Omnichannel strategies require transformation of organizational culture, processes and operations, as well as technologies. A study by Shen et al. identified the quality of channel integration as the main characteristic of the omnichannel [21]. The quality of channel integration is reflected in the consistency of interaction between different environments and includes two dimensions, such as the consistency of process and content. The undoubted achievement of Shen et al. is an empirical study of the impact of factors in using an omnichannel service, including object-oriented beliefs (i.e., the quality of channel integration) and behavioural beliefs (i.e., perceived speed). The results of an online survey of 401 omnichannel users conducted by Shen et al. show that the quality of channel integration significantly affects the perception of fluency of information perception on various channels [21].

2.2 Trends in the Development of the Infocommunication Market in Russia

In Russia, 77% of the total number of households have Internet access. 65% of the adult population in Russia use mobile phones (smartphones) to access the Internet outside of home or work. More than a third of Russians (35%) use the Internet to order goods and services, which is much more popular in the UK (83%), Sweden (78%), and Germany (77%). Quite a lot of Russian Internet users (39%) make online financial transactions. This practice is even more common in Finland (94%), Sweden (91%), and Estonia (90%). In contrast, surprisingly few Japanese Internet users (15%) trust the Internet for financial transactions [22, 23].

The largest network providers still receive large revenues from mobile communications, but there is no significant revenue growth for companies yet. The revenue from mobile services accounts for more than 80% of the total revenue of each of the companies, while the net profit of the companies is low. In 2019, MTS had the highest net profit (127.2 million rubles), and MegaFon has the lowest (5.2 million rubles) [24]. This is due to high commercial and management costs, as well as the high cost of services provided.

According to AC&M research, the growth of SIM card sales in Russia is staggering (Table 1). According to the company, in January–June 2019, operators sold 47.4 million new SIM cards as compared to the first six months of 2018, when operators sold 46.7 million SIM cards [25]. However, experts note that the outflow of subscribers is decreasing by one percentage point in six months, to 18%. This means that the subscriber base of operators is getting better and better.

Table 1. Dynamics of SIM card sales in Russia [25]

Indicator	2016	2017	2018	2019
SIM card sales, mln.	56	54.1	46.7	47.4
Outflow level, %	23	22	19	18

Mobile operators are becoming service companies capable of integrating channels that ensure the formation of an ecosystem. MTS notes that the operator has a stable subscriber base, and the company's revenue is growing mainly due to increased sales of digital products and services of the company's ecosystem. MegaFon has also reported that the number of subscribers is growing, among other factors, due to the development of the company's ecosystem of services [26] (Table 2).

Table 2. Number of subscribers in Russia, mln. people

Operator	2018	2019	Changes	Percentage of subscribers
MTS	78	79.1	1.4	30
MegaFon	75.2	75.2	0.0	29
VimpelCom	55.3	54.6	−0.6	21
T2 RTK Holding	42.3	44.6	2.3	17
Other	5	7.2	2.3	3
Subtotal	255.7	260.7	5.0	100

MTS is the largest mobile operator. In November 2019, the company announced the rebranding and approval of a new development strategy "Customer Lifetime Value 2.0", which is an appropriate response to digitalization and the growth of business requests for new technologies. The strategy also involves organizational changes: the operator identifies four business verticals—Telecom, Fintech, media, cloud services and digital solutions for corporate clients (Table 3).

The company positions itself as an ecosystem of digital services. The range of such services includes traditional telecommunications services, financial services, cloud and digital solutions, and media. New directions developed by MTS: MTS Marketer, Smart

Table 3. MTS' efficiency indicators [27]

Indicator	2015	2016	2017	2018	2019
Current subscribers, mln. people	107.0	109.9	106.5	105.3	79.1
ARPU, $/person	338.0	342.0	343.0	346.0	355.0
Revenue, bln. rubles.	431.2	435.7	442.9	451.5	476.1
EBITDA, bln. rubles	175.5	169.3	179.8	204.6	210.3
Net profit, bln. rubles	49.5	48.5	56.0	65.9	54.2
Cost, bln. rubles	163.3	175.7	169.4	176.3	178.9
CAPEX, bln. rubles	96.1	83.6	76.4	86.5	91.5
Capitalization, bln. rubles	433.9	535.2	551.6	475.6	652.7
Profitability of EBITDA, %	40.7%	38.9%	40.6%	45.3%	44.2%
Net profitability, %	11.5%	11.1%	12.6%	14.6%	11.4%
ROE, %	29.4%	34.8%	46.6%	101.0%	163.9%
ROA, %	7.6%	8.9%	10.2%	7.2%	6.6%
Staff, no. of persons	–	69,322	65,003	65,102	62,500
Labour productivity, mln. rubles/persons/year	–	6.29	6.81	6.93	7.62
CAPEX/Revenue, %	22%	19%	17%	19%	19%

University, MTS Entertainment, Smart Med, Big Data product, WASD.tv, MTS Al products. Thus, MTS uses Big Data Analytics, Al-based solutions, marketing tools, and implements a single ID, end-to-end loyalty programs and CRM in its digital operations.

2.3 IT Solutions Architecture for Building a Platform

The centre of the MTS product ecosystem is the My MTS application, which is used to manage the complex of its products. My MTS is a convenient technology platform for effective interaction with partners and a better customer experience. A feature of the MTS platform business model is that the operator moves away from the integration scheme with partners, developing its own products in various industries.

At the same time, special attention is paid to organizing the experience of seamless customer transition within the ecosystem.

Figure 1 shows the author's vision of the IT solutions architecture necessary for the formation of a platform business model. It should be stated that creating a platform requires not only financial resources, but also a certain initial level of trust of potential participants in relation to each other and the creators of the business platform. It is necessary in order to prevent opportunistic behaviour from becoming too attractive and then typical for its participants. It should be noted that this initial level of trust of business platform users during its operation will grow due to positive feedback from business culture, gradually forming a kind of club business culture.

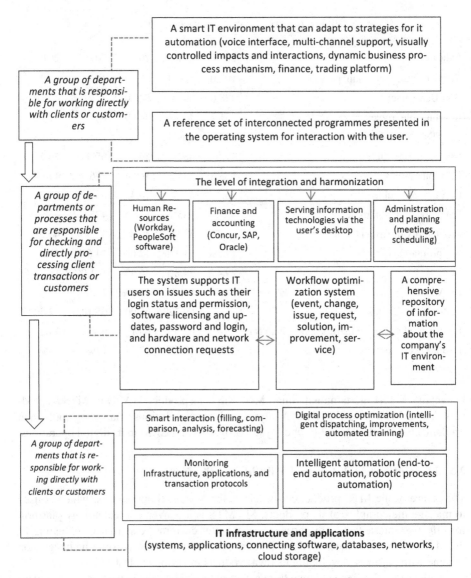

Fig. 1. IT solutions architecture for building a platform

Integrated platforms provide organizations with pre-designed capabilities for integration with critical IT systems. They also usually come with a library of pre-packaged bots that target the most important sources of work in IT, including operations management, security, end-user support, cloud operations, and asset management. Intelligent automation mechanisms can perform various IT tasks. Their extensive repositories of pre-project bots that can handle everything from simple end-user support to machine learning-enabled incident resolution, as well as their wide range of application programming interfaces (APIs) prove their value to many organizations that operate on the principles of platform-based business models.

3   Conclusion

The following main results were obtained during the research:

– Platform-based business models allow you to combine the benefits of using economies of scale with an individual approach to each client. This increases the speed of customer service and reduces costs by eliminating intermediaries. The scope of platform business models lies within industries with a high share of information relative to other factors of production.
– The infocommunication industry is characterized by changing competition between companies and competition between business platforms. For companies with a traditional business model, only narrow market niches remain.
– Mobile operators are becoming service companies that can integrate various channels in order to create a progressive platform business model based on the ecosystem.
– The authors are aware of the limitations of the case study methodology, especially if the study is based on one specific case only. Thus, the dissemination of the results obtained to the infocommunication industry is limited due to the fact that the described innovative business model is really unique and was developed based on the values and culture of MTS and in accordance with them. As for the future research, it would be interesting to trace the relationship of omnichannel integration within the platform business model with the company's ability to create new products and services.

Acknowledgments. This research work was supported by the Academic Excellence Project 5-100 proposed by Peter the Great St. Petersburg Polytechnic University.

References

1. Osterwalder, A., Pigneur, Y.: Business Model Generation: A Handbook for Visionaries, Game Changers, and Challengers. Wiley, Hoboken (2010)
2. Garifullin, B., Zyabrikov, V.: Types of Business Models of Companies in the Digital Economy, vol. 13, p. 83. Publisher "Kreativnaya Ekonomika" (Moscow), Moscow (2019). https://doi.org/10.18334/ce.13.1.39720
3. Otto, B.: Digitale Souveränität: Beitrag des Industrial Data Space (2016). https://doi.org/10.13140/rg.2.2.35125.68321
4. Noll, F., Luke, W., Wappler, M., Oles, M.: Industrial companies in innovation ecosystems. In: 2018 IEEE International Conference on Engineering, Technology and Innovation (ICE/ITMC) (2018). https://doi.org/10.1109/ice.2018.8436300
5. Makarenko, S.A., Sukhina, N.Y., Krymov, S.M., Martynenko, S.V., Adamenko, A.A.: Testing economic systems of capitalist countries by the world economic crisis. Espacios **39**(28), 37–52 (2018)

6. Krymov, S.M., Kolgan, M.V., Suvorova, S.L., Martynenko, O.: Digital technologies and transformation of modern retail. IOP Conf. Ser.: Mater. Sci. Eng. **497**, 012126 (2019). https://doi.org/10.1088/1757-899X/497/1/012126
7. IPP.   https://www.innovationpolicyplatform.org/content/innovative-entrepreneurship. Accessed 14 May 2020
8. Evans, D.S., Schmalensee, R.: Matchmakers: The New Economics of Multisided Platforms, vol. 78, pp. 272–278. Harvard Business Review Press, Boston (2016)
9. Digital Mobility Platforms and Ecosystems State of the Art Report. Project Consortium TUM Living Lab Connected Mobility, pp. 229–238. Technical University of Munich, Germany, July 2016
10. Sui, L.: Strategy analytics: android captures record 88 percent share of global smartphone shipments in Q3 2016. Strategy Anal.: Res. Experts Anal. **28**, 28–35 (2016)
11. Eisenhardt, K.M.: Building theories from case study research. Acad. Manag. Rev. **14**, 532–550 (1989)
12. Hancock, D.R., Algozzine, B.: Doing Case Study Research: A Practical Guide for Beginning Researchers. Teachers College Press, New York (2015)
13. Yin, R.K.: Case Study Research: Design and Methods. International Educational and Professional Publisher, Thousand Oaks (1994)
14. Desfonteines, L., Korchagina, E.: Study of gender structure in the Russian labour market. In: Proceedings of the 33rd International Business Information Management Association Conference, IBIMA 2019: Education Excellence and Innovation Management through Vision 2020, Granada (Spain), 10–11 April 2019, pp. 2216–2221 (2020)
15. Korchagina, E., Naumova, E., Kryukova, K., Bakharev, V.: Research of innovations implementation within the seaport anti-crisis policy. In: E3S Web of Conferences, vol. 135 (2019). https://doi.org/10.1051/e3sconf/201913504074
16. Przhedetskiy, Yu.V., Przhedetskaya, N.V., Borzenko, K.V., Bondarenko, V.A.: Blockchain technologies in healthcare institutions: focus on security and effective cooperation with the government. Int. J. Econ. Bus. Adm. **VII**(2), 92–99 (2019)
17. Bondarenko, V.A., Efremenko, I.N., Larionov, V.A.: Marketing strategy for hotel and tourist complex companies. Int. J. Econ. Bus. Adm. **VII**(1), 388–394 (2019)
18. Nikishkin, V.V., Tverdokhlebova, M.D.: The role of marketplaces in the market of retail trade services. Pract. Mark. **6**(268), 3–8 (2019)
19. Susanto, H., Sucahyo, Y.G., Ruldeviyani, Y., Gandhi, A.: Analysis of factors that influence purchase intention on omni-channel services. In: 2018 International Conference on Advanced Computer Science and Information Systems (ICACSIS) (2018). https://doi.org/10.1109/icacsis.2018.8618249
20. Cao, L., Li, L.: The impact of cross-channel integration on retailers' sales growth. J. Retail. **91**(2), 198–216 (2015)
21. Shen, X.-L., Li, Y.-J., Sun, Y., Wang, N.: Channel integration quality, perceived fluency and omnichannel service usage: the moderating roles of internal and external usage experience. Decis. Support Syst. **109**, 61–73 (2018). https://doi.org/10.1016/j.dss.2018.01.006
22. Russian Statistical Yearbook. 2019: P76 Stat. Collection/Rosstat, Moscow (2019). 708 p.
23. Abdrakhmanova, G., Demyanova, A., Dranev, Y., Gokhberg, L., et al. (eds.): Digital Economy: Pocket Data Book. National Research University Higher School of Economics. HSE, Moscow (2019). 92 p.
24. Nekrasova, T., Leventsov, V., Gluhov, V.: Development of infocommunications services in Russia. In: Galinina, O., Andreev, S., Balandin, S., Koucheryavy, Y. (eds.) NEW2AN/ruSMART -2019. LNCS, vol. 11660, pp. 505–514. Springer, Cham (2019). https://doi.org/10.1007/978-3-030-30859-9_43
25. FY2019 Cellular stats for Russia. http://www.acm-consulting.com/news-and-data/acm-news/110-cellular.html

26. Yearly Financial Report of "MegaFon" (2019). https://corp.megafon.ru/investoram/shareh older/msfo/. Accessed 28 Apr 2020
27. Yearly Financial Report of "MTS" (2019). https://moskva.mts.ru/about/investoram-i-akcion eram/korporativnoe-upravlenie/raskritie-informacii/godovaya-otchetnost. Accessed 28 Apr 2020

Transformation of Online Consumer Behavior Under the Influence of the Pandemic and the Development of Telecommunications

Olga Chkalova[1]([✉]), Inna Bolshakova[1], Natalia Kopasovskaya[1], Natalya Mukhanova[2], and Vladimir Gluhov[2]

[1] Lobachevsky State University of Nizhni Novgorod, Nizhni Novgorod, Russian Federation
{ochkalova,bolshakova,kopasovskay}@iee.unn.ru
[2] Peter the Great St. Petersburg Polytechnic University, Saint Petersburg, Russia
{nmukhanova,vicerector.me}@spbstu.ru

Abstract. The authors analyzed some features of changes in consumer behavior when shopping online in the context of the mass development of modern telecommunications and self-isolation. The study is based on the data of a sociological survey conducted in May 2020 and a comparative analysis of consumer reviews for January–May 2019 and 2020, presented on review aggregator websites. This paper studies the frequency of purchases, the assortment of goods purchased for the first time during the self-isolation, the structure and content of negative reviews about online shopping experience, as well as the opinion of consumers about the possibility of online shopping in the future, when self-isolation is canceled. The main trend in March–May 2020 was the increase in purchases, the average check and the number of orders online. But upon closer examination, one can observe groups of consumers who, on the contrary, have reduced the frequency of purchases on the Internet, have formed a negative or partially negative opinion about this method of purchasing goods, and, as before, are wary of expanding their purchasing activity using modern telecommunications. Online stores should carefully consider the existence of this segment of consumers, while trying to reduce negative user experiences in peak loads and form a loyal attitude to the new forms of trading.

Keywords: Online trading · Telecommunications · Self-isolation · Negative experience · Problems with buying · Assortment · Frequency of purchases

1 Introduction

Over the past years in the world as a whole and in Russia in particular, there has been an increase in online sales. This has led to a number of studies. For example, the conditions for the successful promotion of online retailers were studied in the works of R. Ladhari, MC Rioux et al. [1], A. Zhang, C. Liang and J. Yin [2], K. Anshu and L. Gaur [3], while the factors that enable one to evaluate the quality of Internet commerce are considered in the works of B. Lu, S. Zhang [4], Sudrajat J. Meiryani, Lesmana T. Lusianah

© Springer Nature Switzerland AG 2020
O. Galinina et al. (Eds.): NEW2AN 2020/ruSMART 2020, LNCS 12526, pp. 338–347, 2020.
https://doi.org/10.1007/978-3-030-65729-1_29

[5], Y. Fang and I. Qureshi et al. [6], T. Ade Surya, SAF Silalahi [7], A. Sharma and S. Bahl [8]. Other authors, such as H.T. Keh and E. Shieh [9], S. Prasad and M. Sharma [10], C. Hand et al. [11], T. Hansen [12], P.K. Chintagunta, J. Chu et al. [13], H.H. Wang, N. Hao [14], among others, also studied these factors. The development of consumer loyalty in online trading and the reduction of risks of online shoppers (financial, quality, quantity, etc.) were studied by S. Meents, T. Verhagen [15], I.B. Hong, H. Cho [16], W. Chansanam, U. Detthamrong [17], V. Sfenrianto [18], Z.A. Bulut, A.N. Karabulut [19], S. Kim, J. Kandampully, A. Bilgihan [20], F.S. Khoo, P.L. Teh, P.B. Ooi [21].

According to Data Insight forecasts (November 2019), the total volume of Internet trade in Russia in 2019 increased by 24.62% compared to 2018. At the same time, the average check decreased by 14%, but the number of orders increased by 41%, i.e. the number of consumers and the frequency of purchases increased [22].

The range of products that the consumer is ready to buy online is expanding. The purchasing of the FMCG category goods in 2019 doubled compared to 2018, according to The Nielsen Company [23].

In 2019, stores, retail chains, and logistics intermediaries increased their activity, offering online sale and delivery of food, including perishable goods. In one form or another, the online sale of food products was promoted by federal (Perekrestok, Lenta, METRO, and Auchan) and regional (SPAR) trade enterprises.

Continued growth in 2020 was virtually inevitable. But self-isolation has turned the rapid growth of online retail into explosive. The operational statistics of large retailers immediately confirmed an increase in online sales according to all indicators.

In this situation, it was logical to put forward the following assumption. By the beginning of the pandemic, a significant number of consumers either have experience buying goods online or are sufficiently informed about this possibility. Under self-isolation, online shopping will become for them the obvious (perhaps the only) way of acquiring goods. After the end or weakening of self-isolation, these customers will gain new experience in using Internet communications to buy goods, and, perhaps, will retain the habit of buying some goods online.

Digital transformation of society, enterprises, and households creates conditions for large-scale changes. The achieved level of digital technologies and technical characteristics of machines have been developed to such an extent that new opportunities have opened up for businesses and society [24, 25].

The formation of a digital infrastructure, which includes broadband communication systems and cloud technologies, allows you to find new areas of application and conduct digital business. The advent of smartphones has simplified the customer service process. Consumers are at the center of the digital world and telecommunications services [26, 27].

The development of digitalization is characterized by the digitization of products, that is, there is a strong tendency to move from the consumption of products as such to the use of services. Products and services are becoming more and more personalized, tailored to the individual requirements of the consumer. This trend opens up new opportunities for the development of e-Commerce and accompanying telecommunications services [28, 29, 31].

However, despite being logical enough, this assumption is likely to be too simplistic. It implies a more or less uniform consumer behavior in relation to online retail both before the pandemic and during it.

The purpose of this study is to clarify the features of consumer behavior in relation to online shopping and the directions of its transformation during the pandemic and, as a forecast, after it.

Research objectives: 1) collect and process the opinions of customers regarding the use of the Internet when purchasing various groups of goods in several time ranges: immediately before the pandemic, during the pandemic and (predictably) after the completion or weakening of the isolation regime; 2) confirm, refute or clarify the hypothesis put forward above about the behavior of consumers online during and after self-isolation.

2 Method of Research

The collection of customer opinions was carried out in two directions: a survey through online questioning and a study of consumer reviews published in open sources.

The survey was conducted May 25–30, 2020. 88 people participated in it. The survey did not consider the order of ready-made meals online and the purchase of goods and services delivered online (software, films, e-books, etc.).

The survey was aimed at promptly receiving the opinions of customers at a time when they still clearly enough remember their consumer behavior before the pandemic and during it, rather than at getting a massive amount of data.

The questions were divided by time of events into three periods: before self-isolation; March–May 2020 (period of self-isolation); after completion/weakening of self-isolation (forecast). Since the vast majority of respondents at the time of the survey lived in Nizhny Novgorod and the Nizhny Novgorod Region, where mitigation of self-isolation was started on May 18, 2020, the use of such periods seem justified.

Since an online purchase can be carried out by one of the family members to meet the needs of the whole family, the wording of the questions included the phrase "you or your family members", and the family status of the respondents was clarified: own family, living without a family, living with parents.

The second method was the analysis of public consumer reviews posted on specialized platforms. According to a Data Insight study, 65% of surveyed online buyers began to pay more attention to product reviews over the past year. Regardless of the experience of online shopping, at least 30% of respondents said that they pay most attention to the product reviews on the Internet [30, 32].

For the purposes stated in this paper, consumer feedback aggregators such as irecommend.ru and otzovik.ru were selected. According to the prevailing opinion, these sites rigorously monitor their reviews, preventing both positive and negative cheating.

The authors studied the reviews (total number, as well as the number of positive and negative reviews) of some well-known online services. A comparative analysis was carried out for January–May 2019 and for January–May 2020 with a special emphasis on March–May 2020 (the period of the most rigid self-isolation).

3 Discussion

3.1 Change in the Frequency of Purchases (Table 1)

Prior to the start of self-isolation, 96.59% of respondents had already ordered goods online. All of the few "never bought" answers were given by young people living with their parents. All those living on their own or having their own families had gained online shopping experience before the self-isolation. No one made an online purchase more often than 1 or 2 times a week.

Table 1. Change in the frequency of purchases during the period of self-isolation, %

Frequency of purchases before self-isolation	Frequency of purchases during self-isolation (March–May 2020)					
	Never	Occasionally	1–3 times a month	1–2 times a week	More often than 1–2 times a week	Total
Never	**1.14**	0	2.27	0	0	3.41
Occasionally	9.09	**17.05**	3.41	0	0	29.55
1–3 times a month	2.27	19.32	**27.27**	7.95	4.55	61.36
1–2 times a week	0	0	5.68	**0**	0	5.68
More often than 1–2 times a week	0	0	0	0	**0**	0

Most of the respondents used online stores on a regular basis (1–3 times a month and more often) - 67.04%. It can be assumed that the majority will increase the frequency of purchases during the period of self-isolation. Moreover, in March–May 2020, the majority of respondents were in Nizhny Novgorod and its satellite cities, where various ways of delivering both food and non-food products are fully accessible.

However, we see that

- 18.18% of respondents increased the frequency of purchases (table cells above the diagonal);
- 45.45% of respondents did not change the frequency of purchases (the diagonal cells);
- 36.36% of respondents reduced the frequency of purchases (cells below the diagonal).

In 12.5% of cases, the reduction in the frequency of purchases reached zero. First of all, those who refused to make purchases had only occasionally bought goods online, but in some cases more experienced buyers made the same decision. One of the possible causes of this phenomenon is the understanding by customers of the inevitable problems of online shopping with peak loads on the store and delivery, or the desire to postpone some non-urgent purchases until a more favorable time.

3.2 Change of the Assortment (Table 2)

Among those who made purchases during the period of self-isolation, there are buyers who purchased the same groups of goods as before self-isolation (32.4%), and those who started purchasing some types of goods for the first time under self-isolation (67.57%). The list of product categories purchased for the first time was topped by food products (21.30% of the answers). The rest of the groups of goods purchased online for the first time lined up in exactly the same order as before self-isolation: clothes, shoes, textiles; goods for home and leisure, etc.

Table 2. The proportion of answers confirming the purchase of goods of different groups, % of all answers*

Product group	Purchased before March 2020	First purchased during self-isolation	Product group	Purchased before March 2020	First purchased during self-isolation
Foodstuffs, including	2.82	21.30	Cosmetics	16.94	7.41
Those with standard packaging	1.61	12.96	Furniture	4.03	5.56
No packaging	1.21	8.33	Gardening products	4.03	4.63
Clothing, footwear, textiles	31.05	14.81	Construction materials and goods for repairs	4.84	3.70
Home and leisure goods	17.74	11.10	Other	1.21	1.85
Household appliances	17.34	8.33	Total answers	100.00	100.00

*multiple choice was allowed

During the survey, food purchases made for the first time during the pandemic were divided into two categories: with and without standard packaging. Only 8.33% of the respondents took the risk for the first time, during the period of self-isolation, to order goods online that the consumer usually chooses most carefully in the store hall (vegetables, fruits, meat). The first-time ordered standard packages of milk, cereals, etc. accounted for 12.96% of the responses.

3.3 Getting a New Shopping Experience: Survey Results (Table 3)

The new online shopping experience was both positive and negative. Only 42.2% of those who made purchases in March–May 2020 indicated that they did not encounter problems when using the services of online stores.

Table 3. Problems when buying goods online during the period of self-isolation, % of all answers *

Problem	Percentage	Problem	Percentage
Delivery	28.75	Psychological discomfort	11.25
Return of goods	20.00	Order completeness	5.00
Quality of goods	16.25	Payment	3.75
Website performance	13.75	Прочие	1,25

*multiple choice was allowed

Analyzing the nature of complaints, we can see that they most often have to do with logistic problems (28.75% delivery and 20% return), which became especially acute during self-isolation due to peak loads. However, respondents did not ignore problems that were not directly related to self-isolation. For example, 11.25% noted psychological discomfort from the very fact of buying on the Internet, problems with the virtualized choice of goods (predominantly, clothing and shoes).

3.4 Getting a New Shopping Experience: Feedback Analysis (Table 4)

The impressions of the online shopping process were also studied by analyzing consumer reviews on the Internet (irecommend.ru, otzovik.ru).

Table 4. The structure of consumer reviews of online stores,%

Name of indicator	Wildberries	iGooods
Reviews for March–May 2019 in the total number of reviews for January–May 2019	59,79	45,45
Reviews for March–May 2020 in the total number of reviews for January–May 2020	77,68	86,21
Negative reviews for March–May 2019 in the total number of reviews for January–March 2019	46,64	20,00
Negative reviews for March–May 2020 in the total number of reviews for January–March 2020	65,80	76,00

The study did not take into account data on the popular services Ozon and Sbermarket. In the case of Ozon, the majority of reviews are located on the Yandex.Market platform, where there is no opportunity to study reviews from previous periods. In the case of Sbermarket, the share of negative reviews has changed significantly lately for reasons not related to self-isolation (change of ownership and improvement of work). Therefore, the analysis took into account data on Wildberries (has been functioning for about 15 years) and iGooods (has been functioning for about 5 years).

With the introduction of self-isolation, consumers began to write more reviews. The proportion of reviews written between March and May increased from 59.79% to 77.68% for Wildberries and from 45.45% to 86.21% for iGooods. This serves as an indirect confirmation of the growth in the use of online stores and an increase in consumer dissatisfaction, since it is dissatisfied customers who write reviews more often.

Indeed, the proportion of negative reviews for March–May has increased significantly compared to 2019: up to 65.8% for Wildberries, up to 76% for iGooods.

Analysis of the content of reviews for March–May 2020 shows increased dissatisfaction with the increase in delivery time, unjustified cancellation of orders, lower quality, unfair price increases, canceled discounts, the introduction of paid delivery, and the poor work of call centers.

Buyers, in principle, understand that many of these problems are caused by a sharp increase in demand for online store services, but nevertheless they rarely draw far-reaching conclusions. The following opinion is typical (consumer review dated April 8, 2020, Moscow): "The products are scattered randomly, they suggested replacing many of the ordered products with more expensive ones, the quality of vegetables, fruits, and meat is very different from what was expected… In the most extreme case, I may still order here. But I'll never dare to order meat or vegetables here."

Another interesting opinion is that online services (especially in conditions of self-isolation) deprive consumers of emotional impressions from going shopping (consumer review dated April 19, 2020): "Going shopping [to physical stores] is now a really nice special occasion for me, so all these [online shopping] services are not for me…"

Whenever possible, stores respond to negative reviews, but often it comes down to template phrases, possibly generated by answering bots. Such "communication" causes a feeling of indifference, an impenetrable wall, the inability to solve the problem and, as a result, causes even greater dissatisfaction.

3.5   Consumer Behavior Forecast (Table 5)

Inevitable purchases online during the isolation period can serve as an advertisement for this purchasing option. Even those who had never used the opportunities of online trading before self-isolation said that they might purchase online again in the future. However, the opinions of buyers are far from uniformity.

According to the survey, 36.47% plan to make purchases online occasionally, under special circumstances, 61.36% are going to buy only certain types of goods mainly online and only 3.41% would like to move most of their purchases online.

Both those who previously did not make purchases on the Internet at all, and those who did them occasionally, are cautious and mostly (highlighted in color) predict only rare purchases online in special circumstances (11.36% and 20.45% respectively).

Table 5. Predicted changes in consumer behavior online

Frequency of purchases before self-isolation, % of the respondents	Volume of online purchases after self-isolation (predicted), % of the respondents		
	Will buy most goods online	Will buy some goods mostly online	Will buy online rarely, under special circumstances
Never	0	1.14	**11.36**
Occasionally	0	15.91	**20.45**
1–3 times a month	3.41	**31.8**	3.41
1–2 times a week	0	**9.09**	0
More often than 1–2 times a week	0	**3.41**	0

Those who bought 1–3 times a month or 1–2 times a week predict that they purchase only some products mainly online (31.8% and 9.09%, respectively). That is, the majority of consumers do not want to sharply increase their online purchases.

4   Conclusion

1. A number of consumers reduced the frequency of using online stores during the period of self-isolation waiting for the situation to stabilize. The range of goods first bought by the consumer during this period differs from the usual pre-quarantine range only in increased purchasing of food products.
2. Many buyers who made purchases online in March–May 2020 had a negative experience. In part, customer complaints reflect peak load problems during the isolation period, but a number of consumers relate this experience to online trading in general. About 11% of negative feedback from the respondents is associated with psychological discomfort from purchasing via Internet communications in general.
3. In the minds of a number of consumers, especially those who began to use the services of online stores only during the pandemic, a stereotype is being formed about the low quality of online trading.
4. Buyers are rather cautious about the prospect of active purchases on the Internet after the cancellation of self-isolation. Most of them plan to keep the frequency of their online purchases at about the same level as before self-isolation.
5. In this situation, online sellers should carefully monitor the process of forming negative opinions and promptly eliminate the most common problems, paying attention to building effective communications with the consumer.
6. This research work was supported by the Academic Excellence Project 5–100 proposed by Peter the Great St. Petersburg Polytechnic University.

References

1. Ladhari, R., Rioux, M.C., Souiden, N., Chiadmi, N.: Consumers' motives for visiting a food retailer's facebook page. J. Retail. Consum. Serv. **50**, 379–385 (2019)
2. Zhang, A., Liang, C., Yin, J.: How can dmall do better? discussion on new retail marketing mode based on 4Cs theory. In: Paper presented at the ACM International Conference Proceeding Series pp. 46–50 (2018)
3. Anshu, K., Gaur, L.: E-satisfaction estimation: A comparative analysis using AHP and intuitionistic fuzzy TOPSIS. J. Cases Inf. Technol. **21**(2), 65–87 (2019)
4. Lu, B., Zhang, S.: A conjoint approach to understanding online buyers' decisions towards online marketplaces. J. Theor. Appl. Electron. Commer. Res. **15**(3), 69–83 (2020)
5. Meiryani, Sudrajat, J., Lusianah, Lesmana, T.: Applying E-commerce of web-based quality accounting information system for micro, small and medium enterprises (MSMEs) in services sector. Int. J. Adv. Sci. Technol. **29**(6), 1532–1544 (2020)
6. Fang, Y., Qureshi, I., Sun, H., McCole, P., Ramsey, E., Lim, K.H.: Trust, satisfaction, and online repurchase intention: The moderating role of perceived effectiveness of e-commerce institutional mechanisms. MIS Q. Manage. Inf. Syst. **38**(2), 407–427 (2014)
7. Ade Surya, T., Silalahi, S.A.F.: The effect of e-commerce quality on consumers satisfaction and loyalty: Case study of small and medium enterprises. Int. J. Adv. Sci. Technol. **29**(6), 1404–1414 (2020)
8. Sharma, A., Bahl, S.: Shoppers' inclination towards a website in Punjab: a study on virtual shopping experience. Int. J. Adv. Sci. Technol. **29**(6), 1596–1604 (2020)
9. Keh, H.T., Shieh, E.: Online grocery retailing: success factors and potential pitfalls. Bus. Horiz. **44**(4), 73–83 (2001)
10. Prasad, S., Sharma, M.: Demographic and socioeconomic influences shaping usage of online channel for purchase of food & grocery. Indian J. Mark. **46**(10), 7–21 (2016)
11. Hand, C., Riley, F.D., Harris, P., Singh, J., Rettie, R.: Online grocery shopping: The influence of situational factors. Eur. J. Mark. **43**(9), 1205–1219 (2009)
12. Hansen, T.: Consumer adoption of online grocery buying: A discriminant analysis. Int. J. Retail Distrib. Manage. **33**(2), 101–121 (2005)
13. Chintagunta, P.K., Chu, J., Cebollada, J.: Quantifying transaction costs in online/off-line grocery channel choice. Mark. Sci. **31**(1), 96–114 (2012)
14. Wang, H.H., Hao, N., Zhou, Q., Wetzstein, M.E., Wang, Y.: Is fresh food shopping sticky to retail channels and online platforms? evidence and implications in the digital era. Agribusiness **35**(1), 6–19 (2019)
15. Meents, S., Verhagen, T.: Reducing consumer risk in electronic marketplaces: the signaling role of product and seller information. Comput. Hum. Behav. **86**, 205–217 (2018)
16. Hong, I.B., Cho, H.: The impact of consumer trust on attitudinal loyalty and purchase intentions in B2C e-marketplaces: Intermediary trust vs. seller trust. Int. J. Inf. Manage. **31**(5), 469–479 (2011)
17. Chansanam, W., Detthamrong, U.: Impact of information behavior online towards customer loyalty in mobile applications in Thailand. Int. J. Adv. Sci. Technol. **29**, 654–670 (2020) (4 Special Issue)
18. Sfenrianto, V.: Analyis on factors influencing customer experience of e-commerce users in Indonesia through the application of Chatbot technology. J. Theor. Appl. Inf. Technol. **98**(7), 953–962 (2020)
19. Bulut, Z.A., Karabulut, A.N.: Examining the role of two aspects of eWOM in online repurchase intention: An integrated trust–loyalty perspective. J. Consum. Behav. **17**(4), 407–417 (2018)

20. Kim, S., Kandampully, J., Bilgihan, A.: The influence of eWOM communications: An application of online social network framework. Comput. Hum. Behav. **80**, 243–254 (2018)
21. Khoo, F.S., Teh, P.L., Ooi, P.B.: Consistency of online consumers' perceptions of posted comments: An analysis of TripAdvisor reviews. J. Inf. Commun. Technol. **16**(2), 374–393 (2017)
22. Internet trading in Russia 2019. A study that combines Data Insight reports, as well as public studies and data on the Internet, online purchases, delivery from online stores and customers. http://datainsight.ru/sites/default/files/DI_Ecommerce2019.pdf/. Accessed 01 Jun 2020
23. Ahead of trends: the Russian FMCG online market has almost doubled. FMCG and retail. 21–11-2019. https://www.nielsen.com/ru/ru/insights/article/2019/operezhaya-trendy-rossiyskiy-onlayn-rynok-fmcg-vyros-pochti-vdvoe/. Accessed 03 Jun 2020
24. Krasyuk, I., Kirillova, T., Bakharev, V., Lyamin, B.: Life cycle management in network retail enterprise based on introduction of innovations. IOP Conf. Ser. Mater. Sci. Eng. **497**(1), 012125 (2019)
25. Krasyuk, I., Medvedeva, Y., Baharev, V., Chargaziya, G. Evolution of strategies of retail and technological systems under broad digitalization conditions. OP Conf. Ser. Mater. Sci. Eng. **497**(1), 012124 (2019)
26. Krasyuk, I.A., Kobeleva, A.A., Mikhailushkin, P.V., Terskay, G.A., Chuvakhina, A.G. Economic interests focusing as a basis of the formation of investment policy. Espacios **39**(31), 518–531 (2018)
27. Krasyuk, I., Medvedeva, Y.: Resource support in business analytics of innovative development of trade and technological systems. In: Proceedings of the 33rd International Business Information Management Association Conference, IBIMA 2019: Education Excellence and Innovation Management through Vision 2020. Pp. 8807–8817 (2019)
28. Krymov, S., Kolgan, M., Suvorova, S., Martynenko, O.: Digital technologies and transformation of modern retail. IOP Conf. Ser. Mater. Sci. Eng. **497**(1), 012126 (2019)
29. Krymov, S.M., Kolgan, M.V.: On the transformation the distribution channel structure in the digital business environment. In: Proceedings of the 33rd International Business Information Management Association Conference, IBIMA 2019, Education Excellence and Innovation Management through Vision 2020, pp. 2222–2226 (2019)
30. Ozerov, E.S., Pupentsova, S.V., Leventsov, V.A., Dyachkov, M.S. Selecting the best use option for assets in a corporate management system In: 2017 6th International Conference on Reliability, Infocom Technologies and Optimization: Trends and Future Directions, ICRITO 2017, 2018-January, pp. 162–170 (2018)
31. Pupentsova, S., Leventsov, V., Livintsova, M., Alexeeva, N., Vodianova, S. Assessment of the Internet of Things Projects on the Real Estate Market IOP Conference Series: Materials Science and Engineering **618**(1), 012041 (2019)
32. Research: how to buy online before and during a pandemic. April 24, 2020, 13:37. https://www.retail.ru/rbc/pressreleases/24ttl-issledovanie-kak-pokupayut-onlayn-do-i-vo-vremya-pandemii/. Accessed 02 Feb 2020

Fiber-Optical Communication Line with a System for Compensation of Radiation-Induced Losses During the Transmission of Information

Diana S. Dmitrieva[1], Valeria M. Pilipova[1], Roman V. Davydov[2(✉)],
Elena I. Andreeva[1], Vadim V. Davydov[2,3], and Vasiliy Y. Rud'[3]

[1] The Bonch-Bruevich Saint-Petersburg State University of Telecommunications,
Saint Petersburg 193232, Russia
[2] Peter the Great St. Petersburg Polytechnic University, Saint Petersburg 195251, Russia
davydovrv@spbstu.ru
[3] Department of Ecology, All-Russian Research Institute of Phytopathology, Odintsovo District,
Bolshiye Vyazyomy, 143050 Moscow Region, Russia

Abstract. This research is focused on γ-radiation, the main negative factor which causes significant losses in fiber-optical communication lines. We determine the methods for increasing the relaxation rate of color centers that are formed in an optical fiber under the influence of γ - radiation. Moreover, we develop the design of the fiber-optic communication line with the compensation of radiation-induced losses at the moment of exposure to the optical fiber γ - radiation. The results of experimental investigations are presented.

Keywords: Radiation · Fiber-Optical communication line · Color centers · Radiation-Induced loss · Radiation dose · Optical signal · Compensation

1 Introduction

With the development of scientific and technological progress, the number of industrial enterprises and research laboratories that use radioactive materials in their activities is continuously increasing [1–6]. The reduction in the reserves of natural fuels (oil, gas, coal, etc.) with a constant increase in the amount of energy consumed led to the expansion of the nuclear energy segment, primarily to provide electricity to large cities and industrial centers [6–9]. Therefore, the number of adverse environmental impacts associated with radioactivity increases every year. The most difficult to control among them are precipitation containing radioactive emissions that fall into the soil, which leads to an increase in the exposure dose (radiation level) of various communication systems.

Currently, the use of fiber-optic communication lines (FOCL) is the most effective way of transmitting information [6–8, 10–15]. The number of FOCLs for various purposes used in many fields is increasing every year. The density of their placement is continuously growing [10–17]. The main negative factor that has a significant effect on

© Springer Nature Switzerland AG 2020
O. Galinina et al. (Eds.): NEW2AN 2020/ruSMART 2020, LNCS 12526, pp. 348–356, 2020.
https://doi.org/10.1007/978-3-030-65729-1_30

the optical fiber is radioactivity [1, 2, 6, 7, 16, 19, 20]. When γ - radiation is exposed to an optical fiber, color centers are formed in it, and the fiber becomes darker. The attenuation of the transmitted optical signal increases (radiation-induced losses α_s increase.). With a large dose of D_R and prolonged exposure to radiation, the value of α_s becomes more than 10 dB/km. It leads to loss of information since the signal-to-noise ratio in the photodetector module becomes less than 1.0.

It should be noted that during the operation of a fiber-optic communication line in the area affected by γ-radiation, over time, the radiation dose D_R of the optical fiber only increases. Studies have shown that with an increase in the dose of D_R, the number of color centers increases [19, 20]. That leads to a rise in α_s.

The life of modern FOCLs at various facilities is designed to be 15-20 years [6, 7, 10–18, 21–27]. Thus, it requires the development of additional measures to protect optical fibers from the harmful effects of radioactivity and ways to compensate for the increase in losses. Based on our studies, we present one of the possible FOCL options with a radiation-induced loss compensation system for transmitting information in areas with a radiation level of 0.1 Gy/h and higher.

2   The Methods for Controlling the Relaxation Rate of Color Centers in Optical Fibers

Various studies have shown that a decrease in radiation-induced losses of α_s. in optical fibers can be obtained in several ways. The most frequently used of them is the fabrication of the core of optical fiber from pure quartz (SiO_2) [19, 20]. In some cases, a core made of pure quartz with a special design, for example, PANDA, is used. Various impurities, for example, phosphorus, chlorine, or boron, are introduced into the reflective layer of these optical fibers. All these methods have their advantages and disadvantages. Among the difficulties, it is worth noting the very high cost of pure quartz optical fibers, especially using the special PANDA design. The width of the reflective layer is at least an order of magnitude larger than the core. It requires a large number of expensive impurities. Therefore, the use of such fibers on long trunk lines of communication is not economically feasible. These types of fibers are actively used in satellites, etc. [5, 19, 20].

Also, the use of impurities in the reflective layer (a core made of pure quartz) for additional protection of the optical fiber from γ radiation increases losses, which can reach up to 0.5 dB/km or more. It reduces the efficiency of using FOCL over long distances. Moreover, the use of impurities in the reflective layer increases the likelihood of chromatic dispersion (CD) by more than 30%. It is another additional factor that can lead to loss of information, especially with large volumes of its transmission.

Studies [1, 2, 6, 7, 19, 20] by various scientists have shown that the relaxation processes of the destruction of color centers (restoration of the transparency of the optical fiber) after the cessation of radiation exposure occur very slowly. This process, depending on the D_R value, can be more than 10^6 s. The rate of relaxation processes can be increased by increasing the temperature T of the optical fiber. It is actively used in space systems. For trunk lines, this method is not effective. The rate of formation of color centers increases with constant exposure to γ - radiation with increasing temperature.

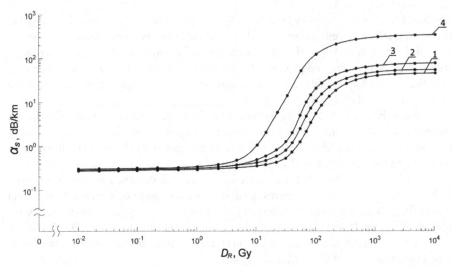

Fig. 1. The dependence of radiation-induced losses α_s of single-mode fiber at a wavelength of $\lambda = 1550$ nm from the radiation dose D_R. Graphs 1, 2, and 3 correspond to the type of core of an optical fiber made of pure quartz (SiO_2) located at the following temperatures T in K: 294.2, 313.4, 328.1. Figure 4 corresponds to the type of core of the SiO_2 - GeO_2 optical fiber (doping 1.5%), located at T = 294.2 K.

Our experiments (Fig. 1) showed that with an increase in T, the value of α_s increases with the same dose of radiation.

An analysis of the results obtained (Fig. 1) shows that the process of formation of new color centers proceeds faster than the destruction of existing color centers with an increase in T; therefore, α_s increases. Also, it is very difficult to control the temperature of an optical fiber in a line at long-haul FOCLs over long distances.

Therefore, we have investigated a method for increasing the relaxation rate of color centers using high-power laser radiation. Figure 2 presents the results of a study of the effect of P_{ex} laser radiation power on changes in the α_s value with time after the termination of the action of γ - radiation optical fiber (irradiation dose of 100 Gy). For research, we used a single-mode fiber (SMF-28) with a SiO_2 - GeO_2 core (doping 1.5%) at T = 294.2 K.

The results show that with an increase in the laser radiation power, the time of the relaxation process, which returns the properties of the optical fiber to its original state, decreases to 10^3 s. It allows us to develop a new method for compensating the effect of γ radiation on an optical fiber using additional high-power laser radiation.

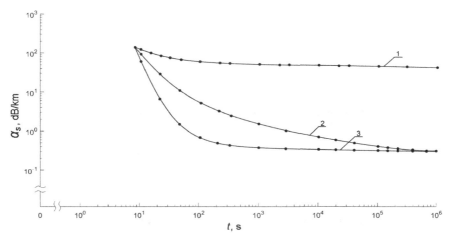

Fig. 2. Dependence of the change in loss α_s from time t at a wavelength of $\lambda = 1550$ nm for single-mode fiber, SiO_2 - GeO_2 core (doping concentration 1.5%). Graphs 1, 2, and 3 correspond to different laser power P_{ex} in mW: 0.4; 10.0; 40.0.

3 Fiber-Optic Communication Line with the Compensation System, Experimental Results, and Discussion

Our experiments and operating experience of fiber-optic communication lines made it possible to develop the following fiber-optic design for the implementation of the new method of α_s compensation. After the electro-optical modulator, an optical signal with $\lambda = 1550$ nm enters through a multiplexer into a single-mode optical fiber. Additional high-power laser radiation at $\lambda = 1310$ nm also enters a single-mode optical fiber through a multiplexer [12, 26, 27]. A multiplexer is installed at the FOCL output, which divides optical signals with different λ into two channels (in one, the signal carrying the information is recorded, in the other, the power of the additional laser radiation P_{ex} is monitored). Figure 3 shows an experimental setup for studying the effect of P_{ex} of additional laser radiation on the relaxation rate of color centers in optical fiber and the quality (introduced additional distortions) of information transmitted over a fiber optic link at $\lambda = 1550$ nm.

For the research, we use a single-mode optical fiber with a SiO_2 core - GeO_2 (doping concentration of 1.5%) and the dose of radiation $D_R = 100$ Gy. Information is transmitted over the fiber in the form of rectangular pulses of different frequencies, duty cycle, and amplitude. Figure 4 shows, as an example, the dependence of the change in α_s from time t (after the termination of the effect of γ radiation on the optical fiber). Rectangular pulses of various durations with a frequency of $f = 1$ GHz are transmitted through the fiber optic link. Additional laser radiation with $\lambda = 1310$ nm with a power of $P_{ex} = 0.3$ W was introduced into the optical fiber.

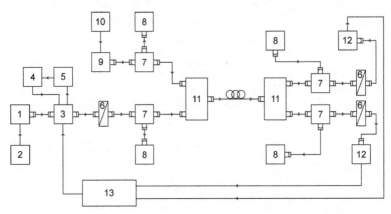

Fig. 3. The structural scheme of the experimental setup: 1 - laser transmitting module ($\lambda = 1550$ nm); 2 - multi-functional power driver; 3- electro-optical modulator; 4 - the device for automatic adjustment of the working point of the electro-optical modulator; 5 - the tool for monitoring the operating point of the electro-optical modulator; 6 - polarizer; 7 - optical divider; 8 - optical power meter; 9 - laser transmitting module ($\lambda = 1310$ nm); 10 - power driver; 11 - multiplexer; 12 - receiving optical module; 13 is a ZVA40 vector network analyzer.

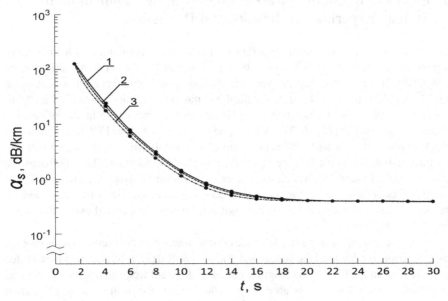

Fig. 4. The dependence of the change in the value of α_s from time t. Graphs 1, 2, and 3 correspond to the pulse duration τ in ns: 0.1; 0.2; 0.8.

The obtained results show that the primary influence on the change in the relaxation rate of color centers (reduction of radiation-induced losses) is exerted by additional laser radiation. Its effect reduces the relaxation time of color centers by several orders of magnitude (depending on P_{ex}) compared with the cases when it is absent in the optical fiber.

Analysis of the results in Fig. 1 and 4 allow us to conclude that there is a point of static equilibrium between the two processes (the formation of color centers and their relaxation). It means that for a specific exposure dose of γ - radiation acting on the optical fiber, there is a value P_{ex} of the optical power of the additional laser radiation. In this case, the value of α_s for a certain period under the influence of γ - radiation on the fiber, for example, for 10^5 s increases insignificantly (less than 2% of its initial value). In this case, we can assume that there is compensation for the negative effect of γ - radiation on the optical fiber.

Our studies have shown that the developed method has limitations on its use. These limitations are related to the P_{ex} values of the additional laser radiation that is introduced into the optical fiber. The use of high power introduces distortions into the signal with information transmitted at λ = 1550 nm. In Fig. 5 shows, as an example, changes in the shape of rectangular pulses (frequency f = 1 GHz) transmitted over a fiber optic link

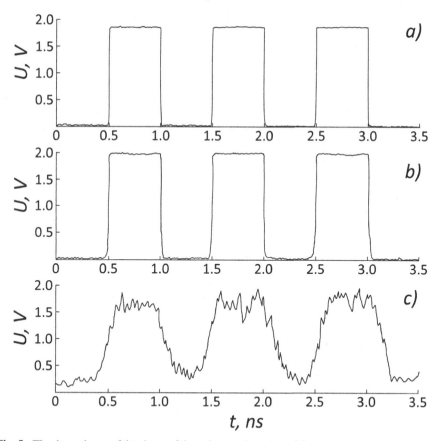

Fig. 5. The dependence of the shape of the pulses on the value of the power P_{ex}. Graphs 1, 2, and 3 correspond to P_{ex} in mW: 200; 400; 800.

when additional laser radiation with different powers of P_{ex} is introduced into the optical fiber.

The obtained results show that, at a high power of additional laser radiation, pulse shape distortions occur. When transmitting information over fiber optic links at $\lambda =$ 1550 nm, especially with compression, this will lead to significant errors in its decryption or complete data loss.

4 Conclusion

The obtained experimental results allow us to conclude that the method we developed for the compensation of radiation-induced losses in the optical fiber provides long-term operation of fiber optic lines up to a specific value of the exposure dose. An essential factor, in this case, is the length of the FOCL section, which is negatively affected by γ - radiation, as well as its position on the trunk line (attenuation coefficient of additional laser radiation in an optical fiber of the order of 0.43 dB/km). This fact must be considered when operating FOCL and making various decisions. Our results confirm this. For example, the use of the method developed by us ensures the operation of FOCL for 20 years, with an exposure dose of about 1.5 mGy/h of an optical fiber section of 2,000 m long. This FOCL section should be located no more than 200 km from the transmitting optical laser module.

The research results showed that for the design of FOCLs in which the method we developed will be used, a new technique is needed at various sites. This technique should consider possible exposure doses of radioactivity, the position of the area of potential exposure to γ - radiation on the optical fiber, and its duration. For this, it is necessary to conduct additional research and calculate what will be a continuation of our work. Currently, there is no such technique in the world.

References

1. Tomashuk, A.L., Filippov, A.V., Kashaykin, P.F., Guryanov, A.N., Semjonov, S.L.: 1.55-μm-light absorption induced by pulsed-X-ray radiation in pure-silica-core fiber: effects of light power and temperature. J. Non-Crystalline Solids **521**, 119504 (2019)
2. Tomashuk, A.L., Filippov, A.V., Kashaykin, P.F., Byshkova, E.A., Guryanov, A.N., Dianov, E.M.: Role of inherent radiation-induced self-trapped holes in pulsed-radiation effect on pure-silica-core optical fibers. J. Lightwave Technol. **37**(3), 956–962 (2019)
3. Nepomnyashchaya, E., Velichko, E., Kotov, O.: Determination of noise components in laser correlation spectroscopic devices for signal-to-noise ratio estimation. In: Proceedings of the 2019 IEEE International Conference on Electrical Engineering and Photonics, EExPolytech 2019, 8906887, pp. 321–324 (2019)
4. Velichko, E., Savchenko, E., Nepomnyashchaya, E., Dyubo, D., Tsybin, O.: Nanocommunication system with a laser activated molecular film. In: Galinina, O., Andreev, S., Balandin, S., Koucheryavy, Y. (eds.) NEW2AN/ruSMART -2018. LNCS, vol. 11118, pp. 649–655. Springer, Cham (2018). https://doi.org/10.1007/978-3-030-01168-0_59
5. Petrov, A.A., Davydov, V.V.: Improvement frequency stability of caesium atomic clock for satellite communication system. In: Balandin, S., Andreev, S., Koucheryavy, Y. (eds.) ruSMART 2015. LNCS, vol. 9247, pp. 739–744. Springer, Cham (2015). https://doi.org/10.1007/978-3-319-23126-6_68

6. Davydov, V.V., Dudkin, V.I., Velichko, E.N., Karseev, AYu.: Fiber-optic system for simulating accidents in the cooling circuits of a nuclear power plant. J Opt. Technol. (A Translation of Opticheskii Zhurnal) **82**(3), 132–135 (2015)

7. Davydov, V.V., Dudkin, V.I., Karseev, AYu.: Fiber – optic imitator of accident situation for verification of work of control systems of atomic energy plants on ships. Opt. Mem. Neural Networks (Information Optics) **23**(3), 170–176 (2014)

8. Ateya, Abdelhamied A., Muthanna, A., Vybornova, A., Darya, P., Koucheryavy, A.: Energy - aware offloading algorithm for multi-level cloud based 5G system. In: Galinina, O., Andreev, S., Balandin, S., Koucheryavy, Y. (eds.) NEW2AN/ruSMART -2018. LNCS, vol. 11118, pp. 355–370. Springer, Cham (2018). https://doi.org/10.1007/978-3-030-01168-0_33

9. Makolkina, M., Pham, V.D., Kirichek, R., Gogol, A., Koucheryavy, A.: Interaction of AR and IoT applications on the basis of hierarchical cloud services. In: Galinina, O., Andreev, S., Balandin, S., Koucheryavy, Y. (eds.) NEW2AN/ruSMART -2018. LNCS, vol. 11118, pp. 547–559. Springer, Cham (2018). https://doi.org/10.1007/978-3-030-01168-0_49

10. Kiesewetter, D., Malyugin, V., Makarov, S., Korotkov, K., Ming, D., Wei, X.: Application of the optical fibers in the system of determining the distance of jump at ski springboard. In: Proceedings – 2016 Advances in Wireless and Optical Communications, RTUWO 2016, 7821845, pp. 5–8 (2017)

11. Koucheryavy, A., Vladyko, A., Kirichek, R.: State of the art and research challenges for public flying ubiquitous sensor networks. In: Balandin, S., Andreev, S., Koucheryavy, Y. (eds.) ruSMART 2015. LNCS, vol. 9247, pp. 299–308. Springer, Cham (2015). https://doi.org/10.1007/978-3-319-23126-6_27

12. Ivanov, S.I., Lavrov, A.P., Saenko, I.I.: Application of microwave photonics components for ultrawideband antenna array beamforming. In: Galinina, O., Balandin, S., Koucheryavy, Y. (eds.) NEW2AN/ruSMART -2016. LNCS, vol. 9870, pp. 670–679. Springer, Cham (2016). https://doi.org/10.1007/978-3-319-46301-8_58

13. Davydov, V.V., Karseev, A.Yu., Nepomnyashchay, E.K., Petrov, A.A., Velichko, E.N.: Fiber – Optic Super – High – Frequency Signal Transmission System for Sea – Based Radar Station. Lecture Notes in Computer Science (including subseries Lecture Notes in Artificial Intelligence and Lecture Notes in Bioinformatics), vol. 8638, pp. 694-702 (2014)

14. Ateya, A.A., Muthanna, A., Gudkova, I., Abuarqoub, A., Vybornova, A., Koucheryavy, A.: Development of intelligent core network for tactile internet and future smart systems. J. Sens. Actuator Netw. **7**(1), 7 (2018)

15. Tarasenko, M.Y., Davydov, V.V., Lenets, V.A., Akulich, N.V., Yalunina, T.R.: Features of use direct and external modulation in fiber optical simulators of a false target for testing radar station. In: Galinina, O., Andreev, S., Balandin, S., Koucheryavy, Y. (eds.) NEW2AN/ruSMART/NsCC -2017. LNCS, vol. 10531, pp. 227–232. Springer, Cham (2017). https://doi.org/10.1007/978-3-319-67380-6_21

16. Ermolaev, A.N., Krishpents, G.P., Vysoczkiy, M.G.: Compensation of chromatic and polarization mode dispersion in fiber-optic communication lines in microwave signals transmittion. J. Phys: Conf. Ser. **741**(1), 012071 (2016)

17. Davydov, V.V., Ermak, S.V., Karseev, A.U., Nepomnyashchaya, E.K., Petrov, A.A., Velichko, E.N.: Fiber-optic super-high-frequency signal transmission system for sea-based radar station. In: Balandin, S., Andreev, S., Koucheryavy, Y. (eds.) NEW2AN 2014. LNCS, vol. 8638, pp. 694–702. Springer, Cham (2014). https://doi.org/10.1007/978-3-319-10353-2_65

18. Friman, R.K.: Fiber-optic Communication Systems. Wiley, New Jersey, 496 p. (2012)

19. Kashaykin, P.F., Tomashuk, A.L., Salgansky, M.Y., Guryanov, A.N., Dianov, E.M.: Anomalies and peculiarities of radiation-induced light absorption in pure silica optical fibers at different temperatures. J. Appl. Phys. **121**(21), 213104 (2017)

20. Kashaikin, P.F., et al.: Prediction of radiation-induced light absorption in optical fibers with an undoped silica core for space applications. Tech. Phys. **64**(5), 701–707 (2019). https://doi.org/10.1134/S1063784219050098

21. Pirmagomedov, R., Kirichek, R., Blinnikov, M., Koucheryavy, A.: UAV-based gateways for wireless nanosensor networks deployed over large areas. Comput. Commun. **146**, 55–62 (2019)

22. Simonov, A., Fokin, G., Sevidov, V., Sivers, M., Dvornikov, S.: Polarization direction finding method of interfering radio emission sources. In: Galinina, O., Andreev, S., Balandin, S., Koucheryavy, Y. (eds.) NEW2AN/ruSMART -2019. LNCS, vol. 11660, pp. 208–219. Springer, Cham (2019). https://doi.org/10.1007/978-3-030-30859-9_18

23. Moroz, A.V., Davydov, R.V., Davydov, V.V.: A new scheme for transmitting heterodyne signals based on a fiber-optical transmission system for receiving antenna devices of radar stations and communication systems. In: Galinina, O., Andreev, S., Balandin, S., Koucheryavy, Y. (eds.) NEW2AN/ruSMART -2019. LNCS, vol. 11660, pp. 710–718. Springer, Cham (2019). https://doi.org/10.1007/978-3-030-30859-9_62

24. Al-Bahri, M., Ruslan, K., Aleksey, B.: Integrating internet of things with the digital object architecture. In: Galinina, O., Andreev, S., Balandin, S., Koucheryavy, Y. (eds.) NEW2AN/ruSMART -2019. LNCS, vol. 11660, pp. 540–547. Springer, Cham (2019). https://doi.org/10.1007/978-3-030-30859-9_47

25. Davydov, V.V., et al.: Fiber-optics system for the radar station work control. In: Balandin, S., Andreev, S., Koucheryavy, Y. (eds.) ruSMART 2015. LNCS, vol. 9247, pp. 712–721. Springer, Cham (2015). https://doi.org/10.1007/978-3-319-23126-6_65

26. Davydov, Roman V., et al.: Fiber-optic transmission system for the testing of active phased antenna arrays in an anechoic chamber. In: Galinina, O., Andreev, S., Balandin, S., Koucheryavy, Y. (eds.) NEW2AN/ruSMART/NsCC -2017. LNCS, vol. 10531, pp. 177–183. Springer, Cham (2017). https://doi.org/10.1007/978-3-319-67380-6_16

27. Davydov, V.V., Dudkin, V.I., Karseev, A.Y.: Fiber – Optic communication line for the NMR signals transmission in the control systems of the ships atomic power plants work. Opt. Mem. Neural Netw. (Information Optics) **23**(4), 259–264 (2014)

Dynamic Range Improvement of Broad-Band Analog Fiber Optic Links with Special Lithium Niobate Integrated Optical Modulators

Aleksei Petrov[1,2], Mikhail Parfenov[1,2], Vladimir Lebedev[2], Igor Ilichev[2],
Peter Agruzov[2], Aleksandr Tronev[2], and Aleksandr Shamrai[2(✉)]

[1] Peter the Great Saint Petersburg Polytechnic University, 29 Polytekhnicheskaya,
195251 St. Petersburg, Russia
alexey-np@yandex.ru
[2] Ioffe Institute, 26 Polytekhnicheskaya, 194021 St. Petersburg, Russia
achamrai@mail.ioffe.ru

Abstract. Two different approaches for dynamic range improvement of broad band analog fiber optic link were considered. They are based on the special lithium niobate modulators which was stabilized in specific working points. The first approach is the laser intensity noise suppression with dual output Mach-Zehnder modulator and balanced photodetector. The high noise suppression was achieved by precise balancing using modulator working point selection and stabilization as well as optical path adjustment. The second approach use a directional coupler modulator which was set to the specific working point corresponding to the minimum of third harmonic and linearized modulation. The requirements to characteristics of the modulators and working point stabilization systems were determined. Experimental demonstration and comparison two types of the photonic links were carried out. The spurries free dynamic range higher than 110 dB/Hz$^{2/3}$ in 3 GHz spectral band was achieved.

Keywords: Microwave photonics · Fiber-optic links · External modulator · Lithium niobate · Spurious free dynamic range

1 Introduction

The technology of integrated optical circuits on lithium niobate substrates is one of the basic ones for the development and production of modern optoelectronic compo-nents, primarily high frequency integrated optical modulators which are the key com-ponents of modern fiber optic telecommunication systems and microwave photonics [1]. So called microwave photonics [2] is the technology which used the optical domain for generation, transmission and processing microwave and millimeter-wave signals. Beside defense applications this field attract a high attention with development and spreading of radio over fiber (RoF) technique [3, 4] which became of a special interest with the emerging of 5G wireless networks. A low noise factor and high dynamic range are the basic characteristics of the fiber optic links determining their performance. Many approaches

© Springer Nature Switzerland AG 2020
O. Galinina et al. (Eds.): NEW2AN 2020/ruSMART 2020, LNCS 12526, pp. 357–363, 2020.
https://doi.org/10.1007/978-3-030-65729-1_31

were proposed for improvement these parameters which are using special modulation formats and integrated optical modulators for their realization [5].

This paper describes two different approaches for dynamic range improvement of broad band analog fiber optic links. They are based on the special lithium niobate modulators which comprise X type waveguide directional couplers. The first approach is the laser intensity noise suppression with dual output Mach-Zehnder modulator and balanced photodetector. The second approach used a directional coupler modulator which was set to the specific working point corresponding to the minimum of third harmonic and linearized modulation.

2 Integrated Optical Modulators

2.1 Dual Output Mach-Zehnder Modulator

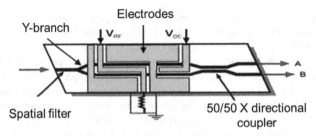

Fig. 1. Configuration of a dual output Mach-Zehnder modulator.

A lithium niobate integrated optical dual output Mach-Zehnder modulator (Fig. 1) [1] was developed and fabricated in the Laboratory of Quantum Electronics at Ioffe Institute. The modulator optical scheme was produced by technology of the thermal titanium in-diffusion [5]. The output X type waveguide directional coupler was precisely adjusted to the 50/50 power splitting ratio using an original technique for the precise photorefractive waveguide trimming [6, 7] and ensured good balancing of modulator outputs. A broad band modulation with frequency bandwidth up to 20 GHz [8] was achieved using travelling wave push pull 50-Ω electrodes.

The quadrature working point of the modulator was set by specially designed electronic system which equalized constant optical power on the different modulator outputs by application of the control DC voltage to the bias electrodes.

The π shift between high frequency modulated signals at the two modulator outputs allows a suppression of RIN and other synphase noises by a balanced detection [2, 9]. The RIN suppression is an especially interesting for low signal applications such as 5G wireless networks

2.2 Directional Coupler Modulator

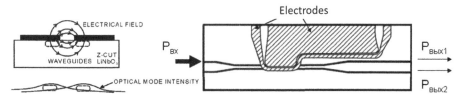

Fig. 2. The directional coupler modulator.

The scheme of the directional coupler modulator is shown on Fig. 2. The principle of operation of the modulator is based on the coupling between two closely spaced optical waveguides. In a typical modulator configuration the interaction length between parallel sections of the waveguides and the distance between them is selected for full coupling. The application of an electric field to interacting waveguides leads to the difference in the propagation constants in parallel waveguides, which violates phase synchronism and reduces the coupling efficiency. The coupling coefficient between the waveguides linearly depends on the applied electric field, thus the optical transfer function of the directional coupler modulator has the form of the sinc function (Fig. 3). The experimental sample of the directional coupler modulator had a configuration with the interaction length of 30 mm and high frequency traveling wave electrodes with the same geometry as on the dual output Mach-Zehnder modulator. The experimental value of the characteristic switching voltage Vs was less than 3 V.

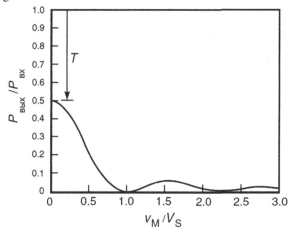

Fig. 3. The optical transfer function of the directional coupler modulator.

The form of the transfer function allows the use directional coupler modulator for a linearization and suppression third-order intermodulation distortion [9]. However, it should be noted that the directional coupler modulator is a sub-octave modulator with a significant level of second-order nonlinear distortion. Experimental dependences of power in different harmonics as functions of bias DC voltage (working point) are shown on the Fig. 4. It can be seen from the graph that different harmonics were suppressed at different working points. We are primarily interested in suppressing third-order nonlinearity (third harmonic).

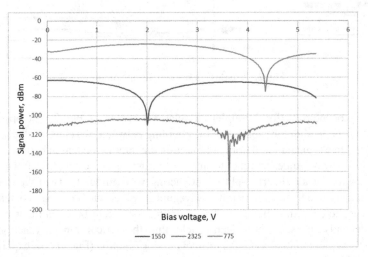

Fig. 4. Suppression of various spectral components at the output of the experimental sample of directional coupler modulator for the modulation frequency of 775 MHz.

3 Dynamic Range Improvement

3.1 Balanced Fiber Optic Link

The scheme of balanced fiber optic link based on the dual output Mach-Zehnder modulator is shown on the Fig. 5.

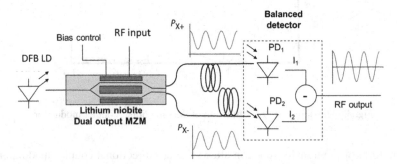

Fig. 5. Balanced fiber optic link with dual output Mach-Zehnder modulator.

In addition to the special modulator high frequency balanced photodetector was developed and produced. It was assembled from two broad band photodiode chips with rather high 30 mA saturation current for operation with high level of optical power. We selected the photodiodes with close response efficiency and similar spectral characteristics that should provide high synphase noise suppression. Observed decrease of the suppression efficiency with the increase of the signal frequency was caused by difference of efficient electric length of the two arms of the balanced detector (Fig. 6).

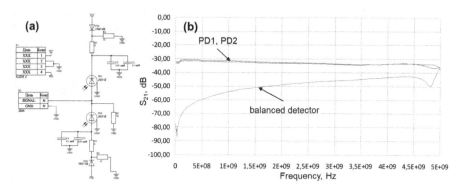

Fig. 6. a) Balanced photodetector. b) Spectral response of separate photodiodes and a synphase noise suppression of the balanced photodetector.

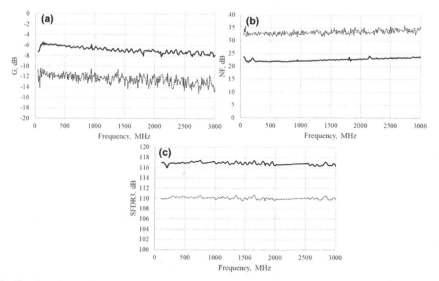

Fig. 7. Experimental results of the balanced fiber optic link testing: a) gain spectral dependence, b) noise figure spectral dependence and c) third order spurious free dynamic range.

Experimental results of the balanced link testing are presented as dependences of key technical characteristics (gain G, noise figure NF and spurious free dynamic range $SFDR_3$) (Fig. 7). A high gain was achieved due to high power of laser diode (100 mW,

1550 nm). The gain was on 6 dB higher for the balanced configuration due to sum of signals amplitudes in the two arms. The noise figure dropped on 10 dB due to gain growth and RIN suppression. Achieved spurious free dynamic range growth was up to the 117 dB/Hz$^{2/3}$ for balanced configuration in comparison with 110 dB/Hz$^{2/3}$ for standard direct detection link.

3.2 Linearization of the Directional Coupler Modulator

As in the balanced link the same high-power DFB laser diode was used in the linearized link with the directional coupler modulator. However due to low transmission in the working point corresponding to the third harmonic minimum the gain was lower on two order of magnitude. Therefore, the noise figure also dramatically rose and was at the level of 40 dB. At the same time third-order intermodulation products were highly suppressed (Fig. 8) and measured third order interception point gave a possibility spurious free dynamic range increasing up to the 120 dB/Hz$^{2/3}$ level.

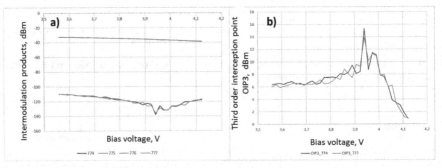

Fig. 8. a) Third-order intermodulation product suppression and b) and the grows of third order interception point at the linearizing regime of the directional coupler modulator.

4 Conclusion

Two types of special lithium niobate integrated optical modulators comprising waveguide directional coupler were used for the dynamic range improvement.

The dual output Mach-Zehnder modulator was applied for balanced microwave photonic link. High link characteristics were demonstrated: the gain about of -6 dB, the noise figure lower than 25 dB and spurious free dynamic range as high as 117 dB/Hz$^{2/3}$.

The directional coupler modulator in the linearized regime could not provide high gain and low noise figure. However high suppression of the third order intermodulation products gave a possibility to reach 120 dB/Hz$^{2/3}$ dynamic range.

Acknowledgments. A. Petrov, M. Parfenov and A. Shamrai acknowledge support by Peter the Great St. Petersburg Polytechnic University in the framework of the Program "5-100-2020".

References

1. Chen, A., Murphy, E.J.: Broadband Optical Modulators: Science, Technology, and Applications. CRC Press, Boca Raton (2012)
2. Urick, V.J., Williams, K.J., McKinney, J.D.: Fundamentals of Microwave Photonics. Wiley, New York (2015)
3. Al-Raweshidy, H., Komaki, S.: Radio Over Fiber Technologies for Mobile Communications. Artech (2002)
4. Waterhouse, R., Novak, D.: Realizing 5G: microwave photonics for 5G mobile wireless systems. IEEE Microwav. Mag. **16**(8), 84–92 (2015)
5. Parfenov, M., Agruzov, P., Il'ichev, I., Shamray. A.: Simulation of Ti-indiffused lithium niobate waveguides and analysis of their mode structure. J. Phys.: Conf. Ser. **741**, 012141 (2016)
6. Parfenov, M.V., Tronev, A.V., Il'ichev, I.V., Agruzov, P.M., Shamrai, A.V.: Photorefractive correction of the coupling ratio of an integrated optical directional x-coupler on a lithium niobate substrate. Tech. Phys. Lett. **45**(3), 187–189 (2019). https://doi.org/10.1134/S1063785019030131
7. Parfenov, M., Tronev, A., Ilichev, I., Agruzov, P., Shamrai, A.: Precise correction of integrated optical power splitters based on lithium niobate substrates by photorefractive effect local excitation. Appl. Phys. B **126**(5), 1–8 (2020). https://doi.org/10.1007/s00340-020-07440-5
8. Lebedev, V.V., Il'ichev, I.V., Agruzov, P.M., Shamray, A.V.: The influence of the current-carrying electrode material on the characteristics of integral optical microwave modulators. Tech. Phys. Lett. **40**(9), 743–746 (2014). https://doi.org/10.1134/S1063785014090090
9. Cox, C.H., III; Analog Optical Link: Theory and Practice. Cambridge University Press, Cambridge (2004)

Reliability and Lifetime Estimations for Field-Aged Optical Cable

Vladimir Burdin[1]([✉]), Vladimir Andreev[1], Anton Bourdine[1,2], Michael Dashkov[1], and Anton Nizhgorodov[1]

[1] Povolzhskiy State University of Telecommunications and Informatics, Samara, Russia
burdin@psati.ru

[2] JSC "Scientific Production Association State Optical Institute Named After Vavilov S.I.", Saint Petersburg, Russia

Abstract. The method for predicting the residual lifetime of a field aged optical cable with based on the test results of its samples taken from a cable line is considered. The test results of the proposed method are presented on the example of four samples of optical cables from cable lines installed in different years. According to the test results, the need to control the strength of the optical fibers of the cable line to predict the lifetime of the optical cable is confirmed.

Keywords: Optical fiber · Optical cable · Delivery length · Fiber-optic line · Field-aged cable · Stress · Strength · Reliability · Lifetime · Prediction

1 Introduction

The task of predicting the lifetime of the cable on communication networks has always been relevant for telecom operators. This is due to the fact that replacing the cable on communication lines is one of the most expensive stages in the reconstruction of a communication network. This is largely determined by the problems of access to land resources and infrastructure. Optical communication cables are no exception. This task became especially urgent for them today, when the lifetime of optical cables put into operation on communication networks in the 90 s approached and even exceeded the optical cable lifetime declared by manufacturers of 25–30 years, which corresponds to estimates obtained on the basis of theoretical models and results of experimental studies [1–4].

There are two main approaches to predicting the reliability of optical cables, of which of which preference is given to cable lifetime estimates [5–7]. At the same time, a comprehensive approach is proposed to determine the optical cable lifetime estimates during the operation of cable lines, including the analysis of cable damage statistics on the line, monitoring data and the results of special measurements of cable parameters, in particular, using a BOTDR [8]. However, even if we know statistics on cable damage on the line, data on monitoring parameters of optical fibers, results of measurements of the distribution of mechanical stresses of cable fibers, etc., the question arises of how to use this data to predict the lifetime of an optical cable.

© Springer Nature Switzerland AG 2020
O. Galinina et al. (Eds.): NEW2AN 2020/ruSMART 2020, LNCS 12526, pp. 364–372, 2020.
https://doi.org/10.1007/978-3-030-65729-1_32

According to the recommendations [6, 7], in order to predict the optical cable lifetime, it is necessary to know two basic quantities. This is the strength of the optical fiber at the time interval of the forecast and the stress that will be applied to the optical fiber in the cable in the future. The stress applied to the optical fiber on the cable line at the time interval of the forecast can be measured using a BOTDR and the methods for measuring the distribution of fiber curvature in the cable [9–13]. According to the measurement data, the stress applied to the optical fibers for the forecast period is evaluated. However, there are no non-destructive methods for monitoring the residual strength of the optical fiber on the cable line today. This forces us to use the estimates obtained as a result of the fiber proof-test [14–18] even before cable was manufacture.

The functions for which the optical cable itself is intended are performed by the optical fiber. All other cable elements must protect the optical fibers from external influences in order to ensure their operability in cable operating conditions. This suggests that the lifetime of an optical cable is determined by the lifetime of the optical fiber in the cable. In this case, to predict the lifetime of an optical cable, you can use the method of predicting the lifetime of an optical fiber based on the results of its tensile tests, taking into account the effects on the optical fiber during cable manufacturing, construction, and then during the operation of the cable line, as testing an optical fiber under load. For this, it is necessary to know the nature of the external action and the stress on the fiber, as well as the time interval during which it is applied. Obviously, for the cable manufacturing process and, in addition, for the construction and operation of cable lines, one can only operate with probabilistic estimates of these parameters, the determination of which requires a large amount of statistical research. One of the variants of the aforementioned approach for predicting the lifetime of an loose-tube optical cable was considered in [19]. The authors examined the main technological processes for the production of optical cable and suggested using estimates of the equivalent values of the stress and the time of its impact on the optical fiber in the manufacture of cable, in the installation of the cable line. An analysis of the nature of the impacts, an assessment of the average values of the stress and the duration of individual technological operations was presented. Based on physical modeling, estimates of the stress on the optical fiber during installation were obtained. An example of predicting the lifetime of an optical cable on a newly built cable line is given. At the same time, the duration of the processes and the stress on the fiber were assumed to be deterministic values. Obviously, this is acceptable for the process of testing optical fiber under load. In this case, the fiber load and loading time are strictly controlled. However, at later stages of cable production, and even more so during the installation and operation of a cable line, these values are random values. As a result, estimates of the strength of the optical fiber in the cable line obtained in this way at the time of the forecast can have a very large error. Accordingly, forecasts based on them will be associated with large errors.

In this paper, we propose a method for predicting the lifetime of optical cables on a cable line under exploitation. As it was proposed in [19] here also the stages of cable manufacture, the installation and exploitation of cable lines were considered as proof-test of optical fiber. This test go on up to the point in time when the optical fiber lifetime prognosis were required. However, in contrast to [19], here the prediction of the field aged optical cable lifetime based on the estimates of strength of optical fibers by the test results of the samples of the aged optical cable taken from the line. This estimates are obtained by the methods described in paper [20, 21].

2 Model of Optical Fiber Lifetime Prediction

Currently, method of optical fiber lifetime forecasts is quite detail description and presented in regulatory documents [6, 7, 20]. To predict the lifetime of an optical fiber, the well-known formula is used, which, as a rule, is written in the following way [6, 7]:

$$
t_a = t_p \left(\frac{\sigma_p}{\sigma_a} \right)^n \left\{ \left[1 - \frac{\ln(1 - F)}{N_p L} \right]^{\frac{1}{m_s}} - 1 \right\},
\tag{1}
$$

Where: t_f – time to failure (lifetime);
t_p – proof test time;
σ_p – proof stress;
σ_a – applied load;
L – fiber length under tension;
L_p – fiber length under proof-test
N_p – proof test break rate;
n – stress corrosion parameter;
m_s – Weibull distribution parameter;
F – failure probability;

Formula (1) can be written as follows [6]:

$$
t_a = \frac{1}{\sigma_a^n} \left\{ \left[\frac{\beta^{m_s}}{L} \ln \frac{1}{P} + \left(\sigma_p^n t_p \right)^{m_s} \right]^{\frac{1}{m_s}} - \sigma_p^n t_p \right\},
\tag{2}
$$

$P = 1\text{-}F$ – probability of fail-safe operation during service life t_f.
From (2), taking into account (3), it follows that [6], as

$$
\beta = \sigma_p^n t_p N_p^{-\frac{1}{m_s}}.
\tag{3}
$$

or

$$
\beta = \sigma_p^n t_p L_p^{\frac{1}{m_s}}.
\tag{4}
$$

Formula (1) was obtained in [16, 21] on the basis of a static model of destruction of an optical fiber from fused silica glass [15, 22], according to which the strength of a silica optical fiber under the influence of a static stress changes as

$$
S_i^{n-2} = S_{i-1}^{n-2} - \frac{\sigma_a^n \Delta t_i}{B},
\tag{5}
$$

where S_{i-1}, S_i is the strength of the optical fiber at the beginning and at the end of the time interval Δt_i, respectively;

σ_a is the load applied to the optical fiber during the time interval Δt_i;

B, n - strength parameters of fused silica glass.

According to [16, 21], the stress parameter of proof-test) can also be defined as

$$\left(\sigma_p^n t_p\right) = B \cdot S_0^{n-2}, \tag{6}$$

where S_0 - is the strength of the optical fiber at the beginning of the test.

It should be noted that at present, as a rule, a more correct two-stage model of destruction of optical fibers made of fused glass is used [17, 18]. However, since the first stage can last for years, and the second takes a fraction of a second, when analyzing the lifetime of an optical fiber in a cable, you can limit yourself to only the first stage using the formula [17]:

$$S\left(t_{min}\right)^{n-2} = S(t_{max})^{n-2} + \frac{1}{B} \int_{t_{min}}^{t_{max}} [\sigma_a(t)]^n dt, \tag{7}$$

for the range of changes t in which the condition $\sigma(t)/S(t) < r$ is satisfied.

Here $S(t_{min})$, $S(t_{max})$ - are the strength of the optical fiber at the beginning and at the end of the time interval $\Delta t = t_{max} - t_{min}$ at time instants tmin and tmax, respectively;

r - is the norm that determines the transition from the first stage to the second;

B, n - are the strength parameters of fused silica glass for the first stage.

For $\sigma_a(t) = const$, formula (7) takes the form (5), but the condition $\sigma(t)/S(t) < r$ must be satisfied. Otherwise, it should be assumed that the optical fiber is destroyed.

3 Prediction of the Field-Aged Optical Cable Lifetime by Estimates of the Optical Fibers Strength of the of its Samples

According to [19], we will consider the stresses applied earlier to the optical fibers in the cable line during cable manufacturing, installation and operation of the cable line as a test of fibers under load. The fiber strength of a field-aged optical cable can be determined from the test results of cable samples taken from the cable line after several years of operation. Then, if the strength of the optical fiber is known after a certain period of operation, taking into account (3)–(4), (6), we obtain the following formula for estimating the optical cable lifetime

$$t_a = \frac{B \cdot S_t^{n-2}}{\sigma_a^n} \left\{ \left[1 - \frac{L_p}{L} \ln(1 - F) \right]^{\frac{1}{m_s}} - 1 \right\}, \tag{8}$$

And from (5) follows the expression for estimating the equivalent stress that the optical fiber in the cable was subjected to in the past

$$\sigma_{eq} = \left[\frac{B \cdot S_0^{n-2}}{\Delta t_i} \left(1 - \eta^{n-2} \right) \right]^{\frac{1}{n}}, \tag{9}$$

$$\eta = S_t / S_0.$$

Known [16] is another form of formula (1)

$$F = 1 - \exp\left(-\frac{L}{L_p}\frac{m_s}{n-2}\frac{B \cdot S_t^{n-2}}{\sigma_a^n t_a}\right), \tag{10}$$

And since we are interested in the probability $F < < 1$, it follows from (10) that, other things being equal

$$t_{at} = t_{a0}\left(\frac{S_t}{S_0}\right)^{n-2}, \tag{11}$$

That is, the service life of the optical cable is reduced during its operation in proportion to the decrease in the strength of its optical fibers in the degree of (n-2).

Figure 1 shows the dependences of the relative decrease in the optical cable lifetime on the decrease in the residual strength of the optical fiber in cable for a number of glass corrosion coefficient values n.

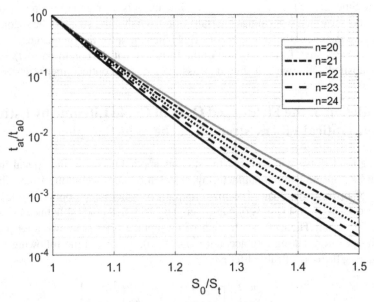

Fig. 1. Dependences of the relative decrease in the optical cable lifetime on the decrease in the residual strength of the optical fiber in cable.

Until recently, estimates of permissible long-term strain of optical fibers were determined from proof tested at levels 0.69 GPa (100 kpsi). However, given the use of the proof test at levels above 0.69 GPa (100 kPsi), the criteria were changed [7, 23].

According to [7], the current recommended criteria are as follows:

- maximum short-term strain on optical fibres is 60% of the proof test strain;
- 0.69 GPa (100 kpsi) proof-tested fibre: Maximum long-term strain: 20% of proof test strain;
- 0.69–1.38 GPa (100–200 kpsi) proof-tested fibre: Maximum long-term strain: 17% of proof test strain;
- there is no recommendation for proof test levels greater than 1.38 GPa (200 kpsi) at the time of publication.

According to (8), the allowable maximum long-term strain of the optical fiber in the cable decreases almost in proportion to the decrease in the strength of the optical fiber and can be determined from the relation

$$\sigma_{at} = \sigma_{a0}\left(\frac{S_t}{S_0}\right)^{\frac{n}{n-2}},\tag{12}$$

Figure 2 shows graphs of the dependences of the estimates of the maximum permissible long-term deformation of optical fibers in a cable from a decrease in their strength relative to the initial one, determined from proof test levels. In the calculations, the proof test level was taken equal to 0.69 GPa, and the corrosion coefficient n = 21.

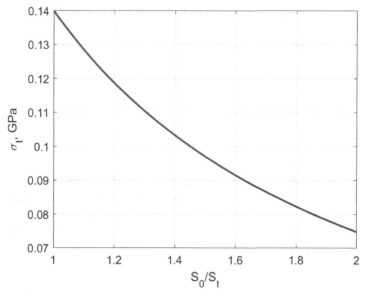

Fig. 2. Dependences of the maximum long time strain of optical fibers in cables on the decrease in the residual strength of the optical fiber in cable.

4   Results of Method Approbation for Field-Aged Optical Cable Lifetime Forecast

In order to test the proposed methodology for predicting the lifetime of a field-aged optical cable from exploited cable lines the short samples of an optical cable 20–25 m long were taken. In total, four samples of a single-mode optical cable from different cable lines were processed. All lines from which cable samples were received were put into operation in the year of cable production. Cable samples were produced, respectively, in 1996, 1998, 2011 and 2017. The first cable sample of 1996 was obtained from the operational stock of cable stored on a drum on a cable court. The remaining three samples were obtained from cable lines laid in cable ducts. In order to exclude instrumental errors, the strength of aged optical fibers was compared with the strength of a reference optical fiber on a reel. This fiber was manufactured in 2019 and not used for cable manufacture. The ratio of the average value of the strength of the optical fibers of the cable sample under test to the average value of the strength of the reference fiber sample was taken as an estimate. Table 1 shows the data obtained as a result of measurements of the strength of optical fibers by the 2-point method [24]. At least 12 measurements were made for each fiber.

Table 1. Test and forecast results for optical cable samples

Cable samle	1996	1998	2011	2017
$\eta_S = S_0 / S_t$	1.27	1.11	1.06	1.00
Maximum long-term strain, GPa	0.112	0.127	0.132	0.140
$\eta_t = t_{at} / t_{a0}$ $(n = 21)$	0.011	0.14	0.33	1.00
lifetime no less, years $(t_{a0} = 30$ years, n $= 21)$	0.32	4.13	9.91	30.00

For the first three samples, the equivalent fiber stress estimates were calculated. The average value of the stress for the studied samples was 0.156% with a standard deviation of 0.0021%. As can be seen, the equivalent stress estimates for different samples are in good agreement. At the same time, they significantly exceed the average values of the loads, which, as a rule, are obtained when measuring on existing cable lines for a cable in a duct 0.03%–0.05%. This confirms the conclusion that it is necessary to control the changes strength of the optical fibers of the cable line to predict the life of the optical cable.

Assuming that the cable service life declared by the manufacturer is 30 years [25], according to formula (11), taking into account the measurement results, we obtain estimates of the remaining service life for the cables of the studied lines. Predicted estimates are also summarized in Table 1.

As follows from the table for optical cables of 1996 and 1998, the total predicted service life at the end of 2019 exceeds 20 years, but less than 25 years. For a cable of

2011 of production it lifetime makes a little less than 18 years. For the sample of the installed in 2017 cable line, no decrease in fiber strength was detected. Accordingly, the predicted cable service life of this line is equal to that declared by the manufacturer. With that, as the calculations showed, in order to increase the lifetime of cables, the samples of which were tested, it is necessary that the maximum long-term stress on the optical fibers in the cable in the future do not exceed the estimates given in Table 1.

5 Conclusion

The paper proposes a methodology for predicting the field-aged optical cable lifetime of a cable line under exploitation. In order to the methodology approbation, we tested four samples of optical cables obtained from lines put into operation in different years. By the test results, the need to control the current value of strength of the optical fibers of the cable line to predict the lifetime of the field-aged optical cable was confirmed and the estimates of optical cable lifetime for samles under test were received.

References

1. Zelenyak-Kudreiko, I.V., Korshunov, V.N., Larin, YuT: The reliability parameters of optical cables. Telecommunication **1**, 25–28 (1994)
2. Petrov, YuM: Reliability of FOCL-VL functioning at low ambient temperatures. Electrosvyaz **3**, 14–15 (1999)
3. Vorontsov, A.S., Korshunov, V.N., Tsym, AYu.: Evalation of fiber optic durability. Telecommunication **2**, 9–13 (1999)
4. Larin, YuT: Optical Cables. Prestige Publisher, Moscow (2006)
5. Larin, YuT: Comparative analysis of two approaches to the reliability of optical cables. Sci. Technol. **315**(2), 3–7 (2009)
6. Optical fibres - Reliability - Power law theory. IEC/TR 62048, 70 (2014)
7. Supplement 59 to ITU-T G-series Recommendations Guidance on optical fibre and cable reliability, G series – Supplement 59, 02 (2018)
8. Koga H., Kuwabara T., Mitsunaga Y.: Future maintenance systems for optical fiber cables. In: ICC 1991 Proceedings, pp. 0323–0329 (1991)
9. Kurashima, T., Horiguchi, T., Yoshizawa, N., Tada, H., Tateda, M.: Measurement of distributed strain due to laying and recovery of submarine optical fiber cable. Appl. Opt. **30**(3), 334–337 (1991)
10. Kurashima, T., Horiguchi, T., Izumita, H., Furukawa, S.I., Koyamada, Y.: Brillouin optical-fiber time domain reflectometry. IEICE Trans. Commun. **E76-B**(4), 382–390 (1993)
11. Sankawa, I., Koyamada, Y., Furukawa, S.I., Horiguchi, T., Tomita, N., Wakui, Y.: Optical fiber line surveillance system for preventive maintenance based on fiber strain and loss monitoring. IEICE Trans. Commun. **E76-B**(4), 402–409 (1993)
12. BOTDR Measurement Techniques and Brillouin Backscatter Characteristics of Corning Single-Mode Optical Fibers. Corning WP4259, 1–9 (2015)
13. Salleh, M.F.M., Zakaria, Z.: Optical fiber bending detection on long distance OPGW using OTDR. Telkomnika **13**(3), 889–893 (2015)
14. Burdin, V.A.: Methods of optical fiber curvature measurement on loose-tube optical cable delivery length. In: SPIE Proceedings, vol. 9807, p. 98071A (2016)
15. Evans, A.G., Wiederhorn, S.M.: Proof testing of ceramic materials an analytical basis for failure prediction. Int. J. Fract. **10**(3), 379–392 (1974)

16. Mitsunaga, Y., Katsuyama, Y., Kobayashi, H., Ishida, Y.: Failure prediction for long length optical fiber based on proof testing. J. Appl. Phys. **53**(7), 4847–4853 (1982)
17. Semjonov, S., Scott Glaesemann, G.: High-speed tensile testing of optical fibers—new understanding for reliability prediction. In: Suhir, E., Lee, Y.C., Wong, C.P. (eds.) Micro and Opto-Electronic Materials and Structures: Physics, Mechanics, Design, Reliability. Packaging. Springer, Boston (2007). https://doi.org/10.1007/0-387-32989-7_18
18. Hanson, T.A., Glaesemann, G.S.: Incorporation multi-region crack growth into mechanical reliability predictions for optical fiber. J. Mat. Sci. **32**, 5305–5311 (1997)
19. Da Silva, A.C., Hirose, F.N., Neto, J.A.M., Furtado, J.M.I.: Optimization of loose tube optical cable manufacture process based on optical fiber mechanical behavior. In: Proceedings of the 50th IWCS, pp. 249–252 (2001)
20. Glaesemann G.S.: Optical fiber mechanical reliability. Review of research at corning's optical fiber strength laboratory. Corning **WP8002**, 1–62 (2017)
21. Mitsunaga, Y., Katsuyama, Y., Ishida, Y.: Reliability assurance for long-length optical fibre based on proof testing. Electron. Lett. **17**(16), 567–568 (1981)
22. Ritter, J.E., Jakus, K.: Applicability of crack velocity data to lifetime predictions for fused silica fibers. J. Am. Ceramic Soc. **60**(3–4), 171–171 (1977)
23. Mazzarese D., Kinard M., Konstadinidis K.: Long term cable reliability design criteria. In: Proceedings of the 62nd International Wire and Cable Symposium IWCS, pp. 363–366 (2013)
24. Matthewson, M.J., Kurkjian, C.R., Gulati, S.T.: Strength measurement of optical fibers in bending. J. Am. Ceram. Soc. **69**(11), 815–821 (1986)
25. Gadonna, M., Griffioen, W., et al.: Reliability of Optical Fibres and Components. Final Report of COST 246. Springer, London (1999). 10.1007/978-1-4471-0545-9

Digital Twin-Based Research on Fiber Optic Current Sensor Behavior and Stability

Valentina Temkina$^{(\boxtimes)}$ ⓘ, Andrei Medvedev ⓘ, and Alexey Mayzel ⓘ

Peter the Great St. Petersburg Polytechnic University (SPbPU), Polytechnicheskaya, 29, St. Petersburg 195251, Russia
temkina.vs@edu.spbstu.ru, medvedev@rphf.spbstu.ru, amayzel@gmail.com

Abstract. Digital Twin technology as an idea of implementing simulation models of particularly every physical entity became universally adopted in the last five years thanks to a huge leap in computer hardware performance and software tools evolution. The early pioneers of Fiber Optic Current Sensors (FOCS) technology in the late 90-th had no access to such an advanced research tool as digital twin of the product being developed. As a result, nowadays FOCS remain undervalued due to its legacy problems including the lack of stability and high cost. However, the Connected World, Industrial Internet of Things open the great opportunities for new metering technologies in power grid. The modern computer simulation approaches helped us in this challenge to bypass the caveats of FOCS, to understand and improve this technology making it more accurate, robust and more competitive in its field.

Keywords: Fiber-Optic Current Sensor · Faraday Effect · Digital twin · Computer simulation · LabVIEW FPGA

1 Introduction

The fourth industrial revolution aims to higher the efficiency of every production by increasing the transparency of every facility and process. Basically, this means first acquiring multiple measurements at every step in the digital form. In power grid, this tendency is implemented with replacing legacy analog voltage and current sensors with digital devices and an ecosystem commonly called Digital Substation technology. These digital measurement devices could be both traditional measuring transformers with analog-to-digital converters (ADCs) or implement other physical phenomena not suited in analog era.

Due to the active introduction of digital substations and the development of Smart Grids in the energy sector, optical current transformers have been developed for several decades [1–3]. This technology has a number of advantages over its inductive analog (electromagnetic current transformers), one of the main of which is the fully dielectric structure of the device measuring part, located in the high voltage region. However, despite all the success of developers of optical current transformers, their application in

© Springer Nature Switzerland AG 2020
O. Galinina et al. (Eds.): NEW2AN 2020/ruSMART 2020, LNCS 12526, pp. 373–383, 2020.
https://doi.org/10.1007/978-3-030-65729-1_33

electrical substations is still limited due to insufficient accuracy, measurement instability and high cost of construction.

Optical transformers that operate basing on the Faraday Effect in a special optical waveguide are being developed to measure the amplitude and spectral distribution of the industrial frequency current in electric networks of 110–220 kV and higher [4–7]. The sensing element of such meter is a spun fiber wrapped around a current conductor. The phase difference between the two circularly polarized light modes is induced in the sensitive fiber under the action of the magnetic field produced by the measured current.

To satisfy the industry demand the FOCS must meet the accuracy class 0.2 and convert the measured values into a digital data stream in accordance with the IEC 61850-9-2 (2011) standard. Therefore, the task of improving the accuracy and stability of such devices is relevant.

We have built the laboratory prototype of the FOCS based on a well-known optical scheme, which is described and studied in detail in [8]. The meter used additional phase modulation by a harmonic signal and digital phase detection based on the ratio analysis of modulation frequency harmonics. We used LabVIEW FPGA and National Instruments hardware platform to rapidly implement control and demodulation functionality into the mock-up. In addition, we have conducted a number of researches of the FOCS laboratory prototype to improve the accuracy and stability of measurements, as well as reduce the cost of the device [8, 9]. Our research demonstrated that the meter measurement accuracy was influenced by a set of external factors, and it was difficult to study the system response to each factor individually in the real prototype. In turn, a computer model of the FOCS will allow us to study the influence of many parasitic factors separately, as well as to check-out the signal processing algorithms, which is also necessary to provide real time high-precision measurements.

2 Modeling Method of the Fiber Optic Current Sensor

Modeling of the FOCS was based on the formalism of Jones matrices. According to this method, each element of the optical circuit can be represented by a 2 × 2 matrix describing the transformation of the polarization state of light when passing through this element. The optical scheme of the FOCS is shown in Fig. 1.

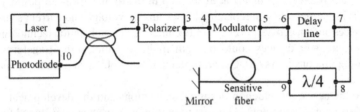

Fig. 1. Optical scheme of the FOCS. The numbers 1–10 indicate the junctions between optical elements or fiber splicing.

The modulator and the quarter-wave plate can be represented by matrices of phase plates in the basis of linear polarizations according the Eq. (1)

$$[K_n] = [K(\varphi_n)] = \begin{bmatrix} e^{-j\varphi_n/2} & 0 \\ 0 & e^{j\varphi_n/2} \end{bmatrix},$$

(1)

where φ_n is the phase difference between the polarization modes formed during propagation through the element. Phase plate matrices for different elements have the same structure, but differ in phases. In the modulator, the phase shift consists of two terms according to the Eq. (2). The first random slowly changing value φ^0_{mod} represents the quasi-static phase difference between the two polarization modes, and the second is variable and is determined by the modulating signal $U_{mod}(t)$

$$\varphi_{mod} = \varphi^0_{mod} + k_U U_{mod}(t).$$

(2)

The quarter-wave plate introduces a phase difference between the two polarization components equal to

$$\varphi_{\lambda/4} = \frac{\pi}{2} + \pi m,$$

(3)

where m is an integer.

Rotation matrices were introduced to account for the rotation of coordinate axes to any element of the optical scheme relative to another element or relative chosen basis according Eq. (4)

$$[R_n] = [R(\alpha_n)] = \begin{bmatrix} \cos \alpha_n & -\sin \alpha_n \\ \sin \alpha_n & \cos \alpha_n \end{bmatrix},$$

(4)

where α_n are the angles at the points where the fibers connect to each other or to elements. It should be noted that in the basis of linear polarizations, the sensitive fiber is also described by a rotation matrix. Since the plane of linear polarization of light turns at an angle $\varphi_F/2$ proportional to the current due to the Faraday Effect, which is identical to the change on φ_F in the phase difference between light modes of circular polarization.

A polarizer transmits only one polarization, which coincides with its own axis and in the ideal case, the matrix of the polarizer has the following form

$$[P] = \begin{bmatrix} 1 & 0 \\ 0 & 0 \end{bmatrix}.$$

(5)

When the light falls directly on the mirror and then reflects off it, the direction of light propagation changes to the opposite. Accordingly, the mirror matrix must be such that a right-handed coordinate system is preserved. To do this, it is necessary to maintain the direction of one of the transverse axes and change the direction of the other to the opposite. Thus, the mirror matrix is a half-wave plate matrix [10]. Let the x-axis keep the direction, and y-axis changes it by 180°, then the mirror matrix can be written as

$$F_{mir} = \begin{bmatrix} 1 & 0 \\ 0 & -1 \end{bmatrix}.$$

(6)

In addition, when the light propagates in the opposite direction through the elements, their matrices must be modified. If the matrix of an reciprocal element in a forward direction is described by an equation

$$B = \begin{bmatrix} b_{11} & b_{12} \\ b_{21} & b_{22} \end{bmatrix}, \tag{7}$$

then in the reverse direction of light propagation through this element, its matrix will have the following form [10]

$$\overline{B} = \begin{bmatrix} b_{11} & -b_{21} \\ -b_{12} & b_{22} \end{bmatrix}. \tag{8}$$

The fiber delay line in the optical circuit of the FOCS must provide such a delay between two orthogonally polarized modes that when light propagates from the modulator to the mirror and back, the phase of the modulating voltage changes sign to the opposite. Therefore, in the case of an ideal delay line, its influence will be taken into account directly in the modulator matrices.

Thus, sequentially multiplying the matrices of each optical element in the order opposite to the direction of light propagation in the scheme, we get the common matrix of the system

$$T = \overline{R_{10}} \cdot \overline{R_2} \cdot \overline{P} \cdot \overline{R_3} \cdot \overline{R_4} \cdot \overline{M} \cdot \overline{R_5} \cdot \overline{R_6} \cdot \overline{F_{dl}} \cdot \overline{R_7} \cdot \overline{R_8} \cdot \overline{F_{\lambda/4}} \cdot \overline{R_9} \cdot \overline{S} \cdot F_{mir} \cdot S \cdot R_9 \cdot F_{\lambda/4} \cdot$$
$$\cdot R_8 \cdot R_7 \cdot F_{dl} \cdot R_6 \cdot R_5 \cdot M \cdot R_4 \cdot R_3 \cdot P \cdot R_2 \cdot R_1, \tag{9}$$

wherein $[R_{1-10}]$ is the rotation matrix by angle α_{1-10}, $[P]$ is the polarizer matrix, $[M]$ is the modulator matrix, $[F_{dl}]$ is the delay line matrix, $[F_{\lambda/4}]$ is the quarter-wave plate matrix, $[S]$ is the sensor matrix, $[F_{mir}]$ is the mirror matrix. The numbers 1–10 indicate the junction of optical elements or fiber splicing in accordance with Fig. 1.

When all the optical elements are ideal and $\alpha_1 = \alpha_2 = \alpha_4 = \alpha_5 = \alpha_6 = \alpha_7 = \alpha_{10} = 0°$, $\alpha_3 = \alpha_8 = 45°$, $\alpha_9 = -45°$, the common matrix of the system $[T]$ is determined by the following equation

$$[T] = \begin{bmatrix} 1 & 0 \\ 0 & 0 \end{bmatrix} \cdot \begin{bmatrix} \cos 45° & -\sin 45° \\ \sin 45° & \cos 45° \end{bmatrix} \cdot \begin{bmatrix} e^{\frac{1}{2}j\varphi_{mod}} & 0 \\ 0 & e^{-\frac{1}{2}j\varphi_{mod}} \end{bmatrix} \cdot \begin{bmatrix} \cos 45° & -\sin 45° \\ \sin 45° & \cos 45° \end{bmatrix}.$$
$$\cdot \begin{bmatrix} e^{-\frac{j\pi}{4}} & 0 \\ 0 & e^{\frac{j\pi}{4}} \end{bmatrix} \cdot \begin{bmatrix} \cos 45° & \sin 45° \\ -\sin 45° & \cos 45° \end{bmatrix} \cdot \begin{bmatrix} \cos \frac{\varphi_F}{2} & \sin \frac{\varphi_F}{2} \\ -\sin \frac{\varphi_F}{2} & \cos \frac{\varphi_F}{2} \end{bmatrix} \cdot \begin{bmatrix} 1 & 0 \\ 0 & -1 \end{bmatrix}.$$
$$\cdot \begin{bmatrix} \cos \frac{\varphi_F}{2} & -\sin \frac{\varphi_F}{2} \\ \sin \frac{\varphi_F}{2} & \cos \frac{\varphi_F}{2} \end{bmatrix} \cdot \begin{bmatrix} \cos 45° & \sin 45° \\ -\sin 45° & \cos 45° \end{bmatrix} \cdot \begin{bmatrix} e^{-\frac{j\pi}{4}} & 0 \\ 0 & e^{\frac{j\pi}{4}} \end{bmatrix}.$$
$$\cdot \begin{bmatrix} \cos 45° & -\sin 45° \\ \sin 45° & \cos 45° \end{bmatrix} \cdot \begin{bmatrix} e^{-\frac{1}{2}j\varphi_{mod}} & 0 \\ 0 & e^{\frac{1}{2}j\varphi_{mod}} \end{bmatrix} \cdot \begin{bmatrix} \cos 45° & -\sin 45° \\ \sin 45° & \cos 45° \end{bmatrix} \cdot \begin{bmatrix} 1 & 0 \\ 0 & 0 \end{bmatrix}. \tag{10}$$

The common matrix of the system connects the output Jones vector, which describes the state of light polarization at the output of the optical circuit, with the input Jones vector, which describes the state of light polarization at the input of the optical circuit, according to Eq. (11)

$$[D_{out}] = [T] \cdot [D_{in}].$$ (11)

Then the intensity of the light beam is calculated like

$$I = \left[D_{out}^*\right]^T \cdot [D_{out}].$$ (12)

Finally, the received intensity is transmitted to the signal processing unit.

3 Computer Simulation of the Fiber Optic Current Sensor

3.1 Building of the Fiber Optic Current Sensor Model in LabVIEW

As the FOCS prototype control and processing algorithms were implemented in Lab-VIEW programming environment the decision was made to develop a simulation model using the same tools. LabVIEW is a graphical programming language that uses graphical images (icons) as functions providing a perfect clarity and traceability of code logic. This made LabVIEW a widely adopted tool for solving various scientific and engineering tasks, including implementation of models of fiber-optic systems [11].

It provided us such advantages as mock-up's code reuse along with ability to add, exclude or replace various elements of the optical scheme without rewriting the program code. In addition, it is not always possible to conduct an analytical solving of the influence of parasitic factors. Prototype measurement error and analysis are significantly complicated by the presence of all disturbing factors simultaneously. In this regard, the proposed FOCS simulation allows to significantly simplify the analysis. It does not require to derivate the analytical formula, it is only needed to set parameters for the model, for example, the frequency and amplitude of the modulation, as well as to set parameters for external influences.

Each matrix in Eq. (10) was modeled as a separate virtual instrument (VI), storing in LabVIEW and being called in the common program for the FOCS model. Figure 2 shows the program code that forms the rotation matrix.

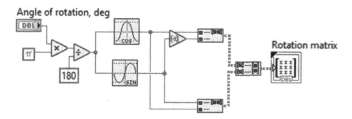

Fig. 2. Program code in LabVIEW for forming the rotation matrix.

Figure 3 shows a part of the common program for the FOCS model. It demonstrates the matrix of circuit elements as VI and their connection in the common program. The

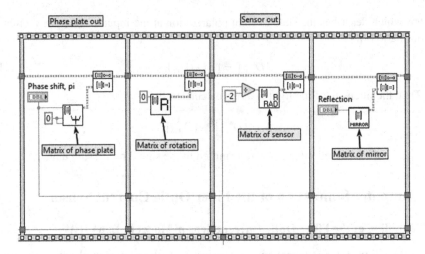

Fig. 3. FOCS modeling in LabVIEW (the part of block diagram).

advantages of this approach are visibility and the ability to add, exclude or replace various optical elements without rewriting the program code, because the matrices of each element are located in separate frames.

The FOCS model used additional phase modulation with a 40 kHz harmonic signal and digital phase detection based on the analysis method of the harmonics ratio of modulation frequency [8]. A harmonic signal with a frequency of 50 Hz was set as a signal simulating an electric current and acting on a sensitive fiber. Thus, the real-time FOCS model generated the raw interference signal that arises at the output of the sensor optical circuit when magnetic field is exposed to the sensor fiber, as well as demodulated signal that characterized this effect (see Fig. 4). This output signal set corresponds to the real laboratory prototype of the FOCS.

Based on Fig. 4, it can be seen that the demodulated signal is identical to the measured harmonic current signal with a frequency of 50 Hz. The developed model, implemented in LabVIEW, describes the actual physical processes occurring in the FOCS. The result of the simulation is fully confirmed by measurements of the FOCS laboratory prototype. In addition, the model can be used for debugging FOCS signal processing algorithms, since it is optimized for both floating-point and fixed-point values, which is necessary for implementing the code on the FPGA.

The FOCS measurement error and its analysis are substantially complicated by the presence of all external parasitic factors at the same time. In this regard, the developed FOCS model will simplify the study. For example, we can add noise to the system, polarizing mismatches at the junctions of fibers, take into account the imperfection of the quarter-wave plate and individually research the influence of each factor on the measurement accuracy.

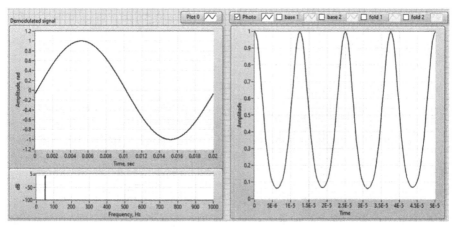

Fig. 4. Interference signal (on the right), demodulated signal and its spectrum (on the left), obtained during the FOCS modeling.

3.2 Influence of Polarization Mismatches on the Accuracy of Fiber Optic Current Sensor Measurements

The case of polarization mismatches occurrence in the circuit element located after modulator and before the sensitive element, namely at point 8 of the FOCS optical circuit, was investigated. For this purpose, we assume $\alpha_8 \neq 45°$ (see Fig. 1).

Using the developed model, the dependence of the measured current amplitude error and the total harmonic distortion on the angle of mismatch at point 8 was obtained (see Fig. 5). The demodulated signal and its spectrum in the ideal case and with polarization mismatch by 10° demonstrated on the Fig. 6.

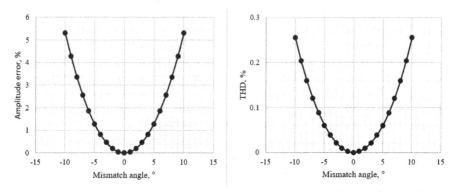

Fig. 5. Current amplitude error vs. Angle of polarization mismatch at point 8 (on the left). The total harmonic distortion vs. Angle of polarization mismatch at point 8 (on the right).

The research showed that the permissible tolerance of polarization mismatches at one of the optical circuit points located after the modulator and before the sensitive fiber

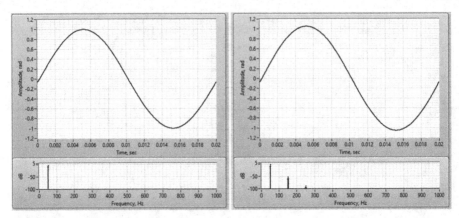

Fig. 6. Demodulated current signal and its spectrum. The angle of polarization mismatch at point 8 is 0° (on the left) and 10° (on the right).

is ±2° to achieve the FOCS accuracy class 0.2. In addition, the average level of the interference signal at the output of the optical circuit decreased by 9% with a mismatch angle of 10°.

3.3   Influence of Quarter-Wave Plate Imperfections on the Accuracy of Fiber Optic Current Sensor Measurements

The fiber quarter-wave plate is one of the most important elements of the FOCS optical circuit and the most difficult element in manufacturing. It is used to convert linearly polarized light modes into circularly polarized modes. This is necessary because the circularly polarized optical radiation is preserved in the sensitive spun fiber. In addition, when reflected from a mirror, modes with circular polarization change the direction of rotation to the opposite. Therefore, when the light passes back through the quarter-wave plate, the x-mode turns into the y-mode and vice versa. As a result, the sensor's current sensitivity is doubled.

A quarter-wave plate is a small piece of birefringent fiber only a few millimeters in size, but the accuracy of the entire huge system depends on it. Because of the research, it was found that the incorrect manufacturing of a quarter-wave plate, expressed in a mismatch in its length, leads to a significant increase in the current amplitude error and the appearance of nonlinear distortions (see Fig. 7 and Fig. 8).

In difference from the effect of polarization mismatches at the points of element junctions or fiber splicing, the quarter-wave plate also affects the contrast of the interference signal at the output of the optical circuit (see Fig. 9). The signal contrast was calculated using the equation

$$V = \frac{I_{max} - I_{min}}{I_{max} + I_{min}} \cdot 100\%, \tag{13}$$

where I is the signal intensity at the optical circuit output.

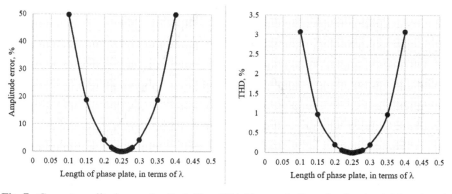

Fig. 7. Current amplitude error (on the left) and Total harmonic distortion (on the right) vs. length of phase plate.

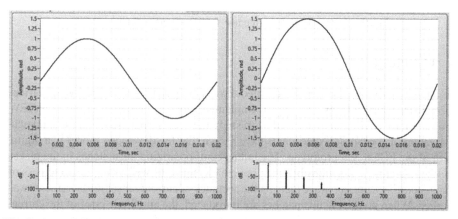

Fig. 8. Demodulated current signal and its spectrum in the case of ideal quarter-wave plate (on the left) and a phase plate with a length of 0.1λ (on the right).

This shows that imperfect quarter-wave plates reduce the signal contrast and thereby limit the dynamic range of the current sensor. It is due to the fact that modes with elliptical polarization are formed at the output of the phase plate. These modes are not converted to orthogonal modes when reflected from a mirror. As a result, when light passes back through the phase plate, the output is again elliptically polarized modes, rather than linear ones [7].

Thus, the permissible tolerance of the error of the quarter-wave plate length is $\pm 0.01\lambda$ to achieve the FOCS accuracy class 0.2. In these error margins the contrast of the interference signal is reduced by only 0.62%.

A similar study was conducted with the FOCS mock-up. The results of the experiments coincided with the simulation results. It confirmed the efficiency of the developed model and the relevance of its application for finding ways to eliminate the overall FOCS errors.

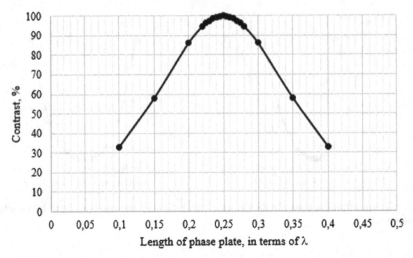

Fig. 9. Contrast of the interference signal vs. length of phase plate.

4 Conclusion

As a result of the research, the FOCS model was developed based on the Jones matrices formalism instead of physical object. Implementation of the model in the LabVIEW programming environment allowed us to study the sensor operation without analytical derivation of formulas. Experiments have shown that the developed model is a digital twin of the FOCS real prototype. The influence of polarizing mismatches in the places of fiber splicing or junctions between optical elements, as well as the incorrectness of manufacturing a quarter-wave plate on the accuracy of current sensor measurements was studied. When polarizing mismatches are introduced, the amplitude error of the current sensor and the non-linearity of the output signal increase. While the imperfection of the quarter-wave plate also affects the contrast of the interference signal at the optical circuit output, and therefore the dynamic range of the device. In order for the FOCS meets the accuracy class 0.2, it is necessary to ensure that the error of junctions between elements is not more than $\pm 2°$ and the error of manufacturing a quarter-wave plate is not more than $\pm 0.01\lambda$. The results of the experiments with the real prototype coincided with the simulation results.

The other advantage of the developed model is the fact that the program code is optimized for implementation on the FPGA but with the benefits of high-level debugging tools. In addition thanks to the LabVIEW features the model appears extremely flexible and reconfigurable to implement alternative FOCS schemes, which allows us to explore the sensor in various configurations.

References

1. Ripka, P.: Electric current sensors: a review. Meas. Sci. Technol. **21**(11), 112001 (2010)
2. De Nazaré, F., Werneck, M.: Hybrid optoelectronic sensor for current and temperature monitoring in overhead transmission lines. IEEE Sens. J. **12**(5), 1193–1194 (2012)

3. Blake, J.N.: Fiber optic current sensor. Patent No. US 6,188,811 B1, Int. Cl. G02B 6/00, G01J 4/00, 13 February 2001
4. Bohnert, K., Gabus, P., Nehring, J., Brandle, H.: Temperature and vibration insensitive fiber-optic current sensor. J. Lightwave Technol. **20**(2), 267–276 (2002)
5. Boev, A., et al.: Fibre-optic current sensor. Patent RU 2437106 C2, G01R 15/24, G01R 19/2, 20 December 2011. Bull. 35
6. Bohnert, K., Hsu, C., Yang, L., Frank, A., Müller, G.M., Gabus, P.: Fiber-optic current sensor tolerant to imperfections of polarization-maintaining fiber connectors. J. Lightwave Technol. **36**(11), 2161–2165 (2002)
7. Przhiyalkovsky, Y., Morshnev, S., Starostin, N., Gubin, V.: Modified sensing element of a fibre-optic current sensor based on a low-eigenellipticity spun fibre. Quantum Electron. **44**(10), 957–964 (2014)
8. Temkina, V., Medvedev, A., Mayzel, A., Mokeev, A.: Fiber optic current meter for IIoT in power grid. In: Galinina, O., Andreev, S., Balandin, S., Koucheryavy, Y. (eds.) NEW2AN/ruSMART -2018. LNCS, vol. 11118, pp. 631–640. Springer, Cham (2018). https://doi.org/10.1007/978-3-030-01168-0_57
9. Temkina, V., Medvedev, A., Mayzel, A., Mokeev, A.: Compensation of fiber quarter-wave plate temperature deviation in fiber optic current sensor. In: 2019 IEEE International Conference on Electrical Engineering and Photonics (EExPolytech), pp. 339–341. IEEE, St. Petersburg (2019)
10. Bhandari, R.: Transpose symmetry of the Jones matrix and topological phases. Opt. Lett. **33**(8), 854–856 (2008)
11. Harun, S.W., Emami, S.D., Arof, H., Hajireza, P., Ahmad H.: LabVIEW applications for optical amplifier automated measurements, fiber-optic remote test and fiber sensor systems. In: De Asmundis, R. (ed.) Modeling, Programming and Simulations Using LabVIEW™ Software, pp. 201–236. InTech (2011)

Self-assembled Biomolecular Films as a New Material for Nano-Telecommunication Devices

Maksim Baranov$^{(\boxtimes)}$ ⓘ, Elena Velichko ⓘ, and Oleg Tsybin ⓘ

Peter the Great St. Petersburg Polytechnic University (SPbPU), St. Petersburg 195251, Russia
baranovma1993@gmail.com, velichko-spbstu@yandex.ru,
tsybin@gmail.com

Abstract. The advances made in telecommunication technologies imply that new functional materials are developed for the components used in advanced electronics. Creating biomolecular films with certain impedance characteristics for telecommunication devices is an urgent task. This paper presents the results of experiments on preparing thin films by dehydration of water-salt solutions of albumin protein on a dielectric substrate. Periodic cellular structures forming in the films during the phase transition were studied. The values of the parameters and the results of the experiments were refined by computer simulation. We reached a conclusion about the significant value of the electric micro-potential, electrical conductivity and the flow of local currents in such processes. Depending on the conditions of formation, various spatial, frequency and energy characteristics of the transmission of electrical signals through self-assembled biomolecular films can be achieved, making it possible to use these films to create devices and elements of advanced electronics and telecommunications.

Keywords: Biomolecular electronics · Biological films · Self-assembly · Telecommunication devices

1 Introduction

As modern semiconductor microelectronics reaches its physical limits, new principles, materials, elements and devices are required to tackle this problem [1–8]. Molecular, and, in particular, biomolecular concepts can be incorporated into the design of new electronic devices [9]. Developing molecular electronics is an urgent task which can be solved by drawing on the unique electrical properties of organic components and their hybrids with solid state electronics. For instance, such systems are characterized by miniaturization, when the surface density of the elements comprising the device can be increased to 10^{13}–10^{14} units per cm^2 in the nanometer layer [10, 11]. Biological molecules are capable of forming complexes and self-assembled layers on the surface of the substrate, storing, converting and transferring energy and information possesses extremely high density in time and space [1, 12].

Practical implementations of biomolecular electronics devices, especially for developing telecommunication technologies, necessitate further studies into physical phenomena in biomolecular structures and clusters, phase transitions and self-assembly

© Springer Nature Switzerland AG 2020
O. Galinina et al. (Eds.): NEW2AN 2020/ruSMART 2020, LNCS 12526, pp. 384–393, 2020.
https://doi.org/10.1007/978-3-030-65729-1_34

processes in thin macromolecular films, and several related physical phenomena. To construct these devices, it is imperative to understand the mechanisms of intra- and intermolecular interactions, charge transfer processes, dynamics of thin liquid films, the influence of external conditions on the biomolecular structure's properties. Electronic properties of biomolecules in thin liquid films are extremely important but still poorly researched [13, 14]. The initial stage of studies into the electrical properties of biological structures has recently been described in Refs. [15, 16]. Molecular electronics prototypes are already available [17, 18].

Stable self-assembled macromolecular films on substrates are the focus of considerable scientific and practical interest for creating the elements of new electronics [1]. Such films show promise as functional materials. The aim of this work is to study the processes by which stable biomolecular films can be obtained from solutions with nonlinear impedance necessary for creating novel telecommunication devices.

We used the methods of optical microscopy and computer simulation to consider self-assembled biomolecular films (Bovine Serum Albumin (BSA), code 4F5S from the Protein Data Bank), obtained under different conditions for dehydration of aqueous and salt solutions. We discovered certain peculiarities associated with creating biomolecular electronics elements with unique properties based on films with dendritic structures [10].

2 Methods

One of the signs of self-assembly are dissipative periodic structures formed in biomolecular films. Optical methods, in particular optical microscopy, make it possible to identify these structures and to establish their parameters, such as the type of structure, size and periodicity of cells or domains. Examples of these structures obtained in preliminary experiments are presented in Fig. 1. Depending on the type of solvent and the parameters of phase transformation, biomolecular films can contain two types of periodic domain structures whose cells are shaped as ellipses twisted in a spiral or dendrites.

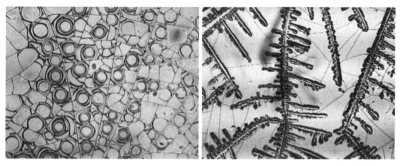

Fig. 1. Examples of typical structures observed in biomolecular films: spiral structure domains, or cells (left); dendrite cluster domains, or cells (right)

Self-assembly processes can be studied both at the macro level, considering biological films formed during dehydration of aqueous solutions of biological fluids, and at the micro level, considering the energy changes during protein folding. Self-assembly processes are characterized by a decrease in the free energy of biological molecules. Protein molecules are combined in ensembles during self-assembly. The principle of energy minimization is preserved for molecule clusters. It is known that self-assembly in proteins is initiated by folding of the α-helix. This process is characterized by a change in the free energy of the molecule

$$\Delta F_\alpha = F_\alpha - F_{ball} = (n - 2)\Delta f_n - nTS_\alpha = -2f_n + n(f_n - TS_\alpha), \quad (1)$$

where f_n is the free energy of hydrogen bonding and the accompanying interactions in the α-helix (rather than describe just the energy, which would be the case in vacuum, f_n includes both energy and the entropy of rearrangements of hydrogen bonds in an aqueous medium), S_α is the entropy loss for one residue creation in a helix.

One of the aspects of synthesizing biomolecular films is solving the stability problem. Stability is understood as the ability of biomolecular films to maintain their structure under external thermodynamic and mechanical influences. The results of numerical computations are described in [19], indicating that the free energy of biomolecular films can be both negative and positive depending on the substrate and plasticizer added to the protein. When free energy is positive, external effects on the biomolecular film may be damaging for filter stability in certain situations.

2.1 Optical Microscopy

We observed the processes of dehydration and self-assembly at the macro level using the method of optical microscopy. We took the bovine serum albumin (BSA) protein (Protein Data Bank code 4F5S) for the study. Experimental samples in aqueous and physiological solutions of protein with a volume of 3 ml were placed in glass cuvettes with a diameter of 2.5 cm, and subsequently dried at a temperature of 308 K for 48 h. Images of the prepared completely dehydrated films were obtained using an Olympus CX 33 optical microscope with an Altami UCMOS10000KPA USB camera connected to it. The images obtained in the experiments had an area of about 0.1 cm^2, a resolution of 1280 × 960 pixels and a depth of 24 bits.

2.2 Computer Simulation

Models of molecular systems were simulated using Visual Molecular Dynamics (VMD). Each of them was a system of four albumin protein molecules (code 4F5S from to the Protein Data Bank database). The minimum distance between the individual sections of the given molecules was about 3 Å. The studies were carried out both in vacuum and in an aqueous cubic volume (TIP3 water model). The distance from the boundaries of the molecules to the edge of the cube was taken equal to 12 Å. To neutralize the electric charge of the system, Na$^+$ and Cl$^-$ ions were added to the solvation cube. Free energy studies were carried out at various concentrations of water in the solvation cube.

Additional experiments were performed filling a water cube with NaCl molecules to achieve the following concentrations: 0.86, 0.43, 0.21, 5.36 × 10^{-2}, 1.33 × 10^{-2}, 3.4 × 10^{-3}, 1.7 × 10^{-3} and 1.7 × 10^{-4} mol/L, which corresponds to 5%, 2.5%, 1.25%,

0.313%, 0.078%, 0.02%, 0.01% and 0.001% volume fractions of NaCl in water as a plasticizer, respectively. Furthermore, a molecular cluster was simulated in physiological solution, where the concentration of NaCl was 0.15 mol/L (0.9%).

Calculations and simulations of biomolecular systems were performed in the NAMD program (NAnoscale Molecular Dynamics) using CHARMM27 force fields. To stabilize the simulated biomolecular systems, the energy of the molecular cluster was minimized in stages at the beginning of each study. Energy was minimized over 5000 Time Steps, which corresponds to 10 ps. Next, the energy of the molecular cluster was calculated for 100 ps at a temperature of 308 K. The time dependences of the energy values were constructed based on these data.

3 Results

3.1 Results of Computer Simulation

Simulation of the free energy dynamics of a molecular cluster consisting of four BSA protein molecules yielded the time dependences of the in vacuum and neutralized water as well (Fig. 2). As can be seen from the graphs, the free energy of the molecular cluster was low time-delayed spontaneously set at a stationary level; notably, it was lower in the water cube than in vacuum. Energy relaxation occurring with slow aperiodic oscillations was consistent with that of a dissipative dynamic system with low electrical conductivity and increased "friction". Apparently, this corresponds to two electrodynamic variants: a strong electric field in a vacuum, shielding of the electric field and its decrease near the cluster surface by polar water molecules.

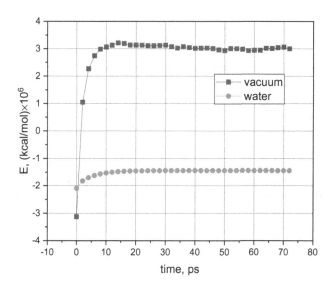

Fig. 2. Free energies of molecular cluster shown as a function of time by two lines, black and red, corresponding to vacuum and neutralized water, respectively (Color figure online)

Due to an increase in electrical conductivity, energy relaxation in water-salt solutions occurred with fast periodic oscillations corresponding to a system with small dissipative losses. Apparently, this is due to an increase in the concentration of dissociated ions and the density of local charge flows near the cluster surface. As an example, Fig. 3 shows the time dependence of the free energy of a molecular cluster in a NaCl salt solution with a concentration of 0.15 mol/L, or 0.9%. The characteristic frequency of vibrational energy relaxation at a temperature of 308 K was about 0.2 THz, which corresponds to the typical vibration frequency of polyatomic particles containing about 10^2–10^3 atoms.

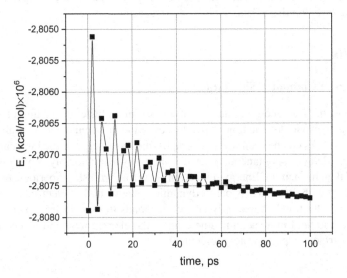

Fig. 3. Free energy of molecular cluster in saline solution as a function of time

It has been established that the frequency of vibrational energy relaxation remains unchanged in water-salt solutions of different concentrations, equal to the value given above. Indeed, the frequency of vibrational relaxation in typical processes depends on the mass of particles, and with a change in salt concentration, the mass of particles should not change significantly.

However, the time of energy relaxation to a steady state varies depending on the salt concentration. As the salt concentration in the solvation cube increases, attenuation occurs faster than with a minimum salt concentration. Figure 4 shows typical time dependences of the free energy of a molecular cluster for salt concentrations of 0.001% and 5%.

We analyzed the energy relaxation times and the steady-state values of the latter, depending on the salt concentration in the molecular cluster. These dependences are presented in Fig. 5.

As can be seen from the graphs, the full value of the dissipation energy is established faster with increasing salt concentration. Besides, the free energy of the molecular cluster decreases with an increase in the concentration of salt in the solution. This corresponds

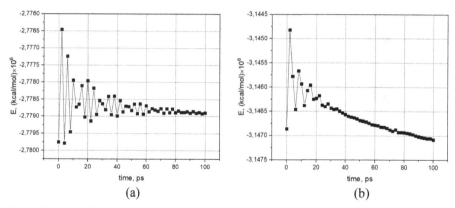

Fig. 4. Free energies of molecular cluster shown as a function of time by two lines, corresponding to n(NaCl) = 1.7 × 10⁻⁴ mol/L (a), and n(NaCl) = 0.86 mol/L (b)

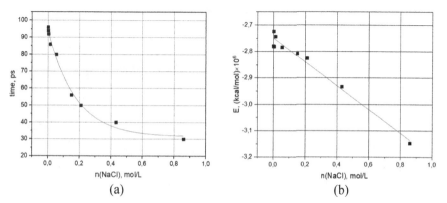

Fig. 5. Dependences of relaxation time and stable energies of molecular clusters shown as a function of NaCl concentration by two lines in (a) and (b), respectively

to a further decrease in the electric field near the cluster surface due to an increase in pH and the electrical conductivity of the aqueous salt solution.

Finally, relaxation of free energy of the molecular cluster indicate that electrodynamic factors play a significant role.

3.2 Results of Optical Microscopy

An aqueous solution of albumin protein was used with different values of the volumetric concentration of protein in the solution: 5%, 2.5%, 1.25%, 0.313%, 0.078%, 0.02%, 0.01% and 0.001%. The area of the film surface was the same for all experiments and was equal to 0.1 cm². Various images were obtained: the most characteristic ones look like quasiperiodic structures consisting of specific cells about 200 nm in size each (Fig. 6).

It can be seen from the images that spiral cells form in the protein film at the highest protein concentration in the initial solution. Dependences on the initial volume of the solution are presented in Fig. 7.

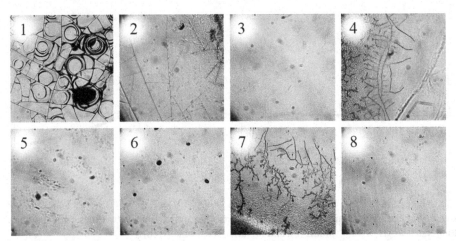

Fig. 6. Images of dehydrated protein films from water solutions with 5%, 2.5%, 1.25%, 0.313%, 0.078%, 0.02%, 0.01% and 0.001% volume fraction of protein (numbered from 1 to 8, respectively)

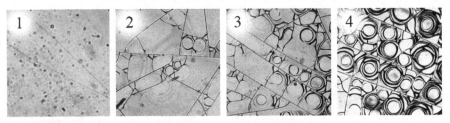

Fig. 7. Images of dehydrated protein films from water solutions with different initial volumes equal to 1 ml, 2 ml, 3 ml, 4 ml (numbered from 1 to 4, respectively)

It was found that the surface density of spiral cells in the protein film increased with a larger volume of the initial protein solution. The effect of pH of the solution is shown in Fig. 8.

The processes of self-assembly in a NaCl-salt solution were studied in the experiments considering the effect of salt concentration on the formation of dissipative structures in biological films. Based on the results of previous experiments, the initial volume of the solution was taken equal to 4 ml, and the protein concentration was more than 5% of the volume fraction. The results of this experiment are presented in Fig. 9.

As can be seen from the images, the concentration of salts in the initial solution has a strong effect on the formation of structures in the films of protein solutions. Note that "regular" fractal dendritic structures are formed at a higher salt concentration in the solution. A different type of dendritic structure is formed at the lowest salt concentration in solution. The dielectric characteristics of biological films with similar structures are discussed in [16].

It can be concluded that, similar to the results of computer modeling and calculation of the free energy of protein molecules in water and water-salt, experiments revealed significant importance of electrodynamic factors. The properties of dehydrated films can

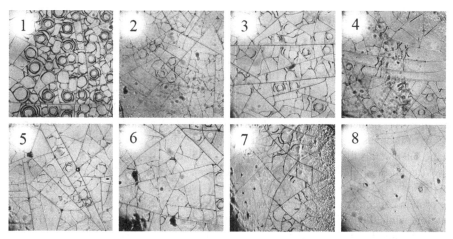

Fig. 8. Images of dehydrated protein films from water solutions with different pH equal to 7.8, 6.8, 5.8, 5.2, 4.9, 4.3, 3.9 (numbered from 1 to 8, respectively)

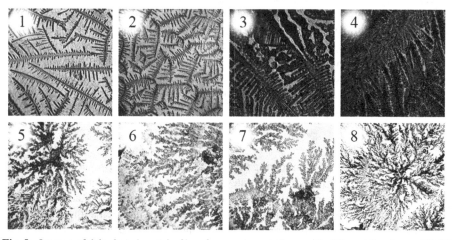

Fig. 9. Images of dehydrated protein films from water solutions with different fractions of NaCl equal to 5%, 2.5%, 1.25%, 0.313%, 0.078%, 0.02%, 0.01% and 0.001% (numbered from 1 to 8, respectively)

be determined by setting the concentration or the pH relative to the isoelectric point, as well as by setting the initial volume of the initial solution of the biological fluid. The largest number of self-assembled cells was formed if the pH values relative to the isoelectric point differed by no more than ±20% in this solution. Given large biases of the pH value in the initial protein solution, spiral cells of irregular, non-elliptical shape are formed first, or they do not exist at all.

3.3   Results and Discussions

Values of free energy of the molecular cluster were obtained by computer simulations of protein molecules in water and water-salt cubes. The study also presents results of experiments on the formation of periodic cellular structures in films of a protein albumin solution. Using the method of optical microscopy, we observed various periodic structures, depending on the initial conditions of the experiment. Fractal-like dendritic structures are characterized by clear phase separation of BSA and NaCl, occurring during drying of droplets of protein-salt solutions; notably, the crystal structures represented by the salt crystals that are located on a protein substrate.

We confirmed that stable biomolecular films can be synthesized when water is added into the protein solution. We discovered that self-assembled structures can be formed if the protein concentration not less than 5% volume fraction is maintained in the initial solution, while the initial volume of the solution is not less than 3 ml, and the pH value of the solution deviates from the isoelectric point by no more than $\pm 20\%$.

Based on analysis of the obtained data, it is logical to assume that mesh-like spiral elliptical and dendritic structures forming due to dehydration of aqueous solutions of protein are electrical in nature. Indeed, the local values and the distributions of electric charges, potentials, and currents were primarily changed in all variations of the experimental conditions used. The formation of fractals during fast phase transitions has well-known equivalents and explanations in the literature [20]. The issue of formation of spiral structures requires additional research. Preliminary, it can be taken that distribution of both electrical potential and field in the volume charge of the domain has a solenoidal structure in kind of cylindrical harmonics.

4   Conclusion

The results of experiments on preparing thin films by dehydration of water-salt solutions of albumin protein on a dielectric substrate are presented. We considered periodic cellular structures evolving in the films during the phase transition. Computer simulation accounting for the energy of the molecular cluster revealed that such a film structure is stable and its free energy and vibrations can be controlled by adding salts to the solution. Significant meaning of the electric micro-potential, electrical conductivity, and the flow of local currents in such processes is suggested. Depending on the specific parameters of synthesis, various spatial, frequency and energy characteristics can be achieved for transmission of electrical signals through biomolecular films. This opens up possibilities for applications of biomolecular films as waveguide filters and other tools for creating elements and devices of biomolecular electronics and telecommunications in the millimeter wave range.

It seems expedient to focus further research on finding the energy of the molecular cluster at temperature fluctuations in an external electric field.

Acknowledgments. The study is supported by Peter the Great St. Petersburg Polytechnic University in the framework of the Program "5-100-2020". We express our gratitude to Tatyana Igorevna Zezina for useful advice in preparing this article.

References

1. Velichko, E., Tsybin, O.: Biomolecular electronics. Polytechnic University (2012)
2. Liu, T.Y., et al.: CMOS-based biomolecular diagnosis platform. In: 2017 IEEE 12th International Conference on Nano/Micro Engineered and Molecular Systems, NEMS 2017, pp. 96–100 (2017). https://doi.org/10.1109/NEMS.2017.8016982
3. Akan, O.B., Ramezani, H., Khan, T., Abbasi, N.A., Kuscu, M.: Fundamentals of molecular information and communication science. Proc. IEEE **105**, 306–318 (2017). https://doi.org/10.1109/JPROC.2016.2537306
4. Bush, S.F.: Nanoscale communication networks (2010)
5. Walsh, F., Balasubramaniam, S., Botvich, D., Donnelly, W.: Synthetic protocols for nano sensor transmitting platforms using enzyme and DNA based computing. Nano Commun. Netw. **1**, 50–62 (2010). https://doi.org/10.1016/j.nancom.2010.04.002
6. Kuscu, M., Akan, O.B.: On the physical design of molecular communication receiver based on nanoscale biosensors. IEEE Sens. J. **16**, 2228–2243 (2016). https://doi.org/10.1109/JSEN.2016.2519150
7. Offenhäusser, A., Rinaldi, R.: Nanobioelectronics - for Electronics, Biology, and Medicine. Springer, Heidelberg (2009). https://doi.org/10.1007/978-0-387-09459-5
8. Baranov, M.A., Klimchitskaya, G.L., Mostepanenko, V.M., Velichko, E.N.: Fluctuation-induced free energy of thin peptide films. Phys. Rev. E **99**, 022410 (2019). https://doi.org/10.1103/PhysRevE.99.022410
9. Gu, K., Onorato, J.W., Luscombe, C.K., Loo, Y.L.: The role of tie chains on the mechano-electrical properties of semiconducting polymer films. Adv. Electron. Mater. **6**, 1901070 (2020). https://doi.org/10.1002/aelm.201901070
10. Liu, Q., Wang, L., Frutos, A.G., Condon, A.E., Corn, R.M., Smith, L.M.: DNA computing on surfaces. Nature **403**, 175–179 (2000). https://doi.org/10.1038/35003155
11. Kahan, M., Gil, B., Adar, R., Shapiro, E.: Towards molecular computers that operate in a biological environment. Phys. D Nonlinear Phenom. **237**, 1165–1172 (2008). https://doi.org/10.1016/j.physd.2008.01.027
12. Dolganov, P.V., Cluzeau, P., Dolganov, V.K.: Interaction and self-organization of inclusions in two-dimensional free-standing smectic films. Liq. Cryst. Rev. **7**, 1–29 (2019). https://doi.org/10.1080/21680396.2019.1586590
13. Velichko, E., Zezina, T., Baranov, M., Nepomnyashchaya, E., Tsybin, O.: Dynamics of polypeptide cluster dipole moment for nano communication applications. In: Galinina, O., Andreev, S., Balandin, S., Koucheryavy, Y. (eds.) NEW2AN/ruSMART -2018. LNCS, vol. 11118, pp. 675–682. Springer, Cham (2018). https://doi.org/10.1007/978-3-030-01168-0_62
14. Privalov, V.E., Rybalko, A.V., Charty, P.V., Shemanin, V.G.: Effect of noise and vibration on the performance of a particle concentration laser meter and optimization of its parameters. Tech. Phys. **52**, 352–355 (2007). https://doi.org/10.1134/S1063784207030115
15. Baranov, M.A., Rozov, S.V.: Study of the dielectric parameters of biological liquids. In: Journal of Physics: Conference Series (2019). https://doi.org/10.1088/1742-6596/1326/1/012006
16. Baranov, M.: Study of dielectric parameters of protein solution, vol. 75 (2019). https://doi.org/10.1117/12.2523338
17. Cuevas, J.C., Scheer, E.: Molecular Electronics: An Introduction to Theory and Experiment (2010)
18. Lyshevski, S.E.: Nano and Molecular Electronics Handbook (2018). https://doi.org/10.1201/9781315221670
19. Velichko, E.N., Baranov, M.A., Mostepanenko, V.M.: Change of sign in the Casimir interaction of peptide films deposited on a dielectric substrate. Mod. Phys. Lett. A **35**, 2040020 (2020). https://doi.org/10.1142/S0217732320400209
20. Golbraikh, E., Rapis, E.G., Moiseev, S.S.: On the crack pattern formation in a freely drying protein film. Tech. Phys. **48**, 1333–1337 (2003). https://doi.org/10.1134/1.1620131

Optical Loss Control in Lithium Niobate Waveguides via Direct Laser Modification of Covered Titanium Film

Aleksandr V. Tronev[1]([✉]) [iD], Mikhail V. Parfenov[1,2] [iD], Nikita A. Solomonov[3], Andrey M. Ionov[4], Sergey I. Bozhko[4], Igor V. Ilichev[1], Peter M. Agruzov[1], and Aleksandr V. Shamrai[1] [iD]

[1] Ioffe Institute, 26 Polytechnicheskaya, St. Petersburg 194021, Russia
trone2008@ya.ru
[2] Peter the Great St. Petersburg Polytechnic University, 29 Polytechnicheskaya, St. Petersburg 195251, Russia
[3] Saint Petersburg Electrotechnical University "LETI", 5 Professora Popova, 197376 St. Petersburg, Russia
[4] ISSP RAS, Academician Ossipyan 2, 142432 Chernogolovka, Russia

Abstract. Laser modification of thin titanium film for precise loss control in lithium niobate optical waveguides was demonstrated. A simple ray model was used for analysis of optical losses induced by interaction of two orthogonal polarization modes of a Ti-indiffused channel optical waveguide in lithium niobate with a thin metal film on the substrate top surface. The theoretical estimations are in a good agreement with experimentally observed increase of the losses 0.95 and 1.05 dB/mm for TE- and TM-polarized modes respectively caused by 5 nm titanium film. Direct laser modification of the titanium film by a 976 nm laser beam with the threshold intensity up to 1 kW/mm^2 was demonstrated. The formation of titanium oxide and titanium nitride during laser modification of the film was discovered via X-ray spectroscopy and explains optical losses reduction. The technique was applied for precise balancing of optical intensities in arms of Mach-Zehnder optical modulator, an associated increase of the extinction ratio from 30 to 48 dB was achieved.

Keywords: Integrated optics · Lithium niobate · Direct laser writing · Thin film

1 Introduction

Lithium Niobate (LN) nowadays become a key material for many integrated optical devices: waveguide couplers, electro-optical modulators, filters, etc. [1] In spite of optical waveguide technologies in LN are well developed, the finite tolerance of waveguide fabrication process makes it possible to use these schemes in specific precision applications, such as quantum network systems [2] and optical sensors [3], only with additional control circuits and distributed feedback systems [4]. In particular, extinction ratio of

© Springer Nature Switzerland AG 2020
O. Galinina et al. (Eds.): NEW2AN 2020/ruSMART 2020, LNCS 12526, pp. 394–399, 2020.
https://doi.org/10.1007/978-3-030-65729-1_35

Mach-Zehnder modulator on LN substrates is limited by the accuracy of waveguide coupler fabrication technology and for the most available devices it is less than 40 dB [5].

We propose a method of precise optical loss adjustment in LN waveguides by forming a nanosized metal cover on the top surface of scheme and its precise modification via local laser illumination at the close of all stages of the fabrication process. Titanium film was chosen as a loading metal cover because of its good adhesion to LN and a significant imaginary part of its refractive index [6] which indicates the good interaction between film and guided optical irradiation. Nanometer thickness of the film changes optical losses for both TM and TE polarization modes due to leakage and surface plasmon polariton excitation [7]. Nanosized thickness of the titanium film allows local oxidation and micromachining by the technique similar to direct laser writing.

2   Materials and Methods

2.1   Theoretical Model

A simple ray model was proposed to evaluate the impact of titanium coating on optical losses in LN waveguides (see Fig. 1).

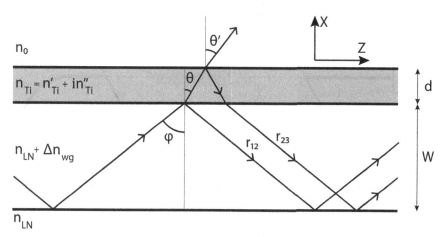

Fig. 1. The ray model of the interaction of optical radiation in a LN channel waveguide with a titanium coating on its top surface.

In the case when thickness of the film is less than the skin layer thickness, optical losses increase significantly because of violation in total internal reflection conditions and radiation leakages over the metal cover. The attenuation coefficient α can be expressed as

$$\alpha = \frac{1 - R_w R_m}{2W \, \mathrm{tg} \, \varphi},\tag{1}$$

where R_m and R_w are reflection coefficients for top and bottom waveguide boundaries, respectively. In case of waveguide propagation $R_w = 1$, because of total internal reflection on waveguide-substrate interface. The value of R_m depends on film thickness and can be written as

$$R_m = \left| \frac{r_{12} + r_{23} \exp(i\delta)}{1 + r_{12}r_{23} \exp(i\delta)} \right|^2,$$

$$\delta = 2\frac{2n_{Ti}d}{\lambda} \cos\theta,$$

(2)

where $n_{Ti} = n'_{Ti} + i \cdot n''_{Ti}$ – titanium film complex refractive index; r_{12} and r_{23} – reflection coefficients for metal film boundaries, which are determined via Fresnel's equations for both orthogonal polarization modes.

2.2 Experimental Methods

To verify the results obtained via the ray model, experimental setup for precise laser modification of nanosized metal film was developed (see Fig. 2).

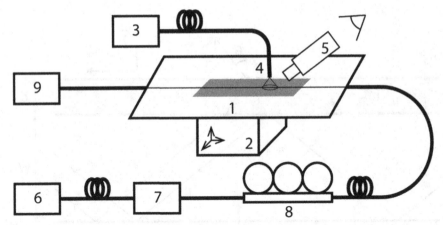

Fig. 2. Experimental setup: 1 – Ti-indiffused waveguide on LN substrate with titanium film; 2 – precision 3-axis stage; 3–976 nm laser; 4 – optical fiber probe; 5 – microscope; 6 – 1550 nm DFB laser; 7 – optical attenuator; 8 – polarization controller; 9 – optical power meter.

Test Ti-indiffused channel waveguide on the X-cut of LN substrate with the 5 nm titanium cover was placed on the high-accuracy 3-axis motor stage. The irradiation from the 976 nm pump laser diode with output power up to 600 mW was supplied to the surface of test scheme via the probe based on optical fiber pigtail. Movement of the test scheme on 3-axis motor stage along a rigidly fixed optical probe with microscope control made it possible to select the area on the circuit for laser modification with the accuracy up to 1 μm. At the same time laser irradiation from 1550 nm telecommunication DFB laser with intensity and polarization control was guided into the input port of scheme and detected on the output port which made it possible to calculate changes in additional optical losses in real time.

To evaluate the impact of titanium film modification on optical waveguide characteristics, the experiment with a chemical etching of titanium film was performed. The examination of surface topography in irradiated areas was made by optical profilometry and scanning electron microscopy. The spectrochemical analysis of the modified titanium cover was performed via the X-ray emission spectroscopy.

3 Results

Laser illumination of 5 nm titanium cover with the threshold intensity over 1 kW/mm formed areas with the increased transparency in visible light, as it shown on the Fig. 3.

Laser film modification caused the decrease in additional optical losses for both TE- and TM- modes of LN waveguide. Table 1 demonstrates that optical losses per unit of length of titanium film obtained from the ray model are enough relevant to the results collected through the experiments of laser modification and chemical etching. Theoretical estimation for additional optical losses was prepared for typical parameters of channel waveguides on the X-cut of LN crystal: $W \approx 7\,\mu m, NA \approx 0.12 \approx \pi\,/\,2 - \varphi[rad]$ and for typical values of LN refractive indexes $n_{LN}^{TE} \approx 2.14$ and $n_{LN}^{TM} \approx 2.21$ for ordinary and extraordinary beams, respectively [8].

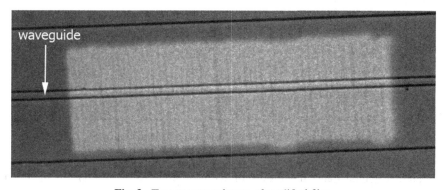

Fig. 3. Transparency change of modified film.

Table 1. Comparison between measured additional optical losses and estimated values.

	Additional optical losses [dB/mm]	
	TE-mode	TM-mode
Theoretical value	**1.04**	**1.27**
Chemical etching	0.95	1.3
Laser modification	1.0	1.4

Optical profilometer and atomic force microscope exploration in the illuminated area demonstrated a build-up of the LN substrate to a height of about 15 nm relatively to the surface of unirradiated titanium cover. Microstructure of the illuminated film region and the variations in the modified substrate height and are shown on Fig. 4 and 5, respectively.

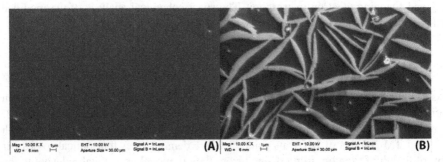

Fig. 4. Scanning electron microscopy of metal film before (A) and after (B) laser illumination.

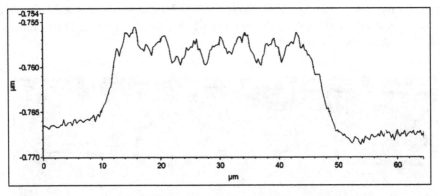

Fig. 5. Substrate elevation in the region of film modification.

Figure 6 demonstrates the results of X-ray emission spectroscopy in modified areas. O1s and Ti2p spectrum lines indicate the formation of titanium dioxide by laser irradiation.

The reproducibility of the obtained results was demonstrated in experiments with different power of laser illumination and different thickness of the titanium film.

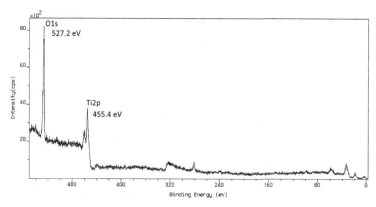

Fig. 6. X-ray emission spectrum of titanium film in the region of laser illumination

4   Discussion

The availability of thin titanium film laser modification for precise intensity control via additional optical losses adjustment in LN waveguides was demonstrated. Titanium dioxide formation and its partial diffusion into the waveguide substrate in the illuminated areas indicate that attached adjustment will be stable.

We applied the proposed method for the extinction ratio improvement of a LN Mach-Zehnder modulator by precise power balancing in arms of its waveguide interferometer. An increase of 18 dB (from 30 to 48 dB) with negligible additional losses was achieved.

Acknowledgement. M. Parfenov and A. Shamrai acknowledge support by Peter the Great St. Petersburg Polytechnic University in the framework of the Program "5-100-2020".

References

1. Bazzan, M., Sada, C.: Optical waveguides in lithium niobate: recent developments and applications. Appl. Phys. Rev. **2**, 040603 (2015)
2. Udd, E., Spillman, W.B. (eds.): Fiber Optic Sensors: An Introduction for Engineers and Scientists. Wiley, Hoboken (2011)
3. Alibart, O., et al.: Quantum photonics at telecom wavelengths based on lithium niobate waveguides. J. Opt. **18**, 104001 (2016)
4. Yamaguchi, Y., et al.: High extinction ratio characteristics of over 60 dB Mach-Zehnder modulator with asymmetric power-splitting Y-branches on X-cut Ti: LiNbO3. Jpn. J. Appl. Phys. **53**, 08MB03 (2014)
5. Chen, A., Murphy, E.: Broadband Optical Modulators: Science, Technology, and Applications. CRC Press, Boca Raton (2011)
6. Palm, K.J., et al.: Dynamic optical properties of metal hydrides. ACS Photonics **5**, 4677–4686 (2018)
7. Il'ichev, I.V., Toguzov, N.V., Shamray, A.V.: Plasmon-polariton polarizers on the surface of single-mode channel optical waveguides in lithium niobate. Tech. Phys. Lett. **35**, 831–833 (2009)
8. Zelmon, D.E., Small, D.L., Jundt, D.: Infrared corrected Sellmeier coefficients for congruently grown lithium niobate and 5 mol% magnesium oxide –doped lithium niobate. J. Opt. Soc. Am. B **14**, 3319 (1997)

Analysis of Mixed Strategies for P2P Streaming Systems

Aminu Adamu[1](✉)[iD], Anna Platonova[2][iD], Irina Yartseva[2][iD],
and Yuliya Gaidamaka[2,3][iD]

[1] Umaru Musa Yar'adua University, Katsina, Nigeria
`aminu.adamu@umyu.edu.ng`
[2] Peoples' Friendship University of Russia (RUDN University), Moscow, Russia
`aaplatonova@list.ru`, `irina.s.yartseva@gmail.com`, `gaydamaka-yuv@rudn.ru`
[3] Federal Research Center "Computer Science and Control" of the Russian
Academy of Sciences, Moscow, Russia

Abstract. With current advancements in communication technologies, video sharing and streaming are increasingly becoming popular among Internet users in applications like social-aware P2P video transmission. Peer-to-Peer (P2P) paradigm was proven to be the promising approach to efficiently deliver streaming services over the Internet. Several P2P-based streaming systems were successfully deployed. In such systems, the basic streaming quality parameters that affect the user Quality of Experience (QoE) are Playback Continuity and Startup Delay. Several research conducted have revealed that buffer filling strategies used in these systems play a key role on the streaming quality. The popularly used strategies are the Rarest First (RF) and Greedy (Gr) strategies, however, studies have shown that RF strategy outperforms Gr strategy in terms of playback continuity and Gr strategy outperforms RF strategy in terms of startup delay. In this paper, a problem of finding an optimal buffer filling strategy in form of mixed strategy was considered. The idea of the mixed strategy is to divide the buffer into two parts via demarcation point and apply one strategy to fill one part of the buffer and then the other strategy is applied to fill the other part of the buffer. Among the derived mixed strategies, an optimal was discovered which provides high probability of playback continuity with low startup delay.

Keywords: P2P streaming · Rarest first · Greedy · Startup delay · Playback continuity

1 Introduction

In recent years, video sharing and streaming over the Internet are increasingly becoming popular. It was forecasted by Cisco that by 2022, IP video traffic will

The publication has been prepared with the support of the RUDN University Program "5-100" (I. Yartseva, original draft preparation; Yu. Gaidamaka, conceptualization). The reported study was funded by RFBR, project numbers 18-07-00576 (A. Platonova, validation) and 20-07-01064 (I. Yartseva, visualization).

O. Galinina et al. (Eds.): NEW2AN 2020/ruSMART 2020, LNCS 12526, pp. 400–414, 2020.
https://doi.org/10.1007/978-3-030-65729-1_36

account for 82% of all IP traffic [1]. Client/server paradigm was traditionally used to deliver streaming services to users, however, considering the rapid advancements in communication technologies and proliferation of end-user devices; scalability, adaptability, fault-tolerance and robustness are the key challenges of client/server-based streaming systems.

A successful alternative to client-server paradigm since the early 2000s is the Peer-to-Peer (P2P) paradigm, where peers share their computational resources and bandwidth with other peers and communicate with each other directly for data sharing and exchange. The P2P paradigm is also part of the Device-to-Device (D2D) communications, which includes many ways to reduce load on networks, e.g. offloading [2].

Despite the fact that the first commercial P2P-based streaming systems [3–6] were successfully deployed in 2010th, this technology is still in demand. Applications related to the Internet of things, such as social-aware P2P video transmission, have added particular relevance to research. Hsu and Tung in [7] proposed a P2P-based streaming architecture for multimedia IoT devices and Silva et al. in [8] also proposed another P2P-based streaming architecture for video conferencing applications. In P2P-based streaming systems, video stream is divided into portions of video data called video chunks (henceforth chunks), and the user streaming application is equipped with a buffer which serves as a temporary storage space for chunks in order to ensure smooth and uninterrupted playback [9]. The video playback process is divided into time slots, the length of each time slot corresponds to the time required to playback one chunk. When a new peer joined a video session, it first begins by filling its buffer; after downloading a reasonable number of chunks enough to be played back for some time; the chunks will start to move to the video player for playback.

The basic quality parameters that directly affect the user Quality of Experience (QoE) in P2P streaming systems are Playback Continuity, Startup Delay and Playback Latency [9]. However, the system's performance based on these parameters depends on some factors such as, the system's chunk downloading strategy, peer selection strategy, overlay construction, video coding and incentive scheme. Therefore, considering these factors, researchers have proposed several ideas to improve the performance of such systems. These ideas are either downloading-strategy-based [10], peer-selection-based [10,11], overlay-construction-based [12], video-coding-based [13,14] and incentive-based [15,16].

This paper aimed at maximizing the probability of playback continuity and minimizing the startup delay in P2P streaming systems. The popularly used chunk downloading strategies in P2P streaming systems are Rarest First (RF) and Greedy (Gr) strategies [17,18]. With RF strategy, peers always tend to download a rare chunk (with few available copies) whereas with Gr strategy, peers tend to download a chunk with closest playback time (those chunks that are about to be played back). In [17,18] results of the strategies' analysis have shown that the probability of playback continuity (playback without pauses) is higher when RF strategy is used to download chunks than with Gr strategy, however, when RF strategy is used, the startup delay is high, unlike the Gr strategy which provides a low startup delay. To achieve the set objects, an optimal buffer filling strategy in the form of mixed strategy was discovered. The idea of mixed strategy is to divide the buffer with total of $M + 1$ buffer positions into two parts via demarcation point x and apply one strategy to fill one part of the buffer and then the other strategy is applied to fill the other part of the buffer.

The rest of the paper is organized as follows. Section 2 presents the related works and a playback model for P2P streaming systems is provided in Sect. 3. Mixed strategies are defined in Sect. 4. Results of the simulation experiments conducted for the analysis of the strategies are presented in Sect. 5 and finally, Sect. 6 concludes the paper.

2   Related Works

Considering the impact of system's overlay construction, peer selection strategy, chunk downloading strategy, video coding as well as the incentive scheme on the streaming quality in P2P streaming systems, several works were done to improve the performance of these systems.

Sina et al. in [10] proposed WidePLive as a P2P live video streaming system. In WidePLive, a low-delay overlay construction mechanism is proposed and the chunk-scheduling scheme contained in WidePLive uses the benefits of Rarest First and Greedy strategies to trade-off between quality parameters. Additionally, priority-based peer selection strategy was proposed in WidePLive to reduce playback latency and startup delay.

Shilpa and Venkatesh in [11] proposed three-stage peer selection strategy in order to manage playback delay experienced by peers in P2P streaming systems. In each stage, peers choose their partners based on parameters such as propagation delay, upload capacity, buffering duration and buffering level.

In [12], Hua et al. have considered an overlay construction and proposed a hybrid P2P network framework called P2P Interactive Streaming Media (PPSIM). PPSIM integrates CDN (Content Distribution Network), P2P network and tree-mesh structure to deliver streaming services. Experiments conducted in [12] have shown that PPSIM framework significantly decreases end-to-end delay, distortion and controls overhead.

Yang et al. in [14] considered long start-up delay as threat to user QoE in P2P streaming systems; therefore, they proposed an approach called Multiple Channels Streaming (MCS). With MCS, multiple parallel channels selected from all channels are linked to the stream of a single channel requested by a peer, as such peers dynamically determine how many and which channels should be selected into the MCS. Although MCS significantly reduces the startup delay, however, it will cause excessive traffic overhead.

Zhang et al. in [15] have claimed that free-riders and redundant streams are the major factors that dramatically degrade playback quality and network performance in P2P streaming systems, therefore, they proposed a distance-driven alliance algorithm which deters free-riding and constructs a multicast tree to reduce redundant streams.

In this paper, a problem of finding an optimal chunk downloading strategy which will maximize the probability of playback continuity and minimize the startup delay was considered. To find the optimal strategy, a mixed approach was used. In the mixed strategy approach, playback buffer is divided into two parts via a demarcation point and one strategy is used to fill one part of the buffer and then the other strategy is used to fill the other part of the buffer. Since the popular strategies are two (i.e. RF and Gr) and buffer is divided into two parts, then there will be four possible mixed strategies, however, for the sake of brevity, only two mixed strategies were presented in the work due to their performance. Among the considered mixed strategies, an optimal was discovered with high probability of playback continuity and low startup delay.

3   A Playback Model for P2P Streaming Systems

In this section, let's consider a playback model for P2P streaming systems. In P2P streaming systems, peer's streaming application consists of streaming machine and a video player. Peer application performs the following functions:

- Downloading of chunks from the server and from other peers;
- Storing of the downloaded chunks in the buffer;
- Uploading the downloaded chunks to other peers;
- Forwarding each of the available chunks in the buffer to the player for playback.

For the exchange of chunks, peers exchange buffer maps. Each buffer map contains information about the chunks a peer successfully downloaded, hence, ready for exchange. A peer can request a buffer map from any of its neighboring peers. After i-peer obtained a buffer map from j-peer, it can download one or some of the chunks advertised in the j-peer's buffer map. A peer could download chunks from one or more neighboring peers simultaneously. Different streaming systems have different chunk downloading strategies defined to dictate the right chunk to download especially when many chunks are available for download. The downloading strategies popularly used are Rarest First (RF) and Greedy (Gr) strategies.

Further, consider a system with N peers and a single video server, which provides only one video stream to the peers and all peers watch and exchange among them only that single stream. The video playback process is divided into time slots, the length of each time slot corresponds to the time required to playback one chunk.

Assume that each subscribed peer in the system has a buffer designed to accommodate M + 1 chunks. Buffer positions are numbered as follows: 0-buffer position (0-position) is designed only to store a fresh chunk, just produced by the server. Other buffer positions m, $m = 1, \cdots, M - 1$ are meant to store the recently downloaded chunks, or the ones to be downloaded in the future time slots. The last buffer position M is to store the oldest chunk that will move to the player for playback in the next time slot (Fig. 1).

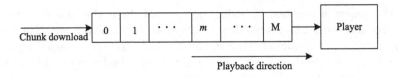

Fig. 1. Playback buffer in P2P streaming system

Let's define the actions performed by peers and the server during each time slot. At the beginning of each time slot, the server selects a peer at random and uploads to its 0-position a freshly produced chunk for the current time slot. Any i-peer not selected by the server in the current time slot will perform the following actions:

– If there are empty positions in i-peer's buffer, it will select at random another j-peer called a target peer from which it will try to download one of its missing chunks. If the target peer by chance has more than one of the missing chunks, then the index of buffer position to which i-peer can download chunk from the target peer is determined by the downloading strategy defined in the system. With RF strategy, i-peer will select and download the youngest chunk (with the longest playback deadline) among the missing chunks, while Gr strategy does the opposite, with Gr strategy, i-peer will select and download the oldest chunk (with the shortest playback deadline) among the missing chunks.
– i-peer will not download any chunk in the current time slot, if:
  • The target peer does not have any one of the missing chunks;
  • All the positions in i-peer's buffer are filled with their respective chunks.

Time slot ends with buffer content shift: chunk in M-position will exit the buffer and shift to the player for playback. Other chunks in other positions will shift one position ahead, towards the end of the buffer; hence 0-position will be free to accommodate the fresh chunk to be produced by the server in the forthcoming time slot. Chunk in m-position will move to the player for playback after $(M - m)$ time slots (Fig. 1). Note that if peer's M-position is filled with a chunk during each time slot, then the peer will experience playback process without pauses; this is what is called *playback continuity*.

Each peer at any moment can either be in online or off-line state. Let $a(n)$ be the n-peer's online indicator, i.e. $a(n) = 1$, if the n-peer is online, otherwise $a(n) = 0$, for simplicity, assume that all peers join and leave the system with equal probabilities $\alpha(n) = \alpha$ and $\beta(n) = \beta$ respectively, $n = 1, \cdots, N$ (Fig. 2).

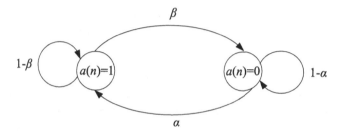

Fig. 2. Peer online and off-line states

Let vector $\mathbf{x}(n) = (x_0(n), x_1(n), \cdots, x_M(n))$ be the state of n-peer's buffer, where $x_m(n)$ is the state of m-position in n-peer's buffer, i.e. $x_m(n) = 1$ if n-peer's m-position is filled with a chunk, otherwise $x_m(n) = 0$, $m = 0, \cdots, M$; $n = 1, \cdots, N$ (Fig. 3).

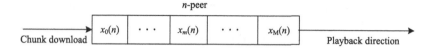

Fig. 3. Buffer state of n-peer

Denote by $p_1(n, m)$ the probability that m-position in n-peer's buffer is occupied (also known as *m-position occupancy probability*) during each time slot. Denoted also by $V(n)$ the probability that buffer M-position of n-peer is filled with a chunk for playback at the end of each time slot. The probability $V(n)$ depends on the downloading strategy used in the system. Therefore, the *Probability of Playback Continuity* can be expressed by Eq. (1).

$$V^\delta(n) = p_1(n, \mathrm{M}) \tag{1}$$

where δ is the strategy used in the system.

A recursive method for the computation of probabilities $p_1(n, m)$, $m = 1, \cdots, M$ based on downloading strategy is provided in [17].

4   Mixed Strategies

In [17,18] it was discovered that RF strategy outperforms Gr in terms of playback continuity i.e. $V^{\mathrm{RF}} > V^{\mathrm{Gr}}$, and with Gr strategy the observed startup delay is shorter than that of RF, hence, it is paramount to find an optimal buffer filling strategy in form of mixed strategy with which peers will experience better playback continuity with short startup delay. The idea of mixed strategy is to divide the buffer with total of M + 1 buffer positions into two parts via *demarcation point x*, $x \in \{0, \cdots, M\}$, and in one part of the buffer a given strategy would be used to fill that part of the buffer, in the absence of chunks to download for that part of the buffer, then another strategy would be used to fill the other part of the buffer.

Since the strategies are two and the buffer is divided into two parts, there will be four possible mixed strategies, however, for the sake of brevity; this paper presents only the best two mixed strategies in terms of performance. In the first mixed strategy, RF strategy would be used for buffer positions $m \in \{0, \cdots, x\}$, if there are no chunks to available to download for these buffer positions, then Gr would be applied to fill the rest of the buffer positions $m \in \{x+1, \cdots, M\}$, let's denote this mixed strategy by $\mathbf{RF}|\mathrm{Gr}_{0\cdots x\cdots M}$ (Fig. 4), it can be noted that in this mixed strategy, RF is marked out boldly, because it is the first strategy to be used.

In the other considered mixed strategy, firstly the Gr strategy would be used for buffer positions $m \in \{x, \cdots, M\}$, if there are no chunks to download for these buffer positions, then RF strategy would be applied for the other buffer positions $m \in \{0, \cdots, x-1\}$, let's denote this mixed strategy by $\mathrm{RF}|\mathbf{Gr}_{0\cdots x\cdots M}$ (Fig. 5), Gr is marked out boldly, because it is the first strategy to be used in this mixed strategy. In both of the mixed strategies the point x is the demarcation point. The demarcation point x of a mixed strategy with which the maximum of the probability of playback continuity is attained is called the optimal demarcation point of that mixed strategy and is denoted by x^*, i.e.

$$x^* : V^\delta(x^*) = maxV^\delta(x), 0 \leq x \leq M, \delta \in \left\{ \mathbf{RF}|\mathrm{Gr}_{0\cdots x\cdots M}, \mathrm{RF}|\mathbf{Gr}_{0\cdots x\cdots M} \right\} \qquad (2)$$

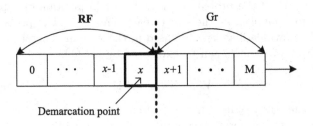

Fig. 4. Mixed strategy $\mathbf{RF}|\mathrm{Gr}_{0\cdots x\cdots M}$

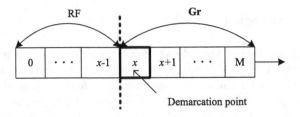

Fig. 5. Mixed strategy $\mathrm{RF}|\mathbf{Gr}_{0\cdots x\cdots M}$

5   Simulation Results

A simulation program was built based on the discrete model presented in [17] in order to analyze the effectiveness of the strategies and finally to find the optimal buffer filling strategy in form of mixed strategy. To this end, let's first analyze a closed system, i.e. a system where $\alpha = 0$ and $\beta = 0$. The system and its parameters are provided by (3).

$$Q = \left\langle N, M, x, \alpha = 0, \beta = 0, \delta \in \left\{ \underset{0\cdots x\cdots M}{\mathbf{RF}|\mathbf{Gr}} , \underset{0\cdots x\cdots M}{\mathbf{RF}|\mathbf{Gr}} \right\} \right\rangle \tag{3}$$

For the closed system, the following problem would be solved

$$\begin{cases} \underset{x}{max} V^{\delta}(x), \\ 0 \le x \le M, \\ 0 \le V^{\delta}(x) \le 1. \end{cases} \tag{4}$$

The search for the optimal demarcation points would be conducted using direct search method for a system with $N = 100$ peers and $M = 40$ buffer positions.

The results obtained have shown that for the defined mixed strategies $\underset{0\cdots x\cdots M}{\mathbf{RF}|\mathbf{Gr}}$ and $\underset{0\cdots x\cdots M}{\mathbf{RF}|\mathbf{Gr}}$ there are set of points x for which $V^{\delta} > V^{\mathrm{RF}}$, $\delta \in \left\{ \underset{0\cdots x\cdots M}{\mathbf{RF}|\mathbf{Gr}} , \underset{0\cdots x\cdots M}{\mathbf{RF}|\mathbf{Gr}} \right\}$, where the maximum value of the probability of playback continuity for mixed strategy $\underset{0\cdots x\cdots M}{\mathbf{RF}|\mathbf{Gr}}$ is achieved at point $x^* = 10$ ($V^{\underset{0\cdots 10\cdots M}{\mathbf{RF}|\mathbf{Gr}}} = 0.99952$) (Fig. 6).

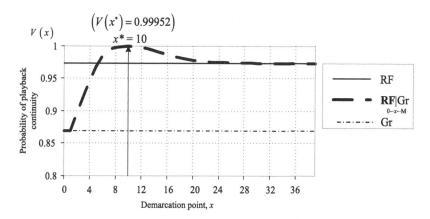

Fig. 6. Optimal demarcation point for the mixed strategy $\underset{0\cdots x\cdots M}{\mathbf{RF}|\mathbf{Gr}}$ (for $\alpha = 0$ and $\beta = 0$)

For mixed strategy $\text{RF}|\underset{0\cdots x\cdots M}{\textbf{Gr}}$ the maximum value of the probability of playback continuity is achieved at point $x^* = 31$ ($V \overset{\text{RF}|\textbf{Gr}}{_{0\cdots31\cdots M}} = 0.99864$) (Fig. 7), however, $V \overset{\textbf{RF}|\text{Gr}}{_{0\cdots10\cdots M}} > V \overset{\text{RF}|\textbf{Gr}}{_{0\cdots31\cdots M}}$. Subsequently, for a closed system the optimal demarcation points for mixed strategies $\textbf{RF}|\underset{0\cdots x\cdots M}{\text{Gr}}$ and $\text{RF}|\underset{0\cdots x\cdots M}{\textbf{Gr}}$ are $x^* = 10$ and $x^* = 31$ respectively (Fig. 6 and 7).

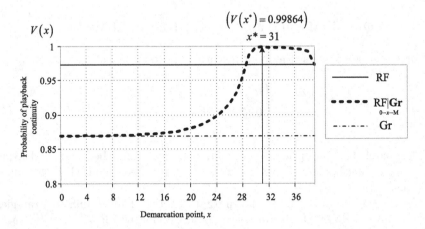

Fig. 7. Optimal demarcation point for the mixed strategy $\text{RF}|\underset{0\cdots x\cdots M}{\textbf{Gr}}$ (for $\alpha = 0$ and $\beta = 0$)

Further, let's analyze the buffer positions occupancy probability $p_1(n, m)$ for the discovered mixed strategies $\textbf{RF}|\underset{0\cdots10\cdots39}{\text{Gr}}$ and $\text{RF}|\underset{0\cdots31\cdots39}{\textbf{Gr}}$. From the graph of the buffer positions occupancy probability $p_1(n, m)$ presented in Fig. 8, it can be observed that for mixed strategy $\textbf{RF}|\underset{0\cdots10\cdots39}{\text{Gr}}$ we have $V^{\text{Gr}} < V^{\text{RF}} < V \overset{\text{RF}|\text{Gr}}{_{0\cdots10\cdots39}}$ (Fig. 8).

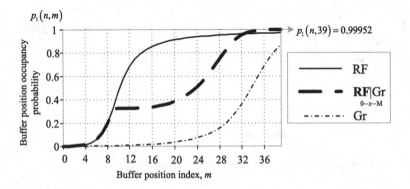

Fig. 8. Buffer position occupancy probability for mixed strategy $\textbf{RF}|\underset{0\cdots10\cdots39}{\text{Gr}}$ (for $\alpha = 0$ and $\beta = 0$)

For mixed strategy $\mathbf{RF}|\mathbf{Gr}_{0\cdots31\cdots39}$ we have $V^{\mathrm{Gr}} < V^{\mathrm{RF}} < V^{\mathbf{RF}|\mathbf{Gr}_{0\cdots31\cdots39}}$ (Fig. 9).

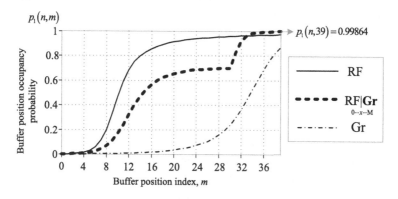

Fig. 9. Buffer position occupancy probability for mixed strategy $\mathbf{RF}|\mathbf{Gr}_{0\cdots31\cdots39}$ (for $\alpha = 0$ and $\beta = 0$)

However, $V^{\mathbf{RF}|\mathbf{Gr}_{0\cdots10\cdots39}} > V^{\mathbf{RF}|\mathbf{Gr}_{0\cdots31\cdots39}}$. The bend in graph of Fig. 8 occurred at point $m = 10$, which corresponds with the optimal demarcation point of mixed strategy $\mathbf{RF}|\mathbf{Gr}_{0\cdots10\cdots39}$, and this is because, with mixed strategy $\mathbf{RF}|\mathbf{Gr}_{0\cdots10\cdots39}$, RF strategy is firstly applied for buffer positions $m \in \{0, \cdots, 10\}$, and in the rest of the buffer positions $m \in \{11, \cdots, 39\}$, Gr strategy is applied. Additionally, the bend in graph of Fig. 9 occurred at $m = 31$, which also corresponds with the optimal demarcation point of mixed strategy $\mathbf{RF}|\mathbf{Gr}_{0\cdots31\cdots39}$, since with mixed strategy $\mathbf{RF}|\mathbf{Gr}_{0\cdots31\cdots39}$, Gr strategy is firstly applied for buffer positions $m \in \{31, \cdots, 39\}$ and for the rest of buffer positions $m \in \{0, \cdots, 30\}$, RF strategy is applied.

Having analyzed the mixed strategies for the closed system, now let's consider an open system, where peers can join the system with probability $\alpha > 0$ and can leave the system with probability $\beta > 0$.

Such system has the following parameters:

$$Q = \left\langle N, M, x, \alpha > 0, \beta > 0, \delta \in \left\{ \mathbf{RF}|\mathbf{Gr}_{0\cdots x\cdots M}, \mathbf{RF}|\mathbf{Gr}_{0\cdots x\cdots M} \right\} \right\rangle \qquad (5)$$

For the open system the following problem would be solved

$$\begin{cases} \underset{x}{max} V^\delta(x), \\ 0 \leq x \leq M, \\ 0 \leq V^\delta(x) \leq 1. \end{cases} \qquad (6)$$

To find the optimal demarcation point $x^* : V^\delta(x^*) = max V^\delta(x)$, $\delta \in \left\{ \mathbf{RF}|\mathbf{Gr}_{0\cdots x\cdots M}, \mathbf{RF}|\mathbf{Gr}_{0\cdots x\cdots M} \right\}$, for open system with $N = 1000$, $M = 40$ and any pair

$(\alpha > 0,\ \beta > 0)$, also the direct search method would be applied. The average number of peers N_{avg} in the system for some pair of $(\alpha > 0,\ \beta > 0)$ is presented in Table 1. It can be observed that for a fixed value $\beta > 0$, as the value of α increases, the N_{avg} also increases.

Table 1. Average number of peers, N_{avg}

α	β		
	0.001	0.01	0.1
0.001	500	90	9
0.005	833	332	47
0.01	909	500	90
0.05	980	833	333
0.1	990	909	499
0.5	998	980	833
1	999	990	909

The results presented in Tables 2 and 3 have shown that for mixed strategies **RF**|**Gr** and **RF**|**Gr** there exist point x^*, for which $x^* : V^\delta(x^*) = \max_{0\cdots x\cdots M} V^\delta(x)$, when $\alpha > 0$ and $\beta > 0$.

Table 2. Optimal demarcation points x^* for mixed strategy **RF**|**Gr** and their corresponding values of probabilities $V(x^*)$ for $\alpha > 0$ and $\beta > 0$

α	β		
	0.001	0.01	0.1
0.001	$x^* = 10$ $V(x^*) = 0.22017$	$x^* = 10$ $V(x^*) = 0.00386$	$x^* = 10$ $V(x^*) = 5.57E - 05$
0.005	$x^* = 9$ $V(x^*) = 0.67846$	$x^* = 10$ $V(x^*) = 0.02016$	$x^* = 10$ $V(x^*) = 8.57E - 05$
0.01	$x^* = 10$ $V(x^*) = 0.86759$	$x^* = 10$ $V(x^*) = 0.19782$	$x^* = 10$ $V(x^*) = 0.00022$
0.05	$x^* = 10$ $V(x^*) = 0.93954$	$x^* = 9$ $V(x^*) = 0.58698$	$x^* = 10$ $V(x^*) = 0.01985$
0.1	$x^* = 10$ $V(x^*) = 0.95749$	$x^* = 10$ $V(x^*) = 0.78801$	$x^* = 10$ $V(x^*) = 0.08268$
0.5	$x^* = 10$ $V(x^*) = 0.97419$	$x^* = 9$ $V(x^*) = 0.80294$	$x^* = 10$ $V(x^*) = 0.26246$
1	$x^* = 10$ $V(x^*) = 0.97580$	$x^* = 10$ $V(x^*) = 0.81758$	$x^* = 10$ $V(x^*) = 0.32508$

Table 3. Optimal demarcation points x^* for mixed strategy RF|**Gr** and their corresponding values of probabilities $V(x^*)$ for $\alpha > 0$ and $\beta > 0$

α	β		
	0.001	0.01	0.1
0.001	$x^* = 31$	$x^* = 31$	$x^* = 31$
	$V(x^*) = 0.20858$	$V(x^*) = 0.00377$	$V(x^*) = 1.14E - 05$
0.005	$x^* = 31$	$x^* = 31$	$x^* = 30$
	$V(x^*) = 0.61515$	$V(x^*) = 0.02146$	$V(x^*) = 4.92E - 05$
0.01	$x^* = 30$	$x^* = 31$	$x^* = 31$
	$V(x^*) = 0.80192$	$V(x^*) = 0.17740$	$V(x^*) = 0.00021$
0.05	$x^* = 31$	$x^* = 30$	$x^* = 31$
	$V(x^*) = 0.87285$	$V(x^*) = 0.53174$	$V(x^*) = 0.01979$
0.1	$x^* = 30$	$x^* = 31$	$x^* = 31$
	$V(x^*) = 0.89203$	$V(x^*) = 0.70102$	$V(x^*) = 0.09789$
0.5	$x^* = 31$	$x^* = 31$	$x^* = 31$
	$V(x^*) = 0.90804$	$V(x^*) = 0.74850$	$V(x^*) = 0.23184$
1	$x^* = 31$	$x^* = 31$	$x^* = 31$
	$V(x^*) = 0.90950$	$V(x^*) = 0.76360$	$V(x^*) = 0.27335$

Results of the analysis of open system as well as closed system have shown that the optimal demarcation point for mixed strategy **RF**|**Gr** $_{0\cdots x\cdots M}$, with which the maximum of the probability of playback continuity is achieved exits and is $x^* = 10$, where for mixed strategy RF|**Gr** $_{0\cdots x\cdots M}$ is $x^* = 31$. Hence, the two mixed strategies were discovered with their respective optimal demarcation points, i.e. **RF**|**Gr** $_{0\cdots10\cdots39}$ and RF|**Gr** $_{0\cdots31\cdots39}$. Note that the previous results of closed system have shown that $V^{\textbf{RF}|\textbf{Gr}}_{0\cdots10\cdots39} > V^{\text{RF}|\textbf{Gr}}_{0\cdots31\cdots39}$, i.e. the probability of playback continuity is higher with mixed strategy **RF**|**Gr** $_{0\cdots10\cdots39}$ than with mixed strategy RF|**Gr** $_{0\cdots31\cdots39}$. Likewise, the results of the analysis of an open system have still shown that $V^{\textbf{RF}|\textbf{Gr}}_{0\cdots10\cdots39} > V^{\text{RF}|\textbf{Gr}}_{0\cdots31\cdots39}$ for $\alpha > 0$ and $\beta > 0$ (Table 2 and 3).

Further, let's analyze these two mixed strategies based on another quality parameter of streaming systems, i.e. startup delay. The goal of this analysis is to find which of the discovered mixed strategies provides the shortest startup delay. The results obtained are shown in Fig. 10 and 11. It can be observed from the graphs that the average startup delay τ with mixed strategy **RF**|**Gr** $_{0\cdots10\cdots39}$ almost tallied with the average startup delay of mixed strategy RF|**Gr** $_{0\cdots31\cdots39}$.

Subsequently the optimal buffer filling strategy has been discovered and is **RF**|**Gr** $_{0\cdots10\cdots39}$, with its application, high probability of playback continuity would be achieved with low startup delay. The success of mixed strategy can be explained as follows: in buffer positions $m \in \{0, \cdots, 10\}$, RF strategy is firstly applied, which allows for rapid increase and distribution of rarely available chunks in the system, in the rest of buffer positions $m \in \{11, \cdots, 39\}$, Gr strategy is applied which maximizes the probability of playback continuity.

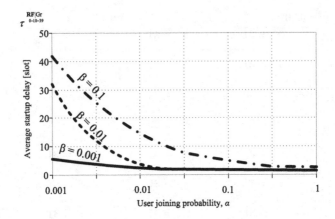

Fig. 10. Average startup delay for mixed strategy $\mathbf{RF}|\mathrm{Gr}_{0\cdots10\cdots39}$

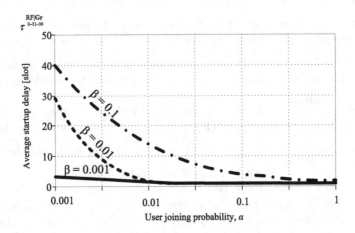

Fig. 11. Average startup delay for mixed strategy $\mathrm{RF}|\mathbf{Gr}_{0\cdots31\cdots39}$

6   Conclusion

In this work, buffering strategies for P2P-based streaming systems were studied. In order to maximize the probability of playback continuity and minimize startup delay, mixed strategies were designed and analyzed. For each of the considered mixed strategies, optimal demarcation points were found. Finally, among the derived mixed strategies, an optimal one which provides higher probability of playback continuity and low startup delay was discovered.

7   Future Work

The optimal demarcation points of the mixed strategies presented in this paper were discovered via direct search method, therefore, in the future, a generalize optimization problem will be considered to enable the discovery of optimal demarcation points for the mixed strategies for any given buffer and network sizes.

References

1. Cisco Visual Networking Index: Forecast and trends, 2017–2022 (2018)
2. Pyattaev A., et. al.: Network-assisted D2D communications: implementing a technology prototype for cellular traffic offloading. In: IEEE Wireless Communications and Networking Conference, WCNC, pp. 3266–3271 (2014). art. no. 6953070
3. PPLive Homepage. http://www.pptv.com. Accessed 20 May 2020
4. PPStream Homepage. http://www.pps.tv. Accessed 20 May 2020
5. QQTV Homepage. http://live.qq.com. Accessed 20 May 2020
6. UUSee Homepage. http://www.uusee.com. Accessed 20 May 2020
7. Hsu, T., Tung, Y.: A social-aware P2P video transmission strategy for multimedia IoT devices. IEEE Access **8**, 95574–95584 (2020)
8. Silva, M.A., Bertone, R., Schafer, J.: Topology distribution for video-conferencing applications. In: 10th International Conference on Networks of the Future (NoF), pp. 90–97. IEEE (2019)
9. Shen, X., Yu, H., Buford, J., Akon, M.: Handbook of Peer-to-Peer Networking. Springer, Heidelberg (2010). https://doi.org/10.1007/978-0-387-09751-0
10. Sina, M., Dehghan, M., Rahmani, A.M., Reshadi, M.: WidePLive: a coupled low-delay overlay construction mechanism and peer-chunk priority-based chunk scheduling for P2P live video streaming. IET Commun. **14**(6), 937–947 (2020)
11. Shilpa, B., Venkatesh, T.: Delay management in mesh-based P2P live streaming using a three-stage peer selection strategy. J. Netw. Syst. Manag. **26**(2), 401–425 (2017)
12. Yang, H., Liu, M., Li, B., Dong, Z.: A P2P network framework for interactive streaming media. In: 11th International Conference on Intelligent Human-Machine Systems and Cybernetics (IHMSC), pp. 288–292. IEEE(2019)
13. Xiyu, P., Cheng, W., Zhonghua, X.: A P2P streaming media segmentation method based on scalable video coding data characteristics. In: 2nd International Conference on Mechanical, Control and Computer Engineering (ICMCCE), pp. 208–211. IEEE (2017)
14. Yang, C., Sun, T., Guan, Y.: On fast channel switching with a parallel multiple channels streaming in P2P systems. In: Computing, Communications and IoT Applications (ComComAp), pp. 386–391. IEEE (2019)
15. Zhang, J., Zhang, Y., Shen, M.: A distance-driven alliance for a P2P live video system. IEEE Trans. Multimed. **22**, 1–10 (2019)

16. Ometov, A., et al.: Toward trusted, social-aware D2D connectivity: bridging across the technology and sociality realms. IEEE Wirel. Commun. **23**(4), 103–111 (2016). art. no. 7553033
17. Adamu, A., Gaidamaka, Y., Samuylov, A.: Discrete Markov chain model for analyzing probability measures of P2P streaming network. In: Balandin, S., Koucheryavy, Y., Hu, H. (eds.) NEW2AN/ruSMART - 2011. LNCS, vol. 6869, pp. 428–439. Springer, Heidelberg (2011). https://doi.org/10.1007/978-3-642-22875-9_39
18. Zhou, Y., Chiu, D.M., Lui, J.C.S.: A simple model for chunk-scheduling strategies in P2P streaming. IEEE/ACM Trans. Netw. **19**(1), 42–54 (2011)

Simulating UAV's Movement
for Servicing User Groups with a
Reference Point in Wireless Networks

Emil M. Khayrov[1] , Nikita A. Polyakov[1] , Ekaterina G. Medvedeva[1,2(✉)] ,
Jiri Pokorny[3,4] , Yuliya V. Gaidamaka[1,2] , and Jiri Hosek[3]

[1] Peoples' Friendship University of Russia (RUDN University), 6 Miklukho-Maklaya
Street, Moscow 117198, Russian Federation
emil.khayrov@gmail.com, goto97@mail.ru
{medvedeva-eg,gaydamaka-yuv}@rudn.ru

[2] Federal Research Center "Computer Science and Control" of the Russian Academy
of Sciences (FRC CSC RAS), 44-2 Vavilov Street, Moscow 119333, Russian Federation

[3] Department of Telecommunications, Brno University of Technology,
Brno, Czech Republic
jiri.pokorny@vutbr.cz, hosek@feec.vutbr.cz

[4] Unit of Electrical Engineering, Tampere University, Tampere, Finland

Abstract. Current cellular networks face outbreaks of an extremely
high demand for communication capacity and coverage during the mass
events. This article discusses a scenario with events in remote areas. It
is expected that the unmanned aerial vehicles (UAVs) equipped with
the directional antennas will become one of the key components of these
networks and provide the solution. It attracts considerable attention in
basic and applied research and commerce for its rapid deployment and
flexible extension of the users coverage, mobility of UAV access points
(APs) and a higher probability of line-of-sight channels. However, it also
creates new issues to be addressed. The critical task is to maximize coverage area with the required quality of service to provide the connection
for the maximum number of users. At the same time, analysis of the performance indicators of such networks, taking into account the mobility
of both access points and users, is challenging. One of the key quality
indicators is the probability of coverage. The aim of this work is to consider two drones' mobility models to cover users with small cells, and to
solve the problem of maximizing coverage probability using the simulation. With a given threshold signal-to-noise ratio, it is shown that using
the particle swarm method as an adaptive navigation algorithm allows
achieving higher coverage probability values as opposed to k-means algorithm. A comparative analysis of adaptive navigation is presented.

The publication has been prepared with the support of the RUDN University Program
"5-100" (E. Khayrov, validation; N. Polyakov, visualization). The reported study was
funded by RFBR, project numbers 18-07-00576 (Yu. Gaidamaka, methodology) and
20-07-01064 (E. Medvedeva, numerical analysis). For the research, the infrastructure
of the SIX Center was used.

O. Galinina et al. (Eds.): NEW2AN 2020/ruSMART 2020, LNCS 12526, pp. 415–425, 2020.
https://doi.org/10.1007/978-3-030-65729-1_37

Keywords: UAV mobility simulation · User group mobility · Coverage probability · Non-terrestrial networks

1 Introduction

In recent years it has been seen the growth of unmanned aerial vehicles' (UAVs) (or drones') employment for wireless networks. It is possible to use them in places where there are no stationary cellular base stations, which contributes to an increase in the quality and possibility of access and provide users broadband access. The usage of drones, equipped with external directional antennas with the ability to amplify the signal, is due to the incredible flexibility and speed of deployment of such a network. Here UAVs act not only as means for inspections, search, and fixing of emergency situations during rescue operations in remote places, but they are also part of the network transport infrastructure [20] and serve as access to data transmission services for users on the ground, during various events on large open areas. This improves the quality of service and reduces the cost of network deployment for the operators. The 3GPP [1] carried out studies aimed at defining the possible role of drone-based communication in the 5G and future 6G networks [4,6,13,19,22,24]. For such cases, the set of indicators – interference, Line-of-Sight (LoS), directional deafness – are affecting signal power and spectral efficiency, as well as traditional indicators, e.g., connection success rate, are analyzed [2,8].

Depending on the radio access technology (WiFi, LTE, mmWave), the estimation of the coverage probability is nontrivial. There are well-known approaches [21,22], which employ several simplified assumptions. One of the main approaches for modeling is the stochastic geometry method, which considers the relative location of the studied objects.

One feature of data transmission using UAVs is the necessity of Line-of-Sight (LoS) between the user and the access point (AP). This strict requirement is compensated by drones' mobility and provides adaptive navigation relative to users, which can significantly improve transmission efficiency and quality of service [15–18,22,23,25,26]. The idea of simulation is to find the most effective method for positioning UAVs taking into account the group movement of users in terms of the coverage probability. We develop the model, which considers a mass event, such as a concert or festival in an open area, where people move in groups, and each group has a reference point or so-called leader [9]. Several UAVs provide the small cells to coverage users and adopt their locations and their groups movement, using particle swarm optimization and k-means.

This paper continues the investigation of UAV-based network and presents the results of constructing a simulation model of user movement in discrete time. In the previous work were considered the individual movements of users and the stationary location of APs on the UAV. Now we are interested in displaying and analyzing the moving crowd of people and changing UAV positions to optimize coverage and provide radio access and maximize such a quality indicator as the coverage probability.

In Sect. 2, we consider the system model and define the movement of users subject to a physical and, in some way, social law – a reference point group mobility – inside a limited open area. Section 3 describes adaptive drone navigation methods in accordance with the k-means [5] algorithm and particle swarm optimization algorithm [10] utilized in each step of the model's run for adaptive drone navigation. In Sect. 4, the performed simulation provides the numerical results based on the evaluation of signal-to-noise ratio (SNR) metric. With this approach, the best simulation result would be the case when all groups and users in groups receive a communication level above a given SNR threshold.

2   System Model

Let us consider a scenario, where the location of UAVs is controlled through the user mobility pattern during a public crowded event organized in an open area without large massive structures or buildings. Let us suppose that users are connected to a several UAVs with a mounted directional antenna are operating as access point and providing wireless radio coverage of the given area. Let us make the set of users $\mathcal{U}$, which is constant over the considered time interval, equal to $|\mathcal{U}| = U$, move within the area in accordance with the Reference Point Group Mobility (RPGM) model [11,15]. It is assumed that each user's mobile device is located at the same height h_u above the ground.

Suppose, the set N_d of drones does not change its height h_d during the movement within the area. The UAV radio coverage is determined by the power of the transceiver antenna and is characterized by the radius R_d, $d = 1, ... N_d$ [18]. The user $u \in \mathcal{U}$ can establish radio connections from the nearest UAV d, $d = 1, ..., N_D$ if the distance between his device and the UAV is $r_{(d,u)}$ does not exceed the radius of the antenna R_d (see Fig. 1).

This user movement scenario assumes that all U users are divided into the N_G groups, $N_G << U$, and the so-called reference point is assigned for each group g, $g = 1, ..., N_G$, which is a user who defines a motion vector for each member within belonged group. In addition, the parameter $r_{\max}$ is set, which determines at what maximum distance from the reference point the users of this group can move. The velocity of users of one group is fixed and is determined by the parameter v_u for all groups, and the reference point obeys the one-dimensional random walk model (e.g., random walk) [14], i.e., the direction of motion is determined uniformly on the interval $(0, 2\pi)$, and the time of motion has an exponential distribution with the parameter τ_u. Our main achievement in this work is the creation of the tool for evaluation the proportion of connected users within coverage area of the UAV with an accuracy of the given user movement patterns and adaptive navigation method. After evaluation the tool conducts a numerical analysis of the obtained values from motion characteristics. To compare UAV motion models, consider the probability metric of coverage of the simulated area, which we will calculate as follows:

$$p_c = \frac{1}{N} \sum_{u \in \mathcal{U}} 1(\gamma_{(d,u)} \geq \overline{\gamma}), \tag{1}$$

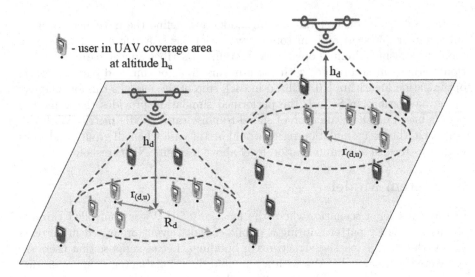

Fig. 1. UAV-based network.

where $\gamma_{(d,u)}$ is the signal-to-noise ratio between the user device u, $u \in \mathcal{U}$, inside the radius the actions of the drone $d, d = 1, ... N_d$, a $\overline{\gamma}$ is the given threshold of the signal-to-noise ratio, which guarantees the quality of the received signal. Since we consider the ideal conditions of a radio transmission channel, the power of the signal received by the user device is modeled using the Friis transmission formula [3].

The modeling task is improving quality of services by increasing the coverage probability. In our system model the probability of coverage depends on the positioning of the UAV, so we analyze and compare UAV adaptive navigation methods to serve users of a wireless network, taking into account both the mobility of groups of people and the mobility of access points. We developed a simulation with the visualization module under the assumption of considered system case. The model takes into account ideal conditions for signal propagation, namely the absence of large-sized obstacles (buildings, trees, power transmission towers) and adverse weather conditions, such as wind and rainfall.

3   UAVs Adaptive Navigation

In our work, we consider two methods of drone navigation: Particle Swarm Optimization (PSO) and K-means. Both of these methods are aimed at maximizing the number of users in the coverage area. The choice of these navigation methods is due to their flexibility and universality. The PSO method is quite accurate and has a wide scope of applications. It determines optimal position for drones (i.e., the location at which the maximum possible number of users are in the coverage area) and relocates them into it. The K-means method is similar to PSO, but it has a special feature: it takes into account the location of other drones during arrangement, and therefore eliminates the mutual signal interference of two drones.

3.1 PSO Navigation Method

According to the Particle Swarm Optimization (PSO) method [10], the drone movement obeys the principle of the best found position in the air from the coverage probability point of view, which changes when users move at a given velocity. Let $F(d) = F(x_d, y_d) = \sum_{u \in \mathcal{U}'} 1(r_{(d,u)} \leq R_d)$ be the function of the number of users $u \in \mathcal{U}'$ located in a cell created by the drone d, where the projection of the drone onto the surface has the coordinates (x_d, y_d). Then, to ensure a new arrangement of one drone by the PSO method, it is necessary to find the center coordinates that satisfy the solution of the following maximization problem:

$$(x_d, y_d) \rightarrow \max_{u \in \mathcal{U}'} F(d) \tag{2}$$

In the case of several UAVs, the solution of problem (2) is carried out among users of the subset $\mathcal{U}'' = \mathcal{U} \setminus \mathcal{U}'$, excluding the users, who were served within the first iteration of the algorithm.

Further, in the simulation area, the number of particles N_p is randomly generated for each of the N_d drones, with coordinates $(x_d^p, y_d^p), d = \overline{1, N_d}$, as well as direction vectors (x_d^v, y_d^v). Each particle also has its own parameter p_{best}, which determines the optimal position of this particle, and the general parameter d_{best} - the optimal global position among all particles. When moving particles at each step of the simulated time, it is recorded in which position they maximize the function $F(d)$. A particle having the most optimal position among all the optimal solutions of other particles is defined as the optimal global solution. In this case, the particles move at each step i of the simulated time according to the following rule:

$$x(i+1) = wx(i) + c_1(d_{best} - x_d^v) + c_2(s_{best} - x_d^v), \tag{3}$$

$$y(i+1) = wy(i) + c_1(d_{best} - y_d^v) + c_2(s_{best} - y_d^v), \tag{4}$$

where $w = 0.5$ is a constant, and c_1, c_2 are random variables having a uniform distribution on the interval $(0; 0.5)$. These parameters play the role of weighting coefficients and allow to adjust the selection of a new particle motion vector. So, for example, if $c_1 = 0$, and $c_2 = 0.5$, then the particle moves towards the best global solution s_{best}.

3.2 Navigation Method of K-Means

The choice of the k-means method [5] is associated with the ability to most effectively reduce the inter-cell interference (ICI) by users, respectively, to increase the parameter of the useful SNR signal based on the algorithm's ability to split the modeling region into non-intersecting clusters, determined by the total number of users and the number of user groups. We assume that the target number of clusters coincides with the number of UAVs.

Initially, users in the simulated area are divided into the number of clusters not exceeding N_d. This happens as follows: N_d points of the plane, indicating the projection of the UAV on the plane, are randomly placed in the area. Further drone movement depends on setting the interval t_{upd}, for which re-application of the clustering algorithm is required, as well as on changing the position of the user group for a given period of time. Those users who have the shortest distance to the center of the UAV under consideration fall into the UAV coverage area (or in the corresponding cluster). The next step is to construct the Voronoi diagram [8] using the obtained coordinates—the centers of the clusters. As a result of the algorithm, the region is divided into several subdomains, in each of which the UAV is most efficiently located. Since the UAV coverage area is approximated by a circle, the task is to place the circle inside the polygon, covering the maximum number of users. When crossing the circumference of the boundaries of a subdomain, its diameter can be reduced (technically this is realized by reducing the antenna power installed on the UAV). Figure 2 shows the difference of the presented methods in the arrangement of 3 drones in a region of size 100×100 m^2 at different moments of modeling.

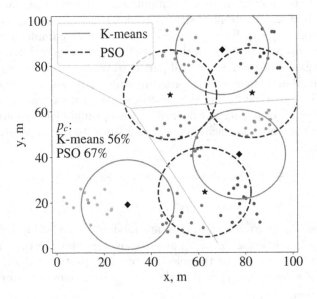

Fig. 2. 2-D projection of drone locations onto the ground. Area size here 100×100 m^2. Other parameters are set to 100 users, 7 groups, 3 drones.

4   Numerical Analysis

We use the physical parameter of the channel and devices from [16] to estimate radius of UAV's small cells by putting this characteristics in the Friis formula. The simulation parameters for mobility models and simulator settings are presented in Table 1. To compare the methods, at the beginning of the simulation we locate $N_U = 100$ users through the area size 100×100 m^2 similarly, but during the simulation time of one experiment, which is 300 s, their location changes randomly according the reference model. To find the coverage probability we collect the metrics (1) after each experiment and divide the sum of probabilities on the total number of experiments. As we already mentioned, due to the random movement of user groups, there is no way to compare drone navigation at any given time. To increase the objectiveness, 100 different experiments were carried out and the final average probability is estimated for each method. The advantage of this simulator is visualization and the ability to view how the position of users and UAVs changes in real time and the effect on the probability of coverage. Figure 3 shows the coverage probability through averaging 100 experiments. We set user velocity $v_U = 0.5$ m/s, implying the scenario in which people leisurely walk, for example, after festival ending.

Table 1. Simulation parameters.

Notation	Value	Description
N_G	5	Number of user groups
N_D	3	Number of UAVs
h_D	20 m	UAV altitude
h_U	2 m	Users altitude
v_D	5 m/s	UAV velocity
v_U	0.5, 1.4 m/s	Users velocity
$\bar{\gamma}$	20 dB	SNR threshold
t_{upd}	5 s	UAV adaptive time slot

Then we considered the case when users move faster, for example, if the concert begins in a few minutes. Thus, we change only users velocity v_U by increasing its value from 0.5 m/s to 1.4 m/s (see Fig. 4). It is observed that plots behave different than in Fig. 3, due to time update interval of the algorithms. It means, when drones are in their positions and waiting for new coordinates to be calculated, users move faster and come out of the coverage area. To improve the coverage probability in that case, drones move to their new positions faster. It can be established by changing t_{upd} value, which determines the interval of applying PSO and k-means algorithm. By changing $t_{upd} = 1$ s, we manage to improve coverage probability, as shown on Fig. 5 for PSO algorithm, and Fig. 6 for k-means algorithm.

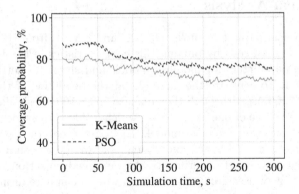

Fig. 3. Average coverage probability through simulations. Users velocity $v_U = 0.5$ m/s.

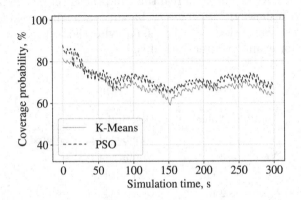

Fig. 4. Average coverage probability through simulations. Users velocity $v_U = 1.4$ m/s.

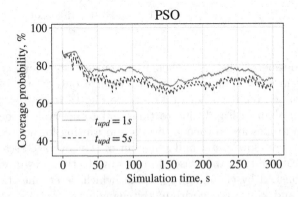

Fig. 5. Average coverage probability for PSO model for different t_{upd} intervals.

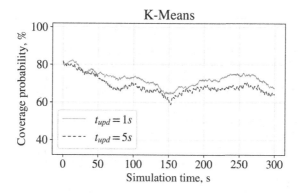

Fig. 6. Average coverage probability for k-means model for different t_{upd} intervals.

5 Conclusions

In this article, we considered two drone navigation methods such as PSO and k-means. We analyzed the dependence of coverage probability on the velocity and time update parameter, and found that with increasing user velocity, the coverage probability becomes lower. The solution of this behaviour requires increasing of drones navigation algorithm frequency of updates. Indeed, by decreasing the parameter t_{upd}, we improved the coverage probability for both models by 3–10%. However, by increasing t_{upd} parameter we also increase computation difficulty and energy inefficiency, which becomes a subject of our future studies.

References

1. 3GPP Study on New Radio (NR) to Support Non Terrestrial Networks. Technical Report 38.811 v15.0.0. Accessed 25 Aug 2019
2. Borodakiy, V., Samouylov, K., Gudkova, I., Markova, E.: Analyzing mean bit rate of multicast video conference in LTE network with adaptive radio admission control scheme. J. Math. Sci. **218**(3), 257–268 (2016)
3. Friis, H.T.: A note on a simple transmission formula. In: Proceedings of the IRE, pp. 254–256. IEEE (1946)
4. Guillen-Perez, A., Sanchez-Iborra, R., Sanchez-Aarnoutse, J., Cano, M.-D., Garcia-Haro, J.: WiFi networks on drones. In: 2016 ITU Kaleidoscope: ICTs for a Sustainable World (ITU WT), pp. 183–190. (2016). https://doi.org/10.1109/ITU-WT.2016.7805730
5. Hartigan, J.A., Wong, M.A.: Algorithm AS 136: a k-means clustering algorithm. J. Royal Stat. Soc. Ser. C. **28**(1), 100–108 (1979)
6. Mozaffari, M., Saad, W., Bennis, M., Debbah, M.: Communications and control for wireless drone-based antenna array. IEEE Trans. Commun. **67**(1), 820–834 (2017). https://doi.org/10.1109/TCOMM.2018.2871453
7. Nain, P., Towsley, D., Liu, B., Liu, Z.: Properties of random direction models. In: Proceedings IEEE 24th Annual Joint Conference of the IEEE Computer and Communications Societies, vol. 3, pp. 1897–1907. IEEE, Miami, FL (2005). https://doi.org/10.1109/INFCOM.2005.1498468

8. Naumov, V., Samouylov, K.: Analysis of multi-resource loss system with state-dependent arrival and service rates. Probab. Eng. Inf. Sci. **31**(4), 413–419 (2017)

9. Kalantari, E., Bor-Yaliniz, I., Yongacoglu, A., Yanikomeroglu, H.: User association and bandwidth allocation for terrestrial and aerial base stations with backhaul considerations. In: IEEE 28th Annual International Symposium on Personal, Indoor, and Mobile Radio Communications (PIMRC), pp. 1–6 (2017)

10. Chopard, B., Tomassini, M.: Particle Swarm Optimization. NCS, pp. 97–102. Springer, Cham (2018). https://doi.org/10.1007/978-3-319-93073-2_6

11. Kumar, D., Srivastava, A., Gupta, S.: Routing in ad hoc networks under reference point group mobility. In: Proceedings - UKSim-AMSS 7th European Modelling Symposium on Computer Modelling and Simulation, pp. 595–598. IEEE (2013). https://doi.org/10.1109/EMS.2013.99

12. Preparata, F., Shamos, M.: Computational Geometry: An Introduction. Springer, Heidelberg (1985)

13. Amer, R., Saad, W., Marchetti, N.: Mobility in the sky: performance and mobility analysis for cellular-connected UAVs. IEEE Trans. Commun. **68**(5), 3229–3246 (2020)

14. Schmidt, A.: Random Walks: The Mathematics in 1 Dimension. https://www.mit.edu/kardar/teaching/projects/chemotaxis(AndreaSchmidt)/random.htm. Accessed 4 Mar 2020

15. Sun, J., Masouros, C.: Deployment strategies of multiple aerial BSs for user coverage and power efficiency maximization. IEEE Trans. Commun. **67**(4), 2981–2994 (2019)

16. Tafintsev, N., et al.: Improved network coverage with adaptive navigation of mmWave-based drone-cells. In: 2018 IEEE Globecom Workshops (GC Wkshps), pp. 1–7. IEEE, Abu Dhabi, United Arab Emirates (2018)

17. Xu, D., Tian., Y.: A comprehensive survey of clustering algorithms. Ann. Data Sci. **2**(2), 165–193 (2015)

18. Zeng, Y., Zhang, R., Lim, T.: Wireless communications with unmanned aerial vehicles: opportunities and challenges. IEEE Commun. Mag. **54**(5), 36–42 (2016)

19. Solomitckii, D., Gapeyenko, M., Semkin, V., Andreev, S., Koucheryavy, Y.: Technologies for efficient amateur drone detection in 5G millimeter-wave cellular infrastructure. IEEE Commun. Mag. **56**(1), 8255736, 43–50 (2018)

20. Pyattaev, A., Johnsson, K., Surak, A., Florea, R., Andreev, S., Koucheryavy, Y.: Network-assisted D2D communications: implementing a technology prototype for cellular traffic offloading. In: IEEE Wireless Communications and Networking Conference, WCNC. art. no. 6953070, pp. 3266–3271 (2014)

21. Ometov, A., et al.: Toward trusted, social-aware D2D connectivity: Bridging across the technology and sociality realms. IEEE Wireless Commun. **23**(4), 7553033, 103–111 (2016)

22. Zhang, L., Zhao, H., Hou, S., Zhao, Z., Xu, H., Wu, X.: A survey on 5G millimeter wave communications for UAV-assisted wireless networks. IEEE Access **7**, 117460–117504 (2019)

23. Chen, M., Mozaffari, M., Saad, W., Yin, C., Debbah, M., Hong, C.S.: Caching in the sky: proactive deployment of cache-enabled unmanned aerial vehicles for optimized quality-of-experience. IEEE J. Sel. Areas Commun. **35**(5), 10461–1061 (2017)

24. Gapeyenko, M., Bor-Yaliniz, I., Andreev, S., Yanikomeroglu, H., Koucheryavy, Y.: Effects of blockage in deploying mmWave drone base stations for 5G networks and beyond. In: Proceedings IEEE International Conference Computer Workshops (ICC Workshops), pp. 1–6. Kansas City, MO, USA (2018)
25. Ghazzai, H., Ghorbel, M.B., Kassler, A., Hossain, M.J.: Trajectory optimization for cooperative dual-band UAV swarms. In: Proceedings IEEE Global Communications Conference (GLOBECOM), pp. 1–7. IEEE, Abu Dhabi, United Arab Emirates (2018)
26. Wu, H., Tao, X., Zhang, N., Shen, X.: Cooperative UAV cluster-assisted terrestrial cellular networks for ubiquitous coverage. IEEE J. Sel. Areas Commun. **36**(9), 20452058 (2018)

Service-Based EMF Monitoring in EMF RATEL System

Nikola Djuric[1]([✉]), Nikola Kavecan[2], Nenad Radosavljevic[3], and Snezana Djuric[4]

[1] Faculty of Technical Sciences, University of Novi Sad, D. Obradovica 6, Novi Sad, Serbia
ndjuric@uns.ac.rs
[2] Falcon-Tech, IT Consulting and Development, Brace Ribnikara 59, Novi Sad, Serbia
[3] Regulatory Agency for Electronic Communications and Postal Services (RATEL),
Palmoticeva 2, Belgrade, Serbia
[4] Institute BioSens, University of Novi Sad, Dr Zorana Djindjica 1, Novi Sad, Serbia

Abstract. The telecommunication services rely on transmission of electromagnetic waves, increasing strength of electromagnetic field (EMF) in the environment, as well as corresponding human exposure to EMF. Thus, such inevitable exposure and their potentially unhealthy effects have been in focus of the general population concerns, requesting and initiating development of systems for daily and continuous EMF monitoring, such is the recently launched, the Serbian EMF RATEL system. This system has been established on spatially distributed wireless monitoring stations/sensors, performing long-term EMF observation over the Republic of Serbia territory, in order to timely inform the Serbian public on present level of EMF and associated exposure. The EMF RATEL system, as the world newest monitoring system, brings a feature of monitoring the EMF contribution from telecommunication services, in several predefined frequency sub-bands. Such service-based monitoring approach, some technical details and analysis/dissemination of measurement results will be presented in this paper, in order to highlight capability of EMF RATEL in prevention, protection and management of EMFs, particularly in the Republic of Serbia.

Keywords: EMF monitoring · Non-ionizing radiation · Wireless sensors network

1 Introduction

The artificially produced electromagnetic fields (EMF) have been extensively used in numerous telecommunication technologies, intensifying their spatial distribution over the wide territory. Accordingly, the daily exposure of humans to EMF become almost unavoidable, triggering deep public concerns [1].

Nowadays, the population works and lives in extensive EMF ecosystem, where it is burdened by the fact that it is exposed to EMF [2], unfortunately, in any daily visited microenvironment [3]. Thus, there are strong and widespread demands for continuous

© Springer Nature Switzerland AG 2020
O. Galinina et al. (Eds.): NEW2AN 2020/ruSMART 2020, LNCS 12526, pp. 426–438, 2020.
https://doi.org/10.1007/978-3-030-65729-1_38

observation and comprehensive investigation of EMF, and more importantly, conclusive scientific evidence/explanation of the EMF influence on health are expected [4].

Consequently, the EMF monitoring campaigns have been widely performed, covering most sensitive parts of the human society [5–7] and considering EMF in various indoor [8] and outdoor surroundings.

Regarding the outdoor environment and established ICNIRP "*Guidelines for limiting exposure to time-varying electric, magnetic, and electromagnetic fields (up to 300 GHz)*" [9], in last decade, the wireless EMF monitoring networks appears as an innovative approach for effective EMF investigation in environment [10–12].

Among those networks, the latest one is the state-of-the-art Serbian EMF RATEL monitoring network [13], which is launched in 2017, by Regulatory Agency for Electronic Communications and Postal Services (RATEL) of the Republic of Serbia.

The concept of EMF RATEL monitoring network is presented in Fig. 1.

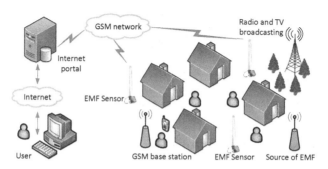

Fig. 1. The concept of EMF RATEL monitoring network.

The EMF RATEL system uses autonomous, wireless monitoring stations (sensors), spatially distributed over the territory of the Republic of Serbia, as shown in Fig. 2.

Monitoring stations are installed in zones of high sensitivity and/or zones of special interest, joined in a unified wireless sensors network. Currently, fifty-one sensors are operable in major Serbian cities, daily performing continuous EMF monitoring [13]. The goal is to reach one hundred installed sensors till 2021.

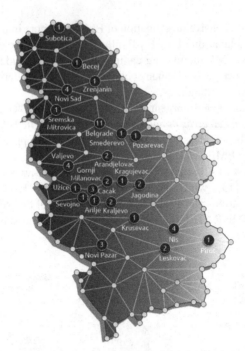

Fig. 2. Current distribution of EMF monitoring sensors over the Republic of Serbia territory.

2 Service-Based EMF Monitoring

The EMF RATEL network is designed as a heterogeneous sensors environment [14], where Narda AMS 8061 monitoring sensor [15], is used for innovative, service-based EMF monitoring. The station hardware and main features are presented in Fig. 3.

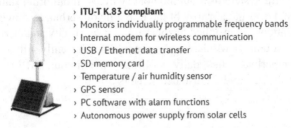

Fig. 3. The Narda AMS 8061 monitoring sensor [15].

This sensor covers frequency range of 100 kHz–6 GHz, supporting simultaneous monitoring in up to twenty programmable frequency sub-bands, within this wide frequency range [15]. Currently, the EMF RATEL performs service-based monitoring in frequency sub-bands presented in Table 1.

Table 1. The EMF RATEL monitored frequency sub-bands.

No.	Frequency sub-band	Telecommunication service
1.	87 MHz–108 MHz	FM radio
2.	430 MHz–470 MHz	Functional radio links
3.	470 MHz–790 MHz	Digital TV (DVB-T2)
4.	790 MHz–821 MHz	Mobile 4G DL
5.	832 MHz–862 MHz	Mobile 4G UL
6.	880 MHz–915 MHz	Mobile 2G/3G UL
7.	925 MHz–960 MHz	Mobile 2G/3G DL
8.	1710 MHz–1780 MHz	Mobile 2G/4G UL
9.	1800 MHz–1880 MHz	Mobile 2G/3G DL
10.	2110 MHz–2170 MHz	Mobile 3G DL
11.	2400 MHz–2500 MHz	WiFi
12.	2520 MHz–2660 MHz	Mobile 4G–NSA 5G UL/DL
13.	3400 MHz–3800 MHz	Mobile 5G DL/UL
14.	5200 MHz–5800 MHz	WiFi

Regarding some specific requirement, the other sub-bands can be selected and programed. However, in all sub-bands, the Narda AMS 8061 perform wideband monitoring, observing contribution of all active EMF sources, which radiate in particular sub-band, in vicinity of this EMF monitoring sensor.

The Narda AMS 8061 sensor is not capable to distinguish the separate contribution of individual EMF sources. Instead, it performs monitoring of cumulative EMF level, i.e. joint contribution of all EMF sources in selected frequency sub-band. Such feature is an imperative, since EMF contribution of telecommunication service can be determined, as an important input parameter for decision makers, responsible for process of environment protection, regarding EMF radiation and related EMF exposure.

3 AMS 8061 Data Transfer in EMF RATEL System

The EMF monitoring sensors are equipped with GSM modem [15], allowing Internet connection over existing mobile telephony network. The measurement results, stored in internal memory of sensor, are wirelessly acquired and transferred to EMF RATEL centralized database [14], as depicted in Fig. 4.

The Narda AMS 8061 sensor communicate with dedicated FTP server, which performs as a centralized data storage hub for EMF RATEL sensors. The measurement results are packed into the ".D61" binary file and transferred with some other data to the FTP personal folder of sensor, shown in Fig. 5.

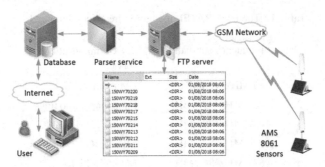

Fig. 4. The AMS 8061 data transfer in EMF RATEL system.

Name	Ext	Size	↓Date
↩..		<DIR>	01/01/1601 01:00 ⌃
BK_D61		<DIR>	01/13/2020 10:00
BK_TXT		<DIR>	01/13/2020 08:00
08_00_03_05_20_	D61	83	05/04/2020 06:00
08_00_03_05_20_	TXT	1	05/04/2020 06:00
8061	CFG	0	05/04/2020 06:00
8061	set	1	05/04/2020 06:00
8061FLD	TXT	1	05/04/2020 06:00
08_00_02_05_20_	D61	83	05/03/2020 06:00
08_00_02_05_20_	TXT	1	05/03/2020 06:00
08_00_01_05_20_	D61	83	05/02/2020 06:00
08_00_01_05_20_	TXT	1	05/02/2020 06:00

Fig. 5. The content example of a Narda AMS 8061 sensor folder on FTP server [14].

Each file in this folder has unique and important role for Narda AMS 8061 station, enabling its proper work. The details can be found in [15].

3.1   The ".D61" Measurement Data File

Regarding all files in sensor FTP personal folder, the ".D61" file can be considered as most important, since it contain measurement data and accompanying events, which are acquired by sensor during continuous EMF monitoring on particular spot.

The AMS 8061 sensor saves its measurement data in format of ".D61" binary file, presented in Fig. 6 [15, 16].

This format is for one record/measurement. However, depending on logging period and sensors scheduled time for sending data to the FTP server, in a single ".D61" file, there can be a number of such records. For example, if sensor performs logging every six minutes, as requested by SRPS EN 50413:2010/A1:2014 standard [17], and sends its data once per day than the ".D61" file will contain two hundred and forty records.

The one measurement result is recoded in format of sixteen bytes, presented in Fig. 7 [15, 16].

Regarding the number of frequency sub-bands, noted as *Number of Bands* (NOB), additional packets of sixteen bytes will follow the first one [15, 16]. In this sixteen-bytes packet format, the sub-band range frequencies are recorded also, as well as Peak and AVG/RMS measured values [15, 16].

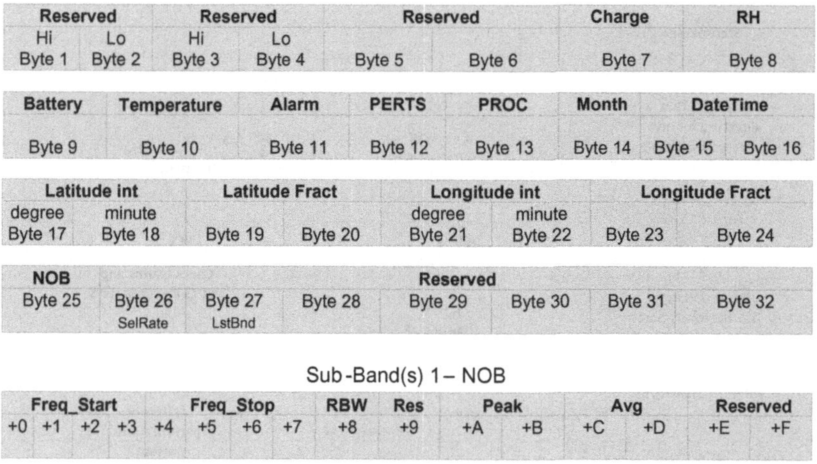

Reserved		Reserved		Reserved		Charge	RH
Hi	Lo	Hi	Lo				
Byte 1	Byte 2	Byte 3	Byte 4	Byte 5	Byte 6	Byte 7	Byte 8

Battery	Temperature		Alarm	PERTS	PROC	Month	DateTime	
Byte 9	Byte 10		Byte 11	Byte 12	Byte 13	Byte 14	Byte 15	Byte 16

Latitude int		Latitude Fract		Longitude int		Longitude Fract	
degree	minute			degree	minute		
Byte 17	Byte 18	Byte 19	Byte 20	Byte 21	Byte 22	Byte 23	Byte 24

NOB				Reserved			
Byte 25	Byte 26	Byte 27	Byte 28	Byte 29	Byte 30	Byte 31	Byte 32
	SelRate	LstBnd					

Sub-Band(s) 1 – NOB

Freq_Start					Freq_Stop			RBW	Res	Peak		Avg		Reserved	
+0	+1	+2	+3	+4	+5	+6	+7	+8	+9	+A	+B	+C	+D	+E	+F

Fig. 6. The ".D61" file format [15, 16].

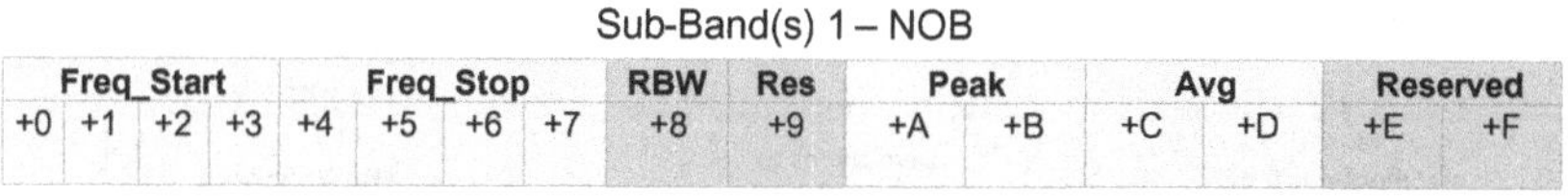

Sub-Band(s) 1 – NOB

Freq_Start					Freq_Stop			RBW	Res	Peak		Avg		Reserved	
+0	+1	+2	+3	+4	+5	+6	+7	+8	+9	+A	+B	+C	+D	+E	+F

Fig. 7. The ".D61" format for one measurement result [15, 16].

3.2 Parser Function for ".D61" Data Files

The ".D61" parser function works on FTP directories, handling ".D61" files, extracting data and storing them into centralized database. At the end, the parser marks processed ".D61" files and returns control for the next FTP directory processing [16].

Regarding EMF RATEL system, each field probe of monitoring sensor [15] has its own parser function, allowing fast adaptation of the management system to the newly used filed probe. Regarding the EHA-2B-01 field probe, used in EMF RATEL AMS 8061 monitoring sensor [15], the parser function follows diagram presented in Fig. 8.

The parser is designed to process ".D61" file by file, extracting data from all records and saving them into appropriate database tables. In case that data saving is not possible for several times, the parser sends urgent error notification to system administrator and aborts its work on particular directory. Later, the control is returned to the top-level puller service, which continue to process the next available sensor directory on FTP server [16].

When saving is successful, the parser marks ".D61" as a parsed one and continue with checking if some alarms or PERTs are present in stored data [16]. If there is any of those events, the report is sent to the system administrator, after which parser finish his work and returns control to the top-level puller service [16].

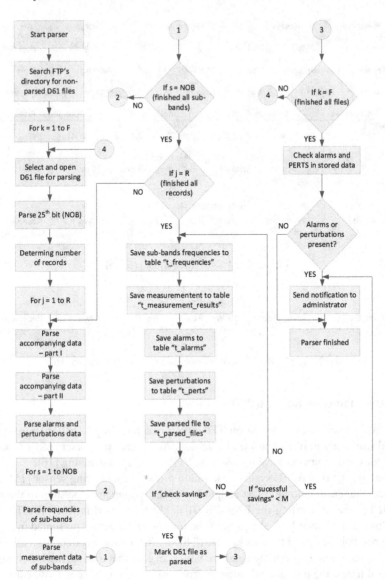

Fig. 8. The flow diagram of the parser function for EHA-2B-01 field probe ".D61" file [16].

3.3 Database Model for AMS 8061 Sensor

Dedicated database model was developed for Narda AMS 8061 sensors, where measurement and accompanying data are stored in tables presented in Fig. 9.

The model reflects the fact that every measurement result is followed by additional information, such as alarms and PERTs [15]. Thus, the "*t_measurement_data*" table is connected with "*t_alarms*" and "*t_perts*", by "*1:1*" relationship, noticing that each measurement result has its own set of alarms and PERTs.

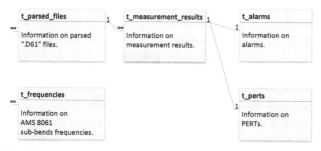

Fig. 9. The EMF RATEL database model for Narda AMS 8061 sensors [16].

Furthermore, only trustworthy information is saved in tables, omitting temperature, humidity and GPS coordinates, since those data are not measured directly with electric field probe dipoles and thus can contain a higher level of uncertainty [6].

The parsed ".D61" files are saved in "*t_parsed_files*" table, which is related to the "*t_measurement_data*" by "*1:∞*" connection, since inside one ".D61" file there can be a number of measurement data records.

Viewing frequency sub-ranges, their start and stop frequencies are saved with each parsed file, for dissemination purposes of measurement results over the EMF RATEL Internet portal [13]. Once pre-arranged sub-bands cannot be changed from record to record, inside the single ".D61" file [15].

At the end, the database hierarchy has been established in a way that each parsed file is saved in central database, regarding security reasons and data recovery. Moreover, all measurement data from specific ".D61" file are connected with its own record in "*t_parsed_files*" table, allowing history tracking and resolving of data belonging.

4   Dissemination of Measurement Results

The EMF RATEL system is intended to transparently and timely inform the public on present EMF levels, using dedicated Internet portal [13], where measurement data are illustrated by time-line graphs, offering the detailed information on EMF fluctuation, as shown in Fig. 10.

User friendly features have been implemented in EMF RATEL Internet portal [13], allowing users to analyze the measurement results per telecommunication service, in selected time period. Regarding convenient work, the users can select/deselect specific service, as shown in Fig. 10.

Besides the sub-band fluctuation, the system can show the lower allowed field limit, regarding the Serbian prescribed field reference values, for the general population [18]. By selecting option "*Show adaptive limit*", it is possible to visualize position of existing EMF levels in relation to the prescribed filed level, as shown in Fig. 11.

However, a number of bonus features can be found on EMF RATEL Internet portal [13], allowing users to work and analyze measurement results, along with saving and printing them for various purpose.

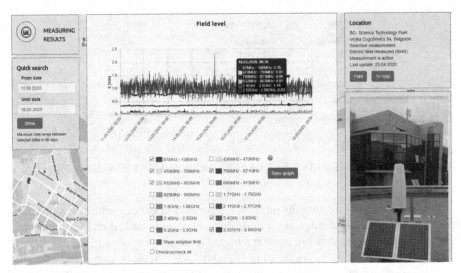

Fig. 10. Dissemination of the service-based EMF RATEL monitoring results.

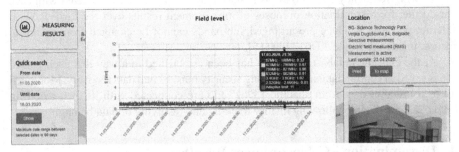

Fig. 11. Comparison of measurement results with most restrictive prescribed reference level.

4.1 Open Data

The EMF RATEL offers acquired measurement results for free use over the national Open Data Portal [19]. The Portal is established on the initiative of the Prime Minister and Office for IT and e-Government of the Republic of Serbia, representing the central hub where data of public interest are gathered, from all Serbian public institutions.

The measurement results are available in machine-readable formats: XML, JSON and CSV [20], as shown in Fig. 12.

In those files, the measurement data are formatted for easy processing, as shown in Fig. 13.

Through this approach, the users can incorporate and process the EMF data in their own research, using various software packages for data processing.

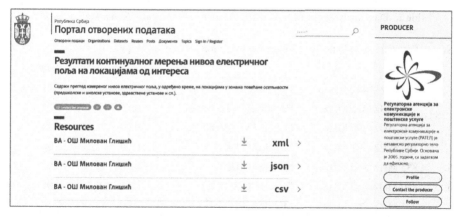

Fig. 12. Part of the Serbian Open Data Portal with results of EMF monitoring.

Location:	BG- Science Technology Park
Address:	Veljka Dugoševića 54
GPS position:	20.50890000, 44.80330000
Sensor type:	Selective measurement
Measurement:	Electric field measured (RMS)
Unit	V/m
Active	Yes

Data and time	87 - 108 MHz	430 - 470 MHz	470 - 790 MHz	790 - 821 MHz	832 - 862 MHz	880 - 915 MHz	925 - 960 MHz	1710 - 1780 MHz	1800 - 1880 MHz	2110 - 2170 MHz
11/3/2019 0:00	0.17	0.02	0.08	0.07	0.01	0.01	0.1	0.01	1.02	0.57
11/3/2019 0:06	0.17	0.02	0.08	0.07	0.01	0.01	0.09	0.01	0.93	0.57
11/3/2019 0:12	0.17	0.02	0.08	0.07	0.01	0.01	0.09	0.01	0.93	0.56
11/3/2019 0:18	0.17	0.02	0.08	0.07	0.01	0.01	0.09	0.01	0.95	0.55
11/3/2019 0:24	0.17	0.02	0.08	0.06	0.01	0.01	0.08	0.01	0.93	0.56
11/3/2019 0:30	0.17	0.02	0.08	0.06	0.01	0.01	0.08	0.01	0.93	0.56
11/3/2019 0:36	0.17	0.02	0.08	0.06	0.01	0.01	0.09	0.01	0.98	0.57
11/3/2019 0:42	0.17	0.02	0.08	0.07	0.01	0.01	0.09	0.01	0.92	0.55
11/3/2019 0:48	0.17	0.02	0.08	0.07	0.01	0.01	0.08	0.01	0.92	0.55
11/3/2019 0:54	0.17	0.02	0.08	0.12	0.01	0.01	0.1	0.01	0.92	0.56
11/3/2019 1:00	0.17	0.02	0.08	0.06	0.01	0.01	0.09	0.01	0.94	0.56

Fig. 13. Data formatting of service-based EMF monitoring results.

4.2 Data Analyses

One of the EMF RATEL AMS 8061 sensors is installed on the Science Technological Park building, as shown in Fig. 10, where it performs monitoring of the electric field strength, every six minutes, as it is required by SRPS EN 50413:2010/A1:2014 standard [17]. The simple analyses of the measurement results is presented in Table 2.

The table shows minimal and maximal detected values per service, as well as more importantly, the average electric filed value, for overall period of monitoring. Those average values reveal that on *"BG – Science Technological Park"* location, the mobile telephony services dominate, as presented in Fig. 14.

However, for the mobile telephony services, the most restrictive Serbian prescribed and allowed electric field reference level is 15.46 *V/m* [17], which is far above of the existing average filed level of any mobile service. This means that this location can be considered as a location with low level of the high frequency electric field, as well as a low EMF exposed location.

Table 2. Data analyses for EMF RATEL location *"BG–Science Technological Park"*.

No.	Frequency sub-band	Telecommunication service	E [V/m]		
			Min	Max	Average
1.	87 MHz–108 MHz	FM radio	0.00	1.65	0.21
2.	430 MHz–470 MHz	Functional radio links	0.00	0.61	0.02
3.	470 MHz–790 MHz	Digital TV (DVB-T2)	0.00	1.45	0.08
4.	790 MHz–821 MHz	Mobile 4G DL	0.00	2.24	0.06
5.	832 MHz–862 MHz	Mobile 4G UL	0.00	0.08	0.01
6.	880 MHz–915 MHz	Mobile 2G/3G UL	0.00	0.10	0.01
7.	925 MHz–960 MHz	Mobile 2G/3G DL	0.00	0.18	0.10
8.	1710 MHz–1780 MHz	Mobile 2G/4G UL	0.00	0.20	0.01
9.	1800 MHz–1880 MHz	Mobile 2G/3G DL	0.00	4.93	1.07
10.	2110 MHz–2170 MHz	Mobile 3G DL	0.00	2.00	1.01
11.	2400 MHz–2500 MHz	WiFi	0.00	0.21	0.02
12.	2520 MHz–2660 MHz	Mobile 4G–NSA 5G UL/DL	0.00	3.28	0.95
13.	3400 MHz–3800 MHz	Mobile 5G DL/UL	0.00	4.48	0.97
14.	5200 MHz–5800 MHz	WiFi	0.00	0.72	0.45

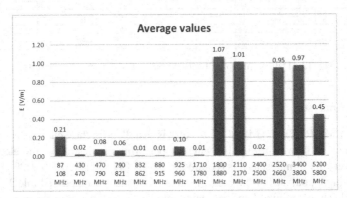

Fig. 14. Averaged field values for location *"BG – Science Technological Park"*.

5   Conclusion

The EMF RATEL monitoring network and its public Internet portal are 24/7 active, timely and transparently informing population on present EMF levels in environment, which is of the wide community interest.

This system is designed as a wireless EMF monitoring network, covering the territory of the Republic of Serbia and it is intended to be a valuable support for the Serbian Government efforts to accomplish systematic EMF monitoring in the environment.

Furthermore, it is anticipated to support EMF prevention, control and management, mostly in upcoming smart-cities ecosystems with intensive EMF radiation in people's living/working surrounding, regarding various telecommunication services.

Also, the EMF RATEL feature of the service-based EMF monitoring will help to clarify doubts on EMF contribution of any particular service, while providing valid technical information in public debate on potential EMF exposure influence on health.

Finally, this system and such feature can serve as a mediator between general population requests for the safe EMF environment and commercial operators that require installation of new EMF sources, in order to improve their service covering.

Acknowledgement. This paper has been supported by the Ministry of Education, Science and Technological Development of the Republic of Serbia, through the project no. 451-03-68/2020-14/200156 – "Innovative scientific and artistic research from the FTS domain".

References

1. Special Eurobarometer 347, "Electromagnetic Fields" (2014). https://data.europa.eu/euodp/en/da-ta/dataset/S843_73_3_EBS347. Accessed 04 May 2020
2. Gajšek, P., Ravazzani, P., Wiart, J., Grellier, J., Samaras, T., Thuróczy, G.: Electromagnetic field exposure assessment in Europe radiofrequency fields (10 MHz–6 GHz). J. Exposure Sci. Environ. Epidemiol. **25**, 37–44 (2015)
3. Sagar, S., et al.: Radiofrequency electromagnetic field exposure in everyday microenvironments in Europe: a systematic literature review. J. Exposure Sci. Environ. Epidemiol. **28**, 147–160 (2018)
4. "Final opinion on potential health effects of exposure to electromagnetic fields (EMF)", Scientific Committee on Emerging and Newly Identified Health Risks – SCENIRH (2015). http://www.ec.europa.eu/health/scientific_committees/emerging/docs/scenihr_o_041.pdf. Accessed 04 May 2020
5. Bhatt, C.R., Redmayne, M., Billah, B., Abramson, M.J., Benke, G.: Radiofrequency-electromagnetic field exposures in kindergarten children. J. Exposure Sci. Environ. Epidemiol. **27**, 497–504 (2017)
6. Kurnaz, C., Engiz, B.K., Bozkurt, M.C.: Measurement and evaluation of electric field strength levels in primary and secondary schools in a pilot region. Radiat. Prot. Dosimetry. **179**(3), 282–290 (2018)
7. Kljajic, D., Djuric, N., Kasas-Lazetic, K.: Comparative EMF monitoring campaign over the campus area of the University of Novi Sad. In: 18th IEEE International Conference on Smart Technologies – EUROCON 2019, July 01–04, 2019, Novi Sad, Serbia, pp. 1–4 (2019)
8. Chiaramello, E., Bonato, M., Fiocchi, S., Tognola, G., Parazzini, M., Ravazzani, P., Wiart, J.: Radio frequency electromagnetic fields exposure assessment in indoor environments: a review. Int. J. Environ. Res. Public Health **16**(6), 955–983 (2019)
9. "Guidelines for limiting exposure to time-varying electric, magnetic, and electromagnetic fields (up to 300 GHz)", International Commission on Non-Ionizing Radiation Protection - ICNIRP (1998). https://www.icnirp.org/cms/upload/publications/ICNIRPemfgdl.pdf. Accessed 04 May 2020
10. Lunca, E., Salceanu, A.: An overview of RF-EMF monitoring systems and associated monitoring data. In: 2016 International Conference and Exposition on Electrical and Power Engineering – EPE 2016, 20–22 October 2016, Lasi, Romania, pp. 418–421 (2016)

11. ITU-T "Monitoring of electromagnetic field levels in Latin America Implementation of Recommendation ITU-T K.83" (2020). https://www.itu.int/dms_pub/itu-t/oth/0b/11/T0B110 000-283301PDFE.pdf. Accessed 04 May 2020
12. Djuric, N., Kavecan, N., Mitic, M., Radosavljevic, N., Boric, A.: The concept review of the EMF RATEL monitoring system. In: 22nd International Microwave and Radar Conference – MIKON 2018, 15–17 May 2018, Poznań, Poland, pp. 1–3 (2018)
13. EMF RATEL Internet portal. http://emf.ratel.rs. Accessed 04 May 2020
14. Djuric, N., Kavecan, N., Kljajic, D., Mijatovic, G., Djuric, S.: Data acquisition in narda's wireless stations based EMF RATEL monitoring network. In: International Conference on Sensing and Instrumentation in IoT Era – ISSI 2019, 29–30 August 2019, Lisbon, Portugal, pp. 1–6 (2019)
15. User's Manual Narda AMB-8061 Area Monitor Selective, 2015. https://www.narda-sts.us/-pdf_files/AMS8061EN-71006-1.22.pdf. Accessed 04 May 2020
16. Djuric, N., Kavecan, N., Mijatovic, G., Kljajic, D., Kasas-Lazetic, K., Djuric, S.: The parser function for D61 files of narda AMS 8061 stations in EMF RATEL monitoring system. In: Fleming, P., Lacquet, B.M., Sanei, S., Deb, K., Jakobsson, A. (eds.) ELECOM 2018. LNEE, vol. 561, pp. 126–136. Springer, Cham (2019). https://doi.org/10.1007/978-3-030-18240-3_12
17. "Basic standard on measurement and calculation procedures for human exposure to electric, magnetic and electromagnetic fields (0 Hz – 300 GHz)", SRPS EN 50413:2010/-A1:2014 (2014)
18. "The rulebook on the limits of exposure to non-ionizing radiation", Official gazette of the Republic of Serbia, no. 104/09, http://www.sepa.gov.rs/download/strano/pravilnik5.pdf. Accessed 04 May 2020
19. The Serbian Open Data Portal. https://data.gov.rs/sr/. Accessed 04 May 2020
20. EMF RATEL measurement data on the National Open Data Portal. https://data.gov.rs/sr/-datasets/rezultati-kontinualnog-merenja-nivoa-elektrichnog-polja-na-lokatsijama-od-inte-resa/. Accessed 04 May 2020

Interaction Between User and UAV with Unreliable Location Information

Gagik Papikyan[1](✉) , Evgeny Mokrov[1] , and Konstantin Samouylov[1,2]

[1] Peoples' Friendship University of Russia (RUDN University), 6 Miklukho-Maklaya Street, Moscow 117198, Russian Federation
{1032172734,mokrov-ev,samuylov-ke}@rudn.ru
[2] Federal Research Center "Computer Science and Control" of the Russian Academy of Sciences, 44-2 Vavilov Street, Moscow 119333, Russian Federation

Abstract. Currently, the demand to the capacity of mobile cellular deployments dictated by modern applications is rising rapidly. This especially holds true for cases where a small area contains great number of users simultaneously like stadium or festival venue. In some of these cases stationary base station can be replaced with timely-deployed UAVs. In this work we consider a scenario of data transmission between a user and UAV. During transmission UAV does not have any information on the user location but has information on its mobility model. Transmitted traffic has certain restrictions on SNR and the main objective is to lower the probability of breaching these restrictions. The current study is a proof of concept for the considered model, aimed to propose and verify the described approach through analysis of the derived results.

Keywords: Signal-to-noise ratio · Mobile base station · Analytical model · Probability density function

1 Introduction

In recent years the idea of using unmanned aerial vehicles (UAV), namely drones, as mobile base stations have become extremely popular. Such development of the industry of UAVs has brought dozens of new scenarios where drones could be used cheaply and efficiently.

The main benefit of UAVs compared to traditional stationary base stations is that it can be deployed on demand and moved to a different location if necessary, making it a flexible solution for sudden bottlenecks. Using UAVs a mobile operator does not have to deploy base stations in areas where traffic rises only occasionally and instead deploy UAVs in these areas as needed, alleviating its expenses.

The publication has been prepared with the support of the "RUDN University Program 5-100" (recipient G. Papikyan). The reported study was funded by RFBR, project numbers 18-00-01555(18-00-01685) (recipient K. Samouylov) and 20-37-70079 (recipient E. Mokrov).

© Springer Nature Switzerland AG 2020
O. Galinina et al. (Eds.): NEW2AN 2020/ruSMART 2020, LNCS 12526, pp. 439–449, 2020.
https://doi.org/10.1007/978-3-030-65729-1_39

However, the utilization of UAVs have several major drawbacks. The main issue is the flight time. The length of autonomous flight of drones is a key factor withholding further development of the area. There is an ongoing research intended to boost battery capacity of drones, as claimed by [11]. The authors of that paper aim to increase the capacity of drone batteries by utilizing lithium-metal battery production technology, replacing the conventional lithium-ion method. Another interesting approach described in [2] is using wireless radio-frequency (RF) power transfer by elaborating upon feasible system parameters and architecture.

Another field of study is inter-drone transmissions as Device-to-Device (D2D) touched upon in papers like [9,10,12], or drone battery efficiency [3,11]. Some papers even focus on modeling movements of UAV groups as a single entity [7]. An ongoing research into new use-cases for UAVs is also conducted by Ericsson in [14].

There are also several papers focusing on LoS and deafness issue, like [5], where a UAV communicates with several users that can block each other in terms of LoS or [6], where authors consider a scenario, where a single UAV, located in an urban area, communicates with a user on the ground, assuming LoS communication is not always possible. In one case authors propose a three-dimensional modelling approach to the deafness problem in case of directional antennas, while in another an approach, based on deep reinforcement learning, is suggested for optimal placement of the UAV. The neural network uses 3D topology map, as well as a map of observed SINR values, and results in four possible actions, making the UAV move in any of fours directions with a constant predefined step size. [8] suggests a UAV trajectory optimisation method, based on solving a convex optimisation problem. Authors focus on utilising mobility of both users and UAVs to maximise the number of served moving users. A traffic-aware adaptive UAV deployment scheme is also proposed in [15], considering a scenario, where drones adapt their positions in a cell relatively to a ground base station, to best serve local hot-spot areas. In the aforementioned work authors consider a situation, where drones have only limited information of real-time user locations in the cell. Authors of [13] focus on fast detection of amateur drones that might be launched from the ground close to drone-free regions of an urban scenario.

In this work we consider a system of a drone, statically located at a certain altitude, and a user, being served by the drone. Random walk is used as user's mobility model [1,4]. The objective being evaluation of the probability of user drop, depending on an Signal to noise ratio(SNR) threshold.

2   A Basic Drone-User Interaction Model

We consider a simple scenario of continuous data transmission between a mobile base station, located on UAV and mobile user. The transmitted data have requirements on SNR that should be complied. Furthermore, in the considered scenario UAV does not have any means to locate user and only has the data of possible user movement model.

Consider a three dimensional euclidean space, where a drone D and a user U are located. The drone is considered to be hovering at a certain altitude h. Let us fix the coordinate grid with drone position at $(0, 0, h)$, so that its position is fixed. Let the user U be initially located directly under the UAV at time $t = 0$. We consider two-dimensional mobility model for user, thus at an arbitrary time t the user is considered to have coordinates $(x(t), y(t), 0)$. Since a user is able to walk not more than a certain distance during a time interval δt, here we consider its coordinates to be random variables $x(t) = \xi(t), y(t) = \eta(t) \sim uniform(a(t), b(t))$. The considered system is depicted on Fig. 1. Further we would use denotations without explicit dependency on t while focusing on system behaviour at a single moment of time.

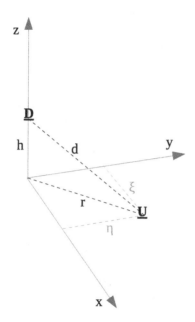

Fig. 1. Mathematical model of drone-user interaction

We consider scenario when drone and user will always have Line of Sight (LoS). This is due to the fact that since base station is located a certain distance from the ground there should not be many obstacles between it and the addressed user. Also, due to the absence of obstacles we can implement Free-Space Path Loss (FSPL) model given in (1) as the default path loss model for the considered model.

$$FSPL(d) = 20 \log_{10} \left(\frac{4\pi\nu d}{c} \right) \qquad (1)$$

Here d is the distance between drone and user position at time t, ν is the data transmission frequency, c is the speed of light, and π is a universal constant. To calculate the FSPL function we need to acquire distance $d(t)$. But first, let's have a look at its projection to the ground plane r. The $CDF(r)$ can be stated as:

$$CDF_r(w) = P\{\sqrt{\xi^2 + \eta^2} < w\} = \int_{-\infty}^{\infty} f_\xi(x) \int_{-\sqrt{w^2-x^2}}^{\sqrt{w^2-x^2}} f_\eta(y)dydx, \quad (2)$$

where $f_\xi(x) = f_\eta(y) = \frac{1}{a+b}$ – PDFs for user coordinates.

The $CDF(d)$ can be stated as:

$$CDF_d(w) = P\{\sqrt{h^2 + x^2 + y^2} < w\} = \int_{-\infty}^{\infty} f_\xi(x) \int_{-\sqrt{w^2-x^2-h^2}}^{\sqrt{w^2-x^2-h^2}} f_\eta(y)dydx,$$
$$(3)$$

where h – drone hovering altitude.

One can notice, that F_d can also be expressed through F_r as

$$CDF_d(w) = \begin{cases} CDF_r(\sqrt{w^2 - h^2}), & w > h \\ 0, & w < h \end{cases} \quad (4)$$

Now that we have d in explicit form and can calculate $FSPL(d)$, we can also write an equation, necessary to obtain $SNR(d)$:

$$SNR(d) = P_t - FSPL(d) - N \quad (5)$$

Here the power of drone's transmitting antenna is denoted as P_t in dB, N is noise, also in dB.

Now we can express $CDF_{SNR}(w)$ like this:

$$CDF_{SNR}(w) = 1 - CDF_d\left(\frac{1}{4\pi\nu d}10^{\frac{P_t-N-w}{20}}\right), \quad (6)$$

It's also possible to consider this model in polar coordinate system. In such a case, an angle ϕ and a radius r will be defining the user's position, and they will also be normally distributed: $PDF_\phi(\psi) = 1/2\pi, PDF_r(w) = 1/R$, where R is the maximum value of r. For this case, distribution functions for distance and its projection would have following form:

$$CDF_r(X_r) = \int_{w<X_r} \int_0^{2\pi} PDF_r(w)PDF_\phi(\psi)dwd\psi = \frac{X_r}{R} \quad (7)$$

$$CDF_d(X_d) = CDF_r\left(\sqrt{X_d^2 - h^2}\right) \quad (8)$$

Now if we consider system dynamic in time, the PDFs of users coordinates can be modified to have an extra parameter t, modeling the time, as was mentioned in the beginning of this section. The idea is that the maximal distance that user can reach increases as time passes. So, for instance, if the considered area is bounded by a square, formed by four points $(-a, -b),(-a, b),(a, -b)$ and (a, b), and if user's speed is given as parameter v units per unit of time, then at time

$t = 0$ units, the user is considered to be right under the drone and nowhere else; at $t = 1$ units, the area where the user can possibly be, is bounded by interval (a', b') on both coordinates, where $a' = \frac{t}{t_{max}} a$, and $b' = \frac{t}{t_{max}} b$. In terms of common sense, if no time passed, user could not change its position, and if only a small fraction of time has passed, the used can not reach the furthest possible point as well. Hence, the corresponding PDFs can be redefined as:

$$PDF_\xi(x,t) = \begin{cases} \frac{t_{max}}{(a+b)t}, & x \in \left[\frac{t}{t_{max}} a, \frac{t}{t_{max}} b\right] \\ 0, & x \notin \left[\frac{t}{t_{max}} a, \frac{t}{t_{max}} b\right] \end{cases} \tag{9}$$

$$PDF_\eta(y,t) = \begin{cases} \frac{t_{max}}{(a+b)t}, & y \in \left[\frac{t}{t_{max}} a, \frac{t}{t_{max}} b\right] \\ 0, & y \notin \left[\frac{t}{t_{max}} a, \frac{t}{t_{max}} b\right] \end{cases} \tag{10}$$

where $t_{max} = \frac{y_{max}}{v}$ in case of 10, and $t_{max} = \frac{x_{max}}{v}$ in case of 9 – is the maximum possible time, in other words, the time, needed for the user to reach the furthest possible point of the considered area, v – user movement speed, x_{max} and y_{max} – maximum coordinates of the user, i.e. the border of the considered area.

In this case the equations for distance and projection CDFs should be modified as follows:

$$CDF_r(w,t) = \int_{-\infty}^{\infty} f_\xi(x,t) \int_{-\sqrt{w^2-x^2}}^{\sqrt{w^2-x^2}} f_\eta(y,t) dy dx \tag{11}$$

$$CDF_d(w,t) = \begin{cases} CDF_r\left(\sqrt{w^2 - h^2}, t\right), & w > h \\ 0, & w < h \end{cases} \tag{12}$$

3   Simulation and Performance Analysis

In this section we present numerical results of both mathematical and simulation model. Initial data of the trials can be seen in Table 1.

Figures 2a and 2b represent plots for CDF_d and CDF_{SNR} are represented for Cartesian coordinate system and Figs. 3a and 3b – for polar coordinate system. For both trials drone was positioned at the coordinate zero-point with altitude h. On Fig. 2a we have considered three cases, where drone is hovering on altitude 25,30 and 100 m. It can be seen that the higher the drone hovers the smaller the considered area becomes. Figure 2b shows F_{snr} for the first of those cases, i.e where drone is hovering at 25 m. The other two cases were omitted, since their behaviour reflects the one of given plot.

In case of radial coordinate system illustrated on 3a – distance CDF and 3b – SNR CDF, the user is moving inside a circle with radius R. Depending on drone's altitude, distance between the user and the drone is either bounded by interval [25, 130] if the drone is hovering on altitude of 25 m, [50,150] when altitude is 50 m, or [100,170] in case of 100 m altitude. One can notice, that the plots on 3a

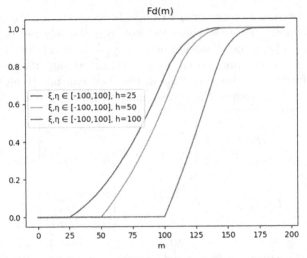

(a) Distance CDF for different drone altitudes

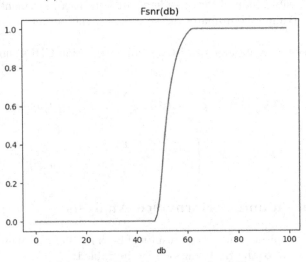

(b) SNR CDF for drone altitude of 25 meters

Fig. 2. Performance metrics for Cartesian system

shift to the right with increasing drone altitude. That can be explained by the fact, that the minimal possible distance is defined by its altitude h, since it is the case where user stands in the closest to drone point on the ground,. i.e. right underneath of drone. According to Figs. 2b and 3b, that SNR for both models belongs to interval [85,110].

It should be noted that both systems exhibit very similar, although not identical behaviour. The similarity is due to the fact that the figures illustrate two approaches of obtaining SNR CDF for the same system. The difference between plots shows space curvature between Cartesian and polar systems.

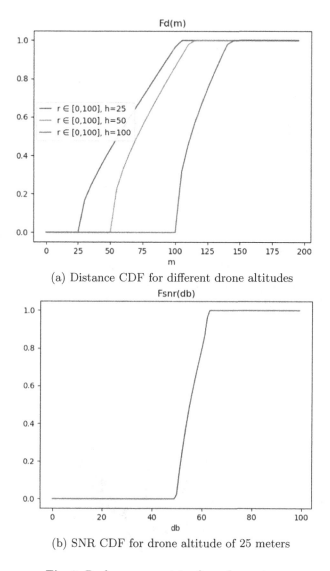

(a) Distance CDF for different drone altitudes

(b) SNR CDF for drone altitude of 25 meters

Fig. 3. Performance metrics for polar system

In case of Cartesian model with parameter t, dropping probability, i.e. probability that current SNR does not satisfy the requirements, was also studied as a function of time and required threshold. The results are presented on Fig. 4. Here the Blocking probability was calculated as a CDF of SNR with respect to t and $SNR*$, $SNR*$ is the threshold, defining acceptable quality of connection. By fixing $SNR*$ at a certain value, the plot on Fig. 4 would illustrate, how blocking probability $P\{SNR(t) < SNR*\}$ changes over time, i.e how probable it is that at certain point of time the quality of connection will become unacceptable.

Table 1. Initial Data

Parameter	Value	Description
a	-100 m	Minimal coordinate a user can have in Cartesian system
b	100 m	Maximal coordinate a user can have in Cartesian system
ν	750 MHz	Data transmission frequency
P_t	20 dBm	Transmission antenna power
N	-100 dBm	Noise power
h	$25, 30, 100$ m	Drone altitude
v	2 m/s	User movement speed
R	100 m	Area radius for polar system

The reason, why for $SNR*$ located in range of 0 to 80 dBm, the probability is zero, i.e the plot is flat, is because there is no way for the user to go far enough from the drone in the observed period of time, to make the quality of connection unacceptable. For the same reason probability for SNR to be acceptable at a late time tends to zero, since the area where user may be located expands with time.

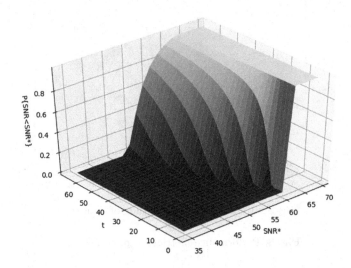

Fig. 4. Dropping probability with respect to time and threshold

For the considered system a simulation model was also developed to acquire the same characteristics as the ones obtained in mathematical in order to proof the model reliability. Simulation model consisted of a single drone and user in a closed region. The drone was located directly in the center of the region, while user was situated directly under drone at the start of the simulation. Then simulator implemented random walk model as user mobility model. According

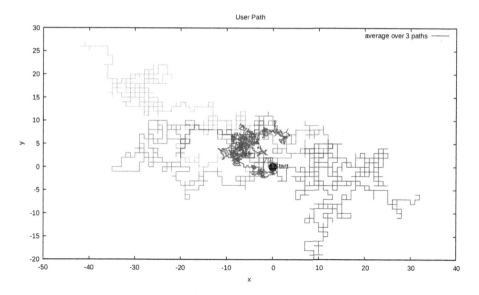

Fig. 5. Mobility model simulation (Color figure online)

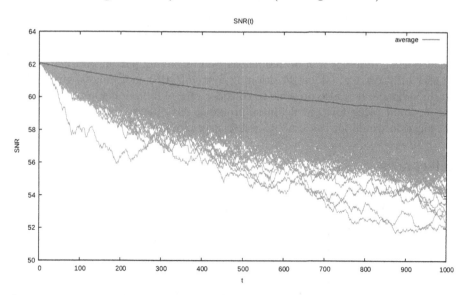

Fig. 6. SNR value for simulation model with 500 trials (Color figure online)

to that model at each moment of time t user randomly chooses one of four directions and moves in a straight line. An illustration of simulation for case of three different trials is presented on Fig. 5. Differently coloured lines illustrate users paths during different trials, red line corresponds to the average position of the user among all the trials. It can be noted, that during each trial user only moves between the nodes of a discreet coordinate grid. This is due to the chosen mobility model. The average value does not belong the aforementioned grid due to the fact that each point of this plot was calculated as average of all the other paths in the trial.

For the described mobility model 500 trials were conducted to acquire the data for average SNR value, the results of these trials are shown on Fig. 6. The lightly colored part corresponds to the results of each trial, while brightly colored line depicts average SNR value. That way we can both observe average as well as approximate variation on this figure. The decreasing nature of the average SNR value obtained in simulation backs up the results, shown on 4, namely, that the probability of drop only rises as time is passed.

4   Conclusion

In this paper we have touched upon a problem of user position in interactions between user and UAV. It was shown that even in case of omnidirectional antennas user mobility greatly impacts system performance. using the constructed model it is possible to determine minimal and average time in which a user can be lost. Also using this model with knowledge of user mobility model and threshold value it is possible to find a point in time at which probability to drop user would go beyond threshold. That time can serve as an approximation of a maximum time available for the UAV to locate user. In further studies we consider using different motion models as well as having partial information on the user location, e.g. Global Positioning System(GPS) coordinates, given with certain variance. It is also possible to consider case of directional antennas, however it would bring forward deafness problem. Also having information of the user location would let the UAV to follow user more effectively.

References

1. Camp, T., Boleng, J., Davies, V.: A survey of mobility models for ad hoc network research. Wireless Commun. Mob. Comput. **2**(5), 483–502 (2002)
2. Galinina, O., Tabassum, H., Mikhaylov, K., Andreev, S., Hossain, E., Koucheryavy, Y.: On feasibility of 5g-grade dedicated RF charging technology for wireless-powered wearables. IEEE Wireless Commun. **23**(2), 28–37 (2016)
3. Galkin, B., Kibilda, J., DaSilva, L.A.: Uavs as mobile infrastructure: addressing battery lifetime. IEEE Commun. Mag. **57**(6), 132–137 (2019)
4. Jabbari, B., Zhou, Y., Hillier, F.: Random walk modeling of mobility in wireless networks. In: VTC 1998, 48th IEEE Vehicular Technology Conference. Pathway to Global Wireless Revolution (Cat. No. 98CH36151), vol. 1, pp. 639–643. IEEE (1998)
5. Kovalchukov, R., et al.: Analyzing effects of directionality and random heights in drone-based mmwave communication. IEEE Trans. Vehicular Technol. **67**(10), 10064–10069 (2018)
6. Krijestorac, E., Hanna, S., Cabric, D.: Uav access point placement for connectivity to a user with unknown location using deep RL. In: 2019 IEEE Globecom Workshops (GC Wkshps), pp. 1–6. IEEE (2019)

7. Kubyshkin, E.P., Kazakov, L.N., Sterin, D.I.: Mathematical modeling of flight reconfiguration of a unmanned aerial vehicles group. In: 2018 Systems of Signal Synchronization, Generating and Processing in Telecommunications (SYN-CHROINFO), pp. 1–4 (2018)

8. Li, G., Zhuang, C., Wang, Q., Li, Y., Xu, X., Zhou, W.: A uav real-time trajectory optimized strategy for moving users. In: 2019 11th International Conference on Wireless Communications and Signal Processing (WCSP), pp. 1–6. IEEE (2019)

9. Liu, X., Li, Z., Zhao, N., Meng, W., Gui, G., Chen, Y., Adachi, F.: Transceiver design and multi-hop d2d for uav iot coverage in disasters. IEEE Internet of Things J. (2019). https://doi.org/10.1109/JIOT.2018.2877504

10. Orsino, A., et al.: Effects of heterogeneous mobility on d2d- and drone-assisted mission-critical mtc in 5g. IEEE Commun. Mag. **55**(2), 79–87 (2017)

11. Patel, P.: New battery tech launches in drones [news]. IEEE Spectrum **55**, 7–9 (2018). https://doi.org/10.1109/MSPEC.2018.8389171

12. Pyattaev, A., Johnsson, K., Andreev, S., Koucheryavy, Y.: Proximity-based data offloading via network assisted device-to-device communications. In: 2013 IEEE 77th Vehicular Technology Conference (VTC Spring), pp. 1–5 (2013)

13. Solomitckii, D., Gapeyenko, M., Semkin, V., Andreev, S., Koucheryavy, Y.: Technologies for efficient amateur drone detection in 5g millimeter-wave cellular infrastructure. IEEE Commun. Mag. **56**(1), 43–50 (2018)

14. Tejedor, A.T.: Drones and networks: ensuring safe and secure operations (2018). https://www.ericsson.com/en/reports-and-papers/white-papers/drones-and-networks-ensuring-safe-and-secure-operations

15. Wang, Z., Duan, L., Zhang, R.: Adaptive deployment for uav-aided communication networks. IEEE Trans. Wireless Commun. **18**(9), 4531–4543 (2019)

Author Index

.

Printed in the United States
By Bookmasters